THE DEVELOPMENT OF THE BALKAN REGION

Acknowledgment
A significant part of this volume is based on research that was
undertaken with the support of the EU's Phare ACE Programme

The Development of the Balkan Region

Edited by
GEORGE PETRAKOS
STOYAN TOTEV

Routledge
Taylor & Francis Group

LONDON AND NEW YORK

First published 2001 by Ashgate Publishing

Reissued 2018 by Routledge
2 Park Square, Milton Park, Abingdon, Oxon OX14 4RN
711 Third Avenue, New York, NY 10017, USA

Routledge is an imprint of the Taylor & Francis Group, an informa business

Publisher's Note
The publisher has gone to great lengths to ensure the quality of this reprint but points out that some imperfections in the original copies may be apparent.

Disclaimer
The publisher has made every effort to trace copyright holders and welcomes correspondence from those they have been unable to contact.

A Library of Congress record exists under LC control number: 00135817

ISBN 13: 978-1-138-70631-6 (hbk)
ISBN 13: 978-1-315-20184-9 (ebk)

Contents

Preface

The Balkan region has been changing in a very fundamental way, under the impact of the interacting forces of integration and transition which are shaping the new European economic landscape. The old structures of internal economic organisation and external economic relations have collapsed, while new economic, political and institutional structures have been, often forcefully and painfully, in the making. As historical and political divides are being removed in Europe, a new economic geography emerges, with several open questions concerning its economic and structural characteristics.

Will western type growth and prosperity levels be eventually reached in the east and the south, or are old divides simply being replaced by new ones with respect to levels of development and fields of specialisation? Will the costs and benefits of east-west interaction in Europe be equally shared by transition countries, or is the process characterised by a selectivity bias with a strong geographical dimension?

Despite early expectations for converging tendencies in a more liberal, market-driven economic environment, the evidence seems to be rather disappointing. It shows that market integration has generated strong pressures and diverging trends which are very clearly observed in the south-eastern part of the new European economic space. It also shows that the Balkan region is identified by unfavourable structural adjustments and those paradigms of integration and transition that face the greatest difficulties and have the weakest performance up to this point.

Indeed, at the turn of the century the Balkans have very little to celebrate for. With the exception of Greece, which is an EU member and has recently managed to comply with the Maastricht criteria for participation in the Economic and Monetary Union (EMU), most other countries have been less fortunate. Especially for some of them the 1990s have been, in the best case, a period of serious and prolonged crisis and, in the worst case, a nightmare.

The ten year old process of transition in Europe has left many important questions without a clear and convincing answer: For example, why did the Balkan countries have to be so different in terms of performance compared to Central Europe? Why did they have to be such a profound case of failure in their transition from plan to market? Are domestic 'policy failures' or unfavourable 'initial conditions' and unfavourable geography responsible for this poor performance? In addition, what has been the policy response of the European Union and what can be done now?

This volume attempts to answer these questions by providing a comprehensive and comparative account of economic performance and structural adjustment in the Balkan region. The volume consists of two parts. The first part includes comparative research work on a wide range of analytical and policy issues, while the second part presents a number of case or country studies. Overall, the volume includes sixteen articles that analyse the economic performance and structure of the Balkan countries, their trade relations in a sectoral and geographical manner, the evolution and distribution of foreign direct investment, the performance of industry, the level and quality of social and technical infrastructure, the domestic policies of transition as well as the European Union policies for the region.

The evidence provided indicates that, should current trends continue in the future, the Balkan region will diverge further from the more advanced European countries, forming a newly expanded and much weaker European periphery. In that respect, mainstream economic thinking of the integration-transition dynamics needs to be re-evaluated, as multi-speed and multi-direction performances generate a more fragmented economic space than the very essence of the European idea may possibly tolerate.

PART I:
ANALYTICAL AND POLICY ISSUES

1 Economic Performance and Structure in the Balkan Region*

GEORGE PETRAKOS
Associate Professor, Department of Planning and Regional Development, University of Thessaly, Greece

STOYAN TOTEV
Deputy Director, Institute of Economics, Bulgarian Academy of Sciences

Introduction

The Balkan region has been changing in a very fundamental way, under the impact of various interacting forces of economic integration and transition that are shaping the new European economic landscape. The old structures of internal economic organisation and external economic relations have collapsed, while new economic, political and institutional structures have been, often forcefully and painfully, in the making. As historical and political divides are being removed in Europe, a new economic geography emerges, with several open questions concerning its economic and structural characteristics (Petrakos et al. 2000, Petrakos 2000). Would western type growth and prosperity levels be eventually reached in the east and the south, or old divides are simply being replaced by new ones with respect to levels of development and fields of specialisation? Would the costs and benefits of the east-west interaction in Europe be equally shared by transition countries, or is the process characterised by a selectivity bias with a strong geographical dimension? Despite neo-classical expectations for converging tendencies in a more liberal, market-driven economic environment, this paper provides evidence that market integration among unequal (and distant) partners generates strong pressures and diverging trends that are very clearly observed in the south-eastern part of the new European economic space. It is shown that the Balkan region is identified by unfavourable structural adjustments and those paradigms of integration and transition that face the greatest difficulties and show the weakest performance up to this point. If current trends continue in the future, the Balkan region will diverge further from the more advanced European countries, forming a new expanded and much weaker European periphery. In that respect, mainstream economic thinking of the integration-transition dynamics needs to be re-evaluated, as multi-speed and mult-direction performances generate a more fragmented economic space than the very essence of the European idea may possibly tolerate.

This article provides a comprehensive analysis of the economic performance, the economic structure and the trade relations of the Balkan countries on a comparative level, allowing us to detect basic trends and developments in the region. On this basis, we evaluate alternative scenarios regarding the prospects of the region in the slowly shaped Pan-European economic order and discuss policy responses to the pressures generated by the interaction between the integration and transition processes. In the next section we examine, on a comparative basis, the economic performance of the Balkan countries, looking at aggregate figures. In Section 3 we look at the structural GDP changes that have taken place in the post-1989 period. In section 4 we compare various indicators of development and in section 5 we examine the structural changes that have taken place in industry. In section 6 we take a look at the geographical patterns of trade relations, and finally, in section 7 we discuss the policy implications of the analysis and draw our conclusions.

The Recent Economic Performance of the Balkan Countries

The first question that naturally arises, concerns the economic performance of the Balkan countries in the post-1989 period. It is already known that all transition countries did not perform equally during this period. In fact, a wide range of performances have been recorded with the relatively more advanced Central European countries having, in general, a better record in all respects (EIU 1996, Petrakos 1997a). On the other hand and in the same period, the European Union (EU) implemented important policies like the Single European Market (SEM) and the policies towards the Economic and Monetary Union (EMU) with various impacts on its member-states. Some countries and regions did better than others, the rule being that the more advanced western European countries and regions outperformed the lagging Southern European ones (CEC 1991).

Wherever it is possible in our analysis, we use EU figures as a measure of comparison with the figures indicating the performance of the Balkan countries. There are two important reasons for doing that. First, the EU economy has been relatively open and exposed to international market conditions for a long period of time. In that sense, its structure and characteristics represent for transition countries a model of a long-term equilibrium and a target to be achieved. Second, the EU is geographically and historically expected, to be the major trading partner of the CEE countries, with all the elements of competition and co-operation that this relationship implies (Petrakos 1997a). In this respect, it is important to compare the performance and structure of the Balkan economies to that of the EU, in order to make an initial evaluation of the characteristics and geographical differences of the on going East-West European integration process.

Examining the basic economic indicators in Table 1, we notice that all transition countries in the Balkans have experienced a deep recession in the post-1989 period. The basic characteristics of this recession are the significant drop in output, the soaring inflation rates during the first years of the transition process and the unprecedented for these countries high and increasing unemployment rates. In 1997, the real GDP level was equal to 87 per cent of the 1990 level in Albania, 69 per cent in Bulgaria, 78 per cent in Croatia, 70 per cent in FYROM, 87 per cent in Romania, 104 per cent in Slovenia and 52 per cent in the FR of Yugoslavia. Half a decade after the reforms, none of the transition economies - with the exception of Slovenia - has fully recovered to the 1990 GDP levels. From all the transition countries, Slovenia, which is also the more advanced, experienced in 1997 a real GDP level slightly higher than its 1990 figure. In contrast, Croatia, FYROM and the FR of Yugoslavia still have real GDP levels significantly lower than the 1990 ones. This picture is depicted in recent figures released by EIU(1998), where the average GDP growth of the Balkan economies for the period 1993-97 has been estimated to be 0.0%, while the respective figure for the Central European ones has been 4.3%[1]. Greece is the only country in the region that experienced a positive GDP growth rate in the 1990-1997 period, although its performance was slightly inferior than that of the EU.

A second characteristic of the early stages of the transition process is the soaring inflation rates that appeared in all countries as a result of

Table 1 Basic Economic Indicators of the Balkan Countries in the Period 1991-1996

Country	Year	Real GDP Growth (%)	GDP Index (1990=100)	Unemployment Rate	Price Inflation
Albania	1991	-27.10	72.90	8.6	36.00
	1992	-9.70	65.83	26.9	226.00
	1993	9.50	72.08	29.0	85.10
	1994	9.40	78.86	19.5	22.60
	1995	8.90	85.88	15.0	7.70
	1996	9.10	93.69	-	12.80
	1997	-7.00	87.13	-	33.20
Bulgaria	1991	-11.70	88.30	11.1	333.50
	1992	-7.30	81.85	16.4	82.00
	1993	-1.50	80.63	12.8	72.90
	1994	1.80	82.08	11.1	96.20
	1995	2.10	83.80	12.5	62.00
	1996	-10.90	74.67	14.1	123.10
	1997	-6.90	69.51	-	1,082.30
Croatia	1991	-20.90	79.10	16.5	123.00
	1992	-11.10	70.32	17.4	665.00
	1993	-0.90	69.69	17.7	1,517.000
	1994	0.60	70.11	17.6	98.00
	1995	1.80	71.37	19.8	2.00
	1996	4.50	74.58	22.0	3.50
	1997	5.30	78.53	-	3.60
Greece	1991	3.10	103.10	7.7	19.50
	1992	0.40	103.51	8.7	15.80
	1993	-1.00	102.48	9.7	14.30
	1994	1.50	104.01	9.6	10.90
	1995	2.00	106.09	10.0	8.90
	1996	2.70	108.96	10.3	8.20
	1997	3.50	112.77	10.0	5.60
FYROM	1991	-9.80	90.20	23.5	115.00
	1992	-13.25	78.25	24.8	1,691.00
	1993	-9.10	71.13	25.6	349.80
	1994	-1.80	69.85	27.3	121.80
	1995	-1.20	69.01	31.6	15.90
	1996	0.70	69.49	42.0	3.00
	1997	1.40	70.47	-	3.60

Table 1 cont.

Country	Year	Real GDP Growth (%)	GDP Index (1990=100)	Unemployment Rate	Price Inflation
Romania	1991	-12.90	87.10	-	174.50
	1992	-8.80	79.44	-	210.90
	1993	1.50	80.63	-	256.10
	1994	3.90	83.77	15.0[a]	136.80
	1995	7.10	89.72	-	32.30
	1996	4.10	93.40	8.5	38.80
	1997	-6.60	87.23	8.8	154.80
Slovenia	1991	-8.10	91.90	8.2	117.70
	1992	-5.40	86.94	11.6	201.30
	1993	2.80	89.37	14.5	32.90
	1994	5.30	94.11	14.5	21.00
	1995	4.10	97.97	13.8	13.40
	1996	3.10	101.00	-	9.90
	1997	3.80	104.84	-	8.30
FR Yugoslavia	1991	-14.20[b]	85.80	21.4	121.00
	1992	-26.20	63.32	22.8	9,237.00
	1993	-30.80	43.82	23.1	116,000,000,000.00
	1994	2.50	44.91	23.2	72,000,000.00
	1995	6.10	47.65	24.6	74.10
	1996	3.50	49.32	-	93.10
	1997	7.40	52.97	-	21.20
EU	1991	3.40	103.40	8.2	5.40
	1992	0.90	104.33	9.2	4.30
	1993	-0.60	103.70	10.7	3.60
	1994	3.00	106.82	11.1	2.90
	1995	2.30	109.27	10.7	2.70
	1996	1.70	111.13	10.8	2.40
	1997	2.60	114.02	10.6	1.80

Sources: EIU (1996, 1997, 1998, 1999) Country Reports, various issues, Economist Intelligent Unit.

EC (1999) European Economy, European Commission.

EIU (1999), Europe 1st quarter 1999, Economist Intelligent Unit.

Eurostat (1997) Statistical Yearbook.

a: Estimate based on a survey by the Romanian National Commission for Statistics (EIU 1996).

b: Social Product growth rates, which differs from GDP in that it excludes Government Services (EIU 1996).

market liberalisation. Although all transition countries experienced some sort of hyperinflation during this period, the worst problems appeared in New Yugoslavia, Croatia and FYROM, that were either involved in the Bosnian war or faced an embargo. As shown in Table 1, some countries managed by 1997 to bring, more or less, inflation under control. This is, however, not the case with Bulgaria, Romania, the FR Yugoslavia and Albania which, due to delayed reforms and political instability, experienced increasing inflation rates or hyper inflation in 1996 and 1997. Recent estimates (EIU 1998), show that the average inflation in the Balkan countries in the period 1993-97 was equal to 131.3 per cent, while the respective figure for the Visegrad countries was 17.1 per cent in the same period. Again here, Greece is the only country in the Balkan region that maintained relatively low and declining price rates throughout this period, although its inflation was still higher than the EU figure.

Declining GDP levels and high inflation unavoidably lead to serious unemployment problems. The Table shows that all transition countries have experienced increasing unemployment rates, which were in general higher than those of Greece and the EU. The highest unemployment rates are found in the countries that were confronted with embargoes or involved in the war (the FR of Yugoslavia, Croatia, and FYROM) and Albania. On the other hand, Bulgaria, Romania and Slovenia have done better in this respect than the other transition countries, with unemployment rates higher, but close to those of the EU and Greece. It is worth noting however, that the course of unemployment over time is rather disappointing, with most countries experiencing increasing rates.

Overall, the performance of the Balkan transition economies in the 1990s shows some similarities and differences that should be recorded. First, all countries had in 1997 real GDP figures that were below the 1990 levels, indicating a recovery process, slower than initially expected. Second, the initial shock of the first three years was in general stronger in countries with a lower level of development and countries that were involved in the Bosnian war or faced an embargo. Third, a multi-speed adjustment process seems to have taken place, with a significant part of the region facing either repeated crises, or significant delays in implementing successful reforms, which made the recovery prospects look weaker.

8

Economic Structure and Change in the Balkan Countries

The ability of the Balkan economies to respond positively to the new economic environment and take advantage of the expected increase and shift in demand, depends to a large extent on the economic structure that they have inherited from the previous political systems and the adjustments that have taken place in this structure because of the reforms. We approach in this section the issue of structural change by examining the sectoral composition of gross domestic product in the region.

In Table 2 we present the sectoral composition of GDP of the Balkan countries and the EU in the early stages of transition and the most recent year (1997) for which there are available data. The general characteristic of all transition economies in the first period[2] is the artificially high share of industry and the low share of services in GDP. This is a general trend found in all the CEE and Former Soviet Union countries (Petrakos 1997a). It is

Table 2 GDP Composition in the Balkan Countries (in current prices)

Country	Year	Primary Sector	Secondary Sector	Tertiary Sector	Total
Albania	1990	40.0	37.0	23.0	100.0
	1997	55.0	22.0	23.0	100.0
Bulgaria	1990	18.0	52.0	30.0	100.0
	1997	18.2	26.8	55.0	100.0
Greece	1990	17.0	26.5	56.5	100.0
	1997	14.0	23.8	62.2	100.0
Romania	1990	18.0	48.0	34.0	100.0
	1997	21.0	40.0	39.0	100.0
Slovenia	1990	5.3	39.6	51.5	100.0
	1997	5.0	38.0	57.0	100.0
FR Yugoslavia	1995	27.0	36.1	36.9	100.0
FYROM	1990	14.8	52.1	33.1	100.0
	1997	12.9	32.0	55.1	100.0
Croatia	1990	10.4	33.6	56.0	100.0
	1997	9.6	25.0	67.0	100.0
EU	1990	3.0	34.2	62.8	100.0
	1997	2.4	32.5	65.1	100.0

Sources: World Bank (1995, 1998).

explained by the position of the Marxist labour theory of value that only the "material sphere" of the economy generates "surplus value" and thus contributes to growth and development. Therefore, most transition Balkan economies had in 1990, shares of industry that approached or exceeded 50 per cent of GDP.

In order to realise how disproportionate these figures are with respect to the realities of a market economy, one has only to compare them with the GDP share of industry in the EU, which was only 34.2 per cent in 1990[3]. The exceptions to this rule were Slovenia and Croatia, the more advanced transition countries in the region, which had modest shares of industry and higher shares of services in GDP.

Another characteristic of the early period is that most transition countries in the Balkans had uncommonly high GDP shares of agriculture, if one judges from the GDP share of agriculture in the EU. Dependence on agriculture is often used as an indication of the level of development, since higher shares of agriculture in GDP are associated with economic structures that correspond to earlier stages of development, while lower shares correspond to more advanced economic structures.

It should be stated here that from all the "peripheral" EU countries (Greece, Portugal, Spain and Ireland) that have in general, a greater dependence on the primary sector than the EU average, Greece is a unique case of a structurally lagging behind country, with a share of the primary sector in 1990 equal to 17 per cent of the GDP, which is about six times the EU average (Petrakos 1997a). This high dependence on the primary sector is unavoidably followed by one of the lowest GDP shares of the secondary and tertiary sectors in the EU. Therefore, we observe that (a) from the spectrum of GDP structures in the EU, Greece has been an outlier with a very high dependence on the primary sector and (b) most of the Balkan transition countries had in 1990 GDP shares of agriculture that were closer to that of Greece, with the exception of Slovenia, which was closer to the economic structure of the EU.

Given those "initial conditions" inherited from the previous economic system, a critical question for the Balkan countries is related to the way they have adjusted their economic structures under the pressures of the transition process. It is now known that structural change in all the CEE countries is typically associated with a reduction in the absolute and relative size of the secondary sector (Petrakos 1997a). Where this adjustment releases resources that are directed to the service sector (forward type of adjustment), we record a positive reaction showing a successful adaptation to the new international environment. However, where released resources are mainly directed to the primary sector (backward type of adjustment), we are faced with a defensive reaction, showing extreme difficulties in dealing with the conditions of the new internal and external economic environment.

Looking at the most recent (1997) data of the sectoral GDP composition in the Balkan countries, we can make a number of important observations with respect to the type of structural adjustment under way. First, the share of industry has declined as expected, but at different rates in different countries. Albania is practically faced with a collapse of its industrial base, while the drop in the other countries has been more modest.

Second, Greece, an EU member, experienced also a decline in its industrial share -from 26.5 per cent in 1990 to 23.8 per cent in 1997. Although specific historical and geographical factors have affected the performance of this country in the entire post war period (Petrakos and Christodoulakis 1997, Petrakos and Pitelis 1997, Lyberaki 1996), it still remains a fact that the contraction of the industrial GDP share is a direct effect of the internationalisation of the economy and the pressures generated by the operation of the Single European Market (SEM) (Petrakos and Zikos 1996). The operation of SEM has intensified competition among firms and regions and has strengthened the competitive advantages of the core regions and countries that house the most efficient European enterprises (Amin et al. 1992, CEC 1991). Lagging behind regions, such as Greece, are suffering directly from the impact of SEM, since they contain the highest share of sensitive sectors (CEC 1990, Camagni 1992), the weakest and most vulnerable productive base, insufficient infrastructure and an overall unfavourable geographical index of strategic location (Petrakos 2000).

Third, all transition economies have experienced a significant decline and have by 1997 industrial shares that are approaching that of Greece. Taking the superiority of Western European industry for granted, especially in the R&D and capital intensive sectors (Landesmann 1995), it may not be unrealistic to expect that in most cases import penetration will further reduce the industrial share in most Balkan transition countries to rates that are closer or even below the Greek share. To the extent that the industrial bases in these countries are unprepared to face the level of international competition required by transition, we may observe a process of decline similar to the one experienced by the Greek industry when the country joined the EU. In that sense, the industrial GDP share of Greece, which continues to decline, may be thought of as a possible scenario of sectoral adjustment that could take place in most Balkan transition economies, if existing trends continue.

Fourth, the GDP structures of the Balkan transition countries have a significantly greater dependence on agriculture than the EU, approaching or exceeding that of Greece. The exception to this rule is Slovenia (and partially Croatia), which along with a number of other transition economies, such as the Czech Republic, Poland, Slovenia and the Slovak Republic, have approached the GDP structure of the EU (Petrakos 1997a), in a way that they exhibited a low GDP dependence on agriculture. This indicates a possible north-south divide in the CEE countries, with the Balkans having a less advanced economic structure than the Central European countries.

Finally, the relatively lower than the EU average shares of the tertiary sector in the Balkan transition economies indicate that certain resources are still employed in industry by virtue of various protection schemes and devices that serve as a buffer to unemployment, until a sustainable strategy of industrial development is formulated and implemented. Although the increase of the GDP share of the tertiary sector in the CEE countries is typically impressive, this is not always the case in the Balkans. With the exception of Slovenia and Croatia (which already had relatively high shares of tertiary sector and experienced a modest or a high increase) and Bulgaria (that started from a relatively low share and indeed experienced a significant increase), the other countries did not do so well. Albania maintains one of the highest shares of agriculture and one of the lowest shares of industry and services in the world, experiencing a definitely backward adjustment to the pressures of transition. Romania on the other hand, has experienced a modest increase of the tertiary sector, as industrial restructuring seems to be at early levels of development.

Overall, sectoral data indicates the existence of a north-south divide among the CEE countries, with the Balkan transition economies having a less advanced economic structure than the Central European ones[4]. While the GDP structure of transition economies like Poland, the Czech Republic and Hungary approach that of the EU, the GDP structure of the Balkan countries tends, in general, to approach that of Greece. Given that within the EU, Greece is a case of a structurally lagging behind country, it appears that in the new, slowly shaped, geography of Europe, the Balkan region has the weakest economic structure. In that sense, it is highly possible to engage in an "unequal integration" process and runs the greatest risk of forming a new, expanded, European periphery.

Indicators of Development in the Balkans

Do economic structures, as analysed before, conform to development indicators in the Balkan countries? The question is crucial, as weak economic structures and negative structural adjustments may be either temporary characteristics of a perhaps prolonged transition period, or more permanent ingredients of their socio-economic base. In Table 3 we present for all the Balkan countries with available data, figures of 1998 GDP per capita in purchasing power parity (PPP) USD, which is an indicator of development taking into consideration cost of living differentials. We also present a number of additional indicators of development such as telephones per 1000 people, road density and infant mortality for the latest year with available data. For comparative purposes, we also include in this table, information for selected advanced EU members economies, like Germany, France, Belgium and the UK. We attempt to evaluate, on the basis of monetary and physical indicators, the degree of the differences existing in the levels of development (a) among the Balkan countries and (b) between the Balkan countries on the one hand and the advanced EU countries on the other.

Examining the data provided, we can make a number of significant observations. First, taking in the first column 1998 figures of GDP per head in PPP USD as an indicator, we find great differences between the Balkan countries. Greece appears as the most developed country in the region with a GDP per head level equal to 13,400 USD in 1998. Slovenia is second in the region with a GDP per head level equal to about 77 per cent of Greece and Croatia is third with a GDP per head equal to 38 per cent of Greece. Romania and Bulgaria are further behind in development levels having a GDP per head equal to about 31 per cent and 30 per cent respectively of the Greek one. On the other hand, Albania appears as an extreme case of underdevelopment, with a GDP per head that is equal to 11 per cent of the Greek one. On the basis of this information, one could argue that, in very broad lines, Slovenia approaches the level of development of Greece measured by GDP per capita, while all the other Balkan countries are lagging behind considerably, with Albania being an outlier with respect to the average picture.

Second, on the basis again of information about GDP per head in PPP USD, all Balkan countries are well behind the more advanced EU countries. Greece, for example, has a GDP per head equal to only 60 per cent of Germany. Slovenia, which comes second, has a GDP per head equal to 46 per cent of Germany. At the other end of the spectrum, Albania has a GDP per head equal to 7 per cent of Germany.

13

Table 3 Indicators of Development in the Balkan and Selected EU Countries

Country	GDP per head in PPP USD	Telephones per 1000 persons	Road Density (Km per million people)	Infant mortality per 1000 live births
	1998	1997	1997	1997
Albania	1,490	23	1,643	26
Bulgaria	4,100	323	4,064	18
Greece	13,400	516	10,207	7
Romania	4,050	167	3,459	22
Slovenia	10,300	364	6,201	5
FYROM		204	2,755	16
Croatia	5,100	335	4,962	9
Germany	22,100	550	7,922	5
France	22,600	575	15,295	5
Belgium	23,400	468	14,093	6
UK	21,200	540	6,326	6

Sources: CIA (1999) and World Bank (1999).

How confident should we feel about the ability of this information to depict reality? Are these differences real or do they largely appear because of distortions in the domestic price formation regimes of the Balkan transition economies? To further examine this issue, we provide in the same table figures of some "physical" indicators of development that are directly comparable. These indicators are telephones per capita, road density and infant mortality that depict the level of social and economic infrastructure of a country.

Starting with intra-Balkan comparisons, we see that the general picture is maintained but the differences are less profound in most cases. Examining telephones per capita, we see that the Slovenian figure is equal to 70 per cent, the Bulgarian figure is equal to 62 per cent, the Croatian figure is equal to 64 per cent and the figure of FYROM is equal to 39 per cent of the Greek one. Albania appears again as an extreme case of underdevelopment, with a figure equal to less than 5 per cent of the Greek one. Examining road density we see that the Slovenian figure is equal to 60 per cent of the Greek one, the Bulgarian equal to 40 per cent, the Romanian equal to 34 per cent and the figure of FYROM is equal to 27 per cent of the Greek figure. Albania again has an extremely low figure that is equal to 16 per cent of the Greek one. Finally, looking at infant mortality which is an indicator of the quality of the health care system (and consequently the health and quality of life of the population), we see that the Slovenian figure is even smaller (that is, better) than the Greek one, the Bulgarian is 2.5 times the Greek one, the Romanian is 3 times the Greek one, while the Albanian figure is almost 4 times the Greek one.

In general, there are two interesting observations that can be made from the examination of these figures. First, there is indeed a divide within the Balkan countries with respect to the level of development, but the differences should not be taken to be as great as the GDP per head figures of the first column of Table 3 indicate, with the exception of Albania. All development indicators show that Albania is an extreme case of underdevelopment in Europe and it has profound differences from all other countries. Second, comparing Greece and the other more advanced countries of the EU with respect to the "physical" indicators, we observe that the existing differences are not as great as indicated by GDP per capita data. In terms of telephones per capita, Greece is doing better than Belgium, while in terms of road density Greece is doing better than Germany and the UK. It is only in terms of infant mortality that Greece appears to be lagging behind the other more advanced EU countries. This, however, is happening by a margin that is narrower than the one indicated by the GDP per capita figures.

These comparisons raise a very important question. If the physical indicators of development (that are related to infrastructure and quality of life) for Greece are not very different from those of the advanced EU countries, why do development levels measured by GDP per capita levels, differ so much? To be exact, why are relatively small differences in physical indicators of development compatible with very large differences in development levels? A possible explanation, that is in line with recent research (Krugman 1994,1995), may be related to the role that geography plays in the development process. Even if infrastructure in Greece was equally good or better than that of the Western European countries, the picture with respect to the levels of development would not be very different. Greece is simply too far away from the major European markets to attract significant mobile investment (CEC 1993) and economic activity that would have a real impact on its level of development. As a result, a small by international standards market size (measured by population) and limited accessibility (measured by large distance) to European markets with a critical size, seem to operate as constraints that diminish the impact of development policies on the level of development.

Overall, the analysis indicates that (a) there are great differences in the levels of development within the Balkan regions, (b) that there are even greater differences between the Balkan regions as a whole and the more advanced members of the EU and (c) that these differences are larger in terms of development levels and smaller in terms of physical indicators, showing the "selective" role of geography in the process of development. With the exception of Slovenia, all the transition economies in the Balkans have considerably lower levels of development than Greece and even lower than the EU. This indicates that convergence towards the EU (again with the exception of Slovenia) will take a lot of time and effort for the transition countries in the region. Taking into consideration the integration experience of Greece (Petrakos and Pitelis 1997) and the type of post-1989 east-west trade relations that dominate (Landesmann 1995, Dodrinsky 1997a), it is very likely that we will observe, at least for a period of time, a divergence process in terms of structural adjustments and development levels (Petrakos 2000).

Industrial Structure and Change in the Balkans

A. Trends in Industrial Employment Shares by Sector

Changes in the industrial structure of the Balkan countries are very important for the type of specialisation the region is going to undertake within the new European economic space. Table 4 presents for those countries with available data and the EU the sectoral composition of industrial employment in the early period of transition and the latest year with available data. Information is available for 9 aggregate sectors that correspond to the ISIC and NACE classifications shown in the first two columns[5]. The aggregate sectors 1-4 are in general capital and technology-intensive, while the sectors 5-8 are in general labour and resource-intensive. Our aim in this section is to examine structural changes in the industrial base of the Balkan countries in order to detect trends of convergence to, or divergence from the EU industrial structure. Although all aggregate sectors have an interest of their own, attention here is focused on sectors 2, 5 and 6 that make up a large share of industrial employment and have significantly different employment weights in different countries.

Aggregate sector 2 can undoubtedly be characterised as the backbone of industry. It includes important industries such as metals, mechanical, electrical and instrument engineering, and transportation. There are two

Table 4 Composition of Industrial Employment in the Balkan Countries and the EU by Sector

				Greece			Bulgaria		Romania		Slovenia		EU
							Composition						
SIC	NACE		SECTOR	1990	1993	1995	1989	1995	1990	1994	1990	1995	1990
/31 2	25/48	1	Chemicals, Rubber and plastic	11.4	12.3	8.7	7.8	11.5	8.7	9.3	8.0	9.4	12.9
35/36/31/32 /38 /34/35 /36/37	2	2	Manuf. of metal articles Mechanical, Electrical and Instrument Engineering Transportation	20.6	18.1	17.8	38.2	32.8	33.0	27.2	38.9	37.7	45.8
	23/24	3	Non-metallic mineral products	6.7	7.0	4.8	5.7	6.5	10.3	10.8	5.3	5.0	4.6
/21 2	21/22	4	Production of metals	2.7	4.0	2.4	5.2	7.8	6.9	8.7	5.8	2.2	3.7
/24 9	41/42	5	Food, Drink and Tobacco	19.6	21.0	18.1	10.8	12.1	7.5	10.1	7.0	8.9	10.7
/26	43/44 /45	6	Textile, Leather, footwear and clothing	28.5	25.8	26.0	16.1	18.2	22.5	21.0	20.2	22.2	10.7
/28	46	7	Timber and wooden furniture	4.3	5.3	114.0	4.7	6.1	2.6	3.3	8.7	7.3	4.1
	47	8	Paper and paper products	5.4	6.6	7.8	2.0	2.8	1.9	2.3	4.8	5.8	6.5
	49	9	Other industries	0.9	0.4	0.3	9.5	2.2	6.8	7.3	1.3	1.0	1.1
			Total	100.0		100.0	100.0	100.0	100.0	100.0	100.0	100.0	100.0

Sources: Own calculations from:
Industrial Surveys, Statistical Yearbook of Greece, 1992, 1995 and Labor Force Survey 1995 (unpublished data).
The Bulgarian Economy, NSI, 1989 and Statistical Reference Book of Bulgaria, 1995.
Annual Statistics of Romania, NCS, 1995.
Statistical Office of the Republic of Slovenia, 1995.
EUROSTAT, 1993.

significant observations that can be made here. First, the Greek share of employment in this technology, knowledge and capital-intensive sector appears very low compared to the EU share and is declining. In fact, it was less than half the EU share in 1990 and dropped to almost one-third in 1993. This picture is clearly in line with previous analysis and highlights on the one hand, the significant divergence of the Greek industrial structure from the Western European one and on the other, the problems and consequences of integration among unequal partners. Second, the employment shares of the Balkan transition economies were clearly greater than the Greek share and closer to the EU share in 1990, but have declined afterwards. A drop of about 6 percentage points has been recorded in Bulgaria and Romania and a very small decline in Slovenia. In general there is a declining trend in the employment share of all the Balkan countries, which, with the exception of Slovenia seem to diverge significantly from the EU share.

Aggregate sector 5, which includes food, drink and tobacco industries, is in general classified as a consumer oriented, labour-intensive industrial sector. Here we observe that Greece has the highest employment share, which is almost twice as large as the EU share. This, in connection with the previous findings about employment shares in aggregate sector 2, should be interpreted as the consequence of an intra-EU specialisation and division of labour, where the weaker members concentrate on labour-intensive or resource-intensive activities, while the stronger ones on capital-intensive and technology- or knowledge-intensive ones. Increasing shares of employment in aggregate sector 5 are also observed in the other Balkan countries, which, however, are at levels lower or equal to that of the EU.

A similar picture appears with aggregate sector 6, which includes textile, leather, footwear and clothing industries, and is also classified as a consumer oriented, labour-intensive sector. Here again Greece has the highest share of employment in the region, which is 2.5 times the share of the EU. All other Balkan countries have employment shares that are much higher than the EU (but lower than Greece) and in some cases, like Bulgaria and Slovenia, rising. Therefore, from the information provided for aggregate sector 6, we see again that within the EU there is a divide in terms of industrial specialisation, with weaker members like Greece specialising more and more in labour and material-intensive sectors. This type of north-south divide, seems to expand geographically in the post-1989 period beyond the EU borders, tending to incorporate most of the transition Balkan countries, as a part of the "southern" economic structure.

B. Convergence-Divergence Trends in the Balkan-EU Industrial Structures

What trends are developing in terms of the industrial structure of the Balkan countries? Do they seem to develop similar structures or not? Do they tend to converge with or diverge from the industrial structure of the EU over time? The industrial structure of the transition economies in the Balkans is characterised in general by substantially higher shares of the intermediate and capital goods sectors than Greece, and lower shares of the consumer and light industry sectors than Greece. Making the comparison with the EU, we see that they have in general lower shares of employment in intermediate and capital goods sectors and higher shares of employment in consumer and light industry sectors. If we concentrate on the sectors of mechanical, electrical, instrument engineering on the one hand and foods and textiles on the other, where Greece and the EU have the most significant differences in their shares, we see that the Balkan transition economies tend to have declining shares in the former and increasing in the latter.

Previous analysis presents a picture where differences and similarities are changing over time. The general feeling from the analysis so far, is that most Balkan transition economies have started from a structure that was closer to the EU than Greece. However, because of the type of sectoral adjustments that the process of transition implies, they have moved away over time from the EU and closer to the Greek structure. To see whether this assertion can be justified in a more formal way, we attempt here to approach these questions by using an index of convergence-divergence. This index, which is also called index of similarity-dissimilarity, is based on the comparison of the sum of the squared differences (SSD_t) of the sectoral employment shares for every pair of countries in the early 1990s and the latest year with available data:

$$SSD_t = \Sigma_i \, [\, a_{it} - b_{it} \,]^2$$

where [a,b] is a pair of countries, i = 1, ...,9, is the number of industrial sectors and t = 0,1 are two time periods: at the beginning of the transition process (0) and the most recent period with available data (1). To the extent that the value of SSD_t for each pair of countries [a,b] is smaller in the last year with available data than at the beginning of the period, that indicates that the industrial structures of these two countries have come closer to each other, or in other words, have shown signs of convergence towards a common structure. In the opposite case, if the value of SSD_t increases over time, then the two countries have diverging industrial structures.

19

In Table 5 we present the SSD_t estimates. Two observations can be made on the basis of these indices. First, verifying the assertions made before in earlier studies (Petrakos and Zikos 1996), the industrial structure of Greece is found to further diverge from that of the EU[6], as a result of the process of economic integration. Second, the industrial structure of the other Balkan countries (including Slovenia), tend to diverge from that of the EU and converge towards that of Greece.

Table 5 Convergence-Divergence Index (SSD_t) of Industrial Structures in the Balkan Countries

Country	Period	Greece	Bulgaria	Romania	Slovenia	EU
Greece	1st		646	423	605	1.039
	2nd		386	341	564	1,107
Bulgaria	1st	646		115	123	208
	2nd	386		101	100	269
Romania	1st	423	115		143	430
	2nd	341	101		257	586
Slovenia	1st	605	123	143		205
	2nd	564	100	257		227
EU	1st	1.039	208	430	205	
	2nd	1,107	269	586	227	

Source: Table 4.

Assuming that the method used to track down structural adjustment processes is reliable, the conclusions of this analysis are rather clear. In terms of industrial structures, the high value of the SSD_t index indicates that Greece has the most distant structure from that of the EU. Although the other Balkan countries are closer to the EU industrial structure, the worrying observation is that the process of transition is associated with a tendency of divergence from it. This indicates that specialisation and trade in Europe retain an inter-sectoral pattern, with European core countries and regions maintaining their specialisation in capital, RDT and knowl-edge-intensive sectors and peripheral countries (comprising the old periphery and a large part of the transition countries) sliding towards a specialisation in labour and resource-intensive sectors, which is not compatible with the structural characteristics of a modern developed economy.

The Geographical Orientation of Trade Relations in the Balkans

It is now recognised that East-West trade relations have experienced a rapid but unbalanced expansion. In the 1992-1997 period, the EU trade surplus with the CEE countries increased by 904 per cent (Petrakos 2000), while in the case of the Balkans, commodity trade statistics indicate an over time increasing trade deficit (World Bank 1998). In addition, some studies (Landesmann 1995, Dobrinski 1997b) indicate that the trade relations of these countries, just like North-South relations, have a predominantly inter-industry character. An aspect of trade relations however, that rarely receives attention concerns the geographical orientation of international trade. As it will be shown in this section, changes in the geographical orientation of trade may affect in various ways the prospects for regional co-operation and development.

In Table 6 we present information about the composition of exports and imports in the Balkan economies, by countries of destination and origin, and for the years 1989 and 1994. The composition of trade in 1989 depicts the situation that existed before transition, while the composition of trade in 1994 (the most recent year with data available for all countries in the Table), has been affected by the transition process. The first part of the Table shows the share of exports of each country that appears in the first column, to each country that appears in the first row for the years 1989 and 1994. For example, in 1989 the share of the Albanian exports to Bulgaria was 10.3 per cent, to Romania 9.1 per cent, to Greece 3.0 per cent, to Slovenia 4.9 per cent, to former Soviet Union countries (FSU) 0.0 per cent, to the Visegrad countries 21.8 per cent, to the other 12 EU countries (except Greece) 11.3 per cent and to other countries 39.6 per cent. The second part of the table shows in a similar way the share of imports of each country that appears in the first column, from each country that appears in the first row in 1989 and 1994.

Examining the information in this table we can make a number of important observations. First, it seems that trade relations among CEE economies (both exports and imports) have declined in significance. For example, while in 1989 the share of Bulgarian exports going to Visegrad countries was 9.6 per cent of the total Bulgarian exports, in 1994 this share dropped to 1.8 per cent. The same is also true for trade relations among CEE and FSU economies. For example the share of Romanian exports to the FSU dropped from 22.6 per cent in 1989 to 6.6 per cent in 1994.

21

Table 6 Share of Exports and Imports (column) to (row)

Share of Imports (column) to (row)

1989	Albania	Bulgaria	Romania	Greece	Slovenia	FSU	Visegrad	EU*	Other	Total
Albania		10.3	9.1	3.0	4.9	0.0	21.8	11.3	39.6	100.0
Bulgaria	0.2		2.0	1.3	1.0	65.2	9.6	4.2	16.5	100.0
Romania	0.3	1.7		1.6	1.7	22.6	8.8	29.0	34.3	100.0
Greece	0.3	0.9	0.6		0.0	1.8	1.1	65.2	30.2	100.0
Slovenia	0.1	0.5	0.2	0.7		13.7	6.6	50.6	27.6	100.0

1994	Albania	Bulgaria	Romania	Greece	Slovenia	FSU	Visegrad	EU*	Other	Total
Albania		0.5	0.0	10.3	0.6	0.0	0.7	56.4	31.5	100.0
Bulgaria	1.3		1.6	7.8	0.9	18.8	1.8	27.8	40.0	100.0
Romania	0.1	1.7		2.3	0.3	6.6	4.2	45.9	38.9	100.0
Greece	2.3	4.4	1.0		0.1	3.8	1.7	54.0	32.8	100.0
Slovenia	0.1	0.2	0.2	0.2		4.6	4.5	58.9	31.3	100.0

Share of Imports (column) to (row)

1989	Albania	Bulgaria	Romania	Greece	Slovenia	FSU	Visegrad	EU*	Other	Total
Albania		7.3	7.0	7.2	4.8	0.0	18.2	15.1	40.4	100.0
Bulgaria	0.5		1.9	0.4	0.9	52.9	11.0	9.8	22.6	100.0
Romania	0.4	2.6		0.5	1.8	31.5	11.8	12.5	38.9	100.0
Greece	0.1	0.5	0.5		0.0	1.6	1.5	64.7	31.2	100.0
Slovenia	0.0	0.4	0.4	0.2		7.9	6.8	56.7	27.6	100.0

1994	Albania	Bulgaria	Romania	Greece	Slovenia	FSU	Visegrad	EU*	Other	Total
Albania		8.4	0.7	24.3	4.7	0.7	1.4	22.7	37.1	100.0
Bulgaria	0.0		1.9	4.8	2.2	31.6	3.3	28.0	28.2	100.0
Romania	0.0	0.9		1.3	0.2	17.9	3.9	46.9	28.9	100.0
Greece	0.2	1.4	0.5		0.1	1.7	0.9	66.2	29.1	100.0
Slovenia	0.0	0.4	0.3	0.1		2.2	6.2	57.0	33.8	100.0

Sources: Own calculations from:
Albania in Figures, Institute of Statistics, 1995.
Statistical Yearbook of Bulgaria, 1990, 1995.
Foreign Trade Statistics of Romania, NCS, 1995.
Panhelenic Exporters Association, 1995.
Statistical Office of the Republic of Slovenia, 1995.

Second, and perhaps more important, trade relations among transition economies in the Balkans in most cases also declined in significance, even when these countries are neighbours. For example, the share of Bulgarian exports to Romania declined from 2.0 per cent in 1989 to 1.6 per cent in 1994.

Third, the trade relations (both exports and imports) of the Balkan transition economies with the rest of the EU (excluding Greece), significantly increased in the same period. For example, the share of the Romanian exports to the EU increased from 29.0 per cent in 1989 to 45.9 per cent in 1994. From the examination of the data, it seems that the trade between Balkan transition economies and the EU in 1994 is greatly affected by the distance intervening between each pair of countries. Albania and Slovenia, who are closer to Italy, have more intensive trade relations with the EU than Bulgaria and Romania.

Fourth, at the intra-Balkan level, the only trade relations that have significantly expanded in this period concern cross-border trade between Albania and Greece, and Bulgaria and Greece. The share of Albanian exports to (imports from) Greece increased from 3.0 per cent (7.2) in 1989, to 10.4 per cent (24.3) in 1994 and the share of Bulgarian exports to (imports from) Greece increased from 1.3 per cent (0.4) in 1989 to 7.8 per cent (4.8) in 1994. Again here, the trade relations of Greece in the Balkans in 1994 seems to be affected by geographical factors, like adjacency and proximity. Relations are more intensive with Albania and Bulgaria and less intensive with Romania and Slovenia. Slovenia of course undertakes a similar process of east-west cross-border intensive trade relations with Italy and Austria.

Fifth, the importance of Greek trade relations with the other EU12 countries has diminished, especially for Greek exports, that have declined as a share of total Greek exports, from 65.2 per cent in 1989 to 54.0 per cent in 1994. This decline in the share of Greek exports to the other EU members indicates a declining ability of Greek products to compete in the Single European Market, despite the fact that barriers to trade and protection schemes and devices have largely been removed (Petrakos 1997b).

Overall, it seems that significant changes have taken place in the geographical composition of trade in the Balkans between the years 1989 and 1994. The basic development is that trade relations have shifted from intra-block to east-west relations. The rapid increase in the east-west pattern of trade is explained by the significant inter-industry type of gains from specialisation and exchange, acquired by all countries involved.

This increase however, in east-west trade relations does not involve all countries equally. Some CEE countries develop closer trade relations with some EU members, the force of attraction being a direct function of market size, development level and geographical factors such as adjacency and proximity. As available reports (EIU 1996, 1997) indicate, the trade of the Balkan transition economies with the EU has developed following this logic. Trade relations are in principle strong with EU countries that are large, developed and nearby. In that respect, it is not surprising that all the Balkan transition countries have developed significant trade relations with Germany and Italy, but not with Spain, the UK, Belgium or the Netherlands.

Intra-Balkan relations have mostly developed along the same lines. Significant increases have been recorded in the cases where trade has an east-west and cross-border character as in the case of Albania and Greece or Bulgaria and Greece. It has been shown elsewhere (Petrakos 1997b), that trade between neighbours has additional benefits besides the well known export-multiplier effect on economic growth. Cross-border trade has in general a larger intra-industry component and as a result it generates fewer external pressures for undesired structural changes in countries that are unprepared to implement a sustainable industrial strategy.

Policy Implications and Conclusions

There are several new elements in the post-1989 Balkan region that this paper has concentrated upon. A significant part of the region still faces repeated crises, political instability or significant delays in implementing successful reforms, that make the recovery prospects of the region look weaker. In addition, most transition countries are found to be with very low levels of development, and tend to slide towards economic and industrial structures that do not conform to that of an advanced modern economy. On this basis, if existing trends continue, the Balkan countries will have to integrate into the EU, with a set of disadvantages that will not favour convergence. Therefore, available evidence indicates that on the emerging Pan-European scale, the existing north-south divide will most likely be maintained, with the Balkan region comprising some of the most backward countries and regions in Europe.

Of course, not all Balkan countries are faced with the same constraints, have the same choices or will follow the same route to European integration. Slovenia, to start with the more advanced transition country in the region, has, by virtue of geography, very clear strategic choices to make. Adjacency to two advanced EU members and a relatively central place with respect to the European core region, make it clear that this small country will look primarily to the north for markets and economic partners. Having a relatively advanced economic structure and being traditionally an open economy will help this country to perform well and resist pressures for inter-

24

industry types of specialisation and a process of integration that leads to structural and economic divergence.

The picture is not that ideal for the other transition economies. Most of them are in varying degrees peripheral with respect to the economic EU gravity centre, have low levels of development and weak economic structures. Integration with the EU will most likely take a north-south character, with inter-sectoral and unbalanced trade relations, that does not lead to convergence with respect to development levels. The strategic options available to these countries with respect to economic relations vary. On the one hand, Albania, FYROM and Bulgaria are (again by virtue of geography) obliged to pay serious attention to intra-Balkan economic relations, since they have common borders only with Balkan countries. The fact that Greece is a member of the EU, makes this option more convincing, as despite their distance from the EU core, they have common borders with an EU member state.

On the other hand, the FR of Yugoslavia and Romania are in a somewhat different position, as they are closer to the European gravity centre, but have borders only with CEE or FSU countries. As a result, their strategic options with respect to economic partners are less focused and their trade relations are expected to be more geographically dispersed. In any case, all transition Balkan economies, to varying degrees and with the possible exception of Slovenia, are expected to develop strong but unbalanced trade relations with the EU, that will be justified on the ground of the technological modernisation of their economies, that however, will tend to increase dependence. Finally Greece, that has discovered neighbours to trade with after several decades of isolation, has a strategic interest in improving intra-Balkan economic relations and promoting the development of a large regional market that is nearby and therefore accessible.

Seeking development strategies and policies for the Balkan region, we must admit, is a difficult assignment. The political realities of the post-war period divided the region into at least four camps and lead most countries to isolation from each other. Being the most fragmented region of Europe (Petrakos 1997c), with so many disputes in the post war period, unavoidably has affected performance, economic structures and development levels and has made transition a more painful process. The disadvantages of fragmentation have been exacerbated by the peripheral position of the region with respect to the major European markets and development centres, which makes economic interaction more difficult (and of a special type) and the spread effects (that are a function of distance) less visible and less significant. As a result, history and geography set up two serious constraints - the first one, hopefully, with a diminishing importance over time - to any efforts for development strategies based on externally driven growth, either in the sense of exports or in the sense of mobile investment.

Of course, external assistance to the region either in the form of the Community Support Framework, the Phare Program, or various other initiatives such as the more recent Stability Pact will continue in the foreseeable future. We should not miss the fact however, that this type of assistance is largely provided in order to offset the aforementioned negative impacts of integration in countries with weak economic structures. Nor should we overlook the fact that until the Kosovo crisis the EU policy bodies had practically neglected the economically and structurally weaker Balkan region in favour of the more advanced Central European countries.

This policy needs to be re-evaluated, especially in the light of the evidence indicating that economic performance in the region is seriously affected by a number of structural deficiencies that make the implementation of reforms more difficult than elsewhere. As the cost of further marginalisation of South-eastern Europe will be in economic and political terms higher in the future and will threaten to reverse the integration and cohesion processes of a Pan-European Union, the EU has a long-term interest in dealing with the new "southern question" in a more focused, decisive and effective manner.

Irrespective of the EU policies and for the time being, however, the only available option to the region as a whole is a strategy of internally driven growth, based on intensive intra-Balkan relations in all fields, including trade and factor movement. This option has two serious advantages. First, it sets in motion regional multipliers based on intra-regional exports and imports that may be an important source of growth over time. Second, smooth relations and increasing intra-Balkan economic activity will lead to a more integrated and accessible economic space that will most likely attract more serious investment projects than the fragmented Balkan economic space today.

Given the fact that small markets mean small business and little attention from international investors, there are good reasons for the Balkan countries to overcome the barriers of their size and "think big", promoting regional co-operation and integration at all levels. Besides, this is one of the lessons of the development history of Western Europe. In addition to a stable macroeconomic and institutional environment, the development of the

26

Western European countries has been based on accessibility to markets large enough to allow industries to operate with efficient sizes, even when the host country has a small domestic market.

Overall, it seems that the best strategic reaction for the region as a whole to the pressures generated by economic integration and transition is based on regional co-operation and regional integration. This strategy will basically overcome fragmentation and will allow for the other advantages of the region, such as its proximity to the new European frontiers in the Black Sea or the Middle East, its pleasant climate, or its low cost base to become more visible and more appreciable. Of course, within this strategic framework each country may follow specialised policies according to its national priorities. As geography would predict, Bulgaria and Romania might focus on their relations with the Black Sea countries, Slovenia may look northwards and Albania may develop closer relations with Italy. The impact of these choices however on their development will certainly be stronger with a less fragmented and more integrated Balkan region than otherwise.

Notes

* This research was undertaken with support from the European Union's Phare ACE Program 1994. An earlier version of this paper has been presented in several workshops and concferences and published in the International Journal of Urban and Regional Research, 24.1, pp. 95-113. As Balkan countries we consider in this paper Greece, a member of the European Union and all the transition countries in Southeastern Europe: Albania, Bulgaria, Romania and the new States in the territory of former Yugoslavia.

1   In this report, Slovenia is not considered a Balkan, but a Central European country.

2   Which basically shows the situation that existed before the reform process had any impact on the economy.

3   Making this comparison, we should bear in mind that the industrial sector of the EU average is technologically more advanced and usually more efficient than that of the Balkan economies.

4   With the exception of Slovenia, that is, however, a small country and does nor change the general picture.

5   The 1995 data for Greece is not directly comparable to the 1990 and 1993 data, as it comes from different surveys. The 1990 and 1993 data come from industrial surveys including all firms with 10 employees or more, while the 1995 data comes from estimates based on a 1.5 per cent sample of a labor force survey. Safe over time comparisons therefore can only be made between the 1990 and 1993 figures.

6   Information about the composition of the EU industrial employment by sector is available only for 1990. Therefore, our estimate is precise only to the extent that the industrial structure of the EU has not changed significantly.

References

Amin A., Charles R. and Howells J.(1992) Corporate Restructuring in the New Europe, *Regional Studies,* 26, 4, pp. 319-331.

Camagni R. (1992) Development Scenarios and Policy Guidelines for the Lagging Regions in the 1990s, *Regional Studies,* 26, 4, pp. 361-374.

CEC (1990) *Social Europe, European Economy,* Commission of the European Communities, Brussels.

CEC (1991) *The Regions in the 1990s,* Fourth Periodic Report, Commission of the European Communities, Brussels.

CEC (1993) *New location factors for mobile investment in Europe,* Regional Development Studies, Commission of the European Commission.

CIA (1999) *The World Factbook,* Central Intelligent Agency, Washington D.C.

Dobrinsky R. (1997a) Bulgaria and Romania: patterns of trade, specialisation in trade with the European Union during the transition from plan to market, Paper presented in the Conference "*Economic Co-operation in the Balkans: A Regional Approach to European Integration*", Phare-ACE Program, University of Thessaly, Department of Planning and Regional Development, Volos, 16-19 January 1997.

Dobrinsky R. (1997b) Multi-speed transition and multi-speed integration in Europe: recent economic developments in the Balkans and their implications, Paper presented in the Conference "*Economic Cooperation in the Balkans: A Regional Approach to European Integration*", Phare-ACE Program, University of Thessaly, Department of Planning and Regional Development, Volos, 16-19 January 1997.

EC (1999) *European Economy,* The EU Economy: 1999 Review, No 69, European Commission.

EIU (1996, 1997, 1998, 1999) *Country Profiles and Country Reports,* Economist Intelligent Unit, various countries.

EIU (1999) *Europe,* Economist Intelligent Unit, 1st quarter 1999.

EUROSTAT (1997) *Statistical Yearbook 1997,* European Commission, Luxembourg.

Krugman P. (1994) *Geography and Trade,* MIT Press.

Krugman P. (1995) *Development, Geography and Economic Theory,* MIT Press.

Landesmann M.(1995) The pattern of East-West European Integration: Catching up or falling behind? , Paper No 212, *The Vienna Institute for Comparative Economic Studies.*

Lyberaki A. (1996) Greece-EC comparative performance at the National and regional level: Why diverge?, *European Planning Studies,* Vol. 4, pp. 313-329.

Petrakos G. (1996a) The regional dimension of transition in Eastern and Central European countries: An assessment, in Jackson and Petrakos (editors), Regional Problems and SME development in transition countries, *Eastern European Economics,* Vol. 34, No 4, pp. 5-38, Special Edition.

Petrakos G. (1996b) The New Geography of the Balkans: Cross-border co-operation between Albania, Bulgaria and Greece, *Series on Transition in the Balkans,* Vol. 1, University of Thessaly, Department of Planning and Regional Development.

Petrakos G. (1997a) Industrial Structure and Change in the European Union: Comparative Analysis and Implications for Transition Economies, *Eastern European Economics,* Vol. 35, No. 2, pp. 41-63.

Petrakos G. (1997b) A European macro-region in the making? The Balkan trade relations of Greece. *European Planning Studies*, Vol. 5, No 4. pp. 515-533.

Petrakos G. (1997c) The Regional Structure of Albania, Bulgaria and Greece: Implications for Co-operation and Development, *European Urban and Regional Studies*, Vol. 4. No. 3, pp. 193-208.

Petrakos G. (2000) The spatial impact of East-West integration in Europe, in Petrakos G. Maier G. and Gorzelak G. (eds.) *Integration and Transition in Europe: The Economic Geography of Interaction*, Routledge, London. pp. 38-68.

Petrakos G. and Christodoulakis N. (1997) "Economic Development in the Balkan Countries and the Role of Greece: From Bilateral Relations to the Challenge of Integration", *Discussion Paper Series*, No 1620, CEPR. University of London.

Petrakos G. and Pitelis C. (1997) Peripherality and Integration: The experience of Greece as a member of the European Union and Implications for the Balkan Economies in Transition, Paper presented in the Conference *Economic Co-operation in the Balkans: A Regional Approach to European Integration*, Phare-ACE Program, University of Thessaly, Department of Planning and Regional Development, Volos, 16-19 January 1997.

Petrakos G. and Zikos S. (1996) "European Integration and Industrial Structure in Greece, Prospects and Possibilities for Convergence", in Paraskevopoulos C. Grinspun R. and Georgakopoulos T. (eds) *Economic Integration and Public Policy*, pp. 247-259, Edward Elgar. London.

Petrakos G. Maier G. and Gorzelak G. (eds.) *Integration and Transition in Europe: The Economic Geography of Interaction*, Routledge. London.

World Bank (1994) *Trends in Developing Countries*, World Bank, Washington D.C.

World Bank (1995) *World Development Report 1995*, World Bank. Oxford University Press, Oxford.

World Bank (1996a) *Social Indicators of Development*, World Bank, The John Hopkins University Press, Baltimore and London.

World Bank (1996b) *World Development Report 1996*, From Plan to Market, World Bank. Oxford University Press, Oxford.

World Bank (1996c) *Trends in Developing Countries*, World Bank. Washington D. C.

World Bank (1998) *World Development Indicators*, World Bank. Washington D. C.

2 Intra-Balkan Trade and Economic Cooperation: Past Lessons for the Future

MARVIN JACKSON

Emeritus Professor, Department of Economics, Katholieke Universiteit Leuven, Belgium

Introduction

This paper provides a historical background to Balkan economic cooperation. Its aim is not only to summarize not readily available information, but also to distill from history possibly lessons that instruct present efforts to promote cooperation in the region and with the EU. What is the statistical record of trade within the region that provides the main quantitative indicator of economic cooperation? How are trade flows related to the level of development of countries within the region? What have been the relative contributions of the Balkan states and their complex of interests and the interests around and outside of the region itself. And does knowledge of political effort to encourage cooperation find a reflection in the record of trade?

The paper begins with a brief analytical overview that is intended to raise questions for the subsequent review of statistical and historical materials. The second section reviews available historical estimates of GDP per capita in order to compare Balkan economic development levels with the rest of Europe and adds calculations of the variations of trade dependency ratios and information on the shares European trade taken by the Balkans. The third section considers statistics on intra-Balkan trade shares in three period, before the First World War, in the interwar period, and in the period from 1966 to 1995. This consideration is limited to total exports and imports of each country and has not been extended as well to the commodity composition of trade, which is admittedly also an important aspect of economic cooperation. This section also seeks to identify factors influencing the trade shares, including the main efforts to establish formal means of Balkan cooperation during the last hundred years. The shares of intra-Balkan regional foreign trade are a main indicator of the intensity of economic interaction, recognizing that there are other aspects such as direct and portfolio investment that are important (but for which comparable data are difficult if not impossible to find). The final section summarizes the main forces affecting cooperation in the past, especially focusing on the interplay of forces inside and outside the region. Are there some lessons for both Balkan cooperation and integration into the European Union? And do they instruct us as the region is more intensively drawn toward the European Union (Jackson 1997).

Reference Points

Before turning to the historical statistical record it is   useful to   review the main findings of economists concerning the known statistical regularities about trade and economic development and the main forces that have affected trade across regions or between pairs of countries. When looking at statistics on the trade of Balkan countries one should have some reference as to whether a given country is trading more or less than might be expected, given its other economic parameters, and whether trade flows between pairs of countries might also be more or less than expected on the basis of what is known of the experience of other countries. Mistaken interpretations of economic statistics are quite common among the uninitiated.

Trade and Economic Development

A country's foreign trade is both a result of and a likely cause of that country's economic size and level of economic development. Both relations have been observed as the common tendencies across large numbers of countries and over long periods going back to the middle of the nineteenth century in countries with available statistics.

In one of the more ambitious studies covering 101 countries from 1950 to 1970, Chenery and Syrquin (1975) found that the ratio of exports to GDP, one measure of overall trade dependence, strongly depends on country population size and moderately depends on the level of GDP per capita. Thus, one can say that the normal expected relationships are for the ratio of exports to GDP falls as country population size increases and increases as GDP increases. Countries with big populations tend to be less dependent on foreign trade than small countries, other things being equal. Countries with higher incomes tend to be more dependent on foreign trade than lower income countries.[1]

Systematic statistical studies also show that the relationship between GDP per capita and trade goes the other way. That is, countries that increase exports tend to have higher growth rates than countries with a lower growth of exports (growth is "export-led"). But the matter is more complicated, as is shown by Sachs and Warner (1995) in estimations of growth equations for a sample of 122 countries for the period from 1970 to 1989.[2] More "open economies" that not only increase exports but also pursue liberal market policies, cut subsidies, and open domestic markets for foreign competition have increased growth rates. Also, such policies leads to convergence of poorer and richer countries by increasing growth rates of the poorer countries more than the richer countries.

Trade between Countries

Another important question is what is it that determines the amount of trade between any pair of countries. Classic international trade theory explains trade between any two countries as the result of different endowments of the factors of production that generates comparative advantages. Given the factor endowments of two countries, trade flows are then determined by transportation costs and size of markets. Such relationship have been tested in so-called "gravity models" which also attempt to measure the negative influence of trade barriers and the positive influence custom unions on trade flows between two countries (for an example applied to Eastern European see Hewett 1976).

Whereas classic trade theory assumes constant returns to scale, recent developments in trade theory and regional economics emphasize the importance of increasing returns to scale, both economies of technology and organization internal to the firm and external economies because of the spatial concentration or agglomeration of suppliers, labor, finance, and technology. With sufficiently low transportation costs, manufacturing industry tends to be concentrated in the regions or places of largest markets which export to other regions or places, resulting in the so-called core-periphery phenomenon (Helpman and Krugman 1985, Krugman 1991). Thus, countries that move first to start production have locational economies of scale and tend to become an industrial core while neighboring countries which have lagged in such development become a periphery with lower incomes resulting from activities that do not benefit from economies of scale.

Also, Helpman and Krugman (1985) observe that as countries become more similar, they tend to trade goods with similar factor proportions. Where product differentiation is important and factor proportions are similar, countries will tend to engage in intra-industry trade. Where product differentiation is important and where factor proportions are different, countries will tend to engage in inter-industry trade.

An Overview of Comparative Development Levels 1913 to 1914

There is admittedly more to the description of comparative development levels than looking at comparative levels of GDP per capita if for no other reason than the chances for distortions and misinterpretation of the numbers. Nevertheless, when one has time to look at only one measure of development, it is widely agreed that GDP is a meaningful indicator of general conditions, especially the productivity of various economies.

Where Are the Balkans Now?

Table 1 considers the current situation in Europe. Its first three columns show different comparisons with the average of EU member countries with data from EBRD that, in turn, draw upon both the World Bank Atlas 1996 and a new round of results from the European Comparison Program (ECP).

The ExRate is based on national data converted to 1994 USD on the basis of average existing annual exchange rates of domestic currencies with the USD. It is known that such exchange rates are defective indicators of relative GDP because the exchange rate can be a distorted view of domestic purchasing power (reflecting the varying the importance of non-traded goods and services in GDP, capital movements, and speculative influences on the market value of currencies). The USD, for example, is under valued compared to European currencies according to the OECD calculations of purchasing power parity (PPP). Purchasing power parity is the ratio of the cost of a common market basket of goods and services in two different currencies.

It is also known that the gap between estimates in current market exchange rates and estimates based on PPP normally varies with the level of GDP per capita, being greater in poorer countries than in richer countries.

The gap or the ratio of the two ways of expressing the value of a given currency in the exchange rate deviation index. One can easily see this in the table.

Table 1 Indicators of Relative European Economic Development

	Relative GDP per Capita 1994			Share of Labor Force in Agriculture	Share of GDP in Agriculture
	ExRate	PPP	PPP*	1990	1994
EU average****	100	100	100	5	2
Italy	93	102	9	3	
UK	89	100	2	2	
Ireland	66	80	14	8	
Spain	64	77	12	3	
Portugal	45	68	18	na	
Greece	37	62	23	16	
Turkey***	15	31	53	16	
Albania**	2	55	55		
Bulgaria	6	23	26	13	12
FYRMacedonia**	4	21	na		
Romania	6	16	20	24	20
Croatia	12	21	16	11	
Hungary	19	35	33	15	7
Slovenia	34	54	6	5	
Czech Republic	15	43	47	11	6
Slovak Republic	11	36	36	12	7
Poland	12	29	27	27	6
Estonia	14	39	21	14	10
Latvia	11	28	17	16	15
Lithuania	7	18	21	18	21

Sources: PPP* calculations are based on EBRD, Transition Report 1996. ExRate, PPP and GDP shares are based on World Bank Atlas 1996. Labor force data are from the World Bank Development Report 1996.

Notes: ExRate is based on conversion of national data to dollars at average annual exchange rates. PPP is based on conversion of national data to dollars according to relative purchasing power ratios.
   * Based on estimates of the European Comparison Program.
   ** No available PPP data for Albania or FYROM.
   *** Turkey from OECD data and estimated for 1994.
   **** Calculated by the author as the unweighted average of 15 member countries.

Estimates of the dollar amount of GDP per capita in terms of PPP are lacking for FYR Macedonia and Albania. The exchange rate deviation index in their cases probably lies somewhere between the extremes of 4 shown by Bulgaria and 2 shown by Turkey. Most likely they would be somewhere in the range 3.0-3.5, but it is best not to speculate because the gap can change abruptly when national trauma occurs, as recently in Albania.

In the case of the two comparisons in terms of PPP, the PPP* comes from a more recent round of the ECP. It features radical declines in the cases of Estonia and Latvia, plus some mild increases in the relative GDP per capita of Romania and Bulgaria. In the Bulgarian case is probably a systematic over estimation of GDP per capita, both currently and in 1992 and 1973 data in Table 2 (Jackson 1991).

Table 2 Relative Levels of GDP per Capita

Countries	Relative to the West European Average					
	1870	1913	1929	1950	1973	1992
West European average	100	100	100	100	100	100
UK	164	145	121	124	103	90
Ireland	89	78	66	64	60	67
Portugal	55	39	35	39	65	64
Spain	69	65	68	43	75	72
Italy	74	72	69	62	89	93
Greece	na	47	55	35	67	59
Turkey	na	28	22	24	23	25
Bulgaria	na	34	27	30	45	23
former Yugoslavia	na	41	31	28	36	22
Romania		41	26	21	30	15
Czechoslovakia	59	60	70	64	60	39
Hungary	64	60	57	45	48	32
Poland			49	44	46	27
Sweden	84	89	89	122	115	97
Russia/USSR	52	43	32	51	52	27

Sources: Calculations based on Jackson (1982 and 1986), and Maddison (1995).

If one includes Slovenia in the Balkans (there are doubtful grounds for doing this), the region's extreme countries, Greece and Slovenia, both have about 60 percent of the EU average GDP per capita. Bulgaria, Croatia, and Romania have 20-25 percent, rather much poorer, while Albania, FYROM, and Bosnia-Hercegovina are even poorer, perhaps about 10 percent. One can only guess that when the FYR (Serbia and Montenegro) have statistics, they will be at about the 20 percent of EU level. What is surprising in the table is to find Estonia, Latvia, Lithuania, and Poland at about the Bulgarian, Croatian, and Romanian levels.

An aspect of lower levels of development seems to be the higher shares of employment and GDP in agriculture. Bulgaria, nevertheless, is relatively poor even with its smaller shares of labor and production in agriculture. And Portugal achieves higher income than Slovenia even though its agricultural shares of labor and production are higher.

Where Have the Balkans Been?

Table 2 assembles historical data from the work of Maddison (1995) to which are added estimates of the Balkan countries in the interwar period (Jackson 1982 and 1986). Maddison's data end in 1992 and are expressed in terms of 1990 dollars of constant purchasing power.

During the period, 1913 to 1950, per capita GDP in the Balkans declined compared to the Western European average. Romania did the worst, followed in this negative sense by Yugoslavia. In comparison, Greece fared rather better and Bulgaria the best at least from 1913 to 1929. The small and less developed countries did better than the larger and slightly more developed countries (Jackson 1982, Lampe and Jackson 1982). Nearly all the countries shown in the table did worse than the Western European average. Not Sweden, clearly, which is a success story.

The period after 1950 shows a different pattern up to 1973. Western Europe has its "growth miracle" into which is pulled Greece. The UK and Sweden seem to be left out. The Central European and Balkan countries share a milder form of catching up, which is most pronounced in Bulgaria. But the view of their relative performance in the table represents figures from Maddison (for the OECD) which have been for some of the known upward biases in the growth rate estimates he uses. Even with such adjustments one must remain suspicious of the figures for 1973; a thorough re-examination of these data are needed.

After 1973 up to 1992, Greece along with Portugal and Spain stop catching up with the Western European average. While this appears as a mild form of relative stagnation, in the former communist-ruled countries, as known, both relative and absolute collapse set in, although it remains to be seen just when, how much, and how much can be quickly recovered.[3] Historically the transition countries, including the Balkans, are the lowest levels recorded in modern times with respect to the West European average.

Table 3 gives a view of merchandise exports as a percentage of GDP over the long run. There is considerable diversity in the experiences of the Balkan countries. Greece and former Yugoslavia, except for 1950, have generally rising exports in GDP, an experience they share with Southern and Central European countries. Bulgaria and Romania appear to reach high ratios in 1973, but their exports figures might be exaggerated.

Table 3 Merchandise Exports as a Percentage of GDP

	1870	1913	1929	1950	1973	1992
Greece	3.3	5.7	3.6	6.3	9.0	
Turkey	9.4	9.2	3.5	3.7	5.7	
Bulgaria	16.7	6.1	5.7	17.3	14.8	
Romania	8.2	10.0	9.2	12.2	7.4	
Yugoslavia	1.6	6.7	3.6	7.7	15.0	
Portugal	5.0	6.0	4.3	6.1	8.4	16.8
Spain	3.6	5.1	5.6	3.4	5.1	11.5
Ireland	24.8	11.5	29.5	69.6		
Czechoslovakia	13.4	10.6	14.1	10.2		
Hungary	8.0	8.4	13.8	17.8		
Poland	5.0	6.2	8.6	7.4		
USSR	2.8	4.3	1.9	2.1	3.4	3.0

Sources: Calculated from data in Maddison (1995) and Jackson (1982 and 1986) with adjustments in 1973 for the over valuation of East European exchanges with respect to the USD.

There are no estimates of the Chenery-Syrquin variety (see next Section) of what might have been considered a "normal expected" ratio of exports to GDP before the Second World War. It is worth repeating that "normal expected" has no normative meaning, but refers to what would be expected on the basis of each country's size and GDP/capita if a regression had been made across a large sample of countries during these years. No doubt the normal curve in the interwar period would have been lower than after 1950 when there were efforts to reduce trade barriers through the GATT, the IMF/World Bank and other international agencies.

After 1950 a number of countries in Table 2 and Table 3 change from market to planned economies. In this case estimates have been done of possible effects of planning and socialist ownership (plus communist policies) on trade dependency. Most estimates show that planned economies have lower than normal overall foreign trade dependency ratios (as measured by the ratio of exports plus imports to GDP). This difference showed up in the coefficient for a dummy variable when the author did regressions for a sample of about 80 countries for the years 1960 to 1985 (Jackson 1987). Table 4 illustrates the differences by using the regression to estimate a "normal" ratio of import/GDP and then compares it with the actual import/GDP ratio for each country in the table.

Of course, some not-planned economies also had below expected trade/GDP ratios and lower than some planned economies - Bulgaria and Yugoslavia, for example, have higher ratios than Spain and Turkey. It was surprising to find Hungary with such low ratios, but it was not a surprise to find Romania, Poland, and the USSR so low.

Table 4 Deviations from Normal Import Dependency (1975 and 1980)*

Countries	1975	1980
Bulgaria	0.95	0.80
Czechoslovakia	0.77	0.63
GDR	0.74	0.60
Hungary	0.56	0.51
Poland	0.70	0.54
Romania	0.66	0.73
USSR	0.46	0.40
Yugoslavia	1.18	0.85
Greece	0.87	0.76
Portugal	1.04	1.29
Spain	0.88	0.79
Turkey	0.69	0.65

Source: Jackson (1987).

* The numbers represent the ratios of the actual imports to a "normal" level of imports which is estimated   on the basis of cross-section regressions using about 80 countries.

There is a major problem in estimating comparable trade data for the former communist-ruled countries. The data in dollars compiled by the United Nations for the former communist-ruled countries are derived by converting the country data which are in special devisa accounting units (such as the so-called convertible ruble, which was never really convertible). Because the devise units were over valued, this caused the dollar figures to be biased upward. Hewitt (1974) figured the over valuation in 1970 was about 20 percent while both Marer (1972) and Vanous (1982) think it was more. The conservative approached is followed by adjusting the 1973 data by multiplying Maddison's figures by 0.80 and the resulting figures might still be over estimated. In 1985, as evidence, Hungary, Poland, and Czechoslovakia applied in their trade data cross rates of about 1.8 rubles per USD, whereas the official Soviet rate was only 0.61 rubles per USD

Table 5 Shares of European Exports

	*1870	*1913	1929	1950	1973	1992
Total Europe	100.00	100.00	100.00	100.00	96.89	100.00
Greece	**0.22	**0.21	0.57	0.37	0.48	0.54
Turkey	*1.51	0.88	0.87	0.65	0.43	0.83
Bulgaria	**0.15	0.88	0.29	0.47	0.87	0.29
Romania	0.98	1.21	1.08	1.22	0.98	0.24
Yugoslavia	**0.18	**0.17	0.87	0.63	0.75	0.79
Portugal	0.68	0.35	0.30	0.76	0.61	1.03
Spain	2.34	1.71	2.54	1.58	1.72	3.16
Ireland	1.40	0.83	0.70	*1.62		
Czechoslovakia	3.78	3.17	1.59	0.62		
Hungary	1.13	1.34	0.89	0.58		
Poland	1.97	2.58	1.68	0.75		
USSR	6.64	7.31	3.00	7.33	5.67	2.30
Other Europe	87.31	87.28	82.21	79.09	80.51	87.26

Source: Author's calculations from Maddison (1996).
Notes: * Percentages in 1870 and 1913 are not comparable with later years because of changes in the countries covered.
    ** Substantially smaller areas than in later years.

(Jackson, Linotte and Zahradnik 1993). This suggests the ruble could have been officially overvalued by a factor of as much as 3. If the 80 percent of Bulgaria's trade which was done with other CMEA countries was reduced by a factor of 3 (or even 2) it would drastically cut Bulgaria's trade dependency and ratio of exports to GDP.

Table 5 gives a historical view of the shares of total European exports of the respective countries. Be warned, for obvious reasons, that the percentages for 1870 and 1913 should not be compared with those for following years when more countries are included in the comparison.

Trade shares in 1992 are lower than they were in 1929 for the Balkan (just equal in Bulgaria's case) and Central European countries. The decline in Romania, like in the case of the Central European countries, is continuous in the long term. Greece and former Yugoslavia show a big decline from 1929 to 1950 and then increases in 1973 and 1992. Transition seems to help them. Bulgaria, again, shows up a special case because of the high apparent share in 1973. If one would reduce its ruble trade to only one-third of the dollars used by the United Nations statistics, then its share would be from 0.35 percent to 0.40 percent and more consistent with the other data.

Intra-Regional Balkan Trade and Efforts at Balkan Cooperation

The Balkans have been subjected to at least four extremely powerful external forces in modern history which have affected their economic relations with each other: (1) their five hundred years of domination by the Ottoman Empire from which they were emerging after 1830, (2) the First World War followed by the collapse of the international trade and payments systems in the interwar period, (3) the imposition of war-time controlled economies in the Second World War followed by the divisions of territory at Yalta, the division of the Iron Curtain, and the imposition of communist policies and control institutions, and (4) the sudden collapse of the communist system, transition, and equally sudden intensification of linkages with the EU. Greece was an obvious exception in the third and fourth stages, having liberalized in the 1950s and in the 1960s having begun integration with the EC culminating in membership in the 1980s.

41

The Development of the Balkan Region

Before the Second World War

The process of "opening" the Balkan economies was linked to their being freed from restrictions on agrarian relations, crafts and manufactures, domestic and external trade that were linked to Ottoman sovereignty which in 1830 gave Greece, two Romanian principalities, and Serbia semi-autonomous status. Full independence came in 1880 at which time an independent Bulgaria also emerged. But the last Ottoman presence from Albania, parts of Serbia, Bulgaria, Romania (on the Black Sea coast), Greek Macedonia and Thrace, and the present territory of FYROM was removed in the second Balkan War (1913) and the treaties ending the First World War (1918).

Opening also required the development of low cost transportation into and within the region for only Greece was effectively connected to the rest of the world and among its own parts by sea transport. The Danube forming a border between Romania and Bulgaria was not bridged until after the Second World War. Although the river offered potentially cheap transportation to the grain regions of Romania and Bulgaria, movement was impeded both in its upper course by the Iron Gates rapids and by silting and shifting channels at its mouth on the Black Sea.[4] The upper course problem remained, while the lower course silting was remedied in 1860 leaving Romania's cheapest transportation leading out of the region and towards West European ports. Only Serbia had the river's access into Central Europe, but that also channeled its trade away from the region.

Railroads came slowly into the region. The first in 1869 connected Bucharest with the Danube river port, Giurgiu. By 1879 connections were made with the capital over the mountains to (Hungarian dominated) Transylvania, west to Turnu-Severin, and northeast to Iasi and towards the Russian border. By 1888 the Orient Express was finished through Serbia and Bulgaria. A line also connected the Danube port, Ruse, with the Varna on the Bulgarian Black Sea and finally the capital Sofia with both ports, Varna and Burgas. Transportation allowed better connections of capital cities and their markets (which were heavily dependent on government expenditures) with the rest of the world than either to other cities in the region or within each country's economy (Lampe and Jackson 1982).

Another factor affecting the region's trade with other countries was customs tariffs. In 1913 average rates did not exceed 25-33 percent for Bulgaria, Romania, and Serbia (calculations of the author in Lampe and Jack-

Table 6 Balkan Intra-Regional Trade Shares (1906 to 1938)

(percent)

	Exports	Imports	Total*		Exports	Imports	Total*
Albania				Greece			
1921-25	23.6	22.3	23.0	1906-11	5.0	8.6	6.8
1926-30	25.1	12.2	18.7	1911-13	10.3	4.9	7.6
1931-34	17.4	12.2	14.8	1921-25	5.7	12.7	9.2
1935-38	14.9	21.3	18.1	1926-30	2.3	17.8	10.1
Bulgaria				1931-34	4.3	15.4	9.8
				1935-38	6.8	14.9	10.8
1906-10	35.0	18.8	26.9				
1911-14	18.9	12.2	15.6	Romania			
1915-18	9.0	18.6	13.8	1906-10	5.9	4.4	5.2
1921-25	25.9	14.7	20.3	1911-14	6.4	3.3	4.9
1926-30	14.3	11.2	12.8	1921-25	12.4	4.2	8.3
1931-34	2.7	7.3	5.0	1926-30	8.7	1.7	5.2
1935-38	1.9	4.8	3.3	1931-34	6.0	2.6	4.3
Yugoslavia				1935-38	7.6	2.8	5.2
1912	16.9	5.5	11.2				
1921-25	8.4	6.7	7.6				
1926-30	9.0	5.1	7.1				
1931-34	6.2	4.0	5.1				
1935-38	5.3	4.6	4.9				

Source: Calculated by the author from official country data.
　　* The total is the simple average of imports and exports.

son 1982). In general they were not higher than in the rest of Europe and would have been low enough to fit the criteria of an "open economy" of Sachs and Warner (1996).

Proposals for cooperation among the Balkan interest groups date back into the Ottoman period and since then there have been numerous calls and proposals for cooperation by individual statesmen and scholars from the region. One of the earliest actions was an effort to form a Balkan League against Ottoman Turkey under the sponsorship of Michael III of Serbia which lasted just two years 1866-68, before his death and Great Power opposition led to its abandonment. The first effort to form a customs union, one between Serbia and Bulgaria agreed to in 1905, was aborted because of Austrian pressure on the Serbs (Lampe 1996). A second

Balkan League in 1912 gained a measure of success in military cooperation against Turkey only to collapse when the second Balkan War broke out against Bulgaria in 1913.

A first view of intra-regional trade shares in Table 6 shows only a short prewar interval before the First World War for Greece (on smaller territory), Bulgaria, Romania's Old Kingdom, and Serbia. Greece's trade share with the region is very small and probably reflects its lack of connections as well as its cheap sea routes everywhere else in the world. Why Bulgaria has such high regional shares in exports is more difficult to explain. Perhaps this reflects its unique position of being more or less in the center of the Balkans. Also, it suggests possible lack of exports demanded in the markets of the rest of Europe.

The First World War and the Interwar Period

Peace of 1918 saw the end of the Habsburg Empire, the region's largest economic and political union of 51 million people. At the same time, the formation in 1918 of the first Yugoslavia (which began as the Kingdom of the Serbs, Croats, and Slovenes) might well be considered the most successful effort at political and economic cooperation in the region so far even though it failed to survive.

Romania also acquired significant new territories in Transylvania and the Banat on the west and north, Bucovina and Bessarabia on the north and east, and in Dobrugea on the Black Sea coast. While the new territories of both countries which had been part of the Habsburg Empire were relatively better endowed with rail transportation than prewar Serbia and Romania, the new states faced major problems in connecting the pieces together and repairing damage, especially to rolling stock, at the very time they were being asked to repay wartime debts. Bulgaria, as the one on the wrong side in the war, faced demands to pay huge reparations that more than mortgaged all of its abilities to generate domestic revenues and the necessary balance of payment surplus. Greece, on its side, faced resettling a million refugees from the war with Turkey in 1922. None of the region's countries had easy access to the financial means for improving transportation systems.[5]

Not surprisingly, Bulgaria even more than the others felt compelled to raise levels of tariff protection giving it by 1927 and 1931 Europe's highest rates for foodstuffs, semi-manufactures, and manufactures. Romania's lower rates still put it at the upper end of the scale of European countries. Yugoslavia's rates were still lower, making it more or less average for Europe.

Looking again at intra-regional trade shares in Table 6, after 1918 compared to before 1913, Greece and Romania tend to have somewhat greater trade shares with neighbors after the war than before in contrast to Bulgaria and Yugoslavia. Greece stands out because its trade shares with neighbors do not fall. Perhaps this reflects its lack of common boundaries before 1918. Also, Greece becomes a special case because of the importance of emigrant remittances in its balance of payments. Possibly the tightening of immigration rules in the US and Western Europe plus the economic crisis forces it into more trade with its neighbors.

In contrast, the intra-regional shares of Romania, Yugoslavia, and Bulgaria fall on into the 1930s. Romania and Yugoslavia both acquired important territories from the dissolved Austro-Hungarian Empire which had strong trade ties with Central Europe. Both also were endowed with important mineral resources which become targets for capital investments and sources of exports with the industrialized countries. All of this might have diverted trade outside the Balkans.

Bulgaria stands out by the extent of the decline in its regional trade. This coincides with a pronounced fall in its total exports/GDP ratio (as shown in Table 3). It also was the most alienated state, having been beaten by the others in the Second Balkan War, on the losing side again in the First World War, having the most difficulties with war and reparations debts in the 1920s, and finally having provided the main resistance to the 1930 proposals for economic cooperation. It was also the most penetrated by special trade relations with Nazi Germany.

There was no shortage of proposals for Balkan cooperation, as a preferred option to special deals with the great powers. Soon after the end of the First World War, a number of prominent Balkan leaders (Titulescu in Romania, Radic in Croatia, Stambuliski in Bulgaria, as well as Papanastassiou, Milonas, and Stephanopoulos in Greece) proposed setting up formal means for cooperation (Wallden 1993, Bookman 1996). A Greek initiative to organize in 1930 the First Balkan Conference in Athens considered a Yugoslav-Romania proposal to create a customs union, which was followed by meetings in Istanbul, Bucharest, and Salonika (Wallden 1993, Lampe 1996). A Balkan Tobacco Office set up in 1932 failed in its attempt to cut excess exports. Bulgaria proved intransigent to wider cooperation with its claims on Macedonian territory and an Aegean outlet. Finally Greece, Yugoslavia, Romania, and Turkey signed an agreement in Athens in 1934, which even provided a permanent Council, a Balkan bank, and legislative coordination. Unfortunately, Italy opposed and when it was supported by France that feared pushing Mussolini into German arms, the Conference weakened and collapsed (Castellan 1992). In fact, it did not succeed practically in overcoming the growing state interference in foreign trade and finance that was promoted especially by growing German influence in the region (Lampe and Jackson 1982, Geschkoff 1940).

The 1930s witnessed a strong shift in exports to Germany/Austria. Bulgaria, in fact, started the shift in the late 1920s and led the way (from 41 percent to 68 percent of its total trade). Greece was also pulled into the German trading orbit with its export share rising from 19 percent to 40 percent followed by Romania with a shift from 17 percent to 32 percent. While Yugoslavia's share rose from 28 percent to 42 percent in 1938, it fell to only 32 percent in 1939. German penetration of Balkan markets was helped by the collapse of the Gold Standard in 1931 and the general resort to exchange controls and clearing agreements for trade. Between 1934 and 1938 an average of 84 percent of Bulgaria's trade was in clearing agreements. For Romania and Yugoslavia the share was about 75-77 percent and for Greece a still dominant 63 percent. Thus, the countries that were enveloped in a Soviet-style foreign trading and payments system after the war already had some significant experience (Lampe and Jackson 1982).

The Second World War and the Cold War

Although the first Yugoslavia was destroyed (principally) by German force, provocation, and unleashing of nationalist extremists, this did not prevent the formation of a second Yugoslavia (Lampe 1996b). During the Second World War in 1942 Yugoslav and Greek Communists proposed a Balkan Union although its real purpose might have been reflected in a remark to the Soviet ambassador by Kerdelj, then Yugoslav foreign minister, that Yugoslavia ought to join the Soviet Union in the future. Stalin is said to have proposed that Tito absorb Albania into Yugoslavia. There was also proposed an extension of the South Slav Union to Bulgaria which was the subject of a Bulgarian-Yugoslav treaty of 1947 (Singleton 1985, Bookman 1996, Detrez 1992). Both ideas failed in Tito's break with Moscow, against the opposition of Great Powers and the failure of Greek Communists to come to power.

New terms for the region were set by Truman's massive aid to Greece and Turkey in 1947-48. At the same time Tito's break with Stalin led to Yugoslavia's expulsion from the Cominform and the severing of trade with the communist block. Tito closed the border for Greek guerrillas in 1949 and soon Yugoslavia also gained American assistance as well as MFN in American markets (Lampe, Prickett and Adamovich 1990). Greece liberalized its foreign trade in 1953, the same year that America brokered the attempted Tripartite Balkan alliance of Greece, Turkey and Yugoslavia (Wallden 1993, 1994). It collapsed in 1955 as a result of renewed Greco-Turkic conflict and the rapprochement between Yugoslavia and the Soviet Union following Khrushchev's visit to Belgrade that same year.

Although eventually Yugoslavia became an observer to the CMEA in 1964, its better relationship with the East did not lead to a return to a Soviet-type system or to a loss of preferential status in the West. Yugoslavia was a founding member of the IMF/World Bank. In 1965 significant market reforms were undertaken, the same year it joined the GATT. In 1970 it was granted general preferences (GSP) by the European Community (the terms of which were significantly improved in 1980 and again in 1987).

Within the region, an opening of Greek trade with Yugoslavia had started after 1952 (Lampe 1996a). A Greek commitment to western markets which began with its own opening in 1953 brought it association status in the EC effective 1961 (Wallden 1994). Turkey's own association agreement came in 1962, although its relations with Greece remained restrained. In the 1960s bilateral relations between Greece and Bulgaria improved (ironically during the military rule in Greece between 1967 and 1974). This was accompanied by further Greek and Bulgarian proposals for formal cooperation mechanisms yet nothing came of these ideas (Clark and Farlow 1976).

Restoration of democracy in Greece came in 1974, a year before the Helsinki Agreements and a general warming of East-West relations. In 1976 Greek Premier Caramanlis organized an Athens Balkan meeting, said to be part of his image-building for the Greek application for full accession into the EC, which was signed in 1980 and effective in 1981. The Athens meeting focused on economic cooperation, but once again Bulgaria was the reticent participant (Albania did not participate). It took nearly four years for Athens to soften Bulgarian resistance. Then expert meetings were held on communications and telecommunications in Ankara in 1979, transport in Sofia in 1980, energy in Bucharest in 1982 and industrial cooperation in 1984 in Belgrade (Wallden 1994). But in spite of a lot of talk and protocol, the meetings led to no important policies or institutional commitments.

47

These were years when some positive measures to reduce barriers should have taken place. Besides Yugoslav international connections, Romania joined the IMF/World Bank in 1974 and in 1975 received MFN status from the U.S. Its contacts with the EC started seriously in 1976 and resulted in 1980 in a five year preferential agreement, which was lost in 1989. Yet, Romania's apparent opening did not lead to liberalization but only to its extreme isolation after being forced to reschedule international debts in 1982-83. In the late 1970s Sofia and Belgrade were quarreling over Macedonia. Tirana broke with Beijing in 1978. Tito died in 1980 and soon Tirana raised the Kosovo issue. Hoxha died in 1985, one year before Milosevic was elected head of the Serbian party and one year before he started real pressure in Kosovo. Turkish-Bulgarian conflict rose in the mid-1980s over the latter's treatment of its minorities thousands of whom went to Turkey where unassimilated they remained a problem. Growing nationalism in Yugoslavia added stress to the increasing failure of its economy and its inability to pay debts. After 1985 Bulgaria became the third communist-ruled country in the region to get into international debt problems. In 1988 Greece also was in political crisis.

The late 1980s would not seem like a particularly good time to make yet another effort at regional cooperation. Nonetheless, in 1988, on the eve of the collapse of communism in the region a Balkan Conference of foreign ministers of six states did meet in Belgrade to consider how greater cooperation could be of mutual benefit (Lampe 1996a). According to Walldin some 20 multilateral meetings were held before the end of 1989, including three at the ministerial level, but again without evident results (Wallen 1994). There was little interest in the regional process it seems (but quite a bit in conference protocal!).

By then the communist system was collapsing in Bulgaria and Romania and followed in Albania in 1990-91. Yugoslavia was seriously weakened. The federal communist party collapsed in January 1990, and war broke out after Slovenia and Croatia declared independence in June 1991. Sanctions were levied against Serbia in November (1991). War came to Bosnia-Herzegovina in 1992. Indecision by the other major powers, particularly the U.S., and Germany's hasty unilateral recognition of Slovenia and Croatia helped to destroy Yugoslavia a second time.[6] The U.S. was forced to recognize Bosnian independence. The uncontrolled collapse of political union once again invited atrocities by nationalist extremists on three sides (Stokes, Lampe and Rusinow 1996, Holbrooke 1998).

The Bosnian War soon brought sanctions against Serbia and a collapse of legal trade flows with neighbors. Greece's road traffic had already been repeatedly disrupted since 1989 by political strikes in Macedonia in support of Greek ethnic Slavs. There were provocations of course even before the Greek economic embargo of Macedonia in 1994 brought a further disruption (for example, President Grigorev's first foreign visit after being elected was to Ankara), but fortunately an American-brokered agreement between Athens and Skopje the same year (Holbrooke 1998).

Since 1989 there has been no shortage of proposals for regional cooperation. Yugoslavia was an original party in the Italian inspired Pentagonale grouping in 1989. A Danube Basin group was also formed in 1989. Turkey initiated the Black Sea Cooperation in 1990. The Adriatic Initiative between Italy and Yugoslavia in 1991 was joined by Greece and Albania. A Capathian-Euroregional group was formed in February 1993 of Hungary, Poland, Slovakia, and Ukraine with hopes that Romania would also join. War provoked Turkey's 1993 failed attempt to organize a Balkan Conference against Serbia (Bookman 1996). The same year, Serbia's Milan Panic proposed setting up a Balkan economic union which also landed on deaf ears. There have also been numerous meetings of Balkan ministers since 1990, but no evident results for regional cooperation (Wallden 1994).

What happened to Balkan intra-regional trade shares during these complex Cold War events? The data for the first years after World War II, when there are difficult problems in obtaining appropriate information, have not yet been compiled. Figure 1 is based on figures from the IMF, Direction of Trade (found in the Annex Tables 1 to 5 and Chart I). Also, whenever possible the incomplete information on the successor states of the former Yugoslavia have been taken from national sources and other papers prepared for this network. After 1992, only the Bulgarian data are adjusted to 1995 with information for Slovenia, Bosnia-Hercegovina, and FYR Macedonia (who knows what trade with Serbia was during the embargo?).

Comparisons with the interwar period. Bulgaria's intra-regional trade shares after 1965 are similar to what they were before 1925 when it was a market economy. In contrast Greek intra-regional trade shares are lower after 1965 than they were in before the war. Perhaps the Common Market pulled its trade out of the region. Romanian regional trade shares seem to be more or less constant in both periods. This also characterizes Yugoslavia, discounting the 1912 figure for Serbia. What "normally expected" trade shares

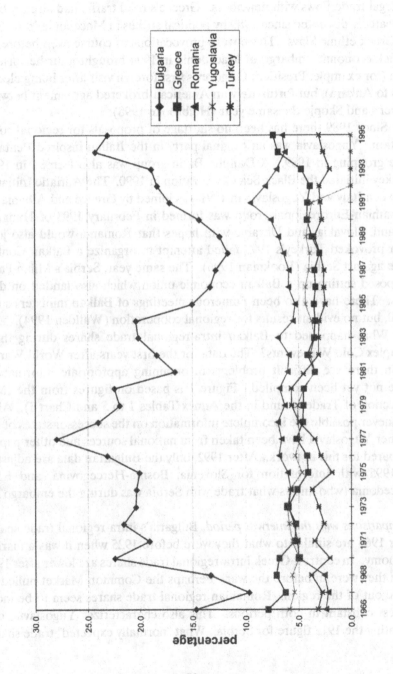

Figure 1 Balkan Regional Trade Shares: Average Percentage of Exports and Imports

would be has not been estimated. Is it possible that different sorts of restrictions were operating before and after the Second World War or are these the normal effects of distance, resource endowments, and economic development levels that are more or less independent of particular politics, institutions, and policies?

Differences across countries. What shows up after 1965 is a remarkable tendency for Bulgaria to have far larger shares of Balkan intra-regional trade than is the case with the other countries. Could this be a result of distance factors - that only Bulgaria is more or less surrounded by other Balkan countries?[7] Up to 1990 its most important Balkan trade partner is Romania, which could reflect their long common border. In reality, not only is the Danube River portion still crossed by only one railroad bridge (Giurgiu-Russe), but also trade under the communists was highly centralized and not conducted by individual traders around the border. In fact, under the communists even borders with other communist countries were a no-mans land. Hence, cross border marketing and cost advantages played no role.

Also, Bulgaria faced specific political barriers in Bulgarian-Romanian trade as was the case with other neighbors. It is a wonder that its trade shares were so high. Bulgaria and Romania had a narrower circle of trading partners than either Yugoslavia or Greece. Romania was not only Bulgaria's most important partner in the region, but turns out to have the second highest regional trade shares of the group (but significantly behind Bulgaria).

It is noteworthy that high shares of trade of Bulgaria and Romania with each other and in the region did not mean high absolute levels of trade with each other. Using a gravity model, Hewitt (1976) found trade between Bulgaria and Romania in 1970 to be only 60 percent of what would be expected had they been market economies with the same per capita income, population, and distance parameters. Romania's trade with its other neighbor, Hungary, was also significantly below the norm for market economies. By contrast, both countries' trade with other CMEA partners was a higher ratio (sometimes a much higher ratio) of "normally expected trade flows". Thus, in spite of the rough 10 percent of trade turnover Bulgaria did with Romania, the share was probably lower than it would have been had these countries both been market economies. Could their central planners find no "bargains" in neighboring countries, or did they overlook or even deliberately ignore neighbors?

Time trends after 1965. By the 1960s the worst of the Cold War's distortions of trade orientations had passed and significant efforts were being made on both sides of the Iron Curtain in Europe to promote trade and economic cooperation. While this might have had the effect of diverting trade from within the region, it could have promoted Greece's role.

Bulgaria's regional trade shares certainly were not reduced, but increased sharply from 1966 to hit a peak in the late 1970s. Then set in a strong decline which lasted until 1989, the year of transition. Is this the collapse of the former trading arrangements and favorable terms of trade with the Soviet Union or transition to markets, or both? If the missing data for Bulgaria trade with Serbia amounted to even a few percentage points then the region certainly has recovered from whatever caused the trade shares to fall in the 1980s.

A similar tendency shows up in the Greek shares of Balkan trade, although they are smaller overall. It is more difficult to see any marked trend in Romanian shares from 1965 up to transition. In the case of Yugoslavia, regional export shares are highest from 1971 to 1980 and then both import and export shares tend to decline. What pushed intra-regional trade shares up generally in the 1970s and then down in the 1980s? Was an unintended result of the Athens Balkan Conference in 1976 involved? And did Tito's death, Bulgarian conflict with Turkey, Greek political crisis, and Romania's debt problems add up to a diversion of trade away from the region? Or is this something coming from the outside? Is trade being diverted rather than pushed aside by intra-Balkan conflicts?

Transition clearly pushes Balkan intra-regional trade shares up in spite of the collapse of Yugoslavia and the Bosnian war. This is partly obscured by the lack of trade for the successor states. With trade officially embargoed it is doubtful if one will ever know the extent of trade with the new FRY (Serbia and Montenegro).

In 1994 and 1995 Bulgaria takes the largest shares ever of Greek imports and exports. Here are the good effects of transition and the freeing up of a once tightly controlled border - a long overdue normalization that should become more robust once Bulgaria's economy starts a sustained recovery. Most likely a similar stimulation of decentralization and marketization has taken place between all partners, with possibilities for multilateral trade that could never be easily managed under the communist system or, for that matter, under conditions of the 1930s.

Nevertheless it is too early to know what will happen if and when a sustained growth of output is once again possible in the whole region. Painful restructuring of industry, public utilities, and the urban infrastructure is needed in all the region except Greece and Slovenia. The transport system was never fully developed to European standards, as suggested by Table 7.

Table 7 The Status of Transportation in 1988

	Road km per km^2 of territory	share of motorways %	Rail km per km^2 of territory
Albania	0.23	0.0	0.018
Bulgaria	0.33	0.7	0.039
Romania	0.31	0.2	0.047
Yugoslavia	0.47	0.7	0.037
Czechoslovakia	0.57	0.7	0.102
Hungary	1.13	0.3	0.082
Poland	1.15	0.1	0.085

Source: Calculations from Hall (1993).

Here the generally lower levels of transportation development in the Balkans compared to Central Europe are clear. What is not shown are the lags of both regions compared to Western Europe. Evidence on the other specific shortcomings in this sector are catalogued in the 1996 issues of EBRD Transition Report and the World Bank Development Report.

Summarizing Balkan Intra-Regional Cooperation in View of the EU Enlargment Process

It is now appropriate to summarize the main forces affecting Balkan intra-regional cooperation, thinking specifically of the variations in the shares of intra-regional trade that have been reviewed in the paper and bearing in mind the main ideas introduced in the conceptual framework. Intra-regional trade shares are affected by both economics in a geographic context and political factors, both internal and external.

A. *Comparative levels of income and growth rates of GDP per capita.* The relatively low levels of income of the region would reduce intra-regional trade shares. On the other hand, if growth rates in the region were higher than in other trading partners, one should observe an increase in trade shares (this might have been the case for some periods before the Second World War and from the mid-1950s to the mid-1970s.

B. *Comparative population size, densities and growth rates.* The total Balkan population is not large compared to surrounding areas of Europe. It (excluding Turkey) roughly equals the population of Turkey or nearby Egypt. Compared to Western Europe it has a low density which tends to diminish the pull force of a given population. Again, this would tend to depress intra-regional trade shares, but if population growth rates were faster than in other trading partners, then trade shares would tend to be pushed up.

C. *Transportation cost (distance and geographic barriers).* While airline distances between population centers are not far and while Balkan countries share long common borders, transportation costs within the region have been relatively high both because of geographic factors (mountain terrain, location of rivers and lack of canal systems, location of ports compared to main population centers) and low levels of transportation system development. The lower cost of moving goods in and out of the region than within the region would depress regional shares. Probably this happened in recent years and have been unfavorable to intra-regional trade.

D. *Locational factors for manufacturing subject to economies of scale.* Economic research suggests that trade in manufactures should increase as a share of total trade in the earlier stages of development, then peak, and possibly decline (as trade in services becomes more important). Thus, at intermediate stages of development factors which might depress intra-Balkan trade in manufactures could also depress intra-regional trade shares. Nevertheless, the advantages of Northwestern and Central Europe as industrial first starters and with large, dense populations which encouraged the location of manufacturing subject to economies of scale did not preclude the interwar development a small, but rapidly growing manufacturing sector in the Balkans (Jackson and Lampe 1982). Of course, during the communist period manufacturing development was pushed by non-market forces (Jackson 1991). Unfortunately, the latter seem to have developed few if any sustainable first-mover advantages for any of the former communist countries (save possibly Russia).

E. *Conventional trade policy factors.* An intra-Balkan custom's union would have promoted intra-regional trade shares in conditions of a market economy. Otherwise, intra-regional trade shares would be affected by differences between intra-regional versus extra-regional tariffs and other trade barriers. Before and after the First World War up to the 1930s, general tariff rates were not higher (except for Bulgaria) than in other European states, but because rates were higher for agricultural products and semi-manufactures than for manufactures, in effect they would have depressed intra-regional trade. In the early 1930s custom tariffs became meaningless.

F. *Domestic politics and the international powers.* The international situation that emerged in 1918 placed large burdens on the still fragile and emerging political systems of the Balkan countries. The typical politician sought to get and hold power. In the 1930s forms of dictatorship prevailed. Internationally the great powers, and particularly re-emergent Germany sought special economic favors and attempted to cultivate their own supporters among the domestic political groups. With one country in the region played off against another and no counter-balancing international force, the political energy given to Balkan cooperation was clearly insufficient.

G. *Systemic factors.* Beginning in the 1930s and without interruption until 1990, currencies were inconvertible and currency controls were evoked. At the same time, foreign trade was managed under clearing agreements. It would have been possible under such arrangements even if the Balkan states would have agreed to have all trade as intra-Balkan trade. But under actual political arrangements, intra-regional trade shares were depressed. This was a combined result of the preferences of powerful trading partners, respectively Germany and the Soviet Union, and of national leaders who sought special advantages by "loyalty" to a great power. Under the communist system there were the further disadvantages of closed borders and highly centralized decision-making that tended to overlook possible bargains with neighbors (Jackson 1987).

One lacks, of course, independent estimates of a gravity model over the long period that has been reviewed so it is difficult to say what might have been "normal intra-regional trade shares" which would result from underlying economic and geographic factors. Rather, factors have been identified which might have increased or decreased intra-regional trade shares over this complicated history.

Turning now to the possible role of the EU in Balkan Cooperation, it is worth stressing the point that systemic factors dominated changes in Balkan intraregional trade shares in the 1980s just as systemic transition problems have played an important role up to now in the1990s. In the 1980s the external environment should have promoted closer cooperation and higher intraregional trade shares, but instead systemic weaknesses in the communist-ruled countries and intra-Balkan political conflicts reduced intra-regional trade shares. Transition since 1989 has witnessed an increase in intra-regional trade shares under conditions that have not been favorable, such as the Bosnian War and the initial fall in levels of production and income in the region, which has been more acute than in Central Europe. What transition has done, albeit too slowly, is to give free market agents a chance to respond to market forces and take advantage of some unused potential as defined by economic and geographic factors. Hence, with their more developed market institutions the Greeks and the Turks have played an initially dominate role in medium-scale capitalist development, although they have faced powerful competition from Germans and Italians, and, in terms of large scale development, multinational companies from all corners of the world.

How fast the unused potential will be used is a big question, as is what will happen afterwards. Stability with open economies in the former Yugoslavia (sans Slovenia) and Albania will determine how fast the used potential will be used up. Then it is likely that a limit will be reached in which structural constraints within the region will remain. These exist in the need to restructure industry and industrial enterprises and to develop an appropriate infrastructure, especially the transportation system.

A new dimension for economic cooperation is clearly offered by the process of the EU's extended presence (beyond Greece's membership and its earlier arrangements with Turkey, Yugoslavia, and Romania) in the region, including its association agreements with Romania and Bulgaria in 1993. In 1992 a non-preferential Trade and Cooperation Agreement was signed with Albania. A 1996 Cooperation Agreement with the FYR Macedonia came into force in 1997. A full custom union was also concluded with Turkey, although the aid provisions of that agreement were held up. There are, of course, three other states in the region - Bosnia and Herzegovina, Croatia, and FR Yugoslavia, which have had no formal relations with the EU. In its recent position paper with respect to these three states the European Commission takes a strong position in recommending these states to conclude a regional cooperation agreement (European Commission 1996). The document says that the subject countries "will have to undertake to adopt reciprocal measures, particularly regarding the free movement of goods and persons and the provision of services, and to develop projects of common interest. Through this regional approach, financial aid from the European Union could be oriented towards jointly defined and cross-border projects."

Furthermore, the document suggests that other states in the region should take an interest and even participate in such agreement. Again, to quote: "Neighboring countries which so wish should be able to be associated in the cooperation by appropriate means." Thus, this document and other policies suggests that the EU takes a strong interest in Balkan regional political and economic cooperation. But there are two rather big problems when one considers the whole set of influences emanating from the EU.

First, some individual countries have a much stronger interest and much more to gain by putting first priority on their bilateral relations with the EU and would want to avoid any negative spillovers which might come if initiatives with neighbors went sour. This surely would be the case with Slovenia, Romania, and Bulgaria (all with European Agreements) that might be trying to differentiate themselves from the "bad actors".[8] This has to be a major consideration with Croatia as well.

Second, considering all interests and all available programs, including the process of EU enlargement (Jackson 1997), what is more likely to happen - development of a stronger Balkan region in which regional markets and spillovers promote economic growth and institutional change or increasing penetration of the Balkans by the rest of Europe, especially stronger neighbors, so that the Balkans become a more or less permanent periphery? The example of Greece integrated as a small semi-isolated country should be instructive in these regards (see Petrakos and Pitelis 1997).

But it is clearly a different world than before 1990 or in the interwar period. Free trade in industrial products for the region appears the consequence of Greece's EU membership, Slovenia's coming accession, the European Agreements of Bulgaria and Romania, and the custom union with Turkey. The Central European Free Trade Agreement has also been extended to Romania and Bulgaria. While agriculture remains a bitter problem in the EU, most countries in the Balkans are or will be participants in the GATT and members of the World Trade Organization. Besides this, the IMF, World Bank, and the EBRD have great leverage.

The region's future can not easily be fathomed with the remaining dangers in Kosovo and Bosnia. Those unsettled conflicts and the continuing sanctions against the Yugoslav Republic (Serbia and Montenegro) are a cancer in the center of the region that can not easily be contained. The region's position is also weakened greatly by conflict between Greece and Turkey, mainly but not only over Cyprus. There is also worry over Turkey's relationship with the EU. One still must ask what can be done if those problems are not immediately resolved?

The network of ties with the EU and other multilateral agreements, as well as evident policies of the international agencies would make it unlikely that much could be gained by some sort of Balkan free trade agreement.

Thus, economic cooperation should be promoted by other means. Much has been said about the need to improve transportation, communication, and other infrastructures. In this case, a promising approach would be to create a Balkan framework through which both international assistance and EU regional-structural assistance could be planned and administrated. No structural assistance for one country in the region should be undertaken without considering possible conflict and complementarity with developments in neighboring countries.

In addition, the EU and the international agencies should give a regional priority to assistance for industrial and financial restructuring, and privatization. The future of major enterprises in one country should be considered within a regional context. Possibly regional consortiums should be promoted in privatization projects. These and other measures by the EU and the international agencies are necessary in order to counter the tendency, all to evident today, for Balkan agents, public and private, to see their relationships with such organizations as a zero-sum game.

Notes

1 These variables also affect the composition of trade. Increasing population tends to decrease the ratios of primary and service exports to GDP, but not shares manufacturing exports that tend to rise with country size up to a maximum of about 5 percent of GDP for a country of 15 million persons. As GDP per capita rises the ratio of primary exports to GDP falls, while the ratio of service and manufacturing exports to GDP rises. The ratios of total exports and total imports to GDP rise more slowly.

2 Their paper also finds these relationship in a more qualitative study going back to the middle of the nineteenth century.

3 The question is how much of the decline in from a demand side shock from which a recovery could be quite rapid and how much is a structural adjustment on the supply side in which capital structures of the former system simply do not meet market demands.

4 The Iron Gates is a constriction in the great river on the lower border of Romania with the former Yugoslavia and is now the site of a jointly constructed dam and hydroelectric generating station.

5 In the early 1920s privatization or a franchise to private investors might have provided a viable solution.

6 Even if a dissolution might have been eventually necessary it could have been negotiated within the framework of internationally recognized agreements and processes to ensure peace and human rights. For a clear review of the diplomatic framework see the early chapters in Richard Holbrooke's book (Holbrooke 1998). Holbrooke was the chief negotiator of the Dayton Accords.

7 Naturally this causes one to wonder if it reflects special ways of reporting data.

8   Also, countries in the region probably would like to avoid association with the adjective, "Balkan", which stirs up prejudice and images of bomb throwing revolutionaries, assassins, and fanatical dictators. Surely a better reference to the region is "South- eastern Europe", which, we note with satisfaction was chosen for the EU document

References

Bookman and Zarkovic, M. (1994), *Economic Decline and Nationalism in the Balkans,* Macmillan Press, London.

Castellan, G. (1992), *History of the Balkans,* East European Monographs, Boulder CO.

CEC (1996), Common principles for future contractual relations with certain countries in South-Eastern Europe. *Report from the Commission to the Council and the European Parliament,* Brussels, 02.10.1996.

Chenery, H., and Syrquin, M. (1975), *Patterns of Development 1950-1970.* World Bank Publication, Oxford University Press: Oxford, New York, London.

Clark, C. and Farlow, R. (1976), Comparative Patterns of Foreign Policy and trade: The Communist Balkans in International Politics. *Studies in East European and Soviet Planning, Development, and Trade,* No. 23., Bloomington in: International Development Research Center, Indiana University.

Cviic, C. (1991), Remaking the Balkans. *Chatham House Papers,* Royal Institute of International Affairs, London.

Detrez, R. (1992). *De Balkan: van Burenruzie to Burgeroorlog,* Hadewijch: Antwerp-Baarn.

Geshkoff, Theodore I. (1940), *Balkan Union, A Road to Peace in Southeastern Europe.* New York: Columbia University Press.

Hall, D. (1993), *Transport and Economic Development in the New Central and Eastern Europe,* Belhaven: London and New York.

Helpman, E. and Krugman, P. (1985), *Market Structure and Foreign Trade,* MIT Press: Cambridge MA.

Hewett, E. (1974), *Foreign Trade Prices in the Council for Mutal Economic Assistance,* Cambridge University Press: Cambridge.

Hewett, E. (1976), A Gravity Model of CMEA Trade. *In Quantitative and Analytical Studies in East-West Economic Relations,* Edited by J. Brada. Studies in Eastern European and Soviet Planning, Development and Trade No. 24. IDRC, Indiana University: Bloomington IN.

Holbrooke, R. (1998), *To End a War,* Random House: New York.

Jackson, M. (1982), National Product and Income Southeastern Europe before the Second World War. *Comparative Economic Studies,* Fall-Winter.

Jackson, M. (1986), Industrial Output in Romania and Its Historical Regions 1880 to 1930: Part II, 1913-1930. *Journal of European Economic History,* Vol. 15, No. 2 (Fall), 231-257.

Jackson, M. (1987), Economic Development in the Balkans since 1945 Compared to Southern and East-Central Europe. *Eastern European Society and Politics,* 1: 3 (Fall).

Jackson, M. (1991), The Rise and Decay of the Socialist Economy in Bulgaria. *Journal of Economic Perspectives,* Fall.

Jackson, M. (1997), What is Likely and What is Better - In, Half In or Out? Reflections on the Balkans and EU Enlargement. *LICOS Working Paper on Transition* No. 62. Faculty of Economics, Catholic University of Leuven, Belgium (forthcoming in Leuven Standpoints).

Jackson, M. and Lampe, J. (1982), A Survey of Evidence on Industrialization in Southeastern Europe, 1900 to 1950: The Cases of Bulgaria and Romania. *East European Quarterly*, XVI:4 (Winter 1982), pp. 1-45.

Jackson, M., Linotte, D. and Zahradnik, P. (1993), Payment Systems and the Recovery of Mutual Trade Between the Central and South-east European Countries and the CIS. *LICOS Working Paper on Transition and Institutional Change in Central and Eastern Europe No. 28.* Leuven.

Kaser, M. (1967), *COMECON: Integration Problems of the Planned Economies*, Oxford University Press, London and New York.

Krugman, P. (1991), *Geography and Trade.* Leuven University Press/MIT Press: Leuven and Cambridge MA.

Lampe, J. (1986), *The Bulgarian Economy in the Twentieth Century*, Croon Holm: London.

Lampe, J. (1996a), *Economic Integration versus Balkan Isolation: Southeastern Europe after the 20th Century*, unpublished paper.

Lampe, J. (1996b), *Yugoslavia as History: Twice There Was a Country.* Cambridge University Press: Cambridge.

Lampe, J. and Jackson, M. (1982), *Balkan Economic History: 1550 to 1950*, In: Indiana University Press, Bloomington.

Maddison, A. (1995), *Monitoring the World Economy 1820-1992*, OECD: Paris.

Marer, P. (1972), *Pricing Patterns in Socialist Foreign Trade.* In International Development Research Center, Bloomington.

Petrakos, G. and Pitelis, C.(1997), Peripherality and Integration: The experience of Greece as a member of the European Union and Implications for the Balkan Economies in Transition. Paper presented at the Conference *"Economic Cooperation in the Balkans: A Regional Approach to European Integration"*, Phare-ACE Program, University of Thessaly, Department of Planning and Regional Development, Volos, 16-19 January.

Sachs, J. and Warner, A. (1996), *Economic Reform and the Process of Global Integration.* Brookings Papers on Economic Activity. No. 1, 1-96, 108-118.

Singleton, F. (1985), *A Short History of the Yugoslav Peoples*, Cambridge University Press: Cambridge.

Stavrianos, L. (1964), *Balkan Federation*, Hamden, Conn: Archeon Press.

Stokes, G., Lampe, J. and Rusinow, D.(1996), Instant History: Understanding the Wars of Yugoslav Succession. *Slavic Review*, 55:1, Spring.136-160.

Turnock, D. (1986), *The Romanian Economy in the Twentieth Century.* Croon Holm: London.

Turnock, D. (1989), *Eastern Europe: An Historical Geography 1815-1945*, Routledge: London and New York.

Vanous, J. (1982), The Real Facts about Czechoslovak Foreign Trade. *Comparative Economic Studies*, 24: Spring.

Wallden, S.(1993), *The Balkan Countries in the International Division of Labour. The European Community and the Balkans*, Proceedings of the Conference, Corfu, Hellenic Centre for European Studies, 2-5 July.

Wallden, S.(1994), *Balkan Co-operation and European Integration.* Hellenic Centre for European Studies, Athens.

Appendix

Table A1 Shares of Bulgarian Trade with the Balkans

	Imports								Exports						
	Albania	Greece	Roman.	Turkey	Yugosl.	Region	Cyprus	Total	Albania	Greece	Roman.	Turkey	Yugosl.	Region	Cyprus
1966	0.0	4.4	0.0	1.3	9.9	0.0	0.0	100.0	0.0	4.6	0.0	2.2	12.7	19.5	0.1
1967	0.0	2.2	0.0	0.9	4.6	7.8	0.1	100.0	0.0	2.8	0.0	1.8	7.0	11.6	0.1
1968	0.0	2.7	0.0	1.4	7.0	11.1	0.2	100.0	0.0	6.2	0.0	2.0	7.2	15.5	0.3
1970	0.0	3.2	5.1	1.0	4.8	14.2	0.2	100.0	0.0	3.2	15.4	1.4	10.7	30.7	0.3
1971	0.0	1.8	5.7	0.9	5.9	14.4	0.2	100.0	0.0	2.9	9.9	1.4	9.7	23.9	0.2
1972	0.0	1.4	9.1	0.9	6.3	17.7	0.1	100.0	0.0	2.7	13.0	0.9	8.8	25.4	0.3
1973	0.0	1.8	9.4	0.9	5.7	17.7	0.2	100.0	0.0	2.6	12.1	1.2	7.3	23.2	0.3
1974	0.0	1.5	7.2	0.6	5.4	14.7	0.1	100.0	0.0	1.6	13.0	1.8	9.5	25.9	0.1
1975	0.0	2.2	6.5	0.5	3.7	12.9	0.2	100.0	0.0	2.5	14.0	3.1	7.7	27.3	0.1
1976	0.0	2.5	6.4	0.5	4.7	14.0	0.1	100.0	0.0	4.4	15.1	5.3	7.4	32.3	0.1
1977	0.0	3.1	11.7	1.1	3.4	19.3	0.0	100.0	0.0	4.7	20.7	3.7	7.7	36.7	0.1
1978	0.0	3.4	9.9	0.7	3.0	17.0	0.1	100.0	0.0	4.0	17.5	1.7	7.7	31.0	0.2
1979	0.0	3.2	8.8	0.4	4.0	16.5	0.1	100.0	0.0	4.1	12.5	4.2	6.6	27.4	0.2
1980	0.0	2.6	9.1	0.5	4.2	16.5	0.1	100.0	0.0	4.0	11.6	5.9	6.9	28.5	0.1
1981	0.0	1.9	5.7	0.4	4.4	12.4	0.2	100.0	0.0	1.5	9.6	2.7	7.2	21.0	0.1
1982	0.0	1.9	7.0	0.7	3.7	13.3	0.2	100.0	0.0	4.2	9.5	2.9	6.9	23.6	0.1
1983	0.0	1.7	8.2	0.8	4.7	15.4	0.2	100.0	0.0	3.4	11.1	5.1	5.3	24.9	0.1
1984	0.0	1.7	7.2	1.0	5.3	15.3	0.1	100.0	0.0	2.7	10.4	6.6	5.8	25.6	0.2
1985	0.0	1.2	5.0	0.2	4.1	10.5	0.0	100.0	0.0	1.2	10.3	3.5	4.5	19.5	0.1
1986	0.0	1.4	5.4	0.4	3.3	10.6	0.1	100.0	0.0	1.3	9.4	1.5	3.9	16.1	0.1
1987	0.0	0.9	5.7	0.3	3.0	10.0	0.1	100.0	0.0	2.4	9.1	0.3	3.8	15.6	0.1
1988	0.0	0.7	4.8	0.6	2.8	8.9	0.1	100.0	0.0	1.5	8.3	0.5	4.0	14.3	0.1
1989	0.0	1.7	4.1	0.6	2.9	9.3	0.3	100.0	0.0	2.2	8.2	0.1	5.1	15.5	0.1
1990	0.0	1.6	3.3	0.3	3.2	8.4	0.2	100.0	0.0	4.1	8.9	1.2	6.1	20.3	0.2
1991	0.0	3.3	2.5	1.3	5.8	13.0	0.2	100.0	0.0	6.6	2.7	3.0	9.0	21.4	0.3
1992	0.0	5.6	1.5	1.7	2.4	11.3	0.3	100.0	0.0	5.8	3.4	7.6	8.6	25.3	0.0
1993	0.0	7.1	2.6	1.6	1.6	12.9	0.2	100.0	0.0	7.6	2.8	7.8	6.7	24.8	0.7
1994	0.0	11.0	2.5	3.3	3.5	20.3	0.2	100.0	0.0	9.3	1.9	5.6	11.3	28.1	1.4
1995	0.0	10.8	1.2	3.6	3.4	19.0	0.2	100.0	0.0	8.5	1.4	8.5	8.7	27.1	2.2

Source: Author's calculations from IMF, Direction of Trade, annuals.
Data for 1966-69 do not include trade with Romania. Data for 1992-95 do not include trade with Croatia, Serbia, and Montenegro.

Table A2 Shares of Greek Trade with the Balkans

	Imports								Exports						
	Albania	Bulgar.	Roman.	Turkey	Yugosl.	Region	Cyprus	Total	Albania	Bulgar.	Roman.	Turkey	Yugosl.	Region	Cyprus
1966	0.0	1.1	0.6	0.5	2.0	4.2	0.0	100.0	0.0	4.6	1.8	0.0	5.2	11.6	0.4
1967	0.0	0.7	0.4	0.3	2.5	4.0	0.0	100.0	0.0	1.9	1.2	0.0	5.5	8.5	0.5
1968	0.0	1.4	1.1	0.2	3.0	5.8	0.0	100.0	0.0	2.3	1.3	0.1	4.8	8.5	0.3
1970	0.0	0.5	0.9	0.3	1.6	3.3	0.0	100.0	0.0	2.3	1.4	0.1	6.6	10.4	0.5
1971	0.0	0.6	0.7	0.3	1.7	3.3	0.1	100.0	0.0	1.3	1.5	0.1	4.5	7.5	0.6
1972	0.1	0.5	0.7	0.5	2.4	4.2	0.1	100.0	0.0	0.9	1.5	0.6	3.4	6.4	0.7
1973	0.1	0.5	1.0	0.6	1.4	3.5	0.1	100.0	0.2	1.0	2.1	1.2	4.1	8.5	0.7
1974	0.1	0.3	0.7	0.6	0.9	2.6	0.1	100.0	0.2	0.9	1.6	0.7	4.2	7.7	0.7
1975	0.1	0.4	0.5	0.0	0.5	1.5	0.1	100.0	0.2	1.4	1.8	0.1	3.1	6.7	0.7
1976	0.1	0.7	1.1	0.0	1.1	2.9	0.1	100.0	0.2	1.3	2.0	0.3	1.7	5.6	0.7
1977	0.1	0.8	0.8	0.0	1.9	3.6	0.1	100.0	0.3	1.5	1.7	0.5	2.9	6.9	0.8
1978	0.0	0.7	0.9	0.1	1.8	3.5	0.1	100.0	0.3	1.5	1.8	0.2	1.8	5.7	0.6
1979	0.1	0.8	0.5	0.2	1.6	3.2	0.1	100.0	0.3	1.5	1.4	0.8	1.8	5.9	0.7
1980	0.1	0.9	0.7	0.1	1.5	3.3	0.0	100.0	0.6	1.2	1.8	0.4	1.8	5.8	0.8
1981	0.1	0.4	0.5	0.2	0.4	1.6	0.1	100.0	0.3	1.2	1.8	0.3	1.7	5.3	0.8
1982	0.1	0.9	0.5	0.2	0.8	2.5	0.1	100.0	0.3	1.0	1.6	0.2	2.8	5.9	0.7
1983	0.2	0.7	0.3	1.2	0.8	3.2	0.1	100.0	0.2	1.0	1.2	0.3	1.2	3.9	0.7
1984	0.1	0.5	0.6	0.3	1.1	2.6	0.1	100.0	0.1	0.9	0.8	1.1	1.3	4.2	0.9
1985	0.0	0.3	0.6	0.2	1.0	2.2	0.0	100.0	0.2	1.0	0.9	1.2	1.7	4.9	0.8
1986	0.5	0.3	0.5	0.2	1.2	2.7	0.1	100.0	0.1	1.0	0.8	0.8	1.3	4.1	0.8
1987	0.1	0.5	0.5	0.3	1.5	3.0	0.2	100.0	0.1	0.6	0.7	1.6	1.0	4.0	0.7
1988	0.0	0.4	0.5	0.4	1.2	2.5	0.3	100.0	0.1	0.6	0.6	1.0	1.1	3.5	1.1
1989	0.1	0.4	0.4	0.8	1.4	3.1	0.4	100.0	0.3	1.0	0.7	1.1	1.4	4.3	1.1
1990	0.1	0.6	0.4	0.7	1.4	3.1	0.3	100.0	0.2	0.7	1.0	1.4	2.2	5.2	1.0
1991	0.1	0.7	0.4	0.8	1.1	3.0	0.2	100.0	0.1	1.0	1.0	1.2	1.9	5.2	1.2
1992	0.1	0.7	0.3	0.6	0.4	2.1	0.2	100.0	0.4	1.8	1.2	1.4	1.0	5.7	1.4
1993	0.1	1.0	0.3	0.7	0.0	2.1	0.9	100.0	1.4	3.3	1.0	1.6	0.0	7.3	1.3
1994	0.2	1.6	0.5	0.8	0.2	3.2	0.3	100.0	2.5	5.2	1.0	1.5	0.3	10.5	1.4
1995	0.2	1.5	0.7	0.9	0.0	3.2	0.3	100.0	2.7	5.7	1.2	1.9	0.0	11.4	0.9

Source: Author's calculations from IMF, Direction of Trade, annuals.

62

Table A3 Shares of Romanian Trade with the Balkans

Year	Imports								Exports						
	Total	Albania	Bulgaria	Greece	Turkey	Yugosl.	Region	Cyprus	Total	Albania	Bulgaria	Greece	Turkey	Yugosl.	Region
1966	100.0	0.0	0.0	0.6	0.3	1.4	2.3	0.1	100.0	0.0	0.0	0.6	0.4	1.7	2.7
1967	100.0	0.0	0.0	0.4	0.3	1.5	2.2	0.0	100.0	0.0	0.0	0.3	0.5	1.4	2.3
1968	100.0	0.0	0.0	0.4	0.6	1.4	2.3	0.1	100.0	0.0	0.0	0.9	0.5	1.4	2.9
1970	100.0	0.2	2.3	0.1	0.2	1.6	4.3	0.1	100.0	0.2	1.3	1.6	0.2	2.2	5.7
1971	100.0	0.2	1.8	0.1	0.2	2.0	4.4	0.1	100.0	0.2	1.3	1.3	0.1	2.9	5.9
1972	100.0	0.3	2.2	0.1	0.3	2.2	5.0	0.0	100.0	0.2	2.0	1.1	0.2	2.5	5.9
1973	100.0	0.2	2.0	0.8	0.3	2.3	5.6	0.1	100.0	0.2	1.8	1.8	0.5	2.1	6.3
1974	100.0	0.2	2.0	0.5	0.1	2.3	5.1	0.0	100.0	0.2	1.8	1.2	0.9	2.6	6.4
1975	100.0	0.1	2.0	0.8	0.1	2.0	5.1	0.0	100.0	0.2	1.4	1.6	1.7	2.5	7.0
1976	100.0	0.2	2.2	0.8	0.5	1.8	5.4	0.0	100.0	0.1	2.2	2.2	1.3	2.8	8.3
1877	100.0	0.2	3.0	0.7	0.3	1.4	5.6	0.0	100.0	0.1	1.9	1.5	1.4	2.6	7.7
1978	100.0	0.2	2.3	1.6	0.7	1.6	6.3	0.0	100.0	0.1	1.7	1.7	2.3	2.5	7.6
1979	100.0	0.2	2.0	0.6	0.4	1.4	4.7	0.0	100.0	0.2	1.8	1.8	2.3	1.9	7.9
1980	100.0	0.2	1.8	0.7	0.5	1.6	4.8	0.0	100.0	0.3	1.4	2.9	2.5	1.5	8.8
1981	100.0	0.2	1.7	0.8	0.4	1.2	4.3	0.0	100.0	0.2	1.6	2.5	1.3	1.2	7.8
1982	100.0	0.2	2.1	0.9	0.7	1.5	5.5	0.0	100.0	0.3	2.0	2.2	1.4	1.0	6.4
1983	100.0	0.4	2.6	0.6	0.8	1.7	6.1	0.0	100.0	0.3	1.6	2.9	1.0	1.1	7.7
1984	100.0	0.3	2.3	0.5	0.7	1.7	5.4	0.0	100.0	0.2	1.7	1.8	0.7	1.0	5.6
1985	100.0	0.3	3.0	0.5	0.5	1.6	5.9	0.0	100.0	0.2	2.2	1.0	1.0	1.1	4.7
1986	100.0	0.4	2.7	0.5	0.3	2.3	6.3	0.0	100.0	0.3	2.3	0.7	2.0	1.5	5.6
1987	100.0	0.3	2.7	0.7	0.4	1.3	5.4	0.0	100.0	0.3	1.9	0.8	2.2	1.1	6.4
1988	100.0	0.4	2.8	0.5	0.4	2.1	6.3	0.0	100.0	0.3	1.6	0.9	2.8	1.3	6.5
1989	100.0	0.4	2.6	0.5	0.6	1.8	5.8	0.0	100.0	0.3	1.9	1.5	2.8	1.7	7.9
1990	100.0	0.2	2.3	0.7	0.9	2.3	6.3	0.0	100.0	0.3	1.8	1.5	2.8	2.4	8.8
1991	100.0	0.1	1.1	1.7	1.6	3.7	8.1	0.3	100.0	0.1	1.4	1.2	3.6	4.5	10.8
1992	100.0	0.0	1.5	1.3	3.0	0.0	5.8	0.4	100.0	0.0	2.7	2.7	5.0	0.0	10.4
1993	100.0	0.0	1.1	1.1	2.3	0.0	4.4	0.2	100.0	0.1	2.1	1.7	5.7	0.0	9.5
1994	100.0	0.0	0.9	1.3	2.1	0.0	4.3	0.1	100.0	0.1	1.7	2.3	4.1	0.0	8.1
1995	100.0	0.0	0.7	1.5	2.4	0.0	4.7	0.3	100.0	0.1	0.9	2.6	4.5	0.0	8.2

Source: Author's calculations from IMF, Direction of Trade, annuals.

Table A4 Shares of Turkish Trade with the Balkans

Year	Imports							Cyprus	Exports						
	Total	Albania	Bulgaria	Greece	Roman.	Yugosl.	Region		Total	Albania	Bulgaria	Greece	Roman.	Yugosl.	Region
1966	100.0	0.0	0.9	0.0	0.7	1.2	2.8	0.0	100.0	0.0	1.1	1.2	0.7	0.6	3.6
1967	100.0	0.0	0.8	0.0	1.1	1.2	3.1	0.0	100.0	0.0	0.7	0.5	1.0	0.3	2.5
1968	100.0	0.0	0.8	0.1	1.1	0.8	2.9	0.0	100.0	0.0	1.1	0.7	1.8	1.1	4.8
1970	100.0	0.0	0.5	0.5	0.4	0.9	2.3	0.0	100.0	0.0	0.5	0.0	0.9	0.4	1.9
1971	100.0	0.0	0.9	0.9	0.9	1.0	3.7	0.0	100.0	0.0	0.4	0.0	0.6	2.2	3.3
1972	100.0	0.0	0.5	1.2	0.5	1.4	3.6	0.0	100.0	0.0	0.4	0.3	0.3	0.7	1.6
1973	100.0	0.0	0.3	0.3	0.4	0.8	1.9	0.0	100.0	0.0	0.5	1.5	0.7	1.6	4.4
1974	100.0	0.1	0.4	0.4	2.1	0.5	3.5	0.0	100.0	0.0	0.5	1.3	0.4	1.7	4.0
1975	100.0	0.0	0.6	0.0	1.3	0.4	2.2	0.1	100.0	0.0	0.5	0.0	0.5	0.5	1.5
1976	100.0	0.0	1.0	0.1	1.8	0.4	3.3	0.0	100.0	0.0	0.4	0.1	1.6	0.5	2.6
1977	100.0	0.1	0.7	0.3	2.0	0.7	3.8	0.1	100.0	0.0	0.8	0.1	1.5	0.9	3.2
1978	100.0	0.0	0.5	0.1	3.8	0.7	5.0	0.0	100.0	0.1	0.5	0.2	3.2	0.9	4.9
1979	100.0	0.1	1.6	0.5	4.6	0.9	7.7	0.0	100.0	0.0	0.3	0.2	1.7	1.4	3.6
1980	100.0	0.1	1.8	0.8	3.4	1.0	7.0	0.0	100.0	0.3	0.4	0.3	2.4	0.9	4.4
1981	100.0	0.1	0.7	0.2	4.1	0.6	5.7	0.0	100.0	0.1	0.2	1.0	1.2	0.5	3.1
1982	100.0	0.0	0.7	0.2	1.2	0.3	2.3	0.0	100.0	0.0	0.3	2.3	1.0	0.4	3.9
1983	100.0	0.0	1.1	0.2	2.0	0.3	3.6	0.0	100.0	0.0	0.4	1.0	1.0	0.3	2.7
1984	100.0	0.0	1.1	0.5	1.1	0.6	3.3	0.1	100.0	0.0	0.3	1.3	0.8	0.3	2.8
1985	100.0	0.0	0.9	0.4	0.6	1.0	2.9	0.1	100.0	0.0	0.1	1.0	0.6	0.4	2.1
1986	100.0	0.0	0.4	0.7	1.0	1.1	3.1	0.0	100.0	0.0	0.2	1.0	0.5	0.4	2.1
1987	100.0	0.0	0.1	0.9	1.6	1.3	3.8	0.1	100.0	0.0	0.1	0.6	0.5	0.2	1.4
1988	100.0	0.0	0.1	0.6	1.3	1.6	3.6	0.0	100.0	0.0	0.2	0.8	0.6	0.5	2.3
1989	100.0	0.0	0.0	0.6	1.5	2.4	4.5	0.1	100.0	0.0	0.2	1.1	0.4	0.7	2.5
1990	100.0	0.0	0.1	0.6	0.9	1.1	2.7	0.0	100.0	0.2	0.1	1.0	0.6	1.1	2.9
1991	100.0	0.0	0.7	0.4	0.9	0.7	2.7	0.0	100.0	0.1	0.6	1.0	0.8	0.6	3.1
1992	100.0	0.0	0.9	0.4	1.1	0.4	2.7	0.0	100.0	0.2	0.5	1.0	1.2	0.5	3.3
1993	100.0	0.0	0.0	0.4	1.0	0.0	1.4	0.0	100.0	0.2	0.6	0.8	1.0	0.0	2.6
1994	100.0	0.0	0.8	0.5	1.0	0.0	2.3	0.0	100.0	0.3	0.7	0.9	1.0	0.0	3.0
1995	100.0	0.0	1.1	0.6	1.0	0.0	2.7	0.0	100.0	0.1	0.8	1.0	1.4	0.0	3.3

Source: Author's calculations from IMF, Direction of Trade, annuals.

Table A5 Shares of Yugoslav Trade with the Balkans

Year	Imports								Exports						
	Total	Albania	Bulgaria	Greece	Roman.	Yugosl.	Region	Cyprus	Total	Albania	Bulgaria	Greece	Roman.	Yugosl.	Region
1966	100.0	0.0	0.9	0.0	0.7	1.2	2.8	0.0	100.0	0.0	1.1	1.2	0.7	0.6	3.6
1967	100.0	0.0	0.8	0.0	1.1	1.2	3.1	0.0	100.0	0.0	0.7	0.5	1.0	0.3	2.5
1968	100.0	0.0	0.8	0.1	1.1	0.8	2.9	0.0	100.0	0.0	1.1	0.7	1.8	1.1	4.8
1970	100.0	0.0	0.5	0.5	0.4	0.9	2.3	0.0	100.0	0.0	0.5	0.0	0.9	0.4	1.9
1971	100.0	0.0	0.9	0.9	0.9	1.0	3.7	0.0	100.0	0.0	0.4	0.0	0.6	2.2	3.3
1972	100.0	0.0	0.5	1.2	0.5	1.4	3.6	0.0	100.0	0.0	0.4	0.3	0.3	0.7	1.6
1973	100.0	0.0	0.3	0.3	0.4	0.8	1.9	0.0	100.0	0.0	0.5	1.5	0.7	1.6	4.4
1974	100.0	0.1	0.4	0.4	2.1	0.5	3.5	0.0	100.0	0.1	0.5	1.3	0.4	1.7	4.0
1975	100.0	0.0	0.6	0.0	1.3	0.4	2.2	0.0	100.0	0.0	0.5	0.0	0.5	0.5	1.5
1976	100.0	0.0	1.0	0.1	1.8	0.4	3.3	0.1	100.0	0.0	0.4	0.1	1.6	0.5	2.6
1877	100.0	0.1	0.7	0.3	2.0	0.7	3.8	0.0	100.0	0.1	0.8	0.1	1.5	0.9	3.2
1978	100.0	0.0	0.5	0.1	3.8	0.7	5.0	0.1	100.0	0.0	0.5	0.2	3.2	0.9	4.9
1979	100.0	0.1	1.6	0.5	4.6	0.9	7.7	0.0	100.0	0.0	0.3	0.2	1.7	1.4	3.6
1980	100.0	0.1	1.8	0.8	3.4	1.0	7.0	0.0	100.0	0.3	0.4	0.3	2.4	0.9	4.4
1981	100.0	0.1	0.7	0.2	4.1	0.6	5.7	0.0	100.0	0.1	0.2	1.0	1.2	0.5	3.1
1982	100.0	0.0	0.7	0.2	1.2	0.3	2.3	0.0	100.0	0.0	0.3	2.3	1.0	0.4	3.9
1983	100.0	0.0	1.1	0.2	2.0	0.3	3.6	0.0	100.0	0.0	0.4	1.0	1.0	0.3	2.7
1984	100.0	0.0	1.1	0.5	1.1	0.6	3.3	0.1	100.0	0.0	0.3	1.3	0.8	0.3	2.8
1985	100.0	0.0	0.9	0.4	0.6	1.0	2.9	0.1	100.0	0.0	0.1	1.0	0.6	0.4	2.1
1986	100.0	0.0	0.4	0.7	1.0	1.1	3.1	0.0	100.0	0.0	0.2	1.0	0.5	0.4	2.1
1987	100.0	0.0	0.1	0.9	1.6	1.3	3.8	0.1	100.0	0.0	0.1	0.6	0.5	0.2	1.4
1988	100.0	0.0	0.1	0.6	1.3	1.6	3.6	0.0	100.0	0.0	0.2	0.8	0.6	0.5	2.3
1989	100.0	0.0	0.0	0.6	1.5	2.4	4.5	0.1	100.0	0.0	0.2	1.1	0.4	0.7	2.5
1990	100.0	0.0	0.1	0.6	0.9	1.1	2.7	0.0	100.0	0.0	0.1	1.0	0.6	1.1	2.9
1991	100.0	0.0	0.7	0.4	0.9	0.7	2.7	0.0	100.0	0.2	0.6	1.0	0.8	0.6	3.1
1992	100.0	0.0	0.9	0.4	1.1	0.4	2.7	0.0	100.0	0.1	0.5	1.0	1.2	0.5	3.3
1993	100.0	0.0	0.0	0.5	1.0	0.0	1.4	0.0	100.0	0.2	0.6	0.8	1.0	0.0	2.6
1994	100.0	0.0	0.8	0.5	1.0	0.0	2.3	0.0	100.0	0.3	0.7	0.9	1.0	0.0	3.0
1995	100.0	0.0	1.1	0.6	1.0	0.0	2.7	0.0	100.0	0.1	0.8	1.0	1.4	0.0	3.3

Source: Author's calculations from IMF, Direction of Trade, annuals.

3 Multi-Speed Transition and Multi-Speed Integration in Europe: Recent Economic Developments in the Balkans

RUMEN DOBRINSKY

President, Centre for Economic and Strategic Research, Sofia, Bulgaria

Introduction

Since the start of economic and political transformation, the economic performance of the transition countries in the Balkan region has been characterised by persistent macroeconomic instability, uneven output performance and lack of consistence in economic policies, leading to repetitive crises. In recent years the contrast to the rapidly reforming central European countries has become increasingly pronounced and now it is widely recognised that the south-eastern European transition countries are laggards in the transformation process; it is even more striking that the Baltic states, which started their reform process later, were, by 1996, definitely more advanced than the Balkan states in many aspects of the reform agenda. This has led a number of observers to put forward the notion of a "multi-speed transition process" in which institutional and economic reforms in different countries are being implemented at a different pace (see for example, UN 1997). Moreover, it has been observed that different reforms within a given country also proceed at a different speed and these speeds also differ across transition countries (World Bank 1996).

What is Specific about Transition in the Balkan Region?

Regrettably, the south-eastern European transition countries tend to be located at the backward end of this increasingly differentiated spectrum; it is even more worrisome that they are continuously falling behind the front-runners and the gap between them and the rapidly reforming countries is

widening. There have been a number of attempts to identify the reasons and to offer plausible explanations for the transition failures of the Balkan transition countries. In a recent survey, Hoey and Kekic (1997) review the analytical explanations for the poor performance of the Balkan countries which have been offered in the literature. They summarise the findings of different authors in a list of ten major causes:
- the deficiencies of Balkan cultures;
- insufficient commitment to the market and to integration with the West;
- the dearth of democratic tradition;
- differential experiences under communism;
- the durability of former communists in power;
- the sizes of the countries and newness of the states;
- the slow pace, or lack, of economic reform;
- the effects of lower income levels and starting conditions;
- the enduring political and administrative legacies of the Ottoman - Habsburg divide;
- the impact of the West.

After analysing these causes, Hoey and Kekic (1997) draw their own conclusion that the most important of the above have been:
- The lasting Ottoman legacy which is apparent in inter-generational transfer of bureaucratic practices and results in lower institutional and political efficiency and, ultimately, in low effectiveness of governments in implementing policy decisions;
- The west European neglect of the region since 1989 and the unequal access to west European markets. The treatment of the Balkans has been much more unfavourable as compared to central Europe in some important aspects such as: offering the countries of the region prospects of economic and political integration with the West; the opening of markets to new products; financial and other forms of aid; diplomatic and political pressures and initiatives.

At the same time, Hoey and Kekic (1997) dismiss the importance of most of the other factors mentioned. Although the two causes mentioned above undoubtedly have played a very important role in determining the differences in economic performance in the Balkans as compared to other transition countries, it is unlikely that they were the sole determinants of the underperformance of the south-eastern European region and of the recently observed transition failures in some countries (Dobrinsky 1997). We would like to point out several other factors which affected both economic policy and the patterns of macro- and microeconomic adjustment in these countries during the first phase of transition. However, it is important to note, that the causes mentioned below had a different degree of significance in the different countries and thus their impact was differentiated across the region. These factors are the following:

The Initial Conditions

In general, it is hard to reject the fact that the initial conditions, at least in some of the south-eastern European countries, were much more unfavourable than those in central Europe. On average, these were generally poorer and less developed countries; they were thus more agricultural (Petrakos and Totev 2000, Mertzanis and Petrakos 1998) and hence, more dependent on products which are considered "sensitive" for western Europe. Many of these countries were characterised by higher levels of inherited macroeconomic imbalances and traditionally loose monetary and fiscal policies. Countries like Bulgaria and Romania and some of the successor states of the former Yugoslavia inherited from the past a very large share (compared to other transition economies) of nonviable enterprises which were hardly fit for restructuring and are due for closure. Among all transition economies, Bulgaria was the country with the highest previous dependence on eastern trade (Totev 1997, Dobrinsky 1997); in addition it inherited an unsustainable level of foreign debt.

Apart from the locational disadvantages, there was much greater political instability in the region. The war in Bosnia and Herzegovina had a negative effect on all neighbouring countries; in particular, this had a negative effect on the perceived risks and the investment climate in these countries. The war also induced negative externalities such as the UN sanctions on Yugoslavia, which had a highly negative effect on third parties as well, and especially on the neighbouring Balkan states (UN 1994).

The Degree of Systemic Weakness

In the course of economic and political transformation in many transition economies, there emerged a number of "systemic weaknesses". These were either: a) weaknesses in the economic structure (such as the existence of inherited large sectors of inefficient enterprises which simply cannot be restructured overnight, as there is a certain limit on the possible speed of restructuring), or b) weaknesses in the institutional infrastructure (deficient or embryonic institutions which create bottlenecks in the functioning of markets and can themselves be reasons for market failures; again this situation cannot be changed overnight).

It appears that the inherent degree of systemic weakness in the southeastern European region on average was much higher than, for instance, in central Europe, both regarding their economic structures and their institutional environment. For example, financial systems turned out to be one of the weakest systemic elements in some of the Balkan transition countries (Bulgaria, Albania, Yugoslavia). In fact in all cases of transition crises or pre-crisis symptoms in the region, the degradation of the financial systems and of the financial markets of the affected countries were central to the overall process. However, systemic weaknesses differ from country to county and also depend on the initial conditions.

Policy Failures and Policy Constraints

The policy making process in the Balkan transition countries was also characterised by a number of detrimental features as compared to the leading reform countries. Policy makers in the region (Bulgaria, Romania, Yugoslavia, Albania) by and large failed to set up the proper (and feasible) reform agenda (leading to macroeconomic stabilisation and self-sustained growth) at the proper time. Serious delays were encountered in most southeastern European countries in the implementation of important elements of the reform agenda (especially structural reforms and systemic transformation). In the worst performing countries there was obvious lack of coherence between long-term and short-term policy goals and misjudgement of the sequencing and speed of reforms.

However, it must also be taken into account that any given society has a limited capacity to process only given "amounts of reform" at a time. This is especially relevant for the Balkan states, due to their traditional lack of democratic traditions, historic lack of experience with market institutions and also historic popular neglect of law and regulation. Policy failures in these countries also reflected the lack of consensus in the society itself over the course of reforms. Needed reforms in the region were also impeded because of a priori individual uncertainty about their outcome: who would gain and who would lose from the reforms (even if it were known that the majority would benefit?). The political constraints were even greater when a priori it was known that (at least in the short-term) a large share of the population would be adversely affected by some reforms (such as the closure of nonviable enterprises). It has been suggested in the literature that when political support of reforms is weak because it affects large interest groups, it is only a crisis that can stage the conditions for the implementation of delayed reforms which are necessary but painful (Drazen and Grilli 1993). All this is equivalent to policy constraints on the reform process and limitations on the speed of feasible reform, which were especially pronounced in some of the Balkan states.

Emergence of "Transition Traps"

This is the danger that - due to unfavourable initial conditions, systemic weaknesses, policy failures or policy constraints, or a combination of these - a country may be locked during the transition into a suboptimal performance path. The transition trap is a vicious circle with limited policy choices allowing to break it from within; in the worst case it leads to a transition crisis.

There may be different causes for the emergence of transition traps. One of them may be the gap between the eradication of the institutions of the centrally planned economy and the feasible speed of establishing the institutional framework of a market economy. This may result in an institutional and regulatory vacuum; in such an environment, corruption and rent seeking flourish whereas the regulatory lacuna may nourish major market failures. The grotesque build-up of the financial pyramids in Albania and the banking crises in Bulgaria and Yugoslavia, as well as the endemic asset stripping of state-owned enterprises in Bulgaria, are examples of this type of development.

Another reason may be the actual degree of built-in "systemic weakness" in a transition economy (e.g. a very large, inefficient sector in the economy, inherited from the past, or a very high foreign debt burden). The existence of a very high degree of "systemic weakness" may generate negative effects of great magnitude which develop more rapidly than the speed of feasible reforms. This was one of the causes of the crisis in Bulgaria.

A policy stalemate caused by lack of political support for the needed reforms (ultimately, by political constraints on the feasible course of reforms) can also be regarded as a cause of (and a form of) transition trap: it leads to blocking of the reform process and thus breeds the conditions for a transition crisis. This occurred in many of the Balkan countries (Bulgaria, Romania, Yugoslavia).

The nature of the transition trap is such that it entails the danger of a "domino effect", i.e. relatively minor disturbances may easily escalate into large-scale market failure(s) and lead to rapid deterioration of the overall economic situation in a country, thus evolving into a serious political crisis. This was how events developed both in Bulgaria and in Albania. The reason for this is again the overall "systemic weakness" of these countries: they lacked both the institutional safeguards against serious disturbances and shocks and the necessary mechanisms to restore equilibrium once the system reaches a state of disequilibrium ("built-in stabilisers"). In such an environment, a crisis can easily be provoked once something goes wrong in the economy.

Lack of Individual Approach in International Assistance

The existence (or the potential for emergence) of transition traps is an issue which may have been underestimated at the outset of reforms, both locally, and by the international community, including the international financial institutions. It appears that there was probably a need for more individualised assistance programs, tailored to the specific conditions and environment in some of the south-eastern European transition countries.

For example, during the 1991-96 period both Bulgaria and Romania reached four standby agreements with the IMF; however, subsequently neither of the two countries managed to finalise any of these agreements successfully, due to failures to meet their conditions. Without trying to vindicate their governments for numerous policy failures, a posteriori one could also question the actual feasibility of the implementation of these agreements, due to the inherent transition traps in the two countries.

As noted, the transition traps are vicious circles which are sometimes very difficult to break from within; on the contrary a more concentrated, upfront assistance package may be rather beneficial (and, sometimes, may be the only way out of a crisis). And, in fact, the current apparent generosity of the new assistance packages that are being negotiated with Bulgaria and Romania (in the wake of the crises in Bulgaria and Albania) is probably an indirect sign of some change from the previous approach to assistance.

Some Implications for the Integration of the Balkan Countries into the European Economy

The detrimental specifics of transition in the Balkan region are likely to have negative implications for the future integration of these countries into the European economy, including accession to the European Union (EU). At this stage it seems most likely that the eventual eastern enlargement of the EU will also take the form of a "multi-speed" process with a highly differentiated speed of accession of the countries holding association agreements at present. Although the EU will open negotiations on future accession to all associated countries, there is a prevailing sense that the speed of these negotiations will vary widely from country to country. The reasons are numerous, ranging from the level of preparedness for accession of individual countries to the capacity of the European commission to handle a simultaneous negotiation process with a given number of countries. The likely implications of this status as well as of the Balkan "specifics" in the transition process discussed above are that the countries of south-eastern Europe (with the exception of Slovenia) will not be among the front tier of transition countries in the first wave of eastern enlargement.

Actually, among the south-eastern European transition countries, there are only three countries having agreements with Europe: Bulgaria, Romania and Slovenia (all of which have also applied for full membership). Although the rest of the countries, namely Albania, Croatia, the FYR of Macedonia and Yugoslavia - or at least some of them - are also possible applicants for association status (and, eventually, at a later stage, for full membership), they are likely to lag further behind in the process of re-integration into the European economy. Indeed, the relations between the south-eastern European countries and western Europe (and, in particular, the EU) seem to be entwined in a kind of Catch-22 situation. On the one hand, the above mentioned western European neglect of the region since 1989 and the unequal access to western European markets was one of the factors that led to the uneven course of reforms and poor economic performance during the first phase of transition. Also, as mentioned above, the role of international financial assistance in general was equivocal and questionable. However, on the other hand, the poor performance record and the lack of notable progress in many important reforms during the last several years in itself is a deterrent to the process of economic integration with western Europe and, in particular, to full membership in the EU. Moreover, with the start of the negotiation process (in which the front runners will undoubtedly receive a disproportionately large share of attention), the wedge between south-eastern and central Europe will grow further. Thus, one of the likely future scenarios is that the multi-speed transition-and-integration process will become even more heterogeneous: the front tier of fast reformers will move even more rapidly in catching up with western Europe and ultimately becoming part of it, whereas the south-eastern European "laggards" will fall even further behind.

Another alternative for the Balkan countries would be to strengthen their regional co-operation, using earlier phases of EU and EC integration as a model. In this way, they will not only benefit from an expanded regional market but will also accelerate the process of synchronisation of their economies and harmonisation of their legislation and regulation with the EU which, in turn, would be beneficial for eventual future EU accession.

References

Dobrinsky, R. (1997), Transition Failures: Anatomy of the Bulgarian Crisis. WIIW Research Reports No. 236, May.

Drazen, A. and Grilli, V. (1993), The Benefit of Crises for Economic Reforms. American Economic Review 83(3), pp. 598-607.

Hoey, J. and Kekic, L. (1997), What's Wrong with the Balkans? Country Forecast Economies in Transition, Regional Overview, 1st Quarter 1997, London: The Economist Intelligence Unit.

Mertzanis, H. and Petrakos, G. (1998), Changing Landscapes in Europe's Economic Structure. Transition, Volume 9, Number 2, April.

Petrakos, G. and Totev, S. (2000), Economic structure and change in the Balkan region: Implications for integration, transition and economic co-operation, International Journal of Urban and Regional Research, Vol. 24, No. 1, pp. 95-113.

Totev, S. (1997), The Bulgarian economy in transition: Possibilities for Balkan regional integration. Paper presented at the Conference "Economic Co-operation in the Balkans: A Regional Approach to European Integration", Phare-ACE Program, University of Thessaly, Department of Planning and Regional Development, Volos, 16-19 January.

UN (1994), World Economic and Social Survey. New York: United Nations Secretariat.

UN (1997), Economic Survey of Europe in 1996-1997. UN Economic Commission for Europe, New York and Geneva, 1997.

World Bank (1996), From Plan to Market. World Development Report 1996, New York: World Bank/ Oxford University Press.

4 Foreign Direct Investment and Western Firms' Internationalization Strategies in the Balkan Countries

YORGOS RIZOPOULOS
ERSI, University of Amiens and ROSES-CNRS, Universite de Paris-I

Introduction

Foreign Direct Investment (FDI) provides resources, creates externalities and recomposes sector and regional specialisation. Production capacities, technologies and know-how are redistributed on a world level through the FDI flows. States take measures to make attractive, and to open their national economy, to the foreign direct investment, at the same time, limiting their own possibilities of action. Old debates concerning the usefulness of FDI seem out of fashion and every country tries to attract foreign investors.

FDI can hardly substitute for internal investment, public or private, but it is also considered a determinant factor of economic development during transition (Blanchard et al. 1991; Dunning 1993). Meanwhile, capital inflows in this region are quite low, except in Hungary, and the attractiveness of different transition economies is unequal. Indeed political, social and economic instability, as well as overall weak performance of the Balkan countries have a negative impact on the amounts invested by foreign companies and, furthermore, determine the nature, the objectives, the degree of involvement, and the modalities of FDI.

The purpose of this article is not to deal with every particular question concerning foreign direct investment in this region, but to provide an adequate theoretical framework to make its distinctive traits intelligible and to analyse FDI during a systemic transformation process. The following two sections stress, in parallel with the impact of the conditions existing in the local markets, the importance of oligopolistic competition and competitive pressures in the "home" (international, national or regional) markets, as a determinant of direct foreign investment in the comparatively less attractive

Balkan countries. The fourth section outlines the recent trends in FDI in this region. It deals especially with the importance, growth, sector structure, regional location and distribution according to the origin country of FDI. Unfortunately, figures provided by official or semi-official sources are often unreliable and contradictory. Consequently, we have to consider existing data as simply indications of general tendencies, what makes illusive on any sophisticated quantitative approach.

The fifth section discusses some points on the nature and motivations of western investors in the Balkan countries. Why do some firms decide to invest in rather unattractive markets? Indeed, it seems that "followers", suffering strong competitive constraints and trying to ameliorate their positions, constitute the majority of foreign investors during the first period of transition in the Balkans. For them, high specific attractiveness may compensate for low global attractiveness. Market penetration is the dominant objective, even if important differences exist among the different countries of the region. The sixth section points out the methods of entry and ownership patterns. Available data reveal the important share in co-operative strategies, although western firms prefer a majority control and show little interest for joint-ventures with big state enterprises. The seventh section deals with the possible negative and positive effects of FDI in the Balkans (resource transfer, contribution to the global performance, competitive and counter-competitive effects...), given their specific characteristics.

The final section poses the important question of Greek FDI in the other Balkan countries, linked to the prospects of economic relations and co-operation with each other. Greece (alone with Turkey) is the only country of this region not engaged in a systemic transformation process. Furthermore, it is a member of the European Union and can constitute a bridge for the European integration of other Balkan countries. On the other hand, its economic performance is weak, relative to western standards, and Greek enterprises may face intense competition in their national and international markets. As "followers", they see a reinforcement in the Balkan region as an opportunity for the amelioration of their global position. Consequently, they can be a vector of regional co-operation and of interdependence of national productive systems. This last section refers to the factors that explain the density of investment flows from Greece to the other Balkan countries (especially Albania and Bulgaria), as well as to the sector composition of Greek FDI; to its limits and constraints.

What Theory for Foreign Direct Investment (FDI) During Transition?

Many areas of economic analysis (theory of the firm, monopolistic competition, capital theory, location theory, international trade theory...) try to interpret overseas investment (Table 1). According to the traditional approaches of international exchange, capital movements are explained mainly by comparative advantage and factors endowment (quantity and quality of labour, capital and subsoil resources). Within this theoretical framework, international investment exploits relatively rare factors of production, characterised by lower cost or better quality[1]. Interesting contributions stress the importance of trade barriers (Mundell 1957, Caves 1981...), technological advantages of exporting capital country (Hirsch 1967 and 1976), product life cycle (Vernon 1966) or combination of comparative advantage and technological advantage (Kojima 1977).

Table 1 Global Attractiveness of the Balkan Countries

FAVOURABLE FACTORS	UNFAVOURABLE FACTORS
Production costs. *New markets.* *Access to new technologies.* *Fiscal facilities.* *Low commercial barriers.* *Insufficient local supply and old products.* *Co-operative attitudes on the part of most local actors.*	*Economic, social, institutional and political instability.* *Small market size.* *Insufficient infrastructure (transport, finance communications).* *Long negotiation procedures, frequent changes of persons, rules of the game and laws.* *Absence of common language and common preoccupations with domestic partners.* *Need to invest in the training of local staff.* *Ignorance of the local context and absence of cultural links.* *Legislative framework on property rights.* *Criminality.*

Another set of models considers the specific characteristics of capital markets to be the main reasons for FDI: interest rate variations and differences, exchange rate fluctuations (Aliber 1970), portfolio and risk diversification (Ragazzi 1973). The investor develops an "efficient" portfolio of investment in which risk-aversion and expected value of returns are balanced. On the other hand, some scholars have applied the transaction costs theory (internalisation) in the field of direct investment (Buckley & Casson 1976, Krugman & Obstfeld 1995).

The variety of theoretical contributions reflects the wide range of motivations existing at the origin of an international direct investment. Notwithstanding the interest of these models and the very existence of foreign direct investment which intend to exploit cost or financial advantages, strictly financial and factors endowment considerations have apparently weak influence on FDI flows during the first period of the systemic transformation process in Central and Eastern Europe. Therefore, such approaches seem to be on the wane and are insufficient to explain FDI in the Balkan countries, and it seems necessary to propose a more adapted analytical framework.

Some alternative models focus on market imperfections which enable oligopolistic advantages. In this framework, foreign direct investment is a by-product of imperfect markets and of actors' strategic action. Competitive advantages or disadvantages and firms' interactions are the main factors explaining international transfer of assets, which seems to constitute an appropriate basis to analyse FDI in the Balkans as well.

Hymer and Rowthorn (1970) have suggested one of the early well known ideas concerning direct investment of American firms in Europe after the Second World War. Their starting point is the hypothesis of an actual international oligopoly and the need to preserve market shares against competitors.

According to Kindleberger (1969), FDI is justified if potential profit abroad is higher than both profit in the national market and the profits of firms in the host country. This means that the investing firm must have some advantages compared to other firms in its national market and compared to local firms (product differentiation, technological or managerial know-how, economies of scale, formal or informal relations with local authorities...). These advantages should be "transferable" abroad and protected by barriers. In other words, the investing firm must have exclusive access to information or knowledge which make possible the exclusive appropriation of a part of the social welfare produced by the firm (Johnson 1970). The creation of entry barriers (Swendenborg 1979, Lipsey & Weiss 1981...) can also be a useful explanation of foreign direct investment, while the eclectic approach focuses on the combination of firm-specific, comparative and oligopolistic advantages (Hirsch 1976, Dunning 1981, Mucchielli 1985).

Furthermore, subsequent work by Vernon (1974) has led to modifications of his initial theory of product life cycle, so as to emphasise the oligopolistic behaviour of firms. During the mature oligopoly stage, product and location strategies are based upon actions and interactions of competitors. Firms set up production activities in their competitors' major markets to strengthen their bargaining position. This hypothesis is very close to Knickerbocker's suggestion that oligopolists follow each other into new foreign markets as a defensive strategy: the followers try to negate any advantage that the first mover might gain (Knickerbocker 1973). According to Cotta (1970), in the conditions of a stable national oligopoly ("leader's" and "follower's" positions cannot easily change), international expansion may provide more advantages than national development. This idea was further developed by Rainelli (1979) and Anand & Kogut (1997). Firms would internationalise their activities in order to obtain a cost or differentiation advantage enabling the amelioration of their competitive position.

Generally, firms also tend to manage uncertainty on the basis of a subjective appreciation of real or potential dangers and opportunities. They react to existing market constraints and try to anticipate future evolutions, through their own perception, decision procedures and organisational capabilities. Indeed, investment decisions are taken in a context of imperfect information and dependence on other actors (competitors, suppliers, customers, state agencies...). When Kindleberger (1969) suggests that the investing firm must obtain a higher profit both in its national market and abroad, he simply reproduces the basic maximisation hypothesis of the neoclassical paradigm, though in a context of bounded rationality (Simon 1983) and eponymous market relations, optimisation strategies are not feasible. Rational calculation of future returns or profit rates is, in most cases, extremely hazardous. Furthermore, the amelioration of profit possibilities very often becomes a secondary objective, when the survival of the firm is in danger because of an unfavourable evolution of its environment or increased uncertainty (new entrants, "cut throat" competition, etc.).

FDI might be considered a necessary condition, not to ameliorate profits, but just to preserve minimum profits or market shares. It might be a defensive action due to a weak competitive position or a constraint imposed upon the firm by its customers. Furthermore, enterprises investing abroad are not necessarily leaders. Advantages, but also disadvantages may motivate a foreign direct investment (Rizopoulos 1991 and 1995a, Maroudas & Rizopoulos, 1995). In this perspective, FDI can be defined as a strategic movement tending to exploit, preserve or acquire specific advantages at the managerial, production, commercialisation, R&D, organisational, relational and financial levels, to compensate for a real or an anticipated advantage loss, and to attenuate (or eliminate) a real or potential advantage of competitors. Combination of several objectives is frequent. One firm may have both technological or organisational advantages compared to the firms of a foreign country and disadvantages compared to other firms in its home market. On the other hand, exploitation of advantages through overseas investment could be parallel to an effort to attenuate competitors' advantages by creating entry or mobility barriers.

Foreign Direct Investment during Transition: The Intensification of Competition in International Markets and the Specificity of the Balkan Countries

In the absence of the systemic constraints that have contributed to the formation of a relatively closed economic area during several decades, the opening of eastern European economies and their progressive integration in the world economy constitutes a new competitive arena for western enterprises. The widening of oligopolistic competition can be a factor of new opportunities (access to specific knowledge and know-how, new markets, economies of scale, cost advantages or possibilities of delocalisation...), but also of new threats linked to the emergence of new competitors and of new networks of alliances which could destabilise current positions in international markets. On the other hand, investment in these countries is relatively risky, given the fluidity and the very bad knowledge of the local markets. Consequently, the opening of Eastern European economies offers new perspectives of profit and, at the same time, aggravates uncertainty. This contradiction seems to have an significant impact on the strategic goals, the ways and the modalities of western investment in these countries.

Balkan economies are an even more specific case. From the point of view of western enterprises, they have some favourable characteristics: insufficient local supply, old products, and an "open oligopoly" structure, given the decline of domestic production, the co-operative attitudes on the part of most local actors, the low level of required initial investment and the low commercial barriers. On the other hand, Balkan countries are less developed than other east European countries: they suffer poor economic performance and infrastructure and, frequently, shortage of necessary skills, especially in the marketing and commercialisation fields. They are also penalised by the relative ignorance of the local context on the part of potential western partners and by a more pronounced bureaucratic behaviour of local authorities (Table 2).

Table 2 FDI in the Balkan Countries (Million USD)

	1991	1992	1993	1994	1995	1996	1997	TOTAL 1991-97
Albania		20	58	53	70	90	48	339
Bulgaria	56	42	40	105	90	109	49 7	939
Croatia			95	102	98	533	348	1,176
FYR Macedonia				24	9	11	16	60
Romania	40	80	94	342	420	265	1,224	2,465
Slovenia		111	113	128	176	186	321	1,035
Total	*96*	*253*	*400*	*754*	*863*	*1,194*	*2,454*	*6,014*

Source: UNCTD 1998.

Some scholars suggest that less attractive countries must offer higher profit prospects to attract foreign investors (Dietz 1991). Indeed, shortages or close relational links can have a positive effect on the potential profit rates of some foreign investors. Meanwhile, low global attractiveness means high uncertainty which has a direct negative impact on the real value of assets. Furthermore, if this consideration may be valuable for a speculator, it seems highly improbable that an established enterprise will adopt such an adventurous strategy developing new activities in a high uncertainty context (except if its involvement does not imply a significant investment). Furthermore, it is very difficult to evaluate empirically potential profit in a genuine uncertainty context.

As stated above, it is an error to consider FDI as a free choice, independent of interaction with other economic actors. Following Kindleberger's arguments (1969), we can consider that FDI is a result of imperfections[2] in products and in factor markets throughout the world which are structural or issue from strategies pursued by firms: market size and growth, oligopolistic market structure, factor endowment, trade barriers, product differentiation, entry and mobility barriers, economies of scale, managerial capacity, specific knowledge and know-how, etc. These imperfections are sources of real or potential competitive advantages very unequally distributed among competitors. As a consequence, some of them are dominant and others dominated, in the various specific markets.

A relatively dominated enterprise or one that has to face a deterioration of its competitive position may agree to take important risks (be involved in less attractive markets) in order to ameliorate its own position by avoiding direct confrontation with more powerful competitors, but without necessarily securing profits higher than those of the local competitors. On the other hand, a leader whose positions are protected by strong entry or mobility barriers (technological advance, differentiated products, control of distribution channels...) would be more cautious. Rational (albeit "limited") calculations on investment return and the will not to aggravate its own uncertainty - given that competitive pressure is relatively weak - may motivate a "conservative" attitude, and exporting or "wait and see" attitudes will be preferred instead of investing. At the beginning of the transition process, a study of the strategies of pharmaceutical groups in Eastern Europe have consolidated this statement (Rizopoulos 1991). Indeed, very few complex industrial co-operation agreements are initiated by leading firms, which generally prefer the simplest forms (licences..), though smaller or less protected pharmaceutical enterprises are more interested in the privatisation process and joint-ventures. In this way, they try to attain a "critical" size, enlarge their markets, reach scale economies, prolong the life cycle of their products or exploit local specific knowledge.

Consequently, direct investment in the less attractive transition countries (and specifically in the Balkan countries) will be realised, to a great extend, by "followers" trying to ameliorate their competitive position or by companies which face a decline of their activity in the western markets. In the tobacco sector, for example, the major Western companies were strongly competing to set up joint ventures with local producers in Eastern Europe, in order to compensate for a relative decline of demand in Western Europe. For such firms, global institutional and macro-economic attractiveness determines the importance, the forms (greenfield, buying a local enterprise, "cherry-picking", joint-venture...) and the relative irreversibility of their engagement but it will not necessarily be a decisive factor concerning the decision of whether or not to be present in these markets. Other parameters, and especially potential competitive advantages related to their own specific position, will probably have a greater influence and can compensate for low global attractiveness by high specific attractiveness.

The Reality of FDI in the Balkans

It is very difficult to obtain reliable data on FDI in the Balkan countries analysed here. Various national and international sources give contradictory figures concerning the number, the value of the capital invested, the sectors and the origin of foreign investment. For the purpose of comparison between countries and for the appreciation of the general tendencies, we use the United Nations data issued from the balance of payments statistics and excluding investment in nature or reinvesting profits (Table 3). National statistics are used for the study of structure by country of origin and by sector.

Table 3 FDI Cumulated Inflows Per Capita (USD)

	1996	1997	Balkan Countries	1996	1997
Transition economies	*124*	*175*	Albania	88	103
Central Europe	529	662	Bulgaria	53	113
Balkan countries	62	104	Croatia	177	250
Baltic countries	254	389	FYR Macedonia	22	30
CIS	44	80	Romania	55	109
			Slovenia	359	520

Sources: UN/ECE and own calculations.

Investment inflows to the transition countries (including CIS) reached 74,534 million USD in 1997, a 41.2% increase compared to 1996. Increase for the Balkan countries was above the average (68.6%), but globally FDI remain weak in this region (6,034 million USD, or 8.1% of the total, against 57.3% for Central Europe). FDI per capita is also very low (104 USD, against 662 USD in Central Europe).

Meanwhile, important differences characterise the Balkan countries. During the period 1990-97, Slovenia receives regular and important FDI inflows, though its share in the region diminishes. Romania seems progressively to have become a major destination of foreign capital since 1995, whereas Bulgaria registers a steady decrease of its relative part up to 1996 and Albania suffers from internal institutional and politico-economic instability[3]. Only Slovenia and, to a lesser extent, Croatia register relatively high cumulative inflows of FDI per capita (Table 3).

Albania

According to the data published by the Albanian Institute of Statistics, 1532 joint ventures and 890 foreign companies were operating up to the end of 1995, compared to 1252 joint ventures and 717 foreign companies existing at the end of 1994. The Albanian Centre for Foreign Investment Promotion (ACFIP) gives another figure: 400 joint ventures and foreign companies up to the end of 1994. One year later, there were 1963 registered joint-ventures (Table 4). 1244 were in trade, 389 in industry, 33 in agriculture and food, 95 in construction, while 202 companies were in services and transport.

Table 4 Distribution of Joint-Ventures in Albania (1996, by number)

Sector	1 employee	2-10 employees	Over 10 employees	TOTAL
Agriculture	7	19	7	33
Industry	131	174	84	389
Construction	30	52	13	95
Services	55	61	5	121
Transport	31	49	1	81
Commerce	535	687	22	1,244
TOTAL	789	1,042	132	1,963

Source: INSTAT, December 1997.

On the other hand, of 1235 registered private operations, independent or in collaboration with private Albanian individuals or companies (Table 5) - whose number tended to increase more quickly than joint-ventures - 781 were in trade, 184 in industry, 12 in agriculture and food, 64 in construction, while 194 companies were in services and transport. The prevalence of small enterprises is a major characteristic of foreign direct investments in Albania (Tables 4 and 5). Following the ACFIP investigations, 1.2% of the total number of projects was above 1 million USD, in 1996.

In 1996, 53% of the total number of joint ventures are Italian (but their percentage in value of capital invested is weaker, about 35%), 27% Greek, 6% German and 2.6% American. Austrians have invested in very few projects but their part in the value of the invested capital exceeds 10%. France, United Kingdom, Turkey and Luxembourg are also important investors. FDI from other Balkan countries is very low, but small enterprises or indi-

Table 5 Distribution of Private Foreign Enterprises in Albania (1996, by number)

Activity	1 employee	2-10 employees	Over 10 employees	TOTAL
Agriculture	8	3	1	12
Industry	82	73	29	184
Construction	41	17	6	64
Services	86	44	7	137
Transport	30	24	3	57
Commerce	451	311	19	781
TOTAL	698	472	65	1,235

Source: INSTAT, December 1997.

viduals from the Yugoslav province of Kosovo and from Romania have invested in Albania. Some Bulgarian and Slovenian firms are involved, in the construction and electronics sectors respectively. The fact that 80% of foreign or joint venture enterprises are Italian or Greek shows the importance of proximity factors. The Italian capital is mainly concentrated in the Western areas of Albania, particularly in towns like Tirana, Durres, Elbasan, Lushnje, Shkoder, Vlore, etc., while the Greek investments are concentrated mainly in the Southern and South-eastern part of Albania, in towns like Korca, Gjirokastra, Delvina and Saranda (Table 7).

Table 6 Structure of FDI in Albania by Economic Activities (1996, %)

Activity	Structure in%
Tourism	34
Light Industry	20
Food and Agriculture	18
Construction	15
Transport	6
Others	7
TOTAL	100

Source: ACFIP investigations, 1996.

Table 7 Sector Structure of FDI in Bulgaria, 1997

Sector	Share of total investment volume
Primary sector	0.4
Industry	55.2
Services	40.4
Transportation and telecommunications	*6.7*
Trade	*17.2*
Tourism	*6.0*
Financing	*9.5*
Construction	*1.0*
Without precision	4.0
Total	100.0

Source: Foreign Investment Agency, Bulgaria.

Light industry (mainly clothes, footwear, and other labour intensive activities), food industry and tourism seem to be the most attractive sectors for foreign investors (Table 6). Mining and oil extraction, as well as banking activities also seem to interest foreign companies. According to the estimates of the ACFIP, 34% of foreign investment operations are in the sector of tourism, 20% in light industry, 18% in the food industry and 15% in construction.

Bulgaria

As far as Bulgaria is concerned, an important increase of FDI inflows in 1997 has followed the decline of 1995 and the quasi-stagnation of 1996, according to the UNCTD data. Information obtained from the Bulgarian Foreign Investment Agency also indicates a growing number of FDI operations (10,061 compared to 4,806 at the end of 1995). Up to the end of 1995, the value of FDI flows grew more slowly than the number of investments and the amount of average investment tended to decrease (see also Bobeva 1996). 73% of them were less than 1000 USD, and about 89% did not exceed 10,000 USD. On the other hand, there were 70 FDI operations of more than USD one million each, which aggregated to 90% of the total FDI stock. Though these proportions do not change dramatically, a significant change took place in 1997, thanks to the two big operations in the chemical and non-ferrous metallurgy sectors performed by the Belgian firms Solvay and Union Miniere.

Table 8 FDI Value Structure in the Bulgarian Industry Including Mining (production of energy not included) - Projects above 100,000 USD, end 1997 (%)

Branch	Share
Food	24.5
Chemicals, plastics and pharmaceuticals	21.6
Cement and construction materials	20.7
Non-ferrous metallurgy	13.4
Machine building and metal products	5.3
Mining	3.4
Electrical and electronic appliances	2.9
Printing	2.6
Paper	1.5
Wood and furniture	1.5
Textiles and clothing	0.7
Other	1.9
TOTAL	100.0

Sources: Foreign Investment Agency and own calculations.

Firms from Western European countries represent the bulk of total FDI inflows (Table 9). At the end of 1997, German firms account for about 21% of the total, followed by investors from Belgium (20%), Netherlands (7.4%), USA (5.9%), Switzerland (5.4%) and Greece (4.8%). Some American companies have invested in Bulgaria through their European affiliates and their real share in FDI stock is certainly underestimated. Greece (6th in terms of FDI value) has the largest number of investments (about 12.7% of the total FDI operations).

With regard to the fields of activity, 37% of total FDI stock was invested in manufacturing at the end of 1995 (Tables 7 and 8). Construction and transport attracted respectively about 1.1% and 5.9%, while trade attracted 17.3% of invested capital. In terms of the number of FDI cases, trade accounted for about 80%, while the weight of manufacturing was less than 5.2%, and those of construction and transport less than 2.6%. Concerning investment in manufacturing, and according to the available data for operations of more than 100,000 USD (total value of about 753 million USD - own calculations), the investments of Solvay and Unions Miniere account for 35% of the total. Various industrial branches (electronics, sanitary products, paper, machinery,...) have attracted foreign investment but the only significant concentration is visible in the food industry with about 25% of the total value. The importance of textiles and especially clothing are certainly under-estimated because the number of operations is of low unitary value (less than 100,000 USD) and figures are not available.

At the end of 1997, FDI in Bulgaria is mostly concentrated in the city of Sofia with about 41.1% of the total FDI value, followed by Barna (19.8%), the region of Sofia (11.3%) and Lovetch (8.39%).

Table 9 FDI in Bulgaria by Countries (31/12/1997)

Countries	Value (million USD)	% of total amount
Germany	261.88	20.9
Belgium	251.94	20.1
Netherlands	92.55	7.4
USA	73.53	5.9
Switzerland	68.03	5.4
Greece	60.21	4.8
Austria	54.63	4.4
Great Britain	50.06	4.0
S. Korea	45.66	3.6
Spain	44.67	3.6
Luxembourg	41.98	3.3
Russia	30.91	2.5
Cyprus	27.18	2.2
Ireland	22.82	1.8
France	16.68	1.3
Turkey	14.81	1.2
Others	69.44	7.6
Total	1251.86	100.0

Source: UN/ECE.

Romania

According to the Romanian Development Agency, the total amount of FDI in Romania reached 3.78 billion USD, which is clearly above the 2.46 billion USD estimated by UNCTD (Table 2). Data indicate that the number of companies with foreign participation is quite important, while the average size of FDI operations and FDI per capita (Table 3) are quite low (see also Ferris et al, 1994). Just a small number of important foreign investments have notable effects on the national economy, even compared to Albania and Bulgaria.

Table 10 Sector Structure of FDI in Romania, 1997 (by value, %)

Sector	Share
Primary sector (mining included)	6.0
Industry	53.0
Services	35.5
Transportation and telecommunications	*4.0*
Trade	*16.0*
Tourism	*4.0*
Financing	*5.0*
Construction	*1.0*
Without precision	6.0
Total	100.0

Source: UN/ECE.

Regarding the sector structure (Tables 10 and 11), almost all companies with foreign participation have declared numerous fields of activity, both in order to be able to make immediate use of any opportunities in the market and to avoid re-registration procedures. In most of the cases, trade is declared as one major activity. Transport and tourism also attract a great proportion of foreign investors. Within manufacturing, machine building, food processing and, to a lesser extent, chemicals and oil production, are the best represented. Textile, transport equipment and electronics/electrotechnics also have a relatively important share. From the point of view of value, some important investments are taking place in the fields of energy and metallurgy.

Table 11 Structure of FDI in Romania by Value and by Industry Including Mining (energy production not included), end 1997

Branch	Share
Machine building	25
Food and tobacco	25
Cement and construction materials	11
Chemicals	9
Mining and oil	7
Textiles and clothing	7
Transport equipment	5
Electric and electronic appliances	5
Metallurgy and metal products	2
Other	4
TOTAL	100

Sources: UN/ECE, Romanian Development Agency and own calculations.

In 1997, FDI in Romania is mostly concentrated in Bucharest with about 56% of the invested capital and about 62% of the incorporated companies. Counties with a substantial share are Dolj (6.4%), Timis (5.6%), Cluj (3.7%), Constanta (3.4%), Bihor (3.1%), Arges (1.9%) and Prahova (1.9%). As to the distribution of investments according to the country of origin, OECD countries have 74% of the invested capital and 51% of the incorporated companies (Table 12). At the end of 1997, Western European countries accounted for 61% of the invested capital and 48% of the FDI cases. Meanwhile, commitments of investors from developing countries increased considerably. Indeed, five countries (Syria, Jordan, Lebanon, Iraq and Iran) accounted together for 26% of the total number of foreign participation in registered FIEs and, in 1996, South Korea's Daewoo Heavy Industries was at the top of the foreign firms with a 156 million USD contribution, in exchange for 51%, in a joint venture with the Romanian carmaker Automobile Craiova. France, South Korea, Netherlands, Germany, USA and Italy were the major investor countries at the end of 1997.

Table 12 Foreign Investors in Romania (15/12/1997)

Country	Capital invested, million USD	% of total amount
France	427.1	12.6
S. Korea	368.3	10.8
Netherlands	294.6	8.7
Germany	290.1	8.5
USA	254.5	7.5
Italy	199.8	5.9
Great Britain	139.4	4.1
Turkey	124.4	3.7
Austria	99.3	2.9
Luxembourg	94.9	2.8
Switzerland	88.4	2.6
Greece	64.6	1.9
Australia	61.2	1.8
Canada	54.4	1.6
Others	839.0	24.7
TOTAL	3,400.0	100.0

Source: Romanian Development Agency.

Slovenia

At the end of 1995 the stock of invested foreign capital had risen to 1,643 million USD (Rojec 1997). Though other transition countries such as Hungary have attracted a much higher volume of FDI, the cumulative stock of FDI per capita, which amounted to USD 520 at the end of 1997, is quite high (Table 3).

Five countries account for as much as 93% of total FDI in 1995 (Table 14). The Slovene-Croatian joint venture in a nuclear power plant, which took place at the time when the former Yugoslavia was still in existence, more or less explains the place of Croatian direct investment. Leaving Croatia aside, by far the greatest volume of invested foreign capital originates from Austria (25.5%), followed by Germany (21.3%), France (10.5%) and Italy (9%). In most cases, foreign investors are small or medium-size firms from one of the nearby EU countries, which are also Slovenia's major foreign trade partners (Rojec 1997). Except for Croatia, FDI from other Balkan countries was very low. There is some investment from Bosnia and Herzegovina and Yugoslavia still dating from the time when the countries together formed SFRY.

Table 13 Branch Structure of FDI in the Slovenian Industry (value, 1996, %)

Branch	Share
Paper	23.5
Electric and electronic appliances	20.9
Transport equipment	17.3
Chemicals, plastics and pharmaceuticals	16.8
Food	9.3
Non-ferrous metallurgy	5.5
Machine building	2.7
Other	4.0
Total	100.0

Sources: UN/ECE and Bank of Slovenia.

Table 14 Cumulative Stock of FDI in Slovenia by Countries, 1995

Countries	USD	%
Croatia	681	26.6
Austria	652	25.5
Germany	546	21.3
France	269	10.5
Italy	230	9.0
Spain	59	2.3
Great Britain	49	1.9
Netherlands	24	0.9
Denmark	23	0.9
Belgium	14	0.6
Other	13	0.5
TOTAL	2,558	100.0

Sources: UN/ECE and Bank of Slovenia.

Table 15 Characteristics of the Activity and Investment Forms

	Greenfield	Acquisition	Joint venture
Labour intensive	+++	---	+/-
Capital intensive (technology largely diffused)	---	+++	+++
Specific (protected) technology	+++	---	---
Well established trademark	+++	+/-	+/-
Need of distribution channels	---	+++	+++
High restructuring costs	+++	---	+/-
Problems of land property	---	---	+++

Source: Rizopoulos 1995a, p. 214.

The largest FDI projects are mainly concentrated in the manufacturing sector and particularly in electrical machinery and appliances, transport equipment, chemicals, paper, food and tobacco. In 1996, manufacturing thus accounts for 74% of all foreign direct investments, and services, 36% percent. This is quite a different situation compared to the other Balkan countries where instability and uncertainty foster small scale investments in low risk activities. Most of the large FDI projects in Slovenia have grown out of previous successful cooperation between the foreign investor and the Slovenian partner/target company and have multiple objectives (market enlargement, access to technological knowledge, re-exporting and cost advantages, trade links with other neighboring countries, etc).

Nature and Motivations of Western Investors in the Balkan Countries

FDI flows in the Balkan countries remain relatively weak compared to the other zones of the world economy or to the other East European countries such as Hungary and Poland. Meanwhile, systemic change has favoured a growing internationalisation of the Balkan economies. Economic liberalisation and reforms have alleviated, at least partially, the constraints burdening entrepreneurial activity under the former regime. So, a significant number (in comparison to the past) of Western enterprises have invested in the Balkan countries since 1990.

We can identify three major categories of investors in relation to size, internationalisation of activities, strategic objectives and previous involvement in the Balkan countries (Rizopoulos 1995a, Maroudas & Rizopoulos, 1995):

- Leading multinational firms with a real global strategy, trying to develop, consolidate or protect their positions and market shares in some specific enlarged international markets. They have to resolve location problems but Balkan the countries are just a piece in this global puzzle and national characteristics are rather secondary parameters concerning direct investment in this region. Food industry provides some good examples (Amylum, Kraft Jacob Suchard, Danone, Coca Cola...).
- Followers, trying to ameliorate their competitive position. They constitute the majority of investors in the Balkan countries and represent very different initial situations (efficient but relatively small or very specialised enterprises, firms suffering from a restricted home market, big groups having difficulties with declining products...). They have in common their interest in specific advantages, in order to exploit or to acquire. For this reason, national market characteristics play an important role.
- The third category is a mixed one. It is composed of both big multinational (Dow Chemical, Siemens...) and small or medium size enterprises (Byk Gulden...) which have developed long- lasting relations (before systemic change) with the region as a whole or with a specific country (for FDI in Bulgaria before 1989, see Maroudas 1995 and Maroudas & Rizopoulos 1995). The opening of these markets has changed (often weakened) their relative position because of new entries. Meanwhile, they benefit from the good knowledge of local context and some extremely important formal and informal relations. On this basis, they adapt their approach and try to develop their activities further. They are often involved in complex operations (privatisation, equity joint ventures...).

As far as specific strategic goals are concerned, we can also identify three major reasons motivating investment in one or several Balkan countries (Rizopoulos 1995a, Maroudas & Rizopoulos 1995 ; see also Dunning 1993 for the "resource seeking" and the "market seeking" FDI):

- Market penetration, the creation of competitive advantages and the elevation of entry barriers. Indeed, the hope to benefit from "first

94

mover" advantages and monopolistic position constitutes a very attractive perspective, especially for "followers". Relatively stable oligopolistic structure of a great proportion of activities (for Bulgaria, see Jones & Meurs 1991) and the disappearance or the difficulties of local firms facilitate market share control strategies of the first movers. Indeed, "contestability" of local markets grows, but high concentration makes possible the immediate control of important market shares. On the other hand, as a great deal of empirical evidence confirms (UN 1988), there is a strong correlation between FDI and the turnover realised in a foreign country. Direct involvement weakens competitors in each particular market.

Sometimes, FDI is the result of customers' delocalisation. Packaging activities and especially production of metal boxes or seals for soft drinks and beer are good examples (the Swiss investment firm Talladium has invested USD 12 million in the Bulgarian enterprise Razvitie, Crown International - affiliate to the Greek 3E - has invested in Romania...).

- Approaching the neighbouring markets (Russia, Ukraine...), which are larger but have a higher element of risk, as well as the other Balkan countries, thanks to the cultural and geographical proximity and to the traditional relations linking them. The purchase of the Bulgarian leader in cement production, Gazobeton, by the German Ytong, as well as the investments of the German brewery Brau & Brunnen, or of a French industrial bakery, constitute some examples. However, the risk of creating parallel distribution channels - because of the differential price policies and structures - with these already existing in Greece seems to dissuade some American multinationals from investing in the other Balkan countries (Lambropoulos 1995).
- Strengthening competitive positions in Western markets through the exploitation of comparative advantages (access to know-how, raw materials, low production costs and re-exporting...). The raw materials for the perfume and cosmetics sector (Asko-G, Marubeni-J...), copper mining (Navan Resources) in Bulgaria, as well as oil production in Albania and Romania, are some examples.

Important differences exist among the Balkan countries. Market control and, to a lesser extent, expansion in other regional markets seem to be the dominant goals of FDI in Bulgaria and in Romania. However, it is possible that the very limited information concerning some simpler forms of the largest defined FDI (especially sub-contracting), leads to an underestimation of cost advantage oriented investment. On the other hand, it seems clear that Albania attracts investors seeking lower production costs in labour intensive activities (clothing, knitwear...) or subsoil resources (oil, mining...), given that the internal market is extremely narrow for reasons of both population and living standards. A sector approach seems necessary to explain some "market" or "cost advantage" oriented FDI. According to G. Graziani (1996), who studies the case of the Italian textile and clothing industry, FDI in Eastern and Central Europe in such labour intensive activities is mainly cost advantage oriented (29% of all Italian FDI in Bulgaria and Romania have been made in the textile and clothing sectors and relocation in the textile industry - relatively more capital intensive - is of lesser importance than in clothing), even though market motivations hold the first place in all FDI operations in Eastern Europe.

Types of Investment

Frequently we can notice a sequence concerning the complexity and the type of involvement of the Western firms. Commercial representations and exports are preferred during the first period of contact with the local context and partners. Afterwards, simple industrial co-operation forms can be adopted (subcontracting, licensing, co-production...) and if co-operation is successful, the Western partner may decide upon a more complex and risky investment (greenfield, acquisition through privatisation, joint-venture). Licensing remains a common practice and "ancient type" agreements (barter) have not disappeared because of capital shortage and financial problems of local partners.

Given that market penetration constitutes the most frequent goal, distributorship (shop networks, improvement of maintenance activities...) is a widespread form of initial involvement since financial and organisational risks are limited. At the same time, distributorship gives the opportunity to evaluate market situation, reliability of local partners and potential of future activities. But even distributorship is restrained to services, tourism and light industry, because of the risks for the company's image in the case of more complex products.

Acceleration of economic reform should favour autonomous direct investment. Meanwhile, co-operative strategies continue to constitute the dominant form of Western investment in the Balkan markets. Indeed, the will to diminish uncertainty, as well as the slow pace of privatisation, favours partnerships with local enterprises. They represent 47% of FDI operations in Bulgaria, 58% in Romania and 71% in Albania during the first five years of transition (Miliarakis 1995). In most cases, joint-venture seems to be the best solution, giving more guarantees to the foreign investor (especially in the case of land property problems) and the possibility of purchasing the local partner if the co-operation is successful (for joint venture advantages and disadvantages in the penetration of foreign markets see Contractor & Lorange 1988, Gomes-Cacceres 1989, Toyne & Walters 1993). Obviously, western firms prefer majority control and show little interest in joint-ventures with big state enterprises.

Preference for local or semi-local trademarks, because of nationalistic feelings or of "best price searching" behaviour is also favourable to partnerships with local firms. However, the share of autonomous direct investment should grow in the case of greater economic and political stability. In any case, the structural characteristics of each activity and of local enterprises largely determine the type of investment (Table 16).

Table 16 Stock of Greek FDI in the Balkan Countries

	Year	Number	Value (USD million)	Position	Total value of FDI (USD million)
Albania	1997	200	52	2	133
Bosnia-Herzegovina	1996	7			
Bulgaria	IX 1997	1,000	120	3	1,200
Yugoslavia	VII 1997	127	390	2	1,080
FYROM	1995	63			
Romania	1997	1,481	70	11	3,052
Total		2,878			

Source: Greek Ministry of National Economy.

Table 17 Stock of Greek FDI in Romania

	1994	1995	1996	1997
Value (USD million)	33.7	50.0	58.4	63.9
Number	1,310	1,510	1,621	1,659

Source: Romanian Development Agency.

Table 18 Inflows of Greek FDI in Bulgaria, 1992-1997 (1,000 USD)

1992	1993	1994	1995	1996	1997	Total
164.1	50,76.8	29,74.8	29,785.7	11,753.2	10,459.1	60,213.3

Source: Bulgarian Foreign Investment Agency.

Table 19 Sector Structure of Greek FDI in Bulgaria, (value, 1997, %)

	Total	Industry	Constr.	Agricul.	Transp.	Telecom.	Tradeï	Tourism.	Finance	Other
Greek FDI	100.0	78.0	2.0	0.1	0.1	1.2	6.2	2.2	5.9	4.3
Total FDI	4.8	6.7	8.9	1.0	0.1	6.5	1.7	1.5	3.8	5.6

Sources: Bulgarian Foreign Investment Agency and own calculations.

Costs and Benefits for the Balkan Countries

The traditional economic theory suggests a number of beneficial effects of FDI for the host countries: competition and, thus, improvement of economic efficiency, resource (capital, technology, managerial skills... transfers, positive balance of payments effects, social and cultural progress...).

It is assumed that FDI during transition is of critical importance for financing the economic adjustment (see also Booth 1994). Through investment in key industries, FDI would contribute to the development of market based enterprises because of the relative capital scarcity in the host countries. FDI would also stimulate demand from smaller enterprises and suppliers would have to invest in technology and improve organisational and managerial practices. Finally, FDI should ameliorate local purchasing power and living standards (multiplier effects), as well as enhance employment and industrial capabilities among the labour force, while imitation and backward and forward linkages could be developed with related industries. Contracts with local enterprises could ensure sustainable development. Equally, FDI should enable local firms to market their products under the brand name of the foreign investor and through their distribution channels. High quality inputs, rationalisation of the production process and managerial experience also constitute some positive effects.

Negative direct or indirect effects are possible too. Major FDI may crowd out local firms, with a loss of entrepreneurial skills and talents. "Cherry picking" can have the same result. On the other hand, foreign investors try to benefit from (or to create) monopolistic situations by acquiring the leading enterprises of one sector (generally, at very low prices, because of the lack of reliable valuations of assets). In the longer run, host countries might get "locked in" their present structure of revealed comparative advantages, based on highly labour-intensive activities, while the exploitation of potential comparative advantages in higher-tech stages of production would be delayed.

On the other hand, a certain share of the national production and exports would strictly depend on foreign investors' decisions and performance, hence, increasing economic vulnerability (especially in the case of plants for the assembly of goods for sale in the local markets). Import of raw materials and semi-finished products might prevent local industry from developing fully. Local enterprises might be obliged to adapt to the foreign investors' needs and some functions, like R&D, might even disappear. Finally, regional inequalities might be strengthened, as these activities tend to cluster around particular zones. Meanwhile, the fact is that in many cases, local firms have no better choice in order to survive. Dunning (1993) suggests that the role of FDI is likely to fluctuate according to both the form and stage of economic development of the host countries.

As far as the balance of payments is concerned, the impact seems to be neutral in the long term (Bellon & Gouia 1977), given that local earning of previous investments is in large part reinvested (in 1995, 60% of the total investment of the American multinationals).

There is no reliable data concerning the contribution of companies with foreign participation to the performance (growth, profits, exports, imports...) of the different Balkan economies. However, according to some studies realised in more "advanced" transition countries (especially in Hungary), companies with foreign participation show better performances compared to the average of national firms. At the same time, the decisions of the new owners concerning: layoffs, closing down of plants, or repatriation of profits by means of tax avoidance, as well as the import of goods and the subsequent deterioration of the balance of payments cause concern among governments and individuals about the long-term consequences of the FDI. It is likely that FDI will have different effects according to the particular conditions prevailing in each country, including the strategic and organisational behaviour of decision-makers. It seems that FDI could play a positive role where there are clear objectives and policies on the part of the local partners (including governments), while providing sufficient assurances for foreign investors.

Positions and Strategies of the Greek Enterprises in the Balkans

Greek enterprises have a very particular position in this region. Their traditional activities (mainly non-durable consumer goods and bulk intermediate products) may face intense competition in their national and international markets. The healthiest among them feel the narrowness of the Greek internal market and tend to acquire positions in international markets. However, they are globally dominated in the world economy because of technological, productive, commercial or financial weakness. Insufficient size, shortage of capital and entry barriers raised by European partners make penetration of the European Union markets very difficult. At the same time, big multinationals try to consolidate their positions in the Greek market (actually very profitable, especially for consumer goods). This means that their competitive positions are, in general, weak, and at risk of losing market shares.

In this context, systemic change in the north neighbouring countries appeared as a good opportunity for expansion. Balkan markets constitute a second best for two main reasons:

- Reinforcement in the Balkan region could ameliorate their global position (scale economies, market enlargement, cost advantages...).
- Powerful multinational groups are not very interested in these countries because of the ignorance of the local context, great political, economic and social uncertainty and very narrow (compared to other world

regions) internal markets. On the contrary, for Greek enterprises these markets are quite important (Bulgaria has almost the same population as Greece).

Greek enterprises have some specific competitive advantages in this region. They are not always at the best technological level, but they have acquired a good knowledge of the advanced management and marketing methods and the functioning of a "market" economy. So, a complementarity with local enterprises, which frequently have a high technological and productive competence, is possible. At the same time, Greek products are considered to have good quality compared to local standards and, at the same time, they are less expensive than comparable Western products. Next, relatively small size diminishes fears of absolute control and suspicion of local partners who can maintain a higher bargaining power would be the case, if it were necessary to contend with big multinational enterprises.

Furthermore, Greek firms are favoured by their proximity and low transport costs. They have a better knowledge of local context and greater adaptability, thanks to their flexibility, and their familiarity with the "rules of the game" of the informal economy, the conditions of high inflation and the weight of an inefficient bureaucracy. Also, the importance of similar perception of the world and of common language - from a semantic point of view -must not be underestimated. Other points which should not be underestimated are historical, religious and cultural traditions which constitute factors that both homogenise and fragment this region (great ethnic mobility and mixture, existence of recent or ancient Greek communities in the other Balkan countries having, sometimes, good positions in the public sector). These factors and the extensive utilisation of European Union programs and financial support, allow the exploitation of their relative competitive advantage compared to local firms. Finally, the relations of Greek firms with several multinational groups indubitably have incontestably an impact (but not always a favourable one) on the investment operations in the Balkans.

Following the dramatic growth of trade between Greece and most of the other Balkan countries (Petrakos 1997), investment activity of Greek enterprises is quite important. Meanwhile, it is very difficult to obtain reliable data on the number of operations or the value of invested capital in the Balkan countries. The Greek Ministry of National Economy provides figures only for the investments accompanied by an official application and the demand for subsidies. For the Balkan economies as a whole (including countries of the former SFRY), 2,878 operations are identified up to the end of 1997, representing a total amount of investment of 632 million USD (Table 16).

About 200 Greek or Greek-Albanian enterprises were operational in Albania at the beginning of 1997, of which more than half have received financial assistance (grants) from the Greek State under the provisions of the (modified) Greek Investment Law. In their great majority, these investments are of very low value. Only 5-7% of Greek investment was designated for existing privatised enterprises. The invested Greek capital in Bulgaria at the end of 1997 was about 120 million USD distributed among approximately 1,000 operations (a number which is significantly higher than the Bulgarian figures and certainly overestimates the actually operating firms). The largest share of operations (about 80%) is entirely Greek owned (and usually very small) enterprises. Yet, the few important industrial investments were joint-ventures with a domestic firm - in almost all cases a private one - and a small share (5-7%) represents privatised State firms. In 1997, only 3.8% of the registered Greek operations in Bulgaria represent an investment above 100,000 USD. The registered level of invested Greek capital in Romania at the end of 1997 was 70 million USD for 1481 operations. In fact, just about 500 Greek enterprises were operational this year.

As far the sector composition of Greek investment is concerned, the bulk of the Greek investment in Albania is concentrated in the food, textile, clothing and tobacco industries, which make up about 74% of the total capital invested (see also Table 20). In contrast, the majority of Greek firms in Bulgaria and in Romania are active in the fields of trade and services. From the value point of view, industry's share is about 78% of Greek investments in Bulgaria. Industrial investment is mainly concentrated in the food and drink industries, as well as in the paper industry, textiles, metal products and packaging. Greek FDI seems correlative to the sector structure of Greek exports to the Balkans (see Petrakos 1997).

It is noteworthy that Greek banks and financial institutions are very active in the Balkan countries. It is obvious that adequate financial infrastructure is a necessary condition for industrial investment. However, it seems that the Greek presence in banking is even more important than the Greek presence in the other economic sectors. Greek banks are involved both in the financing of infrastructures (transports, communications, energy...) and of private investment.

Table 20 Some Greek Direct Investments in the Balkans

ALBANIA

Enterprise	Sector	Value of investment	Other information
ACTION	Clothing	61 million dr.	Koritsa, 212 employees
ADELINE	Clothing	100 million dr.	Koritsa and Pogradets, 800 employees
ALFA	Clothing	n.a.	
ANTECO TEXTILES	Clothing	80 million dr.	Koritsa, 70 employees
APOLLONIA BANK (initial name which will be changed)	Finance	720 million dr.	Tirana
ARCZIPO	Cigarettes	n.a.	
CORDON	Clothing	82 million dr.	Koritsa, 400 employees
GATIC	Clothing, knitwear	n.a.	Gjirokaster
GLOBAL	Fur exports	n.a.	
FANCO	Clothing	200 million dr.	Koritsa, 120 employees
INTER-ALBANIA	Meat products	n.a.	
KAVER-SER	Tobacco treatment	n.a.	
KORCETEX	Clothing	n.a.	Koritsa
MIKAVERAT	Tobacco treatment	360 million dr.	Berat, 15 tons/day
SUPER BETON	Construction materials	n.a.	Agios Saranta, 85 employees

BULGARIA

Enterprise	Sector	Value of investment	Other information
ALPHA EPSILON	Business furniture	n.a.	
ATHINON BANK	Finance	n.a.	
B + G CHIMCO	Coatings	23 million dr.	Sofia, Vratza
BREWINVEST	Brewery	Initial investment: 5.3 billion dr. Total investment: 9.9 billion dr.	Joint-venture of 3E and ATHINAÏKI ZITHOPIIA (affiliate of HEINEKEN) which bought the biggest Bulgarian brewery, based in Stara Zagorka.
CHIOS BANK	Finance	n.a.	Sofia, 25 employees
DELTA	Ice-creams and milk products	2.8 billion dr.	Production and distribution network, Varna, 400 employees
DROMEAS	Business Furniture	n.a.	
ETEM	Metal products	892,000 USD	
FAROS	Training in foreign languages and computers	n.a.	
GERMANOS	Distribution of accumulators	n.a.	
GOODY'S	Fast-food	1.1 million USD	Sofia
IONIAN BANK	Finance	3 million USD	
KATERINA	Textiles	538,082 USD	Pirin

Table 20 cont.

KATSIGIANNIS	Design	1.65 million USD	Sofia
LEVENTIS/3E (COCA-COLA)	Bottling and production of plastic caissons	2.4 billions dr.	Sofia and factories in Bourgas, Plovdiv, Targoviste, Pleven. 1.400 employees
MAILLIS	Packaging materials	207,000 USD	Sofia
MAKEDONIAN-THRACE BANK	Finance	n.a.	
MORTIMOR	Textiles	219,000 USD	
INTRACOM	Telecommunications, production of electronic and computer equipment	5 billions dr.	Joint-venture with MULTIGROUP (Bulgaria)
NEOSET	Home furniture	n.a.	
OLYMPIC	Advertising	72 millions dr.	Affiliate to DDB NEEDHAM. Sofia, 6 employees
PRODECO	Clothing	840 millions dr.	3 factories and a retail network in different cities
SATO	Business furniture	n.a.	
TKM FRUIT	Food and soft drinks	8.55 million USD	

ROMANIA

Enterprise	Sector	Value of investment	Other information
BANCA BUCURESTI (affiliate of ALPHA CREDIT)	Finance	5.62 million USD	Based in Bucharest, agencies in Klouz, Constanza, Arad, Iasi, Baja Mare. 66 employees
BEST FOODS	Food	2.84 million USD	
CROWN INTERNATIONAL (affiliate of 3E)	Packaging (metallic seals)	600,000 USD	Iasi
DELTA	Dairy products	417,000 USD	
ELPEN	Pharmaceuticals and medical equipment	n.a.	
HAMBO	Fast-food	n.a.	
INTRACOM	Telecommunications	4.4 million USD	Organisation of Romanian LOTO, informatization of rails..., Bucharest
MACEDONIAN-THRACE BANK	Finance	n.a.	Bucarest
MOLINO (G-B)/3E	Bottling of soft drinks	n.a.	Iasi, Oradea
PAPASTRATOS + IONIAN TRADING	Tobacco	804,000 uDS	
TITCO	Fuels	6.2 million USD	

At the beginning, there were some isolated movements such as Chios-bank - affiliate of Vardinogiannis group - which invested in Bulgaria mainly to serve the financing needs of its parent company, which is very active in this country (fuels, press, tourism, trade companies...). Meanwhile, other important operations have been rapidly set up: Alpha Credit invested in Romania, as has done the state owned Commercial Bank which considers the Black Sea zone as a priority for expansion. The Ionian Bank (affiliate of the Commercial Bank) has created the Balkan-Ionian Bank, jointly with food processing and construction enterprises, which develops its activities in Bulgaria and in Albania. Attikis Bank, another affiliate of the Commercial Bank, is involved in Albania, as is the National Bank, which has formed a joint Albanian-Greek Bank. The Macedonian-Thrace Bank aims at rapid expansion in the Balkans and is planning to set up a venture capital firm based in Thessaloniki, to assist Greek business investment. Links between Greek banks and international banks (EBRD, World Bank...) seem to play an important role and to favour their expansion in this region. For example, Global Finance and Euromerchant Balkan Fund (Latsis group) are involved in Bulgaria, in co-operation with the EBRD, the International Finance Corporation (World Bank) and some Greek firms having investment plans in this country.

Even though industrial investment is less important in terms of number of FDI cases, some significant operations already exist: Controlled by the Cypriot owned Leventis Group the Greek 3E bottling company, the Coca-Cola franchise-holder for Greece and Bulgaria, has become a very important investor in Bulgaria, with investments of more than 100 million USD, by acquiring majority stakes in five co-operative bottling plants around the country and setting up its own distribution network. It has also invested in a greenfield site outside Sofia, and acquired control of 3P, a plastics manufacturer. 3E has also diversified to beer-brewing (Zagorka), through a joint venture (Brewinvest) with another Greek company (a Heineken affiliate). Molino Beverages, also controlled by Leventis, has invested 78 million USD in three new Coca-Cola plants in Romania, where it has a franchise covering 40% of the population. Delta (dairy products) in Bulgaria and Romania or Fanco (clothing) in Albania also constitute quite important operations (Table 20).

Conclusions and Policy Implications

FDI could be an important element of economic restructuring and adjustment in the Balkans. However, flows and stock of foreign direct investment are still very low. Foreign investors are often surprised by the infrastructure and institutional features of the Balkan countries (insufficient roads, telecommunications, financial organisations or capital markets, but also legal problems, administrative or "lobbying" attitudes, employees' behaviour, working styles or specific relations between the social actors). Furthermore, great uncertainty has a negative impact on FDI operations. It is clear that the rapid dismantling of the former system should create a more favourable institutional framework for foreign investment opportunities. But, alternatively, the instability arising from an excessively rapid reform may discourage FDI (see also Ferris & et al. 1994).

On the other hand, the major objectives of most foreign investors (market penetration or delocation of some labour intensive activities) are not always favourable to productive investment or technology transfers. "Followers" may offer host countries more advantages compared to the "leaders", in return for preferred access to local markets or resources. Meanwhile, only a very limited part of gross fixed capital formation is related to FDI, even though foreign investment in infrastructure can play a great role in economic development. Indeed, following the international experience in this sector (UNCTD 1996), local governments seem to turn more and more to foreign firms for capital and technology, notably in telecommunications. Meanwhile, even if it is a factor of critical importance concerning future development, FDI cannot substitute for local investment.

It is noteworthy that, according to the existing data, there is very little dependence of FDI on GDP growth. For example, although FDI flows in Bulgaria increase rapidly till the end of 1994, there is serious macro-economic disequilibrium and very slow growth. It is equally difficult to find any relation between the growth of the different sectors and the flows of FDI. For instance, a negative evolution of the food industry in Bulgaria does not hinder FDI in this sector. This point is contrary to the conclusions of UNCTD (1996), which argues that economic growth and FDI inflows in the Central and Eastern European economies are closely related. Meanwhile, this same report identifies two major exceptions: FDI related to privatisation and FDI linked to establishing first-mover advantages escape this interrelationship. Given that in most cases FDI operations in the Balkans are not linked to privatisation programs until the middle of the nineties, the important share of first-mover strategies seems to be at the origin of this situation.

FDI could also be a vector of a wider Balkan co-operation. Actually, Greece appears as a major investor in Albania, Bulgaria and, to a lesser extent, Romania. In the short term, the extension of Greek investment seems possible in some specific sectors or activities (the food industry, clothing, textiles, leather, shoes, banking, services and trade, but also transport, telecommunications and energy, provided that there are good relations among states and financial support). In the medium term, the amelioration of the economic situation could favour increased inter-Balkan foreign direct investment and that also means investment from the other Balkan countries in Greece. But for the moment, there is no real economic interdependence among the Balkan countries. Intra-Balkan trade is a small share of total trade and, in some cases, trade with some other countries of the region has decreased. FDI flows among Balkan countries are also very weak and they cannot substitute for FDI from more advanced countries. Given that inter-Balkan FDI depends on the relations of local enterprises with big multinational firms, investment in other Balkan countries might be linked to the global strategy of parent companies rather than to the strategies of local actors.

This general context implies the definition of relevant policy issues. Two public policy orientations seem to be of tremendous importance. Indeed, it is necessary to:

- ameliorate the global attractiveness in order to create better conditions for the FDI in the transitional Balkan countries.
- intensify the FDI flows between the counties of the region.

The first point raises the question of adequate measures to improve attractiveness. Actually, beyond the solution of current political, social and economic crises, attractiveness can not be seen as exclusively linked to the cost of production factors, to public subsidies and to fiscal rules, given that every country in the world proposes this kind of advantages. It is the endogenous organisational, collective and environment dynamics of the local productive systems (behaviour of economic actors, qualification of manpower, density and quality of business relations, dynamics of local capital, innovation...) that determine global attractiveness (see Bellon & Gouia 1997). It is necessary to establish norms and rules commonly accepted by the socio-economic actors and, at the same time, to favour economic growth. In this sense, public policy can not be limited to macro-economic stabilisation and state disengagement. Growth is impossible without local investment, but in the existing conditions, investment is impossible without public support. In this context, there should be some role for industrial policy (see Rizopoulos 1995b). Placed within the neo-classical framework, industrial policy distorts relative prices, impedes flexibility and favour special interest groups against the less organised common interest. Meanwhile, the organisation of markets, the rise of investment and the integration in the European economy seem impossible in the absence of any industrial policy. The choice of priority know-how and competencies, the valorisation of sector specialisation or a relatively harmonious regional development cannot be accomplished by capital markets and private initiative alone.

Moreover, it is doubtful whether there should be dissociation of restructuring and development. Reformers think that restructuring will allow access to the market, but in the absence of effective demand, restructuring makes no sense. As a result, the state must favour economic growth in general, as well as consolidation of specific markets. At the same time, it has to ameliorate the bargaining power of local enterprises so that they may face trade partners and foreign investors, and facilitate integration into the international strategic alliances networks.

Public action must be guided by the necessity to develop learning processes. Hybrid regulation mechanisms should allow the establishment of new relations and the attenuation of the deindustrialization effects. Indeed, it is not certain that the state could play this role in the Balkan countries. Efficient state intervention presupposes that there exists a reasonable capacity to decide in an autonomous way and even to act contrary to some specific interests. This condition is far from obvious. But it must be clear that in the case of state failure, improvement of attractiveness is doubtful.

Together with the amelioration of the global attractiveness of these countries, public policy has to push towards exploitation of the potential advantages of a regional co-operation. Indeed, further intra-Balkan FDI development seems closely related to the political willingness of the different states in this region.

Even though substitution for FDI originating from the rest of the world is not a reliable perspective, a variety of reasons make regional co-operation interesting for the Balkan countries.

Cross Balkan investment and the development of close links among local enterprises can constitute a positive factor as far as the development of an adequate strategic behaviour of local public and private actors is concerned. The ability to form partnerships creates an atmosphere of trust and loyalty. In this sense, negotiation of co-operative arrangements between neighbours can prepare and facilitate the integration into more extended international networks, and intra-Balkan investment flows could be complementary with FDI originating from the rest of the world.

On the other hand, interpenetration of national productive systems and co-operation make economies of scale, technology and know-how exchanges possible, facilitate international expansion of inexperienced firms, and allow quasi-integration advantages by linking the activities of the partners in a "value chain" (Contractor & Lorange 1988). Simultaneously, it makes possible the exploitation of cross-border co-operation, which was non-existent for several decades (Petrakos 1995). In general, creating co-operative irreversibility and mutual dependence is one of the major means contributing to both political stability, and economic performance in this region.

Notes

1   For a discussion see (Graham 1996).
2   Meanwhile, we consider these "imperfections" as the normal state of any market and not as an evil.
3   Because of special conditions created by war, the other countries emerging from SFRY are not analysed here.

References

Aliber R. (1970): A theory of direct foreign investment, in Kindleberger (1970).

Anand J., Kogut B. (1997): Technological capabilities of countries, firm rivalry and foreign direct investment. Journal of International Business Studies, vol. 28, n° 3, 1997, pp. 445-465.

Bellon B., Gouia R. (1997): Les investissements directs etrangers: Nouvelles politiques de developpement industriel, Economica, Paris.

Blanchard O., Dornbusch R., Krugman P., Layard R., Summers L. (1991), Reform in Eastern Europe, The MIT Press, Cambridge, Mass.

Bobeva D. (1996): Foreign investment and small and medium-sized enterprises in Bulgaria, in OCDE: Small firms as foreign investors: case studies from transition economies, Paris, 1996.

Buckley P.J., Casson M. (1976): The future of the multinational enterprise, Macmillan, London.

Caves R. (1981): Multinational enterprise and economic analysis, Cambridge University Press, Cambridge.

Contractor F., Lorange P., eds (1988): Co-operative strategies in international business, Lexington Books, Lexington.

Cotta A. (1970): Les choix economiques de la grande entreprise, Dunod, Paris.

Dietz R. (1991): The role of western capital in the transition to the market - a systems' theoretical perspective, in L. CSABA (ed.): Systemic change and stabilization in Eastern Europe, Dartmouth, Aldershot, pp. 103-123.

Dunning J.H. (1981): International production and the multinational enterprise, George Allen & Unwin, London.

Dunning J.H. (1993a): Multinational enterprises and the global economy, Addison-Wesley, Wokingham.

Ferris S., Thompson R., Valsan C. (1994): Foreign direct investment in an emerging market economy. The case of Romania, Eastern European Economics, July-August, pp. 81-95.

Gedeshi I. (1997): Some characteristics of Foreign Direct Investments in Albania, Albanian Observer, n° 6.

Gomes-Caccere S.B. (1989): Joint ventures in the face of global competition, Sloan Management Review, vol. 30, n° 3, Spring, pp. 17-26.

Graham E. (1996): The (not wholly satisfactory) state of the theory of foreign direct investment and the multinational enterprise, Economic Systems, vol. 20, issue 2/3, pp. 183-206.

Hirsch S. (1967): Location of industry and international competitiveness, Oxford Univ. Press, London.

Hirsch S. (1976): An international trade and investment theory of the firm, Oxford Economic Papers, 28, July, pp. 258-270.

Hymer S., Rowthorn R. (1970): Multinational corporation and international oligopoly: the non-American challenge, in Kindleberger (1970).

Johnson H.G. (1970): The efficiency and welfare implications of the international corporation, in Kindleberger (1970).

Jones D., Meurs M. (1991): On entry of new firms in socialist economies: Evidence from Bulgaria, Soviet Studies, vol. 43, n° 2, pp. 311-327.

Kindleberger C.-P. (1969): American business abroad, six lectures on direct investment, Yale Univ. Press, New Haven.

Kindleberger C.-P. ed. (1970): The international corporation, MIT Press, Cambridge.

Knickerbocker F. (1973): Oligopolistic reaction and the multinational enterprise, Harvard Univ. Press, Boston.

Kojima K. (1978): Direct foreign investment, a Japanese model of multinational business operations, Helm, London.

Krugman P., Obstfeld M. (1995): Economie internationale, De Boeck, Paris-Bruxelles.

Lambropoulos K. (1995): Strategy of Greek business in the Balkans, in Maroudas L., Tsardanidis Ch.: The Greek-Bulgarian relations: Contemporary economic and political dimensions, Papazissis, Athens, 1995, pp. 273-284.

Lipsey R.E. & Weiss M.Y. (1981): Foreign production and exports in manufacturing industries, Review of Economics and Statistics, vol. LXIII, n°4, nov.

Maroudas L. (1995): Direct foreign investment in Bulgaria, in Maroudas L., Tsardanidis Ch.: The Greek-Bulgarian relations: Contemporary economic and political dimensions, Papazissis, Athens, 1995, pp. 151-183.

Maroudas L., Rizopoulos Y. (1995): La Bulgarie dans les strategies d'internationalisation des firmes occidentales, Revue d'Etudes Comparatives Est-Ouest, vol. 26, n° 1, mars, pp. 115-138.

Miliarakis N. (1995): Les investissements directs des entreprises grecques dans les pays des Balkans, memoire de DEA, University of Paris-I.

Mucchielli J.-L. (1985): Les firmes multinationales, mutations et nouvelles perspectives, Economica, Paris.

Mundell R.A. (1957): International trade and factor mobility, American Economic Review, vol. XLVII, n° 3, juin, pp. 321-335.

Petrakos G. (1995): Cross-border cooperation among Albania, Bulgaria and Greece, Final report, ACE contract n° 92-0391-R, Athens.

Petrakos G. (1997): The trade relations of Greece in the Balkans: Structure, evolution and implications for economic cooperation, Conference "Economic cooperation in the Balkans: A regional approach to European integration", University of Thessaly/Phare ACE, Volos, 16-19 January.

Ragazzi G. (1973): Theories of the determinants of foreign investment, IMF Staff Papers, vol. XX, n° 2, July, pp. 471-498.

Rainelli M. (1979): La multinationalisation des firmes, Economica, Paris.

Riche T.X. (1995): Investissement direct etranger dans les PECO, Chroniques Economiques, n° 11, 15 novembre, pp. 427-438.

Rizopoulos Y.(1991): La pharmacie en Europe centrale et orientale: les enjeux de la cooperation industrielle, Courrier des Pays de l'Est, n° 365, La Documentation Francaise, decembre, pp. 3-24.

Rizopoulos Y. (1995a): Competitive constraints and western firms' strategies in Bulgaria, in Maroudas L., Tsardanidis Ch.: The Greek-Bulgarian relations: Contemporary economic and political dimensions, Papazissis, Athens, 1995, pp . 185-217.

Rizopoulos Y. (1995b): Groupes d'interet, action public et dynamique industrielle, in Andreff W.: Le secteur public a l'Est. Restructuration industrielle et financiere, L'Harmattan, Paris, 1995, pp. 105-123.

Rojec M. (1997): The development potential of foreign direct investment in the Slovenian economy, WIIW, n° 235, April.

Simon H. (1983): Models of bounded rationality, 2 vol., MIT Press, Cambridge.

Swedenberg B. (1979): The multinational operations of Swedish firms, an analysis of determinants and effects, Almquist and Wiksell International, Stockholm.

Tarpagos A. (1994): The Balkan penetration of Greek capitalism, Theseis, N° 50, pp. 59-75.

Toyne B., Walters P. (1993): Global marketing management: A strategic perspective, Allyn & Bacon (2nd edition), Boston.

UN (1988): Transnational corporations in world development, United Nations Centre on Transnational Corporations, Geneva-New York.

UN - CEE (1994): East- West investment and joint ventures, Geneva-New York.

UNCTD (1995): World Investment Report 1995.

UNCTD (1996): World Investment Report 1996.

UNCTD (1998): World Investment Report 1998.

Vernon R. (1966): International investment and international trade in the product life cycle, Quarterly Journal of Economics, vol. 80, May, pp. 190-207.

Vernon R. (1974): The location of economic activity, in J.H. DUNNING (ed.): Economic analysis and the multinational entreprise, George Allen & Unwin, London, pp. 89-114.

111

5 Structural Reforms in Southeastern Europe: Demonopolization and Privatization in Albania, Bulgaria and Romania

VESSELIN MINTCHEV
Research Fellow, Institute of Economics, Bulgarian Academy of Sciences.

Introduction

This chapter presents a comparative analysis of the structural reforms in Bulgaria, Romania and Albania. These three countries belong to the "second wave" of emerging market economies (WB 1996). Their decline in GDP and in industrial output is considerably more serious than in Central Europe. They are characterised by fragile macroeconomic stabilisation and modest progress in their structural reforms (EBRD 1996). The chapter treats consecutively the decentralisation and the corporatisation of state enterprises, and the changes in property rights.

The first section of the analysis deals with the decentralisation of state enterprises. The division of the unions of the state-owned enterprises into their constituent parts is demanded by the concentration level in the typical central-planning economies, such as those of Bulgaria, Romania and Albania, as well as by the fact that socialist enterprises have social functions which are uncommon to firms within modern market economies. These issues are correlated with competition policy.

The second section treats corporatisation, in the sense of transformation of disintegrated unions and state enterprises into commercial companies. The issues concerning the restoration of commercial registers and the norms of commercial law are also dealt with. The changes are aimed at the normalisation of company organisation and the creation of the standard forms of individual business and commercial companies.

The third section examines the organic relation between decentralisation and corporatisation of state enterprises and privatisation legislation. The institutions in charge of the changes in the ownership regime are also presented. The section presents a comparative analysis of concrete policies with regard to restitution and "small-scale privatisation", privatisation of big industrial enterprises, and the development of mass privatisation schemes[1].

The analysis uses the emerging "theory of transition" (Andreff 1993, Lavigne 1995, Roland 1996); in particular, the section concerning reform of enterprises and changes in the property rights. Previous comparative studies of the economies of the Balkan countries are also taken into account (Gianaris 1982).

Decentralisation and demonopolisation of centrally planned economies could precede or follow price and foreign trade liberalisation. This is one of the factors determining the transition to a market economy as "heterodox" if changes begin with decentralisation, or as "orthodox" if systemic changes begin with liberalisation.

Corporatisation of state enterprises viewed as transformation of state enterprises into commercial companies is a precondition for privatisation. However, from the point of view of the corporative governance theories, it is a consequence of privatisation.

Privatisation is a political act of change of ownership. These changes can begin with re-privatisation and indemnification of former proprietors. Different methods are applied with the so called "small-" and "large-scale" privatisation. Schemes for mass privatisation disperse the property rights of transformed companies[2] and include in the agenda issues concerning the division of ownership from control and corporate governance.

Decentralisation

One of the dilemmas at the beginning of the systemic economic changes, was whether to begin with the liberalisation of prices and foreign trade, or the dismantling of existing state monopolies. This discussion was topical at the beginning of the Gorbachev perestroika[3].

The choices made at the beginning of the systemic changes by South-Eastern European countries are different. Bulgaria, and later Albania, began their reforms with liberalisation (Mintchev 1995, Totev 1997), Gadeshi and Mara 1997). Romania, on the contrary, began with measures aimed at the decentralisation of the economy (Zaman 1997). That choice determines the transition model. When reforms begin with price liberalisation, as in Poland and the Czech Republic, an "orthodox" character is added to them. If the emphasis is on decentralisation, a "heterodox" aspect is added.

Neither transition model actually exists in its ideal form. In both cases, the "orthodox" (shock therapy) and the "heterodox" (gradualism), the same measures are applied. The difference consists in the sequence and the dose. The delay of structural reforms (and especially of the transformation, privatisation and liquidation of the large-scale unprofitable state companies) in comparison with the price and foreign trade liberalisation, can bring extremely unfavourable consequences, such as the ones that Bulgaria has been experiencing since mid-1996 (UN - ECE 1997), (OECD - CCET 1997).

The combination of economic liberalisation and disintegration of the existing state monopolies has had a negative short- and mid-term impact on trade such as between former CMEA members - Bulgaria and Romania. Conversely, the systemic changes have a favourable influence on their trade with Greece and Turkey (Petrakos and Totev 1997).

In spite of the differences between Bulgaria and Albania, on the one hand, in which systematic transformation began with price and foreign trade liberalisation, and Romania, on the other, where first the enterprise unions in the Regies Autonomes and Commercial Companies were transformed, in all three countries there were important similarities. The size structure of state enterprises necessitated the dismantling of the existing unions and the restoration of the anti-monopoly provisions and the provisions for protection of competition.

Bulgaria

In Bulgaria, the activities of the central administration concerning decentralisation, are considered important elements for the structural adjustment of the economy (Ministry of Industry and Trade 1991). They followed price and foreign trade liberalisation.

At the end of 1989, the concentration in industry in Bulgaria was quite similar to that in Romania. "Big" enterprises, rather than "very big" ones, were prevailing, in the same way as in Romania. The enterprises with 501 to 5,000 employees produced 58.9 percent of the industrial output. The share of small firms (up to 200 employees) was considerable. They constituted 48.0 percent of the total number of firms, and 9.0 percent of the employees in industry work in them. They produced 7.9 percent of the industrial output of the country (Table 1).

Table 1 Industry Structure by Number of Employees and Industrial Production in Albania, Bulgaria and Romania Before the Transition

(percentages)

Enterprise Size (employees)	Share of enterprises			Share of employees			Share of Industrial production		
	Alban. 1980	Bulg. 1989	Rom. 1989	Alban. 1980	Bulg. 1989	Rom. 1989	Alban. 1980	Bulg. 1989	Rom. 1989
>5000*	6.2	0.6	6.8	28.0	10.9	32.9	-	13.0	33.8
501-5000**	53.1	25.7	67.7	57.0	60.8	63.0	-	58.6	60.2
201-500	32.5	25.7	3.6	13.6	19.3	4.8	-	20.5	4.8
200<	8.2	48.0	0.5	1.4	9.0	0.5	-	7.9	1.2

Sources: Romania Statistical Yearbook, 1990, p.428; Statistical Yearbook of Bulgaria, 1992, p. 109 (In the grouping for Bulgaria electricity providing and producing enterprises do not take part); Gadeshi Ilir, Albanian Case Study, p.5.
* - For Albania - > 2000.
** - For Albania - 501 - 2000.

A single Law of Competition (05/1991), including regulations against monopolies and for the protection of competition, was considered a better variant than two separate laws, one for each of these issues, as had been the case before World War II. In accordance with that law, the Commission for Protection of Competition was founded (in June, 1992).

This Law was preceded by the Council of Ministers' Regulation 154 on Decentralisation and Demonopolization (04/1991). Under the Ministers' Regulation, a decision for working out and implementing programmes for the division of the unions of the state-owned enterprises was taken. The deadline for approval of these programmes for the firms in electronics, telecommunications, energy, machine-building, metallurgy, chemical production, grain production and special production was 30 April. The reorganisation and the other activities were to be completed within short time frames. A list of 117 enterprises, having a monopoly status in the system of the former Ministry of Industry and Trade (MIT) at that time, was published. As a result of the anti-monopoly programmes in the MIT system, 139 firms were decentralised by the end of 1991. The decentralisation was completed on the basis of "orders" by the Council of

116

Ministers, based on the Commercial Law. The firms were transformed into 1360 units, of which 898 were limited liability companies, 220 joint stock companies and 3 holdings (Ministry of Industry and Trade 1991). These processes continued throughout 1991 and 1992 (OECD - CCET 1997).

Questions which had not been initially included in the legislative acts were raised in the discussions of and commentaries on, this matter. One of them was the definition of the conditions required for the existence of a monopoly position. It is not reasonable, in an economy the size of Bulgarians, which, besides other factors, is exposed to unfavourable foreign shocks, that local firms covering 35 percent of the national market be considered monopolies as is the case according to the Law on Protection of Competition.

Romania

In Romania large enterprises are predominant: as a relative share of the GDP, as a relative share of the employees, and even in number. Some 95.9 percent of the labour force population was employed in the large (from 500 to 5,000 employees) and the very large firms (with over 5,000 employees) in 1989. They produced 94 percent of the industrial production and constituted 74.5 percent of the number of companies (Table 1). In Romania, the concentration in industry is higher than in Bulgaria and Albania. It is even the highest in Central and Eastern Europe, in branches like mechanical engineering, wood processing and the textile industry (Lhomel 1996a). This is a serious obstacle to restructuring and adjusting the Romanian economy.

Unlike the situation in Bulgaria and Albania, in Romania the systemic transformation was initiated by decentralisation of the big unions (centrals), rather than by price liberalisation. Measures for the division of the large state enterprises and their unions were taken in Romania in 1990. In accordance with the clauses of Law No.15 (Table 2), about 50 of the existing centrals were transformed into more than 300 autonomous public companies and around 7,900 commercial companies. These measures have had some negative results, destroying the existing technological links, and causing a "managerial crisis" because of the change of the top managers (Zaman and Bratu 1997).

Table 2 Corporatisation of Enterprises in Albania, Bulgaria and Romania

	Albania	Bulgaria	Romania
Corporatisation (Changes in the status of state enterprises)	07/1992 Law on State Enterprises 04/1995 Law on Transformation of State-Owned Enterprises into Commercial Companies	1989 Decree on Economic Activity 1991 Law of Establishment of Sole Merchant Companies with State Property	08/1990 Law No.15 on reorganisation of the State Economic Units in Regies Autonomes and Commercial Companies 1993 Government Ordinance No.15
Regulations of the status and activity of companies	11/1992 Law on Commercial Companies;	1991 Commercial Law	- Commercial Code 1991 Law 31
Types of companies	- Limited liability company - Joint-stock company	- Partnership -Limited partnership -Public limited partnership - Limited liability company -Joint-stock company	- Partnership - Limited liability company - Stock company - Joint venture

Sources: Transition Report 1996, Infrastructure and Savings, EBRD, 1996; Trends and Policies in Privatisation, Vol. II No 2, OECD, 1995.

The Competition Act (Law No 21/ 1996) was adopted in April, 1996. This law, like the corresponding law in Bulgaria, includes provisions for protection of competition and provisions against monopolies. It has been in force since 1/01/1997. A Council of Competition and a Copyright Office have been established.

Albania

Albania is not an exception, in regard to the concentration of the government non-financial sector on the eve of reforms. As can be seen in Table 1, in the early 1980s 59.3 percent of the industrial enterprises, employing over 501 people, produced 71.6 percent of the industrial output and constituted 85.0 percent of the industrial labour force. The situation remained unchanged until the beginning of the systemic reforms. This accounts for the measures undertaken for the purpose of demonopolization and decentralisation of the economy. Besides the measures for privatisation and restructuring, measures for limiting the companies with a monopoly position were also included in the strategic programme of the Albanian cabinet for 1992. The processes of decentralisation are viewed, on the one hand, as decentralisation, with respect to the management decision making, and on the other hand, as a division of ineffective structures. Meanwhile, in accordance

118

with the Law on Commercial Companies (Table 2), 5 corporations, including enterprises from the strategic extracting and infrastructure branches, were founded (Gadeshi, Misja and Mara 1997).

In Albania, the Competition Act was adopted in December, 1995. It has introduced procedures against consolidations and mergers. An "Economic Competition Department" was established at the Ministry of Industry.

The processes of decentralisation and demonopolisation of the Balkan economies binder examination are confronted with similar difficulties and restrictions. The high degree of concentration of state enterprises and the lack of experience of the proper institutions in the area of competition policy are among the basic causes of the complicated and inconsistent nature of the decentralisation processes. The corporatisation, and consequently, the privatisation of state-owned companies largely depends on the speed of these processes and the way they proceed with decentralisation.

In spite of the differences in the transition models, these processes have the same direction in Bulgaria, Romania and Albania. This allows for an active exchange of experience and specialists. Initiatives in this respect are undertaken on the part of international institutions. The OECD popularises the experience of Greece and Turkey, as well as that of the Central Europe transition economies in the area of economy deregulation and anti-monopoly provisions and procedures in the above-mentioned three countries. In a long-term perspective, the normalisation of the size structure of economic agents in the Balkan countries under examination can be expected to be a factor encouraging the intensification of regional co-operation and integration.

Corporatisation of the State Enterprises in Bulgaria, Romania and Albania

The corporatisation of state enterprises is interpreted in different ways. It can be analysed both in regard to the division of ownership and control in modern companies, and from the point of view of corporate governance of already privatised companies (Peev and Hare 1995, Tchipev 1997).

At the initial stages of the transition to market economy, corporatisation is viewed normatively - as a transformation of the economic agents formed after the fragmentation of the monopoly structures, into commercial companies. This could either be a single juridical act of the central authorities, which would actually be most reasonable, or a process accompanying the restoration of the Trade Court and Commercial Register (Mintchev 1993).

We examine corporatisation normatively - that is, as a transformation of the status of state enterprises. This is a necessary pre-privatisation measure, and privatisation strategies depend on its implementation and on the dismantling of the unions of state owned enterprises. This issue is still topical for the so called "second wave" emerging market economies to which Bulgaria, Albania and Romania belong. As a result of the implementation of corporatisation the standard organisation of firms emerges as individual entrepreneurs and commercial companies.

The standard organisation of firms is both one of the preconditions for the unification of the institutions and part of the "rules of the game" in transition economies and industrial countries. In a long-term perspective, this can be expected to foster regional development and co-operation in South-Eastern Europe.

Bulgaria

In Bulgaria, one of the first legal regulations and pre-conditions for radical changes in the firm organisation is Decree 56 on Economic Activity (DEA), and the Regulations for its Implementation (RIDEA), which were adopted in 1989 (Table 2). These are "transitional" acts, which preceded, by two years, the price liberalisation in the beginning of 1991 and, by three years, the enforcement of the Privatisation Law. Having in mind these normative decrees, the authors of one of the first programmes about the Bulgarian transition, R. Ran and R. Ut stated that privatisation in Bulgaria has acquired an "initial activating legislating factor"(Ran and Ut 1990). Under the decree, the Commercial Register has been restored and the registration of the existing and newly founded enterprises has been regulated.

After two years, the Constitutional National Assembly adopted the Commercial Code (CC) (06/1991) and the Law on Establishment of Sole Merchant Companies with State Property[1] (LESMCSP) (07/1991) (Table 2). Initially, the Commercial Code replaced the part of Decree 56 referring to the status of firms. Therefore a register was created, duplicating the register already created according to Decree 56. Under the Commercial Code, the economic agents are divided into two standard groups: individual entrepreneurs and commercial societies.

The Commercial Code (Table 2) defines the following forms of commercial companies:

- (general) partnership,
- limited partnership,
- public limited partnership (also known as "limited share-holding partnership"),
- limited liability company,
- joint-stock company.

Table 3 Economic Subjects by Type in Bulgaria (as of 31.12.)

	1993	1994	1995
Private Merchant	273,194	341,818	383,328
Single-person Limited Liability Company	7,711	12,025	17,021
Single-person Joint-Stock Company	392	508	547
Public Partnership	414	418	344
Citizens' Partnership	36,728	36,769	34,439
Public Limited Liability Company	1,189	1,882	2,416
Citizens' Limited Liability Company	11,867	20,005	28,655
Joint-Stock Company	941	1,391	1,983
Co-operative	4,545	5,739	6,495
State Firm (Decree 56)	1,458	1,097	776
Municipal Firm (Decree 56)	1,515	1,036	459
Public organisation firm(Decree 56)	1,558	778	554
Joint Venture with Foreign Capital (Decree 56)	597	878	402
Agricultural Labour Co-operative and Agrofirm	1,760	1,753	1,249
Collective agricultural farming	295	314	216
Branch, Subsidiary	1,926	2,115	2,291
Other local economic subjects	15,298	19,273	19,688
Other	6,453	5797	6109
Total	368,703	454,963	508,429

Source: Statistical References Book, National Institute of Statistics, 1996, pp. 200-201.

Table 3 illustrates the transitional system of commercial registration. It presents the number of companies registered under Decree No. 56 and according to the Commercial Code. The difference in the status of state enterprises according to Decree 56 and the Commercial Code is only superficial. The Commercial Code abolishes the restrictions on the establishment of various kinds of private firms: individual and commercial companies. According to data from the National Institute of Statistics, by 31/12/1995 383,328 (75 percent) of the total number of firms were "individual entrepreneurs"; 28,655 (7,5 percent) were citizens' limited liability companies (collective firms of citizens), etc. By this date 508,429 companies were registered, of which 466,455, or 91 percent, as is shown by Table 4, with predominant private ownership.

Table 4 Economic Subjects by Branches and Ownership in Bulgaria (as of 31.12.1995)

	Predominantly state ownership	Predominantly private ownership
Services	31,713	372,939
Industry	3,798	61,121
Construction	1,106	22,422
Agriculture and forestry	5,367	9,963
Total	41,984	466,445

Source: Statistical References Book, NSI, 1996, pp. 202-203.

Romania

During the last few years a number of juridical acts, determining the "rules of the game" for the transition to market economy in Romania, Bulgaria, and Albania have been adopted. One of the important laws defining the framework of the enterprise reforms is Law No 15/August 1990 (Table 2), concerning the reorganisation of the state economic units (Centrales) in "regies autonomes" (RAs) (autonomous public companies) and commercial companies (CCs) (Zaman and Bratu 1997).

According to Government Decision No 266/June 1993, former state enterprises are transformed into RAs in branches such as:
- electric and thermal power production and distribution;
- exploitation of serviceable minerals;
- the postal system and telecommunications;
- arms, ammunition, explosives and the production of combat techniques.

The transformed enterprises in RAs must be a natural monopoly, produce goods and services of social importance, or be of importance for the defence of the country (Government Ordinance No 15/1993). They are under the control of the Ministry of Industry. A system for subsidising RAs of national interest has been established. This explains why some firms are trying to obtain this status, although there are too many of them, and they are not always in the expedient branch. For a period of three years (1992-95), their number increased from 390 to 448 (of which 83 are of national importance) (Table 5). At the first stage of reforms in Romania, before President Constantinesku came to power, privatisation of the "regies autonomes" was not expected. Prime minister Ciorbea's cabinet is preparing a package of legislative initiatives - a new law to substitute for Law 15 and Ordinance 15, aimed at allowing for the transformation of some "regies autonomes" into commercial companies, as well as their subsequent privatisation.

Table 5 Regie Autonomes, Commercial Companies and Private Entrepreneurs in Romania

	1992	1993	1994	1995
Ras	390	494	486	448
of National Interest	84	79	82	83
Ccs	220,284	323,309	437,710	478,553
- state owned	7,928	8,455	6,963	6,233
- private owned	199,902	308,795	421,676	468,207
Entrepreneurs	144,709	160,416	200,800	224,700
- family enterprises	28,942	32,084	38,346	58,388
- physical persons	115,767	128,332	162,454	166,312

Source: Panorama economique, Revue trimestrielle, No 3. 1996. p.16.

The activity of commercial companies is regulated by Law 31/1991. The commercial register in Romania has been restored by this law. Commercial companies are accountable to councils of representatives of the central administration, whose number has decreased from 7 to 3 members. Finally, the management of the commercial companies is escaping the limited state control (Zaman and Bratu 1997). Depending on the branch, the importance for the national economy, and other criteria, the commercial companies are founded either by a decision of the government or, when they are of local importance, by a decision of the local authority. At the end of 1992, there were 7,928 commercial companies; and at the end of 1995, 6,233.

The forms of commercial companies are:
- Partnerships under a collective name,
- Simple partnerships,
- Joint ventures,
- Stock companies,
- Limited liability companies (Table 2).

The corporatisation of the state enterprises is accompanied by a rapid growth in the number of new private firms: commercial companies and private entrepreneurs (Table 5).

Albania

In Albania, laws regarding the status of state enterprises and their unions are:
- Law on State Enterprises from 07/1992;
- Law on Commercial Companies from 11/1992;
- Law on the Transformation of State-Owned Enterprises into Commercial Companies (04/1995), (Table 2).

Under the new Law on State Enterprises, enterprises determine their production programmes independently. They are managed by executive boards, consisting of 5 or 7 members. Representatives of the trade unions take part in the boards. At the beginning of the transition in Albania, there were 37,558 enterprises, which were state-owned, including 1,797 in industry. In the country, there were around 300 more important enterprises. The largest 32 were under the Restructuring Agency (Gadeshi, Misja and Mara 1997).

In accordance with the Law on Commercial Companies, the state-owned firms from the ore-mining industries and the infrastructure are associated in the following corporation: 1) Energy-Electric Corporation, 2) Oil and Gas Corporation, 3) Albachrome Corporation, 4) Copper Corporation, 5) Albanian Telecommunication. Formally those companies are autonomous. On the other hand, according to the Law on the Transformation of State-owned Enterprises into Commercial Companies (04/1995), the enterprises included in the mass privatisation scheme have been transformed into joint stock companies and limited liability companies (Gadeshi and Mara 1997) (Table 2).

Corporatisation of state enterprises is a precondition for the changes in ownership regime. The restoration of the commercial law norms, however, is relevant to economic agents with predominant private ownership, who are disciplined by the market's "invisible hand". In cases of lack of such, the delay in the changes of the property rights at the time of with-drawal of government from the economy may cause spontaneous process-es of decapitalisation of enterprises, and capture of the savings of the pop-ulation by shadow structures. This is a kind of privatisation in which the underground economy ousts the official economy from an increasing num-ber of spheres. One of the most serious questions of the transition to a market economy in South-Eastern Europe is whether the emerging civil societies in these countries will manage to escape this unfavourable sce-nario.

Privatisation in Bulgaria, Romania and Albania

Dismantling inherited monopoly structures and their transformation into commercial companies is a necessary but insufficient condition for the sys-temic transformation of the property rights regime. Privatisation in Cen-tral and Eastern Europe is a unique and complex process. It is a political act ensuring the shift of property from state to private ownership. It is also one of the aspects of reintegration of formerly centrally-planned economies into the world economy. In this sense, the further development of deregulation and privatisation in the South-Eastern Europe transition economies can be expected to favour the development of the Balkan regional economic cooperation.

The complexity of the privatisation process brings many debates over whether companies should be restructured before privatisation or after it; whether it is justified that the changes in the property rights begin with restitution; and whether the use of the unique schemes for mass privatisa-tion is justified with the so called "large-scale" privatisation. In South-East-ern Europe these broadly discussed issues have special characteristics related to the delayed industrialisation and modernisation of these coun-tries in comparison with Central Europe, as well as to the political insta-bility and ethnic tension which characterises the Balkans.

Some of these features are evident in the institutional framework of the changes in property rights and the different privatisation policies, methods, and first results in the South-Eastern European countries.

Bulgaria

Privatisation in Bulgaria started with radical restitution laws (Table 6) similar to the ones in United Germany, under which the property rights have been given back to non-residents. As of September, 1996, 90 percent of all requests for restitution of ownership have been satisfied. About 22,000 properties totalling approximately USD 200 million were restituted. About half of these were shops which allowed for a considerable expansion of the private sector in trade and services (OECD - CCET 1997).

Table 6 Legislation Initiatives Concerning Property Rights in Albania, Bulgaria and Romania

	Albania	Bulgaria	Romania
Date of adoption of Law on privatisation	08/1991 Law No7512 Permitting and Protecting Private Ownership	04/1992 Law on Transformation and Privatisation of State and Municipal Enterprises	08/1991 Law 58/08 on Privatisation of Commercial Companies
Law/Decree on acceleration of privatisation	04/1993 Decree on Acceleration	06/1994 Amendments and Additions to the Law on Transformation	06/1995 Law No. 55 on the Acceleration of Privatisation
Laws on restitution	1993 Law on Restitution and Compensation	1992 Three Laws on restitution	- Restitution of nationalised housing
Coverage of mass privatisation schemes	97 enterprises	1050 enterprises	I MPS* - 6900 CCs II MPS* - 3900 CCs

Sources: Transition Report 1996, Infrastructure and Savings, EBRD, 1996; Trends and Policies in Privatisation. Vol II No 2, OECD, 1995; Respective Laws on Privatisation.
* Mass privatisation scheme

Since 1992 the Privatisation Agency has been developing privatisation programmes annually, based on the annual privatisation programmes of the branch ministries. The programme for 1996 is as ambitious as those of previous years (Privatisation Agency 1996). So far, their implementation has been less than modest (OECD - CCET 1994, 1995, 1997).

The bulk of the privatisation agreements in 1996 were prepared and contracted by the Privatisation Agency, the Ministry of Trade, and the Ministry of Industry. The fact that different institutions are given the opportunity to initiate privatisation procedures, and the multitude and complexity of the legally stipulated methods of privatisation, cause numerous conflicts of interests and delay in ownership changes. On 31 December 1996, 4,730 decisions for privatisation of state and municipal enterprises were taken, of which 31 percent of the units to be privatised were state-owned. The majority of them were not transformed enterprises. By the end of 1996, 2,355 agreements had been concluded. The total value of the privatised state-owned enterprises was worth around BGL 9,500 million (Table 7).

Table 7 Privatisation of State and Municipal Property in Bulgaria (as of 31.12.1996)

	State property	
	Decisions	Transactions
Commercial companies	887	142
Non-transformed trade companies and separate parts	597	268
	Municipal property	
Commercial companies	63	22
Non-transformed trade companies and separate parts	3,183	1,923
Total (state and municipal)	4,730	2,355

Source: Current Economic Situation, NSI publication, December 1996, p.26.

The commercial companies preferred to conduct sales through negotiations, which accounted for 59.1 percent of the agreements. The remaining 17.7 percent were carried out through tender (public offering). The enterprises that had not been transformed were sold predominantly through public offering (33.3 percent). As far as payment is concerned 69.1 percent of the deals of commercial companies and 47 percent of the transactions of non-transformed enterprises were concluded through immediate payment of the whole sum. The rest of the agreements were effected by paying in instalments (Table 8).

Unlike Romania and Albania, debt equity exchange is largely used in the privatisation process in Bulgaria. In the privatisation agreements the Bulgarian Brady bonds can be used (Brady Bonds, according to the agreement with the London club of creditors dated from 1994), as well as the bonds on the Bad Credits Act - the so called ZUNK-Bonds. According to data from the Agency for Privatisation, in 1995 more than half of the privatisation transactions were concluded by use of Brady Bonds and ZUNKs. In this sense, the Bad Credits Act and the Agreement with the London club creditors are an important aspect of the institutional framework of Bulgarian privatisation, without an equivalent in the other transition economies in the region (OECD - CCET 1997).

Table 8 Share of Privatised Firms by Mode of Selling and Forms of Acquisition in Bulgaria (as of 31.12.1996)

(percents)

	Trade companies	Non-transformed in trade companies and separate parts
Mode of selling		
Auction	1.8	33.3
Competition	17.7	7.6
Negotiations	59.1	10.7
Other	-	48.4
Forms of acquisition		
Lump-sum payments	69.1	47.0
Installment selling	18.4	52.1
Replacement of debt in exchange for property selling	1.9	-
Redemption clause rent	1.4	0.5

Source: Current Economic Situation, NSI publication, December 1996, p.30.

The Bulgarian administration has taken measures aimed at the acceleration of "large-scale" privatisation. Similar steps were also taken in the other two South-Eastern Europe transition economies. In June 1994, the Amendments to the Law on Privatisation (Law on Transformation and Privatisation of State and Municipal Enterprises - 04/1992) were adopted (Table 6). These were formulated as Chapter 8 of the Law, "Privatisation through Investment Bonds". According to these Amendments, every Bulgarian citizen who is over 18 years old and is a resident of the country is allowed to receive privatisation investment bonds of 25 thousand BG Leva, for a payment of 500 BG Leva. Bonds can be inherited or transferred as a lineal inheritance, but they cannot be pledged against collateral loans. They can be used only for buying shares in enterprises announced for privatisation under this scheme.

The developed mass privatisation scheme was initiated in January 1996. More than 3 million Bulgarians purchased their Investment Bonds. 2/3 of them have transferred the vouchers to relatives or to one of the 81 licensed investment funds. In this respect, Bulgaria's experience is unique in comparison to the other transition economies in the region. On the other hand, a survey of the privatisation funds in Bulgaria analysing the relationship between strategies, amount of capital, and establishers of privatisation funds indicates that more than half of them lack a clear strategy (Tchipev 1997). Around 400 thousand Bulgarian citizens participated individually in the auc-

128

tion sessions. The first session for the exchange of investment bonds for shares, owned by 967 enterprises, was held in late 1996.

In the period 1992-96 approximately 20 security auctions registered after the Commercial Code, and a significant number of non-stock exchange financial intermediaries were in operation in Bulgaria. The National Stock Exchange unites the major security auctions. The regulation of its activity, as well as the licensing of non-stock exchange financial intermediaries, is still to be carried out. In regard to this area and the privatisation legislation, Bulgaria falls behind in comparison with the other Central and South-Eastern European transition economies (Mintchev 1993, Tchipev 1997).

Romania

Romania has realised an original scheme for privatisation (Frausum, Gehman and Gross 1994, Gabriele 1995, Zaman and Bratu 1997, Zaman 1997). The restitution is not so radical as in Bulgaria and Albania. The following steps are envisaged: a partial reinstatement of property rights and packages in recompense for about 250,000 residential properties, confiscated after World War II.

The approaches towards the "small" and "large-scale" privatisation are different. A priority use of Management Employment Buy-Out (MEBO) schemes for the middle-sized enterprises is envisaged. More than 80 percent of the book value of privatised state-owned enterprises has been privatised in that way. The first instalment is supposed to be 20 percent and the purchasing credits are to have favourable interest rates (Law No 77, 1994).

The "large-scale" privatisation started with pilot projects through which approximately 30 enterprises were to be offered to the public. The realisation of these projects was delayed for approximately one year. The programme started in August, 1992 and 18 enterprises had been privatised in the framework of the pilot projects by March, 1993 (OECD - CCET 1993).

As has already been noted, the original Romanian scheme for mass privatisation is based on the strategic division between Regies Autonomes and Commercial Companies. The capital of nearly 7,000 commercial companies liable to privatisation is distributed in a ratio of 70 percent to 30 percent between the State Ownership Fund and the five private funds[5].

The State Ownership Fund (SOF) is the country's greatest holder of state property. In spite of the criticism of its activity, it should be considered a positive fact that the property rights on 70 percent of the capital of the commercial companies to be privatised has been delegated to the fund. The fund uses different methods of privatisation: tenders, direct negotiations, MEBO, sales through consortiums, etc.

Four groups of enterprises are included in the fund's portfolio:
- Approximately 50 big enterprises intended for sale in the capital market make up the first group;
- The second group comprises approximately 100 agricultural enterprises: 20 percent of them are given to farmers; the remaining 80 percent are offered through direct negotiations;
- The third group of enterprises consists of two sub-groups: the first sub-group includes 300 companies, up to 49 percent of which are for sale; the second sub-group includes 500 companies; 60 percent of their capital is offered for sale;
- The fourth and most numerous group includes the commercial companies offered solely through the mass privatisation scheme. Besides, the SOF is expected to retain its control over more than 400 strategic enterprises. Here, as well as in Albania, the criteria for determining the strategic enterprises remain obscure.

The fund participates in 4 consortiums: with Creditanstalt, Societe Generale, Standard Charterhouse, and Wasserstein Parella. They prepare the privatisation of about 100-120 big companies. Active negotiations and sales through consortiums are impossible without the concentration of property in the fund. The lack of such an institution in Bulgaria and Albania (before the creation of the Ministry of privatisation in September 1996) restricts their opportunities for the restructuring of big industrial companies and their preparation for sale.

At the realisation of the first Mass privatisation scheme, the National Agency for Privatisation distributed among the adult population, 30 percent of the capital of the commercial companies, possessed by the five private funds. All Romanian citizens have been given 5 certificates of ownership, each one containing 10 coupons. Their price is 100 Lei. (In 1991 100 Lei was 1 percent of the mean monthly salary.) There are approximately 15.5 million beneficiaries of the certificates. The realisation of the first Mass privatisation scheme often involves complicated tasks and problems. The institutionalisation of POFs and capital markets was delayed. The immediate exchange of ownership certificates for shares was not to the benefit of POFs. According to plan, they should finish their activity within 5 years, but in practice they are trying very hard to increase that term. This led to the adoption of the Law for the Acceleration of Privatisation in June, 1995.

According to the Law for Acceleration (Table 6), the second stage of mass privatisation will cover around 3.900 commercial companies. About 49 percent of the capital of strategic enterprises and 60 percent of the remaining enterprises were allotted. The new stage started in August, 1995. The Romanian citizens, having acquired "certificates for ownership" in 1992, without using their total value in privatisation, were supposed to receive the so called "nominal coupons". The total value of certificates and coupons which one individual was given, amounted to 1,000,000 Lei (25 000 Lei - certificates for ownership and 975 000 Lei - nominal coupons). By the middle of 1996, 90 percent of the people entitled to that right had participated in the completion of the scheme. About 85 percent of the participants in the scheme preferred to exchange their coupons directly for shares of enterprises from the mass privatisation scheme. The remaining approximately 15 percent invested their coupons through POFs. This situation is similar to that in Albania (if we ignore the participation in financial structures), where mass privatisation participants also preferred to invest their coupons directly. In Bulgaria, conversely, the bulk of the investors prefer privatisation funds.

The total number of commercial companies privatised in the period 31/12/1992 - 31/12/1996 is 2,842. Their capital amounts to 4,145,141 thousand Lei and they employ 856,980 people (Table 9).

Table 9 Privatisation of the Commercial Companies in Romania
   (31/12/1992 - 31/12/1996)

Years	Number	Assets ('000 lei)	Employed
1992	1	125	72
1993	264	45,799	76,843
1994	595	332,160	181,438
1995	622	1,759,308	316,081
1996	1,747	3,069,125	405,618
Total (1992 - 1996)	2,842	4,145,141	856,980

Source: Institute of National Economy, Romanian Academy of Sciences.

The institutionalisation of the Bucharest Stock Exchange (BSE) and RASDAQ-system (created after the American NASDAQ) has been slow.

The actual law regulating the government securities trade - the Securities and Stock Exchange Law - dates from August, 1994. The BSE was formally opened on 25 June, 1995. It has functioned since 20 November, 1995. At present, 27 companies quote their securities there. RASDAG has approximately 2,700 listed companies of the companies included in the mass privatisation. The shares of 474 are actively traded.

The progress of the Romanian mass privatisation scheme has been slow. In practice, two mass privatisation programmes were implemented -- in 1992 and in 1995. The institutionalisation of the five private funds and of the capital market has barely progressed. This necessitates numerous changes in the list of enterprises for mass privatisation, also, the price of the "nominal coupons" has been updated and harmonisation with the price of the "ownership certificates" has been effected. The above mentioned measures are complex mechanisms for compensation of the State Fund on the part of private funds. The latter do not fulfil their intermediary function. The price of the shares of enterprises with great demand is reduced, etc.

Albania

Privatisation in Albania has been a priority in Government programmes since 1992. The first programme covered the period 1992 to 1994, and the second one, the period 1994 to 1996 (Gadeshi and Mara 1997).

There is a distinction between "small-scale" and "big" privatisation. The "small-scale" privatisation concerns enterprises having up to 0.5 million USD capital and 300 employees. For the purpose of accelerating their privatisation, Decision 248 of the Council of Ministers "Measures for the acceleration of the privatisation of small and medium-sized enterprises" was passed in 1993 (Table 6). The Councils for Privatisation, composed of 22-23 members (about 850 members all over the country) were founded in every district. They controlled the realisation of auctions. Three groups of participants were favoured: 1) former landowners; 2) people repressed for political considerations during the totalitarian regime; and 3) the staff of enterprises to be privatised.

The "small-scale" privatisation has been influenced by the restitution (Law on Restitution and Compensation, 1993), (Table 6), which is as radical as that in Bulgaria. The indemnification of former proprietors (incl. the former landowners) has been estimated at 200 million USD. The allocation of the "privatisation leks", which could be exchanged for shares of enterprises to be privatised began in 1994. They were granted gratis to people who were repressed for political considerations. By the end of 1995, about 17.1 million USD had been paid for time spent in prisons, 12 million USD, as special pensions, and nearly 30 million USD privatisation vouchers. Six months after being shared out, their market price fell to 28 percent of their nominal value.

By April, 1995, 4,397 small and medium-sized enterprises were privatised, including 1,760, or 40 percent, which were bought out by the personnel. The former landowners possessed 1,105, or 25 percent of the above mentioned enterprises and 1,508, or 34.7 percent of the enterprises were owned by Albanian individuals and legal entities. Only 12 of those, belonging to this group, were bought out by foreign investors (Gadeshi 1997).

The large-scale privatisation refers to enterprises with a staff of over 300 people and capital of over 0.5 million USD. By January, 1994, 394 enterprises met these criteria. In fact, 47 of them were closed down, while the production equipment of another 259 was in extremely bad condition (Gadeshi and Mara 1997).

Albania, like Bulgaria, applied a scheme for mass privatisation, which is based on the Czech experience. The vouchers were distributed in three consecutive stages, by the state savings bank. About 1 million Albanian citizens having reached the age of 18 by 1/08/1991 took part in the first stage - in May 1995. As far as their age, is concerned they were included in separate groups (age 18-35; age 35-55; and over 55) and received vouchers with a nominal value of 10,000; 15,000; 20,000 Leks (100, 150, 200 USD) respectively. The second stage of the scheme started in December 1996. The same groups of people, differentiated by their ages, received vouchers to the extent of 40,000; 60,000; 80,000 Leks (corresponding to 400, 600, 800 USD). Following the scheme, the property of 97 big and medium-sized enterprises (5 packages of shares - each one comprising 15-20 enterprises) was transferred. Some 79 of them were completely privatised, while the government maintained the major package of shares in 17, enterprises which were considered to be strategic. The shareholders' capital was dispersed. In most cases, it was owned by the personnel, including both retired and dismissed former employees. The former landowners possessed 51 percent of a single enterprise and about 20 percent of a further 13 (Lhomel 1996c, Gadeshi and Mara 1997).

In the country, three privatisation funds had been granted licences by the end of 1996[6]. Of all the three funds, only the Anglo-Adriatic Investment

Fund is in operation. It opened branch offices in most of the big towns. No more than 30 000 people chose this investment fund. The Anglo-Adriatic Fund was to be quoted at the Tirana Stock Exchange and on the international market. So far the funds have been regulated by the Ministry of Finance, though there is a tendency for these functions to be assumed by the Securities Commission, which was established with the assistance of the British Know How Fund.

The Tirana Stock Exchange was set up in May, 1996. Thirteen dealers were licensed there. Three of them are private; the rest are representatives of the state banking sector. The stock exchange trade, however, is inactive. Government bonds, 12-month t-bills and privatisation vouchers were traded. The bankruptcy of financial structures - VEFA, GJALLICA, KAMBERI, etc. could discredit this process.

The multilateral aspects of the changes in the ownership regime and the deregulation of the economy presuppose the use of various privatisation policies and methods. Restitution is implemented in all three countries, though to different degrees and in different sequence. It is radical in Bulgaria and Albania and of more restricted coverage in Romania. Restitution poses numerous juridical and technical questions which complicate the changes in the property rights.

The "small-scale" privatisation is presently terminating. In all three countries the MEBO-schemes for staff participation in privatisation are widely used. Very often, however, enterprises privatised in that way preserve their status-quo and their problems increase.

Unlike "small-scale" privatisation, restructuring and privatisation of big enterprises, and especially of big industrial enterprises, are confronted with serious problems. Possibilities for acceleration of the "big" privatisation are sought in the unique mass privatisation schemes. Romania is the most experienced of the three countries, though its experience is rather ambiguous. The original scheme developed by Mr P. Roman's administration was modified in 1995. The three-year stagnation predetermined the low credibility in financial intermediaries and a preference for direct participation. The mass privatisation in Bulgaria and Albania is based on the Czech experience. In spite of the contradictions and complexity of the processes, the changes in the three countries are irreversible and unidirectional. This creates preconditions for dynamism of the regional development and integration. Not only small- and medium-sized enterprises, but also newly emerging institutional investors and financial intermediaries, as well as the emerging capital markets are going to have considerable contributions in that respect.

Conclusions

The macroeconomic stabilisation in the South-Eastern Europe transition economies would fail without measures for adaptation and restructuring of the production sector. In this sense, structural reforms are a decisive component of the model of market economy transition. These reforms are aimed at the establishment of an institutional market environment and the increase of competitiveness. They include decentralisation, corporatisation and privatisation of state companies.

Real sector decentralisation in the South-Eastern Europe transition economies aims at normalisation of the size structure of the production system. The systemic reforms in this area are outlined by the fragmentation of existing companies, removing from them the functions that are not typical of a modern enterprise, as well as by the restoration of the anti-monopoly legislation and by the policy for protection of competition. Pure increase in the number of enterprises is not a sufficient proof of the efficiency of these measures. When management teams are changed without justification or when technological links that have been operating for decades are disrupted, there is a danger of intensification of the shock caused by economic liberalisation.

Corporatisation in the sense of transformation and re-registration of state companies after the Commercial Law, creates the preconditions for radical changes in the ownership regime. One of the conclusions that can be drawn is that transformation of state enterprises through a single act is preferable. Thus, time is gained, and the spontaneous processes causing decapitalisation of state enterprises are restricted. For example, Bulgaria's experience shows that so far the cash privatisation of non-transformed enterprises has been proceeding more smoothly. It is risky to apply the norms of commercial law when there is a lack of market economic agents. That creates the conditions for the emergence of the "shady" zone between the government financial and non-financial sectors and the newly emerging private sector.

The changes in property rights can be discredited unless there are clear, simple, and transparent rules and stable institutions. The analysis of the privatisation legislation in Bulgaria, Albania and Romania reveals an inconsistent picture. In striving for privatisation at any price, some legislative acts (such as, for example, the Bulgarian Privatisation Law which comprises 15 privatisation procedures) are made in such a way that their application seems impossible. The same applies to the institutions in charge of the privatisation process. The central administration very hesitantly concedes the property rights to the specialised institutions. And when this is done, as is the case with the Romanian State Ownership Fund, these institutions are burdened with impossible functions that duplicate those of other institutions. In Romania the functions of SOF's duplicate those of the Development Agency in their policy regarding foreign investment; of the Restructuring Agency regarding the application of reinforcement programmes; of private funds regarding mass privatisation; and of the National Agency for Privatisation regarding the methodological ensuring of the privatisation process. This "disease", common to all transition economies, seems to have its most serious consequences in south-eastern Europe.

The changes in the ownership regime create new dynamics in the region. Restitution, "small-scale" privatisation, and the MEBO-schemes create small- and medium-sized enterprises directed towards the markets of neighbouring countries. "Large-scale" privatisation in its cash variation, especially in direct negotiations with strategic investors, is a factor attracting the attention of foreign investors. The voucher variation of "large-scale" privatisation creates the environment for the emergence of capital markets and activates the transfer of state property to private investors, directly, or through the intermediation of privatisation funds. Because of the serious delay of institutional reforms in south-eastern Europe, a number of measures connected with the creation of an environment, adequate for the small and medium-sized enterprises, as well as for the post-privatisation corporate governance of large-scale companies, and for the regulation and liquidity of the capital markets, are yet to be implemented. The appearance of the transition economies in the region will depend on their realisation.

In spite of the differences in the "reform packages" in Bulgaria and Albania on the one hand, and in Romania on the other, all three countries fall in the group of the so called "second wave" of reforming economies (WB 1996). The indecisive pace of the reforms depends on the unfavourable starting positions of the Balkan countries: high macroeconomic instability, unfavourable economic structure, underdeveloped institutional infrastructure (Dobrinsky 1996). After 1995, at a later stage of the transition, the insufficient potential for successful conducting of the market-oriented reforms became more perceptible. Serious non-economic problems and conflicts, such as the war in Yugoslavia, the tension between certain countries, and the internal political instability, also have a negative impact.

The analysis of the processes of decentralisation, corporatisation, and privatisation in Bulgaria, Romania, and Albania reveals the serious systemic weaknesses (Dobrinsky 1996) of their transition. The economic structure in these countries is characterised by an extremely high degree of concentration in industry, as well as by business organisation similar to that of the Stalin type of industrialisation in the 50's and 60's. It is significant that this concerns comparatively young countries, in some of which a form of trade legislation similar to that of the Ottoman Empire continued to be in force in the beginning of the century. The absence of traditions concerning the institutional infrastructure of the market, especially regarding trade legislation, protection of competition, bankruptcy, etc., as well as the unclear property rights (property rights changed several times over a relatively short period of time) seriously restricts the efforts of the reformers in the region. All this proves, once again, the necessity of stimulation of the development of regional economic assistance and co-operation, as well as the necessity of an individual approach of the international financial institutions to the southeast European countries.

Notes

1 Mass (voucher) privatization or privatization through investment bonds is payable/non-payable distribution of state enterprises' shares among the adults in some of the East European countries - including Bulgaria, Romania, Albania. The term "cash" privatisation is used further on as the explanation of the standard (market) privatization procedures.

2 Transformed enterprises are state or municipally owned enterprises registered in accordance with the Commercial code as commercial companies.

3 These issues were widely discussed in Spain after the end of Franco's dictatorship.

4 Sole Merchant Companies with State Property - transformed and non-transformed enterprises with 100 percent state share-holding.

5 The 5 Private Ownership Funds (POFs) are located in 5 different cities, and their assets are differentiated on the basis of sector criteria:
- POF I. Arad. Wood processing and non-ferrous metals;
- POF II. Bacau. Textiles and clothing;
- POF III. Brasov. Naval transport, fishing, tourism, catering;
- POF IV. Bucharest. Glass and ceramics, construction materials, cosmetics, pharmaceuticals;
- POF V. Craiova. Electronics and electrotechnics, footwear and leather goods.

6 1) Anglo-Adriatic Investment Fund;
2) "New Albania";
3) "Oxford".

References

Andreff, W. (1993), La crise des economies socialistes: la rupture d'un systeme, Presses Universitaires de Grenoble.

Dobrinsky, R. (1997), Multi-speed transition and multi-speed integration in Europe: recent economic developments in the Balkans and their implications. Paper presented at the Conference "Economic Cooperation in the Balkans: A Regional Approach to European Integration", Phare-ACE Program, University of Thessaly, Department of Planning and Regional Development, Volos, 16-19 January.

EBRD (1996), Infrastructure and savings. Transition Report.

EBRD (1997), Transition report update.

Frausum, Y., Gehman, U. and Gross, J. (1994), Market Economy and Economic Reform in Romania: Macroeconomic and Microeconomic Perspectives. Europe-Asia Studies, Vol. 46, No 5.

Gabriele, A. (1995), Reform of Property Rights and Corporate Governance Restructuring in Romania. Moct-Most, No 3.

Gadeshi, I. (1997), The Privatisation Process and the Structure of Property in the Albanian Economy. Center of Economic and Social Studies, Tirana, mimeo.

Gadeshi, I. and Mara, H. (1997), Economic transition in Albania and its cooperation with Balkan countries. Paper presented at the Conference "Economic Cooperation in the Balkans: A Regional Approach to European Integration", Phare-ACE Program, University of Thessaly, Department of Planning and Regional Development, Volos, 16-19 January.

Gadeshi, I., Misja, V. and Mara, H. (1997), Restructuring State Enterprises in Albania. In Dimitrov M. ed State Enterprise Restructuring in Bulgaria, Romania and Albania, Gorex Press, Sofia, pp. 243-294.

Gianaris, N. (1982), The Economies of the Balkan Countries: Albania, Bulgaria, Greece, Romania, Turkey, and Yugoslavia, Preager, New York.

Lavigne, M. (1995), The Economics of Transition, From Socialist Economy to Market Economy, Macmillan Press.

Lhomel, E. (1996a), Le tissu industriel roumain. Le Courrier des Pays de l'Est, No 407.

Lhomel, E. (1996b), L'economie roumaine en 1995-1996: entre reprise et consolidation. Le Courrier des Pays de l'Est, No 409.

Lhomel, E. (1996c), L'economie albanaise en 1995-1996: une croissance impressionante mais fragile. Le Courrier des Pays de l'Est, No 409.

Ministry of Industry and Trade, (1991), Real Economy - Analysis and Programme for Acceleration of Economic Reform, Sofia.

Mintchev, V. (1993), Demonopolisation et transformation des entreprises d'Etat en Bulgarie. Feflets et Perspectives de la vie economique, No 3/4.

Mintchev, V. (1994), La privatisation en Bulgarie. Le Courrier des Pays de l'Est, No 392.

Mintchev, V (1995), Macroeconomic Changes, Privatisation and Development of the Private Sector in Bulgaria. In Maroudas L., Tsardanidis Ch. The Greek-Bulgarian Relations: Contemporary Economic and Politic Dimensions, Papazissis, Athens, 1995, pp. 99-122.

OECD - CCET (1993), La Roumanie: evaluation de la situation economique, Paris.

OECD - CCET (1994), Trends and Policies in Privatization, Vol.II No.1, Paris.

OECD - CCET (1995), Trends and Policies in Privatization, Vol.II No.2, Paris.

OECD - CCET (1997), Economic Surveys: Bulgaria, Paris.

Peev, E. and Hare, P. (1995), Corporatization and Control in a Transition Economy. Economic System, Vol. 19, No 4.

Petrakos, G. and Totev, S. (1997), Economic structure and change in the Balkan region: Implications for integration, transition and ecoonomic cooperation. Paper presented at the Conference "Economic Cooperation in the Balkans: A Regional Approach to European Integration", Phare-ACE Program, University of Thessaly, Department of Planning and Regional Development, Volos, 16-19 January.

Privatisation Agency (1996), Information Bulletin No 6.

Ran, R. and Ut, R. (1990), Report on the Project of the Economic Growth and the Bulgarian Transition to Market Economy. Foundation of USA for Bulgaria, Division IV, p.3.

Rizopoulos, Y. (1997), Foreign Direct Investment and Western Firms' Internationalization Strategies in the Balkan Countries. Paper presented at the Conference "Economic Cooperation in the Balkans: A Regional Approach to European Integration", Phare-ACE Program, University of Thessaly, Department of Planning and Regional Development, Volos, 16-19 January.

Roland, G. (1996), Theorie de la transition et processus de changements institutionnels. Conference, Universite de Paris X, Avril.

Tchipev, P. (1997), Bulgarian Mass Privatisation Scheme: Implications on Corporate Governance. Institute of Economics, Bulgarian Academy of Sciences. Discussion Papers, 01, BAS, Sofia.

Totev, S. (1997), The Bulgarian economy in transition: Possibilities for Balkan regional integration. Paper presented at the Conference "Economic Cooperation in the Balkans: A Regional Approach to European Integration", Phare-ACE Program, University of Thessaly, Department of Planning and Regional Development, Volos, 16-19 January.

UN - ECE (1997), Economic Survey of Europe in 1996-1997, New York and Geneva, pp. 75-84.

World Bank (1996), From Plan to Market. World Development Report, Oxford University Press, New York.

Zaman, G. (1997), Bilateral and Multilateral Potential of Romanian Economic Cooperation in the Balkan Region. Final Report, Phare ACE-project 94-0760, "Economic Cooperation in the Balkans: A Regional Approach to European Integration".

Zaman, G. and Bratu, I.(1997), Restructuring State Enterprises in Romania. In Dimitrov, M. ed, State Enterprise Restructuring in Bulgaria, Romania and Albania, Gorex Press, Sofia, pp.131-241.

6 Industrial Performance under Transition: The Impact of Structure and Geography

MARVIN JACKSON
Emeritus Professor, Department of Economics, Katholieke Universiteit Leuven, Belgium

GEORGE PETRAKOS
Associate Professor, Department of Planning and Regional Development, University of Thessaly, Greece

Introduction

Structural adjustment is very often recognised to be a precondition to growth and prosperity, especially for countries or regions that are confronted with a changing international economic environment or enter a different phase of their development cycle. This observation becomes more important in the case of Central and Eastern European Countries (CEECs) that are currently going through the 10th year of a - longer than expected - transition period.

A number of studies have already analysed several aspects of the structural characteristics of transition, on the basis of either sectoral output and employment data, or disaggregated international trade statistics. Although definite answers to many questions will have to wait until more concrete evidence becomes available, there are distinct structural aspects of the transition process that have been highlighted.

First, as the relevant literature expands, it becomes increasingly evident that a group of countries has a systematically inferior transition performance to others. The results of a convergence-divergence model with the use of GDP per capita data for the period 1987-1995, shows that significant divergence trends exist in Europe, which tend to maintain or even intensify an east-west divide with respect to development levels and performance (Petrakos and Christodoulakis 1998). In addition, significant differences exist in terms of performance within the Central and East European countries.

Although mainstream analysis and thinking would point to differences in the pace and speed of the reforms, it has not escaped the attention of the literature that history, structure and geography often play an important role in shaping final outcomes (World Bank 1996). This general observation receives greater attention when it is realised that success and failure in the transition process have a strong geographical dimension (Petrakos 1997, Dubrinski 1997, Petrakos and Totev 1999), as the Visegrad countries in Central Europe have in general a better record than the Balkan countries in South-eastern Europe in both economic performance and structural adjustment indicators.

Concerning changes in GDP and employment sectoral structures in the early transition period, Petrakos (1997), Mertzanis and Petrakos (1998) and Petrakos and Totev (1999) found a clear indication of a North-South divide within the CEE countries. They report that the Balkan region has a significantly greater dependence on agriculture than the EU and a less advanced economic structure than the Central European and the Baltic countries. Although the GDP structure of Poland, Hungary and the Czech Republic approaches that of the EU core, the GDP structure of the Balkan countries seems to diverge from that, primarily due to the relative increase of the importance of the primary sector.

Similar evidence comes from the examination of industrial employment data. Petrakos and Totev (2000) estimated an index of dissimilarity in industrial structures on the basis of employment data for 9 aggregate industrial sectors for Greece, Bulgaria, Romania and Slovenia and the EU. They found that the Balkan transition economies have started from a structure that was closer to the EU, but, because of the type of sectoral adjustments imposed by the process of transition, they have moved away from it over time. The changes under way imply a reduction in the importance of capital and technology intensive sectors and an increase in the importance of intermediate, resource intensive or consumer sectors in proportions that diverge from the EU average structure.

Important evidence for structural change in transition countries is also presented in a group of papers that utilize trade statistics. Landesmann (1995, 1998) provides evidence of a strong "developmental gap" between CEECs and the EU, in a sense that the former tend to develop patterns of specialization away from capital-, R&D-, and skill-intensive sectors and towards labor intensive sectors. This move, which provides strong evidence for an inter-industry pattern of specialization, was found to be much more dramatic in the case of Bulgaria and Romania than in the case of the other CEE economies.

Despite the dominance of the inter-industry (H-O) type of trade, intra-industry trade (IIT) has also increased in CEECs (Landesmann 1995, 1998, Dobrinsky 1995). This is more evident among the more advanced CEECs, such as the Czech Republic and Hungary where the higher indices of IIT occur, providing evidence of an over-time reduced inter-industry type of specialization with the EU. This increase, however, is followed by evidence of a significant "quality gap" between western and eastern products that is likely to persist for a long time (Landesmann 1998). In addition, the increase in IIT may be associated with the intensification of outward processing traffic (OPT).

Although the export structures of CEECs were initially quite similar in many respects, this group is by no means homogeneous with respect to their trade performance vis-a-vis the EU. The Czech Republic and Hungary appear more advanced in their trade restructuring, displaying changes that bring their export performance and structure closer to that of the EU countries (Dobrinsky 1995).

Finally, Repkine and Walsh (1998) examine the evolution of industrial products in four transition countries in the period 1989-95 using a combination of trade and industrial statistics. They find that products and industries with a pre-1989 experience of the EU market have had a better transition performance. On the contrary, non-EU oriented products in the pre-1989 period, had a very difficult transition experience and an inferior performance.

The basic arguments of the literature reviewed have been that: structural characteristics and structural changes are important elements of the transition process which have strongly differentiated among transition countries. Although several papers have implicitly linked structural change with economic performance, there is not, up to this point, any report directly measuring the impact of structural features on some indices of performance in a quantifiable way.

The goal of this paper is to provide empirical and comparative evidence concerning paths of structural change in transition countries and their impact on performance in terms of GDP growth. A significant statistical relationship among structural and performance indicators, will have important implications with respects to (a) the mix of transition policies, (b) the direction of EU policies for transition countries and (c) the "catching up" or "falling behind" prospects of these countries. The rest of the paper is organized as follows: In second section, we present and analyze some aspects of structural change in the industrial sector of seven European transition countries on the basis of both industrial output and employment data, as well as trade data. In third section we report the results of two empirical models, attempting to test the impact of structural factors on economic performance at the aggregate national and the disaggregated-branch level. Finally in the last section we draw our conclusions.

The Structural Aspects of Transition: Evidence from Trade and Industrial Data

How fast and in which way do the productive structures of transition economies change? Do these changes follow a similar or a differentiated pattern? Some answers to these questions have already been provided in earlier work. In this section we are using two important databases[1] in an effort to analyze and present evidence of structural change in a more complete and systematic way. We start our analysis by examining aggregate shifts in GDP and industrial output by country. Then, we look at more disaggregated information, such as the shifts in the sectoral composition of industrial output and industrial employment for the countries for which we have available data. We proceed with the estimation of a number of parameters of structural change, such as the index of structural change, the index of export-import asymmetry, the index of structural dissimilarity, and the index of irregularity in the geographical direction of trade.

In Table 1 we present a GDP index for the 1989-1997 period for seven transition countries. There are two important observations that can be made: First, with the exception of Poland, none of the other transition countries has reached in 1997 the GDP level of 1989. Second, Bulgaria and Romania follow a less steady recovery path, as their GDP has declined again in the last period. Similar trends have been also observed in Albania F.R. of Yugoslavia and F.Y.R of Macedonia (Petrakos and Totev 1999) indicating a weaker performance for the transition countries in Southeastern Europe.

144

Table 1 Comparative Changes in GDP (1989 = 100)

	1989	1990	1991	1992	1993	1994	1995	1996	1997
Bulgaria	100.0	90.9	80.3	74.4	73.3	74.6	76.2	67.9	62.8
Czech	100.0	99.6	88.1	85.2	85.7	88.5	94.2	97.8	98.8
Hungary	100.0	96.5	85.0	82.4	81.9	84.3	85.5	86.6	90.4
Poland	100.0	88.4	82.2	84.3	87.5	92.1	98.6	104.6	111.8
Romania	100.0	94.4	82.2	75.1	76.2	79.2	84.8	88.3	82.4
Slovakia	100.0	99.6	85.1	79.5	76.6	80.3	85.8	91.7	97.7
Slovenia	100.0	95.3	86.8	82.0	84.3	88.8	92.4	95.3	98.5

Sources: EBRD, Transition report 1995, Transition report update (April 1996), Transition report update (April 1998).

In Table 2, we present an index of industrial output for the same transition countries in the period 1989-1997. We observe again that in 1997, none of the CEE countries has reached the 1989 level of output. Moreover, significant differences seem to exist in the adjustment process of the countries. Bulgaria and Romania, which have the greatest losses in industrial output in this period, are also the only countries that again experience reductions in the last years.

Table 2 Comparative Changes in Gross Industrial Ouput (1989=100)

	1989	1990	1991	1992	1993	1994	1995	1996	1997
Bulgaria	100.0	84.0	66.4	62.1	58.3	61.8	58.4	53.6	49.8
Czech	100.0	96.5	75.0	69.1	65.4	66.8	72.6	73.7	77.0
Hungary	100.0	90.4	73.9	66.7	69.4	76.0	79.5	82.2	91.3
Poland	100.0	73.9	68.7	70.5	73.2	77.0	82.4	87.4	93.4
Romania	100.0	76.3	66.5	60.7	61.6	64.0	68.5	71.3	66.6
Slovakia	100.0	96.4	77.7	70.5	67.9	71.2	77.1	79.0	80.6
Slovenia	100.0	89.5	79.1	69.2	67.4	71.9	73.5	74.4	75.4

Sources: EBRD, Transition report 1995, Transition report update (April 1996), Transition report update (April 1998).

Tables 3 and 4 provide two indicators of the relative performance of the industrial sector under transition. The first one shows the relative performance of industrial output compared to GDP in the 1989-1997 period. In fact, it is the ratio of the indices presented in Tables 2 and 1. We observe that industry was hit harder compared to the performance of GDP in all countries. With the exception of Hungary, industrial performance in 1997 was, in all countries, lagging behind that of GDP.

Table 3 Ratio of Change in Industrial Output to Change in GDP

	1989	1990	1991	1992	1993	1994	1995	1996	1997
Bulgaria	1.00	0.92	0.83	0.83	0.79	0.83	0.77	0.79	0.79
Czech Republic	1.00	0.97	0.85	0.81	0.76	0.75	0.77	0.75	0.78
Hungary	1.00	0.94	0.87	0.81	0.85	0.90	0.93	0.95	1.01
Poland	1.00	0.84	0.84	0.84	0.84	0.84	0.84	0.84	0.84
Romania	1.00	0.81	0.81	0.81	0.81	0.81	0.81	0.81	0.81
Slovakia	1.00	0.97	0.91	0.89	0.89	0.89	0.90	0.86	0.83
Slovenia	1.00	0.94	0.91	0.84	0.80	0.81	0.80	0.78	0.77

Source: Tables 1 and 2.

Table 4 Share of Industry in GDP in Current Prices

Industry	1991	1992	1993	1994	1995	1996
Bulgaria	39.6	39.0	32.7	29.9	31.1	31.6
Czech Rep	-	40.2	34.9	33.6	34.1	33.8
Hungary	25.1	23.4	22.5	22.1	23.5	-
Poland	40.2	34.0	32.9	32.2	29.2	27.1
Romania	37.9	38.3	33.8	35.6	34.6	36.0
Slovakia	-	-	30.1	30.1	31.0	28.9
Slovenia	36.0	36.0	29.3	30.4	28.6	27.8

Source: EBRD (1998) Transition Report Update.

Table 4 presents the shares of industry in GDP in the period 1991-1996 for the countries and years with available data. In line with the observations made above, we see that transition has been associated with an over-time significant reduction of the share of industry in GDP. This trend is, to a large extent, natural, given the high shares of industry in these countries in the pre-transition period. These shares were significantly higher than those of the EU (Petrakos 1997, Petrakos and Totev 2000), due to the preoccupation of the labor theory of value with the "material sphere" of the economy.

In 1996, Hungary, Slovenia and Poland had the lowest shares of industry in GDP. The latter two, along with Bulgaria, are those countries that have experienced the largest decline in their industrial shares. On the other hand, Romania and Slovakia, the two countries with the highest share of industry in GDP in 1996, are, at the same time, those that have experienced the smaller decline in the same period.

Summing up our aggregate level evidence, we would say that, in conformity with existing literature, the accumulated transition experience indicates different rates of success among countries, both at the level of the economy and the level of industry. In terms of GDP, some countries have already reached (or are very close to reaching) the 1990 levels, the rule being that Central European countries outperform Southern European ones. In terms of industrial output, the picture is less ideal, although most countries are in a steady recovery path, albeit one that is longer than expected. The exception to the rule here is again the Balkan countries.

Sectoral Shifts in the Composition of Industrial Output and Employment

In Table 5 we present the sectoral shares of industrial output and employment for seven countries for which there is available data in the 1989-96 period. We also present relative productivity indices, measured as a ratio of output over employment shares. The sectors, which are aggregate 2-digit NACE sectors (see Appendix), are also grouped in three general categories that grossly represent consumer, intermediate and capital goods. Starting with the output data, we observe that between the two periods there is a clear trend for the share of capital goods to decline in all countries except Slovakia, while in intermediate and consumer goods the evidence is mixed. Four countries (Bulgaria, the Czech Republic, Poland and Romania) experienced an increase in the share of intermediate goods, while Hungary and Slovakia experienced a decrease in their share. On the other hand, four countries had a decrease of their consumer goods' share in industrial output (Bulgaria, the Czech Republic, Romania and Slovakia), while Hungary and Poland experienced an increase. Making comparisons among countries at the aggregate level, we see that Bulgaria has the lowest share of capital sectors in output, followed by Poland and Romania, while the Czech Republic and Romania have the highest. In intermediate sectors, all countries have, in general, maintained high shares of industrial output, with Bulgaria, Slovakia and Romania having the highest. Finally, Poland is the country that seems to maintain the highest share of output in consumer sectors.

Table 5 Sectoral Shares of Industrial Output and Employment for Transition

Output (current prices)

	Bulgaria		Czech		Hungary		Poland		Romania		Slovakia	
	1990	1995	1989	1996	1989	1996	1989	1996	1989	1996	1989	1996
DA	27.38	20.91	21.53	16.24	20.57	25.63	20.55	25.31	18.55	17.74	14.53	16.28
DB	8.79	5.24	6.56	5.15	7.16	4.15	8.91	7.27	10.40	7.63	5.81	3.94
DC	1.53	1.37	2.59	1.23	2.07	0.88	2.63	1.36	1.84	1.62	2.18	1.54
DD	1.13	1.24	1.67	1.47	0.87	1.66	1.76	3.46	1.54	2.23	2.14	1.77
DE	1.71	3.65	2.64	4.31	3.14	4.52	1.88	5.73	1.70	2.18	5.81	6.33
DF	9.91	24.21	8.08	4.70	5.34	7.63	5.19	4.65	7.74	10.72	9.44	8.84
DG	5.38	9.37	5.20	8.48	11.23	10.03	7.04	7.64	6.68	9.39	8.97	9.89
DH	2.46	2.63	1.66	2.75	2.63	3.84	1.83	3.93	3.32	2.70	3.63	4.52
DI	3.82	3.79	3.88	5.16	3.48	3.63	3.49	4.69	4.58	4.83	5.09	4.29
DJ	9.14	13.41	15.70	21.34	15.50	10.96	14.98	12.11	15.59	17.30	21.79	17.80
DK	5.70	3.65	11.61	9.08	7.56	5.64	7.89	6.94	12.01	8.06	9.08	8.07
DL	12.07	4.89	6.36	5.99	11.81	11.34	15.86	5.13	7.02	4.11	5.27	5.37
DM	5.44	3.48	10.03	10.82	6.35	8.68	6.53	7.93	6.30	8.23	3.63	8.90
DN	5.52	2.16	2.50	3.28	2.28	1.41	1.48	3.84	2.73	3.28	2.62	2.45
TOTAL	100	100	100	100	100	100	100	100	100	100	100	100
A*	46.06	34.56	37.49	31.68	36.09	38.25	37.20	46.97	36.75	34.67	33.09	32.32
B**	30.72	53.41	34.51	42.42	38.18	36.09	32.52	33.02	37.92	44.94	48.93	45.34
C***	23.22	12.03	28.00	25.90	25.72	25.66	30.28	20.01	25.33	20.39	17.98	22.34

Employment

	Bulgaria		Czech		Hungary		Poland		Romania		Slovakia		Slovenia	
	1989	1995	1989	1997	1989	1996	1989	1997	1989	1995	1989	1995	1989	1996
DA	12.05	15.66	7.85	11.11	16.89	19.48	11.93	18.07	7.68	10.86	10.23	10.97	6.78	8.69
DB	15.41	17.25	10.10	10.05	14.84	14.72	14.57	14.31	19.47	17.06	10.94	12.16	15.47	16.13
DC	2.69	3.28	2.71	2.29	4.20	3.59	3.84	2.72	3.68	3.79	4.40	4.90	4.56	4.22
DD	1.92	2.28	1.67	1.91	1.11	2.52	2.13	4.41	2.72	3.51	3.31	3.29	9.15	9.15
DE	2.17	3.07	2.52	3.78	2.77	4.30	2.61	4.01	2.00	2.24	3.66	4.97	4.62	5.30
DF	1.09	1.88	11.82	0.50	0.50	2.64	1.57	0.82	0.96	1.64	1.54	1.34	0.36	0.18
DG	5.13	6.28	2.94	4.74	6.10	6.85	5.69	4.87	5.30	5.75	6.28	5.92	6.40	7.71
DH	2.38	3.24	1.59	3.21	1.50	3.36	2.33	3.67	2.49	2.24	2.49	3.30	1.27	1.95
DI	5.15	5.19	5.64	6.18	4.71	4.80	6.00	6.04	5.10	5.61	6.21	5.71	4.80	5.26
DJ	7.04	12.52	12.88	17.59	10.34	10.37	12.96	11.73	10.49	12.32	9.75	13.40	15.88	13.79
DK	17.89	9.96	16.22	14.59	10.90	8.22	13.13	9.90	17.47	14.74	20.41	15.74	7.49	5.66
DL	16.62	9.39	8.72	9.41	15.31	11.50	11.81	6.45	6.40	5.29	9.88	8.21	14.85	14.92
DM	5.85	7.10	11.77	9.50	6.17	4.44	8.78	7.14	10.05	8.21	6.45	6.31	7.04	5.80
DN	4.59	2.91	3.57	5.15	4.67	3.20	2.67	5.87	6.20	6.75	4.45	3.79	1.32	1.23
TOTAL	100	100	100	100	100	100	100	100	100	100	100	100	100	100
A*	38.84	44.45	28.42	34.28	44.47	47.82	37.75	49.38	41.74	44.21	36.98	40.07	41.91	44.72
B**	20.79	29.10	34.86	32.22	23.15	28.01	28.54	27.12	24.33	27.55	26.28	29.66	28.71	28.89
C***	40.36	26.44	36.72	33.50	32.38	24.17	33.72	23.49	33.92	28.24	36.73	30.26	29.38	26.39

Relative productivity

	Bulgaria		Czech		Hungary		Poland		Romania		Slovakia	
	1989	1995	1989	1997	1989	1996	1989	1997	1989	1995	1989	1995
DA	2.27	1.34	2.74	1.46	1.22	1.32	1.72	1.40	2.42	1.63	1.42	1.48
DB	0.57	0.30	0.65	0.51	0.48	0.28	0.61	0.51	0.53	0.45	0.53	0.32
DC	0.57	0.42	0.96	0.54	0.49	0.25	0.68	0.50	0.50	0.43	0.50	0.31
DD	0.59	0.54	1.00	0.77	0.78	0.66	0.83	0.78	0.57	0.64	0.65	0.54
DE	0.79	1.19	1.05	1.14	1.13	1.05	0.72	1.43	0.85	0.97	1.59	1.27
DF	9.09	12.88	0.68	9.40	10.68	2.89	3.31	5.67	8.06	6.54	6.13	6.60
DG	1.05	1.49	1.77	1.79	1.84	1.46	1.24	1.57	1.26	1.63	1.43	1.67
DH	1.03	0.81	1.04	0.86	1.75	1.14	0.79	1.07	1.33	1.21	1.46	1.37
DI	0.74	0.73	0.69	0.83	0.74	0.76	0.58	0.78	0.90	0.86	0.82	0.75
DJ	1.30	1.07	1.22	1.21	1.50	1.06	1.16	1.03	1.49	1.40	2.23	1.33
DK	0.32	0.37	0.72	0.62	0.69	0.69	0.60	0.70	0.69	0.55	0.44	0.51
DL	0.73	0.52	0.73	0.64	0.77	0.99	1.34	0.80	1.10	0.78	0.53	0.65
DM	0.93	0.49	0.85	1.14	1.03	1.95	0.74	1.11	0.63	1.00	0.56	1.41
DN	1.20	0.74	0.70	0.64	0.49	0.44	0.55	0.65	0.44	0.49	0.59	0.65
TOTAL	1.00	1.00	1.00	1.00	1.00	1.00	1.00	1.00	1.00	1.00	1.00	1.00
A*	1.19	0.78	1.32	0.92	0.81	0.80	0.99	0.95	0.88	0.78	0.89	0.81
B**	1.48	1.84	0.99	1.32	1.65	1.29	1.14	1.22	1.56	1.63	1.86	1.53
C***	0.58	0.45	0.76	0.77	0.79	1.06	0.90	0.85	0.75	0.72	0.49	0.74

* Statistically significant at 1% confidence interval.

* *Statistically significant at 5% confidence interval.

* **Statistically significant at 10% confidence interval.

Source: LICOS industrial database.

In terms of employment, it seems that the sectoral trends are more systematic, as in all countries the consumer sectors increase their share in total industrial employment and capital sectors decrease it. For the intermediate sectors the evidence is mixed, as five countries have increased their share and two have experienced a reduction. It is worth noting that in 1996, consumer goods represent by far the largest sectors in terms of employment in all countries. It is worth noting that trends in sectoral employment are in a direction that do not seem to approach the EU sectoral distribution. As can be estimated from Table A1 in the Appendix, the shares of consumer, intermediate and capital goods sectors in the EU are 33.42%, 29.39% and 37.19% respectively. As a result, transition countries tend to develop an industrial structure which, compared to that of the EU, contains a higher proportion of employment in consumer sectors and a lower proportion in capital sectors.

In terms of productivity, the general trends in all countries are a relatively average but decreasing productivity in the consumer sectors, a relatively high and in some cases increasing productivity in the intermediate sectors and a relatively low productivity in the capital goods sectors.

These trends are in line with the literature (Landesmann 1998), which has indicated a move of transition countries away from technology and skill intensive sectors (which are more or less the capital sectors of this analysis) and towards labour or energy intensive sectors (which are, to a large extent the intermediate sectors of this analysis).

Index of Structural Change

In this section we attempt to measure structural change in a more quantified way. Following Havlik(1995), we define as the coefficient of structural change (CSC) the correlation coefficient:

$$CSC = Cor(X_{it}, X_{it+k})$$

$i = 1,2,...,n$ sectors
$t =$ base year
$k = 1, 2, ...,T$ years after the base year

This index measures for each time period the degree of change of a variable with respect to the base year. High values (close to 1) of the CSC for a given year indicate that the sectoral distribution between the current and the base year are very similar. On the contrary, low values indicate that significant changes have taken place.

149

In Table 6, we estimate the CSC for industrial output and industrial employment, on the basis of the sectoral shares of the 14 sectors of Table 5 for the countries and the years with available data. We also estimate CSC for exports and imports to/from the EU on the basis of 2-digit SITC sectors and compare them with the respective coefficient for intra-EU trade. On the basis of the information provided in the Table we could make a number of observations.

First, on a comparative basis, the countries that have shown clearer signs of change in terms of the structure of industrial output and employment are Bulgaria, Poland and the Czech Republic. On the other hand, most countries show significant changes in the structure of their exports to the EU, with Romania, Hungary, the Czech Republic and Bulgaria having the lowest values of the CSC coefficient. In terms of imports, the countries that have experienced more significant structural change are Slovakia, the Czech Republic and Bulgaria.

It is interesting that all countries, except Slovenia, to one degree or another and for at least one variable, show some signs of change. Slovenia stands out as the only country with very little change in its industrial and trade structure in the post-transition period.

Second, because of their exposure to the international environment, trade structures are more sensitive to change than productive (output or employment) structures and as a result they exhibit a greater propensity to structural change. Although not directly comparable, the CSC coefficient of all countries is lower in the external than in the productive sector of the economies under consideration. This might indicate that structural changes are introduced in the economies largely through trade. Changes are introduced either by imports (for domestic consumption) or exports (by foreign demand) and then spread to the entire economy, ultimately affecting the structure of productive sector with a time lag. To the extent that this reasoning and way of causality is true, and judging from the continuously declining CSC coefficients in trade data, we might expect additional adjustments in the productive sector of all economies under consideration.

Third, the speed of structural change cannot be classified as an a priori positive or negative development, as it seems to be associated with the actual pressure that the specific productive structure of an economy receives through its contact with the international environment. In general, high speed of adjustment should be associated with an unsustainable initial productive structure that under the pressure of the international markets and the domestic policies, may lead to (a) either a successful restructuring or (b) a backwards type of adjustment and a further diverging productive structure.

Table 6 Coefficients of Structural Change

Industrial Output

	Bulgaria	Czech	Hungary	Poland	Romania	Slovakia	Slovenia
1989	-	1.000	1.000	1.000	1.000	1.000	-
1990	1.000	0.999	0.983	0.889	0.988	1.000	-
1991	0.908	0.974	0.951	0.861	0.979	0.999	-
1992	0.906	0.987	0.871	0.816	0.944	0.998	-
1993	0.886	0.987	0.888	0.807	0.907	0.997	-
1994	0.718	0.976	0.904	0.811	0.915	0.992	-
1995	0.716	0.935	0.926	0.808	0.912	0.974	-
1996	-	0.887	0.924	0.801	0.922	0.927	-

Industrial Labour

	Bulgaria	Czech	Hungary	Poland	Romania	Slovakia	Slovenia
1989	1.000	1.000	1.000	1.000	1.000	1.000	1.000
1990	0.884	1.000	0.994	0.998	1.000	0.998	0.999
1991	0.886	0.991	0.980	0.979	0.993	0.999	0.996
1992	0.872	0.970	0.913	0.904	0.984	0.998	0.996
1993	0.852	0.935	0.908	0.882	0.976	0.972	0.987
1994	0.753	0.908	0.908	0.880	0.967	0.937	0.983
1995	0.790	0.906	0.921	0.858	0.962	0.929	0.979
1996	-	0.724	0.940	0.848	-	-	0.976
1997	-	0.718	-	0.830	-	-	-

*Exports**

	Bulgaria	Czech	Hungary	Poland	Romania	Slovakia	Slovenia	EU***
1988	1.000	1.000*	1.000	1.000	1.000	1.000*	-	-
1989	0.897	0.990*	0.994	0.977	0.995	0.990*	-	-
1990	0.864	0.984*	0.989	0.942	0.974	0.984*	-	-
1991	0.715	0.891*	0.971	0.914	0.860	0.891*	-	-
1992	0.589	0.821*	0.934	0.896	0.564	0.821*	1.000	-
1993	0.565	0.709	0.881	0.828	0.568	0.754	0.993	1.000
1994	0.602	0.725	0.828	0.852	0.592	0.761	0.979	0.998
1995	0.618	0.711	0.669	0.821	0.552	0.753	0.948	0.981
1996	0.612	0.609	0.586	0.762	0.528	0.645	0.939	0.988

*Imports**

	Bulgaria	Czech	Hungary	Poland	Romania	Slovakia	Slovenia	EU***
1988	1.000	1.000*	1.000	1.000	1.000	1.000*	-	-
1989	0.955	0.993*	0.943	0.919	0.909	0.993*	-	-
1990	0.943	0.974*	0.944	0.887	0.797	0.974*	-	-
1991	0.675	0.875*	0.869	0.701	0.765	0.875*	-	-
1992	0.552	0.770*	0.786	0.757	0.665	0.770*	1.000	-
1993	0.544	0.737	0.750	0.739	0.709	0.765	0.963	1.000
1994	0.546	0.664	0.729	0.783	0.757	0.671	0.953	0.997
1995	0.545	0.613	0.683	0.722	0.754	0.537	0.941	0.983
1996	0.574	0.586	0.674	0.683	0.750	0.521	0.931	0.987

*Data from 1988-1992 are for Czechoslovakia.
** To/from EU (2-digit SITC sectors).
*** Intra-EU (2-digit SITC sectors) trade.

As a result, speed does not necessarily indicate success, as the direction of adjustment is not measured by the CSC coefficient. On the other hand, a slow pace of adjustment may be associated with two possible (but very distinct) conditions. In the one case, a country may adjust slowly because it already possesses a structure that is more or less compatible with that of the main actors in the international markets, and as a result, competitive pressures do not materialize or do not have a strong sectoral impact. In the other case, a country may adjust its structure slowly because there is still a significant level of protectionism and public intervention in output or labour markets.

In Diagram 1, we plot an index of GDP (1989=100) and industrial output (1989=100) against the coefficient of structural change (CSC) for seven countries and six years with available data. We observe that the fitted line of the diagram has a small but positive slope, which indicates that higher (lower) values of the CSC coefficient are associated with a better (worse) performance in terms of GDP and industrial output.

Interpreting this relationship, we could say that on the average and ceteris paribus the transition countries that experienced rapid structural change are those that had the poorest record in terms of GDP and industrial output growth. On the other hand, the countries that showed a better performance record had, in general, a slower structural adjustment process. This is an indication that in the period under examination, rapid changes have been imposed primarily by international market dynamics on weak industrial structures and are associated more with a defensive and backwards type of adjustment and less with a successful restructuring.

Summing up, signs of significant or slow change should not be a priori associated with positive developments in the productive structure of a country, as the direction of change is a very important factor. The issue of direction of structural change, which is associated with the convergence-divergence prospects of each country to the EU economic structure, will be further examined in a later part of this section.

**Figure 1 The Relation between Performance Indicators
(GDP, Industrial Output) and the CSC**

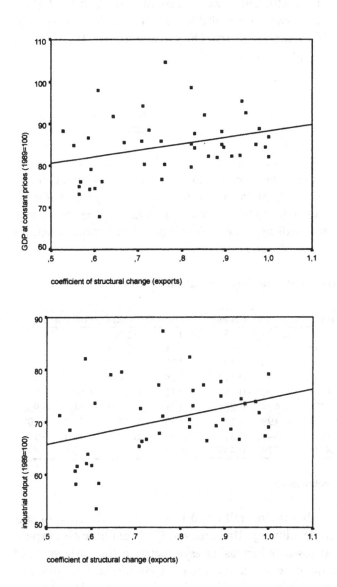

Index of Export - Import Asymmetry

In Table 7 we present a coefficient of asymmetry in trade with the EU for seven countries and nine years with available data. This index is in fact the correlation coefficient between exports (X_{it}) and imports (M_{it}) of each country j at the 2-digit SITC sectoral (i) level:

$$CAS_j = Cor (X_{it}, M_{it}), \qquad \text{where: } j = \text{country}$$
$$i = \text{sector and}$$
$$t = \text{time}$$

This CAS index takes values between zero and one. The lower the value of the correlation coefficient between the exports and imports of a country, the more asymmetric its trade structure is and the more likely it is that trade is dominated by an inter-industry type of relations. On the other hand, high values of the coefficient indicate very similar export and import structures and an intra-industry type of trade relations.

Table 7 Index of Asymmetry in Trade Relations with the EU

	Bulgaria	Czech	Hungary	Poland	Romania	Slovakia	Slovenia	EC
1988	0.276	0.229*	0.225	0.057	0.174	0.229*	-	-
1989	0.246	0.209*	0.225	0.089	0.145	0.209*	-	-
1990	0.243	0.252*	0.320	0.103	0.135	0.252*	-	-
1991	0.169	0.395*	0.330	0.119	0.228	0.395*	-	-
1992	0.169	0.494*	0.400	0.160	0.171	0.494*	0.623	-
1993	0.262	0.647	0.434	0.267	0.158	0.319	0.664	0.996
1994	0.189	0.710	0.499	0.249	0.195	0.461	0.753	0.997
1995	0.136	0.763	0.641	0.336	0.209	0.597	0.800	0.998
1996	0.258	0.824	0.729	0.433	0.228	0.699	0.838	0.997

*1988-92 data are for Czechoslovakia

We observe first, that the overall trend is towards a reduction of sectoral asymmetry in trade, although Bulgaria and Romania have also experienced a visible trend towards increasing asymmetry in the early years of transition. Second, we observe that among all countries, Bulgaria and Romania have the lowest value of CAS in their trade with the EU and therefore are characterized by trade structures that are dominated by the inter-industry type of trade. On the other hand, Slovenia and the Czech Republic, followed by Hungary and Slovakia, have the highest values of CAS and the lowest asymmetry in their sectoral trade patterns with the EU. Finally, Poland seems to take an intermediate position between these two groups, with CAS values indicating that both inter- and intra-industry trade are important elements in its relations with the EU.

The evidence provided in Table 7 is in line with the findings of Landesmann (1995, 1998) and others, who estimate GL coefficients of intra-industry trade and reach the same conclusions with respect to the general trend, as well as the national differences in specialization and trade.

Here however, we would like to advance this issue a little further by examining the relation of asymmetry in trade specialization and aggregate economic performance. Although not explicitly stated, most studies show some concern over the implications of an extreme or strong inter-industry type of trade specialization, for the development prospects of a country. In Diagram 2 we plot two performance indicators (GDP and industrial output) against the coefficient of asymmetry CAS, for seven countries and six years. We observe a clear positive relationship between performance and structural indicators, which implies that countries with a higher CAS (and a higher proportion of ITT) have a better performance than countries with a lower CAS (and a higher proportion of H-O trade).

Although we will come back to this issue at a later stage of the analysis, we regard the following as a likely interpretation of this diagram: Countries that have managed to avoid an excessive inter-industry type of specialization by developing export bases in several economic sectors have had, in general, a better performance in terms of GDP and industrial output growth. This seems to be in line with the experience of the Czech Republic, Slovenia and Hungary, which have the lowest asymmetry in trade and a very good record in terms of growth. It is also in line with the experience of Bulgaria and Romania, which have a very asymmetric export/import structure that seems to be related to their poor performance in the transition race.

Figure 2 The Relation between Performance Indicators (GDP, Industrial Output) and CAS

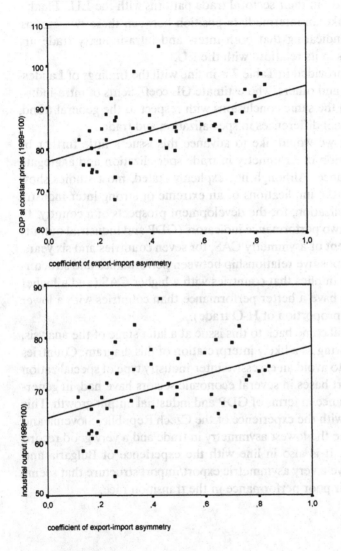

Index of Dissimilarity

A measure of success in industrial restructuring under transition can be the extent to which the productive (or trade) structure of these countries comes closer (converges) or move away (diverges) from the respective structure of the EU. In order to examine this issue, we estimate in this part an index of dissimilarity IDX in sectoral export structures, measured as:

$$^N_{i=1} \text{IDX}_{k,m} = \Sigma \, (s_{ik} - s_{im})^2$$

where s_{ik} is the share of sector i in the exports of country/region k and s_{im} is the share of sector i in the exports of country/region m. High values of this index indicate dissimilar export structures between two countries, while low values indicate similar export structures. An over-time reduction of the index indicates convergence in the export structures of the two countries/regions, while an over-time increase indicates divergence.

Table 8 Coefficients of Dissimilarity in Sectoral Export Structures

	Year	Czech. R*	Slovakia*	Hungary	Romania	Bulgaria	Slovenia**	Poland	EU***
Czech R.*	1988								
	1996								
Slovakia *	1988	0							
	1996	134.78							
Hungary	1988	799.32	799.32						
	1996	244.36	308.19						
Romania	1988	374.56	374.56	388.39					
	1996	*1,076.44*	*799.32*	*957.82*					
Bulgaria	1988	113.23	113.23	919.70	587.95				
	1996	*531.79*	*374.56*	508.15	388.39				
Slovenia **	1992	187.19	187.19	610.04	332.04	158.61			
	1996	138.56	113.23	264.26	*919.70*	*587.95*			
Poland	1988	181.69	181.69	1,331.89	653.34	201.62	326.04		
	1996	179.22	*187.19*	295.27	610.04	*332.04*	158.61		
EU ***	1993	584.75	584.75	1,401.11	654.26	653.80	530.82	401.91	
	1993	140.75	181.69	287.85	*1,331.89*	653.34	201.62	326.04	

* 1988 data are for Czechoslovakia.
** Data are for 1992 and 1996.
***Data are for 1993.

The estimated coefficients of dissimilarity of sectoral export structures for the seven transition countries and the EU are given in Table 8. We observe first, that both convergence and divergence trends can be detected in the period under examination. On the one hand, the Czech Republic, Hungary, Slovenia, Poland and Slovakia tend to develop export structures that converge with each other and the EU, while on the other hand, Romania and Bulgaria tend to develop export structures diverging from most other transition countries and the EU.

Second, the countries that have the export structures closest to the EU in 1996 are the Czech Republic, Slovakia and Slovenia (in this order), while the countries that have the export structures most distant from the EU are Romania (by far) and Bulgaria. In this framework, Hungary and Poland take an intermediate position.

Third, the countries that have made the most visible progress in covering their distance from the EU in the 1988-96 period are Hungary (by far) and the Czech Republic. At the other end of the spectrum lies Romania, which has increased its distance from the EU (and most other countries), as well as Bulgaria, which has maintained its distance from the EU at the same levels.

These developments tend to verify earlier findings (Petrakos 1997, Petrakos and Totev 2000) that structural adjustments in transition economies follow a more or less clear geographical pattern. According to this pattern, the countries in Central Europe tend to follow a more successful adjustment path converging with the economic structure of the EU, while the countries of Southeastern Europe tend to experience less successful structural changes, that either increase or maintain their distance from the EU.

Index of Irregularity in the Geographical Direction of Trade

Geography plays an important role in determining the direction of trade for each country. A recent gravity model estimated by Baldwin (1994) shows that geography is an important factor determining trade flows and patterns. Petrakos(1996) has also shown that distance and geogrraphical features will play an important role in shaping the future pan-European hierarchy of central places, markets and economic relations. Our concern in this part of the paper is: (a) whether the geographical pattern of trade for transition countries is the normal or expected one and (b) whether deviations from the expected or normal pattern of trade have any consequences for the development prospects of these countries.

We first need to define briefly the notion of normal or expected trade patterns. What would be the factors determining the geographical distribution of trade (for example exports) of a given country? Which are the more likely destinations of these exports? Gravity models predict that in an international framework with no major obstacles to commodity flows, exports from a country i to a country j will be a direct function of a country i's productive capacity (measured by GDP), a direct function of country j's market size (measured again by GDP) and an inverse function of the distance between the two countries. Other factors, such as the difference in the level of development between these two countries and the existence of common borders can also be introduced in the model.

Given that trade relations for Central and East European countries in the pre-1989 period were largely determined by political considerations, our concern here is whether and to what extent transition countries have undertaken, in the post-1989 period, a normal type of trade relations. That is, we are interested to know whether the (abrupt in several cases) redirection of trade from the East to the West is largely driven by market forces or by a new set of less detectable, but still existing political type of considerations. To the extent that there is a bias in the geographical pattern of trade relations, we are interested to know whether this has affected economic performance under transition, and in which direction.

We first need to establish the notion of a normal geographical distribution of trade and obtain the estimated parameters of a model that will depict this type of distribution as closely as possible. In order to do that, we claim that the EU is an economic space with no major barriers to interaction. As a result, the countries of the EU are expected to have normal type of trade relations with each other, in the sense that the direction of trade is driven to a large extent by the forces of market size, distance and adjacency.

On the basis of trade data provided by the IMF Direction of Trade Statistics Yearbook (1998), we estimate gravity model equations for each of the years 1991-1997 for the direction of exports of individual EU countries. The gravity model estimated is the following:

$$X_{ij} = A \ GDP_i^a \ GDP_j^b \ DIST_{ij}^{-c} \ ADJ_{ij}^d \ GNPCAP_{ij}^g$$

where X_{ij} is the exports of country i to country j, GDP_i and GDP_j represent the size of the economies i and j respectively, $DIST_{ij}$ is the distance between these two countries measured in minutes of travel time by airplane between the capitals, ADJ_{ij} is a dummy variable taking the value 2 if the two countries have common borders and 1 otherwise and $GNPCAP_{ij}$ is the ratio of the GNP per capita of country i over country j. We expect the market size of the two countries to have a positive impact on exports, distance to have a negative impact, and the existence of common borders, a positive impact. The ratio of the two GNP per capita values measures the differences in the level of development and is expected to have a positive impact on exports, to the extent that a higher level of development gives the country of origin an advantage that should lead to a higher volume of exports. This equation has been estimated in a logarithmic form and the results are presented in Table 9. We observe that the model has a very strong explanatory power and that the estimated coefficients have a statistically significant influence on exports as well as the expected sign.

Table 9 Gravity Model Estimation Results

Dependent Variable : Exports							
Year		Independent variables					R^2	N
	Constant	GDP_i	GDP_j	$DIST_{ij}$	ADJ_{ij}	$GNPCAP_{ij}$		
1991	-6.214	0.728	0.757	-1.023	0.649	0.205	0.90	273
	(-6.59)	(21.96)	(22.81)	(-11.32)	(3.32)	(3.36)		
1992	-6.109	0.720	0.749	-1.016	0.665	0.234	0.89	273
	(-6.44)	(21.73)	(22.59)	(-11.19)	(3.38)	(3.50)		
1993	-5.940	0.720	0.742	-1.030	0.588	0.224	0.90	273
	(-6.60)	(22.98)	(23.65)	(-11.94)	(3.17)	(3.29)		
1994	-6.057	0.717	0.746	-1.015	0.652	0.27	0.90	273
	(-6.48)	(22.30)	(23.17)	(-11.47)	(3.47)	(4.00)		
1995	-6.792	0.734	0.762	-0.952	0.676	0.218	0.90	273
	(-7.26)	(23.13)	(23.99)	(-10.81)	(3.66)	(3.31)		
1996	-2.206	0.617	0.622	-1.275	0.631	0.256	0.83	273
	(-1.87)	(15.21)	(15.32)	(-11.22)	(2.55)	(2.70)		
1997	-4.229	0.753	0.620	-1.245	0.654	0.433	0.80	273
	(-3.06)	(15.85)	(13.06)	(-9.35)	(2.26)	(3.87)		

Our next step is to find what would be the volume of exports of each transition country to other transition countries, to EU countries and to non-EU countries, in an ideal environment where trade is driven by the forces captured by the gravity model. To do this, we use the parameters of the model to estimate X_{ij} which represents the expected or normal pattern of exports by country of origin and destination, should the direction of exports of transition countries follow the same pattern as that of the EU countries. On the basis of these figures, we then estimate for each country (i) an index of irregularity in the geographical direction of exports, which is measured as:

$$\sum_{i=1}^{N} (X_{ij} - \bar{X}_{ij})^2$$

This index measures, in fact, the degree to which the direction of exports of a country is diverging or is different from that predicted by the gravity model equations. A high value of the index is therefore associated with a geographical export structure that is 'irregular' in the sense that it is very different from the one produced by the model. On the contrary, a low value indicates an export structure that is very close to the one predicted by the model. The results of this assignment are given in Table 10.

Table 10 Index of Irregularity in the Geographical Direction of Exports (IIGDE)

Country	1991	1992	1993	1994	1995	1996
Bulgaria	381.17	387.14	786.74	553.99	519.09	415.80
Czech	18.65	10.42	535.32	285.55	402.65	16.26
Hungary	188.36	191.13	712.57	369.89	351.25	39.62
Poland	193.08	266.35	245.52	346.34	35.01	30.90
Romania	251.63	227.84	229.24	233.41	100.04	100.19
Slovakia	18.65	10.42	98.76	98.75	110.37	35.75
Slovenia	32.06	28.65	190.70	200.94	250.85	228.91

We observe, first, that this index shows great variation over time and among countries. Most countries experienced a peak in the index of irregularity in the 1993-1995 period, most likely because of the abrupt reorientation of trade from the East to the West. This peak is normally followed by a significant decline in the value of the index. Second, we observe that in 1996 some countries, such as Bulgaria, Romania and Slovenia, continue to have relatively high index values, while some others have developed over time relatively normal trade patterns. The relatively irregular geographical patterns of trade for Bulgaria, Romania and Slovenia are attributed to the lack of relations with neighboring countries, which has been detected in earlier research work. Petrakos and Totev (2000) have observed in their study of the Balkans that transition countries in the region have nearly eliminated all trade relations with each other in the post-1989 period. This is certainly explained to a large extent by the wars, the conflicts and the tensions that afflict the region, but also by a political decision to cut off the ties with their past and a declared preference for association and interaction with the West.

Trade relations among neighboring countries, however, represent an important component of trade for all developed countries. Moreover, they are considered to be an important component of growth, as they usually have an intra-industry character and allow for the realization of economies of scale in sectors with a significant cross-border interaction. In addition, cross-border trade, because of its intra-industry character, is considered to have a beneficial impact on the economic structure of industry, as it imposes a severe specialization and allows for a greater sectoral variety.

Given these trends in the geographical direction of exports and the discussion above, we would like to examine whether significant irregularities in the geographical direction of trade have any implications for the growth prospects of transition economies. To see that, we proceed our analysis as follows: First we estimate gravity models similar to the ones presented above, for the estimation of the parameters determining the geographical origin of imports (not shown). On the basis of these parameters, we estimate in Table 11 the Index of irregularity in the geographical origin of imports (IIGOI). Finally, we plot these two indices against performance indicators in Figures 3 and 4.

Table 11 Index of Irregularity in the Geographical Origin of Imports (IIGOI)

Country	1991	1992	1993	1994	1995	1996
Bulgaria	500.41	664.85	860.09	586.91	568.02	661.37
Czech	130.94	80.50	565.15	386.40	367.99	116.74
Hungary	244.39	253.29	742.71	427.93	325.92	59.54
Poland	244.55	151.28	288.56	571.38	353.06	235.87
Romania	429.04	360.82	363.70	345.64	322.95	223.59
Slovakia	130.94	80.50	175.79	264.83	554.57	114.00
Slovenia	55.96	164.77	242.80	306.84	247.50	146.67

Starting from Table 11, we observe that irregularities in import structures are in general higher for all countries except Slovenia. The peak of the index is again in the 1993-95 period, while we now have to add Poland to the countries with relatively high irregularity in geographical import structures.

This tendency for a greater divergence of import structures from the values predicted by the gravity model is of course attributed to the increasing penetration of the CEE markets by EU products. It is also related to the bilateral (and not multilateral) type of the Association Agreements, which in many cases implied (at least until recently) serious obstacles to trade among transition countries.

How serious are these irregularities in trade relations compared to those of EU countries? For comparison purposes, we report that the divergence of actual from fitted exports (imports) for EU countries such as France, Germany and Greece in 1996 is 12.0 (12.1), 5.8 (6.4) and 39.3 (9.4) respectively. Indices of irregularity for all EU countries are reported in the Appendix. Obviously, there are significant differences between EU and transition countries, especially in the divergence of actual imports from the fitted values generated by the model.

What are the implications of irregularities in trade relations of transition countries for their prospects for growth and development? How is the documented lack of cross-border trade with each other affecting their economic performance? Diagrams 3 and 4 attempt a first answer to these questions.

We observe that both indices of irregularity in the geographical direction of exports (IIGDE) and irregularity in the geographical origin of imports (IIGOI) have a very clear and negative relationship with performance indicators such as GDP and industrial output. This provides some first indication that the geographical pattern of trade of some transition countries does not facilitate rapid growth, to the extent that the irregularities observed arise from the absence of substantial cross-border relations between neighbouring countries.

Figure 3 Relation between Performance Indicators
(GDP, Industrial Output) and IIGDE

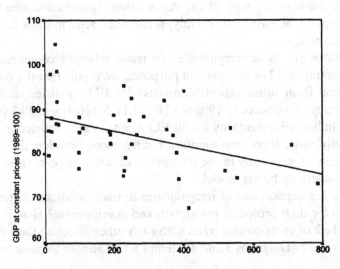

Index of irregularity in the geographical direction of exports

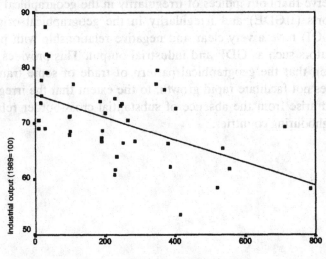

Index of irregularity in the geographical direction of exports

Figure 4 Relation between Performance Indicators (GDP, Industrial Output) and IIGDI

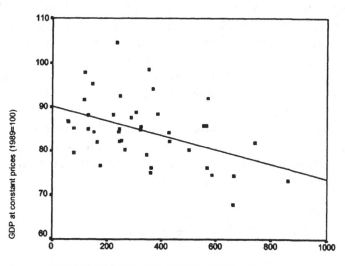

Index of irregularity in the geographical direction of imports

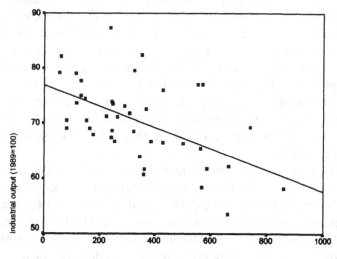

Index of irregularity in the geographical direction of imports

Industrial Performance under Transition: The Impact of Structural Factors

Our analysis in the previous section, as well as the work of others, indicate that some structural aspects of the transition process may operate, for a number of countries as real constraints to their performance in the new economic environment. These factors, to the extent that they appear in a systematic but also geographically selective manner, might be responsible to some extent for the fact that different groups of countries follow very distinct paths of adjustment.

In this part of the paper, we would like to examine whether the relations between industrial performance and industrial structure shown diagrammatically in the previous section can be supported in a more formal way. To this end, we construct an ad hoc model of the form:

$$Y_{it} = b_0 + \sum_{j=1}^{N} b_j x_{itj} + \sum_{j=1}^{M} g_j z_{itj} + e_{it}$$

Y_{it} is an index of industrial output (1989=100), measuring the performance of industry, x_{itj} is a set of structural explanatory variables, z_{itj} is a set of other national factors, e_{it} is a disturbance term, i, t are countries and years respectively and j is the number of variables. The structural factors that are included as explanatory variables in the model are the coefficient of asymmetry (CAS), the index of irregularity in the geographical direction of exports (IIGDE)[2] and the coefficient of structural change (CSC). The model is estimated, pooling information for seven countries and six years (1991-1996) for which we have available data. In some versions of the model we also include GDP per capita and two dummy variables as explanatory variables.

The National dummy groups transition countries as follows: it takes the value of 2 for the Central European countries (the Czech Republic, Hungary, Slovenia, Slovakia and Poland) and the value of 1 for the Southern European countries (Bulgaria and Romania). The time dummy takes the value of 1 for the period 1991-1993 and 2 for the period 1994-1996. The purpose of the dummy variables is first to reduce the variance of the residuals and second to account for important industrial performance differences over time and across (groups of) countries. The results of the model are given in Table 12.

Given the high degree of correlation between some of the structural variables (CAS, CSC) with GDP per capita and the national and time dummy variables (Pearson partial correlation values ranged from .68 to 0.82), we had to run several versions of the model. In general, the results are statistically significant and in the expected direction. Starting from the first column, we observe that the variable of structural asymmetry in trade (CAS), has a positive and statistically significant impact on industrial output. That is, higher values of the CAS index, which imply a lower asymmetry and a higher IIT component in trade, improve the prospects for industrial growth for reasons that have already been discussed.

Table 12 Regression Results

Dependant variable: Industrial output (1989=100)

Independent variables	Estimated Models					
	1	2	3	4	5	6
Constant	4.502*	3.682*	3.828*	4.062	4.277	4.198
	(85.22)	(9.72)	(18.34)	(11.84)*	(61.07)	(61.44)*
CAS	0.054**	-0.018	-	-.044	-	-0.035
	(2.31)	(-0.46)	-	-1.28	-	(-1.37)
IIGDE	-0.052*	-0.034*	-0.036*	-0.028*	-0.027	-0.027*
	(-3.04)	(-3.35)	(-3.36)	(-3.03)	(-2.93)	(-3.06)
CSC	0.121***	0.006	0.022	0.003	0.037	-
	(1.82)	(0.08)	(0.30)	(0.03)	(0.46)	-
GDP per capita	-	0.091**	0.075*	0.018	-	-
	-	(2.18)	(3.27)	(0.45)	-	-
National dummy	-	-	-	0.212*	0.174*	0.233*
	-	-	-	(3.26)	(3.44)	(5.097)
Time dummy	-	-	-	0.098**	0.088**	0.100*
	-	-	-	(2.63)	(2.75)	(3.23)
N	42	42	42	42	42	42
$\overline{R}^2$	0.403	0.457	0.468	0.612	0.613	0.630

*   Statistically significant at 1% confidence interval.
* *   Statistically significant at 5% confidence interval.
* ** Statistically significant at 10% confidence interval.

167

We also observe that existing irregularities in the geographical pattern of trade have a negative, robust and statistically significant impact on industrial performance. High values of the IIGDE variable, associated with serious divergence from normal patterns of trade (due to the CEEC's neglect of cross-border trade with each other and the excessive dependence on trade with the EU, which has a greater inter-industry component) have a negative impact on industrial output growth.

Finally, the positive and significant impact of the coefficient of structural change, indicates that abrupt shifts in the industrial structure of transition countries (that is, low CSC values), are not signs of successful restructuring but of regressive adjustments under the pressure of international markets that eventually seem to restrict growth potentials.

In the second and third column of Table 12 we add GDP per capita as an explanatory variable of industrial performance. The issue under examination here is whether countries with more advanced economies and higher levels of development are experiencing a faster or slower growth of industrial output. This is an important question. If higher levels of development lead to faster growth, then the process of transition is characterized by diverging trends that will eventually add a new divide to those already existing in the European economic space. The results of the model seem to provide some support for this hypothesis, as the coefficient of GDP per capita is positive and statistically significant. We note however that this variable is highly correlated to the CAS and CSC variables, nullifying their impact on industrial output in equations 2 and 3.

In the last three columns of Table 12, we add the national and time dummy variables. Our interest here is to examine whether there are systematic differences between (a) Central and Southern European countries and (b) the early and the more advanced period of transition. The results, as expected, provide evidence that the countries of Central Europe have a systematically superior performance to that of the Balkan countries. They also provide evidence that industrial growth was better in the 1994-96 than in the 1991-93 period.

Conclusions

Summarizing the main points of this paper, we would first argue that there is evidence that some distinct structural aspects of the transition process generate barriers to the recovery and growth of industry. These aspects have emerged largely as byproducts of a specific type of liberalization in trade relations that led to a rapid change in industrial structures, asymmetry in export-import relations and a biased geographical pattern of trade. Our evidence indicates that these factors may explain a significant part of the variation in industrial output across countries.

These findings, along with earlier work cited in this paper, indicate that there may be time for "rethinking" structural policies in transition, mainly understood as an agenda where privatization and liberalization are the top priority issues. As there is already serious concern about the weak relation between mass privatization and firm restructuring and growth in several countries (Nellis 1999), it may be time to focus attention on those issues of the external structure of the economies that in many cases are the real engine of change. In the light of our findings, it may be realized that trade liberalization ought to be more gradual and in pace with domestic liberalization and structural change. Available evidence shows that, in fact, it was too abrupt, exposing many important industries which however were unprepared, to advanced international competition (Gatsios 1996). It may also be realized that excessive trade dependence on the EU and neglect of inta-CEEC (especially cross-border) trade is not a proof of "westernization", but a factor that may jeopardize the long term potential of the industrial sector in transition countries.

The second point that needs to be highlighted is the clear difference in performance between Central and Southern European transition countries. Verifying evidence provided in earlier reports, our analysis shows a systematically inferior performance and structural adjustment for Bulgaria and Romania. These differences would have been greater had Southern countries such as Albania, Bosnia, FYROM or Serbia also been included in the analysis. As a result, a north-south divide within transition countries seems to be well under way, based on significant differences in growth performance, development levels and (as our analysis suggests) the direction of structural adjustment.

This paper has, perhaps, significant implications for policy making, which are, however, difficult to implement. It suggests a different framework for west-east and east-east trade relations which requires a more liberal (on the EU side) and multilateral type of Association Agreements as well as a clear commitment on behalf of transition countries to promote regional cooperation in spheres and sectors where geography and structure indicate that there are important opportunities for mutually beneficial interaction to be explored. However, removing EU barriers to trade in sensitive sectors is politically unrealistic today, because of the existence of strong pressure groups and high unemployment in the EU (Cecota 1995), conditions that undermine a more balanced type of integration. Moreover, regional cooperation, despite the creation and expansion of CEFTA, is undermined by the many tensions, disputes and conflicts among transition countries themselves.

It also suggests that some aspects of the EU policy towards transition countries need to be re-examined, if a permanent marginalisation of the Balkans is to be avoided. In that respect, policies need to focus equally on the forerunners of the transition process and the laggards, finding a new working balance between maintaining a rational incentive structure among candidate states (that is, rewarding success) and keeping the laggards in the race (that is, avoiding marginalisation). In addition, policies need to be more decisive and to take the form of a more generously financed support framework. This is necessary in order to partially offset the impact of the existing type of trade liberalization and to deal with the problems of structural weakness and deficient infrastructure that are more profound in the Balkan region.

Notes

1 The first one is the industrial database constructed by LICOS, including output and employment data for 7 countries and 14 industrial sectors in the period 1989-1995 and the second one is the Eurostat database on trade statistics.
2 Alternatively, the model was also run with the index of irregularity in the geographical orientation of imports (IIGOI). The results were identical and therefore are not reported.

References

Baldwin R. (1995) Paths towards an integrated Europe: problems and prospects, in R. Dobrinsky and M. Landesmann (eds.) *Transforming economies and European integration*, Aldershot: Edward Elgar, pp. 46-54.
Cekota J. (1995) Barriers to European (East - West) Integration, in R. Dobrinsky and M. Landesmann (eds.) *Transforming economies and European integration*, Aldershot: Edward Elgar, pp. 32-45.

Daianu D. (1995) Europe under a double challenge, in R. Dobrinsky and M. Landesmann (eds.) *Transforming economies and European integration*, Aldershot: Edward Elgar, pp. 15-31.

Dobrinsky R. (1995) Economic transformation and the changing patterns of European East-West trade, in R. Dobrinsky and M. Landesmann (eds.) *Transforming economies and European integration*, Aldershot: Edward Elgar, pp. 86-115.

Dobrinsky R. (1997) Multi-speed transition and multi-speed integration in Europe: recent economic developments in the Balkans and their implications, Paper presented at the Conference *Economic Cooperation in the Balkans: A Regional Approach to European Integration*, Phare-ACE Program, University of Thessaly, Department of Planning and Regional Development, Volos, 16-19 January 1997.

Gatsios K. (1996) Eastern European lessons on economic restructuring: a synthesis of the literature, in Scholtes P (ed.) *Industrial Economics for countries in transition*, Edward Elgar, pp. 39-53.

Havlik P. (1995) Trade reorientation and competitiveness in CEECs, in R. Dobrinsky and M. Landesmann (eds.) *Transforming economies and European integration*, Aldershot: Edward Elgar, pp. 141-162.

Jackson M. and Repkine A. (1997) A comparison of structural changes among the branches of industry in seven transition countries, Discussion Paper 64, *LICOS Center for Transition Economics*, Katholieke Universiteit Leuven.

Landesmann M. (1995) The patterns of East-West European integration: catching up or falling behind? in R. Dobrinsky and M. Landesmann (eds.) *Transforming economies and European integration*, Aldershot: Edward Elgar, pp. 116-140.

Landesmann M. (1998) Features of East-West European integration: cost structures and patterns of specialization, Paper presented in the international workshop on: *Competitiveness of the CEFTA countries: measurement and trends in the period of preparation to join the EU*, Bratislava, 17-18 April, 1998.

Landesmann M. and Burgstaller J. (1997) Vertical product differentiation in EU markets: the relative position of East European producers, Research Report No. 234a, *The Vienna Institute for Comparative Economic Studies*.

Mertzanis H. and Petrakos G. (1998) Changing Landscapes in Europe's Economic Structure, *Transition*, Volume 9, No. 2, pp. 12-13, The World Bank.

Nelis J. (1999) Time to rethink privatization in Transition economies? *Transition*, Volume 10, No 1, pp. 4-6, The World Bank.

Petrakos G. (1996) The Regional Dimension of Transition in Eastern and Central European Countries: An Assessment, *Eastern European Economics*, Vol. 34, No 5, pp. 5-38.

Petrakos G. (1997) Industrial Structure and Change in the European Union: Comparative Analysis and Implications for Transition Economies, *Eastern European Economics*, Vol. 35, No. 2, pp. 41-63.

Petrakos G. and Christodoulakis N. (1998) Transition in the Balkans: Patterns of Change and Policies to Overcome marginalisation and Disintegration, Phare-ACE Program *Structural Changes and Spillovers in the East European Reform Process*, Final Report, Imperial College Management School, University of London.

Petrakos G. and Totev S. (2000) Economic Structure and Change in the Balkan Region: Implications for Integration, Transition and Economic Cooperation, *International Journal of Urban and Regional Research* Vol. 24.1, pp. 95-113.

Repkine A. and Walsh P. (1998) European trade and foreign direct investment U-shaping industrial output in Central and Eastern Europe: theory and evidence, Discussion Paper 73, *LICOS Center for Transition Economics*, Katholieke Universiteit Leuven.

Sheehy J. (1995) Economic Interpenetration between the European Union and Central and Eastern Europe, in R. Dobrinsky and M. Landesmann (eds.) *Transforming economies and European integration*, Aldershot: Edward Elgar, pp. 61-80.

World Bank (1996) *From Plan to Market: World Bank Development Report*, World Bank.

Appendix

Table A1 Industrial Sectors and Sectoral Distribution of Employment in the EU (1994)

NACE	Category	Sectoral share
DA	Food, Beverage and Tobacco	12.99
DB	Textiles and Textile Products	6.97
DC	Leather and Leather Products	2.11
DD	Wood Products	2.34
DE	Paper, Printing and Publishing	3.48
DF	Fuel Production	3.46
DG	Chemicals, products, fibers	4.34
DH	Rubber and Plastic Products	4.95
DI	Mineral Materials and Products	4.97
DJ	Basic Metals and Fab products	11.67
DK	Machinery, excluding electrical	11.28
DL	Electrical and Optical Equipment	11.65
DM	Transport Equipment	14.26
DN	Other Manufactured Products	5.53
Total	Total	100.00

Table A2 Index of Irregularity in the Geographical Direction of Exports for EU Countries

	1991	1992	1993	1994	1995	1996	1997
Austria	5.58	7.25	8.52	10.30	9.97	15.20	15.81
Belgium-Lux	4.46	3.52	4.02	3.81	3.68	3.62	3.09
Denmark	5.33	5.50	6.51	7.43	7.32	12.25	12.11
Finland	2.44	2.26	2.74	2.43	3.02	51.32	48.04
France	5.85	6.77	6.83	6.44	6.21	12.00	10.95
Germany	5.40	4.47	3.01	2.59	2.67	5.87	5.84
Greece	10.57	10.97	10.31	17.27	15.88	39.35	43.49
Iceland	24.25	23.11	21.51	13.10	15.01	19.00	18.93
Ireland	8.97	8.83	9.51	9.80	10.22	9.78	121.47
Italy	2.83	2.86	2.34	2.64	2.42	5.71	10.58
Netherlands	6.17	10.20	3.65	3.54	3.41	4.95	5.86
Norway	6.87	9.79	8.79	8.33	6.65	13.36	14.28
Portugal	9.82	6.51	4.10	4.00	3.66	5.17	5.45
Spain	5.52	5.32	2.28	3.13	2.66	7.90	6.26
Sweden	216.47	219.11	212.12	220.64	4.70	8.58	9.04
Switzerland	5.35	5.10	4.72	7.79	8.14	13.88	14.82
U K	3.12	3.25	3.51	3.08	3.19	5.08	6.24

Table A3 Index of Irregularity in the Geographical Origin of Imports of EU Countries

	1991	1992	1993	1994	1995	1996	1997
Austria	10.92	9.97	10.50	8.57	12.24	19,81	22.41
Belgium-Lux	7.00	5.60	6.66	9.13	10.01	7.72	8.91
Denmark	4.82	6.49	6.60	8.12	9.36	13.68	11.76
Finland	5.65	4.71	4.06	4.34	5.71	68.44	68.29
France	3.95	4.55	5.43	5.85	6.99	12.08	13.17
Germany	4.25	3.08	2.37	2.79	3.13	6.42	6.61
Greece	4.11	4.75	3.51	4.92	7.48	9.43	8.92
Iceland	11.06	13.92	10.85	12.14	11.13	16.77	16.58
Ireland	9.94	8.24	9.44	9.19	11.99	12.51	126.67
Italy	5.33	6.96	7.52	8.05	9.19	15.82	32.61
Netherlands	3.22	3.42	3.01	3.81	4.53	6.89	6.76
Norway	5.60	4.49	4.42	4.83	5.52	10.01	9.92
Portugal	7.66	6.32	4.20	4.57	4.36	8.41	9.50
Spain	3.56	3.21	2.59	2.88	2.85	4.80	6.74
Sweden	217.29	220.80	213.85	222.36	158.25	8.55	9.34
Switzerland	3.44	4.71	4.69	5.41	5.85	12.22	15.28
U.K	5.01	4.67	5.14	4.39	4.96	6.57	6.15

7 Infrastructure Comparisons in Transition Countries: A New North-South Divide in Europe?

PANTOLEON SKAYANNIS
Assistant Professor Department of Planning and Regional Development, University of Thessaly, Greece.

Introduction

The predominantly economic restructuring that was attempted in the countries of Central and Eastern Europe during the transition period from the regime of centrally planned economies to that of the free market, included the critical process of infrastructure restructuring and upgrading. The intervention attempted in the field of infrastructure highlights the fact that infrastructure has to be in correspondence to the rest of the production base of the economy. Whereas during the previous regime, in the context of a limited internationalisation of exchange relations, infrastructure corresponded to, hence facilitated, the base of production and the relations in the sphere of exchange, in the currently developing transitional stage this is no longer true. This transitional restructuring period, within the framework of the globalisation process of economic relations and partly of production, leads to a process of necessary adaptation and restructuring of infrastructure as long as the question of how to face the new realities remains.

The intervention in the countries of Central Europe (CE) and the Balkans, especially in those that are about to access the European Union (EU), i.e. mainly the CE countries, is an issue discussed more and more frequently within the EU. To a great extent, this intervention aims to link these countries to the infrastructure networks of the EU in the perspective of integration of European space.

The EU participates in the project of restructuring the CE, Eastern European and Balkan countries in a major way via various programmes such as Phare and Interreg.

175

In this sense, the Community Support Frameworks, by and large comprising infrastructure investment, especially in the "objective one regions", are not the only domain of infrastructure co-financing of the EU. It is evident that the EU financing of infrastructure expands over and above its borders.

The infrastructure intervention in the former socialist countries is attempted within the framework of a general spatial development policy, more specifically of a spatial planning policy of the EU.

After the first attempts to face the European regional planning issues (such as Europe 2000), and under the constantly reshaping conditions and necessities, as well as under the prospective enlargement of the EU and the accession of the CE countries and the Balkans, the EU decided to proceed to a more concrete regional planning policy.

According to the EU, the basic reasons that lead to the development of a new spatial development policy are:

a) the cohesion issue
b) the internationalisation of economic and other processes
c) the necessity to support policies in other sectors

Therefore in the context of the Maastricht Treaty for the European Union, (Maastricht, November 1st, 1993), it was decided that the Economic and Monetary Union (EMU) will by and large be based on the convergence concept which in turn will be built along the following three axes:

a) Economic and Social Cohesion
b) Transeuropean Networks
c) Environmental Policy

However, there is de facto a different level of development among the various regions, at least as far as the above axes are concerned. In this sense, the co-called favoured and less favoured regions appear as a fundamental distinction. Consequently, the necessity of planning appears; hence of regional planning. This necessity raises the question of regional decentralisation that can be based on regional competition and solidarity (which are two contradictory, yet co-existent conditions and concepts). Not only are there intra-EU differentiations, but the newcomer countries in the market economy also have a different level of development. Their constant approx-

176

imation to the EU on the basis of their convergence along the three above mentioned axes, and their real or potential capacity to become member states, converts, in fact, these countries into fields of a strange regional policy to be indirectly applied by the EU. In addition, it converts them into areas where EU influence in a series of socio-economic sectors is heavily exercised. This is especially true for the infrastructure restructuring policy, mainly via the above-mentioned EU programmes.

The claim for funds by these countries, however, causes chain reactions within the EU and puts these countries into an antagonistic situation with the "objective one" countries. At the same time, the CE countries themselves and the Balkans do not enjoy a similar level of development. The differences they have in the field of infrastructure correspond to those they have in their economies.

The issue of infrastructure network development in the prospectively enlarged EU, is not merely a step towards the fulfilment of a cultural obligation, neither is it an element of common and trivial economic assistance to these countries underpinned by the also common and trivial arguments related to the enlargement of the market and the facilitation of transactions at the European level.

In greater depth, there is the question of capital, which attempts to expand and to become integrated into a larger spatial level. This attempt includes both the infrastructure intervention and the pursued predominantly economic but also significantly political results.

The Pan (or Trans) European Networks, being infrastructures, comprise the spine of the structuralisation of a single system of General Conditions of Production. The simultaneous liberalisation of capital and of personal movement provides the necessary complementary conditions so that this system may become functional and "productive". More specifically, as the General Conditions of Production secure the artery function of the production base and achieve the creation of scale economies and a significant economy in the capital circulation expenses (faux frais), the preconditions are set for the profitable development of the production activities. Therefore the flows of constant and variable capital are accelerated, leading to the acceleration of the process of capital rotation, predominantly in the sphere of circulation but also in that of production per se. Given the differential capital development between, on the one hand the western, and on the other, the CE-eastern European countries, the process of the uniform establishment of the General Conditions of Production inescapably leads to the increased possibility of western capital expanding to the central and eastern European space and the Balkans.

This becomes particularly intense in the case of border areas. Characteristic, in this direction, are the concerns that "while the German investments are welcome, the economic linkages developed between the border areas of the Czech Republic and Poland create problems in relation to the submission to Germany of the intentions for economic planning" (Turnock 1997: 22). Furthermore, there are problems with the loss of economic and political control in favour of Germany (Weclawowicz 1996 in Turnock 1997: 22).

The establishment of the General Conditions of Production is materialised via the construction of infrastructure works, which is also carried out under terms and procedures that favour western capital. A paramount role is played here by the construction and engineering capital that are significantly active factors of international capital in the present era of globalisation.

The discussions on the Balkans are particularly significant for Greece, especially because the issue of the Greek spatial policy, through the long yet shallow regional planning, has not up to now probed deeply enough in relation to the position of the country, hence the weak position of Greece in the international infrastructure networks, especially that of transport (Vassenhoven 1993: passim). In addition, the Greek policy of relations with the countries of the CE and EE and the Greek "intrusion" in these countries is not systematically planned (with ranking, priorities, etc.). The importance of this issue for Greece is twofold: on the one hand, infrastructure works can become a factor for the integration of the South European market, which would be beneficial for people of this area. It would also support the accession tendencies of the CE, EE and Balkan countries to the EU. In addition, it would strengthen the wider construction activity to which the Greek construction capital seeks outlets after the decline of its activity in the Arab countries. On the other hand, some of the infrastructure may create a spatial and economic competition between countries or regions in the Balkans. The different propositions, evidently, are based on different interests hidden behind them and aim at the exploitation of the essentially new markets opening (Skayannis 1994: 160-1).

In the Balkans, infrastructure development is currently undergoing a critical phase. The geopolitical restructuring through the challenge of borders and the continuous local warfare in the former Yugoslavia (especially today after the almost complete destruction of the infrastructures of the New Yugoslavia due to the NATO bombing) have not, for the most part, allowed the upgrading and modernisation of infrastructure to the extent that this has happened in the rest of the CE and EE countries. This is true despite the fact that, in any case, the starting point for the Balkan countries, for historical reasons, is at a lower level, compared to that of the CE and EE countries. In addition, it has been observed that older infrastructures have also been destroyed. An example of such phenomena is Albania, where, for instance, road pavements were dismantled in order for tiles to be used for bathrooms.

As reported by the CIA, telephone cable was removed in order to construct fences (CIA 1999). From a series of facts and data presented below one can verify that there is a serious difference between the development of infrastructure in the Balkans and in the rest of the CE countries. It can be argued that this difference establishes a new type of "North- South" spatial divide in the European spatial system.

Some of the most characteristic issues of the Balkans are those of the North-South transport corridors (from North-Eastern Europe to the Mediterranean) and of the West - East. These issues are long existent in the area. Other problems that either emerge or presently recur concern the energy infrastructure of the area; natural gas, as well as telecommunications. Through these problems one can clearly observe the great political and national importance that infrastructure works can assume for all countries involved (Skayannis 1994: 161), especially after the period of local wars.

In the next sections of this chapter a first analytical approach of the very basic technical infrastructures of the Balkans and of CE is attempted. This is carried out by means of the simple indices that are readily available from sources, such as the United Nations, the World Bank, the International Telecommunication Union, the Central Intelligence Agency of the USA, etc. By the structured presentation of these facts, comparisons are attempted between countries, mainly between the Balkan countries as a whole, and the respective sets of countries of CE and EE. It shall be proved from these comparisons that the Balkan countries are still lagging behind the other geopolitical groups of countries.

It should be noted that because of the nature of this analysis, which is "extensive" rather than "intensive", in-depth observations concerning the quality and functional characteristics of the various networks and sectors

179

cannot be made. However, it would be reasonable to assume that the economic and development condition of the Balkan countries, which is generally worse than that of the CE countries, and obviously of the EU, influences the quality and functional characteristics of the various networks. Therefore one expects Balkan networks to be in an even worse situation than that suggested by the quantitative data.

In this sense, the differences, hence the comparison, between the Balkan and the CE countries, in most cases being in favour of the latter, render large and strong interventions critically necessary, provided the bridging of the gap and convergence is sought, so that finally the cohesion of all European regions is achieved.

Transport

The Networks

In the areas under consideration the common land and air transport will be briefly examined. In the tables that follow, the basic facts of the CE and Balkan countries, as well as certain interesting differentiations between these two groups of countries, are presented.

Road network The road network, as is evident from table (1A-app.), is denser (network km./ 1000 sq.m.) in Hungary and Poland, Slovakia, Slovenia, and the Czech Republic (i.e. in the CE countries), and then in Romania, Albania, and the other Balkan countries. The position of Greece, according to this indicator is immediately after Hungary and Poland. It is interesting that the countries of CE have an indicator of 1,176, while the Balkan countries just reach 526 (i.e. more than twice less), while, with the participation of Greece, the Balkans come up to 894. It is a fact that this indicator embodies a reasonable bias toward having higher values in plane (flat) areas, where road construction is relatively easier. To some extent, this is how the lead of Hungary and Poland and the slower development of the Balkans (including Greece) can be explained. The latter are, for the most part mountainous and inaccessible areas. Yet, the same is not true for the length of the paved networks. The small network of Bulgaria is almost all paved (91.9%), as well as those of the Czech Republic (100%), Slovakia (98.5%), and Greece (91.8%). The denser network of Hungary has the lowest percentage of pavement (43%) after Albania (30%). The rural character of the network could explain this.

It is also worth noting that motorways are almost absent from the Balkans, while some are present in the CE countries. As shown in table 1 (A1), of the Balkan countries only Greece, and to a lesser extent FYROM, Romania and Bulgaria have some kilometres of motorways, while the CE countries have more than 200 km each, i.e. as many kms as the Balkans have if put together, excluding Greece.

Table 1 Balkans and Central European Countries
Road Network and Motorways

COUNTRY	Road Network in kms	Density of Road Network (km of network per 1000 sq. kms)	Motorways in kms	Paved Road Network in kms	Percentage of Paved Road Network[1] (1996)
Balkans	277,253	460	246	185,267	58
Balkans +Greece	434,099	592	716	292,673	67
Central Europe (CE)	640,630	1,176	1,881	417,387	65
Balkans / CE	0.43	0.39	0.13	0.44	0.90
Balkans +Greece / CE	0.8	0.50	0.38	0.70	1.03
European Union (EU)	3,529,351	1,120	41,461	3,421,975	96.96
CE / EU	0.18	105.04	4.54	12.20	67.04
Balkans / EU	0.79	41.06	0.59	5.41	59.82

Source: CIA World Factbook 1998.
[1]World Bank World Development Indicators 1998.

As can be seen in Table 1, the comparisons of all road network parameters between the various countries, especially the Balkans, and the EU are staggering. The road network density is marginally higher in the CE countries compared to the EU, but that of the Balkan countries is just higher than 40% of the EU. The CE countries just reach 4.9% of the EU in motorways, while the Balkan countries remain well below (0.59%). The difference in the various percentages of paved roads is also significant. In the CE countries, paved roads are 67.04% of the total road network, while in the Balkans, 60%.

Railway network The railway network, as can be seen in Table A2, is comparable to the road network. The densest network (considering all categories of railway gauge) is in the Czech Republic (120 km /1000 sq. km.) and in Hungary (82.4), while Poland, Slovakia, and Slovenia follow. The sparsest network of Slovenia (59.3) is already denser than the densest of the Balkans, that of Romania (49.3). The density of the network in the Balkans is less than half of that of the CE countries. If Greece comes into the calculations, the situation for the Balkans becomes even worse, as Greece has the sparsest network of all the countries under consideration (just 18.9).

It is also important to examine the electrification of the network. The percentage of electrified network in the total of standard gauge track is highest in Bosnia-Herzegovina (77.9%) and in Bulgaria (65.5%). In this case the Balkans are almost in the same position as the CE countries. 40.6% of the Balkan network is electrified, while the electrification percentage in the CE countries is 42.3%. The inclusion of Greece in the calculations with a mere 36 km of electrified track, keeps the Balkans at a lower percentage (38.2%). Of course, Greece, in the context of the Community Support Frameworks, among other works and expansions of the railway network, is proceeding to double and electrify the railway track along the Patras - Athens- Thessaloniki - N.borders axis. This is despite the fact that, contrary to what happened in the rest of the Balkan countries, in post war Greece, railway development had never been a priority of land transports. Because of the recent wars in the New Yugoslavia, the network of this country is destroyed, while the economies of the other countries still leave open serious questions and have to deal with difficult problems. In these circumstances, it is difficult for these economies to increase investments in the field of rail network improvement and modernisation.

In comparison to the EU, as shown in table 2, the CE countries (that have double the network, both in total as well as in standard gauge compared to the Balkans), just reach 27.43% (total network) and 31.39% (standard gauge network) of the EU, while in the Balkans the figures are 14.34% and 16.84% respectively. The total network in the CE countries is denser than that of the EU, while that of the Balkans reaches 75% of the EU. However, the density and the length of networks do not reflect their degree of modernisation. This is best indicated by network electrification. In this case, relative to the length of the network, the same proportion is kept between the CE countries and the Balkans (2/1), while with reference to the percentage, both the CE countries and the Balkans (which both have a clearly smaller network than that of the EU) are below 90% of the EU.

Table 2 Balkans and Central European Countries
Railway Infrastructure

COUNTRY	Length of Railway Network in kms	Density of Railway Network (km of network per 1000 sq. kms)	Total Length of Standard Gauge Network in kms	Length of Electrified Network in kms	Standard Gauge Electrified Network as a percentage of the Total of Standard Gauge Network
Balkans	24,164	40.10	23,447	9,510	0.41
Balkans +Greece	26,638	36.30	25,012	9,546	0.38
Central Europe (CE)	46,225	84.90	43,689	18,466	0.42
Balkans / CE	0.52	0.47	0.54	0.51	0.96
Balkans +Greece / CE	0.58	0.43	0.57	0.52	0.90
European Union (EU)	168,514	53.00	139,198	65,333	0.47
CE / EU	27.43	160.16	31.39	28.26	89.93
Balkans / EU	14.34	75.62	16.84	14.56	86.30

Source: CIA World Factbook 1998.
World Bank World Development Indicators 1998.

Airport network Airports are more or less normally dispersed (A3). If the airports with paved runways are considered, the densest network is that of Croatia (0.9 airports per 1000 sq. km). Greece follows with 0.5, FYROM and the Czech Republic with 0.4, Slovenia and Bulgaria with 0.3, while all other countries score 0.2, excluding Romania (0.1). In the case of airports, the statistical role of Greece is determinant, because, while the average of the CE countries and the Balkans is 0.2, if Greece is included in the calculations, the Balkans take the lead, achieving an average of 0.3. The relatively highly developed airport infrastructure in the Balkans is due to the fact that the ground relief does not favour land transport, which is linear, for cost reasons. Consequently, an airport, which is point infrastructure, is frequently a compulsory solution. The same applies to Greece for the above reasons, in addition to the large number of islands and for reasons of national security and defence.

Table 3 Balkans and Central European Countries
       Airport Infrastructure

COUNTRY	Airports. (1997 est.)	Airports with Paved Runways	Airport Density. (% ratio of paved airports in the countries' area)	Paved Airports as a Percentage of Total Airports	Airports with not Paved Runway
Balkans	228	146	0.26	64.00	82
Balkans +Greece	306	209	0.30	68.30	97
Central Europe (CE)	201	130	0.20	64.70	71
Balkans / CE	1.13	1.12	1.01	0.99	1.15
Balkans +Greece / CE	1.52	1.61	1.19	1.06	1.37
European Union (EU)	2,673	1,53	0.48	0.57	1,145
CE / EU	7.52	8.51	49.74	113.59	0.06
Balkans / EU	8.53	9.55	50.45	112.28	0.07

Source: CIA World Factbook 1998.

The comparison of the magnitudes of the airports to those of the EU, as shown in Table 3, is also overwhelmingly in favour of the EU. In all cases, i.e. in the case of paved runways, of unpaved runways and in total, the percentages of the countries under consideration do not even reach 10% of the EU. The density of airports is double in the EU compared to these countries, but the percentage of airports with paved runways is smaller in the EU. This is due to the fact that many of the large EU countries (primarily Germany, France, UK and Sweden) have a very large number of small unpaved airports which are obviously used for general aviation purposes.

Conclusions on the Transport Networks

The general picture that the physical infrastructure networks present in the areas under consideration is one of a development cleavage between the EC countries and the Balkans, with the latter lagging behind as far as the land networks are concerned, and with a relative balance in the airport infrastructure. In similar land relief (e.g. in the Balkans) railways are denser as opposed to the road network (in relation to but not in comparison with the EU densities). The same applies to the CE countries. This fact reveals the priority given by the central planning regimes to the mass means of transport, that is par excellance to the railways, and the relative disregard of the parameters concerning the road network (few motorways and low percentage of asphalt pavement, as well as policies not particularly favouring private cars).

The Development of Transport Infrastructure

The basic guidelines for the development of the transport infrastructure of Central and Eastern Europe were decided in 1994 at the second Paneuropean summit of the transport ministers, in Crete. The decision included nine combined high priority transport corridors that would enjoy the support of the EU. Obviously, the European part of the former Soviet Union is considered as a part of the Paneuropean transport system. Three out of the nine corridors of Crete pass through these countries. For the reasons stated above, these new countries participated in the third Paneuropean Conference of Transport held in Helsinki during June 1997.

In order to apply the decisions of the Hessen summit, the EU developed the Phare programme as a multiyear financial tool focussing on investment expenditure. An important part of the infrastructure projects of the CE and Balkan transport network is co-financed by the EU via the Phare programme. Today, up to 25% of the total budget of the Phare programme can be allocated to co-finance infrastructure projects related to the Paneuropean networks. This has a special provision for the Cross - Border Passage Programme which aims to reduce the cross border traffic costs. Multiyear investment programmes for the development of Paneuropean Networks (1995-1999) were agreed upon by all countries and with the involvement of international financial institutions, primarily with the European Investment Bank. The contribution of the Phare programme to the co-financing of infrastructure projects related to the Paneuropean networks amounted to the sum of 190 MECU just for 1996.

It is not surprising, therefore, that the most widely discussed transport problems are those of the Paneuropean corridors. In Greece, the issue of the Egnatia corridor is on the agenda. This corridor is very important for the EU because it can secure east-west trade, irrespectively of the political unrest and upheaval that create problems in the rest of the Balkans. At the same time, this corridor can guarantee low cost proximity to the Black Sea countries (A.Gonzalez-Finat, 1993). The construction of the Egnatia corridor is under way. This motorway has an additional importance because of the spatial restructuring it is likely to cause not only to the Greek, but also to the wider Balkan space. This motorway will be linked to the important transeuropean motorway Helsinki-Alexandroupolis, a part of which will be linked to the Black Sea ring, the realisation of which is even further in the future, and will cut across other major corridors such as the one between Istanbul and Berlin. Obviously, with this sort of linkages and with the fact that it is part of such a network, the Egnatia corridor is not just a motorway for vehicles to move fast, but an axis of a more general spatial organisation. It is a factor for relocation of economic activity, for changes to the relations, magnitudes and organisation of the city network, etc. In this context, the "vertical" linkages of Egnatia to the northern borders of Greece are worth mentioning and are interesting to examine. These, taken from east to west, are: a) Ormenio (GR) - Svilengrad (BUL) - Harmanil (BUL) - Stara Zagora (BUL), b) Komotini (GR) - Nymphaio (GR) - Kirdzali (BUL) - Haskovo (BUL), c) Xanthi (GR) - Echinos (GR) - Smoijan (BUL) - Plovdiv (BUL), d) Drama (GR) - Nevrokopi (GR) - Exochi (GR) - Banska (BUL), e) Serres (GR) - Sidirokastro (GR) - Promachon (GR) - Kleidi (GR) - Kulata (BUL) - Sofia (BUL), f) Evzonoi (GR) - Gevgelia (FYROM) - Titov Veles (FYROM) - Skopje (FYROM), g) Florina (GR) - Niki (GR) - Bitola (FYROM), h) Kastoria (GR) - Crystalopigi (GR) - Bilista (AL) - Korce (AL), j) Ioannina (GR) - Kakavia (GR) - Gyrokaster (AL) - Saranta (AL).

These linkages are expected to contribute to the restructuring of the southern Balkan space, creating an Egnatia-centric structure, and providing the countries bordering on Greece with better access to the Aegean, a fact which is envisaged to be beneficial for the improvement of both their economies and that of Greece. In addition, as these countries develop economically, the linkages will facilitate necessary itineraries that in the future will have less to do with the migration to Greece and more with trade and tourist activity.

The promotion, on the part of Turkey, of the so-called "anti" or "para-Egnatia" corridor is also an important development. Other Balkan counties through which the "para-Egnatia" is proposed to pass obviously participate in this effort. It is obvious that all expect to benefit if the motorway runs through their area. (see Kathimerini 20/1/1994: 60). At the macro level, "para-Egnatia" is an element of a regional planning proposal that reflects an intensive inter-Balkan bargain (P.Skayannis 1994: 161). The "para-Egnatia" corridor has been registered as the eighth Paneuropean corridor in the framework of the Paneuropean network decided upon in Crete. In fact, it is the corridor Durach (AL) - Tirana (AL) - Skopje (FYROM) -

Sofia (BUL) - Plovdiv (BUL) - Varna (BUL). In Plovdiv, it is linked to the Berlin (DEU) - Istanbul (TU) corridor and to the 9th corridor: Helsinki - Alexandroupolis (GR). These arrangements make Bulgaria the node of the important north-south and east-west corridors, and hence increase her strategic role. On the contrary, the largest part of the former Yugoslav space, i.e. the New Yugoslavia and Bosnia-Herzegovina, or even Croatia, as well as a large part of Romania, remain outside of the current Paneuropean corridor planning, and no provision is made for another necessary ring, the Adriatic one.

Telecommunications, Informatics, and Mass Media

Telephony and Mobile Telephony

Telecommunications in the countries of this area are developing at a slower rate if compared to those of Western Europe. This can be seen in Table A4. The most important indicator in basic telephony is that of main telephone lines per 100 inhabitants (telephone penetration). This indicator, irrespective of the degree of network digitalisation, presents the following fluctuation: Besides Greece, which is an advanced telecommunication region having a penetration of 51% (1997), the rest of the countries range from 3.5% (Albania) and 9-10% (Bosnia-Herzegovina) up to 36.5% (the Czech Republic and Slovenia). On average, the Balkans have a penetration of 20.3%, while the CE countries of 26.95%. Greece enables the Balkan average to rise to 25.2%, which still remains lower than that of the CE countries.

The picture in cellular mobile telephony is very similar, irrespective of whether the technology is GSM, DCS or analogue. In the total of mobile telephony most of the Balkan countries have a telephone penetration (connection per 100 inhabitants) of less than 1% (1998). The exceptions are Croatia and the New Yugoslavia, which score 4.07 and 2.26 respectively (in 1998 Greece had 8.91% while the percentage was becoming higher quite rapidly)[1]. On the contrary, the CE countries fluctuate with ratios between 4.4% (Slovenia) and 9.39% (the Czech Republic), thus establishing yet another field where these countries are more advanced than the Balkans.

187

Table 4 Balkans and Central European Countries
Telecommunications Infrastructure (Connections of Standard
and Mobile Telephony)

COUNTRY	Main Telephone Connections in 1000s. (1998)	Main Telephone Connections per 100 inhabitants (1998 and own calculations)	Mobile Telephony Subscribers (1998)	Mobile Telephony Connections per 100 inhabitants (1998 own calculations)
Balkans	11,190.8	20.27	733,400	1.33
Balkans +Greece	16,621.7	25.23	1,671,100	2.54
Central Europe (CE)	17,910.9	26.95	4,159,100	6.26
Balkans / CE	0.62	0.75	0.17	0.21
Balkans +Greece / CE	0.93	0.94	0.40	0.41
European Union (EU)	195,770.1	53.42	77,153,900	20.65
CE / EU	0.09	0.50	0.05	0.30
Balkans / EU	0.06	0.38	0.01	0.07

Source: International Telecommunications Union Basic Indicators 1999.
Note: Own calculations based on population estimates for 1998 for the CE countries from
CIA World Factbook 1998; for the EU from Eurostat.

The comparisons in the field of classic telecommunications (based on table 4) are overwhelmingly in favour of the EU. In basic telephony, the CE countries reach half of the EU penetration, while the Balkans a mere 0.38%. In mobile telephony, the discrepancy is vast. The Balkans, compared to the EU, are below 1%. This means that, if in the EU 20-21 out of 100 inhabitants have a connection, in the Balkans this number is just over 1. Of course, the situation, especially in mobile telephony is easily reversible. This is because mobile telephony is developed by the private sector and undertaken by firms that are quite flexible, as this kind of technology itself is. At the same time, in the absence of modernised and upgraded networks, mobile telephony often becomes a substitute. Despite the disadvantage of higher prices, it can be proven to be a quick solution for many consumers. For this reason, a rapid increase in the region of CE and the Balkans should be expected, to the extent that the wider economic environment improves and allows its wider spread. Investments in modern digital basic telephony networks and associated facilities are taking place at a much slower pace, because of their extent, of the kind of technology and of practical issues such as trench digging.

Mass Media and Informatics

In the field of electronic mass media and of the wider information infrastructure, one can include the traditional indicators related to radios and televisions (TV sets) as well as the ones related to Personal Computers (PCs) and Internet hosts. As can be seen in Table A5, radios per 100 inhabitants are 6% more in the CE countries compared to the Balkans (26.46% against 20.43%). Televisions per 1000 inhabitants, in the Balkans, range from 55 in Bosnia-Herzegovina and 170 in FYROM, to 361 in Bulgaria (Greece has 442). In the CE countries the lowest rate was that of Slovenia (375) which, however, is higher than that of Bulgaria (the highest in the Balkans, excluding Greece). The highest was that of Hungary (444). Despite the fact that the reference years differ, the differentiation between the CE and the Balkan countries is very obvious. In the field of PCs and Internet hosts, magnitudes are indicative; it does not seem that a convincing data collection methodology has yet been established. For example, while Bulgaria and Slovakia seem to have a three-digit number of PCs per 1000 inhabitants, all other countries (including Greece) have a two-digit number or provide no data. However, all EU countries, except the European South, have three digit numbers with Denmark being the most advanced, reaching 304 per 1000 inhabitants.

In the field of Internet hosts, the rate in Slovenia is equally surprising (85.66 connections per 10000 inhabitants). In the Balkans, Bosnia with 0.13 and Albania with 0.32 come last against 2-3.00 in FYROM, the New Yugoslavia and Romania, 6.65 in Bulgaria and 14.08 in Croatia. (Greece has 18.76). In the countries of CE, the lowest rate is that of Poland (11.22) while the other rates are higher. The Balkans score one digit numbers, except for Greece and Croatia which score two-digit numbers. In the EU, all countries reach two or three digit numbers with Greece (18.76) and Portugal (18.26) being the worst and Finland (654) and Sweden (321) the best. In particular, Finland is in an even better position than the US (442).

Conclusion on Telecommunications, Informatics and Mass Media

According to what has been stated so far, it becomes evident that the Balkans are an area that particularly lags behind the rest of the European regions in all indicators (an overview of other indicators such as waiting time to acquire a connection, or for fixing malfunctions reveals a similar picture.

189

(See WB, 1998). This is despite the fact that one should have a lot of reservations related to the methodology data which were collected in the various countries for the information technology sector.

The lagging behind of the Balkans in the field of telecommunications does not cease to render these countries an area of very severe international competition at various levels: first, at the level of investment for system modernisation, and second, at the level of determining who shall become the main telecommunication node of the area. Besides both the exaggerations made and the "dangers" envisaged by the press, the efforts to push Greece aside by the "optical fibre arc" supported by Turkey with the backing of Italy and the participation of other Balkan countries, is a fact. This network is materialised via two agreements; the TBL (Bari - Istanbul, via Tirana, Skopje, Sofia) and the ITUR (Palermo -Istanbul - Odessa and Novorosisk), both bypassing Greece (see "To Vima", 19/12/1993: 64-5) (P.Skayannis 1994: 161-2). The Greek answer comes through the Interreg projects, which link Greece to Italy, as well as through the penetration of the Hellenic Telecommunications Organisation (OTE) and the firms it participates in (e.g.Hellascom), into the Balkan space. In particular, OTE has already made moves to participate in major telecom projects in Romania, and the New Yugoslavia.

Energy

Electric Energy

Production structure according to primary sources The production of electric energy is of paramount importance for modern economies. Its use is indicative of the development level of a country. A first interesting element is that of the production structure according to the primary energy source. This is indicative of the dependencies of an energy system. EU policy today tries to decrease the dependency on oil, keeping its participation in production lower than 15%.

From the point of view of structure, as can be seen in Table A6, the Balkan countries produce electric energy from hydroelectric power in fairly high percentages (Albania 95.2%, Bosnia-Herzegovina 64.5%). Coal comes second, while only Croatia and Greece produce more than 15% of their electric energy from oil (27.7% and 21.5% respectively). Bulgaria is the only country that uses nuclear power for electric energy production (42.4% in 1995). Romania has the most balanced structure, which includes 26.9% production from natural gas. The CE countries have far less production from water, one of the reasons being their geographic relief (which being flatter, does not provide satisfactory scope for this purpose). Yet, they have significant production from coal and nuclear power. The only country in CE for which there is no record of the use of nuclear power is Poland, which, however, is dependent by 97.3%, on coal. It is worth noting that except Hungary and Slovakia which produce 11.9% and 9% of their electricity from natural gas, the percentages of the rest of the CE countries are negligible. This is despite the fact that many kilometres of natural gas pipelines pass through these countries.

As can be seen in Table 5.1. and particularly in Table 5.2., the percentage of energy that is produced from water is, in the Balkans, double that of the EU countries, while that of the CE countries reaches 1/3 of the EU countries. The percentage of energy produced from coal is double in the CE countries compared to the EU countries, while the Balkans exceed the EU by 1.39 times. The EU is stronger in energy production from oil, having a production in percentage terms that is 2/3 larger if compared to the CE and 1/3 larger if compared to the Balkans. In natural gas, the Balkans are

Table 5.1 Balkans and Central European Countries
Sources of Electric Energy (Production in Bil. kwh)

COUNTRY	Production in bil. kwh (1995)	Electricity Production from water[1]	Electricity Production from coal[1]	Electricity Production from oil[1]	Electricity Production from natural gas[1]	Electricity Production from nuclear power[1]
Balkans	158.80	40.91	68.34	10.88	21.44	17.26
Balkans +Greece	200.00	44.46	97.01	19.74	21.52	17.26
Central Europe (CE)	269.50	12.20	197.99	9.14	7.11	42.43
Balkans / CE	0.59	3.35	0.34	1.19	3.02	0.41
Balkans +Greece / CE	0.74	3.64	0.49	2.16	3.03	0.41
European Union (EU)	2306.30	287.27	714.11	224.84	233.02	810.16
CE / EU	11.68	4.24	27.72	4.06	3.05	5.28
Balkans / EU	6.88	14.24	9.57	4.84	9.20	2.13

Source: World Bank (WB) World Development Indicators 1998.
Note: [1] Own calculations based on WB 1998.

**Table 5.2 Balkans and Central European Countries
Production Percentages by Source**

COUNTRY	Production in bil. kwh (1995)	Hydroelectric	Coal	Oil	Natural Gas	Nuclear Power
			(as a percentage of production in 1995)			
Balkans	158.80	25.76	43.03	6.85	13.50	10.87
Balkans +Greece	200.00	22.23	48.51	9.87	10.76	8.63
Central Europe (CE)	269.5	4.53	73.47	3.39	2.64	15.74
Balkans / CE	0.60	5.69	0.58	2.02	5.11	0.69
Balkans +Greece / CE	0.74	4.91	0.66	2.91	4.08	0.55
European Union (EU)	2306.30	12.46	30.96	9.74	10.10	35.13
CE / EU	11.68	0.36	2.37	0.35	0.26	0.45
Balkans / EU	6.88	2.07	1.39	0.70	1.34	0.31

Source: World Bank (WB) World Development Indicators 1998.
Note: Own calculations based on WB 1998 and on b1.

stronger than the EU, while the CE countries are lagging behind the EU. Where the EU is clearly stronger is nuclear power. The EU produces more than 1/3 of its electricity from nuclear power, compared to 11% in the Balkans (all of which is in Bulgaria) and 16% in CE. Thus, the relation formed is 0.31 and 0.45 with the Balkans and CE respectively.

The electric energy production structure seems to be more ecological in the Balkans (higher percentages of water and natural gas and lower of nuclear power, oil dependency lower than 7%), despite the fact that the total production and the per capita magnitudes are clearly lower (see below). It becomes obvious that each country uses the primary energy source that is more available and proves economically more efficient. This accounts in part for the 73% that the CE countries score in energy production from coal. At the same time, it is surprising that the supposedly ecologically aware and sensitive countries of the EU are still by and large dependent on nuclear power, France (77.1% !!!), Belgium and Sweden being the champions.

Electricity capacity, production and consumption As can be seen in Table A7, the electricity capacity and the production of electric energy differ significantly among countries. The per capita figures show that the Balkans have the same capacity as the CE countries, but the CE countries have higher figures in production and consumption. In particular, the electricity capacity is higher in Bulgaria (1.43 million kW/inhabitant), obviously due to the Kozlodui nuclear power station. The lowest level is reached in Albania (0.60). In the Balkans, besides Bulgaria, the only country that has a level of more than 1.00 is the New Yugoslavia (Greece has 0.82). However, the condition and the destiny of the energy infrastructure of the New Yugoslavia is unknown and can not be predicted after the severe NATO bombing that this country suffered during the spring of 1999. Three of the CE countries score higher than 1.00 and, if Kozlodui were not there, the level of the CE countries would exceed that of the Balkans. Thus, the relation of the capacity indicators between the Balkans and CE comes to 1.010. If Greece is also included in the calculations, then the score of the Balkans is lower because Greece itself lags behind the average magnitude of the Balkans.

In the field of energy production per inhabitant (Table A7), the last position is held by Bosnia-Herzegovina (0.48 billion kWh/inhabitant) and Albania follows (1.39), while the first place is held by Slovenia (6.33) and the second by the Czech Republic (5.88). The Balkan countries reach 2.83, which becomes 3.0 once Greece (which alone has 3.95) is included in the calculations. This number (3.0), however, is still lower than that of the CE countries, the equivalent number of which is 4.09. So, at the production level, the CE countries exceed the Balkans and form a relation of 7-7.5/10.

The picture of the consumption of electric energy corresponds to that of production. Bosnia-Herzegovina has the lowest consumption (0.51 kWh/inhabitant) followed by Albania (1.31), while Slovenia (5.76) comes first and the Czech Republic (5.07) comes second. Bulgaria (4.8) is an exception in the Balkans, while Greece (3.7), being second after Bulgaria in the Balkans, still remains at a low to medium level when compared to the CE countries that clearly supersede the Balkans.

As can be seen in Table 6, in the fields of electricity capacity and production of electric energy, both in absolute and per capita terms, the EU does better than the Balkans and the CE. In the field of electricity capacity per capita, the Balkans and the CE are almost equal, but their magnitudes come to 7/10 of the EU. In the field of production per capita, the CE countries are better than the Balkans, but they all lag behind the EU. The Balkans produce 46% and the CE 66% of the respective per capita production in the EU. In the field of electricity consumption per capita, the Balkan countries range from 506 to 4,821 kWh, the CE countries from 3,360 to 5,759 (see Table A7), while the EU countries start from 3,072 in Portugal and 3,720 in

Table 6 Balkans and Central European Countries and European Union Electric Energy: Capacity and Production

COUNTRY	POPULATION (1995)[1] est.	Capacity in mil.kW (1995)[2]	Capacity[2] per inhabitant[1] (1995)	Production in bil. kWh (1995)[3]	Production per inhabitant (1995)[3]
Balkans	56,148,000	55.12	0.98	158.80	2.83
Balkans +Greece	66,591,000	63.72	0.96	200.00	3.00
Central Europe (CE)	65,812,000	63.97	0.97	269.50	4.09
Balkans / CE	0.85	0.86	1.01	0.59	0.69
Balkans +Greece / CE	1.01	1.00	0.98	0.74	0.73
European Union (EU)	371,582,760	506.32	1.36	2,306.30	6.21
CE / EU	0.18	0.13	0.71	0.12	0.66
Balkans / EU	0.15	0.11	0.72	0.07	0.46

Sources: [1]Council of Europe (CoE). Recent Demographic Evolution in Europe 1998 Eurostat Demographic Statistics 1996.
[2]CIA World Factbook 1998.
[3]World Bank World Development Indicators 1998.

Greece, to reach 13,518 in Luxembourg and 15,996 in Sweden (see Table B1). The picture clearly shows the slower rates of the Balkans in a field that is considered to be classic for the indicators of prosperity and development.

Natural Gas

The production of electric energy from natural gas is cheap and ecological, compared to other methods and primary production sources. As is the case with all primary sources, all countries are not endowed with natural gas[2], so natural gas transport is required, via pipelines.

Natural gas pipelines installed in a country can serve the needs of that country (as is the case in Greece), or they can serve through traffic that has a third country as its destination (as happens with the CE countries through which pipelines coming from Russia-Siberia and heading to Western Europe pass).Therefore, the length of pipelines is not a conclusive indication of the natural gas sector development, yet it remains quite suggestive. In this field, the CE countries have triple the total length of the Balkan countries (excluding Greece). As can be seen in Table A8, FYROM has no pipelines, Albania has 64 km, while the largest network is that of Romania, which alone has more than half of the pipelines in the Balkans. Despite the through traffic, Romania, as mentioned above, uses natural gas to produce electricity, by 26.9%. The CE countries have more pipeline kilometres: the smallest network is that of Slovenia while the largest is that of Poland, which has more than half of the pipeline network of all the CE countries (the area of Poland is of course the largest in CE). Yet the production of electricity from natural gas in this country is practically zero. Overall, there are 29,792 km of pipelines in the CE countries, in contrast to 10,374 in the Balkans (excluding Greece). Even if pipeline lengths are calculated in terms of network density (i.e. considering the area of the several countries), the difference remains at the ratio of almost 1:3 (17/55).

Table 7 Balkans and Central European Countries and European Union Natural Gas: Pipelines and Consumption

COUNTRY	Natural Gas Pipelines in kms (1992)[1]	Density of Natural Gas Pipelines kms/area	Total of Natural Gas Consumption (1995) in terajoules[2]	Per capita natural gas consumption (1995) in megajoules[2]
Balkans	10,374	17	1,168,061	20,803,25
Balkans +Greece	10,374	n.a	1,170,050	17,570,69
Central Europe (CE)	29,792	55	1,312,748	19,946,94
Balkans / CE	0.35	0.31	0.89	1.04
Balkans +Greece / CE	0.35	n.a	0.89	0.881
European Union (EU)	181,086	57	12,632,115	33,995,43
CE / EU	0.16	0.96	0.10	0.59
Balkans / EU	0.06	0.30	0.09	0.61

Sources: [1]CIA World Fact book 1998. and own calculations.
[2]UN 1995 Energy Statistics Yearbook.

According to Table 7, the pipeline length in the EU is multiple that of the Balkans and CE. The EU pipeline density is triple that of the Balkans and almost the same as that of the CE countries. The EU per capita consumption is larger than that of both the Balkans and the CE.

The natural gas consumption in the EU is ten times more than that of the Balkans and CE, while the per capita magnitude of the EU is almost 40% larger than that of the two other groups of countries. Of the Balkan countries, as can be seen in Table A8, Romania has the largest per capita natural gas consumption (35,592 mj/c). Bulgaria (22,557) and Croatia

(19,973) follow. The rest of the countries follow with a significant difference, while Greece (190) still remains slightly better than Albania (138) and FYROM, which has no network. It should be noted, however, that Greece has very recently completed the major part of its trunk network, while industrial connections and city networks are currently being constructed, creating a very promising environment for natural gas utilisation in many urban and industrial sectors. The CE countries have much larger magnitudes, ranging from 10,744 in Poland to 41,233 in Slovakia. Yet their average does not supersede the Balkans which are influenced by the very large magnitudes of Romania.

However, this per capita consumption does not supersede that of the EU average. Of course, there are EU countries, such as Greece, which recently have been constructing their network, or which have small networks, such as Portugal, Spain, and Sweden. The use of natural gas has been established and has prevailed in most western European countries for a long time. For example, the per capita consumption in Holland is 102,419 mj/c, in Luxembourg 63,271, in Great Britain 49,867, etc. (In comparison, the US figure is 88,614).

From this analysis, it can be derived that the Balkans still have an inadequate network, while the CE countries, despite their slightly lower average, are in a better network development position, but are also well behind the EU.

The Issue of the Greek Energy Policy in the Balkans

Energy co-operation in the Balkans has been an issue of discussion and common effort, but has not progressed much apart from the links of the electric systems and the power imports and exports among other countries. Other fields that co-operation could develop are the exploitation of deposits, the common hydroelectric power stations, the compatibilisation of networks, etc. (see E.Pournarakis 1987). Any policy, however, must have as its target the systematisation of rationalisation, resource economising and autonomy increase (P.Skayannis 1994: 209).

The energy problem at a Balkan level is also related to the link of the EU networks to the Balkan ones and also to the link of the Greek and the Turkish network (see indicatively, I. Kathimerini 23/1/1994: 62) (P.Skayannis 1994: 162). The question of the link with Turkey is considered to be part of the general planning targets of the Public Power Corporation in Greece, and could prove beneficial for Greece to the degree that Turkey's link to Europe passes exclusively through Greece. Otherwise, this link could become, for Greece, just a channel for energy import and a domain of dependency (I. Kathimerini 19/12/1993:50). At the same time, it has to be stressed that because of the wars in the former Yugoslavia, the former Yugoslav network has been divided into two parts (north and south). Greece, being obviously linked to the southern part (now FYROM), is not properly linked to Western Europe and until 1994 could import electric power only from Bulgaria (and via Bulgaria from Romania and Russia) and Albania. The link with Bulgaria has problems because the Bulgarian network has the central and east European functional characteristics. In order for Bulgaria to maintain an energy surplus, the old and dangerous Kozlodui nuclear power station has to be in operation (it produced 42.4% of the country's electricity in 1995) (P.Skayannis 1994: 209; updated).

During the period between 1990 and 1975, Greece was importing 0.5-1.0% of its electricity from Albania at low prices. Albania was then considered to have high quality electricity, produced from hydroelectric power stations. However, the Albanian power system now requires technical assistance. It needs hardware such as transformers, and co-operation in the construction of hydroelectric power stations (there have been discussions about the construction of a dam at the position Batlion on the Aoos river³). The Albanian power system needs modernisation. Italian interests had, by 1993, already undertaken the modernisation of 25% of the distribution network at Tirana. Potentially, the Greek Public Power Corporation could co-operate closely with the Albanian KESH. There could be mutual benefits from co-operation in the areas of studies, construction, training, distribution, etc. (Th. Xanthopoulos 1993). This small "dependency" on Albania is not so important as to create future problems. Yet, given the instability in this country, because of which reliability cannot be guaranteed, this "dependency" could cause some functional complications (P.Skayannis 1994: 209).

It is characteristic that all moves described above are discussed within a framework with which the EU is in agreement. For the majority of the European partners these moves constitute alternative, and to a certain degree pursuable, proposals worth materialising. Of course, these proposals sometimes come in conflict with, or function in a complementary way with, the Greek proposals already expressed in the context of the Com-

197

munity Support Frameworks and other European Initiatives. What becomes obvious is the strategic role that is attributed to infrastructure networks, in order for comparative advantages to be acquired, and for the securing of control positions, i.e. of power and authority against others (P.Skayannis 1994: 162).

Social and Research Infrastrucure and Achievement

In the field of social infrastructure, in this chapter, only a few magnitudes of tertiary education and health are examined.

Education

In 1995, expenditure for public health as a percentage of Gross National Product (GNP), ranged in the Balkans between 5.5% (FYROM) and 3.2% (Romania) (see Table A9). The CE countries, during the same year, ranged from 6.1% (the Czech Republic) to 4.4% (Slovakia). It is very interesting that the former Yugoslav countries (excluding the New Yugoslavia and Bosnia-Herzegovina for which there are no data) had quite high percentages (higher than 5%). Of the CE countries, only the Czech Republic and Hungary had higher percentages. The higher percentages in the EU, as can be seen in Table 2B-app, were achieved by the Scandinavian countries. Denmark, Sweden and Finland had 8.3%, 8% and 7.6% respectively. The lowest percentages were those of Greece (3.7%), Germany (4.7%) and Italy (4.9%). Excluding Scandinavia, the percentages of the EU countries are similar to those of CE, but evidently the Balkans lag behind.

Similar are the 1995 data concerning the expenditure per student in tertiary education, as a percentage of GNP per capita (see Table A9). Generally, the Balkan countries have lower percentages than the CE countries, which have better than or similar to the figures of the EU. For example, Hungary and Sweden spend almost the same per student (more than 76%), while the "worst" country, Slovenia, has 38%, which is just two units less than the best Balkan percentage, that of Romania. Similarly, the last of the EU countries, Spain (18%), Italy (23%), France (24%) Portugal (25%) and Greece (29%) are the countries of the South.

Health

In the field of expenditure for public health, as can be seen in Table A9, the Balkan countries had, during 1990-1995, a worse performance than the CE countries, which proportionally spent almost the same or a slightly higher percentage of their GDP for public health than the EU countries. Excluding Croatia and FYROM (which reach 7-8.5%), the Balkan countries achieved half of these percentages, i.e. 3-4%. It is worth noting that, judging by Croatia and FYROM, the performance of the former Yugoslav countries was fairly high (There are no data for the New Yugoslavia and Bosnia-Herzegovina, while Slovenia was also high, having a percentage of 7.4%). Thus, it seems that this sector was quite developed in Yugoslavia. The CE countries ranged at levels similar to or higher than those of the EU countries (Denmark 5.3% and Germany 8.2%, the Czech Republic 7.7% and Hungary 6.8%). The indicator of hospital beds per 1000 inhabitants is also important. The picture for the year 1994 is similar to the above. The Balkan countries are 1-2 units behind the CE countries, which are marginally better than the EU countries. In comparison to the EU, the Balkan countries are at the same level as the "worst" EU ones. In the field of medical doctors per 1000 inhabitants, the Balkan countries, during the same indicative year, were also behind the CE countries. However, contrary to the other indicators, the CE countries here are also behind the EU, yet not significantly. In comparison to the EU countries, the Balkans, in this field, are in a similar position to the last of the EU countries. For example, the UK, which has the lowest indicator in the EU (but one of the most advanced medical sciences world-wide and a very good health system), has 1.5 doctors per 1000 inhabitants (see Table B2), a rate almost equal to that of Albania (1.3). This awkward coincidence is related to the investments that historically were made in the sector of health, to the research, the high specialisation of the assisting personnel (nurses and other para-medicals) and more generally to the technology used and the efficacy and efficiency of the sector and the health system as a whole.

Scientific and Technology Infrastructure and Achievement

Three indicators are examined in this field: a) the number of scientists and engineers in Research and Development (R&D) per million inhabitants (1981-1995), b) the expenditure for R&D as a percentage of GNP (1981-1995), and c) the volume of high technology exports as a percentage of the exports of manufactured goods (1996).

In the field of scientists and engineers in R&D, in quantity terms, the Balkans successfully compete with both the CE countries and the EU. As can be seen in Table 10A-app, Bulgaria has the highest percentage (4,240 per million of inhabitants) and FYROM the lowest (1,258). Greece is in a significantly lower position (774). This is excluding Albania and Bosnia-Herzegovina, for which there are no data. The CE countries range between 1,000-2,000, excluding Slovenia which reaches 3,000. In comparison, the EU countries, excluding Greece (774) and Portugal (599) range between 1,098 (Spain) and 3,714 (Sweden). In the field of R&D expenditure as a percentage of GNP, there are no adequate data for the Balkans. However, the CE countries are not up to the level of the EU. The "best" of the CE countries is Slovenia with 1.5% while the majority of the EU countries have higher percentages. Yet, even in this case the South lags behind. Greece (0.5%), Portugal (0.6%), Spain (0.9%), and Italy (1.3%) have low percentages as do Ireland (1.4%) and Austria (1.5%). The 9 remaining EU countries have a higher percentage than Slovenia. Unfortunately, inadequate data exist for the Balkans, concerning the third indicator, the volume of high technology exports as a percentage of the exports of manufactured exports. The CE countries are once more lagging behind if compared to the EU. The "best", Hungary (19%), is better than Portugal (12%), Greece (13%), Italy (15%) and Spain (17%), while all other EU countries have higher percentages than the CE countries.

Conclusion on Social and Research Infrastructure and Achievement

From the examination of the magnitudes related to the social, technical and scientific infrastructure and achievement, it can be derived that in the fields of education and particularly of tertiary education and of health, the CE countries compete with the EU and often supersede its rates, while the Balkans lag behind both. In the field of R&D scientists, exports and expenditure, the EU has the lead while the Balkans have a relatively significant percentage of human capital. These conclusions reflect the post-war policies, when the regimes of central planning paid special attention to the social sectors. It is characteristic that the analysis above, where dealing with expenditure, takes into consideration only the public sector. The calculation of private expenditure, at least in the field of health, and in part in the field of education, would prove the EU to be the leading force.

In the field of science, even taking into account the minimal data existing for the Balkans, one could risk the conclusion that the relatively satisfactory production of scientists does not reflect itself in related expenditure nor in the export of technology goods. This simply means that there is a problem of modernisation of the production processes and of restructuring in the direction of production differentiation towards new products, as well as of the need for an effort to create a more innovative environment. A more general observation would be that in these fields there is a consistent trend of slower development in the European South compared to the rest of the countries in the EU.

General Conclusions

This chapter has made clear how the Balkans are at a lower level of development than the CE countries and, by and large, than the EU. One could argue that in the context of Eastern Europe (excluding the former Soviet Union) a North-South division has developed, similar to that of Western Europe. However, like the western division, the eastern one owes its existence to a long historical process, but has eventually intensified and has reached unprecedented levels at the turn of this century. In order for these conclusions to become clear, Table 8 presents some simple and common indicators whereby the EU is taken as a basis, represented by 100.

From the field of transport it is derived that in order for the Balkans to reach the EU and the CE levels, the priorities should be the paving of the road network, the construction of new linkages and the upgrading of part of the network to motorways. At the same time, modernisation and electrification of railways and higher density and drastic modernisation of the airport network are also important priorities.

In the field of telecommunications the Balkans are far behind the EU. The question is not mobile telephony (where the gap is even larger), but standard telephony, which comprises the telecommunication backbone of a country. The lagging behind of both the Balkan and the CE countries is presumably due to the delays that these countries had in the adoption and development of digital technology in everyday applications. The result was that while the "eastern countries" for some time after the Second World War managed to compete with the "western countries" quite successfully, at some point they failed to keep pace with digital revolution in technology. This was

Table 8 Comparison of Basic Infrastructure Development Indicators

	CATEGORY	Balkans	CE Countries	EU
1.	Road Network			
1.1.	Density	41.1	105.0	100.0
1.2.	% Paved Main Road Network	59.8	67.0	100.0
2.	Railway Network			
2.1.	Density (standard gauge)	75.6	139.2	100.0
2.2.	% Electrification (standard gauge)	86.3	89.9	100.0
3.	Telecommunication Network			
3.1.	Main Connections per 100 Inhabitants	37.9	50.4	100.0
3.2.	Mobile Telephony Connections per 100 Inhabitants	7.0	30.0	100.0
4.	Energy Network			
4.1.	Electricity Production per Inhabitant	45.6	66.0	100.0
4.2.	Natural Gas Consumption per Inhabitant	61.2	58.7	100.0
5.	Education			
5.1.	Public Expenditure as a percentage of GNP	74.0	92.1	100.0
5.2.	Public Expenditure per student in tertiary education as a percentage of GNP per cap	86.3	124.5	100.0
6.	Health			
6.1.	Public Expenditure as a percentage of GDP	85.6	107.2	100.0
6.2.	Hospital Beds per 1000 inhabitants	81.2	102.6	100.0
7.	Science and Technology Infrastructure			
7.1.	R&D Expenditure as a percentage of GNP	67.8	65.5	100.0

Source: Own elaboration of this paper's data.

obviously because of different priorities and ranking in scientific research and application policy. Because of the chain reactions this entailed, it was one of the reasons why the "eastern" countries were left behind to such an extent that in order for them to catch up, huge expenditures are required for their modernisation. This is not only true for the field of telecommunications in the narrow sense, but for almost all the directly and indirectly technology- related sectors.

In the field of energy, the Balkans lag behind in electricity capacity, production and consumption, as well as in the natural gas network development. Yet one can observe the better composition of primary energy sources, such as lower nuclear power dependency and higher hydroelectric power generation. The Balkans are favoured by nature, so in the energy sector they can easily achieve more if they take advantage of their natural resources, such as hydrocarbon deposits, coal, waterfalls, etc. In this sense, they do not need to seek refuge in nuclear power. On the contrary, they can make existing nuclear power stations redundant.

In contrast to the technical infrastructure sectors, where a general lagging behind of the CE countries and most importantly of the Balkans is observed, the quantitative magnitudes of the social infrastructures are better for the countries of former central planning. Public expenditure of the CE countries in education, tertiary education and hospital beds is still greater than in the EU; even if not in all cases, the gap, compared to other indicators, is smaller. This convergence, however, should not become a reason for wrong assessments: the qualitative parameters in some cases are significantly different because of the more general conditions of social sector development and of the dependency of these sectors upon many other factors such as investment in education, research, etc, or even tradition. The Balkans, when compared to the other two country groups, lag behind in these sectors, yet not as far behind as in other sectors, if the quantitative magnitudes are examined. However, the question of quality, where there are no available data and a commonly accepted methodology of measurement, still remains. In the field of research and technology, the Balkans also need to make a significant effort, in order to catch up with the levels of the other countries.

Strategic planning in the Balkans should particularly foster the field of technical and social infrastructures as essential constituents of the General Conditions of Production and of the General Conditions of Labour Force Reproduction. This is necessary in order to achieve the substantial convergence of magnitudes with those of the developed countries, so as to take advantage of the opportunities that today have the potential to emerge in the various economy sectors.

It is self-evident that the EU should play the role of development catalyst in the planning for the regeneration of the Balkans, as it has both the capacity and the experience. The target should be the substantial convergence of the Balkans with the EU, so as to gradually access the common market and the rest of the EU institutions, in a way that is beneficial for them, with the prospect of being part of the economic and monetary union. Already, in the context of the Interreg and Phare programmes (the latter includes the Cross-Border Co-operation Programme), there is an effort which, however, should expand and intensify. In the framework of the EU, the role of Greece should be critical and decisive. This is because the proximity of Greece to the Balkan countries, and its sensitive geopolitical position, cannot allow for any kind of apathy in facing these developments. Any step of planning for these countries concerns Greece indirectly and more often than not, directly. For this reason Greece seeks to be present in all phases of planning for the New Balkans, starting from the monitoring of needs, through the future evaluation of the materialised projects, having gone through the phases of planning and materialisation.

Notes

1   By April 2000, the number of mobile telephony connections in Greece already amounted to more than 4 million, i.e. 37%. Similar developments, indicative of the speed of mobile telephony intrusion, have happened to other countries.
2   Worldwide, the area most endowed with natural gas is Siberia.
3   The Aoos river is shared by Albania and Greece.

References

Central Intelligence Agency (1999) *The World Factbook 1998.* USA: CIA.
Council of Europe (1998) *Recent Demographic Evolution in Europe 1998.*
European Commision (1995) *Europe 2000*+Co-operation for Spatial Planning in Europe. Luxembourg: OOPEC.
Eurostat (1996) *Demographic Statistics.* Luxembourg.
Gonzalez-Finat, A. (1993) "Transeuropean Transport Networks and Spatial Development". International Conference: *Greece in Europe: Regional Planning and Policy towards 2000.* Athens: Technical Chamber of Greece. December.
Pournarakis, E. (1987) *The Possibilities for a Multiparty Economic Co-operation in the Balkans. Energy and Transports.* Issues of Programming 34. Athens: CPER.
Rietveld, P. (1993) "Transport and Communication Barriers in Europe". In Cappellin, R. and Batey, P.W.J (eds) *Regional Networks, Border Regions and European Integration.* London: Pion.
Skayannis, P. (1994) *Infrastructure Programming Policy.* Athens: Stamoulis.
Turnock, D. (1997) "Cross-border co-operation as a factor in the development of transport in Eastern Europe". *Trent Geographical Papers.* No1. UK: The Nottingham Trent University. January.
United Nations (1997) *1995 Energy Statistics Yearbook.* Department for Economic and Social Information Analysis. Statistics Division. New York.
Vassenhoven, L. (1993) "Regional and Physical Planning: the European strategy of Greece". International Conference: *Greece in Europe: Regional Planning and Policy towards 2000.* Athens: Technical Chamber of Greece. December.
World Bank (1998) *World Development Indicators.* USA: The World Bank.
World Bank (1999) *World Development Report: Knowledge for Development.* USA: The World Bank

Xanthopoulos, Th. (1993) *Greek-Albanian Co-operation in Electric Energy Production.* I Kathimerini   p.50, 19 December. Athens.

I Kathimerini, 20/1/1994: 60 (Daily newspapper, in Greek).
To Vima, 19/12/1993: 64-5 (Daily newspapper, in Greek).

Appendix

Table A1 Balkans and Central European Countries, Road Network and Motorways

COUNTRY	Population July 1998 (CIA est.)	Area in 1000 sq.kms	Road Network in kms. (CIA 1996 est.)	Density of Road Network (km of network per 1000 sq. kms)	Motorways in kms.	Paved Road Network in kms	Percentage of Paved Road Network (WB 1996)	Normalised Road Index (WB 1996)
Albania	3,330,754	27.4	18,000	657	0	5,400	30.00	110
Bosnia-Herzegovina	3,365,727	51.2	21,846	426	0	11,425	52.30	NA
Bulgaria	8,240,426	110.5	36,720	332	0	33,746	91.90	99
Croatia	4,671,584	56.4	27,247	483	0	22,206	81.50	NA
FYROM	2,009,387	24.9	10,591[2]	426	133	5,500	63.80	79
New Yugoslavia	11,206,039	102.1	49,525	485	0	28,873	58.30	NA
Romania	22,395,848	230.3	153,170[1]	665	113	78,117	51.00	108
Balkans	55,219,765	602.9	277,253	526	246	185,267	58.00	-
Greece	10,662,138	130.8	117,000	894	470	107,406	91.80	155
Balkans+Greece	65,881,903	733.7	434,099	592	716	292,673	67.00	-
Czech Republic	10,286,470	78.64	55,489	706	423	55,489	100.00	NA
Hungary	10,208,127	92.3	158,633	1,718	420	68,370	43.10	147
Poland	38,606,922	304.5	374,990	1,231	258	245,243	65.40	156
Slovakia	5,392,982	48.8	36,608	750	549	36,059	98.50	NA
Slovenia	1,971,739	20.26	14,910	736	231	12,226	82.00	100
Central Europe	66,466,240	544.55	640,630	1,176	1,881	417,387	65.00	-
Balkan/CE	0.831	1.107	0.433	0.391	0.131	0.444	0.90	-
Balkans+Greece/CE	0.991	1.347	0.678	0.503	0.381	0.701	1.03	-

Sources: CIA World Factbook 1998.
World Bank World Development Indicators 1998.

Notes: 1: CIA 1995 est.
2: CIA 1997 est.

Table A2 Balkans and Central European Countries, Railway Infrastructure

COUNTRY	Population July 1998 (CIA est.)	Area in 1000 sq.kms	Length of Railway Network in kms.	Density of Railway Network (km of network per 1000 sq. kms)*10³	Total Length of Standard Gauge Network in km	Length of Electrified Network in kms	Standard Gauge Electrified Network as a percentage of the Total of Standard Gauge Network
Albania	3,330,754	27.4	670[2]	24.453	670	0	0
Bosnia-Herzegovina	3,365,727	51.2	1,021[2]	19.929	1,021	795	0.779
Bulgaria	8,240,426	110.5	4,292[2]	38.824	4,047	2,650	0.655
Croatia	4,671,584	56.4	1,907	33.806	1,907	769	0.403
FYROM	2,009,387	24.9	922[4]	37.094	922	232	0.252
New Yugoslavia	11,206,039	102.1	3,987[4]	39.036	3,987	1,341	0.336
Romania	22,395,848	230.3	11,365[1]	49.34	10,893	3,723	0.342
Balkans	55,219,765	602.9	24,164	40.078	23,447	9,510	0.406
Greece	10,662,138	130.8	2,474[5]	18.914	1,565	36	0.023
Balkans+Greece	65,881,903	733.7	26,638	36.305	25,012	9,546	0.382
Czech Republic	10,286,470	78.64	9,440[3]	120.033	9,344	2,688	0.288
Hungary	10,208,127	92.3	7,606[3]	82.37	7,394	2,207	0.298
Poland	38,606,922	304.5	24,313[3]	79.843	22,243	11,648	0.524
Slovakia	5,392,982	48.8	3,665[3]	75.102	3,507	1,424	0.406
Slovenia	1,971,739	20.26	1,201[3]	59.291	1,201	499	0.415
Central Europe	66,466,240	544.55	46,225	84.886	43,689	18,466	0.423
Balkan/CE	0.831	1.107	0.523	0.47	0.537	0.515	0.960
Balkans+Greece/CE	0.991	1.347	0.576	0.43	0.573	0.517	0.903

Sources: CIA World Factbook 1998.
World Bank World Development Indicators 1998.

Notes: 1: CIA 1994. 2: CIA 1995.
3: CIA 1996. 4: CIA 1997.
5: CIA αχρονολόγητο.

Table A3 Balkans and Central European Countries, Airport Infrastructure

COUNTRY	Population July 1998 (CIA est.)	Area in 1000 sq.kms	Airports (CIA 1997 est.)	Airports with Paved Runways	Airport Density (% ratio of paved airports in the countries' area)	Paved Airports as a Percentage of Total Airports	Airports with not Paved Runway
Albania	3,330,754	27.4	9	5	0.2	55.6	4
Bosnia-Herzegovina	3,365,727	51.2	26	9	0.2	34.6	17
Bulgaria	8,240,426	110.5	34	34	0.3	100.0	0
Croatia	4,671,584	56.4	71	51	0.9	71.8	20
FYROM	2,009,387	24.9	16	10	0.4	62.5	6
New Yugoslavia	11,206,039	102.1	48	18	0.2	37.5	30
Romania	22,395,848	230.3	24	19	0.1	79.2	5
Balkans	55,219,765	602.9	228	146	0.2	64.0	82
Greece	10,662,138	130.8	78	63	0.5	80.8	15
Balkans+Greece	65,881,903	733.7	306	209	0.3	68.3	97
Czech Republic	10,286,470	78.64	66	33	0.4	50.0	33
Hungary	10,208,127	92.3	25	15	0.2	60.0	10
Poland	38,606,922	304.5	83	68	0.2	81.9	15
Slovakia	5,392,982	48.8	13	8	0.2	61.5	5
Slovenia	1,971,739	20.26	14	6	0.3	42.9	8
Central Europe	66,466,240	544.55	201	130	0.2	64.7	71
Balkan/CE	0.831	1.107	1.134	1.123	1.014	0.989	1.155
Balkans+Greece/CE	0.991	1.347	1.522	1.608	1.193	1.056	1.366

Source: CIA World Factbook 1998.

Table A4 Balkans and Central European Countries, Telecommunications Infrastructure (Connections of Standard and Mobile Telephony)

COUNTRY	Population July 1998 (CIA est.)	Telephones (CIA 1993 est.)	Main Telephone Connections in th. (ITU 1998)	Main Telephone Connections per 100 inhabitants (ITU 1998)	Main Telephone Connections per 100 inhabitants (own calculations based on ITU 1998)	Mobile telephones per 100 inhabitants (ITU 1998)[8]
Albania	3,330,754	55,000[1]	115.7	3.71	3.47	0.09
Bosnia-Herzegovina	3,365,727	727,000[1]	331.9	9.03	9.86	0.69
Bulgaria	8,240,426	2,773,293	2,681.1[6]	32.26	32.54	0.84
Croatia	4,671,584	1,216,000	1,558.0	34.77	33.35	4.07
FYROM	2,009,387	125,000[1]	407.8[6]	19.87	20.29	0.60
New Yugoslavia	11,206,039	700,000[1]	2,319.4	21.81	20.70	2.26
Romania	22,395,848	2,600,000	3,776.9[6]	16.73	16.86	0.89
Balkans	55,219,765	8,196,293	11,190.8		20.27	1.33
Greece	10,662,138	5,571,293	5,430.9[6]	51.61	50.94	8.91
Balkans+Greece	65,881,903	13,767,586	16,621.7		25.23	2.54
Czech Republic	10,286,470	3,349,539	3,741.5	36.39	36.37	9.39
Hungary	10,208,127	2,160,000[4]	3,095.3[6]	30.42	30.32	6.95
Poland	38,606,922	8,200,000[3]	8,812.3	22.76	22.83	4.98
Slovakia	5,392,982	1,362,178[2]	1,539.3	28.63	28.54	8.65
Slovenia	1,971,739	691,240[5]	722.5[6]	36.40	36.64	4.70
Central Europe	66,466,240	15,762,957	17,910.9		26.95	6.26
Balkan/CE	0.831	0.520	0.625		0.752	0.21
Balkans+Greece/CE	0.991	0.873	0.928		0.936	0.41

Sources: CIA World Factbook 1998.
International Telecommunications Union Basic Indicators 1999.

Notes: 1: CIA undated, 2: CIA 1992 est.
3: CIA 1996 est. 4: CIA 1996 Jan.
5: CIA 1997 est. 6: ITU 1997.
7: Own calculations based on ITU number of connections and on July 1998 CIA population estimates.
8: Total magnitudes based on own calculations.

Table A5 Balkans and Central European Countries, Mass Media and Information Infrastructure

COUNTRY	Population July 1998 (CIA est.)	Population 1995 (CoE est.)	Radios (CIA est.)	Radios (CIA) per 100 inhabitants (CoE)	TV sets (CIA 1993 est.)	TV sets per 1000 inhabitants (WB 1996)	Personal Computers per 1000 inhabitants (WB 1996)	Internet Hosts per 10000 inhabitants (WB 1997)
Albania	3,330,754	3,167.500[8]	577.000[3]	18.22	300,000	173.00	-	0.32
Bosnia-Herzegovina	3,365,727	4,570,000[8]	840,000[1]	18.38	1,012,094[1]	55.00	-	0.13
Bulgaria	8,240,426	8,427,500	-	-	2,100,000[2]	361.00	295.2	6.65
Croatia	4,671,584	4,779,000	1,100,000	23.02	1,520,000[1]	251.00	20.9	14.08
FYROM	2,009,387	1,957,000	369,000[4]	18.86	327,011[1]	170.00	-	2.15
New Yugoslavia	11,206,039	10,535,000	2,015,000[1]	19.13	1,000,000[1]	185.00	-	2.72
Romania	22,395,848	22,712,000	4,640,000[4]	20.43	4,580,000[4]	226.00	5.3	2.66
Balkans	55,219,765	56,148,000	9,541,000	16.99	10,512,421	-	-	-
Greece	10,662,138	10,443,000	-	-	2,300,000	442.00	33.4	18.76
Balkans+Greece	65,881,903	66,591,000	-	-	12,812,421	-	-	-
Czech Republic	10,286,470	10,299,000	-	-	-	406.00	53.2	47.66
Hungary	10,208,127	10,375,000	6,000,000[5]	57.83	4,380,000[7]	444.00	44.1	33.29
Poland	38,606,922	37,879,000	9,900,000[7]	26.14	9,400,000[7]	418.00	36.2	11.22
Slovakia	5,392,982	5,269,000	915,000[6]	17.37	1,200,000[6]	384.00	186.1	20.47
Slovenia	1,971,739	1,990,000	596,100[5]	29.95	454,400	375.00	47.8	85.66
Central Europe	66,466,240	65,812,000	17,411,100	26.46	15,434,400	-	-	-
Balkan/CE	0.831	0.853	-	-	-	-	-	-
Balkans+Greece/CE	0.991	1.012	-	-	-	-	-	-

Sources: CIA World Factbook 1998.
World Bank World Development Indicators 1998.
Council of Europe (CoE), Recent Demographic Evolution in Europe 1998.

Notes: 1: CIA undated. 2: CIA 1990 est.
3: CIA 1991 est. 4: CIA 1992 est.
5: CIA 1993 est. 6: CIA 1995 est.
7: CIA 1996 est. 8: Population 1993.

Table A6 Balkans and Central European Countries, Sources of Electric Energy (Production in Bil.kwh)

COUNTRY	Population July 1998 (CIA est.)	Area in 1000 sq.kms	Production in bil. kwh 1995 (WB)	Hydroelectric Power as a percentage of production 1995 (WB)	Coal as a percentage of production 1995 (WB)	Oil as a percentage of production 1995 (WB)	Natural Gas as a percentage of production 1995 (WB)	Nuclear Power as a percentage of production 1995 (WB)
Albania	3,330,754	27.4	4.40	95.2	0	4.8	0	0
Bosnia-Herzegovina	3,365,727	51.2	2.20	64.5	35.5	0	0	0
Bulgaria	8,240,426	110.5	40.70	3.1	43.1	3.6	7.9	42.4
Croatia	4,671,584	56.4	8.90	59.4	2.7	27.7	10.1	0
FYROM	2,009,387	24.9	6.10	13.1	86.3	0.6	0	0
New Yugoslavia	11,206,039	102.1	37.20	30.2	63.7	2.4	3.7	0
Romania	22,395,848	230.3	59.30	28.2	35.1	9.8	26.9	0
Balkans	55,219,765	602.9	158.80	25.76	43.03	6.85	13.5	27.4
Greece	10,662,138	130.8	41.20	8.6	69.6	21.5	0.2	0
Balkans+Greece	65,881,903	733.7	200.00	22.23	48.51	9.87	10.76	8.6
Czech Republic	10,286,470	78.64	60.60	3.3	74	1	0.8	20.2
Hungary	10,208,127	92.3	34.00	0.5	29.5	16.3	11.9	41.2
Poland	38,606,922	304.5	136.70	1.4	97.3	1.1	0.2	0
Slovakia	5,392,982	48.8	25.60	19.1	22.6	4.7	9	44.6
Slovenia	1,971,739	20.26	12.60	25.6	34.3	2.3	0	37.8
Central Europe	66,466,240	544.55	269.50	4.53	73.47	3.39	2.64	114.35
Balkan/CE	0.831	1.107	0.589	5.69	0.56	2.02	5.11	0.24
Balkans+Greece/CE	0.991	1.347	0.742	4.91	0.66	2.91	4.08	0.07

Sources: CIA World Factbook 1998.
World Bank (WB) World Development Indicators 1998.
Council of Europe (CoE) Recent Demographic Evolution in Europe 1998.

Table A7 Balkans and Central European Countries, Electric Energy: Capacity, Production and Consumption

COUNTRY	Population 1995 (CoE est.)	Capacity in mil.kW (CIA 1995)	Capacity (CIA) per inhabitant (CoE) (1995)	Production in bil. kWh (WB 1995)	Production (WB) per Inhabitant:10 (CoE) 1995	Consumption per inhabitant in kWh (CIA 1995)
Albania	3,167,500[3]	1.89	0.60	4.40	1.39	1.31
Bosnia-Herzegovina	4,570,000[3]	2.34	0.51	2.20	0.48	0.51
Bulgaria	8,427,500	12.09	1.43	40.70	4.83	4.82
Croatia	4,779,000	3.59	0.75	8.90	1.86	2.31
FYROM	1,957,000	1.37	0.70	6.10	3.12	2.58
New Yugoslavia	10,535,000	11.78	1.12	37.20	3.53	3.01
Romania	22,712,000	22.06	0.97	59.30	2.61	2.41
Balkans	56,148,000	55.12	0.98	158.80	2.83	-
Greece	10,443,000	8.61	0.82	41.20	3.95	3.72
Balkans+Greece	66,591,000	63.72	0.96	200.00	3.00	
Czech Republic	10,299,000	13.85[1]	1.34	60.60	5.88	5.07
Hungary	10,375,000	6.98	0.67	34.00	3.28	3.42
Poland	37,879,000	33.50[2]	0.88	136.70	3.61	3.36
Slovakia	5,269,000	7.12	1.35	25.60	4.86	4.70
Slovenia	1,990,000	2.52	1.27	12.60	6.33	5.76
Central Europe	65,812,000	63.97	0.97	269.50	4.09	-
Balkan/CE	0.853	0.862	1.010	0.589	0.691	-
Balkans+Greece/CE	1.012	0.996	0.984	0.742	0.733	-

Sources: CIA World Factbook 1998.
World Bank World Development Indicators 1998.
Council of Europe (CoE), Recent Demographic Evolution in Europe 1998.

Notes: 1: CIA 1994. 2: CIA 1997 est.
3: 1993 population.

Table A8 Balkans and Central European Countries, Natural Gas: Pipelines and Consumption

COUNTRY	Natural Gas Pipelines in kms. (CIA 1992)	Density of Natural Gas Pipelines kms/area	Total of Natural Gas Consumption (UN 1995) in terajoules	Per capita natural gas consumption (UN 1995) in mcgajoules
Albania	64[2]	2	468	138
Bosnia-Herzegovina	90	2	10,740	3,009
Bulgaria	1,400	13	191,941	22,557
Croatia	310	5	89,980	19,973
FYROM	0	0	0	0
New Yugoslavia	2,110[1]	21	66,000	6,438
Romania	6,400	28	808,932	35,592
Balkans	10,374	17	1,168,061	20,803
Greece	-	-	1,989	190
Balkans+Greece	10,374	-	1,170,050	17,571
Czech Republic	5,400[1]	69	263,040	25,630
Hungary	4,387[2]	48	384,128	38,010
Poland	17,000[3]	56	414,252	10,744
Slovakia	2,700[1]	55	220,100	41,233
Slovenia	305[1]	15	31,228	16,222
Central Europe	29,792	55	1,312,748	19,947
Balkan/CE	0.348	0.314	0.890	1.043
Balkans+Greece/CE	0.348	-	0.891	0.881

Sources: CIA World Factbook 1998.
UN Energy Indicators 1997.

Notes: 1: CIA undated. 2: CIA 1991.
3: CIA 1996.

213

Table A9 Balkans and Central European Countries, Social Infrastructures

COUNTRY	Public Expenditure for Education as a % of GNP (WB 1995)	Expenditure per student in tertiary education as a percentage of GNP per capita (WB 1995)	Public Expenditure as a percentage of GDP (WB 1990-95)	Hospital Beds per 1000 inhabitants (WB 1994)	Medical Doctors per 1000 inhabitants (WB 1994)
Albania	3.4	36	2.7	3.0	1.3
Bosnia-Herzegovina	-	-	-	2.0	0.6
Bulgaria	4.2	21	4.0	10.2	3.3
Croatia	5.3	-	8.5	5.9	2.0
FYROM	5.5	-	7.3	5.5	2.3
New Yugoslavia	-	-	-	5.4	2.0
Romania	3.2	40	3.6	7.7	1.8
Greece	3.7	29	5.5	5.0	4.0
Czech Republic	6.1	41	7.7	7.4	2.9
Hungary	6.0	73	6.8	9.6	3.6
Poland	4.6	42	4.8	6.3	2.3
Slovakia	4.4	39	6.0	7.1	2.8
Slovenia	5.8	38	7.4	5.8	2.2

Source: World Bank World Development Indicators 1998.

Table A10 Balkans and Central European Countries, Science and Technology Infrastructure

COUNTRY	Scientists and Engineers in R&D per million of inhabitants (WB 1981-95)	R&D Expenditure as a percentage of GNP (WB 1981-1995)	High Technology Exports as a percentage of manufactured goods exports (WB 1996)
Albania	-	-	-
Bosnia-Herzegovina	-	-	-
Bulgaria	4,240	1.7	17
Croatia	1,977	-	17
FYROM	1,258	-	-
New Yugoslavia	1,476	-	16
Romania	1,382	0.7	7
Greece	774	0.5	13
Czech Republic	1,285	1.3	14
Hungary	1,157	1.0	19
Poland	1,083	0.9	11
Slovakia	1,922	1.1	16
Slovenia	2,998	1.5	16

Source: World Bank World Development Indicators 1998.

Table B1 European Union, Capacity, Production and Consumption of Electric

COUNTRY	Population 1995 (Eurostat)	Capacity in mil.kW (CIA 1995)	Capacity (CIA) per inhabitant (Eurostat) (1995)	Production in bil. kWh (WB 1995)	Production (WB) per inhabitant (CoE) 1995	Consumption per inhabitant in kWh (CIA 1995)
Austria	8,040,000	15.65	1.94	55.1	6.82	6.90
Belgium	10,131,000	13.59	1.33	73.6	7.22	7.31
Denmark	5,216,000	10.60	2.00	36.8	6.95	6.43
Finland	5,099,000	14.14	2.75	63.9	12.41	13.18
France	58,020,000	102.94	1.75	489.3	8.33	6.84
Germany	81,539,000	109.73	1.34	532.6	6.49	6.15
Greece	10,443,000	8.61	0.82	41.2	3.92	3.72
Ireland	3,588,000	3.62	0.98	17.6	4.77	4.67
Italy	57,269,000	57.19	0.99	237.4	4.12	4.51
Luxembourg	407,000	0.14	0.33	-	-	13.52
Holland	15,423,000	20.09	1.28	81.1	5.18	4.97
Portugal	9,912,000	8.83	0.89	32.2	3.23	3.07
Spain	39,177,000	39.58	1.01	165.6	4.21	4.03
Sweden	8,816,000	35.46	4.01	147	16.61	16.00
United Kingdom	58,504,000	66.15	1.12	332.9	5.63	5.55
EU	371,583	506.32	1.36	2306.3	6.21	-

Sources: CIA World Factbook 1998.
World Bank World Development Indicators 1998.
Council of Europe (CoE), Recent Demographic Evolution in Europe 1998.
Eurostat Demographic Statistics 1996.

Table B2 European Union, Social Infrastructure

COUNTRY	Public Expenditure for Education as a % of GNP (WB 1995)	Expenditure per student in tertiary education as a percentage of GNP per capita (WB 1995)	Public Expenditure in Health as a percentage of GDP (WB 1990-95)	Hospital Beds per 1000 inhabitants (WB 1994)	Medical Doctors per 1000 inhabitants (WB 1994)
Austria	5.5	32	5.9	9.4	2.6
Belgium	5.7	35	7.0	7.6	3.7
Denmark	8.3	55	5.3	5.0	2.9
Finland	7.6	46	5.7	10.1	2.7
France	5.9	24	8.0	9.0	2.8
Germany	4.7	35	8.2	9.7	3.3
Greece	3.7	29	5.5	5.0	4.0
Ireland	6.3	38	5.4	5.0	2.0
Italy	4.9	23	5.4	6.5	1.7
Luxembourg	-	-	-	-	-
Holland	5.3	44	6.7	11.3	2.5
Portugal	5.4	25	4.5	4.3	2.9
Spain	5.0	18	6.0	4.0	4.1
Sweden	8.0	76	6.0	6.5	3.0
United Kingdom	5.5	44	5.8	4.9	1.5
USA	5.3	23	6.6	4.2	2.5

Source: World Bank World Development Indicators 1998.

Table B3 European Union, Capacity, Science and Technology Infrastructure

COUNTRY	Scientists and Engineers in R&D per million of inhabitants (WB 1981-95)	R&D Expenditure as a percentage of GNP (WB 1981-1995)	High Technology Exports as a percentage of manufactured goods exports (WB 1996)
Austria	1,604	1.5	24
Belgium	1,814	1.7	-
Denmark	2,647	1.9	25
Finland	3,675	2.3	23
France	2,537	2.5	31
Germany	3,016	2.6	25
Greece	774	0.5	13
Ireland	1,871	1.4	62
Italy	1,303	1.3	15
Luxembourg	-	-	-
Holland	2,656	1.9	42
Portugal	599	0.6	12
Spain	1,098	0.9	17
Sweden	3,714	3.5	31
United Kingdom	2,417	2.2	40
USA	3,732	-	44

Source: World Bank World Development Indicators 1998.

8 Fragmentation or Integration in the Balkans? Strategies of Development for the 21st Century

GEORGE PETRAKOS
Associate Professor, Department of Planning and Regional Development, University of Thessaly, Greece

Introduction

Recent reports by international organisations and a number of studies (Petrakos and Totev 2000, Jackson and Petrakos 1999) have indicated that among transition countries in Europe, the Balkan countries have an inferior economic performance and structure compared to the Central European ones. The available data seems to indicate that the Balkan countries have not been able to recover from the shock of transition from centrally planned to market economies, despite the fact that this process has lasted for nearly 10 years. A number of Balkan countries in transition have experienced repeated economic crises during this period that have caused a serious divergence from the record of the other European transition countries.

There is already a number of propositions that explicitly or implicitly compete in their attempt to account for differences in performance among transition economies in Europe and especially for this inability of the Balkan transition countries to follow the Central European ones (Petrakos and Christodoulakis 1998). The most widely shared explanation relates poor outcomes with delayed and non-persistent policies of privatisation and market liberalisation. Although everybody would agree that poorly designed or implemented policies cannot have significant results, it can be the case that properly designed or implemented policies do not have significant results either, if other background factors have an offsetting influence. The exclusive reliance on "policy failures" to explain diverging patterns of performance does not leave ground for a convincing answer to the question why all lagging behind European countries in the transition process happen to be in the South.

Searching for alternative explanations, we have to take into consideration first the evidence provided in the literature and the propositions (some times speculative) about the factors that have produced such a differentiated outcome in various transition countries. A non-exclusive list of these factors would include: (a) "Policy failure" explanations, according to mainstream economic thinking, that attribute poor transition performance to delayed reforms and non-persistent policies of privatisation and market liberalisation, (b) "Market failure" explanations that consider the "shock therapy" of massive privatisation, liberalisation and deregulation in the absence of appropriate institutional arrangements as the primary factor explaining repeated crises in a number of transition countries, (c) Explanations pointing to different initial conditions with respect to the structure of the economies and the enterprises, as well as to different initial conditions with respect to infrastructure and human capital development, (d) Explanations pointing to different conditions with respect to geographical features such as centrality, adjacency, proximity and accessibility of major European markets and different ranking in the new European economic order that affect capital mobility, attraction of higher functional order activities and diffusion of technology and know-how, (e) Explanations related to institutional differences and differences in historical experience with market mechanisms and operations.

The transition countries in the Balkans are not the only ones in the region that face serious economic difficulties and challenges. Greece on the one hand, despite being the most developed and stable economy and the only member of the European Union (EU) in the region and despite recent progress, is facing serious structural problems in its economy. It is in fact the only EU country that has not met the Maastricht criteria and therefore is for the moment left outside the EMU. On the other hand, Turkey, despite its significant size and strong potential for growth and development, is also plagued by a number of very serious economic and structural problems.

For the residents of the Balkans, these disappointing facts are in absolute contrast with their pride and own vision of their identity, the diverse environment and resources of the region, its historical and cultural heritage and the fact that large parts of the region were for centuries the civilisation and development centre of the known world. In the minds of many people there is a question why in the post-1989 European architecture the Balkan region has been such a profound case of failure and why from all possible development paths, the one that eventually materialised seems to be the worst?

Without ignoring the importance of the other factors mentioned before, this article provides an additional explanation of this diverging performance. It is argued here that the prevailing fragmentation and conflict in the Balkan region, as well as the existing ethnic rivalry and regional instability are major factors that significantly impede growth, structural change, economic progress, transformation and development. In the following sections we present a number of theoretical propositions and analyse some basic economic characteristics of the Balkan region related to market size, development potentials, trade relations and foreign direct investment. On the basis of these characteristics we will attempt in the concluding section to highlight the costs and benefits of the options available to the individual countries in the region with respect to regional conflict or regional co-operation.

Geography and Development: the Questions we Fail to Ask

In this section we address some issues concerning the geography of development and relate them to the prospects and possibilities of the Balkan countries to reverse existing trends in their economic performance. We do that by asking the following set of questions: (a) Is it possible for a country engaged (in one way or another) in a regional conflict to prosper? (b) Is it possible for a country to prosper in a depressed and unstable region? (c) Is it possible for a country to grow and develop without having economic relations with its neighbouring countries? (d) Is it possible for the Balkan region to really converge - even in the distant future - towards the EU economic standards without eliminating first all sources of tension and conflict among Balkan countries?

Economic theory offers an analytical framework, which helps us to understand some neglected aspects of international relations and provide an answer with some policy value to these questions. In this section we are going to examine: (i) the role of rationally formed expectations and positive or negative externalities in the expansion of economic activities, (ii) the role of internal and external economies of scale for economic efficiency and competitiveness, and (iii) the role of regional trade multipliers for growth and development. The analysis of these issues will provide a basis for the discussion of the preceding questions.

The Development of the Balkan Region

Expectations, Uncertainty and Externalities

It is argued here that fragmentation and conflict impedes economic growth for at least three interacting reasons. First, it generates uncertainty and does not allow economic agents to plan for the future and commit themselves to specific economic activities, as their expectations about the future are formed not on the basis of competitive advantages, specialisation and available opportunities, but on the basis of political factors and external forces that are largely independent from market processes and unpredictable.

Therefore, political instability, social - ethnic unrest and unsolved frictions with neighbouring countries over ethnic minorities or territorial disputes, are factors generating serious uncertainty to markets and economic activity. Their immediate impact is to cancel running or planned (domestic or foreign) investment projects, while their long-term impact is to put at serious risk the prospects of the country for growth and development.

Moreover, a country can be affected by the negative externalities of a regional crisis, even if it is not directly involved. The war in Serbia and Kosovo has affected Greece, by reducing tourism, trade and investment activities in the country and imposing longer transportation routes for its exports to EU markets. In addition, and this is equally serious, the expectations of people and firms about the future have become less optimistic, despite the significant progress of the economy.

Overall, instability and conflict in a region will affect negatively all countries, regardless of their actual involvement, as expectations are formed on the basis of risk aversion, not the specific conditions prevailing in each country. Negative expectations about the future, may affect in a very direct way the real economy today, if economic units cancel or postpone their activities and take defensive positions. This, may have a "domino" effect to all countries in the region, its magnitude being a function of proximity and intensity of relations with the area and the parties involved in the conflict.

Internal and External Economies of Scale

Second, market fragmentation, the result of socio-political fragmentation, generates serious inefficiencies in the productive sector of each country, as several industries, in order to operate efficiently and be competitive, require internal and external economies of scale, not available in small markets. Internal economies of scale are attained when industrial firms have a sufficient size and production level, which guarantees that resources are combined efficiently and therefore output has a competitive price. Therefore in order for industrial firms to benefit from economies of scale, they must operate in large national markets, or be able to promote their products in a larger geographical market that exceeds national borders. External economies of scale are attained when industrial firms develop dense inter-firm relations with other firms operating in the same sector (joint R&D programs, labour force training programs, subcontracting joint supplies, etc.) or in forward and backward related sectors (supplier-producer and producer-consumer relationships). In order for a firm to benefit from external economies of scale, the national productive base must be rich in productive activities (a condition that cannot be met by small economies) or open to co-operation with other nearby economies.

As a result, small economies are required to be open and allow their firms to operate in a larger geographical market. For firms operating under economies of scale, neighbouring countries are the best markets for their products. This is because consumers in neighbouring countries usually have similar preferences implying an easier and deeper market penetration. In addition, adjacency and proximity between two countries implies a lower transportation cost.

Regional Multipliers, Intra-Industry and Intra-Regional Trade

Third, fragmentation and conflict in a region is a major obstacle to growth and development, as it restricts the operation of regional multipliers and does not allow for the benefits of regional interaction and export-led growth to be fully realised. The concept of regional multiplier is based on two conditions: First, trade is more intensive among neighbours because of the benefits of similar preferences and lower transportation cost. Second, this intensive interaction implies that high growth rates in one country can be quickly transmitted to neighbouring countries due to increasing demand for imports. Therefore, growth in one country can partly be driven by exports to expanding neighbouring economies that experience a fast increasing demand. Generalising this argument, it becomes obvious that in a region with no major obstacles to communication and interaction, each country: (a) benefits from the progress made in the other countries and (b) contributes to that progress and the overall progress of the region.

In addition, international economic theory and evidence indicates that trade among neighbours is the most beneficial type of trade, because of its sectoral structure and composition. The critical issue here is whether two countries (or groups of countries) tend to specialize and trade products that belong to different industries (inter-industry type of trade) or tend to trade more intensively products within the same industry (intra-industry type of trade). Several studies have shown that the inter-industry type of trade is suitable only for countries with comparable levels of development. This is because in the case of trade between a developed and a developing country, the first will specialize in capital and technology-intensive products, while the second will necessarily specialize in labor or resource-intensive products, missing the opportunity to industrialize and therefore missing the opportunity to develop. Also the inter-industry type of trade relations are considered to cause, in several cases, severe adjustments to the productive base of a country as some sectors shrink and some others expand, a process that is not always free of social friction.

On the other hand, trade within the same industry is not associated with major structural adjustment (as adjustment takes place within the industry or even within the firm) and it usually characterizes neighboring countries with similar levels of development and similar tastes. In addition, intra-industry trade allows for the expansion of economic relations in a more diversified manner, without exerting pressure for a strict specialisation that would perhaps require severe structural adjustments in the countries involved. This leaves some room for restructuring policies in order to reorganise productive resources within sectors, maintaining existing specialisations and avoiding major sectoral shifts of resources that could generate structural unemployment and reduce the diversity of the production base. It is not a coincidence that all developed countries have the highest share of their trade taking place within sectors and in addition taking place with neighbouring countries.

To sum up, intra-regional or cross-border trade, or trade among neighbours is essential for the growth and development of a country for the following reasons: (a) It allows for a higher volume of trade and therefore for export-led growth due to similar consumer preferences and lower transportation cost, (b) it allows small economies to benefit from economies of scale in industrial production, by providing a larger geographical market that is easily accessible and (c) it allows for a sectoral structure of economic relations (intra-industry), that does not threaten the diversity of its productive base.

The Evidence we Need to Consider

Any effort to understand the potentials of the Balkan region and the development options and strategies available to individual countries, depends necessarily on a set of basic information concerning the relative standing of each country and the region in the broader European context. In Table 1 we present information about population, area, Gross Domestic Product (GDP) and Gross National Product (GDP) per capita for all Balkan countries and the EU. The information is presented in absolute figures and also as a share of the EU figure. Starting with population, we observe that with the exception of Turkey and Romania, the other Balkan countries are relatively small or very small in size, especially if one compares with the total population of the EU. Three countries (Albania, FYROM and Slovenia) have a population size that is less than 1% of the total population of the EU. When however all Balkan countries are considered as a group, the picture changes considerably. The total population of the Balkan region amounts to 132 million people, which is equal to about 35% of the population of the EU.

Table 1 Market Size and Development Level of the Balkan Countries (1997)

Countries	Population		Area		GDP		GNP/head	
	million	%	th. m^2	%	Million USD	%	USD	%
Albania	3	0.80	27	0.86	2,276	0.03	750	3.21
Bosnia	4	1.07	51	1.63	3,260	0.04	785	3.36
Bulgaria	8	2.14	111	3.54	9,484	0.12	1,140	4.88
Croatia	4	1.07	56	1.79	19,081	0.24	4,610	19.73
FYROM	2	0.53	25	0.80	2,061	0.03	1,090	4.66
Greece	11	2.94	129	4.11	119,111	1.47	12,010	51.40
Romania	23	6.14	230	7.34	35,204	0.44	1,420	6.08
Serbia	11	2.94	102	3.25	15,147	0.19	1,429	6.12
Slovenia	2	0.53	20	0.64	17,905	0.22	9,680	41.43
Turkey	64	17.09	770	24.56	181,464	2.25	3,130	13.39
Balkans	132	35.25	1521	48.51	404,993	5.01	5,221	22.34
EU	374	100.00	3,135	100.00	8,082,297	100.00	23,367	100.00

Sources: World Bank (1998-99), CIA (1997), EBRD (1997).

Examining the size of the territory of each Balkan country separately, the picture is similar. Turkey and Romania possess a significant area, followed by Greece, Bulgaria and Serbia. The other countries possess very small territories, the smallest being those of Slovenia and FYROM. When however the Balkan region is considered as a whole, the picture changes considerably, as it covers an area that is equal to about 48% of the area of the EU.

Turning now to the economic figures of the Table, we see that the general picture is very different. With the exception of Turkey (which has the larger GDP) and Greece, that have in relative terms a significant economy, the other countries in the region have to a large extent very small and insignificant economies. It is very indicative that all together the eight (8) Balkan countries in transition have a .GDP level that is smaller than the GDP level of Greece alone and of course of Turkey. Comparing the size of the Balkan economies as a whole to that of the EU, we get a disappointing figure. The size of the economy of the 10 Balkan countries put together is equal to only 5% of the size of the EU economy. Even more disappointing are the figures related to GNP per capita that measure development and welfare levels. With the exception of Greece and Slovenia, all the other countries have GNP per capita figures that are less than 20% of the average figure of the EU. Some countries like Albania, Bosnia, FYROM and Bulgaria have welfare figures that are not considered acceptable for European countries. Greece is the only country in the region with a GNP per capita figure that exceeds the 50% of the EU average.

To summarise, despite its potential (given by population and territorial size), the importance of the Balkan economy (given by GDP) and its weight and significance (given by GNP per capita) are very limited in the European context. Some countries are unsustainablly small in terms of population and economic activity and insignificant in terms of development levels. This is not necessarily a problem in an integrated regional economic space. However, the small economies of the region operate in a politically fragmented and in some cases frictional or even hostile regional environment. This intensifies the problems of inefficiency in their productive base, making it unsustainable in the new gobalised economic environment.

In Table 2 we present information about the flows and stock of Foreign Direct Investment (FDI) in the Balkan transition countries, the transition countries in Central Europe[1], Greece, Turkey and the EU. The information is presented in million USD and in figures per capita. Looking at inward flows first, we observe that the Balkan transition countries received in 1997 only 28% of the FDI going to transition countries in Central Europe, despite the fact that these two groups have a similar size in terms of population. We also observe that Turkey, despite its population and GDP size, has received an insignificant amount of FDI in the same year. Comparisons among countries or groups of countries are equally dramatic when we look at per capita flow figures. Greece, the only country in the region enjoying relative stability and the only member of the EU, has the highest FDI per capita flow figure, which is close to 50% of the EU figure. Among transition countries, the Balkans have a per capita figure that is less than half the Central European one. Finally, Turkey is a destination of a relatively insignificant amount of foreign investment in 1997.

Table 2 Inward Flows and Stock of Foreign Direct Investment in the Balkans, the Central European Countries and the EU (1997)

Area	Inward Flows		Stock	
	million USD	per capita	million USD	per capita
Balkan Transition Countries	2,455	55.30	7.494	312.77
Central European Transition countries	8,556	125.20	40,401	736.31
Greece	1,500	136.36	21,864	1987.64
Turkey	606	9.47	6,431	100.48
EU	108,172	288.84	1,195,643	3192.64

Source: Estimated from United Nations (1998).

Looking at accumulated (stock) FDI and FDI per capita figures, the picture is similar. The Balkans are a less frequently chosen destination than Central Europe, while Turkey is in an inferior position. Greece, is the only country in the region that stands out with an FDI stock per capita figure that is equal to 62% of the EU figure.

Why are these figures important and what do they really mean? FDI flows or stock indicate the attractiveness of a country or a region to international investors. Therefore, the first point of this Table is that international investors (small and large private foreign firms, multinational corporations or even foreign public sector firms) are, under present conditions, less willing to invest in the Balkans than in other competing destinations like the countries in Central Europe. The only exception to this rule is Greece, a politically stable country and a member of the EU. Taking into consideration that the vast size of the region and its low cost production base[2] is a real advantage for foreign firms operating in global markets, there must be some other offsetting factors hindering the expansion of foreign firms in the region. These factors are the fragmentation of the region in many small, unstable and at times conflicting countries. As it has been discussed before, fragmentation implies small and insignificant market sizes, while conflict implies an uncertain business environment. These two factors are the most important ones in explaining the absence of FDI in the region.[3] The limited amount of FDI in the region has several negative effects, as foreign capital is an important supplement to domestic capital formation and its in several cases the avenue of technological progress and structural change in host economies. It is not accidental that all countries, even the most advanced ones, have adopted special promotion programs and openly compete with each other in order to attract a significant volume of FDI. As the economy becomes more and more globalised, FDI will play an increasingly more important role for the development, technological advancement and structural change of host countries. The fact that the Balkans run a real danger to be left outside this trend, is a measure of the marginalisation of their economy with long term consequences for growth and prosperity in the region.

In Table 3 we present information concerning the trade relations of each Balkan country[4] with all the others and the EU. In Table 4 we present information about the share of exports and imports of a selected group of Western European and Balkan countries with their neighbours. All exports and imports data are for 1997. Starting from Table 3, we observe that several Balkan countries, despite being neighbours and despite similarities in development levels, culture and consumer preferences, have insignificant trade relations. For example, Bulgaria exports only 2.0% of its total exports to FYROM and only 1.4% to Romania. Similarly, Turkey exports only 0.7% of its total exports to Bulgaria and 1.1% to Greece. The countries with the lowest share of intra Balkan trade relations are Turkey, Romania and Greece with a share of 4.2%, 7.9% and 11.2% respectively of total exports going to the other Balkan countries and a share of 2.7%, 4.6% and 3.7% respectively of total imports coming from other Balkan countries. The countries with the highest shares are Croatia, FYROM and Bulgaria with a share of 30.3%, 25.9% and 23.1% (11.4%38.2% and 9.8%) of their exports (imports) going to (coming from) other Balkan countries. It is worth noting that geography affects intra-regional trade, as the more perimetric countries with respect to the Balkan region, like Turkey and Romania, have the lowest intra-regional interaction. On the contrary, central Balkan countries like FYROM and Bulgaria have a higher intra-regional interaction. It is also worth noting that all countries (except FYROM) have higher export than import shares with the other Balkan countries, because of their dependence on imports from developed countries.

Table 3 Trade Relations among Balkan Countries

Share of exports to Balkan Countries													
Countries	Albania	Bosnia	Bulgaria	Croatia	FYROM	Greece	Romania	Serbia	Slovenia	Turkey	Balkans	EU	Total
Bulgaria	0.5	0.1		0.3	2.0	8.8	1.4	0.0	0.2	9.9	23.1	45.0	100.0
Croatia	0.1	15.0	0.2		1.8	0.3	0.3	0.0	12.2	0.2	30.3	51.3	100.0
FYROM	1.1	0.1	1.9	3.5		1.7	0.4	10.1	4.7	2.5	25.9	43.1	100.0
Greece	1.7	0.0	2.0	0.2	0.4		1.9	0.3	0.2	4.5	11.2	54.7	100.0
Romania	0.0	0.1	0.7	0.2	0.1	2.1		0.2	0.2	4.2	7.9	56.6	100.0
Slovenia	0.1	3.4	0.2	10.0	1.8	0.3	0.3	1.3		0.4	17.8	63.6	100.0
Turkey	0.2	0.1	0.7	0.1	0.3	1.1	1.4	0.2	0.1		4.2	46.7	100.0
Share of imports from Balkan Countries													
Countries	Albania	Bosnia	Bulgaria	Croatia	FYROM	Greece	Romania	Serbia	Slovenia	Turkey	Balkans	EU	Total
Bulgaria	0.0	0.0		0.2	0.6	4.9	1.4	0.0	0.2	2.5	9.8	41.9	100.0
Croatia	0.0	1.5	0.2		0.5	0.3	0.3	0.0	8.3	0.3	11.4	59.4	100.0
FYROM	0.2	0.1	5.3	4.7		2.0	0.7	11.4	9.1	4.7	38.2	41.5	100.0
Greece	0.1	0.0	1.5	0.1	0.1		0.7	0.0	0.1	1.2	3.7	67.9	100.0
Romania	0.0	0.1	0.5	0.1	0.0	1.7		0.1	0.2	1.9	4.6	52.5	100.0
Slovenia	0.0	0.3	0.2	5.0	0.6	0.2	0.2	0.4		0.5	7.3	67.4	100.0
Turkey	0.0	0.0	0.8	0.0	0.1	0.9	0.8	0.1	0.1		2.7	51.0	100.0

Source: Estimated from IMF (1998).

Looking at Table 4 we observe that significant differences exist between Western European and Balkan countries with respect to the share of exports and imports with neighbouring countries. Austria, for example, has 59.2% of its exports going to neighbouring countries and 60.6% of its imports coming from neighbouring countries. Similarly, Belgium and Luxembourg have 46.9% (49.9%) of their exports (imports) going to (coming from) neighbouring countries. On the other side of the spectrum, Greece and Romania have 8.1% and 4.7% (2.8% and 4.2%) respectively of their exports (imports) going to (coming from) neighbouring countries. Obviously, in understanding the real magnitude of these differences, one has to take into consideration several factors such as the size and the development level of neighbouring countries, or the existence of the Single European Market among EU members. Nevertheless, it remains a fact that intra-regional and cross-border trade in the Balkans is very limited compared to the other countries and regions in Europe.

These figures indicate that the Balkans, besides their perimetric location in Europe (Petrakos 1997a), are found today in a unique unfavorable situation resulting from distorted economic relations, as in several cases their borders are meant to be barriers to communication and trade with neighboring countries. This type of "border condition" where borderlines in the region operate as barriers to economic and social relations, is a rare situation in the history of international relations (Petrakos and Christodoulakis 1997).

Table 4 Trade Relations of Selected Countries With their Neighbouring Countries

	Exports to neighbouring countries as a share to total exports	Imports from neighbouring countries as a share to total imports	Total
Austria	59.2	60.6	*100.0*
Belgium-Luxembourg	46.9	49.9	*100.0*
France	43.7	42.9	*100.0*
Switzerland	41.8	54.8	*100.0*
Greece	8.1	2.8	*100.0*
Bulgaria	22.1	9.4	*100.0*
Croatia	28.4	12.4	*100.0*
FYROM	14.8	19.0	*100.0*
Romania	4.7	4.2	*100.0*

Source: Estimated from IMF (1998).

This condition, along with perimetric position in the European economic space generates an overall unfavorable index of geographic location, with serious long-term implications for the economic structure and performance of the region. The "missing factor" in the trade relations among neighbors generates a significant reduction in the trade potential of the region, limiting market accessibility for exporting industries and limiting the prospects for export-led growth.

Because of these conditions, the trade relations of the Balkan countries have necessarily taken an inter-industry character with the more advanced and distant countries of Western Europe (Landesmann 1998), with a serious impact on the industrial structure of the region. As we have already seen, international economic theory indicates that trade with neighboring countries is more intensive and usually takes an intra-industry character, implying greater room for more industries to develop. This is because international specializations are not mutually exclusive and the division of labor takes place within and not between sectors (Petrakos 1997b, Petrakos 1999). Therefore, the lack of trade relations among Balkan countries pushes them further towards an inter-industry type of specialization with the technologically more advanced western European countries that is rather unfavorable for the prospects for industrial development in the region. In that respect, the old and recent "border conditions" in the region have generated a "missing factor" in trade relations that in its turn has imposed additional constraints on the already weak structure of the Balkan economy.

Overall, it is claimed here that the performance of the Balkan economies has been affected by their artificial division in the pre- and post 1989 period and the consequent restrictions imposed on the structure and level of the external economic relations of the region. Although there is no direct empirical evidence to support it, we are confident that a simple spatial trade model would predict for each Balkan country a very different level and structure of trade than the existing one, should barriers to trade with neighboring countries had not been imposed.

Conclusions: Can we Make the Right Choices for the Future?

This paper has not intended to provide arguments about the essence of the so many disputes and conflicts among ethnic groups or countries in the Balkans. Our contribution is in a different direction. We have tried to show that fragmentation and conflicts have a serious cost for all countries in the region and not only those directly involved every time in a dispute or a war. As a result, it is to the best interest of the people and the governments in the Balkans to take seriously under consideration these costs and examine in a more thorough and informed way the available options. In doing so, they have to look less often at their divided past and more often at the possibility for a common future. Other countries, such as Germany and France, or Germany and UK that have fought in the past many bloody wars, did that after the Second World War, and they have enjoyed for half a century the benefits of stability and prosperity. Learning from others, has always been a recipe for success, if one is careful enough to chose the right examples.

In examining available options, people and governments in the Balkans also have to take a closer look at their immediate environment and the prevailing integration trends in Europe. As we move with a faster pace towards a global economy, being part of a large economic union is a vital condition for survival and prosperity, especially for small countries. Under certain conditions, it is very likely that in two decades all European countries will be members (in fact regions) of the strongest economic organisation on earth:

the European Union. Given that this is the declared strategic goal of all European countries that are not currently EU members, three points deserve consideration by policy and opinion makers in the Balkans. First, under existing conditions with respect to ethnic tensions and disputes, it is highly unlikely that any other Balkan country (except Slovenia) will ever join the EU. Second, even if one or two more Balkan countries eventually manage to become members, their benefits from membership will be lower and their costs higher, if large parts of the Balkan region remain outside the Union. Third (and perhaps more important), existing tensions and conflicts about borders and ethnic groups will become more or less irrelevant with membership in a larger, stronger, integrated and internally open European Union.

If these points make sense, then it is relatively easy to highlight the two distinct options available to the people and governments in the Balkans. On the one hand, stands the option of solving existing differences in accordance with the "national interests" of each country. This option may require the intensification of the disputes and it is understood by the parties involved as a zero-sum-game. Some win and some loose. Our earlier analysis, however, has shown that although there will certainly be losers at the Balkan scale, it is highly unlikely that there will be any winners at the European scale. The Balkans may have a different balance of powers, or different borders, but they will still be fragmented, perhaps devastated by the conflict, poorer than ever and outside the EU. If their strategic goal is still EU membership, it is clear that this option leads to a no-win situation.

The other option implies an understanding that the common interests and goals of the countries in the region are much more important than the issues that divide them. In that sense, it is a more difficult choice, as it requires a change in the prevailing perceptions of the people of each country for their neighbours. This option promotes regional co-operation on the understanding that: (i) this is a better framework to discuss differences, (ii) it promotes (the so much needed) regional stability and (iii) the unsolved issues of today, might be largely irrelevant in the broader European context of tomorrow. This option leads to an all-win situation, to the extent that all countries meet their strategic goal to become members of the EU and offer its stability, institutions and prosperity to its people.

The second option has an additional advantage, as it is in line with the declared vision of the EU for a larger and non-exclusive Europe. This coincidence of intentions generates a unique historic opportunity to create an open, stable and prospering economic space from the Atlantic to the Black Sea and from the North Sea to the Mediterranean. This could be the most valuable contribution to the next generation. The United States of Europe are not a more difficult project today than it was the United States of America two centuries ago. Then, as in America, the Mediterranean, which is the Sun Belt of Europe, will gradually attract quality resources and activities that will allow for a fast convergence to the development levels of the West and the North. To make a precarious comparison, it could become the California of Europe. For the people in the Balkans, this is the best available way to regain the prestige and the pride of their glorious (but distant) past.

This option requires that the EU undertakes two important steps. First, it invites all Balkan countries to join in the foreseeable future the EU, and works hard and consistently for the homogenization of their status through an en-block association agreement that will take into consideration the peculiarities of the region and be more generous than the existing ones with Bulgaria and Romania. This policy is a cornerstone for the future of the Balkan region and it is the only one that allows in the long run the unification of the Balkan and European space and the better accessibility and connection of Southern with Northern and Western Europe. Secondly, it implements an EU strategic development plan for the Balkan region at various spatial, operational and sectoral levels with a special emphasis on the issues of intra-regional cooperation and integration. This development plan should include effective transportation and telecommunication networks that will allow the integration of the Balkans and reveal the special weight of Southeastern Europe as an emerging regional market with significant size, and a strategic advantage for the expansion of the EU economic relations in the Black Sea region, Eastern Mediterranean and the Middle East.

Notes

1   The Czech Republic, Hungary, Poland and Slovakia.
2   Labour cost in the Balkan countries is the lowest in Europe.
3   Other factors that have been found in the economic literature to have an impact on the direction of FDI are proximity or adjacency of host countries to the large and more developed EU markets, as well as cultural affinity.
4   Except Albania, Bosnia and Serbia, for which there is no reliable information.

References

CIA (1997) *The World Factbook 1997*, Central Intelligence Agency, Washington DC.

EBRD (1997) *Transition Report Update*, April 1997, European Bank for Reconstruction and Development, London UK.

IMF (1998) *Direction of Trade Statistics Yearbook*, International Monetary Fund, USA.

Jackson M. and Petrakos G. (1999) Regional differences in the impact of EU integration on the industrial structure and competitiveness of CEFTA countries, paper prepared for the Phare ACE P96-6071-R project: *Competitiveness of CEFTA countries: measurement and trends in the period of preparation to join the EU.*

Landesmann M. (1998) Features of East-West European integration: cost structures and patterns of specialization, Paper presented in the international workshop on: *Competitiveness of the CEFTA countries: measurement and trends in the period of preparation to join the EU*, Bratislava, 17-18 April, 1998.

Petrakos G. (1997a) "The Regional Structure of Albania, Bulgaria and Greece: Implications for Cross-Border Cooperation and Development", *European Urban and Regional Studies*, Vol. 4, No 3, pp. 193-208.

Petrakos G. (1997b) "A European Macro-Region in the Making? The Balkan Trade Relations of Greece", *European Planning Studies*, Vol. 5, No. 4, pp. 515-533.

Petrakos G. (1999) "La Greece et les Balkans: Geographie perdue et retrouvee", *Revue d' Etudes Comparatives Est-Quest*, Vol. 30. No. 4, pp. 177-199.

Petrakos G. and Christodoulakis N. (1997) "Economic Development in the Balkan Countries and the Role of Greece: From Bilateral Relations to the Challenge of Integration", Discussion Paper Series No 1620, *Centre for Economic Policy Research* (CEPR), London.

Petrakos G. and Christodoulakis N. (1998) "Transition in the Balkans: Patterns of Change and Policies to Overcome marginalisation and Disintegration", Phare-ACE Program *Structural Changes and Spilovers in the East European Reform Process*, Final Report, Imperial College Management School, University of London.

Petrakos G. and Totev S. (2000) "Economic Structure and Change in the Balkan Region: Implications for Integration, Transition and Economic Cooperation", *International Journal of Urban and Regional Research*, 24, 1, pp. 95-113.

United Nations (1998) *World Investment Report 1998*, Trends and Determinants, USA.

World Bank (1999) *World Development Report*, Knowledge for Development 1998/99, Oxford University Press. USA.

9 European Policies for the Reconstruction and Development of the Balkans

ANGELOS KOTIOS
Assistant Professor, Department of Planning and Regional Development, University of Thessaly, Greece

Introduction

The Balkan countries are in transition, and are participating, each at a different pace, in the new European structures which are being shaped after the collapse of the bi-polar world. This transition concerns a special group of countries, which, in relation to the other Central and East Europe (CEE) countries, have certain special characteristics. First, they lack a true communist experience. But they also lack experience with the functioning of a developed capitalist system as well. They have a comparatively lower level of development and a weaker economic structure than the larger, more distant economic and technological centers of Central and Northern Europe (Petrakos and Totev 2000). They have a number of internal political problems, some of which have not been resolved since the fall of the Ottoman Empire (Agh 1998). These special characteristics have a negative impact, both on the process of their transformation, as well as on their integration into West European structures.

Relations between the Balkans and the European Community (EC), the so-called Euro-Balkan cooperation, have also exhibited some special features over time; referring to them should contribute to a better understanding during the evolving formation of these relations. These characteristics include the following:

First, the relations between the countries in this area and Western Europe have always been, and continue to be, determined by international and national political parameters. For example, during the bi-polar era with the related political and economic division of Europe, special cooperative relations were established with the EC through association agreements with Greece (1962) and Turkey (1963), which then evolved into EC membership for Greece and membership in the tariff union for Turkey. Already, following the European Council Meeting in Helsinki (December 1999), Turkey has been considered a candidate state for accession into the EC. In addition, as early as 1980 the former Yugoslavia became the third Balkan country to start special cooperation relations with the EC. Because Yugoslavia had always pursued a neutral position between the East and the West, it was not fully integrated into the eastern socio-military and economic system. As a result, in 1983, the EC and Yugoslavia signed an Agreement for Cooperation. This agreement included, among other things, economic, technical and financial cooperation, special conditions for bilateral trade (e.g. preferential status without reciprocity for industrial products, lower duties on agricultural goods, etc.), collaboration in the labor sector and the institution of a Cooperation Council. For political reasons relations with the other countries of the area (Bulgaria, Romania and Albania) were much less developed.

Second, as a result of national and international parameters, relations between the Balkan countries and the European Union (EU) have traditionally suffered from an intense fragmentation. The Balkans as a defined geographical space has, historically, never been a homogeneous political and economic entity with respect to the application of European Community foreign economic policy. Differences in internal policy and economic structure among the Balkan countries, as well as different orientations in their foreign affairs and especially foreign economic policy, divergences in the levels of economic growth, and finally divergent national choices and targets, have decisively defined the intensity and extent of their cooperation with the institutions of the West European economic union.

The collapse of the bi-polar world, and the institutional and structural-political changes in the former Yugoslavia which led to the creation of new independent states in the Balkans, have created new conditions pertaining to Euro-Balkan cooperation. Two countries of the eastern Balkans (Bulgaria and Romania), as well as other countries in the western Balkans (e.g. Albania and FYROM), are pursuing a transition to a western type of parliamentary democracy and a mixed economy, with an emphasis on market mechanisms. Thus they have shifted their foreign political and economic orientation towards the West. They now aim at the development of close relations with the EC, and a gradual incorporation into western mechanisms of cooperation and integration. Through the development of cooperation with the EC, these countries seek to strengthen democratic processes and to establish an irrevocable independence from the former Soviet Union (Lippert 1990). At the same time, as in the case of the other countries in accession, these countries anticipate the economic benefits of technical and financial support, including direct European investment, as well as the opening of a large, unified internal European market for their exports. Accession to the EC is their final objective, their national target and their socio-political vision.

In contrast to this other new states of the area, such as the Federal Republic of Yugoslavia (FRY), Croatia and Bosnia-Herzegovina, have been involved primarily in war activities, political conflicts, interior crises and civil wars, due mainly to existing national minorities. Developments in these countries have obviously not only deterred conditions for cooperation with the EC but have also brought about, especially in the case of the FRY, a greater or lesser involvement of EC country members in the war in Kosovo, with the resulting imposition of economic sanctions and a trade embargo.

Therefore, Euro-Balkan relations that were gradually shaped after the establishment of the European Community in 1957, are now evolving into cooperation with some of the Balkan countries and confrontation with, or separation from, others. The analysis and prospects for those relations is the core of the present analysis. First, a concise description and evaluation of EC policies designed to support the processes of systemic transformation of the Balkans is attempted. Second, the existing institutions of cooperation as well as their basic economic influences are described. The position of the countries of this area in the ever-developing expansion of the EC to the east is the second part of the analysis. The war in Kosovo was the proximate reason for the reappraisal and re-determination of EC Balkan policies, as well as for the introduction of new support mechanisms for the reconstruction and the integration of this area into Europe. The recording of the conclusions of the analysis and suggestions towards a new strategy of cooperation in the Balkans, in conjunction with the role that the EU is asked to assume, make up the last part of this study.

European Balkan Policy in the 1990s: Main Characteristics and Problems

A. EU Measures to Support the Transition Process

The transformation process of the transition countries of Central and Eastern Europe (CEE), as well as the course of their integration into the west-

237

ern institutions of cooperation, implies that great structural and institutional adjustments must be made. These adjustments in turn will have an economic, social and political impact. To reduce the cost of adaptation and to enable a smooth harmonization of the socio-political and economic systems of the CEE countries with those of the West, the EC has developed and, since 1989, applied a number of support measures. In order to assist the transition countries of the Balkans, the EC is using the Phare and OBNO-VA Programs, and at the same time is activating cooperative funding mechanisms through the European Investment Bank (EIB) and the European Bank for Reconstruction and Development (EBRD). There is also aid granted on a bilateral level on behalf of the country members of the EC. Table 1 contains the total amount of aid given to the Balkan countries to support the process of their transformation and to cover urgent humanitarian needs.

Table 1 1991-1999 EU Assistance to South-Eastern Europe
(Allocation in millions of Euro)

Beneficiary country	European Community	Member States [1]	EIB	EU TOTAL
ALBANIA	816.73	712.80	46.00	1,575.53
BOSNIA-HERZEGOVINA	2,061.87	507.90	0.00	2,569.77
CROATIA	353.76	1,165.90	0.00	1,519.66
FEDERAL REPUBLIC OF YUGOSLAVIA	471.80	712.40	0.00	1,184.20
FYROM	403.89	178.20	60.00	642.09
Regional Co-operation	462.15	0.00	0.00	462.15
TOTAL A [2]	4,570.21	3,277.20	106.00	7,953.41
ROMANIA	1,813.20	3,069.40	1,134.50	6,017.10
BULGARIA	1,480.50	754.80	751.00	2,986.30
TOTAL B	3,293.70	3,824.20	1,885.50	9,003.40
TOTAL A+B	7,863.91	7,101.40	1,991.50	16,956.81

1 Provisional figures; figures on 1998-1999 are not included as only provided by LUX, I, SV, DK, UK, EL, SF.
2 These figures include Phare, Obnova, Media, Democracy & Human rights, Demining, Humanitarian aid, Food security and Macro-assistance.
Financial perspectives 2000-2006 (indicative allocation): Albania, Bosnia-Herzegovina, Croatia, Federal Republic of Yugoslavia and FYROM approx. 5 billion Euros. Romania and Bulgaria 6.2 billion Euros
Source: European Commission, DG External Relations.

Through the Phare Program, the EU offers necessary know-how, including consulting and training, to a wide range of public, private and non-governmental organizations. In addition it funds studies, subsidizes capital, and gives necessary guarantees, credit and finances, often in cooperation with other international organizations, for infrastructure projects. However, it does not aim to serve macroeconomic goals, nor to cover the balance-of-payment or budget deficits of the countries in transition. The latter kind of support has been undertaken by specialized international organizations and banks (International Monetary Fund, World Bank, European Investment Bank).

According to the first evaluation report of the Phare Program (European Commission 1997), the above sectors were funded at a level of 6.636 billion ECUs from 1990 to 1996 (1997: 7.7 billion ECUs). As shown in Table 2, from 1990 to 1996 there were also reallocations of resources among sectors. During the first years of the transformation process there were large amounts granted for critical aid, for the restructuring of agriculture and for the support of the emerging private sector economy. In the period 1994-1997 more emphasis was put on infrastructure and the development of public administration.

Table 2 Phare Priorities, 1990-1993 and 1994-1996

	1990-1993		1994-1996	
	MECU	%	MECU	%
Critical aid	337.7	10.3	180.0	5.4
Agricultural restructuring	392.8	12.0	85. 5	2.6
Private sector	876.4	26.7	611.2	18.2
Human resources	431.0	13.1	434.4	13.2
Social development	213.8	6.5	108.5	3.2
Environment and nuclear safety	325.9	9.9	215.0	6.4
Infrastructure (incl. Cross-border)	280.0	8.5	1, 208.1	36.1
Public administration	164.5	5,0	275.2	8.2
Democratisation	34.0	1.0	66.4	2.0
Multidisciplinary	229.6	7.0	157.2	4.7
TOTAL	3 ,285.7	100.0	3 ,350.5	100.0

Source: European Commission 1997.

The incorporation of a country into the Phare Program was at first dependent upon political and economic conditions. For example, the supply of EC aid through the Phare Program was tied to the process of democratization, as well as the transformation of internal economic systems. Thus, due to the existence of this framework of principles and terms, and because of the different stages of internal adjustment of the Balkan countries, there was not a simultaneous incorporation of these countries into the Program. Bulgaria was incorporated into Phare in 1990, Albania and Romania in 1991. Because of the civil war in Bosnia-Herzegovina and the political friction between the Former Yugoslavian Republic of Macedonia (FYROM) and Greece, these countries did not started participating in the Program until the beginning of 1996. Croatia and the Federal Republic of Yugoslavia (FRY) have not yet profited from Phare, first, because of their bilateral conflict (Kraina, East Slavonia), second, because of their involvement in the Bosnia-Herzegovina war, third, because of their policy towards their ethnic minorities and, finally, because of deficiencies in their processes of internal democratization. In the case of FRY all economic relations with the EU have been cancelled because of the NATO military intervention and a continuation of the pre-existing political status of Serbia.

Technical and financial assistance through Phare is of major significance for the participating countries of the Balkans, which, in comparison with the other CEE countries, present the greatest problems of political and economic transformation. Tables 3, 4 and 5 describe the sector allocation of resources as a percentage of total national programs (Table 3), the allocation of funds of the Program by country (Table 4), and the total number of commitments, contracts and payments made per country (Table 5), for the period 1990-96. The first conclusions drawn are that the absorption of the approved funds by the Balkan countries is about the average of all the 13 Eastern European recipient countries, and that their allocation is roughly proportional to the size of their populations. For example, the commitment of funds to Bulgaria, for the period studied, equaled 538.2 million ECUs. This amount represents 8.4% of the total commitments of the Program, and compares to the 8% that Bulgaria represents of the total population in the recipient countries. The percentages of funds committed to Romania and FYROM were less than the percentages of their populations in the total of Phare partner countries. Only in the case of Albania was the percentage of funds (5.8%) considerably higher than the percentage represented by its population (3.1%) (see Dauderstadt).

Table 3 Country Distribution of National Programme Commitments, 1990-1996

Countries	Total Phare commitments 1990-1996, MECU	Country population (millions)	Share of Phare funds (%)	Share of population (%)
Poland	1,388	38.5	30.8	36.6
Hungary	684	10.3	15.2	9.8
Czech Rep.	429	10.3	9.5	9.8
Slovakia	207	5.3	4.6	5.0
Slovenia	91	2.0	2.0	1.9
Romania	726	22.7	16.1	21.6
Bulgaria	539	8.4	12.0	8.0
Estonia	130	1.5	2.9	1.4
Lithuania	179	3.8	4.0	3.6
Latvia	132	2.5	2.9	2.4
Albania	385	3.3	5.8	3.1
FYROM	110	2.0	1.6	1.9

Sources: European Commission 1997, own estimations.

Table 4 National Programme Sectoral Allocations of Phare Assistance
(in percentage)

	BG	CZ	ES	HU	LE	LI	PL	RO	SR	SL	CA	Other
Administration and public institutions	4	6	22	7	13	10	6	3	7	9	10	6
Agricultural restructuring	10	2	2	11	1	3	14	11	8	0	0	0
Democracy-Civil society	1	0	0	0	0	0	0	1	0	0	0	8
Humanitarian, critical aid, food	5	0	0	0	0	0	0	11	0	0	7	5
Education, training, research	14	10	12	18	11	11	15	16	18	17	17	7
Environment-nuclear safety	12	2	3	11	5	2	8	2	1	0	19	11
Infrastructure	35	56	22	15	12	29	29	20	15	19	28	0
Private sector												
Development and regional integration	13	13	20	32	24	23	21	20	33	24	18	17
Social development, public health	6	8	2	6	9	4	4	6	10	7	0	5
Multidisciplinary	0	3	17	1	26	18	2	10	8	24	0	42
Total	100	100	100	100	100	100	100	100	100	100	100	100

Note: (BG) Bulgaria; (CZ) Czech Republic; (ES) Estonia; (HU) Hungary; (LE) Latvia; (LI) Lithuania; (PL) Poland; (RO) Romania; (SR) Slovak Republic; (SL) Slovenia; (MC) Multi country.

Source: European Commission 1997a.

Table 5 Commitments, Contracts and Payments by Country of Phare Program (1990-1996)

	Commitments MECU	Contracts MECU	%	Payments MECU	%
Albania	385.0	262.2	68	237.1	62
Bosnia	177.3	122.3	69	87.9	50
FYROM	110.0	85.9	78	75.7	69
Poland	1389.5	862.9	62	858.5	62
Hungary	683.8	461.8	68	459.0	67
CSFR	232.2	228.4	98	226.0	97
Czech Rep.	284.0	96.1	34	105.9	37
Slovakia	130.9	73.0	56	70.0	53
Lithuania	179.0	108.7	61	65.7	37
Estonia	130.3	65.1	50	38.2	29
Latvia	132.0	82.9	63	49.5	38
Romania	726.1	491.0	68	406.3	56
Bulgaria	538.2	341.4	63	308.2	57
Slovenia	91.0	90.3	99	88.3	97
MCPs	704.2	486.8	69	373.0	53
Horizontal Programmes	742.6	474.1	64	323.6	44
Total	6,636.1	4,301.8	65	3,727.2	56

Source: European Commission 1997.

As far as the sector priorities were concerned, Bulgaria gave more emphasis to infrastructure (35% of the overall financing), education and training (14%), development of the private sector (13%), environment (12%) and the agriculture sector (10%). Romania, on the other hand, gave priority to infrastructure (20%), the development of the private sector and regional development (20%), education and training (16%), agriculture (11%) and critical aid (11%). In the case of Albania the aid was mainly expended on the development of the financial sector (32%), critical aid (20%) and the development of infrastructure (19%).

At this point we should mention the distinct cooperation of the EU with Bosnia-Herzegovina (European Commission 1998a). Following the Dayton agreement (12.11.1995) to terminate the war, the World Bank and the European Bank for Reconstruction and Development (EBRD) worked out a program for the reconstruction and rebuilding of this country. The program arranged for a total free aid of $5 billion for the period 1996-1999. The contribution of the EU was $1 billion, administered through the Phare Program ("Essential Aid"). It was a critical aid program aimed at rendering humanitarian aid, as well as at reconstruction activities and the support of sectors like transportation, education, housing, agriculture, energy, water, telecommunications etc. On the other hand, the EU initiative OBNOVA (European Commission 1999a) focused on the reconstruction of Bosnia-Herzegovina, Croatia, FRY and FYROM (Regulations 1628/96, 2240/97 and 851/98). The particular targets of this initiative were economic development, the rehabilitation of civil society and cooperation among the Republics of the Former Yugoslavia within the sphere of the regional approach that the EU has followed in the area of the Western Balkans (EU Council 1998). Finally, the Balkan countries that are candidates for accession into the EU are participating in programs concerning education, training and employment as well as the SME's, research and development.

Three countries that have signed special cooperation agreements with the EU have received financial assistance from the European Investment Bank (EIB). This support has been in the form of loan guarantees or in the form of long term loans with interest rates lower than those applicable from the open capital market. The countries of CEE, and therefore the cooperating Balkan countries, are able to receive loans from the EIB to improve their macroeconomic situation (e.g. balance of payment assistance) on condition that they will apply these loans to programs for macroeconomic stabilization. In addition, there are loans available for investments in infrastructure, as well as loans to different banks of the CEE for the support of the SME's and the market economy.

Based upon Decision 97/256/EU (14.4.1997) of the Council, the total amount reserved for the funding of these countries is 3.520 million ECU's for the period 1997-2000. In early 1998, the Board of Trustees of the EIB bound 3.500 million ECU's as funding assistance within the framework of a pre-accession strategy for the countries of CEE which are accession candidates. Furthermore, the cooperating Balkan countries received loans as well as loan guarantees for the development and reconstruction of their infrastructure in transportation, telecommunications and energy, with emphasis on European networks. Very often EIB activities complement Phare Program activities as well as those of the EBRD and the World Bank. Euratom may also approve loans for the security and improved functioning of existing nuclear power plants. Bulgaria, as well as the Ukraine and Russia, which operate unsafe nuclear power plants, have already received such support.

The European Bank for Reconstruction and Development (EBRD) offers immediate funding for private sector activities, for reconstruction and privatization, as well as for the infrastructure necessary to support these activities. Furthermore, it supports the creation and development of private economy institutions. The main types of funding are in the form of loans, participations and guarantees. In order to increase total investment resources, the Bank emphasizes co-funding as well as technical support. Thus, up to the first half of 1998, Albania had received a total funding of 74.3 million ECUs (9 investment programs) and 7.09 million ECUs for technical assistance from the EBRD (EBRD, 1997, 1998a). Bosnia-Herzegovina had received 73.6 million ECUs (11 investment programs) and 11.1 million ECUs for technical assistance (EBRD 1997, 1998b), Bulgaria 340 million ECUs (28 investment programs) and 6.8 million ECUs for technical assistance (EBRD 1997, 1998c). Romania had received 1.257 million ECUs (41 investment programs), amounting to 11.4% of the total funding of the bank, and 29 million ECUs for technical assistance (EBRD 1997, 1998c), FYROM 163 million ECUs (9 investment programs) and 3.8 million ECUs for technical assistance (EBRD 1997, 1998e), Croatia 434.9 million ECUs (23 investment programs) and 3.5 million ECUs for technical assistance (EBRD 1997, 1998f). Funds from these loans were invested mainly in infrastructure, development of the banking system, industry, energy, telecommunications and tourism.

B. Contractual Relations as a Basic Integration Policy Instrument

Trade and economic cooperation agreements Immediately after the collapse of really existing socialism and the centralized East European or COMECOM system of labor division in 1989, the CEE countries sought entry into the West European system of economic cooperation and integration, and, more particularly, the development of closer relations with the EU. Given that these countries were not members of the most important economic organizations of world economic order (e.g., the World Trade Organization, the OECD, etc.), their new economic relations with the EU had to be based upon bilateral relations.

The EU, which already regulates its trade relations with all developing countries in the framework of more or less preferential agreements, has reacted positively to the challenge of this opening, and the western orientation of the CEE countries in general, by signing agreements on trade and economic cooperation with them. In the case of ten countries, including Bulgaria and Romania, these agreements were later replaced by new Accession Agreements ("European Agreements"). However, the original agreements on trade and economic cooperation with Albania (from 1992) and FYROM (from 1997) are still in effect. These agreements were based mainly on certain general political and economic principles, such as respect for the principles of democracy and human rights as they have been described in the Final Act of Helsinki and the Paris Charter for a new Europe, respect for minorities and the principles of good neighboring, transition to a market economy, respect for the principles of the Bonn Conference for Economic Cooperation in Europe, and respect for mutual interest and non-discrimination (EU 1992, 1997). The main goals of these agreements, beyond the strengthening of bilateral relations, were support for the transformation process, the strengthening of economic development, promotion of harmonized trade development, regional and sector diversification, regional cooperation, and the establishment of new types of trade and economic relations.

Within the framework of trade cooperation, the EU offered to open its markets for industrial products, excluding from totally free market access certain special products, such as iron, steel, textiles and processed agricultural products, for which there remain tariffs and/or quotas. They also excluded agricultural products for which there were common market organizations in the EU from full import liberalization. Furthermore, the EU reserved the right to impose anti-dumping and anti-subsidy tariffs, as well as additional safety measures, i.e., the right to re-impose trade protection measures in cases where the increase of imports from the cooperating countries would severely affect community production. The cooperating countries, on their behalf, offered the EU most favored nation clauses, excluding the special case of liberalization of imports from neighboring countries necessary to develop regional integration. In addition, these countries established the convertibility of their currencies to facilitate their transactions with the EU. In order to protect new industries or to support reconstruction of existing ones, the cooperating countries were also allowed to introduce additional new measures for trade protection.

Economic cooperation refers to matters such as industry, agriculture, mining, fishery, infrastructure, economic policy, transfer of technology and know-how, energy, transportation, research and development, tourism, the environment, the financial sector and the Phare program. The Cooperation Council was responsible for the administration of this cooperation.

"European Agreements" for cooperation between the EU and the countries of the Eastern Balkans The agreements on trade and economic cooperation, the so called "first generation" agreements, despite their indisputable importance especially for trade development, covered a very limited range of issues and were less favorable than the preferential and beneficial terms of the agreements with other countries (e.g., the Lome Agreement with African, Caribbean and Pacific countries, and the agreements with Mediterranean countries). They also lacked a specific target, or final stage, such as EU accession. Thus, with the progress of the transformation process, it became obvious that the above agreements did not suffice for the attainment of ambitious goals such as the gradual integration of Western and Eastern Europe. Beyond that, the accession prospect could function from the very beginning as a motive for reconstruction and adjustment, and as an incentive for social tolerance and self-discipline in the economies and societies suffering the transition (Kramer 1991).

The EU, whose political and economic interests in the area of Central and Eastern Europe are important, was asked to respond with a second generation of agreements, which would not only allow for closer cooperation but which would, at the same time, serve as an "accession waiting room".

In 1993, two countries of the Eastern Balkans (Bulgaria and Romania) signed accession agreements with the EU (EU 1994a, 1994b). These countries, unlike the countries of the Western Balkans, avoided involvement in military conflicts, avoided intense internal unrest and political tensions with neighboring countries, and succeeded in establishing democratic systems. Both these accession agreements, similar in content, presupposed the adoption of a series of political and economic measures. Each contracting party was asked to respect the basic terms mentioned in the first part of the agreement, such as the principles of mutual interest, reciprocity, political and economic freedom, the establishment of a political system that would be based on the rule of law and a respect for human rights. Political pluralism and a multi-party political system with free and democratic elections, application of the principles and provisions contained in the Final Act of OSCE, the development of a market economy and a commitment to free trade in accordance with the principles of the WTO were further obligations to the contracting parties. The agreements recognized that the final goal of the associated countries of the Eastern Balkans (as applicable in the case of the other associated countries of the CEE) was accession to the EU, and that this agreement would contribute to the realization of that goal.

The more specific targets of the agreements are (EU 1994a, 1994b):
• The creation of an appropriate framework for political dialogue between the interested parties that would allow the development of close political relations.
• The gradual establishment of a free trade zone between the EC and the two Balkan countries, which would ultimately cover all trade.
• Support for and enlargement of trade, and the attainment of balanced economic relations between the contracting parties so as to accelerate the dynamic economic development and prosperity of these two countries in the Eastern Balkans.
• The functioning of the agreements as a basis for economic, financial, cultural and social cooperation, as well as for the rendering of Community aid.
• Support for the effort of the two countries of the Eastern Balkans to develop their economies and to complete the establishment of a market economy.
• The development of a necessary framework for their gradual integration into the European Community. Towards this end they would adopt new rules, policies and practices.
• The establishment of new institutions able to guarantee the effectiveness of the association.

Through an institutionalized political dialogue the EU is seeking the integration of the associated countries of the Balkans into the community of democratic countries, an increase in the convergence of their stances on international issues, the strengthening of security and stability, etc. The political dialogue in the framework of the association agreements is to take place at the level of country leaders and governments, at the ministerial level (Association Council), at the level of higher administration staff, at the level of experts, etc.

As far as trade cooperation is concerned, the target of free movement of goods is to be materialized through the creation of a free trade zone during a transitional period of ten years. During these years the EU will accept a partial application of the reciprocity principle and equal market access. Thus, following enactment of the agreement, the EU would revoke all restrictions on imports from the associated countries. Certain special goods, such as iron, steel, textiles, clothes and the majority of agricultural goods, would be exempted from full release. For the latter there are certain marginal cases of free exports in effect. Special protocols define the terms and conditions of importing these goods into the EU.

The associated countries are bound by the Agreements to liberalize their imports from the EU gradually over ten years. This applies mainly to tariff barriers, given that quotas and currency limitations will be revoked once these agreements are in effect.

In very special cases and for a limited period of time (5 years) the associated countries of the Balkans may increase their trade protection, solely through the increase of the relevant import tariffs. Relevant special cases deserving protection are infant industries, i.e. newly founded ones, which, in the beginning, must be protected against outside competition, and also sectors under reconstruction or facing severe problems of adjustment. The maximum increase of import duties from existing levels is not allowed to exceed 25%.

The EU reserves the right to impose anti-dumping measures, as well as measures against subsidized imports from the associated countries. In addition, in cases where goods are imported into the EU at an ever increasing rate so as to cause or threaten to cause serious damage to local EU producers of similar or immediately competitive products, EC authorities reserve the right to activate the enabling clause of the Agreement, i.e., the right to a unilateral re-imposition of import barriers.

Because of the importance of the public sector the Association Agreements favor a mutual opening of markets for public procurements and contracts on the basis of the principles of non-discrimination and reciprocity, according to the relevant law of GATT /WTO. The associated countries of the Balkans must fully open their markets by the end of the 10-year adjustment period. During this time they are obliged to grant EC enterprises all rights derived from the most favored nation clause. Given the desire of associated countries for future accession into the EU, the Association Agreements foresee a gradual adaptation of national law in the two eastern Balkan countries and the adoption of EC law in the following sectors: tariffs, company and banking law, taxation law, intellectual property rights law, worker safety, financing, services, competition, health protection, as well as people, animal and plant life protection, consumer protection, income taxation, technical standards, nuclear protection, transportation and the environment.

Economic cooperation refers mainly to EC support of certain sector policies in the associated countries. Thus, for example, industrial cooperation supports industrial reconstruction, the establishment of new enterprises, transfer of technology, etc. For the promotion and protection of investments there are bilateral agreements for the protection of foreign investments, avoidance of double taxation, the transfer of capital, support for deregulation, for planning and participation in trade exhibitions, etc.

The agricultural sector is of vital importance for development and employment in both Bulgaria and Romania (European Commission 1998c). Here, cooperation is directed at support for private producers, the creation of distribution networks for agricultural goods, innovations in agricultural infrastructure, the improvement of productivity and health, etc.

These conditions of association unquestionably provide a necessary institutional framework for the development of close cooperation and integration between the EU and the two countries of the Eastern Balkans. They cover almost all bilateral issues, as well as those relating to technical and economic assistance in the specific economic sectors of both countries. As very clearly stated, the Association Agreements have an intermediate and transitional, as well as functional character leading to full membership.

At this point certain general comments should be made relating to the importance of these agreements for the Balkan countries as well as for the EU.

First, the political and economic terms and conditions of the Agreements are undoubtedly a means for rapid institutional adjustment and social acceptance of these difficult reforms. Second, the prospect of accession provides an incentive for the attainment of a domestic political, social and economic consensus in these Balkans countries, since accession to the EU (as well as to other institutions of Western cooperation) is defined as a national goal of high priority.

In addition, trade cooperation should, to a large degree, create the conditions for geographic and sector diversification of external trade between the associated countries, and should intensify their bilateral trade relations as well. As far as the quantitative dimensions of the time-limited preferential treatment of EU imports from its associated partners are concerned, certain existing limitations should be noted (Bruecker 1997, Weise und Bruecker 1997, Henriot and Inotao 1998). For example, the liberalization of imports of industrial products into the EU is not complete. As already mentioned, certain industrial products have never had free access to the Common Market. These products are still liable to quota limitations, import taxes, surveillance and technical approval, and they are the very ones where the associated Balkan countries have comparative advantage and which make up the bulk of their exports (World Bank 2000). In this way the possibilities for these Balkan Countries to exploit their competitive advantage are seriously limited. This is applicable to the greatest degree in the case of agricultural products, for which the import barriers are still quite high. Almost all the Balkan countries still continue to have an extensive agricultural sector, the development of which is of great importance to the overall success of their economy and employment. High West European trade protectionism in agricultural products (Messerlin 2000), in combination with their agricultural export subsidies, not only present obstacles to the export of Balkan agricultural products, but also to the loss of third country export markets, such as those of the former COMECON partner countries. It should also be mentioned that the average protectionism of the Balkan countries regarding imports of agricultural products is less than that of the EC, which results in serious deficits in bilateral agricultural trade at the expense of these Balkan countries.

The importance of preferential treatment for these Balkan countries is effectively limited by two additional factors:

First, the overall effect of the elimination of EC tariffs on the great majority of industrial products coming from the associated countries should not be considered to have been especially important, given that the size of the tariffs ranged only from 4% to 9% (Bruecker 1997, Weise und Bruecker 1997).

Second, the associated countries of the Balkans are not the only countries that enjoy the privilege of "managed" free access to the EC market. Indeed, the same privileges have been granted to another eight countries in Central and Eastern Europe, most of which are more competitive than the Balkan countries. These countries are also geographically closer to the developed markets of Northern and Central Europe, with which they are reviving their traditional relations. In addition, tariff union agreements, either association or cooperation agreements, were signed many years ago by the EC with most of the countries of the Mediterranean basin. Their export structures as well as their conditions of access to the internal EU market are similar to those of the newly associated partners of the Balkans. To the list of the countries with preferential access to the European Market we should also add the countries of Africa, the Caribbean, and the Pacific (ACP), which for the last 25 years have enjoyed most preferred access to the EU (99% of their exports have been fully freed of tariff or other quota limitations). There are in addition other developing and industrial countries whose exports have to a large extent been freed from restrictions within the framework of the Community System of Generalized Tariff Preferences (European Commission 1999b). Finally, free access to the EU market for industrial products and most services has been granted to the countries of EFTA (Switzerland, Norway, Iceland and Liechtenstein). Thus, it can be said that the associated countries of the Balkans have a relatively better access to the EC market only when compared to the countries of Latin America and the developing countries of Asia.

All the above greatly limits the impact of preferential treatment on Balkan exports into the European Union. In addition, liberalization of imports into the EC may be further reduced through the application of defensive measures, (e.g., anti-dumping tariffs, or application of the escape clause to reduce possible damages to community producers that might result from a sudden increase in imports of particular goods, etc.).

Finally, we should underline the fact that the development of trade does not depend solely on the bilateral institutional framework, but also chiefly on real economic factors such as: production structure, competitiveness, development of GDP and market demand, exchange rates, foreign direct investments (increasing importance of intra-firm trade), etc.

The list of issues and goals for economic cooperation embodied in the "European Agreements" is the longest that has ever been included in association agreements between the EU and third countries. Here it is not only the content of the list per se, as much as it is the kind and extent of its materialization (Kramer 1991). The economic cooperation of the Balkan countries is clearly of greater importance than the promotion of the "four freedoms", and this is true because for the countries in transition certain prerequisites must be established, (such as infrastructure, restructuring, improvement of human capital, administration, modernization, new investments, transfer of technology and know-how, macroeconomic stabilization, etc.). Only then can those "freedoms" be promoted, freedoms which would allow the realization of the benefits of economic integration, but freedoms that would be attained only at the cost of an overall increase in competition.

The recent EU approach to the Eastern Balkans: from association agreements to accession negotiations Among the group of ten countries of the CEE that have submitted accession applications to the EU are Bulgaria (application dating from 14-12-1995) and Romania (application dating from 22-6-1995). The new process of enlargement of the EU comprises two stages of negotiations: (a) the pre-accession period, and (b) the period of accession, itself. The two Balkan countries are in a second group that started negotiations in January 2000. The pre-accession period, to which the two Balkan countries above belong, is designed to help countries speed up the process of meeting the political and economic criteria for accession (the Copenhagen Criteria).

Within the framework of Agenda 2000: Vol. II, the Council has defined the elements of the pre-accession strategy (EU 1999b). The institutional framework for this strategy consists of the European Agreements, participation in Community programs, the means of application of the Community's "acquis" (without the right of joint decision), and the new institution of Accession Partnership. The goal of the Accession Partnership is to establish a common framework of priorities for further action. These priorities have been pinpointed by the Council for the countries which are candidates for accession to the European Union. They outline the available economic means that will help those countries satisfy the priorities and terms that will be in effect once aid is rendered.

The partnership relation for accession is the framework for a series of policy making instruments, which can be used to support the candidate countries during their preparation to become full members. These instruments include, among other things, a national program for the adoption of the "acquis" which each country must draw up, and which include a new set of priorities for evaluating economic policy.

Within the framework of the Accession Partnership with Bulgaria and Romania (EU 1998b, 1998c), the Council has already announced the decisions pertaining to the principles, priorities, intermediate targets and terms included in the Accession Partnership (Decision of the Council 98/266/EK for Bulgaria and 98/261/EK for Romania). During 1998 both countries submitted their national programs for the adoption of the "acquis", which were examined within the framework of the anticipated bilateral contacts with Community authorities.

The pre-accession strategy focuses on the enlargement of existing institutions and, more specifically, on the creation of new ones able to support the adaptation of enterprises to Community patterns (European Commission 1999b). The attainment of intermediate targets foreseen by The European Agreements and agreed on within the framework of the Accession Partnership is a precondition for financial aid, aid which has been enlarged and restructured within the framework of the pre-accession strategy. The Phare Program, whose resources continue to increase, continues to be the most important financing means. Thus, according to the decision of the European Council in Berlin (24th and 25th March 1999), pertaining to the new budgetary prospects of the Union for the period 2000-2006, the highest annual financing for Phare will amount to 1,560 million Euros, and will be used (in the case of the ten candidate countries of the CEE) for institution building (30%) and investments (70%). In addition, the Council has foreseen an increase in the size of the programs and a greater decentralization of administration in favor of the recipient countries. Also, according to the suggestions of Agenda 2000, the Berlin Council has adopted two new financing mechanisms for all ten candidate countries of CEE: the Special Accession Program for Agriculture and Rural Development (SAPARD) and the Instrument for Structural Policies for Pre-Accession (ISPA) (EU 199a).

To assist candidate countries to adapt to the rules and mechanisms of the Common Agricultural Policy (CAP), and to develop their own agricultural sector, the Community will offer (2000-2006) 520 million Euros annually (European Commission, 1998g). For implementation of policies in the environmental and transportation sectors (European Commission 1998f) the Community will offer 1,040 million Euros per annum. This is undoubtedly a substantial increase over the aid given so far. Commitments for the entire seven years amount to a total of 21.840 billion Euros, whereas the overall aid for the support of the transition for the seven years up to the end of 1997 amounted to 7.7 billion ECUs. This notwithstanding, the aid is much less than the aid received by the areas of Target 1 of the EU within the framework of its economic and social cohesion policy. This is true not only in absolute numbers, but also as a percentage of GDP, as well as per capita income.

At this point there are three important questions to be addressed: First, what is the role of the Balkan countries in the new enlargement process of the Union? Second, what are the prospects for their accession? Third, what are the expected repercussions of this accession?

To answer the first question: The only transition Balkan countries in the pre-accession stage are Bulgaria and Romania. Albania and FYROM are far from this stage, since these countries are only now preparing to sign the stabilization and association agreements. Bosnia-Herzegovina are much further from joining the EU. They must get beyond the problems of the civil war, must arrive at a stabilization of new institutions, and, above all, must re-establish trust between the two parts of the country (the Confederation of the Croats and the Muslims on the one hand and the Serbian Republic on the other). This will probably take a good deal of time to accomplish, and an intensification of efforts will be required. Resolution of the problem of ethnic minorities, the return of refugees, and the democratization of political institutions will largely determine the future of the FRY and Croatia.

The fact that the two transition Balkan countries (which had already submitted an accession application to the EU) are participating in a second round of accession negotiations is a result to their inability to fulfill the criteria posed by the European Council of Copenhagen (1993). According to these criteria, accession of a candidate country to the EU pre-supposes the following:

• The prior attainment of stability in those institutions that guarantee democracy, the rule of law, human rights, and respect and protection of ethnic minorities.

• The existence of a functioning market economy, as well as an ability to face the pressures of competition and of market forces once inside the Union.

• The ability to assume the obligations of the political, economic and monetary union.

In October 1999 the Commission published its second scheduled report concerning the progress that each candidate country had made (European Commission 1999c). As far as the political criteria of Copenhagen are concerned the report concludes that Bulgaria and Romania have fulfilled these basic criteria. In Romania there were serious efforts made to achieve proper respect and protection for the Hungarian minority, as well as to restore children to their families. However, much needs to be done in both Romania and Bulgaria towards fighting corruption, creating a normal justice system, as well as ensuring protection under the Roma rights.

In contrast to the political situation, the two former socialistic countries of the Balkans are in an inferior position economically, as compared to other CEE candidate countries (Jackson and Petrakos 1999). The macroeconomic situation in the two countries reflects basic economic weaknesses

(UN/ECE 1999). Both countries have an extremely low GDP as a percentage of the Community average (Bulgaria 23%, Romania 31%, 1997). The GDP of both countries is much lower than in 1989 (Petrakos and Totev 2000). In other words, instead of economic growth and convergence, Bulgaria experienced a dramatic decline in its GDP in 1996 and 1997, though there was an increase in 1998. Romania, after 1997, has presented a steady decline. Common for both countries are the problems of foreign debt, deficits in the balance of payments, a low percentage of GDP in investment, a low inflow of foreign capital for direct investments, a large proportion of the GDP, and a much larger proportion of total employment in agriculture, etc. On the other hand, both countries have increased their trade with the EU considerably, even though they are well behind the other candidate countries.

As far as the Copenhagen Criteria are concerned, the Council reports that Bulgaria cannot yet be viewed as a functioning market economy. It has, nevertheless, succeeded in adopting the necessary measures for a reestablishment of macroeconomic stability and monetary stabilization through the establishment of a Currency Board. However, much more is required, for example, in the freeing up of price formation, in the liberalization of trade, in structural policy, and in the creation of an institutional and economic framework. Also, because of the structural problems of the country, its lack of infrastructure, modern technology and qualified human resources, its inflated state sector, the weakness of its financial sector, etc., the Bulgarian economy is not considered to have fulfilled the criteria for competitiveness. From this perspective Romania is even further behind.

As to the second question concerning the prospects for accession of the candidate Balkan countries to the EU, the answer is not at all optimistic. The two Balkan countries in transition are far from fulfilling the economic criteria. In both countries the process of restructuring is progressing at a very slow pace. System rigidities, a large, counterproductive and over-indebted public sector, delay in privatization, a large external debt, corruption, outdated infrastructures, etc., are only some of the factors that have thrown the two countries into the vicious cycle of underdevelopment.

The economic and technical assistance rendered by the EU is not able by itself to   deal with these problems. An annual net inflow of 1-2% of GDP for these countries is more than counterbalanced by declines in GDP (6.6%, for Romania in 1997, 10.9% for Bulgaria in 1996, and 6.9% for Bulgaria in 1997). It is estimated that in order to attain 75% of the average Community GDP by 2015, the Bulgarian economy would need to increase by 10.1% annually and the Romanian economy by 9.2%. In the present circumstances these growth rates are quite unrealistic. If the GDP in the EU were to increase annually by an average of 2.5%, and in the Balkans by 3.5%, it would take more than 100 years to cover the per capita income difference (Welfens 1999, Siebert 1997, Fisher, Ratna and Vegh 1998). This means that real convergence would require more than an increase in the transfer of resources (e.g. Community development assistance, aid from other international organizations, foreign direct investments, etc.) Effective internal reforms and structural adjustment, as well as an increase in national saving for investment would also be required.

Thus, one may conclude that, given strict application of the criteria and under the present circumstances in the two candidate Balkan countries, there is no way of estimating the exact time of their accession to the EU. Accession to the EU will depend mainly on their internal efforts. The best development assistance policy is in vain if the internal prerequisites do not exist.

C. Shortcomings, Deficiencies and Inadequacies in the Applied Measures

The overall conclusion reached from the above short analysis is that the Euro-Balkan co-operation has not realized its targets and ambitions. Despite the efforts made and the means used, the transition Balkan countries continue to face important problems, not only in their economic transformation, but also in the establishment of firm democratic institutions. Even worse, the whole area is in a state of fluidity and insecurity, with limited prospects for development, and with regional conditions that have deteriorated even more following the war in the FYR.

All this is happening at the same time that the other former socialistic countries of the CEE are transforming and growing to such a degree that the accession of five of them to the EU seems possible by 2002. Therefore, we can see a gradual divergence among the countries in transition. The development gap between Western and Eastern Europe is rapidly evolving into a chasm between Central and Southeast Europe (World Bank, 2000). Thus, the development gap between Albania, FYROM, Bulgaria, Romania and Bosnia-Herzegovina, on the one hand, and Slovenia, Hungary and The Czech Republic, on the other, is becoming larger than the gap between the latter and the EU.

Obviously, the question arises about the causes of this new divergence. One group of reasons is related to the application of the European co-operation policy. More specifically, because of the conditionality of the assistance and because of the geopolitical and economic interests of certain EU member countries, EU policies have given more emphasis to the stabilisation, transformation and development of Central European Countries. Thus, even though the starting conditions that existed in the various CEE countries were different, the EU ignored this differentiation during the planning and application of its assistance policy. The Community also indirectly exacerbated these differences by giving equal treatment to countries with unequal conditions. The strict application of the principle of conditionality led to a less favourable treatment for the Balkan countries (as far as time and content of co-operation were concerned).

For example, the aid provided through the Phare program depended on political and economic criteria, which, because of the comparatively worse starting conditions in the Balkan countries, were difficult to materialise concurrently with the other CEE countries. The result was that most of the Balkan countries participated in this program after some delay (or not at all due to political tensions and crises). The amount of aid depended mainly on the size of the population and not on internal needs. Furthermore, at the beginning of the transformation process (1990-92) the EC simply disregarded the fact that the Balkan countries had huge deficits in their balance of payments, a high negative rate of development and the lowest per capita income of all the CEE countries. It also ignored the comparatively higher cost of the re-orientation of their external economic relations. Before 1989 the Balkan countries were largely dependent on trade with non-western European countries (e.g. Bulgaria with the countries of the former Soviet Union, FYROM, and Bosnia-Herzegovina, and Croatia with the FYR), or were closed economies (e.g. Albania, a state with an extremely closed economy).

At the same time the financial aid was not only insufficient compared to the magnitude of the needs, but was also broken down into too many projects, with very few multiplication effects and with high management and information costs. Nor did trade co-operation entail full liberalisation of entry for all the exports of the Balkan countries. An important percentage of the exports from the Balkan countries, and especially of those from the Western Balkans is subject to controls and limitations such as quotas and anti-dumping tariffs (World Bank 2000). Meanwhile, the actual preferential element of the bilateral trade co-operation is of limited value, given that, as mentioned above, most countries of the world already enjoy preferential access to the common market to a greater or lesser degree. For example, because of their comparatively higher competitiveness, the transition countries of Central Europe are much more favoured by the European policy of trade co-operation, while also enjoying more favourable conditions of access to the markets of the EU member countries (e.g. lower transportation costs, more developed infrastructures with cross border connections, revival of old economic, cultural and religious relations, etc.).

On the basis of inflexible terms and conditions, the non-differentiated EU approach to the CEE countries actually produced disparate results. The EU obviously did not perceive well the special circumstances of the Balkan countries, (e.g. the problems of ethnic minorities and nationalism, as well as the importance of the Balkans for the stability, security and economic well-being of all Europe), and failed from the very beginning to develop a regionalized approach. Instead, for example, the EC, finding itself in the process of strengthening its economic and political integration (e.g. negotiations for the Maastricht and then for the Amsterdam Agreements, establishment of a monetary union, etc.) accepted and, to a certain degree, exacerbated the tendencies of disintegration of the former Yugoslavia.

The above-mentioned undifferentiated, yet dissimilar treatment by the EU of the Balkan countries per se (Gligorov, Kaldor and Tsukalis 1999) has created a pyramid of relations. On the bottom of this pyramid are found the least developed countries (e.g. Bosnia-Herzegovina, Albania, FYROM), in the middle are found Bulgaria and Romania, then Turkey, and at the top, Greece. The FYR and Croatia have been outside the pyramid during the 1990s. What this means is that the EU has closer relations with the more developed Balkan countries, and less intense relations with the less developed countries of the region. The latter are simply left to cope with a vicious cycle of underdevelopment and political instability. As a result of this kind of co-operation policy, the EU has been not able to contribute substantially to the breaking of the vicious cycle in which these poorer Balkan countries have been entrapped. Nor have they been able to help promote a new era of peace, stability and prosperity in the region.

The second and most important group of reasons for the lack of progress in the Balkans concerns the countries themselves. As we have already mentioned, the best co-operation policy and transfer of resources, per se, is not enough to launch a country into the orbit of dynamic development. A country must also strive hard to create the necessary conditions for the liberation of its productive forces and the attraction of direct foreign investments (i.e., political stability, legal security, democratic institutions, good governance, functioning price mechanisms and competition, macro-economic stability, a stable and clear institutional framework, realistic exchange rates as well as normal functioning of the markets for goods, labour and capital). Unfortunately, the former socialistic countries of the Balkans are slow to create the above conditions. Therefore, it is not through mere chance that they are well behind the other CEE countries in all the basic economic measures, including, most importantly, in the attraction of foreign investors. On top of this, some Balkan countries (e.g. Bosnia-Herze-govina, Croatia, FYR), instead establishing a market economy and creating new democratic structures which would allow peaceful co-existence among their different minorities, gave priority to the creation of "ethnically cleansed" nation states, with all the well known consequences.

Finally, the Balkan countries have failed to promote co-operation amongst themselves on a political and economic level. Most of them have pursued integration into West European Structures, while at the same time downgrading the importance of creating new Balkan regional co-operation to encourage development through the safeguards of regional stability and peace.

Europe's Reaction in the Aftermath of the Kosovo War

A. The "Wake-up-Call Effect" of the Kosovo War

The crisis in Kosovo exposed the weaknesses of the European co-operation and integration policies of the 1990s, while also exposing the particularities of the area, which had existed even before the NATO military intervention. The direct and indirect costs to the Balkan countries of this crisis, as well as the involvement of the EU, itself, in the war, has emphasised, apart from the above, the importance of the area for European stability, security and pros-perity. For example, at the Special Council of General Affairs in Luxem-bourg (8.4.1999), it was acknowledged that European stability and well-being could not be disconnected from developments in the countries of Southeast Europe (EU Council 1999a). An even livelier Commissioner, Chris Patten, expressed this new EU realisation at the Washington Conference for the Reconstruction of the Balkans (September 1999). He emphasised that "...either Europe exports stability to the Balkans - or the Balkans will export instability to the rest of Europe" (Patten 1999).

By the beginning of the Kosovo crisis, the Balkans had become the main topic of discussion in the EU, in International Organisations (e.g. UN, NATO, OSCE, IMF, World Bank, EBRD), and in other institutions of multilateral or plurilateral economic co-operation (e.g., OECD, ILO, the G 24, the Paris Club, SECI, BSEC).

The Special Council of General Affairs, mentioned above, asked the European Commission to urgently investigate the upgrading of contractual relations between the EU and Albania and FYROM. The upgrading of these relations, as well as the signing of association agreements, was discussed on 27.4.1999 during a meeting between the EU Troika and the Ministers of Foreign Affairs of Albania and FYROM (EU 1999c, 1999b). In addition, both the Special Council on General Affairs on 8.4.1999, as well as the Council on General Affairs on 26.4.1999 (EU Council 1999b), emphasised the necessity for a comprehensive EU intervention in the region after the end of the crisis. This new intervention would be in the form of a Stability Pact. According to the conclusions of the Special Council on General Affairs on 8.4.1999: "South Eastern Europe needs a Stability Pact which would open the door to a long term political and economic stabilisation process. Such a broad based strategy could take advantage of existing regional initiatives" (EU Council 1999a). At the same meeting it was agreed to organise an International Conference on Southeast Europe in Bonn on 27.5.1999. This conference would invite the participation of relevant international organisations and banks, as well as interested countries, to discuss regional stability and the participation of these countries in Euro-Atlantic structures.

B. The Stability Pact for Southeast Europe as a Global Policy Framework

During its EU Presidency, Germany submitted its suggestions (on 9.4.1999) for a Stability Pact in Southeast Europe (Auswartiges Amt 1999). The German plan acknowledged the importance of stability in Southeast Europe for the stability and security of all Europe. It also defined as its goals: the avoidance of violent conflicts in this area in the future, the creation of proper conditions for democracy and a market economy, the establishment of regional co-operation and, finally, the accession of Balkan countries into Euro-

Atlantic structures. The adoption of the Stability Pact occurred at the International Conference of Cologne (10th June 1999), in which all of the interested countries and organisations participated. The basic aim of this conference was to sign bilateral as well as multilateral contracts and intergovernmental agreements, and to ensure their consistent application, in order to overcome structural, political and economic deficiencies, and to reduce or eliminate the potential for conflict in this area.

The Stability Pact consists of eight sections (Stability Pact 1999). The first section states that the participating countries and organisations are bound to co-operate closely to safeguard peace and stability, and to promote the development of Southeast Europe.

The second section outlines the principles and rules of the Pact. The participating countries are bound to the principles and rules of the United Nations Charter, the Final Act of Helsinki, the Paris Charter, OSCE, etc., and agree to respect human rights and the principles of good neighbouring. The Balkan countries participating in the Stability Pact agree to continue their democratic and economic reforms, to promote bilateral and regional co-operation among themselves, and to work towards their accession to the Euro-Atlantic structures.

The third section refers to the targets of the Pact. Generally, the participants agree to support the efforts of the countries in the region to accelerate the attainment of peace, democracy, and a respect for human rights, as well as the attainment of economic prosperity and stability in the region. The more particular aims of the Pact are directed to the avoidance of tensions and crises in the Balkans, the establishment of democratic systems, the creation of market economies and regional economic co-operation, the fighting of crime and corruption, the safe return of refugees, etc. They also emphasise the intention to co-operate directly with the government of Montenegro, and under certain conditions (e.g. democratisation) with Serbia.

The fourth section defines the mechanisms and the instruments of the Pact. In order to materialise the Pact's goals the participants agree to create a "Southeast Europe Regional Discussion Group", which will supervise the course of implementation of the Pact and will be responsible for the promotion and attainment of its targets. The Stability Pact provides for a co-ordinator who will chair the "Regional Group". At the same time it establishes three specialised "working groups": (a) a working group for democratisation and human rights, (b) a working group for economic reconstruction, development and co-operation, and (c) a working group for security issues. For all the above groups the members will be those who participated in the Pact, as well as other interested parties who will serve as full members or observers.

The fifth section of the Pact defines the offices and terms of co-operation among the members. At this point the leading role of the EU is acknowledged, not only for the initiation of the Pact, but also for its implementation. This section also stresses the significance of the efforts and initiatives of the EU for the support of the countries of the region and for the development of contractual relations. More specifically, it gives testimony to the Community strategy for the development of new type of relations among the countries of the Western Balkans. Through the Pact the EU is offering the prospect of accession to the countries of the area on the basis of the Amsterdam Pact and the Copenhagen criteria. Finally, this section defines the functions of all the participating countries and international organisations.

The sixth section stresses the significance of regional co-operation for the stability of Southeast Europe, as well as the useful role of initiatives such as the Organisation for the Black Sea Economic Co-operation (BSEC), the Central European Initiative, the Southeast Europe Co-operation Initiative (SECI), etc.

The seventh section of the Pact describes how international development assistance is rendered. The developed countries and the competent international organisations are bound to support the reconstruction, stabilisation and integration of the region and the Pact makes an appeal to the international community to participate in this effort. It also welcomes the common initiative of the EU and the World Bank for the co-ordination of international assistance. The co-ordination and responsibility for the organising of donor conferences belongs to the EU and the World Bank.

Finally, the eighth section of the Pact defines the function, the working procedures and the role of the different " Working Groups". The main aims of "Working Group II" are: the promotion of co-operation among the Balkan countries, as well as co-operation between them and third countries; the promotion of free trade areas and the development of cross border transportation; support for energy availability and conservation; assistance in the development of infrastructures and for the establishment of deregulation and of transparency, support for the private sector and for the sustainable rehabilitation of refugees, support for environmental issues and for participation in the co-ordination of international development assistance.

The Stability Pact is the first comprehensive regional approach by the international community for the Balkans and it is a product of EU initiatives. The Pact is a long-term programming framework for co-operation and is not one more autonomous international institution. It aims at mobilising and co-ordinating existing agencies of the international community. In other words the Pact is not a new international organisation with its own structures and mechanisms of implementation. The application of measures to help the Balkan countries is the responsibility of the participating countries and organisations. The Pact only offers a special forum for encouragement and energising, a dialogue framework and a channel for action. In addition, the Pact is an expression of the newly formed international concept for coherent and integrated global policies to support peace, freedom, stability, reconstruction and development in the Balkans (Biermann 1999).

There is certainly a great distance between the Pact's ambitions and very broad goals and the limited and vague means which can be employed to achieve these goals and ambitions. The Pact does not refer to specific quantitative targets, does not contain concrete actions and projects and does not record commitments for financial assistance. Furthermore, it does not define the circle of the aid recipient's national, regional and sector targets and allocations. Therefore, the Pact is not a unique approach, nor a coherent plan for the reconstruction of the area, but is rather a political program of hopes and desires, and a framework for potential and voluntary agreements and actions. It is up to the will of the participants to define its effectiveness through periodic, special conferences.

Ten months after its adoption, the Stability Pact had not managed to promote any significant portion of its ambitious plans. If we exclude certain agreements, such as the agreement among the countries of the area to move forward with certain internal reforms that would support local and foreign investments (Investment Compact Agreement), the initiative to fight corruption (Anti-Corruption Initiative), the agreement concerning the mass media (Media Carter) and the establishment of the Working Group on Trade Liberalization and Facilitation, the results were rather limited. This delay could probably be attributed to the fact that the international community gave emphasis to the solution of more important problems in postwar Kosovo. An important step, however, was taken towards the implementation of the proclamations of the Pact at the Donors Conference in Brussels on the 29th and 30th of March 2000. Forty-seven countries and 36 international organizations participated in this conference.

Three reports concerning the strategic approach to the development of the Balkans were produced at the conference: one by the World Bank ("The Road to Stability and Prosperity in Southeastern Europe: A Regional Strategy Paper"), one by the EIB on work to be done on infrastructures ("Basic infrastructure Investments in Southeastern Europe Regional Project review"), and one by the EBRD on the development of the private sector ("International Financial Institutions Regional Private Sector Initiatives in Southeastern Europe"). The financing of three packages was agreed upon by all the participants: a Quick Start Package, whose application is scheduled to begin in the first year (by 31.3.2001), a Near Term Package, to last for 2-3 years after the first package is completed, and a Medium Term Package, for the period after that.

The projects of the Quick Term Package, with a cost amounting to 1.7 billion Euros, and with pledges by the donors for 2.4 billion Euros, will cover a number of activities from all three Working Groups of the Pact (see Table 6). In addition, the conference defined the programs of the two other packages along with their financial needs, even though there remains a great need for detailed analyses and estimates for the Medium Term Package. At this point we should mention that Kosovo and Montenegro are included in the group of recipient countries. Also, it should be mentioned that the Programs of the Near Term Package, and even more those of the Medium Package evidence important financial gaps.

C. The New European Regional Approach: The Stabilization and Association Process for the Countries of the Western Balkans

Following a proposal made by the European Council (26.5.1999), the EU adopted a new regional approach for the Western Balkans, the so-called "Stabilization and Association Process" (SAP). This approach aims at the protection of peace and stability, the fostering of economic development, and the improvement of the conditions for the region's accession into European structures. In other words, it is a new attempt to transcend previous individual and fragmented approaches by applying decisions and statements of already existing EU proposals which are aimed at an overall regional approach (e.g. the Regional Approach of the General Affairs Council of 26 February 1996, Conclusions of European Council Meetings in Vienna, December 1998). This new strategy recognizes that whatever differences these countries may have among themselves, they also have common and interrelated problems that require a total regional approach.

The SAP is considered by EU officials to be their most important contribution to the attainment of the aims of the Stability Pact. The basic instruments of the SAP are:

• The Stabilization and Association Agreements (SAA). These are similar in content to the "European Agreements". They presuppose the fulfillment of well-defined political and economic terms (Application of Conditionality, Annex III, to the Council of General Affairs' Conclusions - Luxembourg, 29-30 April 1997). Included in these terms is the obligation of the FYR, Croatia and Bosnia-Herzegovina to apply the agreements of Dayton and Paris, as well as to contribute to the promotion intra-regional co-operation. In order to be effective the SAAs must be tailor-made to the special situation of each partner country. Before the opening of negotiations there must be a report (feasibility study) prepared for each individual country concerning the fulfillment of political and economic terms. For FYROM a report has already been made. This report has reached some very positive conclusions, thus launching the opening of negotiations (March 2000). On the other hand, the report for Albania has concluded that it is well behind in fulfilling certain political and economic criteria. Finally, signing a SAA does not require that a country had previously signed a "first generation agreement" (i.e. a trade or/and economic co-operation agreement) or a "European Agreement".

• Not signing a SAA, however, does not deprive the countries of the area of the ability to enjoy, even to a lesser extent, other benefits of the Community's preferential trade treatment through, for example, Autonomous Trade Preferences; the receipt of financial, technical, economic and critical aid; and/or political co-operation and dialogue, even when they do not fully comply with the necessary political and economic prerequisites.

Special treatment by the EU of the whole region of the Western Balkans, the most fragile area in all Europe, after a period of ten years may be considered as a positive development. The prospect of association first and accession later, serves as an incentive for these countries to introduce faster reforms such as democratization, rule of law, respect for human rights and ethnic minorities, a market economy, as well as the development of intra-regional co-operation.

The custom shaping of the SAA's will allow the intervention means to

Table 6 Summary of Funding Requirements in Euros for the Stability Pact Quick Start Package

	Euro
Cross-Table Initiatives	
Activities	**TOTAL**
Anti-corruption Initiative	1,800,000
Trauma and Reconciliation in SEE	2,500,000
Social Development Initiative	860,000
TOTAL	5,160,000
Working Table I	
Activities	**TOTAL**
Human Rights and Minorities	6,950,223
Good Governance	
Public Administration	1,555,700
LocalGovernment	1,253,800
Ombudsman	229,000
Gender	896,368
Media	11,827,300
Parliamentary Exchange	869,740
Education	11,601,842
Szeged Process	1,500,000
SUBTOTAL	36.683.973
Refugees/Displaced Persons [1]	218,400,000
TOTAL	255,083,973
Working Table II	
Activities	**TOTAL**
Infrastructure [2]	1.131,000,000
Private Sector Development [3]	290,000,000
Investment Compact	2,000,000
Environment	19,550,000
Vocational Education and Training	6,532.000
TOTAL	1,449,082,000
Working Table III	
Activities	**TOTAL**
Defense and Security	67.021,487
Justice and Home Affairs	10,796,118
TOTAL	77,817.605
Aggregate Total	
Activities	**TOTAL**
Cross Table Activities	5,160,000
Working Table I	255,083,973
Working Table II	1,449,082,000
Working Table III	77,817,605
TOTAL	1,787.143,578

1 162.9 M. Euros will be financed by the European Commission, 20 M. Euros by the Netherlands (for minority returns in BiH), 17 M. Euros by Germany, 18.5 M. Euros by the US. Other bilateral pledges are expected at the Conference.

2 The EIB report includes three categories of projects: Projects for Quick Start amounting to EURO 1.131M. Euros. Near term Projects amounting to 2.735 M. Euros and Medium Term Projects (no figures given).

3 EBRD report includes two categories of projects: Projects for Quick Start amounting to 290 M. Euros and Near Term Projects amounting to 150 M. Euros.

Source: EU and World Bank, http://www.seerecon.org.

be adjusted to the different internal conditions and needs, without creating discrimination and fragmentation. The prospect for integration into the structures of the EU is open to all the countries of the region. The fulfillment of political and economic terms, and the fostering of cooperation between the EU and any one country, is expected to cause demonstration effects, and to influence positively the efforts of other countries in the region. The possibility of developing somewhat closer relations with the EU, without the full materialization of conditionality, may enable the Balkan countries to enter more quickly into Stabilization and Association Agreements (World Bank 2000).

Further Steps for the Fuller Integration of Southeast European Countries into the EU

All the above proposals, ideas and initiatives illustrate vividly the particular Balkan circumstances. They demonstrate the importance of the Balkans for overall European stability, and even more the need for a total solution to the problems of the region. Furthermore, any solution must take place within the framework of a multilateral initiative, in which Europe would play the leading role. Fortunately, there seems to be a convergence of opinion as to the direction of a future regional approach. The main objectives of this approach are: support for democratization, economic reconstruction and restructuring, and the accession of the Balkan countries into European and international institutions.

Of major importance in the economic field is the future development and formation of Balkan relations with the EU, to be assisted by international financial assistance or by what is commonly known as a small "Marshal Plan" for the Balkans. At this point we should emphasize that the relations of the Balkan countries in transition with the EU are much more important than any international financial assistance. These relations cover a wide spectrum of themes (e.g. trade, economic, technical, institutional, political and cultural co-operation, etc). Therefore closer Euro-Balkan relations may offer overall support for the transition process, and create realistic conditions for economic growth (e.g. access to a large market, without which countries with small, open economies cannot develop; the introduction of institutional reforms and modernization; etc.). For example, financial assistance from the EU is mostly in the form of grants. In addition, as mentioned above, the EU is a reference point, and the ultimate destination towards which all attempts at political and economic reform in the Balkans are directed.

International financing organizations generally offer loans on rather attractive conditions, which, if used only for consumption purposes, undermine the future development and stability of the recipient countries. Therefore, financing through the international organizations should be considered as a necessary but not sufficient condition for a sustainable economic development, as has been verified by the experience of most developing countries. Thus, in order to establish the conditions for a full integration of the Balkan countries into Europe, the following are required (apart from the above mentioned actions and initiatives).

A. Enhancement of Contractual Relations and Strengthening of Trade Integration

The prospect of signing a SAA between the EU and the countries of the Western Balkans without a prior signing of first generation agreements for some of them (e.g. Croatia, Bosnia-Herzegovina, FYR), plus entrance into the "waiting room" for accession is certainly a positive response by the EU to the problems of the region. Apart from the positive impact of the prospect of association, the SAA has covered all the important sectors of co-operation by offering asymmetric trade relations (i.e. the ability of the Balkan partners to delay the opening of their markets to imports from the EU). These are useful tools for promoting bilateral integration.

Most countries of the Western Balkans do yet not fulfill all the political and economic criteria for the signing of an SAA with the EU. Considering the fact that the negotiations and ratification of such agreements by the national parliaments of the EU member countries is a particularly time-consuming process (taking up to 3 years), the EU could offer full trade liberalization for Balkan exports of industrial and processed agricultural products, and a substantial increase in the quotas for unprocessed agricultural goods. The further opening of the EU market could take the form of autonomous trade preferences on the basis of bilateral agreements. The low percentage of EU imports from the transition Balkan countries (less than 1% of the total Community imports) means that there will not be any strongly felt consequences for EU producers (Gros 1999).

In order to avert any trade diversions, the trade preferences of the EU should be applied equally to each of the recipient countries of the Balkans.

The rate of liberalization of the external economy of the Balkan countries should not be faster than the liberalization of their internal economy, as has been the case with Bulgaria and Romania. Otherwise, external competition will annul the effectiveness, or increase the cost of internal state intervention. Thus, internal liberalization must progress faster than external liberalization, so that the economy is able to face external competition.

At this point, two more specific questions may be posed for further investigation: First, the question of regional economic integration in the Balkans, and, second, the issue of the accession of the Balkan countries to the international trade order.

Economic integration within the Balkans is at a very low level. For example intra-regional trade is on average small, at 12-14% of the total (World Bank 2000). On a bilateral level there have been several specific attempts at trade integration, such as the agreement for the creation of a Free Trade Area (FTA) between Croatia and Slovenia, Croatia and FYROM, Slovenia and FYROM, FYROM and Bulgaria, and FYROM and FYR (before the embargo). None of these agreements has the endorsement of the WTO, in other words, these agreements have not been "multi-lateralized". If we exclude Bulgaria and Romania, no other transition Balkan country is a full member of the WTO, although all of them have applied for membership.

This, combined with the different rate at which trade relations have been established with the EU, has resulted in multiple trade regimes. In such a small region as the Balkans this causes uncertainty and reduced transparency. It also causes discriminatory treatment for non-participating countries. This further fragments the Balkans, and keeps them from taking full advantage of regional economic integration. Meanwhile, the Balkan markets are small. They have low per capita incomes and great similarities in their structures of production. They lack cross-border trade infrastructures and experience continuing political frictions. Thus, the economic advantages of intra-regional economic integration in the Balkans would not replace the benefits of integration with EU. Nonetheless, a more intensive regional economic integration could have a positive impact on political stabilization and co-operation. (Gligorov, Kaldor and Tsoukalis 1999, Dauderstadt 1999, World Bank 2000.)

The importance of regional economic integration is recognized in the Stability Pact. Also the European Commission considers the establishment of a regional free trade area and closer regional economic cooperation as prerequisites for integration into the EU, and as a condition for the signing of SAA's (World Bank 2000, p. 61).

Such a regional integration policy could take the form of a Free Trade Area (Southeast Europe Free Trade Area, SEFTA) or a tariff union (Southeast Europe Tariff Union, SETU). The President of the European Commission, Mr. Pronti, also has suggested the creation of a Balkan tariff union and its future absorption into the EU (World Bank 2000, p. 61). Albania, FYROM, Bulgaria, Romania, Croatia and Bosnia-Herzegovina could participate initially, and, at a later stage (after its democratization), the FYR. A SETU would not only promote the static and dynamic advantages of regional integration and attract foreign investments, it would also be an important step towards political dialogue and political co-operation in the region. At the same time, the EU could proceed in signing a "European Agreement", or an SAA, with the SETU replacing existing bilateral agreements among individual countries. The future enlargement of the EU towards Southeastern Europe would absorb all of the SETU. Very likely, certain countries in the region would not see their participation in a SETU in a positive light. These are countries which already have more advanced relations with the EU (e.g. Bulgaria and Romania), or which, for historical, geographical and political reasons, reject their Balkan identity (e.g. Croatia). However, the previous upgrading of conventional relations with the other countries of the area would restore the balance and would equalize the prospects of accession to the EU. Even more, because of its substantially higher level of development and competitiveness as compared to the other Balkan countries in transition, Croatia could be excluded from the SETU in order to avoid intense development divergences and competitive asymmetries within the SETU[1]. In order to promote the above idea, the EU could supply technical and economic assistance. Also the EU could support cooperation and the development of cross-border infrastructures. It could establish a Development Fund for the SETU countries and declare that, in the second stage of the enlargement, all the SETU countries would access en block, something which, in any case, could not take place before the year 2015. Also, the adoption of the community's "aquis" by all the Balkan countries would indirectly contribute to the harmonization of their economic systems and to the creation of similar institutional frameworks in the member countries of SETU[2].

The suggestion by CEPS (the Centre for European Policy Studies) (CEPS1999, Gros 1999) for the establishment of a tariff union between transition Balkan countries and EU, should be considered as second best. First, the creation of a Tariff Union, as the example of Turkey has shown, is a particularly time-consuming process. Second, the adoption by the Community of external trade status for the Balkan countries would greatly increase external competition for the Balkans, just at the moment when they are restructuring and reconstructing their economies. On the other hand, co-operation through a bilateral Tariff Union (between the EU and the Balkans) would be less helpful than a "European Agreement" (or an SAA). The latter would contain elements of a preferential trade treatment as well as more extended economic and financing co-operation. Even more, within the SETU framework, or even irrespective of it, a Balkan Monetary System with fixed exchange rates could be established. This would avoid competitive devaluations and would free up long-term capital movements. The Balkan countries could either bind their currency exchange rates to the Euro through a "Currency Board" (see the latest successful case of Bulgaria and the very drastic reduction of inflation in that country), or they could agree to institute other exchange rate systems (e.g. "crawling peg" or "managed floating")[3].

At the same time, all the Balkan countries should become members of the WTO, the Bretton Woods Agreement, and OECD. They should seek access into the WTO as developing countries, in order to enjoy the special status and the privileges provided for its less developed member countries (Langlammer and Luecke 1999). The other members of the Stability Pact, in addition to the EU, could in turn offer the Balkan countries autonomous tariff preferences.

B. Increase of Financial Assistance and the Proposal for a New "Marshal Plan" for Southeast Europe

As mentioned above, the financial assistance given in the 1990s was insufficient to deal with the magnitude of the economic problems, especially under the political conditions existing in the area. The same was true for the decision of the Brussels Funding Conference. The breaking of the vicious circle of underdevelopment and political instability in the Balkans would presuppose an integrated approach, as well as a generous and cohesive plan for financial assistance. Reconstruction would imply the re-creation of destroyed fixed assets, which would, in turn, enhance the potential for economic growth in the primary stages. In contrast, funding for the Balkan countries (with the exception of Bosnia-Herzegovina and FRY), has been aimed primarily at the restructuring of their inefficient production systems, a process that has entailed the partial destruction of the fixed assets created during socialism. To a certain degree this explains the negative growth rates which appeared during the primary stages of the transformation process in all the former socialistic countries. Beyond this, there is a much larger comparative deficit in technology and know-how in the Balkan countries, as well as a deficit in other institutions and in experience with democracy and the market economy.

For all the above reasons, financial assistance to the transition Balkan countries within the framework of a "small Marshal Plan" must be proportionately more substantial than the assistance allocated to the destroyed countries of Western Europe during the period 1948-52 under the U.S. Marshal Plan. It should be mentioned that under this Plan, certain countries received high annual assistance for up to five years (e.g. Greece about 8.8% of its annual GDP, Austria 7.2%, Holland 5%, Ireland 3.4%, France 2.5%, Turkey 2.3%, Denmark 2%, etc.) (Kostrzewa, Nunnenkam and Scmieding 1990). Thus, as in the case of the American Marshal Plan, it would be preferable to offer a substantial amount of assistance in a comparatively short period of time in order to give a positive shock to the economy and, thus quickly create the proper conditions for development. Financial assistance offered in small amounts for a prolonged period of time merely acts as a pain reliever.

The Balkan countries need funding mainly for investments in infrastructure, for investments in the three sectors of production, as well as for the modernization of the state and the public administration. Assistance allocated to the Balkan countries during the 1990s was rather limited. This was particularly true for those countries neighboring Kosovo, which also are the poorest. Assistance allocated in 1999, for example, was aimed more at the easing of the consequences of the Kosovo crisis and less at the assistance for a strategic plan for reconstruction and development (Table 7). In order to increase national savings, this assistance should to some degree emphasize co-funding. Let us not forget that American assistance under the Marshal Plan was not totally free. The Community's experience with the planning and implementation of its Structural Funds could be used as an example.

Table 7 Overall EC Assistance to Kosovo's Neighbouring Countries in 1999 (in millions of Euro)[1]

	Albania	Bosnia-Herzeg.	Croatia	FRY	FYROM	Multi-County	TOTAL
PHARE + OBNOVA	118.5	146.0	15.0	23.5	68.7	2.8	374.5
Humanitarian Aid (ECHO)	7.0	56.4	5.0	7.6	-	182.0	258.0
Food Security (DGVIII)	5.7	-	-	-	-	-	5.7
Balance of payment Support (DG II)	20.0	60.0	-	-	-	-	80.0
EIB	n.a.	n.a.	-	-	-	-	0.0
Other Actions		10.0	1.4	0.5	0.5	2.0	14.4
Total EC Assistance	151.2	272.4	21.4	31.6	69.2	186.8	732.6

1 Indicative allocation.

n.a. = not available.

Source: European Commission - DG 1A.

Suggestively (see Table 8), by considering the amount of assistance by the American Marshal Plan to Greece (8.8% of the annual Greek GDP for four years), assistance to the Balkan countries (except the FYR and Kosovo, for which the amount required for its complete reconstruction cannot be estimated exactly) should amount to $28.584 million and should be allocated over a short period of time (e.g. 4-5 years). Based on the percentage of assistance by the Marshal Plan to all the recipient countries (2.1% of GNP for all the recipient countries annually), a total amount of $6.820 billion should be committed. If we take into account the percentage of assistance of the Community to the cohesion countries (about 3% of the GDP annually), the amount would increase to a total of $9.744 billion. In the latter two cases, the amount of assistance might not equal the real needs of the Balkan countries.

Table 8 Alternative Funding Scenarios for Balkan Countries Based on a "Marshal Plan" Percentage (1948-52) and EU Structural Policy (in mil. $)

Countries	Total GDP (1998)	Scenario 1 8,8% GDP	4 years	Scenario 2 2,1% GDP	4 years	Scenario 3 3%GDP	4 years
Albania	2,500	220	880	52	208	75	300
FYROM	3,650	321	1,249	77	308	109	436
Bosnia	3,800	334	1,338	80	320	114	456
Croatia	20,500	1,804	7,216	430	1,720	615	2,460
Bulgaria	12,780	1,125	4,498	268	1,072	383	1,532
Romania	38,165	3,358	13,434	801	3,204	1,145	4,580
TOTAL	81,395	7,162	28,615	1,708	6,832	2,441	9,764

Scenario 1: On the basis of annual transfers under the "Marshal Plan" in Greece (8,8% of Greek GDP).
Scenario 2: On the basis of annual transfers under the "Marshal Plan" in all recipient countries (2,1% of their GDP).
Scenario 3: On the basis of annual transfers of EU cohesion countries.

The criteria for the geographical allocation of financial assistance should be based on the level of development and the political and social problems of the recipient countries (as was the case with the American plan).This would allow a bigger development push in the less developed Balkan countries. We should also consider the fact that the consequences of the crisis in Kosovo vary widely from country to country. Thus, based on the criteria of: (a) the level of development (b) the intensity of the consequences of the crisis and (c) the more general political and economic conditions existing in each of the Balkan countries, a first indicative approach concerning the financial needs of each country is offered (Table 9). For the six Balkan countries, and for a period of at least five years (2000-2004), the allocation of substantial extra assistance is suggested. After this period of time assistance would return to existing levels. The lowest recommended financial assistance for the six countries would total 21.425 billion Euros (Albania 1.250 billion, FYROM 1.825 billion, Bosnia-Herzegovina 3.800 billion, Croatia 3.075 billion, Bulgaria 3.634 billion and Romania 9.541 billion Euros). The situation in the of FYR (including Kosovo) is different because of heavy war damages and the urgent need for its fast accession into the international community. Therefore, the assistance to this country should be higher than to the other countries, and should, at a minimum, amount to

15% of its 1998 GNP, for a total of 11.932 billion Euros for the first five years following the war.

Table 9 Proposed Funding Assistance

Countries	Total GDP (1998) in mil. Euro	Per capita Income (1998) in Euro	GDP decrease Due to crisis (%)	Annual funding Assistance % GDP	Annual funding Assistance in mil. Euro	Total 5 years Funding In mil. Euro
Albania	2,500	750	2	10	250	1,250
FYROM	3,650	1,765	5	10	365	1,825
Bosnia	3,800	1,187	5	10	380	1,900
Croatia	20,500	4,500	1	3	615	3,075
Bulgaria	12,780	1,554	2	6	767	3,834
Romania	38,165	1,696	0.5	5	1,908	9,541
FYR	15,910	1,510	25	15	2,386	11,932
Total					6,671	33,355

Sources: WIIW and own estimations.

Apart from this, these countries suffer from the pressing problems that the accumulated foreign debt creates. Thus these debts should be politically restructured within the framework of the Club of Paris (for the public debt), the Club of London (for the banking debt), as well as within the framework of international banks and financial organizations. Otherwise, the net capital inflow will be very low. The conversion of this debt to a long term (at least ten years), with a remission period (at least two years) is of vital importance.

At this point we should stress that the anticipated assistance by the EU, especially in the case of accession of a country to the first circle, will widen the gap among the CEE countries. Thus, for the period 2000-2006, for example, 58.070 million Euros is proportioned against 61 million people in the six candidate countries (following a possible enlargement in 2002), while only 15.600 million Euros would be offered to the seven Balkan countries, two Baltic countries (Lithuania and Latvia) and Slovakia, with a total population of 67 million people, and with a much lower average per capita income and a lot more transformation difficulties.

The Marshal Plan of 1948-52 was funded solely by the USA, given that at that time there were no other countries that could put up any funds. (This plan was probably not as costly as might appear, since the USA imposed a kind of industrial, agricultural and general export promotion policy by tying the use of assistance to the import of American products.) The European funds for reconstruction and development of the Balkans could derive from the restructuring of funds from the Phare program and the two new structural actions for accession candidates (22.400 million Euros for the 2002-2006 period). A total amount of about 8 billion Euros should go to the six Balkan countries, if we were to consider population as a criterion for allocation (the population of the 6 Balkan countries amounts to 37% of the population of the CEE countries). In addition, if the five central European countries were ultimately to become members of the EU in 2002, then the total framework of financial assistance for non-EU members of the CEE countries (the "outs") would increase substantially, given that the additional cost of the new enlargement has already been guaranteed (58.070 million Euros for the years 2002-2006). Should the EU allocate funds from the Phare program and both of its new structural initiatives on the basis of the level of development of each CEE country, as well as on the basis of the degree of difficulty of the transformation process, combined with the fact that the assistance would be allocated over seven years (2000-2006), then the total amount of assistance for the Balkans would reach about 10 billion Euros. This amount could increase substantially (e.g. by 4-5 billion Euro's annually), should the EU increase the annual percentage of its own committed resources by 0.3% of the community GDP, which would still leave a significant margin before reaching the upper limit of 1.27% (CEPS 1999). In any case, further assistance of at least $10 billion by other G 24 or other third-party countries, as well as loans from the EIB, the World Bank Group, the EBRD and the IMF, would have to be added to Community assistance, if the needs of the six and the FRY (as well as Kosovo), are to be covered.

In order to avoid overlapping coverage, contradictory targets, or discriminatory treatment, funding of the reconstruction and development of the Balkan countries should be implemented on the basis of an overall strategic plan for the region, as well as one for each country separately. Otherwise, as the experience since 1996 in Bosnia-Herzegovina has shown, as well as that gained from the 10 months following the war in Kosovo, any financial assistance given will be characterized by a lack of coordination, by fragmentation, by overlapping, by connections (of bilateral assistance to national export goals), by a misallocation of resources, and by an attack only on the symptoms. On the other hand, the most generous financial assistance policy will always be highly ineffective if the recipient countries don't manifest requisite political stability, good governance, macroeconomic stability, economic freedom and a well-functioning market system. For this reason, stress should be given to the creation of appropriate new institutions and to administrative reforms in the Balkan countries. Also, Balkan enterprises should be preferred over the enterprises of donor countries where public procurements and contracts associated with the implementation of assistance projects are concerned. In addition, the phenomenon of "rent seeking", i.e., giving up productive activities and pursuing access to foreign aid funds, should be discouraged (Dauderstadt 1999).

Finally, we should take into consideration that, contrary to the first years following World War II, the countries of the Balkans have to restructure and adjust to an intensely internationalized economic environment with an ever-increasing free circulation of products, services, capital and other factors of production. The integration of the countries of the region into the new international economy offers opportunities and challenges as well. These include opportunities for fund raising and the attraction of foreign direct investments, for the exploitation of comparative and dynamic advantages, for the import of technology and know-how, for the introduction of institutional reforms, etc. Challenges include such things as intensive external trade and investment competition, a growing number of international financial crises, and the restricted ability to exercise an autonomous economic policy. All of this should be carefully considered during the planning and implementation of the widely discussed policies for the restructuring of the Balkan countries in transition.

Notes

1 Quite indicative is the fact that in 1998, in spite of the problems that the conflict with Serbia and the war in Bosnia-Herzegovina caused to Croatia, its per capita GDP was at least five times larger than that of Albania, and three times as much as Romania's.

2 Certainly the trade benefits resulting from the opening of the large European market to the exports from the Balkan countries in transition are much more important than those resulting from the Southeast Europe Tariff Union (SETU). The economies of those countries have been continuously oriented towards the EU. Already, their trade with the EU is about ten times as much as the trade among themselves. This does not necessarily imply that there are not important margins for the further development of intra-regional trade within the framework of SETU and its integrated market of roughly 63 million people. Of major importance would be another SETU which would include the new countries in the region that have resulted from the breakup of the former Yugoslavia, as this would rehabilitate former close economic relations. This suggested SETU would undoubtedly support the development of the area, though its main importance would be

to improve political co-operation and stability. At the same time, a SETU is not being suggested as a substitute for the European integration of the Balkan countries, but as a complement.

3 In its proposal for the establishment of a post-war system in Southeast Europe, CEPS (The Center for European Policy Studies) recommends binding the national currencies of the Balkan countries in transition to the Euro as an interim solution (until the Euro circulation). This would take place in the framework of a currency system (Currency Board) that would be in effect until the replacement of national currencies with the Euro ("Euroisation"). In order to cover the necessary reserves of the Balkan Central Banks, CEPS suggests that the EU put up interest free reserves, and cover the cost (interest) of the loans through the Community budget (CEPS 1999, Gros 1999). At this point, however, we should stress that this particular exchange rate system would entail the total loss of national control over monetary policy, which could, as the Argentine case has shown, cause a strong recession because of the reduction in internal monetary liquidity. For this reason, some have suggested that the Currency Board be avoided, and that a better solution would be a system of fixed rates with wide margins of fluctuation (e.g., plus or minus 15%), along with the ability to realign official parities (Orlowski 1998).

References

Agh, A. (1998) *Emerging Democracies in East Central Europe and the Balkans*, Cheltenham and Northampton: Edward Elgar.

Auswartiges Amt (1999) *Ein Stabilitatspakt fur Sudeuropa*, Bonn.
[http://www.auswaertiges-amt.de/6_archiv/inf-kos/hintergr/stabdt.htm]

Biermann, R. (1999) The Stability Pact for South Eastern Europe - potential, problems and perspectives, *Center for European Integration Studies, Discussion Paper*, C 56, Bonn.

Bruecker, H. (1997) Europaische Union: Osterweiterung beschleunigt Konvergenz, *DIW Wochenbericht 14/97*, Berlin.

CEPS (1999) A System for Post-War South East Europe, *Working Document* No. 131, Brussels.

Dauderstadt, M. (1999) Neuordnung und Wiederaufbau in Sudosteuropa, *Friedrich Ebert Stiftung, Politikinformation Osteuropa 81*, Bonn.

EBRD (1997) *Technical Cooperation Commitments*, London.
[http://www.ebrd.com/english/opera/Tc/go8.htm]

EBRD(1998a) *EBRD activities in Albania*, London.
[http:/www.ebrd.com/english/opera/Country/albafact.htm]

EBRD (1998b) *EBRD activities in Bosnia and Herzegovina*, London.
[http://www.ebrd.com/english/opera/Country/bosnfact.htm]

EBRD (1998c) *EBRD activities in Bulgaria*, London.
[http://www.ebrd.com/english/opera/Country/bulgfact.htm]

EBRD (1998d) *EBRD activities in Romania*, London.
[http://www.ebrd.com/english/opera/Country/romafact.htm]

EBRD (1998e) *EBRD activities in FYR Macedonia*, London.
[http://www.ebrd.com/english/opera/Country/fyrmfact.htm]

EBRD (1998f) *EBRD activities in Croatia*, London.
[http://www.ebrd.com/english/opera/Country/croafact.htm]

European Commission (1997) Phare: *Une Evaluation Interimaire, Rapport de Synthese*, Brussels.

European Commission (1998a) *Evaluation of the Phare "Essential Aid" Programme for Bosnia and Herzegovina*, Brussels.

European Commission (1998b) *Proposal for a Council Regulation (EC) on Community Support for Pre-accession Measures for Agriculture and Rural Development in the Applicant Countries of Central and Eastern Europe in the Pre-accession Period*, Doc. 598PC0153, Brussels.

European Commission (1998c) *Agricultural Situation and Prospects in the Central and Eastern European Countries, Summary Report*, Working Document, Brussels.

European Commission (1999a) *What is OBNOVA?*,
[http://europa.eu.int/comm/dg1a/obnova/index.htm]

European Commission (1999b) *Amended Proposal for a Council Regulation (EC) on Coordinating Aid to the Applicant Countries in the Framework of the Pre-accession Strategy*, Doc. 598C0551, Brussels.

European Commission (1999c) *Regular Report from the Commission on Progress towards Accession by each of the Candidate Countries, Composite Paper*, Brussels.

EU Council (1998) Council Conclusions on Conditionality, *Bulletin EU 4-1998*, Brussels.

EU Council (1999a) *(special) General Affairs, Council Conclusions-Kosovo, Luxembourg (08-04-1999)*,
[http:europa.eu.int/news/kosovo2-en.htm]

EU Council (1999b) General Affairs, Provisional Version, Press Release, Luxembourg (26-04-1999), Nr. 7561/99.

EU (1994a) Europe Agreement establishing an Association between the European Communities and their Member States, of the one part, and the Republic of Bulgaria, of the other part, *Official Journal No. L 358, 31/12/1994*, pp. 2-222.

EU (1994b) Europe Agreement establishing an Association between the European Communities and their Member States, of the one part, and Romania, of the other part, *Official Journal No. L 357, 31/12/1994*, pp. 2-189.

EU (1999a) *Berlin European Council 24 and 25 March 1999, presidency Conclusions*, Press release, Brussels (25-03-1999), Nr. sn 100.

EU (1999b) EU *Troika-Macedonia: Political Dialogue Meeting/Joint Statement*, Press release: Luxembourg (27-04-1999), Nr. 7565/99.

EU (1999c) EU *Troika- Albania: political Dialogue meeting/ Joint Statement*, Press release: Luxembourg (27-04-99), Nr. 7546/99.

Fisher, St., S. Ratna and C. A. Vegh (1998) How Far Is Eastern Europe from Brussels?, *IMF Working Paper 98/53*, Washington, D.C.

Gligorov, Vl., M. Kaldor and L. Tsoukalis (1999) *Balkan Reconstruction and European Integration*, The Hellenic Observatory, The European Institute, LSE, The Centre for the Staudy of Global Governance, LSE and The Vienna Insitute for International Economic Studies.

Gros, D. (1999) An Economic System for Post-War-South Europe, *Companion paper to the CEPS Working Document* No. 131, CEPS, Brussels.

Henriot, A. and A. Inotao (1998) What Future for the Integration of the European Union and the Central and Eastern European Countries?, *BRIE Working Paper 127*.

Jackson, M. and G. Petrakos (1999) Opening to the EU, Competitiveness and Structural Change in the Industry of Transition Economies, *Phare-ACE Project P-96-6071-R*, Volos.

Kohler, W. (1998) Fifty Years Later: A New Marshall Plan for Eastern Europe?, Working Paper No. 9814, *Institut Fuer Volkswirtschaftslehre, Linz University,* Linz.

Kostrzewa, W., P. Nunnenkamp and H. Schmieding (1990) A Marshall Plan for Middle and Eastern Europe, *The World Economy,* Vol. 13, No. 1, pp. 27-49.

Kramer, H. (1991) *Die "Europaeischen Abkommen" fuer die Assoziation der mittel- und suedosteuropaeischen Staaten mit der EG: Ein Baustein der neuen Architektur Europas?,* SWP-IP2710, Ebenhausen.

Langhammer, R.J. and M. Luecke (1999) WTO Accession Issues, *Kiel Working Paper No. 905,* Kiel Institute of World Economics, Kiel.

Lippert, B. (1990) Etappen der EG-Osteuropapolitik: Distanz-Kooperation-Assozierung, *INTEGRATION, 13, Jg., 3/90,* pp. 111-125.

Messerlin, P. (2000) *Measuring the Costs of Protection in Europe,* Institute for International Economics, Washington, D.C.

Orlowski, L. T. (1998) Economic Conditions of Accession of the East European Transforming Economies to the European Union: A Policy Proposal, in I. Zloch-Christy (ed.), *Eastern Europe and the World Economy,* Cheltenham and Northhampton: Edward Elgar, pp. 123-151.

Patten, Ch. (1999) *Remarks, Conference on Economic Reconstruction in the Balkans,* Washington, September 24.
[http://www. Seerecon.org/Calendar/patten.htm]

Petrakos, G. and S. Totev (2000) Economic Structure and Change in the Balkan Region: Implications for Integration, Transition and Economic Cooperation, *International Journal of Urban and Regional Research,* Vol. 24, No. 1, pp. 95-113.

Siebert, H. (1997) Reintegrating the Reform Countries into the World Economy, *Kiel Working Paper No. 829,* Institut fuer Weltwirtschaft, Kiel *Stability Pact for South Eastern Europe, 1999.*
[http://www.seerecon.org/KeyDocuments/KD1999062401.htm]

UN/ECE (1999), Economic Survey for Europe.

Welfens, P. J.J. (1999) Economic Aspects of the Eastern Enlargement of the European Union, *Bericht des BIOst Nr. 7/99,* Koeln.

Weise, Ch. H. Bruecker u.a. (1997) Ostmitteleuropa auf dem Weg in die EU, *DIW Beitrage zur Strukturforschung, Heft 167,* Berlin.

World Bank (2000) *The Road to Stability and Prosperity in South Eastern Europe: A Regional Strategy Paper,* Washington, D.C.

PART II:
CASE STUDIES

10 Peripherality and Integration: The Experience of Greece and its Implications for the Balkan Economies in Transition

GEORGE PETRAKOS
Associate Professor, Department of Planning and Regional Development, University of Thessaly, Greece

CHRISTOS PITELIS
Associate Professor, Department of Economics, University of Athens, Greece and Director, Centre of International Business and Management, University of Cambridge

Introduction

The purpose of this paper is to present the integration experience of Greece, a country that is peripheral to the European Union (EU) centre in both geographical and economic terms. This experience may be useful to the other Balkan countries with similar characteristics, which entered in the early 1990s a phase of restructuring, marketization and openness of their economies, in their effort to gradually integrate with the EU. In the next section, we present the basic theoretical issues of the integration and convergence literature. In section 3 we analyse, using time-series and cross-section data, the most important aspects of the economic performance and structural change of Greece, using the EU as a measure of comparison and discuss its integration experience, especially during the last 20 years. Finally, in section 4 we draw our conclusions and discuss policy implications for the Balkan transition economies.

Economic Integration and Convergence

The early theory of international trade indicated until recently, that trade between countries can be beneficial to all parties involved, provided that they specialise in products where they face the least comparative disadvantage (Ricardian Theory), or the lowest opportunity cost (Heckscher-Ohlin Theory). Few exceptions for protectionism were allowed, notably in cases of "infant industries". These benefits of specialisation and exchange, that occurred in the form of lower production cost and higher consumption and welfare levels for all parties, have been the ground on which free-trade policies and policies of economic integration have been justified. Simply stated, the formation of trade and economic unions among countries in a geographical region (for example Europe), based upon the elimination of tariffs and all barriers to trade and factor movements, will be to the advantage of all participating country-members.

In recent years, this belief has been seriously questioned on various grounds. First, the economic development of Japan and the countries of the Far East has been based on building competitive advantages rather than relying on existing ones and on reliance on managed, as opposed to free, trade (Pitelis 1994).

Second, recent developments in the theory of international trade question the assumption of efficiently operating, perfectly competitive markets and explicitly recognise the existence of imperfectly competitive markets and increasing returns. Under these conditions, it is possible that countries with high return industries can do better than others, raising the possibility for strategic trade policies practised by governments. These policies, that can take the form of subsidies, tax relief, and protectionism in support of domestic firms that generate positive externalities, make the extreme pro-free trade position unattainable (Krugman 1986).

The "new" theory of international trade has further implications related to issues such as the EU enlargement, integration and convergence. It is now widely recognised that imperfect competition can result in adverse effects, namely in an uneven distribution of benefits from trade, including the possibility of some countries being net losers (Krugman 1987, 1991, 1994). This uneven distribution of benefits can come about through the existence of excess returns in imperfectly competitive industries, as countries with high return industries can benefit at the expense of others.

Further problems identified by Krugman include adjustment costs and income distribution problems, the latter arising, for example, when trade leads to increases in unemployment in some countries. Moreover, such problems are likely to be accentuated as a result of enlargement. In the case of the EU, the original member states were very similar in terms of economic structure and level of development, with trade being mainly intra-industry. Such trade is characterised by small adjustment costs (Grimwade 1989). Enlargement has given rise to inter-industry trade, with a more conventional specialisation in labour-intensive, low technology production on the one hand and high-tech, capital- or skill-intensive industries on the other. This is likely to be associated with substantial adjustment costs and implies the possibility of significant costs in terms of unemployment for some partners.

The problems of imperfect competition can be further accentuated in the case of transnational corporations (TNCs). The inherent mobility of such firms has increasingly resulted in situations where national states have to "bid" for such investment by "their" and "foreign" TNCs. In this competitive struggle, the winners will be those states that will be able to offer the best bargain to TNCs in terms of overall expected benefits. Considerations of labour costs, technology, infrastructure, market size, political stability, etc. (CEC 1993), become all important here, suggesting that some states may emerge as consistent losers in this competitive struggle. It is also evident today that labour costs are becoming a decreasing part of overall production costs. Economies of time through, for example, just-in-time production, can instead lead to substantial reductions in costs of production (Best 1990, Best & Forrant, 1996). This may tend to reduce the attractiveness of lower labour costs to TNCs vis-a-vis other factors. As lower labour costs is typically the characteristic of less-developed countries, the emerging new conditions may tend to remove a source of competitive advantage from such countries. This, may tend to reduce their bargaining power vis-a-vis TNCs. Moreover, the elimination of trade barriers seems to alter the spatial behaviour of TNCs, reinforcing on a larger scale the importance of geographical factors such as adjacency, centrality or market accessibility and a more ordered spatial organisation of activities at the European level (CEC 1993). Overall, these factors may tend to imply fewer investments by TNCs in such countries and more "bad deals" over such investments.

A parallel to this literature, which is concerned with the EU experience, pays more attention to the various "endowments" available to the EU member states engaged in the process of integration. It indicates that the dynamics of integration may take the form of a "cumulative" process, having an overall unfavourable impact on the performance of the less developed countries and regions. In the first place, it has been argued that the operation of the Single European Market (SEM) will intensify competition among unequal firms and strengthen the competitive advantages of the core regions that house the most efficient European enterprises (CEC 1991, Amin et al. 1992). As a result, lagging states and regions may suffer directly from the implementation of SEM, as they contain the highest share of sensitive sectors (CEC 1990, Camagni 1992), the weakest and most vulnerable economic base and an overall unfavourable geographic index of strategic locations (Petrakos and Zikos 1996). In addition, policies towards economic and monetary union (EMU), may have a disproportionately adverse effect on the weaker member states, by largely depriving them of the means of fiscal policy and the means of monetary and exchange rate policy, that allow them to compete with the more efficient members of the EU (Camagni 1992).

In addition, it has been claimed more recently (Petrakos and Christodoulakis 1997, 2000) that the trade relations and the integration prospects of a country can be seriously affected by its geographical position and the geopolitical conditions prevailing in the region. In this argument, a peripheral country engaged in an integration process among distant and unequal partners will tend to develop trade relations that are unbalanced and with a strong inter-industry character. In addition, if geopolitical realities do not allow trade with the neighbours, then it is very likely that trade relations will have an unfavorable impact on the industrial structure of the country. Trade theory indicates (Gruber and Lloyd 1975, Greenway and Milner 1986, Grimwade 1989) that trade with neighbouring countries is more intensive and usually takes an intra-industry character, implying greater room for more industries to develop, as international specialisations are not mutually exclusive and the division of labour takes place within and not between sectors. Therefore, the strong reliance of a peripheral country on trade with distant and more advanced partners is likely to result in unfavourable effects for convergence: contraction of capital- or technology-intensive industrial sectors with serious adjustment costs and inefficiently small industrial firms, as the small size of the country and the lack of accessible nearby markets with a critical size, does not allow industrial firms to benefit from economies of unit costs.

To summarise, imperfect competition and strategic trade policies, competitive bidding by states and the spatial behaviour TNCs, as well as unequal initial "endowments" and geography, are all factors which, at least in principle, may operate in ways that hinder convergence within Europe.

The EU Integration Experience of Greece

Greece joined the EU in 1981[1] after a long period of accession, with mostly political arguments in support of this decision[2] and, arguably, quite unprepared to deal with the economic consequences of membership. This decision was taken by the New Democracy (Conservative) Party that was in power in the period 1974-1981, despite the strong criticism and opposition of the other (mostly Socialist and Communist) parties of the Parliament. Today the political rhetoric and debates of the late 1970s over EU membership seem distant and rather irrelevant, as a more pragmatic and less ideological approach has prevailed with regard to the place of Greece in the international economic environment[3]. However there is still a lot of scepticism about the implications of (the timing of) membership on the economy, as increasing competition seems to have led to an initially at least, negative effect on the industrial base of the country. Although Greece has recently managed to meet the Maastricht criteria for participation in the Economic and Monetary Union (EMU), the decline in its manufactuiring base, and rising unemployment in the 1980s and the early 1990s may be considered to be symptoms of a limited ability of the economy to compete in the European market. Voices of concern might have been stronger and louder, had significant assistance not been provided to the less advanced regions of the EU in the form of the Community Support Framework (CSF I, II and III).

In this section we present information about the structure and performance of the Greek economy in comparison with the EU average in key statistics, such as GDP growth rates, GDP structure, industrial structure and trade relations. In most cases we cover a relatively long period of time and take a comparative approach. Since Greece has joined the EU in 1981, our purpose here is to compare over time the performance of the Greek economy to the EU average, paying particular attention to the performance of the economy in the post-1981 period. On the basis of these statistics, we attempt a preliminary evaluation of the impact of the EU integration process on Greece and provide some explanations that may be useful to transition economies in the Balkans.

The Development of the Balkan Region

A. The Performance of the Greek Economy

The performance of the Greek economy in the last four decades is shown in the next Tables and Figures. Table 1 and Figure 1 present the annual percentage change of real GDP, labour productivity, industrial production and total gross fixed capital formation, for the period 1961-2000. We observe that Greece has in all indicators a considerably better performance than the EU average in the 1960s and the 1970s[1], but a weaker performance than the EU in the 1980s and the early 1990s. Real GDP has been growing in Greece with an average rate of 8.5 percent in the 1961-1970 and 4.6 percent in the 1971-1981 period, better than the EU average, which was 4.9 percent and 3.0 percent respectively for the same periods. In the 1980s however this picture changed and Greece (growing with an average rate of 0.7 per cent) had a weaker performance than the EU (that experienced a 2.4 percent growth rate), a trend that continued also in the early 1990s. Interestingly, the performance of Greece compared to the EU average, declined immediately after Greece became a member of the Union. After 1995, however, Greece resumes again growth rates that are higher than the EU average.

Similar trends are also observed in all the other variables of Table 1. For example, labour productivity has been growing in Greece (EU average) with a 9.3 percent (4.6 per cent) rate in the 1961-1970, a 3.9 percent (2.7 per cent) rate in the 1971-1980, a -0.3 percent (1.9 per cent) in the 1981-1990 and a 1.5 percent (1.7 percent) in the 1991-2000 period. Industrial production has increased in Greece (EU average) with a rate of 1 percent (1.9 per cent) in the 1981-1990, and 1.5 percent (1.7 per cent) in the 1991-2000 period. Similarly, Gross Fixed Capital Formation has increased in Greece (EU average) with a rate of 8.4 percent (6.0 per cent) in the 1961-1970 period, 2.8 percent (1.6 per cent) in the 1971-1980 period, -0.4 percent (2.6 per cent) in the 1981-1990 and 4.4 percent (1.9 per cent) in the 1991-2000 period. It appears that over time, the performance of Greece can be divided into three periods: the period 1961-1980 where Greece is doing better than the EU average, the period 1981-1995 where Greece is doing worse than the EU average and the period after 1995 where Greece seems to resume again higher growth rates in all indicators. It is interesting to note that in the 1981-1990 period, Greece was in a unique situation with a performance in all four indicators that is not simply worse than the EU average, but also worse than any other single member State of the EU (EC 1995).

Table 1 GDP, GDP Per Person Employed, Industrial Production and Gross Fixed Capital Formation at 1995 Market Prices

(Annual percentage change)

YEARS	GDP in PPP at 1995 market prices		GDP in PPP at 1995 market prices per person employed		Industrial production construction excluded		Gross fixed capital formation at 1995 prices	
	Greece	EU15*	Greece	EU15*	Greece	EU15*	Greece	EU15*
1961	13.2	5.4	12.8	4.6	-	-	13.2	9.9
1962	0.4	4.7	1.4	4.4	-	-	5.1	5.7
1963	11.8	4.8	13.4	4.7	10.1	-	-6.5	4.6
1964	9.4	5.9	10.9	5.4	10.8	-	19.3	9.3
1965	10.8	4.3	11.5	4.1	8.6	-	15.6	4.1
1966	6.5	3.9	7.5	3.9	15.6	-	5.4	5.0
1967	5.7	3.4	7.0	4.3	4.8	-	-1.3	3.9
1968	7.2	5.2	8.5	5.3	7.7	-	23.1	5.9
1969	11.6	6.1	11.9	5.2	11.9	-	16.5	6.8
1970	8.9	4.9	9.0	4.1	10.2	-	-2.4	5.3
1971	7.8	3.3	7.5	3.1	11.4	-	11.6	3.2
1972	10.2	4.5	9.6	4.3	16.0	-	23.8	4.3
1973	8.1	6.0	7.0	4.5	15.3	-	6.8	6.0
1974	-6.4	1.9	-6.5	1.4	-1.4	-	-32.7	-2.2
1975	6.4	-0.6	6.3	0.3	4.4	-	10.1	-4.6
1976	6.9	4.5	5.6	4.5	10.4	-	7.1	1.7
1977	2.9	2.7	2.1	2.3	2.0	2.5	12.3	1.2
1978	7.2	3.0	6.8	2.6	7.6	2.2	12.5	1.6
1979	3.3	3.6	2.2	2.5	6.1	4.8	5.2	3.0
1980	0.7	1.3	-0.7	1.0	1.0	0.3	-15.2	1.9
1981	-1.6	0.1	-6.4	1.1	0.8	-1.7	-9.8	-4.7
1982	-1.1	0.9	-0.1	1.7	1.0	-1.4	-2.3	-1.7
1983	-1.1	1.7	-1.6	2.4	-0.3	0.9	5.2	-0.1
1984	2.0	2.3	2.2	2.1	2.3	2.2	-15.9	0.9
1985	2.5	2.6	0.0	2.1	3.2	3.3	9.5	2.7
1986	0.5	2.8	0.2	2.1	-0.3	1.9	-0.5	4.3
1987	-2.3	2.8	-2.2	1.5	-1.2	2.1	-6.0	5.5
1988	4.3	4.3	2.6	2.6	5.0	4.4	6.7	8.8
1989	3.8	3.5	3.4	1.8	1.8	4.0	7.1	7.0
1990	0.0	3.0	-1.3	1.2	-2.4	3.1	5.0	3.8
1991	3.1	1.7	5.6	1.5	-1.0	-0.3	4.8	-0.5
1992	0.7	1.2	-0.7	2.5	-1.1	-1.2	-3.2	-0.3
1993	-1.6	-0.4	-2.5	1.6	-2.8	-3.4	-3.5	-5.9
1994	2.0	2.8	0.1	2.8	1.2	5.0	-2.8	2.6
1995	2.1	2.4	1.2	1.7	1.8	3.3	4.2	3.3
1996	2.4	1.6	2.8	1.3	1.2	0.4	8.4	1.8
1997	3.4	2.5	3.8	1.8	1.3	3.8	13.2	3.3
1998	3.7	2.6	0.3	1.3	7.1	3.4	8.0	5.6
1999	3.4	2.1	2.1	0.9	2.2	1.0	7.8	4.7
2000	3.8	3.0	2.4	1.8	2.7	3.3	8.3	5.3

Sources: European Economy 1999 The EU Economy: 1999 Review, No. 69, European Commission. Tables 10,11, 12, 20.
* The data for the period 1961-91 include only West Germany.

Figure 1 GDP at 1995 Market Prices

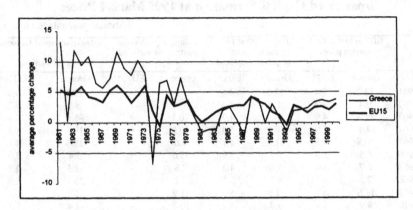

GDP at 1995 Market Prices Per Person Employed

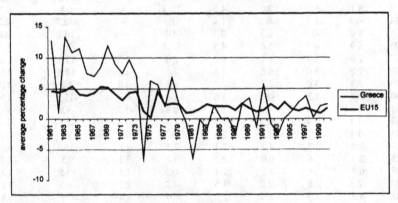

Industrial Production, Construction Excluded

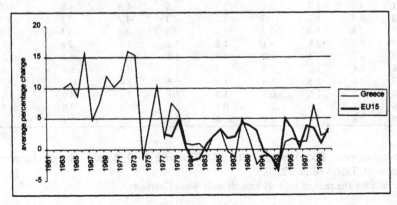

Gross Fixed Capital Formation at 1995 Prices; Total Economy

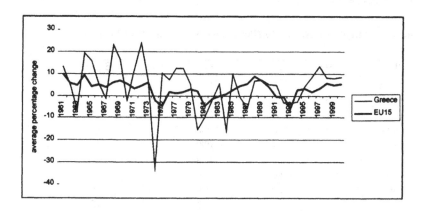

Source: Table 1.

What we have here, is a case of a country that although in the 1960s was placed among the fastest growing OECD economies, in the 1980s it was ranked last among the EU economies. As a result of the sharp decline of the growth rate of output, the economy was unable in the 1980s to create a sufficient number of new jobs, despite the expansion of the public sector. The unemployment rate increased from 2.2 percent in the 1971-1980 period to 6.4 percent in the 1981-1990 period and to 9.2 percent in the 1991-2000 period exceeding after 1998 the average rate of the EU (Table 2). It can be observed in Diagram 2 that the unemployment rate increased rapidly in the early 1980s (with EU membership) and the early 1990s (with the introduction of the Single European Market), to decline only marginally after 1998.

The per capita GDP in Greece, as compared to the EU, has also declined in the 1980s. Table 3 and Diagram 3 present two indicators of the relative position of Greece. The first indicator gives the ratio of the Greek to the EU GDP per capita measured in ECU and the second gives the ratio of the Greek to the EU GDP per capita measured in purchasing power system (PPS)[5].

Both figures show similar trends. Relative GDP per capita in Greece, measured in ECU, increased in the 1960s, reaching its highest value in 1977 and decreased thereafter, reaching its lowest point in 1987. In the 1990s there was again a (slower this time) increasing trend. In 2000, however, relative Greek GDP per capita in ECU was equal to 52.1 percent of the EU average, a figure that is still lower than that of 1977 (55.6 per cent), or 1970 (54.8 per cent) level.

Table 2 Unemployment Rate (Percentage of civilian labour force)

YEARS	Greece	EU15*	YEARS	Greece	EU15*
1960	5.6	2.3	1981	4.0	7.4
1961	5.5	2.1	1982	5.8	8.7
1962	4.8	1.9	1983	7.1	9.1
1963	4.8	2.0	1984	7.2	9.7
1964	4.6	1.9	1985	7.0	9.9
1965	4.8	2.0	1986	6.6	9.8
1966	5.0	2.0	1987	6.7	9.7
1967	5.4	2.6	1988	6.8	9.0
1968	5.6	2.7	1989	6.7	8.3
1969	5.2	2.4	1990	6.4	7.7
1970	4.2	2.3	1991	7.0	8.1
1971	3.1	2.6	1992	7.9	9.2
1972	2.1	2.8	1993	8.6	10.7
1973	2.0	2.6	1994	8.9	11.1
1974	2.1	2.7	1995	9.2	10.7
1975	2.3	3.9	1996	9.6	10.8
1976	1.9	4.6	1997	9.8	10.6
1977	1.7	4.9	1998	10.7	9.9
1978	1.8	5.1	1999	10.3	9.2
1979	1.9	5.3	2000	9.9	8.6
1980	2.7	5.8			

Sources: European Economy 1999 The EU Economy: 1999 Review, No. 69, European Commission. Table 3.
* The data for the period 1960-91 include only West Germany.

Figure 2 Unemployment Rate; Total

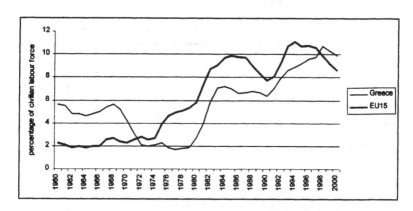

Source: Table 2.

Table 3 GDP of Greece at Current Market Prices Per Head of Population (EU-15=100)

YEARS	ECU	PPS	YEARS	ECU	PPS
1960	41.8	43.6	1981	51.8	68.5
1961	43.6	46.9	1982	56.1	66.8
1962	42.0	45.1	1983	52.3	64.7
1963	43.6	48.5	1984	52.8	64.3
1964	44.9	50.3	1985	50.0	64.1
1965	47.6	53.6	1986	43.4	62.6
1966	49.3	55.0	1987	40.8	59.6
1967	49.9	55.9	1988	42.6	59.7
1968	52.0	57.1	1989	43.5	59.9
1969	54.1	60.3	1990	43.3	58.3
1970	54.8	62.9	1991	44.5	59.4
1971	54.2	66.3	1992	45.6	62.0
1972	52.1	69.4	1993	47.0	63.9
1973	53.6	70.8	1994	47.4	64.7
1974	55.3	65.1	1995	48.6	65.8
1975	52.5	69.3	1996	50.5	66.7
1976	55.0	70.2	1997	52.3	65.6
1977	55.6	69.5	1998	51.0	65.8
1978	55.1	71.7	1999	52.8	66.8
1979	55.1	70.8	2000	52.1	67.2
1980	49.9	70.0			

Sources: European Economy 1999 The EU Economy: 1999 Review, No. 69, European Commission, Tables 8 and 9.

Note: The data for the period 1960-91 include only West Germany.

**Figure 3 GDP at Current Market Prices Per Head of Population
(in ECU; EU15=100)**

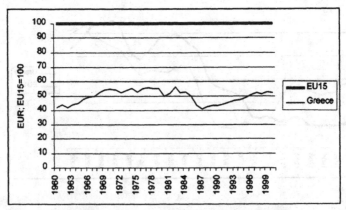

**GDP at Current Market Prices Per Head of Population
(in PPS; EU15=100)**

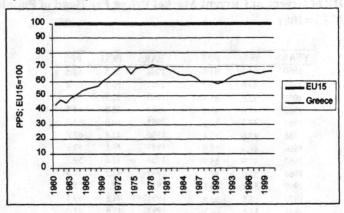

Source: Table 3.

Similar, albeit less profound changes appear with the examination of the relative GDP per capita of Greece when taking into consideration its purchasing power. The variation in this figure is smaller and the ratio of Greek GDP per capita to the EU average is in general higher than the one measured in ECU, especially from the 1970s and thereafter. The basic trend however is maintained as the figure increased up to 1978 and decreased in the period 1979-1991, to increase again in the period thereafter. Thus in

2000, the average income in Greece could command or purchase goods and services equal to 67.2 percent of those that could be purchased with the average income in the EU. This figure, however, is still lower than the 1978 level (71.7 per cent), which was the highest in the entire period[6].

B. The Sectoral Structure of the Greek Economy

In Table 4 and Figure 4 we present information on the sectoral structure of economic activity for Greece and the EU, measured by value added, in the period 1983-1995. We observe that there are a number of significant differences between the two economic structures. First, Greece appears to be a unique case for Western Europe with a share of primary sector equal to 14.2 percent of GDP in 1995, that is five times greater than the EU average, which equals 2.3 percent in the same period. In addition, this high share appears to be a permanent feature of the Greek economy, characterising the entire period 1983-1995.

Table 4 Value Added (%) of Agriculture[1], Industry[2] and Services[3]

	Agriculture		Industry		Services	
Years	EU15	Greece	EU15	Greece	EU15	Greece
1983	3.7	16.9			59.1	53.3
1984	3.7	17.6			59.6	53.2
1985	3.4	17.3	36.5	29.3	60.0	53.5
1986	3.5	16.2	35.7	30.0	60.9	53.8
1987	3.3	15.8	35.1	28.8	61.6	55.4
1988	3.1	16.4	35.1	28.3	61.8	55.2
1989	3.2	16.3	34.9	28.0	62.0	55.7
1990	3.0	14.5	34.2	28.0	62.8	57.4
1991	2.8	16.4	33.4	26.9	63.8	56.8
1992	2.6	14.8	32.4	26.3	65.0	58.9
1993	2.4	13.8	31.4	25.9	66.3	60.4
1994	2.4	14.9	31.3	25.0	66.4	60.1
1995	2.3	14.2	31.3	23.7	66.3	62.0

1: Agriculture, Forest and Fishery.
2: Fuel and power, Manufacturing, Construction.
3: Market and non-market services.

Sources: EUROSTAT Statistical Survey 1995 and EUROSTAT Yearbook 1997.

Figure 4 Value Added (%) of Agriculture, Industry and Services in the EU and Greece

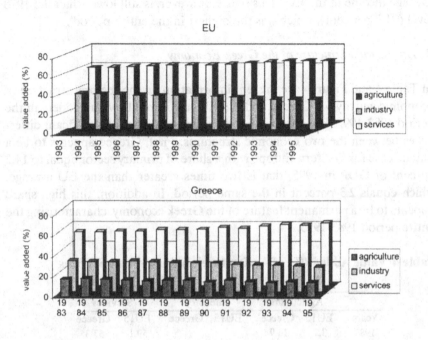

Source: Table 4.

Second, comparing the Greek share of industry in GDP to that of the EU average we observe that although both figures decline over-time, the Greek share is consistently lower than the share of the EU by a margin equal to about 6 percentage points. Third, the share of services in GDP is increasing over time for both Greece and the EU, but the share of Greece is consistently lower than the share of the EU by a margin equal to about 6 percentage points.

Overall, Greece shows a high dependence on agriculture that is not compatible with the profile of other developed countries. The composition of its industry by sector and size also seriously diverges from the EU average (see Tables 5 and 6). Finally, its services have a composition that is by no means similar to that of the EU either, as small-scale retail trade and personal firms of self-employed professionals tend to dominate them[7].

Table 5 Industrial Employment in Greece and the EU-15 by Sector 1985, 1997

ISIC3	EU		Greece	
	Composition			
	1985*	1997**	1985	1997
Food products (311) Beverages (313) Tobacco (314)	10.65	11.67	19.41	22.88
Textiles (321) Wearing apparel except footwear (322)	9.44	8.27	26.39	21.63
Leather products (323) Footwear except rubber or plastic (324)	1.77	1.76	3.54	2.91
Wood products except furniture (331) Furniture except metal (332)	4.32	5.18	3.47	4.17
Paper and products (341) Printing and publishing (342)	6.81	7.75	5.13	5.96
Industrial chemicals (351) Other chemicals (352) Petroleum refineries (353) Misc. petroleum and coal products (354)	7.86	7.95	7.56	9.26
Rubber products (355) Plastic products (356)	4.28	4.93	3.40	3.69
Pottery, china, earthenware (361) Glass and products (362) Other non-metallic mineral products (369)	4.45	4.63	6.75	7.50
Iron and steel (371) Non-ferrous metals (372)	5.52	4.24	3.69	3.40
Fabricated metal products (381)	8.48	10.16	6.25	5.95
Machinery except electrical (382) Professional & scientific equipment (385)	12.73	11.73	2.30	2.73
Machinery electric (383)	11.02	9.96	4.40	4.03
Transport equipment (384)	11.49	10.46	6.67	5.17
Other manufactured products (390)	1.18	1.32	0.83	0.55
Total	100.00	100.00	100.00	100.00
Labour-intensive	*36.84*	*38.14*	*58.78*	*58.10*
Intermediate	*29.57*	*31.14*	*27.65*	*29.81*
Capital or RD-intensive	*33.58*	*30.72*	*13.57*	*12.10*

Source: UNIDO 1999.
* except Germany 1991.
** For the following EU countries there are no data for 1997: Belgium (1992), Germany, Italy and Luxembourg (1994), and Austria, France, Ireland, Netherlands and Spain (1996).

Table 6 Average Employment in Enterprises With One Employee Or More in the Country Members of the EU, 1990

Countries	Industry
Germany	36
The U.K	20
Italy	18
France	33
Spain	17
Belgium	32
Portugal	20
Denmark	31
Luxembourg	51
Netherland	49
Greece	5
EU	27

Source: EC 1994.

C. The Structure of Greek Industry

While in the 1960s manufacturing activity in Greece was the vehicle of development, in the 1980s and the early 1990s its dynamism seemed to have been exhausted. This is shown in the declining average annual growth rate of the industrial production, which from 10.1 percent in the 1961-1970 period fell to 1.0 percent in the 1981-1990 and 1.5 percent in the 1991-2000 period. At the same time, the share of manufacturing in GDP has declined considerably, alongside a declining competitiveness of the Greek industry. This is expressed domestically with the rapid increase of imports and internationally with the sluggish performance of exports (Giannitsis 1984, Petrakos and Zikos 1996).

The decline of Greek manufacturing in the last period is also expressed with the concentration of investment and employment towards traditional activities and the contraction of the intermediate and capital goods sector. Table 5 provides information on the composition of Greek and EU industrial employment for 1985 and 1997 by main ISIC sectors. The examination of this data reveals that different sectors had a different weight in the industrial employment in Greece and the EU in the 1985-1997 period. In general, capital, RTD and technology intensive sectors have a considerably lower share in the total industrial employment in Greece (12 per cent) than in the EU (30 per cent) in 1997. On the contrary, labour intensive or light-industry sectors have a significantly higher share in industrial employment in Greece (58 per cent) compared to the EU (38 per cent).

As it can be seen in Table 5, the structure of the Greek industry does not show any signs of convergence towards that of the EU in the 1985-1997 period. On the contrary, it maintains high shares of employment in traditional sectors such as food, textiles and clothes, a condition which in general, characterises earlier stages of industrial development. At the same time, on the international markets, traditional industries tend to shift towards developing countries that appear to have significant labour cost advantages and compete for a larger share of the market.

As a result, the process of integration and internationalisation has generated a position where Greece has, on the one hand, a disadvantage compared to other industrial EU countries in competing on markets of high-tech, RTD and differentiated products and, on the other hand, a disadvantage compared to low cost countries in competing on traditional markets of labour-intensive and standardised products. This double pressure might have been an important factor related to the decline of industrial activity and its concentration upon inwards looking sectors that often have a local character.

Industrial activity in Greece takes place in very small, by international standards, production units (Petrakos and Zikos 1996). In 1988, for example, 93.5 percent of the industrial firms employed 1-9 persons, being classified as light manufacturing or handicraft units, and this share remained almost unchanged for the last 20 years. As a result, the average size of firms has remained for the entire period equal to the very small figure of 5 employees per firm, which, as Table 6 indicates, is by far the lowest in Europe. Among the EU countries, Luxembourg, Netherlands, Germany, France and Belgium (in that order) have the larger average firm sizes, while Portugal, Spain, Italy and Greece the smaller. This suggests that, with the possible exception of the UK, a North-South or a core-periphery divide exists in the EU, with respect to national industrial structures. Overall, the countries of the "core" (that include Netherlands, Luxembourg, Germany, France, Denmark and Belgium) have larger firms with an average size that, depending on the country, ranges from 51 to 31 employees per firm, while the countries of the "periphery" (that include Spain, Italy, Portugal and Greece) have smaller firms with an average size that ranges from 20 to 5 employees per firm.

D. The Trade Relations of Greece with the EU and the World

In Table 7 and Figure 5 we present data about the total and intra-community exports and imports of Greece as a share of GDP for the period 1960-2000 and make comparisons with the respective EU figures. Looking first at the total exports of goods and services as a share of GDP, we observe a consistently inferior performance of Greece when compared to the EU. The share of total exports to GDP in 1960, was 12.3 percent for Greece and 19.6 percent for the EU. The same share was 18.4 percent for Greece and 33.1 percent for the EU in 2000. As Figure 5 shows, the Greek exports as a share of GDP increase (roughly speaking) in the pre-1981 and decline in the post-1981 period. As a result, the difference in export performance between Greece and the EU increases steadily after 1981.

The situation is similar with respect to intra-community exports of goods, as a share of GDP. The Greek exports as a share of GDP have been growing at a slower pace than the average EU figure and the gap becomes over time wider. As it can be seen in the Table and the Figure, this difference increased from about 5 percentage points in 1960 to about 8 percentage points in 1990 and 12 percentage points in 2000, indicating the declining ability of Greek exports to penetrate the EU markets.

Turning to imports of goods and services, the situation is very different. Total Greek imports as a share of GDP show a similar trend and are very close to the EU average figures, throughout the period examined. The same is also true for the intra-community imports of Greece, that, as a share, are very close to the EU average.

Table 8 and Figure 6 present export/import ratios of Greece with the EU, the rest of the world and total trade for the period 1960-2000. The export/import ratio measures the value of exports of Greece that correspond to a dollar of imports. A ratio greater than one indicates that every dollar of imports in Greece is more than matched by Greek exports. Therefore, higher than one values indicate a positive balance of trade, while lower than one values indicate a negative balance of trade. Another way to interpret this ratio is to think of it as the degree of relative penetration of a foreign market by Greek products.

Looking at the export/import ratio in Table 8 and Figure 6, we can make a number of observations: First, the Greek export/import ratio is consistently smaller than one for the entire period and all groups (EU, rest of world, total). Second, roughly speaking, the export/import ratio of Greece

Table 7 Exports and Imports of Goods and Services and Intra-Community Exports and Imports of Goods at Current Prices

(Percentage of GDP at market prices)

YEARS	Exports of goods and services National accounts definition		Imports of goods and services National accounts definition		Intra-Community exports of goods Foreign trade statistics		Intra-Community imports of goods Foreign trade statistics	
	Greece	EU15*	Greece	EU15*	Greece	EU15**	Greece	EU15**
1960	12.3	19.6	15.8	19.3	2.3	-	8.4	-
1961	11.9	19.1	15.4	18.8	2.1	-	8.3	-
1962	10.4	18.5	16.1	18.6	2.8	-	9.9	-
1963	11.2	18.4	16.6	18.9	2.6	7.7	9.4	7.9
1964	9.6	18.5	18.1	19.2	2.7	8.0	9.3	8.1
1965	9.5	18.7	18.5	19.2	2.5	8.2	9.9	8.3
1966	11.7	19.1	17.0	19.3	2.6	8.2	9.7	8.5
1967	11.2	19.1	16.5	18.9	3.1	8.0	9.1	8.3
1968	9.9	20.1	17.0	19.6	3.1	8.7	9.6	8.8
1969	9.6	21.0	16.9	20.7	3.0	9.5	9.1	9.7
1970	9.8	21.8	16.5	21.6	3.2	10.0	9.8	10.1
1971	10.1	22.0	16.5	21.3	3.0	10.0	9.4	10.1
1972	11.3	22.0	17.6	21.2	3.4	10.4	9.5	10.4
1973	14.5	23.2	21.9	23.0	4.6	11.3	10.0	11.3
1974	18.0	27.1	23.2	28.2	5.2	12.7	9.6	12.7
1975	17.9	25.1	23.1	25.0	5.0	11.4	10.7	11.5
1976	17.7	26.3	22.8	27.0	5.0	12.6	10.7	12.6
1977	17.6	26.7	22.6	26.8	4.4	12.6	10.7	12.6
1978	17.1	26.3	21.3	25.4	4.7	12.4	9.9	12.4
1979	19.1	27.0	22.3	27.3	4.2	13.3	9.9	13.3
1980	24.7	27.2	27.7	28.7	5.2	13.3	9.6	13.2
1981	27.4	28.7	28.2	29.2	4.3	13.1	10.5	13.0
1982	22.1	28.7	27.1	29.0	4.5	13.4	10.8	13.4
1983	21.2	28.9	27.2	28.5	5.6	13.7	11.6	13.6
1984	21.5	30.7	26.5	30.0	6.7	14.5	12.0	14.4
1985	20.6	31.1	26.7	30.1	6.3	14.9	12.6	14.8
1986	22.6	27.9	27.5	26.3	7.7	13.5	14.3	13.9
1987	23.0	27.3	26.7	26.2	8.1	14.1	14.8	14.0
1988	20.6	27.2	25.7	26.6	5.6	14.2	12.4	14.1
1989	20.3	28.4	27.4	28.1	7.6	15.0	15.7	14.9
1990	18.7	28.1	28.0	27.5	6.5	14.5	15.9	14.6
1991	18.0	28.0	27.0	27.0	6.4	13.8	15.2	13.8
1992	18.8	26.1	26.5	26.1	6.8	13.4	15.6	13.4
1993	17.7	26.6	25.4	25.4	5.5	12.7	14.8	12.1
1994	18.1	27.9	24.0	26.6	5.3	13.6	14.5	12.9
1995	17.6	29.7	24.9	28.0	5.7	14.6	15.4	13.8
1996	17.5	30.1	25.5	28.1	5.3	14.6	15.2	13.8
1997	17.8	31.9	25.9	29.7	4.8	15.5	14.7	14.4
1998	17.6	32.0	25.5	30.2	4.4	15.8	14.1	14.7
1999	17.8	31.9	25.5	30.7	4.4	15.7	14.0	14.7
2000	18.4	33.1	26.4	31.9	4.4	16.2	14.6	15.2

Sources: European Economy 1999 The EU Economy: 1999 Review, No. 69, European Commission, Tables 36, 38, 40, 42.

* EU data in the 1960-91 period include only West Germany.

** EU data in the 1960-90 period include only West Germany.

301

Figure 5 Exports of Goods and Services as a Percentage of GDP at Current prices. National Accounts Definitions

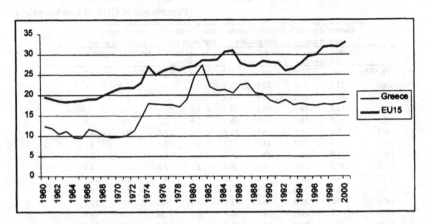

Imports of Goods and Services as a Percentage of GDP at Current Prices. National Accounts Definitions

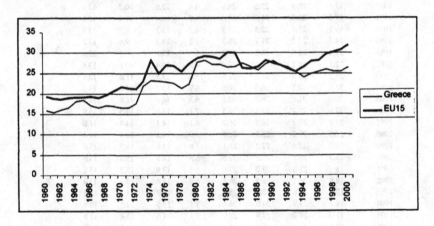

**Intra-Community Exports of Goods as a Percentage of GDP.
Foreign Trade Statistics**

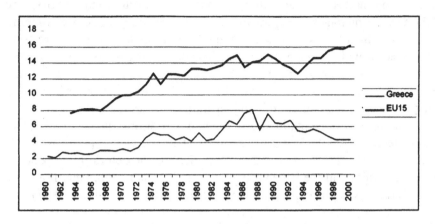

**Intra-Community Imports of Goods as a Percentage of GDP.
Foreign Trade Statistics**

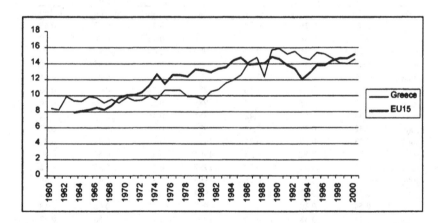

Source: Table 7.

303

with the EU (but also total trade) is increasing in the 1960s and early 1970s and decreasing in the late 1980s and the 1990s. The constantly declining figure during the last 15 years indicates that for each ecu of imports from the EU, Greece manages to export products of a declining value over time. In 2000 the value of Greek exports to the EU were equal to only 30 percent of the value of its imports, a figure well bellow the 56 percent figure of 1984 (which is the highest in the entire period). Third, in the 1990s the export/import ratio of Greece with the rest of the world is either increasing or significantly and consistently higher than that with the EU.

The observations made above indicate that during the last period, two opposite processes took place with respect to the Greek performance in international markets. On the one hand, there is the deteriorating position of Greek exports in the EU markets and, on the other hand, there is a more successful export performance in the non EU markets (Petrakos 1997).

Table 8 International Trade of Greece 1960-2000

	EU15	Rest of World	Total		EU15	Rest of World	Total
Year	Exp./Imp.	Exp./Imp.	Exp./Imp.	Year	Exp./Imp.	Exp./Imp.	Exp./Imp.
1960	0.27	0.29	0.28	1981	0.41	0.57	0.48
1961	0.25	0.38	0.32	1982	0.42	0.44	0.43
1962	0.28	0.46	0.35	1983	0.48	0.44	0.46
1963	0.28	0.49	0.36	1984	0.56	0.45	0.50
1964	0.29	0.45	0.35	1985	0.50	0.39	0.45
1965	0.25	0.36	0.30	1986	0.54	0.45	0.50
1966	0.27	0.43	0.34	1987	0.55	0.41	0.50
1967	0.34	0.54	0.42	1988	0.45	0.43	0.44
1968	0.32	0.37	0.34	1989	0.48	0.44	0.47
1969	0.33	0.37	0.35	1990	0.41	0.41	0.41
1970	0.33	0.32	0.33	1991	0.42	0.36	0.40
1971	0.32	0.31	0.32	1992	0.44	0.39	0.42
1972	0.36	0.40	0.38	1993	0.37	0.45	0.40
1973	0.46	0.37	0.42	1994	0.37	0.58	0.43
1974	0.54	0.39	0.46	1995	0.37	0.56	0.43
1975	0.47	0.38	0.42	1996	0.35	0.56	0.42
1976	0.47	0.37	0.42	1997	0.33	0.58	0.41
1977	0.41	0.39	0.40	1998	0.31	0.57	0.40
1978	0.47	0.41	0.44	1999	0.31	0.57	0.41
1979	0.42	0.38	0.40	2000	0.30	0.56	0.39
1980	0.54	0.45	0.49	-	-	-	-

Sources: European Economy 1999, No. 68. European Commission, Tables 38, 39, 42, 43 and own calculations.

Figure 6 Exports/Imports of Greece with EU15, Rest of the World and World

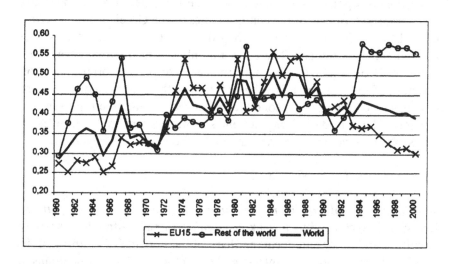

Source: Table 8.

Interpreting these figures it appears that the competitiveness of the Greek economy in the EU markets is lower and declining, while its competitiveness in the other markets is at higher levels and increasing. Higher competitiveness on these markets seems to be affected by the new economic environment of the post-1989 European space. This new environment has allowed economic relations with neighbouring and nearby countries, an option that for many decades had not been available to Greece (Petrakos and Christodoulakis 1997, 2000).

It is also interesting to observe in these figures the following: Despite the existence of the single European market and the fact that the Greek products do not face tariff or non-tariff barriers in the EU, their ability to penetrate the EU market is lower, compared to the world and the rest of the world markets, where certain trade barriers exist. This may be an indication of the difficulties of integration among basically unequal and distant partners.

Some Explanations for the Performance of Greece in the EU

In the previous part of the analysis we have examined, on a comparative basis, important aspects of the characteristics of the Greek economy, giving an emphasis on its performance during the last 20 years, since Greece has been a member of the EU. There are a number of factors that have affected positively or negatively this performance. We present briefly the most important of those in the following order: first, the factors that have exerted a negative impact on economic performance and their presence is stronger in the period of divergence and second, the factors that have exerted a positive impact and are associated with the period of convergence.

A. The Period 1981-95: Why Diverge?

Unfavourable initial conditions and integration among unequal partners. Greece is characterised by a weak economic structure with a high share of agriculture and a low and declining share of industry in GDP. From all the other Southern European country-members of the EU, Greece maintains by far the highest dependence on agriculture. In addition, industrial activities are concentrated in traditional labour-intensive and light-industry sectors and take place in, very small by international standards firms. The last point is worth some consideration, as the average industrial firm in Greece has a size that is less than the one fifth of the size of the average industrial firm in the EU. These structural characteristics along with profound deficiencies in technical and social infrastructure, indicate that the 'initial conditions' of the integration process were highly unfavourable for Greece. The internationalisation of the economy imposed in several instances structural adjustments that were deeper, longer, more painful and in some instances of a backward type. Clearly, the point (and the time) of arrival depends on the point of departure. As a result, it is safe to claim that Greece became a laggard in the integration race in part because it started from an inferior point compared to most other EU countries.

In many important ways, the process of EU integration for Greece was a process of integration among unequal partners. Several studies (including those of the European Commission) have already indicated that the dynamics of integration may have an overall unfavourable impact on the performance of the less developed states of the EU. Because of its weak industrial structure, Greece appears over time, with a limited ability to compete in international markets, as shown by the export/GDP ratio, which is by far the lowest in the EU. It also appears with a limited ability to compete in its domestic markets that are successfully penetrated by the more efficient and experienced enterprises of the advanced EU countries. Overall, it can be argued that the weak economic and especially the weak industrial structure of Greece were not in a position to adapt successfully to the new economic environment of the country, leading to a divergence from the EU average in the 1980s.

Domestic political conditions with respect to the EU, the US and TNCs in the 1980s. The 1980s were a period of serious political tensions and conflicts in Greece. The traumatic experience of a military dictatorship in the 1967-74 period widely believed to be US-supported, the Turkish invasion in Cyprus (which the international community failed to prevent) and the practices of some TNCs generated strong anti-US, anti-EEC and anti-TNCs feelings in large parts of the population. These feelings were very common among government officials that belonged to the Socialist Party, which was in office in the period 1981-1989. Although these feelings were rarely transformed into specific action (although inaction proved to be an equally serious problem), it is clear that the process of integration with the European economy and the European institutional structures started in an especially unfavourable political environment. As a result, it is safe to claim that Greece has been a "victim" of the unwillingness and inability of its government to play the game of the pursuit of competitiveness (a bad word in Greece until very recently). Not only has it been done little in the 1980s by way of restructuring the economy, but European and "foreign" TNCs have been turned away by anti-TNCs, anti-US and anti-EU rhetoric. In contrast to what happened latter in Portugal and Spain, the political conditions that prevailed in the 1980s did not allow Greece to take advantage of its low cost base and attract foreign capital.

The expansion of the public sector. Another explanations about the factors that have caused the declining performance of the Greek economy in the last 15 years points to the public sector. The public sector in Greece increased considerably in the 1980s. While in 1980 total expenditure and total revenues of the general government were equal to 26.6 and 26.5 percent of GDP respectively, in 1990 the same figures increased to 42.5 and 32.9 percent respectively (European Economy 1999). This significant expansion of public spending and public employment can be explained on both political and economic grounds. On the political side, the Socialist Party that was for a first time in office opened the doors of the public sector to thousand new employees for two reasons. First, because politically this was the right thing to do. Secondly, because this was considered to do justice to a large segment of the population, which for political reasons was "excluded" from the public sector for several decades. One economic ground, this expansion of the public sector was necessary to offset the decline of industrial employment and to absorb the expanding - due to strong urban migration flows - labour force.

Nevertheless, the expansion of the public sector in the 1980s and its strong intervention in the economy is now considered to be (Alogoskoufis 1993) an important factor responsible for the sluggish performance of the economy for two reasons. First, because it generates deficits that are inflationary and drive the real interest rates up, discouraging private investment and slowing down the growth rate of the economy. Note that the public debt of Greece, despite serious reduction efforts on behalf of the Government is still over 105 percent of GDP. Secondly, because the public sector was arguably less productive than the private one, and (as) the structure of incentives for public employees did not always emphasize efficiency, while bureaucratic mechanisms and regulations interfered with market operations. Athanassiou and Pitelis (2000) provide econometric evidence in favour of the idea that the public sector exerted a negative and significant effect on Greek manufacturing performance.

The inefficient use of structural funds provided by the EU. The implementation of the First Community Support Framework (1989-1993) for Greece was associated with a lower than desired impact on GDP growth and registered, in fact, the lowest impact among all EU countries with comparable development problems (Economou 1997, Georgiou 1994, Lyberaki 1996). While the impact of CSFI on the annual GDP growth rates of Spain, Portugal and Ireland is assessed to be 0.7%, 1.0% and 0.7% respectively, for Greece it is only 0.3%. These differences exist despite the fact that the EU contributions per head for Greece were comparable to those for Portugal and greater than those for Spain. Factors that might explain the failure of CSFI to have a substantial impact on GDP growth in Greece include, first, the fact that the operational programmes of the CSFI were actually not much more than mere lists of unrelated programs, that were selected by clientist political processes. Second, the programs were dominated by small projects. Such fragmentation satisfied political needs or popular demand, but had only marginal economic effects. Third, several of the projects had small budgets and remained incomplete after the end of the Programme, having neither economic nor functional impact. Finally, "soft" initiatives, networks, innovative actions and supportive services that encourage synergies and joint efforts were largely absent from the the CSFI.

The role of economic geography. A recent explanation of the performance of the country (Petrakos and Christodoulakis 1997, 2000) argues that Greece has been confronted in the post-war period with a uniquely unfavourable situation, not found anywhere else in Europe. This situation resulted from the interaction of (a) a peripheral location in South-eastern Europe, away from major markets and the European development centre, (b) a physical isolation from the other western European countries due to the lack of common borders with them, and (c) the fact that the only borders of the country were along the "iron curtain" and as a result they were, due to the post war realities, meant to be real barriers to communication and trade with neighbouring countries. This type of "border conditions", where practically the entire continental border-line of the country operated as a barrier to economic and social relations with all neighbouring countries, forcing the main bulk of economic relations of the country to be with distant and more developed partners, is a rare situation in the history of international relations.

Theoretical and empirical research has shown the importance of geographical factors such as adjacency and proximity in trade relations (Krugman 1994, Peschel 1992). As a result, the "missing factor" in the trade relations of Greece might have contributed to a reduction in the trade potential of the country, limiting market accessibility for exporting industries and limiting the prospects for export-led growth (Petrakos and Christodoulakis 1997, 2000).

Because of these conditions the trade relations of Greece took an inter-industry character with the more advanced and distant countries of Western Europe (Petrakos 1997), with a serious impact on the industrial structure of the country. Trade theory indicates (Gruber and Lloyd 1975, Greenway and Milner 1986, Grimwade 1989) that trade with neighbouring countries is more intensive and usually takes an intra-industry character, implying greater room for more industries to develop, as international specialisations are not mutually exclusive and the division of labour takes place within and not between sectors. Therefore, the lack of trade relations with the other Balkan countries, pushed Greece further towards an inter-industry special-isation with the technologically more advanced western European countries[8] that was unfavourable for the industrial development of the country.

B. The Period 1996-2000: Why Converge?

Before concluding this section, it is necessary to briefly discuss the impres-sive U-turn of Greece with respect to economic performance in the late 1990s. Indeed, Greece has recently managed to meet all the criteria for its participation in the EMU and in addition is one of the fastest growing economies in the EU. Despite the past record of the 1980s and the early 1990s, its growth rate has been consistently superior to that of the EU average in the second half of the 1990s. In addition, the prospects of the economy as reported by international organisations are especially opti-mistic. Although there are certainly many factors that have contributed to this performance, in our view the following three factors had the stronger impact.

Sound macroeconomic policies. After nearly two decades of serious macro-economic imbalances, and after failing to take part in the first round of EMU, Greece managed in the late 1990s to stabilise its economy. Under the threat for a permanent marginalisation within the new EU structures, the Greek government managed to implement a stabilisation program that reduced public spending from 45.7 percent of GDP in 1995 to 40.2 percent in 1999. This allowed for a reduction in inflation and interest rates, which lead to higher GDP growth. We should note however that "austerity" pro-grams are not popular and cannot last for very long, as they have serious social consequences. The most serious one is the increase in unemployment. Indeed, unemployment in Greece, which remained at relatively low levels in the 1980s, increased from 6.4 percent in 1990 to 10.3 percent in 1999 (European Economy 1999), partly because the public sector was not any more able to offset the losses of the continuously declining industrial employment. Under these difficult conditions, stabilisation policies man-aged to succeed because their adverse impact on sensitive social groups was partly offset by the EU structural funds and the new economic environment in the post-1989 Balkan region.

Improved supply-side policies and better implementation of CSF II. The post-1995 period is also characterised by the first serious attempt to develop a supply-side competitiveness strategy. In the context of a "consensus-based" industrial strategy, this focused on horizontal measures and the identification and development of firm clusters. Various clusters are now up and running with varied success. The combination of the achievement of consensus among social partners, alongside the development of clusters and the overall comprehensiveness and consistency with the EU, of these supply-side measures appears to have contributed to the overall improvement of the industrial climate and industrial performance. At the same time, and in part relatedly, the funds of the Community Support Framework (CSF) II in the period 1994-1999 were used more efficiently than those of the earlier period. Structural funds had, according to the European Commission reports (EC 1999a, 1999b), a significant impact on GDP growth and a better internal structure. According to some estimates, the annual impact of structural funds in the period 1994-99 was equal to 1 percent of GDP, a figure significantly higher than the 0.3 percent of the 1989-93 period. This improvement is partly attributed to the fact that funds in the 1994-99 period were substantially higher than the 1989-93 period. It is also attributed to a considerable "learning by doing" and "catching up" process involving the structure and implementation of the CSFs in Greece. The projects became larger, with a greater value added for the economy and screening, approval, monitoring and evaluation procedures improved considerably.

The new regional environment. In the 1990s, and especially in the second half of the decade, the immediate (in the geographical sense of the word) environment of Greece changed dramatically. The country gradually resumed economic relations with its neighbours, so that in 1997 over 11 percent of the Greek exports were directed to transition countries in the Balkans. This development provided new opportunities for export led growth. In addition, because exports to Balkan countries have a higher intra-industry component and concentrate in sectors complementary to those exporting to the EU, inter-regional trade improved the diversification of the industrial base of the economy. Indeed, new sectors (and firms), which due to strong competition were not able to successfully enter the EU market in the past, found an opportunity to expand their activities by exporting to neighbouring countries.

On the other hand, labour immigration has resulted in cost related advantages and has rather improved the efficiency of the labour intensive

311

sectors of the economy and especially agriculture. Finally, in this new environment many Greek firms found the opportunity to go international by expanding their production or retail activities in neighbouring countries. Several Greek FDIs (a term not existing in the 1980s) have stories of success to tell, which in many cases include successful restructuring and high profitability. Overall, Greece has benefited and continues to benefit from the new economic environment in the Balkans. Higher levels of interaction in terms of trade and FDI generate incomes on both sides of the borders that lead to multiplier and spillover effects, which lead to greater long-term benefits for all the countries in the region.

Implications for the Balkan Economies in Transition

We have examined in this paper the performance of Greece as a member of the EU, taking a comparative approach with respect to its previous record and with respect to the average EU figures. We believe that our analysis has several important policy implications for the Balkan economies in transition, which have to be discussed.

First, given the fact that the decision to internationalise their economies and integrate in the long run with the EU, has been taken on the basis of both economic and political considerations, a question arises about the type of this integration process. It has already been indicated (Landesmann 1995, Jackson and Petrakos in this volume) that inter-industry (H-O) trade relations is already taking place between the CEE and the EU countries, with the former specialising in resource- and labour-intensive products and the latter in technology-, capital- and human-capital intensive products. This form of specialisation and trade could over time affect seriously the industrial structure of these countries. The experience of Greece has shown that a north-south form of integration between unequal partners may intensify existing structural problems and under certain conditions it may lead to divergence, instead of convergence, in terms of economic performance and standards of living.

A first implication of this analysis is that, as the first decade has already shown, the process of internationalisation and integration of the Balkan economies in transition, will be a difficult and painful one, given the structural and institutional problems they face. To the extent that this process takes on the same form as in the case of Greece (or worse), it will generate severe pressures to their economic and especially industrial bases. This pressure will take on the form of intensive competition on the international and domestic markets, by the more advanced Western European enterprises, that may have over time, a triple impact: (a) an overall decline of the industrial share in output, well below existing levels, (b) a relative contraction of technology and human capital intensive sectors and a concentration of activities upon labour and resource intensive ones, and (c) increasing trade deficits in manufacturing products that will more than outweigh possible trade surpluses in agricultural products and raw materials, or fuel. This generates a real danger for a new divide in Europe, where over time the "Southeast" will replace the "South", in forming gradually the new European periphery.

Second, sound macroeconomic policies and efficient use of international funds can have a significant contribution to the growth prospects of transition countries. Although the "initial conditions" of Balkan countries have predominantly affected their performance during the early transition period, we should not be left with the impression that the process is hopelessly deterministic. On the contrary, domestic policy responses do matter and will hopefully have an increasing role in the future. The Greek experience shows, however, that stabilisation policies are more easily implemented when their adverse side effects at the social level are counterbalanced by other positive developments. These positive developments can be the appropriately used international assistance provided by the EU and the "Stability Pact", as well as productivity and competitiveness-enhancing supply-side policies.

Finally, the experience of Greece has shown the important role of geography in trade relations and development. Lack of economic relations with neighbouring countries may lead to a serious trade dependence on more advanced industrial ones, with adverse implications for the industrial structure of the economy. As a critical market size for many industrial sectors is usually not attained within national boundaries, cross-border relations become essential for the survival of industrial sectors that have not yet restructured or possessed the level of technological know-how to compete at the more advanced Western European markets.

Notes

1   Greece was the 10th member of the EU (then called European Economic Community, EEC) following West Germany, France, Italy, U.K., Ireland, Belgium, Luxembourg, the Netherlands and Denmark. Two more countries, Portugal and Spain, joined the EU in 1986 and three more, Sweden, Finland and Austria in 1995. Also, West and East Germany united in 1991, adding to the EU a population of about 16 million. In the analysis that follows all references to EU are for the EU15.

2   The most commonly stated argument in support of membership was then that as a part of the EEC, the country would be in a better position to deal with (a) Turkish aggression and expansionism and (b) maintain democratic rules in the country.

3   The process of reforms in the former centrally planned countries and the apparent end of cold war, has arguably helped to eliminate internal divides over the desirability of joining the EU.

4   This is true with the exemption of 1974. In this year economic indicators have been affected, by the oil crisis, by the Turkish invasion to Cyprus and the fall of the military junta in Athens.

5   The first measure is based on the exchange rate of drachma with the ECU and is affected by the performance of the economy in international markets. The second measure takes into consideration domestic price levels and is a better indicator of the relative purchasing power of income per capita.

6   Note, however, that the two figures may not be strictly comparable, due to changes in the way measured in the meantime.

7   To some extent, the increase of the share of the tertiary sector can be seen as a defensive adjustment, as the economy moves away from activities exposed to international competition and towards mostly non-tradable activities with a local character.

8   This may explain why from all the EU countries, Greece has the lowest share of intra-industry trade.

References

Alogoskoufis G. (1993) How to escape crisis?, *Economikos Tahidromos*, No 2025, 25-2-93, pp. 29-32 (in Greek).

Amin, A., Charles, R., Howells, J. (1992) Corporate Restructuring in the New Europe, *Regional Studies*, 26, 4, pp. 319-331.

Athanassiou E. and Pitelis, C. (2000) "Deindustrialisation and the case of Greece", mimeo, University of Cambridge.

Baldwin R. (1994) Towards an integrated Europe, *Centre for Economic Policy Research*, London.

Best, M. (1990) *The New Competition: Institutions of Industrial Restructuring*, Policy Press, Cambridge.

Best, M. and R. Forrant (1996) Creating Industrial Capacity: Pentagon-Led versus Production-Led Industrial Policies, in J. Michie (ed) *Creating Industrial Capacity*, Polity Press.

Camagni, R. (1992) Development Scenarios and Policy Guidelines for the Lagging Regions in the 1990s, *Regional Studies*, 26, 4, pp. 361-374.

CEC (1990) Social Europe, *European Economy,* Commission of the European Communities, Brussels.

CEC (1991) The Regions in the 1990s, *Fourth Periodic Report,* Commission of the European Communities, Brussels.

CEC (1992) New location factors for mobile investment in Europe, Final Report, *Regional Development Studies,* No 6 Commission of the European Communities, DG XVI, Brussels.

EC (1995) *European Economy,* Annual Economic Report for 1995, No 59, European Commission.

EC (1999a) Sixth Periodic report on the social and economic situation and development of the regions in the European Union, European Commission, Directory General for Regional Policy and Cohesion.

EC (1999b) *The 10th annual report on Structural Funds* (1998), European Commission, [http:// www.inforegio.cec.eu.int/wbdoc]

Economou, D. (1997) The impact of the First Community Support Framework for Greece: The anatomy of failure, *European Urban and Regional Studies,* Vol. 4, No. 1, pp. 71-84.

EUROSTAT (1995) *Statistical Yearbook 1995,* European Commission, Luxembourg.

Georgiou G. (1994) The Implementation of EC Regional Programmes in Greece: A critical Review, *European Planning Studies,* Vol. 2, No. 3, pp. 321-336.

Giannitsis T. (1984), International specialisation and division of labour between Greece and NIC, *CEPR,* Athens.(G).

Greenway, D. and Milner, C. (1986) *The economics of intra-industry trade,* Oxford, Blackwell.

Grimwade, N. (1989) *International trade: new patterns of trade, production and investment,* Routledge, London.

Grubel, H. and Lloyd, P. (1975) *Intra-industry trade: the theory and measurement of international trade in differentiated products,* Macmillan, London.

Krugman P. (1986) Introduction: New Thinking about Trade Policy, in Krugman P. (ed) *Strategic Trade Policy and the New International Economics,* MIT Press.

Krugman P. (1987) *Is free trade passe? Economic Perspectives,* Vol. 1, No. 2, pp. 131-144.

Krugman P. (1991) Increasing Returns and Economic Geography, *Journal of Political Economy,* Vol. 99, pp. 483-499.

Krugman. P. (1994) *Geography and Trade,* MIT Press.

Landesmann M. (1995) The pattern of East-West European Integration: Catching up or falling behind? , *Paper No 212,* The Vienna Institute for Comparative Economic Studies.

Peschel K. (1992) European Integration and Regional Development in Northern Europe, *Regional Studies,* 26, 4, pp. 387-397.

Petrakos G. (1996a) The regional dimension of transition in Eastern and Central European countries: An assessment, in Jackson and Petrakos (editors), Regional Problems and SME development in transition countries, *Eastern European Economics,* Vol. 34, No 5, Special Edition, pp. 5-39.

Petrakos G. (1996b) The New Geography of the Balkans: Cross-border co-operation between Albania, Bulgaria and Greece, *Series on Transition in the Balkans,* Vol. 1, University of Thessaly, Department of Planning and Regional Development.

Petrakos G. (1997a) A European macro-region in the making? The Balkan trade relations of Greece, *European Planning Studies,* Vol. 5, No. 4, pp. 515-533.

Petrakos G. (1997b) Industrial Structure and Change in the European Union: Comparative Analysis and Implications for Transition Economies, *Eastern European Economics*, Vol. 35, No 2, pp.41-63.

Petrakos G. and Christodoulakis N. (1997) "Economic Development in the Balkan Countries and the Role of Greece: From Bilateral Relations to the Challenge of Integration", *Discussion Paper Series No 1620*, CEPR, London.

Petrakos G. and Christodoulakis N. (2000) "Greece and the Balkans: The challenge of Integration", in Petrakos, Maier and Gorzelak (eds) *Integration and Transition in Europe: The Economic Geography of Interaction*, London: Routledge, pp. 269-294.

Petrakos G., Zikos S. (1996) "European Integration and Industrial Structure in Greece, Prospects and Possibilities for Convergence", in Paraskevopoulos C., Grinspun R. and Georgakopoulos T. (eds) *Economic Integration and Public Policy*, Edward Elgar, London, pp. 247-259.

Pitelis C. (1994) Industrial Strategy: For Britain, in Europe and the World, *Journal of Economic Studies*, Vol. 21, No 5, pp. 1-92.

11 The Bulgarian Economy in Transition: Possibilities for Balkan Regional Integration

STOYAN TOTEV
Deputy Director, Institute of Economics,
Bulgarian Academy of Sciences

Introduction

Like the rest of the Central and East European Countries (CEEC), Bulgaria started the transition from central planning to a market economy at the end of 1989. The market economy mechanisms, however, did not automatically begin to operate after the planned economy system was abandoned. A point was reached when the old system was no longer active, but the market mechanism had not been activated yet.

As a result of the political changes, long-term accumulated economic problems emerged and brought the country into a sharp economic crisis. The socialist governments that dominated the overall development until the beginning of 1997, proved that they had practically not abandoned the centrally planned economy approaches and views. Their policy was oriented towards the stabilisation, rather than the changing, of the old structures. Their intervention was limited mainly to attempts at maintaining ineffective production. In other words, their economic policies did not solve problems, but often tried to postpone solutions for the future, when the negative effect of their inaction would be stronger. This led to the emerging of considerable macroeconomic disproportion and to an economic crisis, which deeply affected all sectors of economic life. Thus, in the period 1996-1997, the Bulgarian economy reached a critical level and Bulgaria remained one of the countries in transition that was still badly in need of external assistance.

With the implementation of the Currency board in Bulgaria in mid 1997, the problems concerning the monetary policy and financial stabilisation were solved. The far harder problems of foreign investment attraction and achieving stable economic growth are still ahead.

The overall goal of this paper is to investigate the Bulgarian economic development and potential during transition, the problems of the integration process, and solutions towards more adequate economic policy. For this purpose, we shall try to determine the adaptability of the Bulgarian social and economic development to the changing conditions. We attempt to characterise the economic structure of Bulgaria on different levels of aggregation, which we use as a basis for the identification of production specialisation and the expected economic and trade advantages.

This paper tries to accomplish the following tasks: (i) to identify the specific economic problems of Bulgaria, addressing the last 10 years of transition; (ii) to outline the economic conformity of the sector and branch composition under the new market conditions, including trade potential and comparative advantages; (iii) to examine to what extent the country's loss of the former Council for Mutual Economic Assistance (CMEA) market can be balanced through development of Balkan regional economic relations; (iv) to analyse the linkages between regional integration and the development of relations with the EU.

The presentation is organised as follows:

In the next section, a historic preview is made, as an attempt to outline the specificity of Bulgaria's development. The third section presents the socio-economic basis of the transition period. The fourth section analyses the economic development on different aggregation levels - identification of production specialisation.

From the fifth to the seventh section, are analysed; the structural changes and branch effectiveness, the agricultural development, trade potential, comparative advantages, and the possible future economic development scenarios in a short and a long-term perspective. Special considerations of the linkages with the EU are discussed.

In the eighth section an attempt is made to answer the question of how successful have been the last 10 years of transition are for Bulgaria. The last section summarises and provides some conclusions.

Historical Review

Bulgaria is a centrally located country on the Balkan Peninsula. All the countries that Bulgaria borders on are Balkan: Romania on the North, FR of Yugoslavia and FYR of Macedonia on the West, Greece and Turkey on the South. To the East of Bulgaria is the Black Sea. The mountain "Stara Planina" (Old Mountain), also called the "Balkan", which traverses Bulgaria from West to East, gave the name Balkan Peninsula to the region.

The territory of Bulgaria has 111,000 km^2, with a population of 8.2 million (at the end of 1997) and a population density of 74 persons per km^2. The share of the urban population is 68 percent. In the new European context, Bulgaria can be referred to as a middle-sized European country.

The modern history of Bulgaria started in 1878, when the country shook off its Turkish yoke. Since then, Bulgaria has had a difficult fate - the country took part in five wars connected with territorial changes, refugee flows, etc. In the years following World War II, the country fell totally under the economic and political influence of the Soviet Union. Now, after starting the transition period, when the population finally decided that the country should regain its place as a European country, Bulgaria fell into such a severe economic crisis as had never happened before in recent Bulgarian history, even in the times of war.

A retrospective view of Bulgaria's economic development prior to World War II could help to explain the present economic situation more fully.

Bulgaria before the Central Planning

Reliable information on the economic development of Bulgaria is available from the beginning of the 1920s (Lampe and Jackson 1976). Bulgaria had a fairly good rate of economic growth after World War I in comparison with the other Balkan countries, which were at a similar level of development, and with similar economic structure (Thompson 1993). The overall picture of Bulgarian economic development shows that before World War II, Bulgaria approximated the level of some of today's developed European countries, whereas the post-war development resulted in marked retardation, which placed the country in an unenviable position in comparison. In other words, the great difference between the present Bulgarian economic level, and those of the West European countries is, above all, due to its post World War II development[1].

Before the period between the two world wars, Bulgaria was a country with the lowest per capita income compared to the other Balkan countries - Romania, Greece and Yugoslavia. After that, the economic development became rapid and stable and until 1939, from being a country with the lowest income per capita, Bulgaria left Romania and Yugoslavia behind. Bulgaria outstripped Romania in the mid-1930s and Yugoslavia by 1939, and even overtook Greece on the eve of its occupation (Totev 1992). Parallels of this

kind cannot be absolutely accurate, but the dynamic of Bulgaria's development justifies the assumption that, from a backward country in comparison
with the other Balkan countries, Bulgaria managed to reach the leader,
Greece.

Bulgaria as a whole managed to maintain a positive balance of trade,
due both to the export of agricultural production and to its economic policy
of replacing imports with domestic production (Table 1 and Table 2). It
must be taken into account that all this happened in the Great Depression
period, when the country also had to pay war reparations and external loans.

**Table 1 Composition of Trade by Categories of Goods (Kingdom of
Bulgaria)**

(precentages)

Products	1935-1939 Import Average	1935-1939 Export average
Livestock	0.5	17.6
Agriculture	0.6	31.7
Vegetable oils, fats	1.6	3.2
Food, Beverages, Tobacco	1.7	39.6
Other Manufacture	91.6	7.2
From them:		
metals, ores	(21.3)	(0.3)
chemicals	(14.5)	(1.9)
leather	(3.0)	(0.0)
Others	4.0	0.7
Total	100.0	100.0

Sources: Statistical yearbook of Kingdom of Bulgaria, 1940, pp. 505 - 507.
Statistical yearbook of Kingdom of Bulgaria, 1940, pp. 499 - 501.

Table 2 Total Export and Import (Kingdom of Bulgaria)

(thousands Swiss. Francs)

Years	1935	1936	1937	1938	1939
Total export	121,251	171,977	264,159	293,160	322,829
Total import	111,309	127,170	258,334	255,294	272,421
Export/Import %	108.1	122.9	100.7	113.0	116.7

Sources: Statistical yearbook of Kingdom of Bulgaria, 1940, pp. 505 - 507.
Statistical yearbook of Kingdom of Bulgaria, 1940, pp. 499 - 501.

In this respect, an analysis of the trade structure of the Kingdom of Bulgaria before World War II can illustrate the country's trade orientation in the years when the economy was, to a great degree, closer to a market one (Table 2 and Table 3). This illustration is indicative enough to allow certain general conclusions.

Table 3 Bulgarian Export by Countries before World War II

Years	1935		1936		1937		1938		1939	
	Exp.	Imp.	Exp.	Imp.	Exp.	Imp.	Exp.	Imp.	Exp.	Imp.
Western countries From them:	78.4	81.1	84.1	81.5	81.7	81.2	83.7	80.0	87.8	82.7
nowadays EU	77.4	79.5	81.5	79.1	77.9	79.9	80.3	76.2	84.4	80.2
Other countries from them:	21.6	18.9	15.9	18.5	18.3	18.8	16.3	20.0	12.2	17.3
Eastern Europe USSR	12.5	16.3	8.9	15.7	12.2	16.5	11.9	17.7	9.6	15.3
Balkan Countries	0.0	0.2	0.0	0.1	0.0	0.0	0.0	0.0	0.0	0.1
	4.6	4.6	4.6	4.6	4.3	4.3	5.5	5.5	5.5	5.5
Total	100.0	100.0	100.0	100.0	100.0	100.0	100.0	100.0	100.0	100.0

Source: Statistical yearbook of Kingdom of Bulgaria, 1940.

- Bulgaria kept a high positive trade balance.
- Bulgarian exports and imports conformed a great deal more to the market criteria (they responded to the actual comparative advantages of the economy).
- Western European countries were the main markets for Bulgarian goods. Exports to Germany were around 50 percent; about 25-30 percent was exported to the rest of the developed Western countries.

One explanation for the successful rates of economic development during the inter-war period may be sought in the policy of adequately and flexibly adapting the economy to the changing conditions and in the utilisation of the economic advantages. It may definitely be asserted that the economic policy allowed no groundless decisions, as happened in the later planned economy period.

In spite of the impressive economic results obtained up to the beginning of World War II, significant structural changes were not achieved. The opening stage of industrialisation contributed to a high growth rate, but, at the same time, created serious problems. The development started with restricting imports and stimulating the self-sufficiency of industry (Jackson and Lampe 1983). This is typical for a country in the initial stages of industrialisation. The efforts to stimulate labour intensive development preserved the extensive character of small-sized farms and firms - mainly based on crafts (Totev 1944). Only a few enterprises were sufficiently large and specialised to be able to achieve economies of scale. However, the economic policy managed to maintain a high economic growth rate and a positive foreign trade balance. Such an economic policy was effective for a short, but not for a long-term, period. As a result, at the end of the 1930s, approximately 55 percent of Bulgaria's gross national product (GNP) was produced in the agricultural sector and 80 percent of the active work force was occupied in this sphere (Table 4). This development isolated the country from the world markets in many respects after the Great Depression and the country was literally forced to ally itself with Germany.

Table 4 Composition of National Income in Kingdom of Bulgaria (1924 - 1945)

Years / Branches	1924	1929	1934	1939	1944
Rural Economy	60.0	57.4	50.9	52.1	61.1
Arts and Crafts	7.2	6.8	7.1	6.4	5.3
Industry	5.5	5.4	7.2	8.6	6.6
Transport and Communications	2.6	2.6	3.5	3.4	2.4
Trade	7.6	7.6	6.3	10.1	9.4
Insurance and capital	2.6	3.9	4.2	3.9	2.7
Real Estate	3.5	5.3	6.8	4.1	1.7
Free profession, services	2.4	2.2	2.1	2.8	2.4
Salaries and Others	8.6	8.8	11.9	8.6	7.9
Total	100.0	100.0	100.0	100.0	100.0
Employed in Kingdom of Bulgaria					
Total employed - thousands	2848.9	3168.7	3229.6	3466.7	3760.9
Share of Empl. in agr. sector (%)	82.7	82.6	84.8	82.3	82.6
Indices of national income (total and in the agrarian sector)					
Indices of Nation. Income	47.0	66.3	78.4	100.0	90.1
Indices of agrarian sector	54.1	73.0	76.6	100.0	105.7

Sources: Statistical yearbooks of Kingdom of Bulgaria - different issues.

Bulgaria in the Central Planning Period

We now turn to investigate the degree to which the country's development was typical of the planned economy and to what extent it was influenced by specific Bulgarian factors. We found it interesting to establish the continuities and the differences of the country's development, before and after central planning, in order somehow to explain the behaviour of the policy making authorities during the transition period.

For a country with a market economy, as was the case of Bulgaria up to World War II, the share of government regulation and ownership was quite significant. Perhaps for this reason, Bulgaria was characterised by the most powerfully centralised planning along the lines of economic development protection, with the biggest government ownership amongst the centrally planned countries. The high rates of growth in the years of planning were again the result of extensive development and not of a modern form of industrialisation.

Even when economic policies have similar goals, the type of economic system in action brings about substantial differences. The main contradiction in its development was that the central planning influenced the economy in such a way that Bulgaria was left far behind the other Western countries. This lagging behind strongly affected its agriculture. Until World War II, Bulgaria had focused mainly on agriculture. Later on, the country went to the other extreme, and this sector remained underprivileged, even when compared with the other former socialist countries.

Prior to World War II, economists reasonably considered that one main problem of the Bulgarian countryside, which had to be solved, concerned the over-populated rural areas (Thompson 1993). Since then, one assumption has dominated: namely that the rural population could and should be used as an unlimited source of labour force to feed industry.

Before World War II, Bulgarian industry was based mainly on small firms. This fact provoked an opposite reaction which went to extremes in order to develop heavy industry. The engaging of the whole economy in the achievement of this goal brought support to manufacturing enterprises, which functioned as losers for many long years. Heavy industry branches were declared a development priority area and protected against the possible advantages of light industry and agriculture.

Although there were certain short-term benefits from the close economic commitment to the Soviet Union, similar to the one to Germany during the 1930s, this created an atmosphere of reticence and one-sidedness. The business transactions were mainly bilateral clearing agreements, as before, due to the fact that the Bulgarian economy could not develop under the beneficial environment of international competition. This was the main reason why the country became isolated internationally, without any possibilities of reacting adequately and flexibly to the changing conditions. The artificial conditions created by the planned economy caused problems, which were particularly clear at the turn of the 1980s and 1990s and led to the collapse of the Bulgarian economy. Its prerequisites and preconditions were rooted primarily in the recent past.

The development of the planned economy created a greenhouse effect in which the indicators could be directed in such a way as to follow the centralised decisions without contradicting the basic economic postulates[2]. The price policy of the centrally planned economy was such that the economic indicators were set up so as to prove the economic sensibility of the development. The structure of the capital stocks as well as that of labour followed the tendency of change in the production structure. For the capital stocks this relation is much closer, and this is easily explained by the capabilities of the centrally planned economy to follow and use directly the economic laws for production effectiveness by way of forming non-market prices, and using other economic levers of centralised management. Thus we came to a production decrease of the "ineffective" agriculture, although Bulgaria was, and still is, a country with favourable climatic and other features, defining agricultural effectiveness.

As Greece is a neighbouring country with a market economy, the comparison between some indicators of Greece and some of Bulgaria can enrich our economic analysis. The differences in the structural changes between Bulgaria and Greece are mainly determined by the high relative share of industry in Bulgaria. As a result of this, the structures of the other main sectors in Bulgaria are influenced, and to a certain degree distorted -this is especially valid for agriculture. The employment structure by sectors of both countries had much in common during the 1960s, and although it has been changing in one and the same direction, the difference has generally increased (Table 5).

Table 5 Employment Composition by Basic Sectors for Bulgaria and Greece

Years	1961		1971		1981		1989		1995	
Sectors	Bulgaria	Greece	Bulgaria	Greece	Bulgaria	Greece	Bulgaria	Greece	Bulgaria	Greece
Agriculture	52.4	53.9	33.9	40.6	23.5	30.7	18.6	25.3	23.4	20.4
Industry	30.7	19.1	40.1	26.5	44.5	29.0	46.6	27.5	34.9	23.2
Service	16.9	27.0	26.0	32.9	32.0	40.3	34.8	47.2	41.7	56.4
Total	100.0	100.0	100.0	100.0	100.0	100.0	100.0	100.0	100.0	100.0

Sources: Economic of Bulgaria, National Statistical Institute, different issues, Statistical Yearbook of Bulgaria Concise, Statistical yearbook of Greece, different issues, National Accounts of Greece, NSSG, 1996.

The Demographic and Labour Market Characteristics of Transition

After 1989, as a result of the negative natural growth and the emigration processes, a stable population decrease is observed. Generally speaking, the transition to the market economy involves a deterioration of the population indicators in Bulgaria - birth rates fall sharply, mortality rises dramatically[3]. This process, together with the emigration of young people to Western countries and of part of the Turkish minority to Turkey, has led to a population decrease in the last ten years by approximately 800,000 (close to 10 percent of the population). The observed trends of low fertility, high mortality and a high emigration level naturally caused a rapid process of population ageing.

The contemporary social and economic policies do not lead to the solution of the demographic problems that will continue to exist at least in a short and mid-term perspective. The demographic regression in Bulgaria will have a significant negative impact on the economic conditions. This is a serious factor which economists in Bulgaria neglect, but it will have an especially unfavourable influence because of the critical economic situation of transition[4]. The artificial urbanisation process in Bulgaria, being a result of the extensive industrialisation, is now reflected in the negative natural growth rate of the last 6 years. The demographic forecasts foresee that this negative natural growth rate will be maintained for at least three decades.

The ageing of the population proved to be one of the most negative factors of the economic development, placing the country in a most unfavourable starting position, when compared to all other CEECs. At the end of 1998, the average age of the population was 39.4 years (37.3 years for the urban and 43.8 for the rural population). The average life expectancy in 1998 was 70.5 years (for males - 67.1 and for females - 74.3). The general age structure changes (main age structure 0-15, 16-64, and 65 and more years) measured by the Euclidean distance indicator d (Hristov 1999), rises from d = 3.89% for the period 1965-85, to d =7.93 percent for 1985-2000 The relative share of the number of persons under working age is 17.6 percent, those of working age - 57.7 percent and over working age - 24.7 percent[5]. The average share of the population under working age in the last three years decreases by approximately 0.5 percentage points per year.

Unemployment and the falling living standard are the two character-istics of the countries most acutely experiencing the transition. The fig-ures of absolute unemployment, according to the National Statistical Institute (NSI), moved as follows: increasing from 65,000 persons at the end of 1990, to 419,000 persons in 1991, coming to 626,000 persons in 1993. After that it is decreases for two years - 489,000 persons in 1994 and 424,000 persons in 1995. From then on, the number of unemployed varies approximately by half a million: 1996 - 478,770; in 1997 - 523,100; 1998 - 465,200; March 1999 - 538,300 and July 1999 - 497,200.

The rate of unemployment at the end of 1995 was 11.1 per cent. This indicator covers the so-called "registered unemployment", which underes-timates real unemployment. A survey based on a sample of 24,000 non-institutional households, presented quite a different picture - 564,600 persons unemployed for June 1995 which indicates a rate of 15.7 percent. Although statisticians accept that this sample investigation overestimates the real unemployment, it is expected that its numbers are closer to the real rates. The official rate of unemployment for the last years is as fol-lows: 1996 - 12.5, 1997 - 13.7, 1998 - 12.2, March 1999 - 15.9 and July 1999 -13.0. With the coming winter period, a rise of the rate of unemployment can be expected, a rise which is observed every year.

In 1997-98, with the advancing structural reform, it was expected that the unemployment rate will rise by at least 5-6 percentage points. Since this did not happen, the conclusion can be that again the real structural reform was not fully implemented.

Economic Development in Transition

At the end of 1990, every sector of economic life, without exception, was deeply affected by the crisis. In 1998 the GDP decline was 38 percent, when compared to the level of 1989. For two years 1994-95, a certain stabilisation of production was apparent. This process continued up to the end of 1995. It is hard to estimate to what extent the increase in 1994, with 1.8 percent, and with 2.1 percent in 1995, was real, and to what extent it was the result of not counting the price changes (underestimating the real deflator of GDP). After all, the sharp GDP decline in 1996 (10.1 percent), proves that the increase in these two years was, if not artificial, at least temporary, and was not the result of a real recovery. In 1997 the GDP decline was 8.9 percent, followed by moderate growth in 1998 with 1.8 percent. Again it is debatable to what extent the growth of the GDP with 1.8 percent is actual, or which part of it is due to the inclusion of some household activities not accounted for until then.

A major factor determining the transition economies' adaptability is the conformity between economic structures and market conditions. Irrespective of the fact that the economic policy in all CEECs gave priority to heavy industry, this was possibly the most widespread in Bulgaria[6]. Without being an industrial country, Bulgaria has one of the highest relative share of industry (Petrakos and Totev 2000).

In Bulgaria, no significant changes regarding the structural adaptation of industry have been observed during the past transition years. In contrast to the other countries and especially to the ones from the Visegrad group, the changes in the broad sector structure of Bulgaria can not be easily defined as real structural adaptation, because this adjustment is the result of decreasing production in all sectors. Structural adjustments are, to a lesser degree, the outcome of in-flows of employed and capital stocks from one sector to another, rather than of the uneven collapse of production in all sectors. The changes noticed in the broad sector structure are a result of the more significant decline of the industrial branches in comparison with services and agriculture.

Significant changes in the GDP structure by broad sectors can not be expected in a short-term perspective (2-3 years). Most probably such changes will be observed after 5-7 years. The 1989 level of output in a mid-term perspective is expected to be outstripped by services, reached by agriculture but there are not enough reasons to expect that industry in a mid-term perspective will reach the level of the pre-transition years.

327

The changes in the number of employed is expressed mainly in the decrease of the number of employed in industry, which is, however, lower than that of production. As a result of that, a sharp decrease of labour productivity is observed. So it can be expected that employment will continue to decline even when production increases in order to compensate for the decline in labour efficiency in recent years. The tendency for a decrease of employment in agriculture, when compared to the pre-transition period, remained, while productivity also decreased, although not so sharply. It is estimated that from 1989 on, those actually employed decreased by around 30 per cent.

It can be stated that most of the producers adapt very slowly to the new conditions or sometimes even act inadequately. Pseudo market conditions dominate in the country whereby the economy is not yet subordinated to efficient resource use and allocation requirements or compliance with the market conditions. Another specific feature is connected with the so-called economy of self-sufficiency. Unemployment, inflation and low earnings spread out this process to unbelievable forms. The above statement leads more and more to the conclusion that the first steps of the market economy in Bulgaria have a specificity of their own.

Structural Changes and Branch Effectiveness

At the level of the main economic branches, the structural changes are also dominated and defined by the changes in industry (Table 6). The decrease of industrial production has strongly influenced transport and trade. Construction is experiencing controversial effects. On the one hand, the transition to market prices increased its efficiency, while on the other, being dependent upon the overall economic development, it is suffering from the present general depression. The construction branch is expected to become especially effective in a mid-term perspective when the revival of the economy begins.

Trade, transport and communications may now be added to the sectors currently enjoying advantages. The communications and trade branches, in a short and mid-term perspective have prerequisites for favourable development. An important role in this respect will be played by foreign investments and the process of privatisation will especially favour the branch of trade. In spite of its obvious comparative advantages, agriculture failed to materialise them and is still unable to do this. Nevertheless, in the mid and especially in the long-term perspective, this will be the branch that will have good development prospects.

Table 6 Composition of Gross National Product and Value Added by Main Branches *

(current prices)

Branches	Years 1980	1989	1991	1992	1993	1994	1995	1996	1997	1998
Agriculture & Forestry	19.3	11.5	28.8	18.2	17.9	20.8	22.2	24.1	37.4	32.1
Industry	51.3	58.9	47.0	49.1	45.2	41.8	42.3	40.5	35.9	38.0
Construction	9.1	9.1	4.9	9.0	9.7	8.6	8.5	6.7	4.0	5.7
Transport	6.6	7.5	5.5	7.9	8.4	7.7	6.7	8.8	7.5	8.1
Communication	0.9	1.4	3.0	1.8	2.9	3.0	2.2	2.9	3.2	4.4
Trade	9.8	8.7	7.2	14.0	15.9	18.1	18.1	17.0	12.0	11.7
Residual	3.0	2.9	3.6	-	-	-	-	-	-	-
Total	100.0	100.0	100.0	100.0	100.0	100.0	100.0	100.0	100.0	100.0

Sources: National Statistical Institute, Statistical Yearbooks, different issues, Statistical Reference book, 1999 and own calculations.
* Up to 1991-- Gross National Product. Value Added from 1992 to 1996.

Changes in Industrial Branch Structure During Transition

One important question about the role of Bulgarian industry is whether the GDP share of industry (which is comparable to that of the Western countries, including the Central European Countries in transition) is efficient. Petrakos (1997) (see also Petrakos and Christodoulakis 1997), determines this share as high and inefficient in the context of the newly emerged European north-south economic divide. This gives rise to the next question - to what extent the industrial branch structure in Bulgaria corresponds to the real competitiveness of the industrial branches.

We are going to examine whether the observed insignificant differences between the proportion of heavy industry/light industry by industrial branches for the CEECs, to those of the Western countries (Jackson and Repkin 1997) also imply that in Bulgaria the heavy industry concentration is not high. Or vice versa, in the case of Bulgaria, the concentration of heavy industry could be accepted as high, since the comparative advantages and the branch structure competitiveness are different from those of the other

Central European countries in transition. We should try to prove that the way of industrialisation in Bulgaria was entirely in disagreement with the requirements of the rational distribution and exploitation of resources and that the registered structure at the end of the 1980s was far from the one that the country should have had if the structure had been formatted under market conditions.

Because it is quite important to answer these questions within the context of an economic analysis, the investigation of the structural changes at the level of the main industrial branches remains of considerable interest. The differences in the rates of growth among the industrial sub-branches were considerably higher up to 1989, and were caused by the artificial priority development of some of them - more precisely of the mechanical engineering & metal processing industry and mainly of the electrotechnical & electronic industry (see Table 7 and Minassian 1992). It is interesting to note that these are the branches that were most damaged in the first transition years, mainly because of the loss of the CMEA markets.

Table 7 Indices of Industrial Output by Branches

(constant 1970 prices)

Branches / Years	75	80	89	90	90*	91	92	93	94	95	96	90 / 90*	%
Electrical & Thermal Ind.	129.6	190.0	236.4	260.9	236.4	242.0	220.3	194.3	195.7	181.8	199.8	204.4	97.7
Coal Industry	93.4	106.6	110.4	123.0	113.2	80.0	103.8	98.9	101.2	96.0	100.7	117.5	141.5
Ferrous Metallurgy	167.7	227.2	259.1	269.4	164.6	126.0	90.0	82.1	104.0	132.6	144.4	135.9	130.6
Non -ferrous Metallurgy	-----	100.0	118.5	117.9	88.2	92.0	63.9	61.7	72.0	79.7	74.6	81.4	95.9
Mech. & Metal process. Ind.	182.1	257.3	351.3	377.5	311.1	190.0	247.9	191.9	142.8	136.5	140.2	123.8	163.7
Elect. & Electronic Ind.	262.1	493.1	916.6	13052	939.7	----	582.6	362.7	333.6	312.5	328.4	354.3	----
Chemical & Oil process Ind.	171.0	267.3	374.9	369.7	276.9	128.0	228.2	189.4	166.1	225.8	264.2	295.4	216.3
Construction Ind.	166.9	231.1	251.7	240.1	193.3	92.0	122.3	100.3	97.0	109.5	116.4	126.8	210.1
Timber & Wood process.Ind.	134.9	156.2	181.0	193.1	171.7	55.0	140.5	122.4	106.6	113.3	116.1	118.7	312.2
Pulp & Paper Ind.	175.9	211.7	250.2	248.3	202.1	150.0	145.3	131.4	125.7	139.7	162.2	141.4	134.7
Glass & China Ind.	149.9	202.3	223.0	233.7	234.2	122.0	190.9	156.0	153.4	186.7	195.7	241.9	191.9
Text & Knitwear Ind.	141.4	180.1	210.7	244.9	241.5	116.0	166.6	144.7	120.0	121.8	109.4	114.4	208.2
Clothing Ind.	138.1	154.8	188.9	209.3	233.2	77.0	195.4	163.0	134.1	142.3	137.6	172.8	302.9
Leather, fur & Footwear Ind.	139.5	154.3	207.6	280.5	239.8	77.0	205.7	181.5	152.5	150.1	129.7	145.1	311.4
Printing Ind.	122.2	197.6	215.1	262.6	269.7	----	292.3	303.1	395.9	468.0	416.1	326.2	----
Food Ind.	135.5	157.9	178.6	180.3	162.3	122.0	128.2	109.4	80.0	70.1	71.2	73.0	133.0
Total	154.7	205.8	254.5	286.5	238.4	140.0	185.9	156.4	139.9	153.5	161.8	167.9	170.3

Sources: NSI.

* Own calculation based on tables from Minassian G. (1992).

In Table 8, the ranking of the industrial branches according to the indices of: industrial output, producer's prices, number of employees, changing of the share of the industrial output, and labour productivity, are presented[7].

Table 8 Industrial Branches Ranked by Selected Indicators

	a*	b*	c*	Share of the Industrial output		d*	Share of the Employment		e*	f*	g*
Years				89	96		89	96			
TOTAL	10.5	8.5	9	100	100	12.5	100	100	10.5	9.5	10.5
Electrical & Thermal Ind.	6	3	2	3.5	10.0	2	2.4	5.2	8	2	6
Coal Industry	3	6	6	1.2	2.3	4	3.2	4.8	5	4	3
Oil & Gas extraction Ind.	9	7	1	0.0	0.1	1	0.0	0.2	18	14	7
Ferrous Metallurgy	12	1	5	2.8	5.8	7	2.7	3.7	14	3	13
Non-ferrous Metallurgy	7	2	3	2.2	5.6	8	2.9	3.9	6	5	9
Mech.Eng. & Met.Prod. Ind.	17	13	16	17.6	9.8	16	23.1	21.6	15	12	17
Electrical & Electronic Ind.	18	16	17	15.8	4.3	17	14.4	7.9	10	16	18
Chemical & Oil Ind.	5	5	7	14.6	27.2	6	7.6	10.6	4	6	5
Construction Ind.	14	11	12	3.1	2.5	15	3.9	3.7	11	11	15
Timber & Wood Ind.	8	14	19	2.6	2.6	10	4.4	5.6	9	7	8
Pulp & Paper Ind.	10	8	8	1.1	1.6	3	1.1	1.8	16	13	10
Glass & China Ind.	2	9	4	0.7	1.6	5	1.6	2.4	1	1	2
Text. & Knitwear Ind.	15	15	14.5	5.1	3.4	13	7.9	7.6	12	15	14
Clothing Ind.	4	18	14.5	2.1	1.4	9	4.2	5.6	2	18	4
Leather & Footwear Ind.	11	12	10	1.4	1.3	11	2.3	2.8	3	9	11
Printing Ind.	1	4	13	0.4	1.1	12	0.7	0.8	17	17	1
Food Ind.	13	10	11	21.1	19.2	14	11.5	10.8	7	10	12
Other branches of Ind.	16	17	18	4.7	0.2	18	6.1	1.0	13	8	16

Source: Own calculations from NSI information.
* the highest indices have rank 1.
Key: a - The rank of indices of the industrial output (1996/1989 constant prices).
    b - The rank of producer's prices indices of the industrial output (1996/1990).
    c - The rank of indices of change of the share of the industrial output (1996/1989 - current prices).
    d - The rank of indices of employees in the state sector (1996/1989).
    e - The rank of indices of industrial output (1996/1995 - constant prices).
    f - The rank of indices of employees in the state sector (1996/1995).
    g - The rank of the ratio of the indices of labour productivity 1996/1989.

The structural changes in industry have increased during the years (1989-95)[8]. Generally, these changes were expressed in a slight decrease in the shares of the typical light industry branches, which, according to the market conditions, should have competitive advantages over the typical branches of heavy industry[9]. This change shows that the real shifts resulting from the adaptation to market conditions have still not been made inside the industrial branches. Ferrous metallurgy, non-ferrous metallurgy, and the chemical & oil processing industry have increased their relative share by approximately 20 percent (to some extent these changes are a result of the increase of output also caused by situational factors)[10]. These are the branches that are least influenced by the reform. Light industry is the sphere where privatisation processes take place; for that reason, its sub-branches are expected to have higher effectiveness as a whole, but in practice the light industry share in GDP is diminishing.

The Spearman rank correlation between column a and column d of the table is 0.66. Having in mind the expectation of a very close relation between output and employment, the estimated coefficient can be accepted as being not high. Spearman's rank correlation between column e and column f is only 0.42, a level which is definitely insignificant. So, it can be maintained that on the aggregation of industrial branches, the employment rates are not following the output rates closely. Data show that conformity between the output rates and employment rates is higher within the light industry branches.

Comparison of columns a and g shows for which branches employment is adapted better to labour productivity - food industry and textile industry are the best, and the worst are ferrous and non-ferrous metallurgy[11].

The rank coefficient between columns a and b indicates to what extent output changes correspond to changes of the producer price indices. The calculated rank coefficient of 0.52 shows a weak relation. This coefficient can be accepted as insignificant, having in mind the big differences of the producer price indices. The rank correlation between columns b and c defines the relation between the change of the producer prices and the change of the output share - the estimated rank coefficient of 0.78 shows a significant relation. In other words the structural changes are due rather to changes of the indices of the producer prices than to the real changes of output. This is also proved by the relatively low rank coefficient 0.55 between columns a and c.

The lack of significant structural changes, which could have been resulting from the newly settled market conditions, is demonstrated by the fact that the branches that have a positive increase in 1994-95 are entirely from the sphere of heavy industry. In this respect, one should mention the following statement "If Bulgarian exports continue to be energy intensive, or even increase in energy intensity (the situation up to 1995), it could be taken as a sign of lack of progress in privatisation and hardening of budget constraints" (Wyzan 1995 p. 14). In 1996 a slightly reversed tendency is noticed - better performance of the branches of light industry compared to those of heavy industry. This is an indicator that up to 1995, it is still not possible to speak about the start of industrial structural reforms.

Sources of Changes in the Industrial Branch Structure

The domestic market liberalisation and the legal regulation expressed in the form of subsidies are factors determining the high ranks in column c for the electrical & thermal industry and for the coal industry. For the first branch, the domestic market liberalisation plays the main role, while for the second branch, the legal regulation factor is basic. These "energy - intensive" branches are, to a lesser degree, influenced by the present crisis first, because of the fact that producer prices make the energy import non-competitive and second, because of the social policy concerning coal mining. These branches are not attractive for foreign investments and even if they are partly privatised, they will be the last in the order.

The high ranks of the ferrous metallurgy branch (see indicators b, c and d) are entirely due to the state's legal restrictions and regulations. In this branch with the greatest production decrease, the highest employment is preserved. This branch benefits from the cheap labour and the neglect of environment regulations in Bulgaria[12].

The international market plays a basic role for the chemical & oil processing industry and the non-ferrous metallurgy, thus determining their structural changes, a fact proven by their relative expansion when compared with the overall loss of markets for industry. So the liberalisation of prices, and what is even more important, the more tolerant environmental restrictions in Bulgaria favoured the development of these branches. In this sense, one can say that state legal restriction and regulations play an important role for them[13].

For foreign investors, the chemical industry is probably the most attractive branch and the privatisation process in this sphere will move in tandem with more investments - in this respect the chemical industry definitely has the highest comparative advantages within the branches of heavy industry. Non-ferrous metallurgy is competitive in the external markets, mainly because of the natural resources and the low cost of labour.

For the branches of heavy industry such as mechanical engineering & the metal processing industry, and the electrical & electronic industry, the changes in the external prices in international markets as a result of the loss of CMEA markets is the main factor leading to the production decline. In these high technology branches, there is a decrease in the other transition countries as well, but for Bulgaria this decrease, is the biggest. These branches show the highest decrease not only for heavy industry, but also for industry as a whole, which is a result of their lack of competitiveness. They need serious new investments in order to improve their competitiveness. Since this possibility is limited, their chances for future development are not well grounded.

The overall economic stagnation had a negative impact upon the construction industry and the timber & wood processing industry, while the liberalisation of prices was in their favour. These branches also benefit from using cheap labour and from the possibilities of attracting foreign investment, especially in the case of the timber & wood industry.

The main differences between Bulgaria and the other countries in transition with respect to the formation of heavy industry structure are especially evident in light industry. These differences are the result of the low technological level in Bulgaria, if compared to the other countries; the inability to focus adequately on new markets; and the lack of any preferential policy on the part of the state with respect to these branches.

State regulations and restrictions have not been differentiated among the various branches of light industry so as to give preference in terms of budget subsidising. This, along with the definite disregard for light industry for the sake of heavy industry, led to an uncontrollable production decline.

In spite of its higher potential for adaptability, light industry suffered from the loss of the former Soviet Union markets and is now strongly dependent on barter transactions, which further enhances the influence of conjuncture. Indicative in this respect is the development of the food industry, which in the other countries in transition is defined as a "winner branch" but in Bulgaria is in severe crisis (Economic Bulletin for Europe 1994). The food industry[14], independently of its obvious comparative advantages, which it would have had in a real market environment, suffers from depressed internal consumption, and is slowly orienting itself towards new foreign markets[15]. The possibilities for such an orientation are narrowed by the lack of investments and also by the relatively low technological level of the capital stocks. In this regard, heavy industry had a potentially better position. Although it is expected that light industry will easily attract foreign direct investments (first, because of being more competitive in the external markets and second because of the small and medium size firms which are typical of its branches) - small enterprises are more relevant for the initial flows of foreign direct investments (Meyer 1995).

It is expected that light industry will definitely be more competitive than heavy industry, especially in a long-term perspective (10 and more years). These expectations are based on cheap labour cost, trade and foreign investment possibilities and natural resources. Therefore, the leaders are expected to be the food industry, the clothing industry, and the glass & china industry, together with the chemical industry. The textile & knitwear industry and the leather & footwear industry are not so competitive, because of the great import from other less-developed countries. The production of the pulp & paper industry and the printing industry are strongly related to internal demand and the possibilities for their development are limited.

Expected Sectoral Trends in Bulgarian Industry

We shall attempt to estimate the expected changes in the effectiveness of the industrial sub-branches (see Table II), taking into consideration: the changes in the factors of production and their way of use; foreign investments; the marketing possibilities of production; total sales on the foreign and internal market; material consumption, as well as the indicators used by Landesmann and Szekely (1995).

Those branches that do not require high investments and those with higher labour consumption will be more competitive in the short-term[16], and limitations for material consumption will be strong. A decrease of the high energy consumption per GDP unit is expected, which will allow the branches, especially those that are energy consuming, to be guaranteed with resources at the present production level of the electrical & thermal industry. Consequently, their competitiveness will be ensured - for the short and mid-term period.

The presence of highly qualified personnel will allow the country to compete successfully with other developing countries - this effect may be expected for a mid-term and mainly for a long-term period. The light industry branches will benefit from the privatisation process in a short-term perspective. In the short and mid-term perspective, the low environment restrictions will favour some of the heavy industry branches.

Table 9 Industrial Branch Projection Development

	Short Term	Medium Term	Long Term
Electrical & Thermal Ind.	=	=	=
Coal Industry	=	-	-
Ferrous Metallurgy	-	-	=
Non-ferrous Metallurgy	+	=	=
Mech. Eng. & Met. Prod. Ind.	-	-	-
Electrical & Electronic Ind.	-	-	=
Chemical & Oil Ind.	+	+	+
Construction Ind.	=	+	=
Timber & Wood Ind.	+	=	=
Pulp & Paper Ind.	=	=	-
Glass & China Ind.	+	+	+
Text. & Knitwear Ind.	-	=	=
Clothing Ind.	+	+	+
Leather & Footwear Ind.	=	=	+
Printing Ind.	=	=	+
Food Ind.	=	+	+

Key: + effective development.
 = neutral state, stabilisation of production.
 - the development is ineffective.
* For the branches oil & gas extraction ind. and other branches of industry any forecast will be very risky and unreliable.

It can easily be foreseen that in Bulgaria, future structural changes can be expressed in the increase of light industry efficiency and the decrease of heavy industry, and respectively, the increase of the relative share of light industry on account of heavy industry (Petrakos and Totev 2000). The transition years showed that these changes will come into effect comparatively slowly, and not according to the initial expectations. The dynamics of these changes will obviously depend on the speed of the implementation of reforms. From among the heavy industry branches, in a short-term perspective, only the chemical industry will be able to outstrip the 1989 level of output. Without exception, the rest of the branches of heavy industry will not reach this level soon, while for the mech. & metal processing industry and the electrical & electronic industry, as well as the coal industry, there are no reasons in the foreseeable future to expect that this level will be reached. In a mid-term perspective most of the light industry branches will regain the production level from the end of the plan period, and if this should happen for the food industry, it will undoubtedly be a success.

The main question concerning industrial development is the extent to which it is influenced by factors which can be accepted as general for most branches (influencing all enterprises in the given branch in the same direction) and by factors connected to the management of the enterprises in those branches. Jackson (1997) drew our attention to this interesting problem: "it is important to know if output is declining mostly (or entirely) in the marginally least efficient enterprises, or to what extent the decline is tending to occur across most or all enterprises in the branch".

It can be claimed that the decrease in industrial branch effectiveness is a result, not so much of differences in enterprise management, as of the influence of "outside" general factors, although for light industry branches, differences in management are a factor playing a more significant role. The share of the medium and small firms in light industry determines the greatest adaptive capacity under appropriate management, which leads to a greater variance of the final results. The available information in this field is not rich, since it is based on case studies or on samples whose size did not allow us to make statistical reliability tests. With a certain reservation, we can draw our conclusions, using some available information[17]. Since in light industry, the deviation across branches is much higher, it appears to explain that the decrease might be due to managerial objectives. Having in mind that the shadow economy is more widespread in light industry, it can be expected that the reversibility expressed by a stable increase of the output will occur in light industry branches.

Agriculture in the Transition Period

The negative features of the economic development in Bulgaria during the centrally planned economy may be attributed, to some extent, to the neglect of agriculture as a part of modern economic development. The long misunderstanding in Bulgaria of the role of this sector resulted in a loss of attraction for agriculture, in a demographic crisis and in other negative effects. As a consequence, after the mid 1970s a slump in agricultural production started. In 1990, agricultural production was at its lowest compared to 1960 and possibly for the entire period after 1939. The amount of per capita national income in agriculture is a proof of this. No matter how uncertain a comparison for such a long and dissimilar period might be, the fact that in approximately comparable terms, the national income yielded by agriculture in 1990 was twice lower in per capita figures than in 1939, speaks for itself[18].

Indicative of the state of Bulgarian agriculture is the considerable dependence of production on climatic conditions and other situational factors. This is typical for a weak agriculture, and determined the decline that occurred in those years when certain crops were two times lower than normal.

On the sector level, the development of agriculture during transition is an illustration of the pace of reform so far. The results declare it unsuccessful with respect to the changes made during that period. Price liberalisation proved to be necessary but it was not sufficient to create a radical reform in this field. It stimulated agriculture, but obviously, one cannot rely only on this factor. The development of the economy showed, so far, that one can not speak at all of a preferential policy for agriculture, a policy which agriculture needs badly, especially in such a transition period[19]. Thus, the changes in agriculture, which are to occur sooner or later and which will intensify in the future, are only postponed, as the population already suffers their negative effects. Depopulation, resulting from migration of young people, and low birth-rates, characteristic of the whole country, results in strongly negative population growth, which places most agricultural regions in a critical position.

The development of agriculture has another important aspect for the country's economic development, which has been given hardly any attention in discussions and publications in Bulgaria - the impact of the agricultural reform processes on the potential future integration with the EU.

One of the difficulties that Western economists considered to be a main obstacle for the faster integration of transition economies, is the harmonisation of the national agricultural policy and the CAP (Common Agriculture Policy) followed by the EU countries (Timothy, Tangermann and Walkenhorst 1996). According to their expectations, after the CEECs join the EU, the overall increase of the GDP for the EU will be about 3 percent, and that of agricultural production, about one third (Tangermann and Josling 1994). In this light, the adaptation of an agricultural policy will be one of the decisive factors for the acceleration or delay of our integration with the EU (Timothy, Tangermann and Walkenhorst 1996).

In this respect, the other transition economies adopted special programmes for financing agriculture, aimed at their easier future adaptation to the EU CAP. For these countries, such measures were expressed in price protecting agrarian policies, and were also accompanied by significant subsidies for this sector. In Bulgaria nothing has been done in this direction, and the expectations are that the difficulties in this area will be most significant for our country (Andreeva 1996). Foreign credits and investments in Bulgarian agriculture were also not made in such a way as to have any significant positive impact (Agricultural Policy and Trade Developments in Bulgaria in 1993-94, 1994).

As a result of the process of support and protection of agriculture, the Central European countries presently have an agrarian and trade policy which is more or less in conformity with the CAP requirements. This also explains the fact that our trade agreement with the EU, concerning agricultural trade, is significantly more unfavourable for Bulgaria than for these countries (Yotzov 1997).

From what has been said, it is natural to conclude that in Bulgaria, agriculture is the sector that needs the strongest preferential economic policies, which should be implemented as soon as possible, and that no other economic or non-economic issues should be given priority.

Changes in the Bulgarian Trade Orientation

The deformation of Bulgaria's trade during the planned economy is reflected in the loss of markets at the beginning of the 1990s and the drastic decrease of the turnover. The CMEA's dissolution in the early 1990s affected Bulgaria most negatively, compared to the other CEECs (Bulgarian Economy of Today and Tomorrow 1992) (Wyzan 1995). The trade turnover of Bulgaria was most significant with the CMEA member countries, and it was, at the same time, oriented mainly towards the USSR (Table 8, see also Dobrinsky 1997a).

The two countries that suffered the most serious geographical and political changes among the member countries of the CMEA, were the GDR and the USSR. Whereas the changes in the countries from the Visegrad Four were influenced more by the loss of the GDR as a partner, Bulgaria, having an extremely high turnover with the USSR, was affected significantly by the loss of markets and trade relations with the USSR. This difference had a strong negative impact on Bulgaria's economy in another sense too. The good relations of the Visegrad Four with the GDR helped them later to re-orient easily towards Germany and the EU (Table 10). The loss of the markets of the USSR for Bulgaria could not be compensated for because of the economic and political instability in the CIS (Former Soviet Union countries), as well as because of their new ambitions to re-orient themselves towards Western markets. The geographical situation of the countries from the four Visegrad countries also facilitated their trade relations with Western countries.

The orientation of Bulgaria entirely towards the CMEA countries, especially for export, was very strong - 85 percent of the total exports (Table 10), of which 65 percent to the USSR. The structure of foreign trade by groups of countries has changed significantly in the period after 1990.

Table 10 East Europe: Reorientation of Trade Flows from Russia to Germany

Years Countries	1988 Export	Import	1993 Export	Import	1994 [a] Export	Import
The share of trade with Germany from the total trade						
Bulgaria	1.0 [b]	5.0	6.0 [b]	2.3	7.7	14.0
Czech Republic	7.7	9.3	26.9	25.1	34.1	28.9
Hungary	10.9	13.9	26.6	21.6	28.2	23.1
Poland	13.1	13.3	36.3	28.0	34.3	27.5
Romania	6.6 [c]	2.2 [c]	14.3	16.5	15.6	19.1
The share of trade with Russian Federation from the total trade						
Bulgaria	62.5	53.5	19.4	36.2	10.5	18.3
Czech Republic	33.4 [b]	31.0 [b]	7.5	14.0	6.1 [d]	13.5 [d]
Hungary	27.6	25.0	15.3	22.2	12.8 [d]	16.6 [d]
Poland	24.5	23.3	7.2	10.7	5.9	6.1
Romania	21.7	31.6	9.2	15.9	4.5	14.5

Sources: National Statistical Institute and other sources.
Comment: The data for Russian Federation for 1988 respond for the Former Soviet Union.
Key : a -- January - June.
    b -- Czechoslovakia.
    c -- 1989.
    d -- CIS.

For export, a decrease for the former CMEA countries is present. From nearly 85 percent in 1989, their relative share falls to close to 20 percent in 1998 and this fall is most noticeable for the share of the CIS: from approximately 65 percent, it is now down to 12 percent. These changes in the export structure are mainly in favour of the increase of the share of the exports to the EU countries with 43 percentage points (in 1998 up to 50 percent), as well as in favour of the increase of the exports to the Balkan countries.

In the process of searching for new markets and economic relations, a basic question which economists have raised, is to what degree the existing relations of the Bulgarian economy with the framework of the CMEA, have been the result of the non-market mechanisms of the planned economy. A generally shared view among Western economists is that the dissolution of the CMEA will be followed by the creation of some kind of future form of this market, which will more or less restore the trade volume of the centrally planned economy period (Tangermann and Josling 1994). Of course, a country can not leave effective markets voluntarily, but the binding of Bulgaria to the CMEA was not a product of market relations. In any case, the satisfactory pre-existing economic and cultural relations will favour the maintenance of good trade relations with these countries, but from now on, they will be accomplished on the basis of market interrelations.

Now it is more realistic to expect that Bulgaria will turn to really existing partners - these are, in the first place, the Western countries, where Bulgaria has maintained, traditionally good trade relations with Germany: the Balkan countries; and in addition, with most of the former CMEA countries, in particular Russia and the Ukraine (Totev 1992).

During the transition period, a certain reorientation of trade by countries can be observed (Table 11). This reorientation is a result of different factors, but especially of the general decrease in turnover, some positive trend being already visible, especially though the fact that the former one-sided commitment of the country is no longer at work[20].

The new orientation towards the Western countries may be attributed to the operation of the market mechanisms. The loss of the CIS market is not a direct result of the market mechanisms but is more a result of the political and economic processes in these countries that lead to the destruction of stable trade relations. There is conclusive evidence that with the economic and political stabilisation in these countries, Bulgaria is recovering its export to this destination.

Table 11 The Ten Largest Bulgarian Export Markets in 1988, 1995 and 1998

(share of the trade in percentages)

No	1988 Country	Share	No	1995 Country	Share	No	1998 Country	Share
1	USSR	62.5	1	Russia	10.2	1	Italy	12.7
2	GDR	5.2	2	Germany	8.6	2	Germany	10.5
3	Czechoslovakia	4.6	3	FYR Macedonia	8.4	3	Greece	8.9
4	Poland	4.1	4	Italy	8.3	4	Turkey	8.0
5	Iraq	2.7	5	Turkey	7.4	5	Russia	5.4
6	Libya	2.3	6	Greece	7.0	6	Belgium	3.6
7	Hungary	2.0	7	Ukraine	3.6	7	France	3.4
8	Romania	2.0	8	USA	3.1	8	Spain	2.8
9	Cuba	1.8	9	France	2.9	9	Ukraine	2.7
10	FRG	1.0	10	UK	2.8	10	USA	2.6
	Total top 10	88.3		Total top 10	62.3		Total top 10	60.6

Sources: Export and Import, 4/98, NSI publication and Dobrinsky 1997a.

The product structure in foreign trade underwent serious changes, especially in the transition years. The export of agricultural products significantly increased its share. The branches of heavy industry such as the mechanical engineering & metal processing industry and the electrotechnical & electronic industry have strongly decreased their exports (Table 12). They found markets in the CEECs and especially in the CIS. The balance by products illustrates the country's potential for export of certain products for this period. Positive export is achieved for agricultural products, metal products, and the chemical industry and, to a certain extent, light industry products (Dobrinsky 1997a). In spite of the changes in the country's trade structure, it is far from reaching its best potential (Wyzan 1995).

Table 12 Composition of Export by Industrial Branches

(percentages)

Years	1989	1991	1992	1993	1994	1995	1996
Industry - total	100.0	100.0	100.0	100.0	100.0	100.0	100.0
Electrical and thermal power industry	0.2	2.7	0.2	0.6	0.3	0.5	0.4
Coal industry	0.0	0.0	0.0	0.0	0.0	0.0	0.0
Oil and gas extracting industry	0.0	0.0	0.0	0.0	0.0	0.0	0.0
Ferrous metallurgy (incl. ore extraction)	2.0	3.6	8.2	10.5	12.2	11.5	8.7
Non-ferrous metallurgy (incl. Ore extraction)	-	-	-	-	-	-	-
Mechanical engineering and metal process. Ind.	33.3	18.8	14.7	11.4	13.8	12.2	10.7
Electrical and electronic industry	29.4	13.3	7.5	5.9	5.4	4.1	4.6
Chemical and processing industry (incl. Rubber)	10.9	29.3	24.1	27.1	27.5	27.4	29.5
Industry of building materials	0.4	0.7	1.6	1.4	1.7	1.8	1.6
Timber and wood processing	0.8	1.7	2.9	3.3	3.3	2.8	2.5
Pulp and paper industry	0.2	0.4	0.7	0.9	1.2	1.3	1.3
Glass, china and earthenware industry	0.2	0.5	0.7	0.7	1.0	1.1	1.6
Textile and knitwear industry	1.6	3.1	3.6	3.5	3.8	3.5	4.1
Clothing industry	1.5	1.1	3.6	3.4	3.1	3.3	4.1
Leather, fur and footwear industry	0.9	0.9	2.8	3.1	3.1	2.6	3.1
Printing and publishing industry	0.1	0.1	0.1	0.0	0.1	0.1	0.1
Food industry	12.8	19.4	20.1	17.8	18.2	17.9	17.2
Other branches of industry	0.0	0.0	0.0	0.0	0.0	0.0	0.0
Residual	5.7	4.4	9.2	10.4	5.3	9.9	10.5

Source: National Statistical Institute and Statistical Yearbooks, different issues.

Import to Bulgaria is, to a large extent, influenced by exports and the development of the economy. In a period of crisis, the import of mineral products, which comes mainly from the CIS, is preserved. When there are no investments, trade, with the production of the mechanical engineering & metal processing industry, falls sharply, and, in fact, it has decreased relatively and absolutely for the last years (Table 13).

The production structure of the foreign trade of Bulgaria is very unstable. For an economy that is in recession, the export of products is predetermined by situational factors. Barter deals, especially with the CIS, are a regular practice. This determines the great changes in the export structure throughout two consecutive years.

Bulgarian exports to the EU are higher, as a rule, in goods of low manufacturing degree. The share of "high value added" flows is much higher in imports from the EU but it is decreasing for some of the most sophisticated investment goods and intermediates, due to the transitional depression. Bulgaria performs better than the CEEC average in the sectors of food and some other primary goods.

Table 13 Composition of Import by Industrial Branches

(percentages)

Years	1989	1991	1992	1993	1994	1995	1996
Industry – total	100.0	100.0	100.0	100.0	100.0	100.0	100.0
Electrical and thermal power industry	4.0	14.3	3.9	1.2	0.1	0.5	0.3
Coal industry	3.5	12.9	3.9	2.5	1.8	1.8	6.1
Oil and gas extracting industry	0.0	0.0	0.0	0.0	0.0	0.0	0.0
Ferrous metallurgy (incl. ore extraction)	7.1	4.7	4.6	6.1	6.7	4.8	0.6
Non-ferrous metallurgy (incl. ore extraction)	0.0	0.0	0.0	0.0	0.0	0.0	0.0
Mechanical engineering and metal processing industry	50.8	26.4	24.2	21.1	19.1	19.1	20.9
Electrical and electronic industry	10.7	5.6	10.4	9.0	11.3	10.4	11.5
Chemical and processing industry (incl. Rubber)	10.4	15.9	29.7	37.1	33.8	36.6	29.7
Industry of building materials	0.9	1.1	0.7	0.9	1.2	1.1	1.3
Timber and wood processing	0.6	0.5	0.9	1.5	1.5	1.7	1.1
Pulp and paper industry	1.9	4.9	2.7	2.2	3.2	4.3	4.6
Glass, china and earthenware industry	0.2	0.2	0.5	0.5	0.5	0.6	0.8
Textile and knitwear industry	3.4	4.4	4.6	4.4	5.8	6.2	8.5
Clothing industry	0.2	0.5	0.8	0.7	0.6	0.6	0.7
Leather, fur and footwear industry	0.5	0.3	2.5	1.8	2.1	2.2	3.6
Printing and publishing industry	0.3	0.1	0.3	0.2	0.2	0.3	0.4
Food industry	5.5	8.2	10.3	10.8	12.1	9.8	9.7

Source: National Statistical Institute and Statistical Yearbooks, different issues.

The highest concentration of specialised exports in the case of Bulgaria is observed in SITC 2 (beverages and tobacco) (Dobrinsky 1997a). It can be maintained that the revealed comparative advantages can be expected to be in the primary sector and light industry where the food, clothing and textile industries will play a major role[21].

Possible Future Scenarios of Bulgarian Trade with the EU

The trade balance with the EU is negative for the whole period of transition. The so called "sensitive" industrial and agricultural goods, including textiles and clothing, metals, etc., are differentiated on separate lists and their import is regulated by the EU independently of other goods (this is part of the Association Agreement signed by Bulgaria and the EU). The slowest and most restricted of all is the liberalisation process of trade in agricultural goods, since they are most sensitive for the EU with its CAP. About a quarter of Bulgaria's exports to the EU consist of agricultural products and food. The most competitive export, consisting of agricultural goods, is still most restricted. So the negative trade balance with the EU will remain as long as Bulgarian export is facing severe trade restrictions, protectionism and other distortions like CAP. This is rather unfavourable for Bulgaria, since agricultural and textile goods represent more than 20 percent of its exports to the EU, and metals, about 7 percent (Yotzov 1997). At least in a short and mid-term perspective, the Bulgarian competitive products will be those that fall into the group of the so-called "sensitive goods". Bulgarian exports can find very narrow niches in the EU market which obeyed these "sensitive goods"; so establishing these barriers, the EU determines a permanently negative trade balance with Bulgaria. As was mentioned before, the negative trade balance with the EU is expected to rise with the real start of the structural reform of industry. So the success of the structural reform is somehow determined by the Bulgarian export possibilities to the EU market, and mainly by those of agricultural goods.

The EU authorities should consider taking the following steps with reference to what would be the best alternative for the EU and for Bulgaria:
- supporting the Bulgarian economy with financial credits, whose effects on the economy are not obvious, have no lasting impact and thus, as a rule, do not stimulate the economy in the expected way or, to choose the alternative;
- helping the Bulgarian economy to be stabilised in a more natural way by improving the conditions of Bulgarian exports to the EU market.

This alternative should also be understood by the Bulgarian authorities in order to make efforts, not only to find credits, but to try to improve the Bulgarian agreements with the EU so as to make them similar to those signed by the EU with the Visegrad countries. It should also be recognised by the Bulgarian authorities that the development of trade offers an opportunity for developing other economic relations, typical of the integration processes and that their effect will become evident at a later stage.

The main question that arises in regard to Bulgarian incorporation into the EU is whether agriculture and light industry will be obstacle sectors for the future. It is very difficult to answer this question with certainty: having in mind the EU CAP policy and the GATT agreement, they will play the role of obstacle sectors for the EU. On the other hand, this will be the sector in Bulgaria which, compared to the industrial branches, can adapt better to the market economy, and will not create difficulties for the future incorporation into the EU structures. There is another reason which contributes the non-acceptance of agriculture and light industry as obstacle sectors for the future integration into the EU. Bulgaria has its markets in the CIS countries and it is expected to resume its exports of such products as before. The exports of food even now occupy significant shares in Bulgarian exports to Russia, whereas food items are not so well represented in the exports to other markets. This means that a great part of Bulgarian exports will not be aimed at Western markets even after Bulgaria joins the EU.

According to Landesmann and Szekely (1995), exports are expected to decrease in the "over-represented" share of agriculture in the CEECs, with the accession to the EU. This process will probably not occur so obviously in Bulgaria, because the country is facing great difficulties with its industrial exports.

After the eventual incorporation of the country into the EU, two opposite trends are likely to occur: on the one hand, a decrease of employment in the primary sector as a development typical of the EU countries in general [the forecasts for employment in agriculture indicate that it will decrease both in the EU countries and in the CEECs (European Union Agriculture to 2005 under Alternative Policy Options 1995) and, on the other hand, the opposite tendency of increase in employment in agriculture as a result of a change in the relative share of industry. Indicative in this respect is the sector structure in Greece, where the country's incorporation into the EU resulted in a decrease of employment in industry (Petrakos and Pitelis 1997). In Greece this development, however, did not bring about any employment increase in agriculture, because the potential of the services sector was, and still is, significant. In Bulgaria, the tertiary sector cannot be expected to develop as fast as in Greece, and for this reason, the decline in industry, connected with our future joining of the EU, can result in employment increase in the primary sector.

The revealed comparative advantages of the country (Balassa 1965) and the traditional export potential predetermine, to a large extent, the export commodity structure. The theoretical conclusions are that liberalising trade among countries with different economic development levels should increase trade specialisation (Landesmann 1996). Following the presented three types of inter industry trade (Sodersten and Reed 1994), it can be expected that Bulgarian trade with the EU will be mainly the Heckscher-Ohlin type of export, with comparative advantages resting largely on factor endowments, which in Bulgaria can be referred to the natural resources of local origin (agriculture) and cheap labour force (Timothy, Tangermann and Walkenhorst 1996).

In a short - and even in a mid-term perspective, Ricardo goods type of trade will play a significant role, where comparative advantage depends largely on production conditions related to the primary sector. It can be expected that the share of the Ricardian type of trade will be replaced, in time, with the Heckscher-Ohlin type of export, over a mid and a long-term period. Concerning the import from the Western countries according to this classification, the technological type of trade will be characterising the flows to Bulgaria.

Bulgaria after Ten Years of Transition

At the end of 1999 Bulgaria completes ten years of transition. Naturally this fact raises a number of questions. Where is the country after these ten years, what was lost and what was gained in these years; after ten years of transition, how many more remain?

What did the country not manage to achieve during these years: In contrast to other countries like Poland, Hungary and the Czech Republic, Bulgaria could not combine the economic decline with real positive structural changes.

The conclusions, which can be made in respect to the changes in the structure by basic sectors, are as follows:

- No clear tendency towards real structural changes by basic sectors was present until 1996. This shows that up to this moment, structural reform aimed at the sectoral adaptation of the Bulgarian economy has not been realised and if this process has begun, it has been in a completely initial phase.

- A sharp increase of the share of agricultural production is observed in 1997. Such a development can be explained only with the start (a real one this time) of the structural reform in respect of the basic economic sectors. The second and more important conclusion is that this development defines a defensive type of structural adaptation, where the economy encounters serious difficulties in its development (Petrakos and Totev 2000). It is obvious that Bulgaria is no exception compared to the rest of the South Eastern European countries, where the structural reform is also of a defensive type, and this will outline their further slowdown in comparison with the rest of the Central

European countries in transition.

In spite of the fact that the country's export structure changes to a great degree, conforming to the comparative advantages of the Bulgarian economy, these changes did not reflect the corresponding changes of the production structure, a process that is observed in the other countries in transition.

The main attributes of market functioning state institutions were not achieved and Bulgaria can be used as an example of a "lower institutional and political efficiency.... and of weaknesses in the institutional infrastructure"(Dobrinsky 1997b).

A number of circumstances determine the low FDI in the country. The average level of investment as a percentage of GDP in Bulgaria is at the average 2-3 times less than the same index in the emerging Central European markets. The Kosovo crisis created risk factor attitude and economic problems for the region as well.

A permanent tendency of negative trade balance is observed in the last years. It is typical for all countries in transition but in contrast to them, for Bulgaria this is not a result of an increase of the FDI and, what is more important, the share of the typical consumer goods in Bulgarian import is too high.

What did the country manage to achieve during these years? A very important factor for the ongoing economic and social processes in Bulgaria is the fact that the society already comes to the consensus that there is no other alternative for future development apart from the market economy. The Bulgarian population gave up the illusion of easy, rapid and prosperous development. From now on it will be difficult for any government to receive necessary social credit for its activity without proving that it will provide real reform.

With the implementation of the Currency board in Bulgaria in 1997, the desired financial and monetary stability was achieved. Inflation for the last two years was as follows: 1998 - 1.0 percent, 1999 - 1.2 percent. Another result of the Currency board was the regaining of the foreign investor's confidence. A rise in prices and stability were also achieved in respect of the Bulgarian Brady bonds.

To a great extent, questions like trade liberalisation, privatisation processes and even demonopolisation are already resolved, although not so successfully concerning the privatisation processes. In the last two years the share of the prices guaranteed by the state decreased from 50 percent to just 15 percent. Another positive tendency is the decrease of the share of the economy of self-sufficiency which can be used as an indicator for increasing the market behaviour of the population.

It can be maintained that state policy is now aimed at obtaining maximum access to external markets for Bulgarian exports. During the last two years a corresponding processes of removing the difficulties posed to foreign traders is also observed.

Were these 10 years of transition lost for Bulgaria? What has been said above shows that the country did not manage to perform like the Central European countries. Having in mind that the population in countries like Bulgaria, Romania and Albania was not as prepared for the changes as the ones in Poland, Hungary and the Czech Republic, it is not appropriate for this to be expected. This is the reason why during the ten years of transition, a lack of consensus in society over the course of long-term and short-term policy goals was manifested. This, in most cases, resulted, not in the solution of the problems, but in their postponement for the future. As was mentioned above, society is now prepared for real reform. This allows one to assert that these ten years of transition were not lost. Bulgaria needed these ten years of transition so as to go through its catharsis.

What are the prospects for Bulgaria now? A main indicator of the difficulties which the country is facing in 1999, is the decrease of exports. The decline of exports for the first six months of 1999 is 23 percent; for July, compared with July of the previous year, it is 19.0 percent. This decline is present, together with the fact that the trade balance for 1998 was significantly negative.

A stable decrease of industrial production is observed during the last year. Only for the last six months of 1999, it accounts for minus 12.4 percent; for July compared with July of the previous year, the decrease is 16.1 percent. Profits from sales decline by 13.7 percent for the first 6 months of 1999. A negative rate of the added value is observed during the last year.

Table 14 Rate of the Value Added by Main Branches

(previous quarter=100)

Quarter	1998 I	II	III	IV	1999 I
Agriculture & forestry	115.6	108.4	100.7	93.2	115.0
Industrial	122.3	110.1	96.1	93.0	90.8
Service	101.5	94.0	95.9	110.7	99.2
Transport	89.5	87.3	87.3	98.5	84.1
Trade	116.9	102.2	108.8	102.2	93.3

Sources: Bulgarian economy during the first half of 1999; Agency for economic analysis and forecasts.

Unstable markets in the country and abroad, insolvency of clients, financial problems, unstable economic environment, competitive imports, etc. are the main reasons for this decline.

Legislation and law enforcement are still not providing the necessary legislative confidence to foreign investors. In some cases, even local administration is erecting barriers to foreign investors and businesses with its unwillingness to implement the legacy. Another barrier for every internal and external initiative is corruption, which exists at every economic level. All this provides a fruitful environment for the shadow economy, which is estimated to be not less than 30 percent.

Under the new circumstances after the Kosovo crisis, there is real danger that the delicate recovery process is reversed and that Bulgaria now falls into the so-called cycle of systematic weakness (Dobrinsky 1997b). Although a lot of international institutions declared their readiness to support the restoration process, the Balkan countries, and particularly Bulgaria, express fear that the international reply will again be far from the necessary one, as it was for the last decade of Balkan conflicts.

For Bulgaria the losses due to the crisis are connected mainly with the necessity to re-route its traditional export corridors. Regardless of the fact that the Kosovo crisis is over, these traditional routes through Yugoslavia will remain unstable - the Danube River is still not open for transport. This makes Bulgarian exports more costly and non-competitive and there are a number of other obstacles as well. The imports to the country are also facing similar difficulties.

The other main losses are connected with the withdrawal of investors' interests from the region. A specific significant negative consequence for Bulgaria comes from the decrease of the number of tourists, which is again due to the influence of the Kosovo crisis.

Thus, in addition to a difficult economic situation before the crisis, in its future economic development, Bulgaria will be burdened additionally by the consequences of the Kosovo crisis. All the above mentioned economic distortions will have significant impact on the Budget and the Balance of Payment, which are expected to face serious difficulties in the near future. Up to the present, an important source for the Budget has been the revenues from privatisation, but this source will be exhausted after the year 2000. For the year 2001, when the External Debt payments will be approximately 40 percent higher than those of the previous year, this source will actually not exist.

All those objective and subjective circumstances during the ten years of transition led the country on the eve of the year 2000, to a difficult economic situation when the greater part of the economic reform is still ahead.

Final Remarks and Conclusions

The main impression about Bulgaria's economic development is that the authorities associate economic reform only with monetary policy. Financial reform represents the only sphere where real shifts are taking place in Bulgaria - this is the first stage and to a certain extent, the easiest. It has been defined solely on the basis of current financial needs. Therefore it will not be a mistake to say that economic reforms were implemented mainly in the financial sector.

The implementation of market mechanisms in a country like Bulgaria also results in a strong displacement of long-term policies by short-term ones. This appears as a trend in the economic policy, not only at a micro level but also at macro level. The postponement of the solution of the structural disequilibrium places the economy in a increasingly difficult situation, also making a future solution questionable, which limits the economic potential for future development.

The economic and social development shows that the strategic question of the formation of adequate sector structure is still left in the background. The transition proved that these would come into effect comparatively slowly.

Low elasticity of Bulgarian foreign trade to the new exchange rates and of foreign trade at a macroeconomic level can be observed. Nevertheless, the maintenance of an overvalued national currency has a negative impact on the trade balance: it provoked a decline in exports and a decrease of the investment potential can be observed. This is especially obvious as foreign investors regard Bulgaria as a risk country.

The development of the trade possibilities with the EU will determine the trade balance since it is expected that with its structural reforms, Bulgaria will need more sophisticated products (including investment goods), which will originate mainly from the EU countries. This determines the agro-food products access to the international market and specifically to the EU, as crucial for Bulgarian trade and, as a result, indirectly for Bulgaria's structural changes, particularly for economic reform.

Bulgarian agriculture needs real support during the transition period. The idea that agriculture should be completely subjected to market mechanism regulations should be changed. No matter when the country is incorporated into the EU, effective economic development will be achieved only after development of the agricultural sector reaches its full potential.[22] Bulgarian authorities should recognise that Bulgaria, in spite of the changes during the planned economy period, remains strongly dependent on its agricultural development; the population also remains connected, to a great degree, with the village and its traditions.

International bodies should understand that well-timed financial and other support, mainly facilitating exports, especially of agricultural products, will give the possibility to Bulgaria to begin overcoming its problems. Financing some infrastructure projects - especially a second bridge over the Danube River (corridor No 4), and softening export quotas and barriers, etc., in a more rational way, will help the economy fight the negative consequences of the Kosovo crisis. Provision of some preferencial treatment of Bulgaria in respect of its participation in the processes of economic recovery of the Kosovo region; that is, providing international aid to Kosovo and the region when possible through firms and institutions of the South Eastern European countries will also be of help.

The question that the government must answer is how to follow internal and external economic policy, responding to the real economic situation of the country. The economic development of Bulgaria during transition did not give advantages to the country in the new competitive environment, challenged by the Visegrad countries. In this respect, Bulgaria should clearly define its priorities as well as its regional orientation for their implementation, an orientation which obviously will be aimed, to a great extent, at the Balkan region, and especially at Greece as an EU country, as well as at the Arab countries. As a less attractive country, Bulgaria, for the time being should offer higher profit prospects in order to attract foreign investors, and this means higher rates of return for the Bulgarian market.

Something that all the Balkan countries should do in the near future is to change the picture of risk and uncertainty, which foreign investors have for the region. The great question, which arises after the Kosovo crisis, is whether the Balkan countries will learn a lesson from the repeated Balkan conflicts.

Notes

1. In 1928-1930 the exchange rate of the dollar to the lev (Bulgarian currency) was such that the national product amounted to about 1.5 percent of that of the USA. An equal pro portion before starting the transition period would require the exchange rate of the lev to be at least 10 times better in favour of the lev. In 1937 the purchasing power of the wages of industrial workers (a wage close to the average for the country), was equal to that in Italy and higher than that in Portugal (Berov 1974).

2. One of the goals of the centrally planned economy pursued by Bulgaria was to prove its efficiency in comparison with the market economies (Totev and Tzanov 1994). This led to the declaration of rates of economic growth that did not correspond to the actual economic development (Minassian 1992). See also Table 7.

3. In Bulgaria there are considerable differences between the demographic indicators for urban and rural population. Minority groups have specific influences especially on birth rates and the infant mortality rate.

4. A very specific feature of the demographic processes is the emigration of young and capable people to the Western countries at a time when the transition to the market economy badly needs such people. This is one of the reasons for which, not only the economic, but also the democratization processes of the country are negligible if compared with the other Central European Countries in transition. The genetic consequences of such an emigration will become evident much later.

5. In Bulgaria, the share of the working age population is formed by women 16 to 55 years of age and men 16 to 60 years of age.

6. This structure was also a result of the former USSR's policy aimed at creating in its satellite countries' economies, provisions that could allow rapid re-orientation to wartime conditions - a policy to which Bulgaria proved to be most susceptible.

7. The national economy branches and the sub-branches of industry are formed in accordance with the Bulgarian classification of branches of national economy, rev. 86 (CBNE'86). The data provided from the NSI for the years 1997 and 1998 are not fully compatible. This is the reason why the analyses of Industrial sub-branches level use data up to 1996.

354

8   As Jackson and Repkin (1997) indicate, under structural changes we understand the changes of output, employment and producer prices.

9   Light industry in the countries in transition where economic reform is applied in reality has definitely better indicators of economic development compared to those of heavy industry.

10 In this specific case, this is mainly a result of the budget subsidies, non-market formation of some prices and the political and economic situation, including the war in Bosnia and Herzegovina.

11 For the sub-branch of the oil & gas extraction industry the volume of production is negligible, which determines its situation at this stage of development.

12 For example among the countries in transition, Bulgaria has the highest emission of SO_2 per capita (see table 3.2., Transition Report infrastructure and savings, 1996).

13 There is no alternative to the further development of environmental protection but expectations for its promotion in the coming years are unjustified if we take into account the extremely difficult situation of the Bulgarian economy. The socio-economic adjustment of society is such that ecological problems will give way to economic ones.

14 As opposed to the other CEECs, in Bulgaria, during the plan period, the food industry was not subsidized more than the other branches (Jackson and Repkin 1997).

15 The decline in the food industry is actually much stronger than the average for industry, due to the fact that, during the planned economy period, this was a branch where the reported production corresponded, to a greater degree, to the actual volume of physical production. The actual decline of production after 1990 in the branches where higher growth rates had been artificially declared is smaller (see the last column of Table 7 and Minassian 1992).

16 Because of investment limitations and unemployment, the branches that need highly technical equipment will have lower competitiveness.

17 The data are collected for the Phare-ACE research project, session 1995 "Ownership Control and Firm Performance in Albania, Bulgaria and Romania". The sample covered more than 100 enterprises in 1995.

18 National Statistical Yearbooks published by NSI - different issues.

19 It is obvious that privatization (restitution) is an important factor for the reform of agriculture but it can not solve its problems alone.

20 Commitments have always been a bad choice for Bulgaria - not only during the planned economy period, but also in the period before World War II.

21 A question linked to prices is associated with the formation and the structure of domestic prices and their reflection on trade possibilities and the revealed comparative advantages. The difference between value added to domestic prices and value added when revalued in terms of world prices, is estimated in order to obtain additional information on the comparative advantages of the Bulgarian economy by sectors and branches (Monke and Pearson 1989) (Tsakok 1990). The data does not allow a precise quantitative estimation and for this reason, results are interpreted by ranking the relative differences between domestic prices and import prices. They provide a sufficient basis to claim that within the present structure of internal prices, agricultural production has the highest comparative advantages. Next comes the chemical industry. After that come some of the sub-branches of light industry, such as the food industry, the clothing industry and others.

22 "In many countries problems in the agricultural sector spilled over to the rest of the economy and brought crises in industry, the trade balance and the government budget. It became increasingly clear that weak agriculture could not support a strong industry..." (Tzakok 1990).

References

Agricultural Policy and Trade Developments in Bulgaria in 1993-1994 (1994), Paper prepared to be discussed at the Ad hoc Groups, 12 -15 September.

Andreeva, M. (1966), Pre-Accession Agricultural Policy of Bulgaria - Closing the Price Gap with the EU. Presented at the Wye Seminar Series, Wye College, 1 May.

Balassa, B. (1965), Trade liberalisation and "revealed" comparative advantage. The Manchester School of Economic and Social Studies 33 (2), pp. 99-123.

Berov, L. (1974), Bulgarian Economic Development during the Centuries, Profizdat, Sofia.

Bulgarian Economy of Today and Tomorrow (1992), Book 2, ed. G. Minassian, Sofia.

Dobrinsky, R. (1997a), Bulgaria and Romania: patterns of trade, specialisation in trade with the European Union during the transition from plan to market. Paper presented at the Conference "Economic Cooperation in the Balkans: A Regional Approach to European Integration", Phare-ACE Program, University of Thessaly, Department of Planning and Regional Development, Volos, 16-19 January.

Dobrinsky, R. (1997b), Multi-speed transition and multi-speed integration in Europe: recent economic developments in the Balkans and their implications. Paper presented at the Conference "Economic Cooperation in the Balkans: A Regional Approach to European Integration", Phare-ACE Program, University of Thessaly, Department of Planning and Regional Development, Volos, 16-19 January.

Economic Bulletin For Europe (1994), Prepared by Secretariat of the Economic Commission for Europe Geneva, Volume 46, UN, New York and Geneva.

European Union Agriculture to 2005 under Alternative Policy Options (1995). Working Paper 1, Prepared by Economics (International) Divisions, February.

Hristov, E. (1999), Indicators of Aggregate Structural Differences (Changes), Statistics, 2/1996, p. 14, Sofia.

Jackson, M. (1997), Restructuring or Structural Change in Industry of Transition Countries: a Review of Issues. Working Paper 63/1997, The Leuven Institute for Central and East European Studies, Katholieke Universiteit Leuven.

Jackson, M. and Lampe, J. (1983), The evidence of Industrial growth in Southeastern Europe before the Second World War. East European Quarterly, Volume XVI, No. 4, January.

Jackson, M. and Repkin, A. (1997), A Comparison of Structural Changes among the Branches of Industry in Seven Transition Countries. Working Paper 64/1997, The Leuven Institute for Central and East European Studies, Katholieke Universiteit Leuven.

Lampe, J. and Jackson, M. (1976), An Appraisal of Recent Balkan Economic Historiography. East European Quarterly, Volume IX, No. 2.

Landesmann, M. (1996), Emerging Patterns of European Industrial Specialisation: Implications for Trade Structures, FDI and Migration Flows. Paper Presented at the Workshop on Emerging Market Organization and Corporate Restructuring in Central and Eastern Europe, Vienna, 16-18 February.

Landesmann, M. and Szekely, I. (1995), Industrial restructuring and trade reorientation in Eastern Europe, Cambridge University Press.

Meyer, K. (1995), Direct Foreign Investment, Structural Change and Development. Can the East Asian Experience be replicated in East Central Europe? London Business School, Discussion Paper, Number 16.

Minassian, G. (1992), Bulgarian Industrial Growth and Structure: 1970-89. Soviet Studies, vol. 44, No. 4.

Monke, A. and Pearson, S. (1989), The Policy Analysis Matrix for Agricultural Development, Cornell Univ. Press.

Petrakos, G. (1997), Industrial Structure and Change in the European Union: Comparative Analysis and Implications for Transition Economies. Eastern European Economics, March - April, 1997/vol. 35, No. 2.

Petrakos, G. and Christodoulakis, N. (1997) "Economic Development in the Balkan Countries and the Role of Greece: From Bilateral Relations to the Challenge of Integration", Discussion Paper Series No 1620, CEPR, London.

Petrakos, G. and Pitelis, C. (1997), Peripherality and Integration: The experience of Greece as a member of the European Union and Implications for the Balkan Economies in Transition. Paper presented at the Conference "Economic Cooperation in the Balkans: A Regional Approach to European Integration", Phare-ACE Program, University of Thessaly, Department of Planning and Regional Development, Volos, 16-19 January.

Petrakos, G. and Totev, S. (2000), Economic structure and change in the Balkan region: implications for integration, transition and economic co-operation, International Journal of Urban and Regional Research., Vol. 24, No. 1, pp. 95-113.

Sodersten, B. and Reed, G. (1994), International Economics. Published by the Macmillan Press, LTD, Printed in Great Britain by Antony Rowe Ltd., Chippenham, Wiltshire (third edition).

Tangermann, S. and Josling, T. (1994), Pre-accession agricultural policies for central Europe and the European Union. Final Report for DG I of the European Commission, University of Gotingen, 12 December 1994.

Thompson, S. (1993), Agrarian Reform in Eastern Europe Following World War I: Motives and Outcomes. Paper presented at the Winter 1993 ASSA/AAEA Meetings in Anaheim, CA, January 6.

Timothy, J. and Tangermann, S. and Walkenhorst, P. (1996), Agricultural Implications of CEEC Accession to the EU. Working Paper No. 1/2, Series of the Joint Research Project, Foreign Direct Investment and Trade in Eastern Europe: The Creation of Unified European Econom:y the Agricultural and Food Sectors.

Totev, A. (1944), Landwirtschaft und industrie in ihrer wechebeiziehung. Schriften des Instituts fur Landwirtschaftliche Betriebslehrebslehre, University press, Sofia.

Totev, S. (1992), The Development of the Bulgarian Economy after the First World War - Continuity and Differences. Bulgarian Quarterly, Spring, Sofia, p. 108.

Totev, S. and Tzanov, V. (1994), Price-Wage Dynamics and Structural Changes in Bulgaria. Research Memorandum ACE Project, MEET II, University of Leicester, No 2, April.

Transition Report, (1996), Infrastructure and savings, published by EBRD.

Tsakok, I. (1990), Agricultural Price Policy - A Practitioner's Guide to Partial-Equilibrium Analysis. Cornell University Press, Ithaca and London, p. 113-126.

Wyzan, M. (1995), Bulgaria's Trade Relations With Its Balkan Neighbors: What They Are and What They Could Be. Paper presented at the conference, Redefining Regional Relations in Southeast Europe: Political Challenges and Economic Opportunities, held in Nicosia, March.

Yotzov, V. (1997), Foreign Trade between Bulgaria and the Balkan Countries. Paper presented at the Conference "Economic Cooperation in the Balkans: A Regional Approach to European Integration", Phare-ACE Program, University of Thessaly, Department of Planning and Regional Development, Volos, 16-19 January.

12 Economic Transition in Albania: Possibilities for Cooperation with Balkan Countries

ILIR GEDESHI
Center of Economic and Social Studies, Tirana

HEKURAN MARA
Center of Economic and Social Studies, Tirana

Introduction

The purpose of this study is to review the economic situation eight years after the start of transition towards the market economy in Albania, some characteristics of the path followed, and the necessity of cooperation with the Balkan countries. More than in any other post-socialist Balkan country, transition in Albania started from the traditional socialist model. The systemic rupture did not flow as a normal evolution but as a process dominated by economic collapse and political instability, which took the form of widespread destruction, chaos and revolts.

Albania's structural reforms and privatization have often been formal. This is a result of the prevalence of a political-ideological objective against economic efficiency, in order to gain support from some international institutions, and to gain local social support. Such "reforms" did not solve the problem of managing and recapitalizing enterprises, which is necessary for changing their behavior and for creating new economic dynamics. The attempt to change was accompanied by a deep depression of industrial production and the creation of new disequilibriums in the structure of the national economy.

From the social point of view, these new negative phenomena climaxed in 1997 with a massive revolt and political chaos.

In March 1999, the Albanian economy suffered another blow caused by the arrival in Albania of about 500,000 Kosovar refugees who were forcefully driven out of their homes due to implementation of the policy of ethnic cleansing pursued by the Miloshevic regime. After the solution of the Kosovo crisis and the establishment of the Stability Pact for the Balkans, new prospects opened for the Albanian economy.

As long as internal financial and managerial resources are not available, foreign direct investments are important for reform of the economy. Until the end of 1998, the stock of foreign direct investments per capita in Albania was low and concentrated in two or three sectors. This is the result not only of the real progress of transition but also of the relatively small size of the Albanian market of 3.4 million consumers. Therefore, the cooperation among Balkan countries is expected to facilitate this penetration as well as the integration of Albania and other transition countries of the region into the European Union.

A Brief Review of the Socioeconomic Conditions

Geography and History

Albania is situated in the South Western Balkans. Its area is 28,748 square km of mainly mountainous relief in the internal part of the country and of plains in the coastal area. The largest part of the country has a mild Mediterranean climate, with average annual rain fall of 1,300 mm, distributed mainly in the autumn, winter and spring.

The population of Albania in 1998 was about 3.4 million inhabitants, with an average age of 25 years. About 60 percent of the population live in the countryside and 40 percent in towns.

The Albanians, descendants of the Illyrians, are one of the oldest peoples in the Balkans. After continuous fights for freedom, they managed to gain independence and their own government on 28 November 1912.

During the Second World War, Albania organized a resistance on the side of the Allies and was liberated in November 1944. After the liberation, the process of establishing a social economic system based on a Stalinist socialist model started. This process went on until the end of 1990. In the late 1970s, Albania, driven by ideological motives, followed a policy of self-isolation. In December 1990, after its students' movement, Albania accepted political pluralism and the market economy, which marked the start of social and economic reforms.

Features of Demography

According to the latest census (1989), the population of Albania almost tripled in nearly half a century (1945-89). This growth was the result of high birth-rates and low death rates. Consequently the annual natural growth, as a result also of its absolute growth, rose from 30.1 in 1950 to 60.7 in 1989 (Statistical Yearbook of Albania 1990).

The high rates of natural growth have brought about a significant change of the population structure in favor of young ages as far as age groups are concerned. Thus in 1985, 62 percent of the total population was below 30 years of age.

The transition process towards a market economy was accompanied in Albania by spontaneous internal and external migration phenomena, not encountered since the end of the Second World War. Although official exact data are not available, it is assumed that during 1990-98, more than 400,000 Albanians mainly below the age of 30, have left the country (Misja 1996). As far as internal migration is concerned, it is very intensive in the poorest mountainous areas of the North-East of the country and it is caus-ing an uncontrolled population movement towards the plain and the major cities, while there is no creation of new jobs.

From the viewpoint of its ethnic structure, the population of Albania is generally regarded as homogeneous. According to the data of the latest cen-sus (1989), the Albanians constitute 98 percent of the total population, the Greeks 1.85 percent or 58,758 and the Macedonians 0.15 percent or 4,697 persons (Misja 1996).

As far as the educational level during the last 50 years is concerned, the population of Albania underwent significant changes. Whereas in 1938, the bulk of the population (over 80 percent) was illiterate, in 1989 the percent-age of educated people 10 years of age and older, had reached 91.8 percent. Actually 44.3 percent of the population of 19 years of age is considered to have secondary and higher education (Albania 1995).

Land and Natural Assets

Albania is distinguished as a mountainous country, where, besides moun-tainous areas, there is a coastal line of 316 km, along which lie the most fer-tile plains. In 1989 the arable land covered approximately 714,000 hectares, of which farmed land constituted 82.3 percent, fruit trees, 8.5 percent, olive trees, 6.4 percent and vineyards, 2.8 percent. Corn, industrial crops, and vegetables prevailed.

Albania possesses renewable and non-renewable energy resources. From the first group, potential reserves of hydroelectric power alone, amount to 20 billion kW/h per year. Of the second group, the following resources are being exploited: oil, natural gas and coal. The known oil reserves are: 69.9 million tons, natural gas 12.8 billion cubic meters, whereas coal represents 760 million tons, which is mainly low quality.

The Albanian soil is rich in solid minerals like chrome, copper and ferro-nickel, which are found in abundance. Besides the above, small amounts of other minerals have been discovered, like nickel silicates, bauxite, magnesites, zinc, etc. The chrome reserves known so far are 37 million tons, copper, 50 million tons; iron and nickel 266 million tons. Albania is rich in non-metal minerals like cement, marble, asbestos, gypsum, clay, bitumen gravel, kaolin, ground salts, etc. It possesses in total, 40 kinds of liquid and solid minerals and in 1989 9 million tons of minerals were extracted. Mineral assets have started being exploited since the 1930s.

Main Features of the Transition to a Market Economy in Albania

Features of the Old Economic System

With the first pluralist elections of 1991 Albania gave up the socialist system. This historical change opened the way for democratic transformations and prepared the ground for the transition from the planned economy to the market economy.

The economic and social system which prevailed in Albania until the end of the 1980s, was set up as a socialist model of the Stalinist type with some additional layers. The whole economic and social life of the country had two pillars:

- The absolute rule of social property everywhere and on everything in the form of government and co-operative property. This led to the accelerated disappearance of private property, beginning in the mid 1960s, and with the suppression of any kind of initiative in both urban and rural areas; in production, trade, banking, services and any other private activity.

- The centralised and strictly planned direction of the economy, performed by the government. Such directing produced its positive results for a certain period until the mid 1970s, as long as the Albanian economy was developing in an extensive way and while new production branches and sectors were created (Mara 1991).

Industry, the main element of government property, was built up entirely after 1945. Based on the Soviet model of industrialisation, development priority was given to heavy industry, as opposed to light industry, agriculture or other branches and sectors of economy.

The Albanian economy was characterised by an incoherent financial system with administered prices and massive subsidies from the state, which penalised the efficient enterprises and perpetuated the inefficient ones. During the 1980s, budget subsidies for enterprises with losses increased and in 1990, they exceeded the enterprise transfers (profit tax, amortisation) into the state budget.

Under the pressure of the policy of full employment of a population which increased at rapid rates, the enterprises of the Albanian economy were forced to employ the surplus labour force, which, under the conditions of the existing technology, amounted to 25 percent of the employees (Luci and Mara 1991).

The conservative structure of the Albanian economy deepened further as a result of an autarchic economic policy guided by ideological motives, especially after the split with China in 1978. From 1950 to 1978, 44 percent of the total volume of investments in the Albanian economy were made through foreign credit (Luci 1991). In the 1980s, foreign credits and foreign investments were prohibited by constitutional Law.

Macroeconomic Stabilization

At the end of the 1980s, the country was on the verge of economic collapse. This threat became a reality only during 1991, when the old structures of centralized management were almost totally destroyed and the economy was left without command. The plan did not exist any more, whereas the market had not been created yet. Neither a plan, nor a market was left, but just a state of chaos which was further aggravated by fierce political conflicts, strikes and the absurd dissemination of physical destruction through robbery, ruin, burning, etc., of a part of the social property. The general economic state of the country until mid 1992 is displayed by some of the classic macroeconomic indices:

- The brutal fall of the industrial production level: over 40 percent in 1991 and 60 percent in 1992, whereas some branches of industry did not function at all. Even agricultural production suffered a decrease of 24 percent as a result of the spontaneous dissolution of the former agricultural co-operatives and the destruction of the state system of agricultural input supply and of product trade.
- Great unemployment. At the end of 1992 unemployment reached the number 394,000 or 26.5 percent of the labour force.
- The unprecedented budget deficit - over 25 percent of the GDP during 1991, and 60 percent during the first half of 1992. This was caused by the rapid increase and lack of control over the budget expenses when the income was not being realised.
- Great foreign debt, created as a result of commitments of the National Bank of Albania to inappropriate foreign currency transactions and the deficit in the balance of payments - 254 million USD at the end of 1990, 498 million USD in 1991 and approximately 638 million USD in 1992 (Transition Report Update 1996). This situation made it impossible to draw credit from foreign financial institutions after 1991.
- Hyperinflation: at the end of 1991 inflation was 104.1 percent, whereas in April 1992 it reached 170 percent.
- Rapid devaluation of the national currency - the Lek. In 1990, 1 USD was equal to 8.9 Leks, in December 1991, 25 Leks, whereas in April 1992, 1 USD reached the equal of 106.5 Leks.
- Deep deficit in the balance of foreign trade, as a result of export decrease and import increase. In the year 1991 the deficit reached 72 million USD and in 1992, 101 million USD (INSTAT 1996).

Under this economic situation in Albania, there emerged two concepts regarding the transition towards the market economy. The first one supported the beginning of transition from "zero level", whereas the other supported the idea of a gradual process. The political force in power inclined towards the first concept. The new Government, also following the recommendations of some international institutions like the International Monetary Fund and the World Bank, undertook an economic reform with elements of shock therapy. Its main elements were: prompt liberalisation of prices, trade, the exchange rate and restrictive monetary policy.

In the accomplishment of this objective, in August 1992, the Albanian Government liberalised the wholesale and retail commodity prices. As a result, the liberalised prices increased approximately 10-12 times.

The second element of this policy, the complete opening of the national economy to international competition, was implemented by abolishing the remaining administrative and tariff obstacles.

The main objective of the economic stabilisation program was the reduction of inflation below 20 percent in 1996 (Meksi 1993). In this case, the most difficult part would consist in reducing the budget deficit as the main inflation-promoting source. As a result of the measures taken for the reduction of state expenses, the budget deficit fell to 20 percent of GDP at the end of 1992, and fell even further to 16 percent of the GDP in 1993, to 14 percent in 1994, and to 12 percent in 1995.

This policy caused the deep and long-term depression of industrial production, which, according to some estimates of the International Monetary Fund, continued until the beginning of 1995, to be followed by a long period of stagnation. Meanwhile, as a result of immediate exposure of the national economy to foreign competition, under the conditions of an old technology, a decrease in demand and budget constraints, some branches of industry such as the metallurgical, the chemical and the paper industry, were destroyed or reduced to their minimum activity. Consequently, employment in the state sector was reduced to half. This tendency continues (Nati 1995) under restructuring, privatisation and the administrative reform, as surplus labour is not being absorbed at the same rates by the private sector. A survey conducted in Tirana in 1993 showed that the number of really inactive persons, i.e. people that do not look for work, although they are within working age, was twice as great as that of the recorded unemployed (Albania 1995). In the meantime, as a result of the demographic growth of 2.2 percent during the period 1970-80, 60,000 young people enter every year the labour market.

As a result of the rapid growth of daily consumer goods prices compared to the average nominal salary in the state sector, the real average salary in 1994 as compared to that of 1990 has declined by -16.3 percent.

The effect of these two trends has increased poverty and social disparities. Transition has caused severe problems in vast strata of population, such as the unemployed, the retired, families with many children, etc. In an interesting study, Caroline Van Rijceghem (1994) of the International Monetary Fund indicates that during 1991-93 the urban population living below the poverty level (consuming less than 2,000 K.kal. per capita per day) increased from 6 percent to 25-30 percent. But this poverty is alleviated by migration and social assistance. Other data indicate that in 1996, 143,500 families benefited fully or partially from economic aid from the state. In 1997, this figure rose to 145,900 families and after that, decreased a little in 1998 to 137,700 families (INSTAT 1999).

Another feature of the Albanian reform is its extroversion (Samson 1996). This means that local consumption is much higher than production: the difference is covered by private remittances of Albanian emigrants and by aid from international organisations. From 1991 to the end of 1993, Albania received general foreign aid of one billion USD from the EU (Langer 1995). Foreign currency remittances of economic emigrants abroad have contributed to the financial stabilisation as well. Although accurate data are not available, it may be assumed that these remittances during the period 1991-98, have reached, on an annual average, the amount of 400 million USD.

The question arising in this case is the management of financial flows. This is another institutional aspect of the reform. The first risk is that because of the lack of microeconomic restructuring, the economic flows are not stimulating the local production but are focusing on the import of consumer goods, thus increasing the trade deficit and the foreign debt. The second risk is that because of the lack of an efficient banking system, capable of mobilizing and investing the savings of the population, the financial flows will "freeze" in the informal investment companies.

Until the end of 1995 the policy of macroeconomic stabilization was considered by some international institutions to be a "success story", despite the contradictory results. Thus, at the end of 1995, four years after the implementation of this policy, inflation dropped to 6 percent, the budget deficit fell to 12 percent, the exchange rate was almost stable during the years (1993-95), the foreign debt of 500 million USD inherited from the previous system was settled by paying only 20 percent of it, whereas the remaining part was written off. However, if some other evaluation criteria (Kolodko 1992) are applied, broader than the ones already mentioned, we shall see that industrial production continued to decline until the year 1995; the trade deficit was growing, whereas massive unemployment had decreased mainly as a result of illegal emigration to neighbouring countries.

During 1996, deterioration of the macroeconomic indicators may be noticed. Inflation increased to 17.4 percent, the budget deficit was 250 million USD, the trade deficit reached 690.12 million USD, the exchange rate, 105.7 Lek per USD and economic growth was lower than during 1995. The deepening of these trends and the collapse of the informal financial sector led the country to a new economic collapse and to social explosion, which took on the form of a popular revolt and political chaos.

The most evident aspect of this crisis was mainly the collapse of the informal financial institutions which started by the end of 1996. These institutions, which included private companies, individuals and charity foundations, offered return rates at 8-25 percent per month against 1 to 2 percent offered by the banks. They were operating in the entire territory of Albania and during a period of 2-4 years had collected the savings of 1/3 of the total number of Albanian families, estimated at 1.2 billion USD. High interest rates, applied by the informal financial market, encouraged an artificial consumption growth through imports beyond the real possibilities of the economy and temporarily alleviated the social cost of transition. The high interest rates could not be provided only by real economic activities and without illegal activities that included money laundering and pyramid schemes. The pyramid schemes, besides the negative macroeconomic consequences and encouragement of parasitism, have discouraged the investment of savings in real economic activities, thus hurting economic growth.

Among other factors, the deterioration of the macroeconomic situation is the result of the backwardness of the institutional reform (restructuring, privatisation of large enterprises, reform of the banking system) or the depth of progress towards the market economy. If we use a specific synthetic indicator of transition worked out by the EBRD (1996) to measure the institutional changes, Albania holds the 21st place, behind the top countries, the Czech Republic and Hungary, and behind the other Balkan countries (Slovenia, Croatia, Bulgaria, FYR of Macedonia, Romania).

Structural Reforms

The objectives of "shock therapy" and liberal policy were not only quantitative. They also included qualitative changes through structural reform. The first element was privatisation and development of the prevalent private sector in the economy, as the most important institutional change in the transition to the market economy. This was being carried out by the intertwining of two processes:

- the privatisation of the state enterprises by way of explored techniques, and
- the creation and expansion of new enterprises with foreign or domestic capital.

The institutional basis of the process of privatisation was established by the Law "On sanctioning and protection of private property, free initiative, independent private activities" which was passed by the first pluralist Albanian parliament in August 1991. As a consequence of the creation of this law, the National Agency of Privatisation was formed. This agency is the main institution assigned with the function of transferring the state property to private property.

The features of privatisation in Albania at the time of writing are:
- Rapid privatisation, with quantitative objectives, such as: "by 1999, over 90 percent of the GDP will be yielded by the private sector" (Kopliku 1996).
- Total privatisation of the economy, in order to reduce the state sector to a minimum.
- Privatisation, then restructuring, in order not to lose time. As a rule, restructuring and investment in the existing enterprises are undergone by the private owners, upon privatisation.

The whole strategy is guided by the concept that the more rapid and the more radical the privatisation process and the contraction of the public sector, the more irreversible the post communist transition and the higher the economic growth (Glozheni 1995). At a time when capital was scarce and speed was accepted as a primary criterion, the implementation of this strategy would also condition the choice of the main privatisation method, especially of the privatisation of large state enterprises.

Under these circumstances, privatisation with vouchers, as a quick tool, better suited this strategy. At the same time, it solved the problems of both lack of capital and lack of capitalist entrepreneurs. It was accepted by the population and was supported by international institutions.

Small and Big Privatization

In Albania, as in other Balkan countries in transition, the implementation of the privatisation program was being carried out in two phases:

The first phase includes the privatisation through the auction of small and medium enterprises of production and services. In Albania, enterprises with assets valued up to 150,000 USD are called small enterprises. Medium enterprises are those with assets valued from 150,000 to 500,000 USD, or those with up to 300 employees. By the end of 1993, there were approximately 1,600 small and medium state enterprises in Albania.

Referring to some partial data, only during the period 1993 - April 1995, when the process of privatisation was accelerated, 4,397 small and medium sized enterprises, were privatised. Of these, 1,760 or 40 percent were privatised by the employees; 1,105 or 25 percent by the former owners; 1,508 or 34.7 percent were privatised by Albanian individuals or legal entities; and only 12 enterprises or 0.3 percent were privatised by foreign capital.

A study carried out in the privatised enterprises at the beginning of 1995 revealed that in many of them, there has been no growth of economic efficiency (Mara and Gadeshi 1995). Other sources emphasise that in over 64 percent of the small and medium privatised enterprises 40-50 percent of their capacities have not yet been put into operation (Xhepa 1996a). This shows that the quantitative aspect of privatisation is highly appreciated, while the qualitative aspect, which has directly to do with management and restructuring, is neglected.

The second phase included the privatisation of large strategic and non strategic enterprises. It started in May 1995. Characteristic of this phase was the implementation of mass privatisation techniques. Large enterprises are those with assets valued at over 500,000 USD and with over 300 employees. In January 1994 there were 394 big enterprises, 47 of which were not operating.

The privatisation of the big enterprises started to be implemented in 1995 through: free distribution of privatisation vouchers exchangeable for shares of the state enterprises to be privatised, according to the Czech pattern, to all members of the urban residents over 18 years of age. The distribution of privatisation vouchers started in May 1995 and will be carried out in two rounds.

The majority of people who benefited from privatisation vouchers during the first round, preferred to sell them on the free market. The circumstances leading to this action were insufficient information regarding the financial situation of public companies in auction and the lack of knowledge about where to invest. In June 1995 the vouchers were sold for 25 percent of their nominal value; in June 1996 for 12 percent, and in March 1997 for 1 percent. Until the end of 1996, 97 big enterprises were privatised with privatisation vouchers.

Only a small portion of the population, approximately 30,000 people or nearly 2.7 percent of beneficiaries, have deposited their privatisation vouchers in the Anglo-Adriatic Investment Fund. This is the only investment fund operating in Albania and has promised to distribute dividends once and twice a year. Two other investment funds licensed in October 1996 are not yet operational. Unlike those of the other transition countries, the investment funds did not take part in the first round of privatisation.

Private sector agriculture represents an important element in the private sector of the Albanian economy. This sector was created through the privatisation of arable land. Initially the land was distributed for use but without the right of sale. At the end of 1995, more than 98 percent of the arable land at the disposal of the former co-operatives, had been distributed. During the years 1993-94, the land of former state farms was distributed for use to its former employees. In the year 1995 "The law on land sale and purchase" was approved. With the completion of land privatisation in the villages, where 2/3 of the population still live, 440,000 small private farms have been created with an average land area of 1.4 hectares (Osmani 1995). But small private farms with insufficient land area constitute an obstacle for the development of modern agriculture.

Today, several years after the start of the privatisation process in Albania, 70 percent of the economy has been privatised and 85 percent of the GDP is yielded by the private sector, with a prevalence of small enterprises. By the end of 1998, this sector, not including agriculture, employed 120,000 persons, while the private sector, as a whole, provided over 80 percent of exports (INSTAT 1999). In this framework, the accomplishment of the privatisation of the trade network and part of the services, of the means of transportation and of 200,000 residential apartments, has been relatively rapid. Nevertheless, the main objectives of privatisation have not yet been achieved at the foreseen levels. In spite of the fact that 60 percent of the state enterprises were privatised by the end of 1998, they employed only 50 percent of the work force, and possessed only 25 percent of the total assets.

The Structure of the Albanian Economy

The Structure of the National Economy until 1990

As a result of the Soviet-type and rapid industrialization policy, a diversified economy was produced by the end of the 1980s. The structure of this economy was dominated by industry, which produced 41 percent of the GDP. Regardless of the progress achieved during the last 40 years (1950-90), Albania continued to be the poorest country of Europe. In 1990 the GDP per capita was about 800 USD.

By the end of the 1980s, the Albanian economy presented both a backward and a conservative structure. According to the old doctrine, heavy industry prevailed in the structure of industrial production, which, by the end of the 1980s produced 54 percent of the total production and 56 percent of the total volume of export, and employed 45% of the total number of industry workers (Mara 1991a). In the beginning of 1970, new branches like the mechanical, metallurgical and chemical industries started being developed in the structure of the Albanian economy.

As far as the consumer goods industry goes, the light and agri-food industries played the main role and produced 41 percent of the total industrial production of the country. These two branches of industry employed 46 percent of the total numbers of industrial workers and they provided 85 percent of the total volume of consumer goods.

By the end of the 1980s, Albanian agriculture produced 36 percent of GDP and employed 40 percent of the active population (Mara 1991a). The contribution of the main branches of agriculture to agricultural production is as follows: agriculture 61.5 percent, livestock 32 percent and forestry 6.5 percent. The area of cultivated land was 714,000 ha, while 409,000 ha, or 57.3 percent of the cultivated land was under irrigation. Motor power in agriculture amounted to 1.38 million HP, and 158 kg of chemicals and fertilizers were used per 1 ha of cultivated land (Statistical Yearbook of Albania, 1991).

Transportation, trade and service were also part of the structure of the Albanian economy. Up to the end of the 1980s, Albanian statistics were based on the Marxist concept, which almost excluded the service sector from the creation of national income. Only 18 percent of the total number of the country's workers were employed in this sector and this fact indicates the insufficient development of the sector to meet the current demand.

The Changes in the Structure of the Albanian Economy during the Period of Transition (1991-98)

The process of transition of the Albanian economy towards the market economy was accompanied by significant changes in property structure, size of enterprises, production structure and employment.

The redistribution of property rights and of foreign direct investments are totally changing the property structure inherited from the previous system and have promoted the birth of entrepreneurial capitalism (small enterprise). The current forms of property are state, privatised, private de novo, joint ventures, foreign enterprise, etc. By the end of 1998, the private sector economy included 56,453 active enterprises, of which 41,910 or 74.2 percent were individuals and 14,543 or 25.8 percent were legal entities (INSTAT 1999).

The dynamic of private sector enterprise creation indicated by annual start-ups continuously grew until 1994 and decreased significantly in 1995 and 1996 (INSTAT 1997). This was mainly due to lack of credit and the unfavorable conditions and constraints of the banking system. Other factors which discouraged investments in the private sector were speculative activities and the operation of an informal credit system which, from 1995 on, offered very high return rates.

The size of enterprises in the private sector measured by the number of employees is small. By the end of 1998, 79 percent of enterprises in the private sector employed 1 employee, 19 percent employed 2-10 employees, and only 2 percent of them, or 1,136 enterprises, had over 10 employees (INSTAT 1999). In 1998, the average number of employees in private sector enterprises was about 2 employees. The perspective of economic growth of the private sector requires a higher concentration level of production than the current one.

The large number of private sector enterprises should not be emphasized as long as they have a low level of capitalization. The sectors that have developed more rapidly are trade (29,370 enterprises, or 52 percent); services (10,042 enterprises, or 17.7 percent) and transport (8,199 enterprises or 14.5 percent). However the industrial enterprises constitute only 9.5 percent of the total, and most of them belong to the industries of textile-garment, leather-footwear, timber and construction material (INSTAT 1997).

The economic reform led to significant changes in the GDP structure, as well as in the proportions among sectors, branches and sub-branches, (Table 1). A peculiarity of structural change is the fact that it took place in the condition of a drastic fall of production that was differentiated according to sectors and branches. The fall has been deeper and longer in industry. According to some overestimated figures of the Ministry of Finance, industrial production by the end of 1998 was 27 percent of the level of 1989. Since 1992, a relative rise has started in agriculture, construction, and trade. It has not yet reached the level of 1989. By the end of 1998, agriculture produced 54.2 percent of GDP (35.5 percent in 1989); industry 12.4

percent, (41.3 percent in 1989); construction 12.5 percent (6.9 percent in 1989); transportation 3 percent and other branches, 18 percent. Thus industry, from a leading branch until the end of 1980's, went down to the third place.

Even the structure of industrial production has changed significantly. The extracting industry, which in 1989 produced 18 percent of industrial production, was characterized by a drastic reduction of production, as well as by a close-down of some of its sub-branches. This depression also continued during 1997. The prospective re-activation of these branches, especially through foreign capital investments, would make the structure of the economy more rational and would speed up its integration into the world economy. Even the new branches of industry, respectively the mechanical and chemical ones, are in a profound crisis.

The light and the food industries are also marked by a drastic reduction in production. The main reason for this was the increase of demand for imported goods after the immediate opening of the economy. Under the conditions of backward and obsolete technology, Albanian industry was not able to compete with foreign products, particularly in quality and variety.

The structure of gross agricultural production is characterized by the rapid development of livestock and growth of its specific weight. This is due to the high efficiency of livestock in meeting farmers' needs and sales in the market. In agriculture, the most significant changes have encompassed the area of land cultivated with vegetables, corn, potatoes and forage, as well as the increase of the vegetable yield.

Under the conditions of general economic depression, it is the construction sector that is showing a robust growth, thus giving an impetus to the production of construction materials like cement, brick, tiles, prefabricates, etc., although it is far from the level of 1989. This explains the growth of imports of some construction materials.

The new structure of GDP is characterized by considerable growth of the service sector, (Table 1). From 16.2 percent of GDP in 1989, it rose to 21 percent in 1998. The majority of the employees of this sector are concentrated in services like retail trade, restaurants, bars, etc. The demand in this sector is met mainly by emigration remittances and the high interest rates of the informal financial system till 1996.

Table 1 GDP and GDP Composition

	1994	1995	1996	1998
	At Current Prices (bln Leks)			
1. Agriculture	100,754	125,434	144,830	249,645
2. Industry	23,112	26,943	34,311	56,974
3. Construction	17,722	23,622	31,352	57.589
4. Transport	6,213	8,118	9,009	13,798
5. Services	36,593	45,677	61,496	82,862
Total	184,393	229,793	280,998	460,866
	Composition, %			
1. Agriculture	54.6	54.6	51.5	54.2
2. Industry	12.5	11.7	12.2	12.4
3. Construction	9.6	10.3	11.2	12.5
4. Transport	3.4	3.5	3.2	3.0
5. Services	19.8	19.9	21.9	18.0
Total	100.0	100.0	100.0	100.0

Sources: Ministry of Finance 1997; Albania in Figures, INSTAT, 1999.

The Foreign Economic Relations of Albania

Albanian Foreign Trade

The period of transition toward the market economy in Albania also was associated with considerable changes in the sector of foreign trade. These changes can be seen in both the organisation and the structure of export-import goods as well as in the new geographical orientation of the trade flows. The liberalisation of foreign trade has been in interaction with the macro-economic stabilisation and restructuring of the economy.

Up to the end of the 1980s, Albanian foreign trade had been totally planned and centralised and it did not undergo any partial reforms as was the case with the other countries of Eastern Europe. The whole of Albanian foreign trade had been a state monopoly and had been carried out by certain specialised enterprises. Regardless of the starting point, the liberalisation of foreign trade has been almost total and immediate and was accomplished by using shock therapy. Actually, due to the rapid privatisation of small and medium enterprises, over 80% of the total volume of foreign trade is realised by the private sector (INSTAT 1999).

An Import Oriented Economy

Under the conditions of a relatively closed economy, the ratio of the Albanian trade turnover to GDP during the 1980s fluctuated between 15 and 20 percent. This ratio was close to that of Romania but much smaller than those of Bulgaria and the former Yugoslavia (Bleyer, et al. 1992). In 1998, the ratio was about 33 percent of GDP. This is explained by the rapid increase of import resulting from the immediate opening of the economy in the conditions of a drastic fall of GDP during the first transition years, as a result of the deep economic depression.

The volume of the trade turnover, after a significant fall in the first transition years, increased in 1998, amounting to 1.001 million USD (Table 2). This is mainly due to the increase of imports. In 1998 exports reached 206.47 million USD and imports 794.61 million USD (INSTAT 1999). In the same year, exports per capita were 61 USD while imports were 234 USD. This indicates that the Albanian economy during the transition years was more and more oriented towards imports, causing a rise in the trade deficit. In 1998, the percentage of import coverage in relation to exports was 26 percent, from 42 percent in 1991. As a consequence, the economy passed from an equilibrated trade balance during the 1980s to a deficit trade balance that tended to increase significantly during 1991-98. In 1998 the trade deficit reached 588.14 million USD or 19.2 percent of the GDP from 72 million USD or nearly 6.2 percent of GDP in 1991 (INSTAT 1999). The financing of the foreign trade deficit was mainly covered by the remittances of the Albanian migration and foreign aid.

Table 2 Albanian Exports and Imports (000 USD)

	1991	1992	1993	1994	1995	1996	1997	1998
Export	51,740	77,860	122,470	141,390	201,620	207,500	141,331	206,533
- Private sector	-	-	65,950	67,840	119,870	166,700	-	-
- Public sector	51,740	77,860	56,520	73,550	81,750	40,800	-	-
Import	124,040	179,200	421,140	548,330	649,910	895,700	619,872	794,823
- Private sector	-	-	294,940	429,060	525,890	742,590	-	-
- Public sector	124,040	179,200	126,210	119,270	124,010	153,110	-	-
Export + Import	175,780	257,060	543,610	689,720	851,530	1,103,200	761,203	1,001,356
Trade Deficit	-72,300	-101,340	-298,670	-406,940	-448,290	-688,100	-478,541	-588,290
Aid	-	-	150,450	53,910	62,880	18,284	43,631	-

Source: Albania in Figures, INSTAT, 1999.

The Structure of Foreign Trade Flows

The structure of Albanian foreign trade has reflected the changes of the productive structure of the economy, both during the old economic system and at present. During the 1980s, Albanian exports were dominated by raw materials, while in imports, processed goods, machinery and raw materials for industry prevailed.

The Albanian Institute of Statistics has published some partial but not detailed data for various countries on the structure of import-export goods according to the Harmonized System and SITC classification, only for the period 1994-98. According to these data, the main group of export goods is "textiles and footwear", the specific weight of which changed from 39 percent in 1994 to 53 percent in 1998. This constitutes a new trend in the structure of goods for Albanian export. Most of the goods that are produced with the client's material or by joint ventures with foreign investors, are destined for the markets of Western Europe, mainly Italy and Greece.

Meanwhile, the group "minerals, fuel and electricity" which ranked third in exports at the beginning of 1998 with 11.2 percent, suffered a relative and absolute reduction in the total export. Compared to the period prior to transition, the reduction is profound and this explains the total fall in exports. In 1989, Albania exported 185 million USD "minerals, fuel and electricity", while in 1998, it exported about 23 million USD or eight times less.

As far as imports are concerned, the first place belongs to the group "food, beverages and tobacco", according to the Harmonized System. This group constituted 28.3 percent of the total imports during 1998. This is an expression of a drastic reduction in farm and industrial production during the first transition years. The majority of goods in the group "food, beverages and tobacco" are imported from Italy and some Balkan countries like FYR of Macedonia, Bulgaria and Greece.

The second place in imports belongs to the group "textiles and footwear" with 17.1 percent of imports in 1998. Some of them are processed, then re-exported to the country of their origin. The third place in imports belongs to the group "machinery, equipment and spare parts" with 15.6 percent of the imports in 1998. In comparison with the pre-transition period, the structure of this group has changed.

Regional Structure of Foreign Trade

With the opening of the economy, the foreign trade of Albania underwent significant changes in so far as its geographical allocation is concerned. At present it is oriented towards European countries, which represent over 90 percent of the total volume of foreign trade. Its main partner is the EU, with which in 1998 the trade represented about 85 percent of the total volume of both export and import (INSTAT 1999). Compared to 1991, there has been a significant increase on the side of the EU countries. The increase is due to the reduction of the specific weight of the countries of Central and Eastern Europe and the other countries of the world. By the end of the 1980s, according to the classification of that time, 33 percent of the volume of Albanian foreign trade was conducted with the industrialised countries of Western Europe, 54 percent with the countries of the CMEA and 13 percent with the developing countries (Statistical Yearbook of Albania, 1991).

In the framework of EU countries, Italy is the main Albanian trading partner. This is due to geographical vicinity as well as to the old economic and cultural links. Also Italy, as a developed industrial country specialised in new branches of industry, is able to meet all the needs of Albania for investments and consumer goods. In 1998, this partner accounted for 60.1 percent of the total volume of exports and 44.1 percent of imports (INSTAT 1999).

The Balkan countries in 1998 took up 35.9 percent of the total volume of Albanian foreign trade (Table 3). Among the Balkan countries, Greece stands in the first place in exports as well as in imports, being, at the same time, the second trading partner of Albania (29.2 percent in imports and 19.8 percent in exports). This link becomes more powerful, if we take into account that Greece is the second biggest foreign investor in Albania. Besides, after 1990, 350 thousand Albanians have emigrated to Greece (Misja 1998). Their remittances to Albania are afterwards recycled in other Balkan countries through imports.

Other important partners from Balkan countries are FYR of Macedonia, Bulgaria and Turkey. The increase of trade with these countries is due to the increase of imports. This is explained by the drastic reduction of domestic production in Albania and by the inflow of the remittances of immigrants, which has significantly increased the importing capacity of the country, the importance of geographical vicinity, and the relatively low prices of food-stuffs and other consumption goods, especially in Bulgaria and the FYR of Macedonia. Since 1992, two other countries, Croatia and Slovenia, have increased their trade with Albania in an equilibrated, progressive and sustainable way. Meanwhile, there has been a drastic fall in the trade with Romania and at present Albanian exports are insignificant when compared to 1989.

Table 3 Exports, Imports and Trade Balance of Albania with Other Balkan Countries (million USD)

Countries		1991	1992	1993	1994	1995	1996	1997	1998
Bulgaria	Export	4.67	1.95	0.86	0.77	0.19	0.04	0.02	0.09
	Import	0.79	3.79	30.96	48.99	52.09	35.51	16.91	22.05
	Trade balance	3.88	-1.84	-30.10	-48.22	-51.90	-35.47	-16.89	-21.96
Greece	Export	5.04	12.89	21.94	14.58	30.81	27.36	28.92	40.92
	Import	9.75	7.27	87.91	140.54	174.03	187.23	164.71	231.72
	Trade balance	-4.71	5.62	-65.97	-125.96	-143.22	-159.87	-135.79	-190.80
Croatia	Export	-	0.22	1.24	0.67	2.13	1.43	5.93	1.24
	Import	0.56	1.19	6.79	2.61	13.26	2.53	3.71	-
	Trade balance	-0.34	0.05	-6.12	-0.48	-11.83	+3.40	-2.47	-
FYROM	Export	-	0.59	13.93	6.59	8.00	6.47	3.72	3.09
	Import	0.18	20.87	14.44	16.50	18.8	12.75	10.50	-
	Trade balance	0.41	-6.94	-7.85	-8.50	-12.33	-9.03	-7.41	-
Romania	Export	1.24	0.04	0.20	0.07	0.08	0.14	0.05	0.25
	Import	3.10	0.72	2.91	3.83	3.47	21.23	1.87	3.38
	Trade balance	-1.86	-0.68	-2.71	-3.76	-3.39	-21.09	-1.82	-3.13
Slovenia	Export	-	0.23	1.69	0.91	3.27	2.67	1.76	2.51
	Import	3.84	5.09	10.00	10.47	9.30	13.09	-	-
	Trade balance	0.23	-2.15	-4.18	-6.73	-7.80	-7.54	-10.58	-
Turkey	Export	0.21	-	1.67	1.51	12.51	6.55	1.30	1.12
	Import	11.24	4.22	14.68	27.24	26.68	39.15	27.29	26.59
	Trade balance	-11.03	-4.22	-13.01	-25.73	-14.17	-32.60	-25.99	-25.47
Yugoslavia	Export	6.03	2.86	-	0.23	-	0.36	0.61	-
	Import	0.25	0.78	0.79	-	-	-	-	-
	Trade balance	-0.42	-0.18	-	-	-	-	-	-
Total	Export	17.19	18.78	41.53	25.33	56.99	44.66	42.06	49.83
	Import	24.88	16.74	162.36	246.92	285.38	325.9	236.14	311.83
	Trade balance	-7.69	2.04	-120.83	-221.59	-228.39	-281.24	-194.08	-262.00

Sources: Albania in Figures, 1996, INSTAT, Tirana, May 1999.

As a conclusion, the Albanian foreign trade relations have become polarised between Italy and Greece, during the first years of transition, or expressed in a wider sense, between the areas, the EU and the Balkans. Greece plays the role of a pole in Albanian foreign trade with Balkan countries since in 1998, 75.6 percent of the Albanian Balkan trade is realised with this country. It is worth mentioning that Albanian export to Greece is stable and increasing, and this is due to the re-exporting of goods produced by joint ventures with Greek capital.

Foreign Direct Investments in the Albanian Economy

The liberalisation of the economy in Albania opened the road to foreign investments that should help to accelerate its integration into the world economy. These investments could play a positive role in the Albanian economy because they would bring in fresh capital, modern technology and western experience in the field of marketing and management. Meanwhile, they would help in the economic restructuring, in the acceleration of the privatisation process, in job creation, in export growth, and in trade deficit reduction.

In a survey conducted during 1995, nearly 50 privatised industrial enterprises in Tirana, Durres, Fier, Korca and Gjirokaster indicated that one of their main problems was rehabilitation and modernisation of technology (Mara and Gadeshi 1996). In the circumstances when the new entrepreneurs lack financial capital and when the present banking system is incapable of mobilising and utilising with efficiency the savings of the population, which are estimated to reach hundreds of millions USD (Bundo 1996), foreign direct investments are regarded as one of the means for technological modernisation. Meanwhile, the speed of microeconomic restructuring and growth of efficiency is much higher in privatised enterprises that have solved their control problem and have foreign capital participation, than in local state-owned or private enterprises. This experience is evident throughout Central and Eastern Europe (Richet 1995).

In order to protect and guarantee the security that Albanian law provides to foreign investors, Albania has become a member of the Multilateral Investment Guaranteeing Agency (MIGA) and of the International Center of the Settlement of Investment Disputes (ICSID). The Albanian government has signed investment promotion and protection agreements with 15 countries of Europe (Germany, Italy, England, etc.), the USA and others, as well as 7 agreements for elimination of double taxation. Also in January 1993, the Center for Foreign Investment Promotion was established. This is a public institution subordinate to the Council of Ministers, with the objective of maximising the introduction of foreign capital for the development of priority sectors of the Albanian economy.

From 1991 to 1998, the stock of foreign capital invested in Albania was about 384 million USD or 113 USD per capita (Table 4). Compared to other countries of Central and Eastern Europe, the flow is relatively small, not mentioning the EU countries or some of the developing countries. According to some authors, the level of foreign direct investments per capita represents the best synthetic indicator of transition progress because it reflects the attitude of the international capital markets toward the political, social and economic stability of the recipient country (Samson 1996). The proportion of the flow of direct cumulative investment to GDP in Albania in 1998 was about 8 percent. Flow of foreign direct investments increased especially after the passing of the law "On Foreign Investments" in 1993, and it decreased after the 1997 unrest.

Table 4 Foreign Direct Investment in Albania

Mln. USD	1992	1993	1994	1995	1996	1997	1998
Foreign direct investment	20	58	53	70	90	48	45
Cumulative FDI	20	78	131	201	291	339	383

Source: Bank of Albania, 1999.

Unfortunately, the available data regarding the number of joint ventures with foreign capital diverge. According to the Institute of Statistics, by the end of 1998, there were 3,094 joint ventures and foreign enterprises in Albania, most of which operated in trade and services (INSTAT 1999). By the end of 1998, 26,698 employees, or 24 percent of the total private sector employees, were employed by these enterprises (INSTAT 1999). The majority of them are small enterprises with very few employees and only a small percentage of them employ more than 10 persons.

From the point of view of territorial allocation, over 90 percent of foreign enterprises and joint ventures are located in the Western and South-Eastern part of the country, respectively in the towns of Tirana, Shkodra, Durresi, Vlora, Gjirokaster, Korce and Saranda. This coincides with the geography of Italian and Greek investments in Albania. Tirana stands in the first place with 70 percent of the total number, or with nearly 60 percent of the invested capital. Such concentration of foreign direct investments accounts for new job positions, higher salaries, development rates and social problems, and, therefore, has necessitated a regional policy which would promote foreign investment in the less developed areas of the country (Xhepa 1996b).

The strategy of foreign capital in Albania was to establish commercial contacts with local partners. Then it went on with simple forms of industrial cooperation (production by order, co-production, etc.). If the cooperation was successful, it passed to direct investments (joint ventures, greenfield, acquisition through privatisation). Until 1993 western firms, as a result of insecurity and the slow pace of privatisation, have preferred to set up joint enterprises with state capital but with the objective of future full control over the enterprise. In many cases they have maintained a waiting and hesitating position, thus leaving the plan of investments unrealised. Until the end of 1993, 70 percent of the operations were joint ventures with state-owned enterprises, whereas 30 percent were total foreign private investments and ventures in cooperation with Albanian private companies or persons. From 1995 on, when the Albanian Government declared the privatisation of state shares in joint ventures, the foreign investor asked for the purchase of this share in order to have absolute control. According to a survey conducted in November 1996 by the Institute of Statistics in industrial enterprises with over 10 employees, out of 476 industrial enterprises interviewed, 62 were joint ventures, and 26, foreign enterprises. In 82 percent of 98 foreign or joint venture enterprises of the industrial sector, foreign investors possess more than 51 percent of the capital.

In the cases when the foreign investor has the majority or the absolute control of the enterprise, it is observed that the speed of microeconomic restructuring is much higher than in local enterprises or enterprises with minor participation of foreign capital (Mara and Gadeshi 1995). The latest experience with Central and Eastern European Countries indicates that there exists a strong correlation between privatization techniques (assets purchase or privatisation through vouchers) and foreign direct investments. It is due to the fact that privatisation through vouchers by the enterprise workers themselves (Russia) or by outsiders (Czech Republic) limits the role of foreign capital (Richet 1995).

From the point of view of the country of origin, 50 percent of joint ventures are set up with Italian capital, 20 percent with Greek capital, 17 percent with German capital, 13 percent with American, Austrian, French, English, Turkish, etc. capital (Vokshi 1996). The fact that 70 percent of the foreign or joint venture enterprises are Italian or Greek indicates that foreign direct investments in Albania, in contrast to the other countries of Central and Eastern Europe, have a neighborhood investment character (Gadeshi and Ditter 1996). The Italian capital that clearly dominates is mainly concentrated in the Western areas of Albania, particularly in towns like Tirana, Durres, Elbasan, Lushnje, Shkoder, Vlore, Fier, etc.

The Greek direct investments are concentrated mainly in the southern and south-eastern part of Albania, in towns like Korca (26.4 percent), Saranda (22.9 percent), Gjirokastra (16.1 percent) and Delvina (4.6 percent) (Petrakos 1996). This is explained by the fact that these areas are near the Greek border and have had traditional economic and cultural links, and it is exactly in this area that the Greek minority is concentrated. Meanwhile, Greek capital is making efforts to expand to other areas of the country. According to Petrakos, a characteristic of the Greek direct investments is that they have been subsidised by the Greek Government, according to the Law "On Greek Development and Investments". Greece is perhaps the only country in the world that provides financial support to its citizens for investments in Albania. In 1994, 64 percent of the 100 Greek or Albanian - Greek enterprises benefited from grants from the Greek government. Another characteristic of the Greek investments is that 93 percent of them are new enterprises and only 3-7 percent are privatised enterprises (Petrakos 1996). Greek investments are concentrated in the sectors: agri-food industry, light industry (textiles, garments, leather, etc.), and tobacco processing (in the towns Berat, Fier, Elbasan, Korce, Gjirokaster). These investments constitute 73.8 percent of the invested Greek capital, and 70 percent of the Greek investments financed by the government until the end of 1994. In the beginning of 1996, the National Bank of Greece and some other banks were licensed to open branches in Tirana. Greek investments are estimated to have created 7,000 job positions (Petrakos 1996), the majority of which are in agriculture and the light industry sectors (tobacco, textiles, garments).

From the sectoral distribution point of view, if we refer to invested capital until the end of 1994, direct foreign investments are focused on tourism (hotels and restaurants) with 34 percent; light industry 20 percent; construction 15 percent; agri-food industry 18 percent; transport 6 percent (Vokshi 1996). The first four sectors make up 80 percent of the foreign direct investments in Albania.

In light industry, investments are engaged in the production of garments, footwear and other commodities that require much intensive labor. According to a survey of the Institute of Statistics, 40.7 percent of the foreign or joint venture enterprises belong to the textile and garment industry, 12.2 percent to the industry of leather and footwear, and 5.1 percent to the timber industry (Gadeshi and Progri 1997). Therefore, we conclude that over 50 percent of the number of industrial foreign and joint venture enterprises are concentrated in branches that require much intensive labor. By the end of 1996, enterprises of textiles-garments and leather-footwear employed 6,545 persons, or 61 percent of the total number of employees of interviewed foreign or joint venture enterprises. This sector utilises the relatively cheap but trained labor force of Albania. According to the survey, during 1996 the average monthly wage in joint ventures or foreign enterprises was about 78 USD, from 72 USD during 1995 and 59 USD during 1994. These figures are higher than those in the state sector. Meanwhile, the survey cases indicate that the production yield in these enterprises has grown as a result of better management.

The existence of joint ventures in this sector, or the existence of "new forms of investment" explains the new trend in the structure of Albanian exports. In 1996, nearly 50 percent of the total value of Albanian exports was made up of textile and footwear products (INSTAT 1996). The survey shows that 50 out of 52 enterprises of the textile-garment and leather-footwear industries exported their products and 41 of them, all their output. These products are destined mainly for the Greek and Italian markets and are then re-exported to other countries of Western Europe. All the inputs are imported from abroad except for the labor, which is Albanian. The analysis of these data indicates that foreign direct investments contribute to the restructuring of foreign trade as well as to its flows. According to the export-import data, the trade exchanges of Albania with Italy and Greece have grown during the 1990s.

Another sector is that of the agri-food industry, which was dominated by the processing of local raw materials of agricultural origin. The products of this sector are primarily destined for the local market, making them competitive in quality and price. According to the above survey, enterprises of the agri-food industry constitute 11.2 percent of the joint ventures or foreign enterprises of the industrial sector and employ 10.4 percent of the total number of their employees. The most important investment in this sector is undoubtedly the 7 million USD investment of Coca-Cola.

Foreign capital is becoming increasingly present in construction, which is the most dynamic and profitable sector of the Albanian economy. Various Italian, Greek and Turkish firms have invested in the construction material industry (bricks, cement, marble, etc.), as well as in the construction of various objects. Here, it is worth mentioning the investments of the Italian firms Albanova and VolAlba in brick production in Lushnja, Albit Mermer (Italy) and Market Petra (Greece) for the production of marble plates, construction firms Wolfgang Endrich (Germany) in Durres, Torcello (Italy) in Saranda, Interbeton (Greece) in Saranda, etc.

In tourism, foreign investments are engaged in setting up hotels and restaurants, both in the big cities and in the coastal area of Albania. Since the very beginning of the economic opening of Albania, foreign investors have shown great interest in this sector with great investment potentials. In 1998, revenues from tourism are estimated at 70 million USD, whereas according to some forecasts, during the first decades of the next century, this sector will produce most of the revenues of the Albanian economy.

Until the end of 1995, signed contracts with foreign investors in the sector of tourism amount to 154 million USD. Here we can mention the construction of the "Europa Park" Hotel in Tirana with a value of 22 million USD by the Austrian firm Rogner; the reconstruction of the "Tirana" Hotel with a value of 12 million USD by the Italian firm Di Vincenzo Estero, both financed by EBRD; the construction of a new hotel by the Kuwaiti firm Al Kharafi, with a value of 32.5 million USD; the construction of tourist villages in Ksamil, Llogora, Orikum, Golem, etc. Meanwhile, the EU has invested, through a one million USD project for the development of small-scale tourism in the South of Albania.

Taking into consideration the well-known and potential resources that Albania possesses, big foreign companies like Shell (Netherlands), Agip (Italy), Occidental (USA), Deminex (Germany), Chevron Overseas (USA), OMV (Austria), Coparex (France), Hamilton (England), Na-Naftaplin (Croatia), Fountain Oil (Norway), etc., are given concessions and have started oil and gas explorations off-shore and on-shore. Up to the end of 1994, these firms had invested 105 million USD. A major interest is also shown by foreign capital, particularly by the German, Italian, Japanese and Canadian capital, and various contracts have been signed to discover and exploit the mineral resources of chrome, copper, zinc, etc.

In the banking system until the end of 1998 there were two foreign banks operating with joint capital with the National Commercial Bank of Albania, the Italian-Albanian Bank with the participation of the Banco Di Roma and the Islamic Arabic-Albanian Bank. The National Commercial Bank of Albania has 40 percent of the capital in each of the Banks. Very soon other foreign banks will start operating in Albania, such as the National Bank of Greece, Ionian Bank, Pireus Bank, International Commercial Bank (Malaysia), American Bank of Albania, Dardania Bank (Kosova), First Investment Bank (Bulgaria), etc.

Alongside these, other international organizations, such as the World Bank, the EBRD and other donors, have started to invest in sectors like infrastructure, telecommunications, water supply, electricity, irrigation systems, roads, ports and airports, etc.

Conclusions

The favorable geographic location of Albania, which is a gateway to the Balkans, in the context of East-West relations, the natural resources, the qualified and young labor force and a liberal law on foreign investments are encouraging factors for foreign capital. Regarding these positive factors and the low stock per capita of foreign direct investments, a question arises: Why is there, such a low level of foreign direct investments in Albania?

Part of the answer would be: the late start of foreign direct investments (1991), the lack of knowledge of the country on the part of foreign investors as a result of the long self isolation of Albania, factors that have remained from the old system (lack of infrastructure, the old production apparatus, lack of competition), or the image of the country in the first transition years. Another part of the answer will be given by the analysis, in a wide sense, of the elements of country attractiveness.

If we consider the investment climate up to 1995, the situation appears favorable compared to 1992 and to that of other countries in transition. But, starting from 1996 all macroeconomic indicators worsened. Therefore, we come to the conclusion that after the investment climate, the country risk remains one of the main obstacles for foreign investments in Albania.

Another disadvantage is the relatively small size of the domestic market, which is conditioned by the small population (3.4 million) and by the low buying capacity of approximately 700 USD per capita per year (Kopliku 1996). In these circumstances, the growth of cooperation between Albania and other countries of the Balkans is, not only desirable, but also constitutes a good perspective for foreign direct investments, which can export their products to a Balkan market of more than 80 million consumers.

There are many hypotheses for economic regional integration like: the

Balkan countries, the Visegrad countries, the Bridge area, the former CMEA, the former USSR, the whole region of Central and Eastern Europe, etc., as a predecessor of European integration from the Atlantic to the Urals. The last idea, developed by Steinherr (1993), of course, belongs to the next century. We know from the integration theory of Balassa that the economic integration of the Balkan countries, a desirable but not realistic hypothesis for the moment, requires some conditions like: stabilised, restructured and privatized market economies; coordination of economic policies between member countries; stable and major trade exchanges concentrated between one or two countries with bigger economic potential than the members of the future union, etc. But all these criteria are difficult to implement in a region where the present or potential conflicts may hinder the coordination of economic policies, etc. That is why the idea of an economic cooperation between the Balkan countries is more realistic than that of integration (Gadeshi and Ditter 1997).

Under these circumstances, the government should apply an active policy aiming at the attraction of foreign investments. The government exerts a positive influence on the strategy of firm location by means of its macro-economic policy, build up of material and non-material infrastructure, industrial policy, and image creation by cooperation with other countries. Consequently, the government develops a long term specialisation policy (Cohen 1996).

References

Albania 1994 (1994), IMF Review, Washigton.
Albania 1995 (1996), Human Report development, UNDP, Tirana.
Albania in figures (1996), INSTAT, Tirane, Maj 1996.
Andreef, W. (1994), Le controle des entreprises privatisees dans les economie en transition. Congres A.F.S.E. 1994, Paris, 29 et 30 september.
Andreef, W. (1995), Les privatisations a l'Ouest, un modele exportable? In the book Gerraqui D., Richet X. (sous la direction de), Strategies de privatisation, L'Harmattan.
Andreef, W. (1996), Les multinationales global, La Decouverte, Paris.
Berisham, S. (1994), Rritja e shpejte ekonomike, objektiv madhor, kombetar i P.D. dhe forcave demokratike ne teresi. Fjala ne Keshillin Kombetar te P.D., Rilindja Demokratike, 28 qershor (in Albanian).
Blejer, M., Mecagni, M. and Sahary, R., etal. (1992), Albania: From isolation toward reform. International Monetary Fund, Occasional Paper 98, Washington DC, September.
Bufi, Y.(1997), Strategjia e privatizimit. Zeri i Popullit, 3. 9. 1997 (in Albanian).

Bundo, S. (1996), Fajdeja ka lidhje me bankat bosh. INTERVISTA, 14-20 tetor 1996 (in Albanian).

Buxhuku, G. (1996), Strategjia detyra primare e Ministrise se Privatizimit. Rilindja Demokratike, 1. 9. 1996 (in Albanian).

Chavance, B. (1995), La fin des systemes socialistes, L'Harmattan, Paris.

Cohen, E. (1996), Les Etats sont-ils encore souverains dans l'ordre economique? Problemes economiques, No. 2.415-16, 15-22 Mars 1996.

Drach, M. (1984), La crise dans les pays de l'Est, La Decouverte, Paris.

Enterprises in Central and Eastern Europe (1996), Eurostat.

Gadeshi, I. and Ditter, J-G (1996), Investimet Direkte te Huaja ne Shqiperi dhe perspektiva e tyre. Ekonomia dhe Tranzicioni, 1996, No. 4 (in Albanian).

Gadeshi, I. and Ditter, J-G.(1997), Investimet Direkte te Huaja ne Shqiperi dhe domos-doshmeria e kooperimit Ballkanik. Ekonomia dhe Tranzicioni, 1997, N° 1 (in Albanian).

Gadeshi, I., Progri, V.(1997), Disa karakteristika te ndermarrjeve te perbashketa ne sektorin industrial. Working Paper (in Albanian).

Gjata, A.(1996), Foreigns banks become interested. Albanian Observer, 1996/3.

Glozheni, N. (1995), Privatizimi - Proces i domosdoshem, i ligjshem e transparent. Rilindja Demokratike,23.8.1995 (in Albanian).

INSTAT (1995), Tregu shqiptar i punes ne tranzicion, Tirane, shtator (in Albanian).

INSTAT (1996), Repertori i ndermarrjeve ekonomike, 1991-95. Tirane, korrik 1996 (in Albanian).

Kolodko, G. (1992), Stabilisation, recession et croissance dans les economies postsocialistes. Economie prospective internationale, 1992, No. 51.

Kontrata e PD me Shqiperine (1995), Botim i Gazetes. Rilindja Demokratike, Tirane, Prill (in Albanian).

Kopliku, B. (1995), Jemi bere shembull i reformave te sukseshme. Rilindja Demokratike, 7. 12. 1995 (in Albanian).

Kopliku, B. (1996), Vizion per politiken ekonomike te PD deri ne vitin 2000. Rilindja Demokratike, 12. 4. 1996 (in Albanian).

Kornai, J. (1980), Du socialisme au capitalisme. L'exemple de la Hongrie, Gallimard, Paris.

Langer, A. (1995), Tranzicioni drejt shtetit te se drejtes. Zeri i Popullit, 14. 2. 1995 (in Albanian).

Luci, E. (1994), Structural changes in the Albanian economy during the period from 1960 to 1990. Estratto da Problemi demo-economici dell'Albania a cura di Luigi Di Comite e Marisa A. Valleri, Quaderni Mediterranei 1, Bari.

Luci, E. and Mara, H.(1994), Problems and perspectives of the Albanian economy viewed from the aim of establishing a market economy. Estratto da Problemi demo-economici dell'Albania a cura di Luigi Di Comite e Marisa A. Valleri, Quaderni Mediterranei 1, Bari.

Main Economic Indicators (1997), INSTAT, mars 1997.

Mancellari, A., Duka, R. and Xhilqri L. (1996), Privatizimi masiv ne realitetin shqiptar. Ekonomia dhe Biznesi, Fakulteti i Ekonomise, Buletini 1 (in Albanian).

Mara, H.(1991), Struktura e ekonomise shqiptare. Probleme e perspektiva ne kuadrin e inte-grimit evropian, Konference nderkombetare ne Prishtine. Evropa dhe shqiptaret, Prill, 1991 (in Albanian).

Mara, H. and Gadeshi, I. (1995), Privatizimi i ndermarrjeve shteterore dhe efektiviteti i tyre. Ekonomia dhe Tranzicioni, 1995/2 (in Albanian).

Meksi, A. (1993), Programi afatmesem i Qeverise per zhvillimin ekonomik te Shqiperise me 1993-96. Rilindja Demokratike, 26. 11. 1993 (in Albanian).

Meksi, A. (1996), Shqiperia 2000, mireqenie dhe dinjitet. Rilindja Demokratike, 23. 7. 1996 (in Albanian).

Misja, V. (1996), Probleme te emigracionit nderkombetar. Raport Studimi, Tirane.

Misja, V., Luci, E. and Vejsiu, Y. (1991) Ekonomia e industrise dhe efektiviteti i investimeve, Shtepia Botuese e Librit Universitar, Tirane (in Albanian).

Nati, A. (1995), Politika buxhetore dhe pagat. In the book Permiresimi dhe Zhvillimi i Politikes se Pagave ne Shqiperi, Tirane (in Albanian).

Osmani, M. (1995), Tranzicioni, problemi bujqesor dhe shteti. Rilindja Demokratike, 31.7.1995 (in Albanian).

Petrakos, G. (1996), The New Geography of the Balkans: Cross-border cooperation between Albania, Bulgaria and Greece. Series on Transition in the Balkans, Vol. 1, University of Thessaly, Department of Planning and Regional Development.

Progri, V. (1995), Statistikat e pagave ne sektorin buxhetor. In the book Permiresimi dhe Zhvillimi i Politikes se Pagave ne Shqiperi, Tirane 1995(in Albanian).

Richet, X. (1995), Transnational Corporation, Direct Foreign Investment and Attractiveness of Central European Economies in Transition. Paper presented at the Conference Industrial Organisation and Entrepreneurship in Transition, 5-8 June 1995, Albena - Varna, Bulgaria.

Samson, I. (1996), Albania experience among transition trajectories, Working Paper, Grenoble.

Shahollari, L. (1996), Dukuri, probleme, krahasime ne lidhje me papunesine ne Shqiperi gjate tranzicionit: 1991-95. Ekonomia dhe Tranzicioni, Nr. 1, 1996 (in Albanian).

Statistical Yearbook of Albania (1991), Ministria e Ekonomise, Drejtoria e Statistikes, Tirana.

Steinherr, A.(1993), Essai d'analyse de la nouvelle Europe de l'Atlantique a l'Oural. In the book J. L. Mucchielli, F. Celimene, eds. Mondialisation et regionalisation : un defi pour l'Europe, Economica, Paris.

Tabaku, B. and Salko, D. (1996), Mbi mundesite e investimit te bonove te privatizimit. Ekonomia dhe Tanzicioni, Korrik-Shtator 1996 No. 3 (in Albanian).

Transition Report Update (1996), European Bank for Reconstruction and Development.

Van Rijckeghen, C. (1994), Price liberalization, the Social Safety Net, Income Distribution, and Poverty, 1990-93. IMF Review, Washington.

Vokshi, M. (1996), Kapitali i huaj dhe roli i tij ne reformen ekonomike. Ekonomia dhe Biznesi, Buletini 1, 1996, Fakulteti i Ekonomise (in Albanian).

Xhepa, S. (1996a), Ekonomia ne programet e ardhshme te zhvillimit. Rilindja Demokratike, 13.4.1996 (in Albanian).

Xhepa, S. (1996b), Hartimi i nje strategjie ne marketingun e nje vendi. Teze doktorate, Universiteti i Tiranes, Tirane (in Albanian).

Xhillari, L.(1996), Reforma ekonomike dhe privatizimi masiv ne Shqiperi. Teze doktorate, Universiteti i Tiranes, dhjetor 1996 (in Albanian).

13 Romania: Transition and New Conditions for Regional Cooperation

MARVIN JACKSON
Emeritus Professor, Department of Economics, Katholieke Universiteit Leuven, Belgium

Introduction

This paper reviews Romania's obviously difficult transition. Like its neighbor, Bulgaria, it has not done well either in economics or in politics. Thus, the judgment of the European Commission doubting their capacities to undertake soon the challenges and responsibilities of EU membership is justified. But this point is not as important as the investigation of the causes of their problem and the possible remedies. Here the author of the paper would stress two interaction forces. One, somewhat impersonal, arises out of the countries common history and location in a region on the European periphery. The other would stress the character of institutions and the nature of outlooks and motivations given to individuals who must solve the political and economic problems. If history and location pose great problems for transition in this region, it stands to reason that it is also important to reshape institutions so that individuals can rise to the occasion. If people, political and business leaders, in the region remain fatalistic, as they often have been (and understandably so) how are the negative forces of history and location to be overcome? That question is not answered in this paper, but it has always been upper most on the author's mind in this and other research on the region.[1]

Geography, History and Demography

Geography

The total area of Romania is 238,391 square kilometers of highly varied topography. Mountains, in a number of cases going over 2,500 meters, cover 31 percent, hills and plateaus another 36 percent, and 33 percent plains and meadows.

The mountains moving at first from north to south divide the historical regions of Transylvania to the west and Moldova to the east and then have a roughly ninety degree turn to the west now separating Transylvania to the north from Wallachia to the south.

Most of the southern border with Bulgaria is the Danube River, which turns to the north and then forms a small portion of border with the Ukraine before exiting the Black Sea. The county opens on to the Black Sea where the major port of Constanta, linked by canal with the Danube, provides sea and ocean linkages. To the west and starting approximately at the so-called Iron Gates, the former rapids of the Danube which are now a major hydroelectric and river management facility with the former and now the present Yugoslavia is a border through the historic region of the Banat, which turns into the border with Hungary that curves north and east eventually meeting the Ukrainian and then the Moldovan borders.

The plains of the left bank of the Danube and those of the Moldovan historical region provide the major areas of grain and oil seed production, while the hills of Dobrogea turning into the Black Sea coast provide what was a rich fruit growing region. The topography and the agriculture of Transylvania and Banat are more varied, but historically providing higher yields. While Transylvania has a more mild climate, the other regions are dominated by continental air movements and have both very cold winters and very hot summers. Also, there are often unpredictable late frosts in the spring and early frosts in the autumn and highly variable precipitation in all seasons. Thus, while the topography and sunlight favor agriculture, climate introduces high uncertainty.

The country has had rich forests which were abused both in the later communist years and during the transition period. The best known mineral resource is petroleum and associated natural gas, which unfortunately has faced both declining yields and a lack of discovery of new reserves. Recent governments, both before and after transition, have sought off shore exploration on a larger scale. There are also extensive deposits of lignite and brown coal, much of a high sulfur content. Also, there has been exploitable ferrous, gold, silver and bauxite ores, as well as great reserves of salt. The country is also rich in mineral waters.

History

Romania's Romance language owes its origins to the occupation of the lower Danube area by Roman legions and settlers, who were assimilated by local peoples. The language survived through numerous invasions, including

Slavs and various tribes out of Asia. Medieval Romanian boyars rose to princedoms in Moldova - in the east, Wallachia in the south, and Transylvania in the northwest only to bow at various times to the greater Hungarian, Habsburg, Ottoman, and Russian imperial authority. The Wallachian and Moldovan principalities managed union under one prince and then achieved full independence from Turkey in 1878.

Having joined the Allies, Romania emerged from the First World War much enlarged with areas of the Banat, Crisana and Maramuris, and Transylania in the west and north from Hungary; Bucovina in the northeast from Austria, Bessarabia from Russia in the east, and Southern Dobrogea in the southeast from Bulgaria. The new areas, except for the latter, contained a majority of Romanians, most of whom were Orthodox. Still problems of assimilation of the new territories, which included such difficulties as linking technically different railroad and banking systems, complicated interwar politics so no headway economically was made before the Great Crisis. According to the author's estimates the Romanian national product in 1929 just about equaled the national product on the equivalent territories in real terms (Lampe and Jackson 1982). As elsewhere in Europe, the 1930s saw a great increase in protectionism and efforts to promote domestic industry through import substitution. Whether the promoted industrialization would have survive in an open world economy is an unanswered question, given the Soviet imposition of its system on Romania after the Second World War.

During the Second World War Romania was an Axis ally, providing a large force on the Russian front. After the war, it lost Southern Dobrogea (back) to Bulgaria, and both Northern Bucovina (now part of Ukraine) and Bessarabia (which was divided between Moldova and Ukraine) to the Soviet Union. After first following an orthodox Soviet line, Romanian communist leaders succeeded in promoting a version of national communism in which they not only resisted integration into CMEA and the Warsaw Pact, but also led them to closer relations with the West, culminating in the early 1970s with memberships in GATT, the IMF, and the World Bank. But then it retreated into ever stronger policies of self-sufficiency in an attempt to promote a cult of Ceaucescu's personality that pushed to the extreme in the 1980s when international debt service could no longer be maintained. Under an extreme autarchy, both regional cooperation and the population's living standards suffered.

Demography

As in land area, Romania just about matched the former Yugoslavia in population size. In the Ceaucescu years a draconian program of birth promotion was pushed on the population. It first took the form of a surprise elimination of legal abortion and outlawing of contraceptive devices, which of course resulted in a wave of unwanted births (and high deaths in birth and infancy). Then as the population slowly found its own ways of avoiding maternity, the regime began a system of interrogation of the sexual habits of couples in the child bearing ages. No wonder then that fertility rates have fallen below population reproduction levels. Having reached about 22 million, the population under emigration and low birth rates is slowly declining (Table 1).

As late as 1985 half of this population lived in rural places making the country one of the regions least urbanized. The rural share still stood at 45 percent of the total in 1985. As elsewhere in Europe, the population is rapidly aging. The capital, Bucharest, has a rich history and is one of the major urban centers in Southeastern Europe. Its population of over 2 million accounts for 16.5 percent of the country's total. Scattered around the country are 11 other cities of from 200,000 to 999,000 persons which in total account for another 26 percent of total population. Thus, there is a potential for developing a variety of population agglomerations capable of supporting major economies of scale.

Romania unfortunately does not have an adequate transportation system either in quantity or quality and is poorly connected to neighboring countries. Perhaps the best developed connection is the access by water transport of Bucharest to the Black Sea. But to the south, by contrast, Romania shares with Bulgaria just one bridge across the long border of the Danube.

The one interwar census in 1930 recorded a German minority of over 800,000 and also a large Jewish one, both of whom largely left the country in the postwar period. The latest census of 1992 counted about 120,000 Germans and 9000 Jews by nationality, but only 99,000 and 1000 by mother tongue (Yiddish in the latter case). But the largest minority was and is Hungarian, officially 1,625,000 or 1,639,000 depending on how one would count and now the second largest minority are Gypsies, 401,000 or 167,000. Romanians are 89.4 or 90.7 percent of the total. It might also be pointed out that Romanian speakers are the numerically dominant population in

Moldova and that others are scattered into the territories beyond in the adjoining territories of the former Soviet Union.

Transition: Politics, Institutional Change, and Policy

Overview of Politics since December 1989

Although Romania was the one former communist country where political transition began in violence, the underside of events that led to the deposition of long time dictator, Nicolae Ceaucescu, remain unclear. Popular demonstrations in December in the Banat city of Timisoara grew into a full-scale uprising in Bucharest in which the party headquarters was seized on the 22 of December. Ceaucescu and his wife attempted to flee, were captured, and executed after a military trial. It seems certain that some factions of the party, centered on former Politburo member, Ion Iliescu, had been involved in some form of conspiracy and their immediate take over of state power in the name of the National Salvation Front has all of the substance of a coup d'etat. Very possibly this group also orchestrated the violence through associated members of the Securitate, Romania's secret police.

The NSF, with Iliescu and the younger political technocrat, Petre Roman, initiated the first steps in political and economic liberalization, although especially in the latter case the emphasis was on restricting market forces to the spontaneous initiatives of small scale traders and craftsmen. Iliescu, especially, cited supposed cases of state capitalism with planning and heavy regulation as the model for Romania to follow.

The NSF and Iliescu as president claimed a wide margin of victor in the first post-communist election of May 1990, although it is clear there was behind the scenes manipulation by the former nomenclatura and security forces, especially outside of the main cities. Roman became the prime minister, but soon strains developed between his more reform oriented followers and the conservatives of Iliescu. Roman was forced out of office during the miners' intervention in September 1991. The two groups in the NSF split formally into two parties. In the second elections of September 1992 Iliescu's party won slightly over a quarter of the seats in both houses of parliament while Iliescu himself was re-elected president. Although his new choice as prime minister, Nicolae Vacaroiu, was not formally a member of Iliescu's party, he served carefully and faithfully the president until new

393

more democratic and reform minded forces were elected in November 1996.

During these four years, as will be evident by the following summaries, the Romanian government generated many programs for economic reform, often with the help of international agencies. Yet, as was most often discovered by the World Bank or the IMF, there was great success in simulating reform while continuing to support the bulk of former state enterprises with one form or another of financial subsidies. The kindest evaluation of these policies would attribute them to a desire to protect Romania workers from massive unemployment. The more likely objective was the continuation of efforts to allow the bulk of the former nomenclatura and also new friends of Iliescu and those around him to find safe and secure places either in the new regulatory bureaucracy or for the more ambitious a secure place in the newly forming "capitalist class" of the country. The consequences show up in the statistics as minimal authentic privatization and avoidance of restructuring of the major loss making enterprises of the old system. Also, the means of financing the subsidies necessary were to play havoc with the meeting of IMF targets for financial and budgetary reforms. In fact, in late 1996 in an effort to gain voter favor the strings were loosened by the National Bank and the government. It goes without saying that the new political regime starting in 1997 faced an uphill struggle in meeting new reform mandates.

In the new elections, Emil Constantinescu, who had opposed Iliescu in 1992, and continued to head up the chief opposition group, the Democratic Convention, was elected Romanian president. The DC also won the largest number of seats in parliament and formed a governing coalition with parties in a group led by Petre Roman (who became president of the senate) and the Hungarian minority party. An ambitious fast-track economic and political reform program was launched with renewed IMF and World Bank support. Additional advice and material assistance came from bilateral sources and the EU. Although some important progress is noted below, the new forces have proven to be politically weak. After much infra-coalition and infra-party quarreling, in December 1997 Roman's party withdrew from the government and with others demanded the resignation of the prime minister, Victor Ciorba. The IMF refused to disburse the third tranche of a $410 million stand-by loan because the government failed to put through basic reforms. In March 1998 Ciorba resigned and final in April a new government with the original support forces was formed by Radu Vasile. The Wall Street Journal (April 13, 1998) quotes the World Bank representative to Romania as saying that the months of squabbling "has destroyed Romania's credibility to carry out reforms ...[and] led to a continued downturn in the economy". Thus, the paper is being finished at a time of continued sense of political and economic crisis.

Liberalization and Markets

Market imperfections As it was stated in the introduction to this paper, it is obviously impossible to judge the performance of transition economies as if this is the test of a well established market system with only the usual quantity and quality of market distortions. From the first, often timid steps to liberalize domestic entry and prices up to the present all transition countries have highly distorted market environments in which even the most experienced business manager would move in directions that might reduce output, raise prices, increase unemployment, and other actions which would reflect negatively in the macroeconomic data. The distortion of actions of individual economic agents would be even greater for those lacking experience and perhaps also with unclear mandates because of the lack of clear ownership and governance rules and policies. Judgment of what is going on in such cases should place a great emphasis on whether market and ownership distortions are being reduced once the state embarks on transition.

In Romania's case the evidence suggests that far more than the average level of market distortion has accompanied its transition process. This is due, first of all, to the weakness of historical and locational market forces in the general society, something that Romania shared with Bulgaria and other Balkan countries. But possibly even more important was the long period from the NSF's first take over of state power to the fall of the Iliescu regime during which no opposition managed to challenge those who sought to establish a form of state capitalism dominated by the old forces of communism who supported Iliescu and whose interests in turn were protected by him. Finally it is also clear that the other political forces in Romania have dangerously weak political and administrative abilities. They can neither unite around an appropriate economic mandate nor manage well the existing institutions of economy. Of course, their problems are made worse by the six years of Iliescu rule during which the opportunists and the incompetent could learn the tricks of survival. The main elements of distorted markets need to be reviewed.

Wage controls and incomes policies The old system of detailed wage fixing was applied until February 1991. At that time, Law 14/1991 introduced annual contract bargaining between workers and management. Free negotiations applied only to privately-owned (majority) companies. State-owned companies, i.e., most of those in industry, were still subjected to a complicated constraint of incomes policy. Allowable wage increases were referenced to base occupational groups. Wage increases greater than those brenchmarks were heavily taxed.

Starting January 1992 the system was simplified to encourage elimination of excess labor (at that time the unemployment rate rose rapidly see Table 1). Overall wage bills of enterprises in excess of stated limits were taxed between 20 percent and 500 percent. The allowable increases are linked to changes in the prices of subsidized goods, plus a formula linked to the consumer price index. Indexation was 50 percent from November 1991 to November 1992 and then 65.5 percent.

Collective bargaining became the rule in the next two years, although with continuing political interference. During 1995 and 1996 real wages and productivity grew almost in step. In July 1995 the government, the employers' association and the trade unions signed an agreement on the stipulation of a minimum wage, in which the government promised to revise the gross minimum wage every six months. In mid-1997, the minimum wage was 225,000 lei or about 30 USD per month. Real wages in the state sector grew much faster than productivity, especially in the most subsidized sectors of food production and energy, while wages in the private sector did not keep pace with productivity gains. In 1997, ceilings were imposed on wage increases in loss-making state enterprises and in the autonomous state utility companies (the regies autonomes).

The impact of wage changes has been magnified by employer contributions to Romania's social security system through a payroll tax amounting to 32.5 percent of the wage sum. Employees pay 1 percent of the wage sum. Social security rates have risen substantially since 1991. In addition, all companies are subject to a 1.5 percent tax on their turnover.

Price policy and liberalization Decontrol of wholesale and retail prices began in November 1990 when the government claimed to have freed half of the prices in the consumer basket. Still in July 1991 about 30 percent of wholesale prices were controlled by the ministry, some 12 percent of retail prices were fixed, and another 25 to 50 percent had controlled margins.[2]

Decision 776 of November 1991 devalued and unified exchanges rates. The action provided considerable government influence in price setting:1) Price maximums were set for 24 industrial goods according to the relevant international price at the exchange rate prevailing at the time. Unfortunately no provision was made for adjustment in case of changes in the exchange rate so prices quickly lost any connection with international price relatives; 2) The Ministry of Agriculture was given authority to establish state procurement prices for cereals and livestock, a practice continued until the new government in 1997; 3) price changes for more than 100 goods produced by fewer than three producers are subject to approval by the Ministry of Economy and Finance or by another designated authority; 4) prices of all goods had to be registered with the ministry and a 90 day notification of price changes required (subsequently reduced to 30 days); and 5) a 30 percent limit was put on margins above wholesale costs.

Price liberalization picked up again in 1993 as consumer subsidies were phased out, mark-up limits were eliminated (in June) and the number of consumer goods under direct price control dropped to five. By 1995, according to the EBRD, the share of administered prices had fallen to 3 percent of consumer goods and services. Nevertheless, prices for oil, other energy and some agricultural products remained controlled until early 1997. Foodstuffs subject to price administration accounted for 17 percent of the average household consumption market basket. These price controls have now been lifted. Energy prices were doubled at the beginning of 1997, and are expected to be at world market levels by the end of that year.

The effects of price controls must be seen in combination with other market distorting measures, especially inflation, import restrictions and tariff measures. According to a 1993 World Bank report, "Continued high rates of inflation combined with ad hoc government price intervention, distort relative prices, so that they no longer reflect domestic scarcity costs or relative prices in the international market".[3] Prices have been further distorted by the lack of financial control and domestic competition. A thorough empirical study of relative prices during this period is badly needed if any one seeks a proper evaluation of transition reforms and especially the role of developing markets.

Taxes and subsidies In July 1990 the former system of mandatory profit remittances to the budget and highly variable turnover taxes was changed to more market oriented systems. Tax reforms were implemented as revenues in 1990 dropped by the equivalent of 10 per cent of GDP.

The main direct taxes introduced at that time were a variable profits tax (rates of 30 and 45.5 percent) and incomes tax. Profits tax reductions were granted for new companies, reinvested income, and foreign investments. The 1990 reforms also introduced an "individual wage tax" to replace the old system's "wage fund tax" which was levied on the total enterprise wage bill. As of mid-1994, the enterprise profit tax was levied progressively at rates of 6 to 45 percent, whereas personal income was taxed from 5 to 60 percent. The government has made proposals that would set the corporate tax rate at 38 percent (25 percent for agriculture) from January 1995, and took to parliament during the summer of 1994 a draft law which would index the profit tax base to inflation. A special tax regime was defined for foreign investors.

The main indirect tax was a turnover tax of up to 30 percent. At the wholesale-level an excise tax of up to 70 percent was applied. The 1992 rates of the excise tax varied from 25 percent to 60 percent. The excise tax is paid on both domestic and imported goods, the latter on the basis of import value plus duties. It is market distorting in a few cases where items are not provided domestically, such as automobiles having an engine over 1500cc or color TV sets with wireless remote controls. A value-added tax was introduced in the summer of 1993, replacing the turnover tax. The value added tax is a flat 18 percent with basic consumer goods and exports exempted.

Three categories of commodity subsidies were applied to: 1) a number of extractive industries for strategic purposes, 2) a number of consumer goods for social purposes, and 3) other products as a consequence of price regulation. The communist system employed large subsidies through food producers in the case of most food products and it has taken a long time to phase out such market distortions. They were reduced 25 percent in May 1992 and differentiated reductions were made in September 1992. More cuts were made in May 1993 on food, electricity, and transportation. Finally practically all subsidies at this level were eliminated early in 1997.

Subsidies in the extractive industry have remained. According to principles announced by the former government, such subsidies were to be applied strictly by products and would not vary with the economic performance of the producer. Such principles would reduce market distortions if applied. Otherwise, the subsidy system would appear to distort markets only in some cases, such as chemical fertilizers. The budgeted sums available to industry were only 3.7 percent of the reported value of industrial output in 1991. Nevertheless, larger off-budget subsidies have also been available through the foreign exchange system and the system of finance. After rising sharply in the initial years of transition, total government outlays on subsidies and transfers dropped from 22 per cent of GDP in 1992 to 14 percent in 1993.

Foreign trade arrangements   In February 1990 the former foreign trade monopoly was abolished and the dual exchange rate both unified and devalued (from 16 to 21 lei/$US).[4] Trade licenses were issued automatically and most quantitative controls were removed and on the import side replaced with a low tariff (see below). By the end of 1992 the number of licensed traders increased to about 30,000, including many large producing companies that trade on their own account. Still, most trade in machinery and industrial materials remained in the hands of state owned companies. Estimates of the amount of exports and imports done through the private sector are given below.

Most licensing requirements for export and import were eliminated in May 1992, leaving quantitative import restrictions for a few products related to public health or security. There were no duties on exports and the tariff treatment of imports was fairly liberal. According to the GATT, a total of 12.80 billion lei export subsidies were provided Romanian exports in 1991. In 1992 some 2.0 billion lei of subsidies were used to provide incentives to offset Romania's debts in transferable Rubles to former CMEA partners. Other direct export subsidies were not granted in 1992.

Other programs to benefit exporters include: draw-back of import tariffs, preferential interest rates, export insurance and guarantees, export promotion and marketing assistance. The systems of allocation of these benefits is not known. Nevertheless, under transition conditions it is likely that exporters with political influence will have even more access to favorable treatment than in a more mature democratic, market system.

Indirect subsidies are probably the more important in Romania's case. Several possible cases can be noted. A number of commodities have benefited from energy and raw materials that were priced in terms of over-valued lei exchange rates or whose prices lagged behind the current inflation. Such inputs would then be under priced, compared to the market, while the outputs could be exported for current prices and exchange rates. This would exaggerate the rate of profitability of exports. The best examples would be petrochemicals, iron and steel products, and possibly wood and textile products. There are also possibilities that the system of export licenses and quotas can be manipulated. The system took a long time to be liberalized. On occasion so called temporary export bans were used.

Exporting is still not fully "marketized". In 1992 some 18 percent of exports were in clearing, barter and countertrade, involving both private and state companies. In addition, the share of exporting undertaken by non-private agents varied significantly across product groups. This added considerable possibilities beyond the state ownership of production and production subsidies, discussed under "market distortions", to the use of informal export subsidies by supporting of loss-making export operations. According to this hypothesis, the possibilities of export subsidies through foreign trade markups would be quite high in the cases of metals, machinery, alcoholic beverages, petroleum products, fertilizers, and paper.

With the transition from the former system of state trading monopolies and centrally determined import-export quotas, a relatively liberal import customs tariff came into effect in early 1990. Because of the combined effects of the many other distortions in the Romanian economy it is doubtful if the duty rates have been until possibly in 1997 a determining factor in whether goods were imported or not.

A new and current tariff was introduced on January 1, 1992. It is based on the Harmonized Commodity Description (HS) and comprises 5,018 positions at the six digit level. Duties, which are only ad valorem, are provided in one column for imports from countries having most favored nation (MFN) treatment and in other columns for the European Community, the European Free Trade Agreement, and General System of Preferences. When weighted according to 1991 imports, the average duties in former schedules were about 7 percent compared with a higher 11.7 percent under the new schedules. As would be normal, the duty levels are also escalated according to degree of processing. The highest duty rates were applied to tobacco, textiles, clothing, musical instruments, photographic supplies and footwear.

Tariff exemptions have been provided in the case of foreign capital contributions in kind, as well as raw materials and subassemblies necessary for commercial companies with foreign investment. Also, in 1992 temporary duty reductions were introduced on an MFN basis for 2,271 commodities (at the six digit level). According to the GATT, about 45 percent of imports in value terms benefited from these reductions in 1992. In addition, some 45 commodities received duty exemptions on the basis of a tariff quota.

There were no other import quotas and no application of minimum import prices. There were two cases of surcharges to the normal rates. Beginning August 1992 a fee of 0.5 percent of both exports and imports was levied in order to provide funds to modernize the customs system. A temporary safe-guard surcharge was applied on 23 lines, which were to be discontinued at the end of 1992. Some trade carried on with the former Soviet Union was sub-jected to a barter agreement and was exempted from the tariff.

In the case of government procurement, the only official preference granted to domestic suppliers is in the case of tenders based on World Bank credits, in which case a 10 percent preference is allowed. Quotas, antidump-ing, countervailing duties, and restrictions for balance-of-payments reasons are permitted, but have not been a practice.

Most licensing requirements were eliminated in May 1992. The weight-ed average tariff in 1993 was 11.7 percent, with a maximum of 40 percent. Restrictions existed for arms, drugs, and items affecting health. There was a 30 percent dumping duty on alcohol, vehicles, TVs, and video recorders imposed between May and October 1993.

Export quotas on raw materials were imposed for reasons of conserva-tion and on drugs for price support reasons. Occasional export bans on food, fruits, and wood products, Reduced export licensing requirements were introduced in June 1993.

The foreign exchange system One of the main impediment to reducing mar-ket distortions through the foreign trading system has been the shortage of foreign exchange brought on by an awkward, often revised foreign exchange regime. This became evident under the new system when the combination of fixed rates and domestic price controls led to excess demand and a rapid depletion of foreign exchange reserves.

In November 1990, a dual exchange rate was introduced in which an official rate of 35 lei/USD was applied along side a commercial interbank rate that was supposed to float. Exporters were required to surrender 50 percent of their proceeds at the official rate to the State Currency Fund which financed imports of basic food and energy at that rate. The official rate fell to 60 lei/USD in April 1991, while the commercial rate fluctuated from 180 to 225 lei/USD. The hoped for stimulus to exports is said to have been diminished by the expectation that all foreign exchange receipts would have to be surrendered before the end of the year. Exporters were encour-aged to understate export receipts in order to hold unrecorded foreign cur-rency accounts.

A year later in November 1991 the dual rate system was dropped. In January the unified exchange rate was devalued to 180 lei/USD and all foreign exchange accounts and receipts required to be surrendered. A new rate would be set by daily interbank auctions managed by the National Bank. An effort to divert more foreign exchange by exporters is suggested by the 66 percent increase in exports in December 1991.

In 1992 the unified exchange rate should have eliminated the off-budget subsidies to food and other raw material imports since the exchange rate would henceforth be passed on into import prices. In practice, however, price adjustments were delayed by Decision 776 (see above) while liquidity pressures increased on many enterprises. In any case there was reported more quantity rationing of foreign exchange, while exporters increased efforts to divert proceeds abroad.

In May 1992 exporters were once again allowed to retain 100 percent of their foreign exchange earnings in the banks. Daily auction and exchange institution rates were restricted to adjustments of 5 percent and 2 percent respectively. Even then, however, rates were sometimes kept unchanged in the face of excess demand. Later in the autumn, the minimum required to enter the auction market was lowered and the 5 percent adjustment restriction lifted.

In spite of some immediately favorable effects on reserves, later in 1992, reserves again fell. Large spreads also developed between the auction rate and the open rate, reaching 30 percent, even though the rate fell to about 450lei/USD. By October 1993 official rates fell to over 1000 lei/USD, while street rates went over 1800 lei. The rate in early 1998 rose to over 8000 (Table1).

By mid 1994, the lei was virtually fully convertible for the purpose of foreign trade transactions and for capital and profits of foreign investors. Residents could purchase up to USD 500 per year for tourism abroad. In April 1994 the interbank foreign exchange rate was unified with the rate quoted by the so-called "bureaux" as the interbank market was freed of administrative intervention after a large gradual depreciation during the first quarter. The exchange rate of the leu has been qualified float against the dollar, with limited capital controls.

In early 1997 the exchange rate was freed from previous de facto regulation, and convertibility of the Romanian leu established in July as part of adopting Article VIII of the IMF Agreement. The exchange rate was unified after the removal of restrictions on the interbank foreign exchange market, which had led to overvaluation and dual exchange rates in 1996. The adjustment process and the liberalization of prices resulted in depreciation of the leu some 30 percent in real terms early in 1997, but later it stabilized and now is floating.

The financial system The usual two-tier banking system was created in December 1990, with commercial functions spun off to the Romanian Commercial Bank. Three other commercial banks were created from the postal saving bank, the development bank, and the foreign trade bank, all state-owned. Private banks began operations in 1990. Five foreign banks have branches in Bucharest.

In 1991 the government bought 90 percent of the banks non-performing claims and then canceled the loans, the total nominal value of which was 7.5 percent of the 1991 GDP. Another injection of state capital took place in 1992 through which three state-owned banks received the equivalent of 0.8 percent of GDP. There were also highly negative real interest rates and large spreads between lending and deposit rates during much of 1991-93. These practices by both Romania and Bulgaria have been strongly denounced by the IMF as leading to the expectation on the part of banks and enterprises of a continuing loose budget constraint.

Financial transfers are probably the source of the greatest distortions in the Romanian economy. Although interest rates were liberalized in April 1991 there was little response, partly because commercial banks had access to cheap money from the State Savings Bank. They practiced selective credit rationing to favored clients. According to a report by the consultants, McKinsey & Co., the economy suffers from "massive cross-subsidization between different companies and sectors, a lack of financial discipline and an inadequate circulation of foreign exchange."[5]

Early in 1992 deposit rates started to rise, reaching 70 percent (Table 1), but the State Savings Bank continued to provide funds at 50 percent. Still, most enterprises have been hard pressed and many have simply stopped paying suppliers and the banks. At the same time, neither suppliers nor the banks have found it in their interest to use the credit laws to foreclose on assets, because to do so would face them with collecting mostly worthless debt. By the end of 1991, gross credit arrears reached 40 percent of enterprise turnover (and enterprises listed credit and financing as their major problem).[6]

Table 1 Overview Indicators for Romania

	1990	1991	1992	1993	1994	1995	1996	1997
Output and expenditure			(percentage change)					
GDP at constant prices	-5.6	-12.9	-8.7	1.5	3.9	7.1	4.1	-6.6
Private consumption	-	-	-7.5	0.9	2.1	19.1	6.8	-6.5
Public consumption	-	-	2.2	2.7	11.7	0.7	7	-2.3
Gross fixed investment	-	-	11	8.3	19.6	11.2	4	-2
Exports of goods & services	-	-	2.9	11.1	19	32.7	2.3	5.9
Imports of goods & services	-	-	7.5	4.4	2.8	44.9	11.3	-6.4
Industrial gross output	-23.7	-22.8	-21.9	1.2	3.1	10	8.2	-5.2
Agricultural gross output		-8.6	-12.2	13.4	3.2	4.5	1.8	2.3
Composition of output	(percent of GDP)							
Industry	40.6	37.9	38.3	33.8	35.6	34.6	36	-
Agiculture	21.8	18.9	19	21	19.8	19.9	19.1	-
Employment	(percentage change)							
Labor force (end-year)	-1	1.8	-1.8	-3	0	-7.1	-0.3	-0.5
Employment (end-year)	-1	-0.5	-3	-3.8	-0.5	-5.2	0.8	-0.8
	(percent of labour force)							
Unemployment[1]			6.2	9.5	9.5	7.4	6.1	7
Prices and wages	(percentage change)							
Consumer prices (annual average)	5.1	161	210	256	137	32	36.1	155
Consumer prices (yearend)	37.7	223	199	296	62	28	56.9	151.6
Government sector	(percent of GDP)							
General government balance[2]	1	3.3	-4.6	-0.4	-1.9	-2.6	-3.9	-4.5
General government expenditure	38.7	38.7	42	34.2	33.9	34.5	33.7	31.4
Monetary sector	(percentage change)							
Broad money (end-year)	22	101	80	141	138	72	66	48.9
Domestic credit (end-year)	7.5	122	35	131	114	92	88	66.3
	(percent of GDP)							
Broad money	59.6	46.7	28.9	9.1	21.5	25.4	28.9	24.9
Interest and exchange rates								
Interbank interest rate (up to 30-day)	3.8	19.5	43.6	86.4	62.4	41.5	46.9	59
Treasury bill rate (3 months)						45	55	98
Deposit rate (one year)	-	-	38	52	62	38	47	60
Lending rate (one year)	-	-	53	129	83	59	71	70
	(lei per USD)							
Exchange rate (end-year)	34.7	189	460	1276	1767	2578	4035	7958
Exchange rate (annual average)	22.4	76	308	760	1580	2033	3083	7224
External sector	(million USD)							
Current account	-1656	-1181	-1518	-1239	-516	-1732	-2600	-1900
Trade balance[3]	-1743	-1254	-1373	-1130	-483	-1605	-2494	-1414
Exports[3]	3364	3241	4286	4882	6067	7882	8061	8540
Imports[3]	-5107	-4495	-5659	-6012	-6550	-9487	-10555	-9875
Foreign direct investment, net	18	37	73	97	347	404	415	998
Gross reserves (end-year)[4]	524	695	826	995	2086	1579	2103	3436
Total external debt-stock	1140	2131	3240	4249	5509	6710	8480	10400
	(in months of current account expenditures, excluding transfers)							
Gross reserves (end-year)[4]	1	1.5	1.5	1.7	3.1	1.6	2.2	3.6
	(in months of current account revenues, excluding transfers)							
Debt service	0.2	2.3	8.9	6.2	8.7	11.5	14.8	-
Memorandum items								
Population (millions end-year)	23.2	23.2	22.8	22.7	22.6	22.6	22.6	22.6
GDP (billion lei)	858	2204	6029	20036	49768	72560	109515	249750
GDP per capita (in USD)	1257	1187	859	1159	1324	1573	1437	1521
GNP per capita (in USD) at PPP[5]	-	-	3542	3698	3931	4312	4591	-

1) Registered unemployment.
2) General government includes the state, communes, and extrabudgetary funds.
3) Data from the balance of payments.
4) International reserves of monetary authorities.
5) PPP quotations are from the OECD Short-Term Indicators Transition Economies, 3, 1997.

At the end of 1991, the government and the National Bank arranged what was supposed to be a one time "global compensation" which allowed commercial banks to extend credit in order to liquidate company arrears, with such credits secured by the state or by the assets of the debtors. The immediate effect of the compensation program was to reduce arrears to 25 percent of their former level. Also, there was an attempt to increase credit discipline. Nonetheless, the basic problems of falling production and unrestructured companies remained so arrears rose by mid-1992 to 25 percent of turnover. By September, however, inflation appeared to have reduced debt-stock values relative to turnover so that the ratio fell to about 15 percent.[7]

In the first years of transition one encountered unconfirmed reports of "non-profit foundations" having been set up in order to permit financial transfers among enterprises at a local level. It is believed that these could be used to enable forms of "nomenclatura privatization". How large are the potential market distortions resulting from them is unknown.

Commercial banks are in principle free to set their interest rates. The interbank money market was formally established in 1994. Until recently distortions arose from directed credits, which were channeled through the state-owned banking system and from the issuance of treasury bills to the state-owned banks that were then refinanced by the National Bank., in the absence of a functioning secondary market. The second half of 1996 was characterized by artificially low, often negative real interest rates. According to IMF calculations, the quasi-fiscal subsidies provided by the NBR amounted to 2.6 percent of GDP in 1996.

Such practices are supposed to have been abolished since early 1997 with the new governing regime. This plus price liberalization triggered an increase in real interest rates. Attempts to introduce a secondary market for treasury bills have been under way.

Industrial concentration and monopoly regulation The Transformation Law of 1990 expressed goals of breaking up existing monopolies and of creating competing companies within existing branches of industry. Until 1997 there was not, however, an agency to enforce competition or oversee mergers, etc. A law of January 1991 (Law 11/1991) does define a series of unfair practices, but a proper competition law was lacking.

A comparison of industrial concentration statistics for 1992 by the author showed that Romanian had much higher concentration than Poland, the former Czechoslovakia, and Hungary. Romania's huge enterprises were comparable to those of unreformed Czechoslovakia in 1989.

Romanian employment concentration by branches showed significant variation in mid-1992. Besides food processing, the number and size structure of companies in textiles, and leather goods suggested ample potential for competition. But the high level of aggregation made it difficult to judge other sectors. Very large firms with more than 5000 employees have more than 50 percent of total branch employment in wood processing (3 firms with 68 percent), metallurgy (9 firms with 56 percent), and transport equipment (13 firms with 52 percent). Also, there is high concentration in oil refining, chemicals, and plastic-rubber. These branches have low potential for domestic market competition. Another major barrier to competition has been amply use of the so-called "regie autonome" or regulated state companies with monopolies in strategic areas of the economy.

In none of the cases is there much known about formal or informal coordinating structures within branches or sub-branches. No regulatory or investigative agency existed until 1997. The chances of immediately having competitive behavior on the part of the former nomenclatura, who dominate present management, is equally low. Competition, when it comes, is likely to be a process depending on de novo privatization or new start ups and foreign investors. A law regulating competition took effect in January 1997. A Competition Council has been established and became operational to investigate alleged monopoly concentrations. No record of its actions has been encountered so far for this research.

Changing Property Rights

Privatization

Effective markets and restructuring of enterprises are unlikely to be done without significant changes in property rights in the direction of private ownership. Also, significant help must come from abroad in the form of direct foreign investments, joint ventures, and various forms of cooperation between Romanian and foreign enterprises. A quantitative view of privatization is found in the next three tables and a qualitative description of the process follows (see Table 2, Table 3 and Table 4).

The initial legal framework for privatization includes the following actions:[8]

- General enabling of private enterprise in 1990.
- Law 15/1990 which required the conversion of former SOEs into over 6300 "commercial companies", most of which are joint stock companies

with 100 percent state share ownership and about 800 "regies autonomes" in defense, energy, mining, railways, etc.
- The Privatization Law (Law 58/1991).
- The Foreign Investment Law (Law 35/1991).

Table 2 Sectoral Labor Force by Ownership Categories (end of 1995)

(1000 persons)

	Total	Public	Mixed	Private	Cooperative	Community
Total	9493	4194	304	4815	166	14
Agriculture	3187	181	80	2926	*	*
Forestry	78	68	2	8	-	-
Industry	2714	1937	144	555	77	1
Construction	479	180	14	281	4	-
Trade	988	207	27	695	65	*
Transporation	458	352	8	96	2	-
Communications	98	94	*	4	-	-
Finance	71	39	20	10	2	-
Real estate & other	324	163	5	153	3	-
Pulbic administration	131	130	-	-	*	-
Education	437	427	1	9	*	*
Health	333	326	-	7	-	*
Other	195	90	3	71	19	12
			Structure			
Total	100.0	44.2	3.2	50.7	1.7	0.1
Agriculture	100.0	5.7	2.5	91.8		
Forestry	100.0	87.2	2.6	10.3		
Industry	100.0	71.4	5.3	20.4	2.8	0.0
Construction	100.0	37.6	2.9	58.7	0.8	
Trade	100.0	21.0	2.7	70.3	6.6	
Transporation	100.0	76.9	1.7	21.0	0.4	
Communications	100.0	95.9	4.1			
Finance	100.0	54.9	28.2	14.1	2.8	
Real estate & other	100.0	50.3	1.5	47.2	0.9	
Pulbic administration	100.0	99.2				
Education	100.0	97.7	0.2	2.1		
Health	100.0	97.9	2.1			
Other	100.0	46.2	1.5	36.4	9.7	6.2

Source: Calculations from the Romanian statistical yearbook, 1996.

Land Soon after the Land Law of 1991 the government claimed more than 90 per cent of farmland was distributed in small plots to farmers (up to 10 ha. per family). Research done by the author to review a Commission study of Romania's agriculture clearly showed the government claims to be highly distorted, qualitatively and quantitatively. In 1997 the European Bank for Reconstruction and Development (EBRD) in its annual Transition Report put the figure at only 83 percent; even that figure may be high. The law did not mean that families immediately received land to farm or that the scale of farming was fragmented. Actual possession of land for farming was delayed by conflict over claims, efforts to push peasants into "co-operative" operations around former collective farms, and lack of formal titles sometimes due delays in land surveys and setting up cadasters (or land records). Privatization of state farms and other state facilities, and of up- and down-stream organizations connected with agriculture has been slow and controversial. In 1997 a new land law came into force establishing improved regulation for the leasing of land.

Table 3 Ownership and Size of Industrial Enterprises

	1990	1991	1992	1993	1994	1995
Number of enterprises						
Total	2241	9909	17085	23858	33824	35070
Public ownership	1683	2069	2116	2514	2182	2064
national industry	1612	2011	2058	2117	1808	1642
local industry	71	58	58	397	374	422
Mixed ownership			35	107	244	256
Private ownership		7100	14207	20599	30844	32323
Cooperative ownerships	558	740	727	638	554	427
Number of employees						
Total	3702	3409	3093	2900	2717	2615
Public ownership	3365	3084	2783	2549	2290	1959
national industry	3297	3053	2762	2478	2214	1895
local industry	68	31	21	71	76	64
Mixed ownership			31	32	65	145
Private ownership		48	105	186	271	433
Cooperative ownerships	337	277	174	133	91	78
Employees per enteprise						
Total	1652	344	181	122	80	75
Public ownership	1999	1491	1315	1014	1049	949
national industry	2045	1518	1342	1171	1225	1154
local industry	958	534	362	179	203	152
Mixed ownership			886	299	266	566
Private ownership		7	7	9	9	13
Cooperative ownerships	604	374	239	208	164	183

Source: Calculated from Romanian statistical yearbook.

The large livestock growing operations were largely excluded from privatization. These large operations had been highly subsidized and were inefficient. Soon they encountered trouble and could hardly attract needed foreign investments. At the same time, individual and small scale operators soon began to provide the bulk of animal products for the market. The state also retained

Table 4 Private Sector Share of Various Activities

	1995	1996	1997
GDP	52.0	58.0	-
Industrial production	24.5	33.0	-
Agricultural production	86.1	86.3	88.9
crops	88.1	87.6	89.4
livestock	83.2	84.4	87.9
Construction	70.8		-
Investment	39.7	40.2	-
finished residential space	85.5	87.0	-
Transportation (ton km.)	54.4		-
Foreign trade	-	-	-
exports	41.3	51.5	55.1
imports	45.3	48.5	52.4
Wholesale trade	63.4		-
Retail sales	74.3	74.4	70.4
food products	77.7	77.5	-
non-food products	72.7	67.4	-
Commercial services	58.2	67.4	67.1

Source: Calculated from Romanian statistical yearbook.

ownership in the large agricultural intermediaries as well as in national distributions and storage companies. Privatization and restructuring of these entities is a priority of the new reform program.

Property restitution A draft law granting limited restitution rights to former owners of around 250,000 residential properties confiscated after 1945 by the former communist regime was passed by the Romanian senate in June 1994, but encountered great opposition in the lower house of parliament. Amendments to the law on property restitution, granting more rights to claimants have been announced for later 1997.

Small-scale privatization The rapid increase in small private companies, typical of other transition countries, took place in Romania. Of the 362,000 reported in October 1992, 188,000 were family associations (individual proprietorships) and 174,000 were commercial companies. Less than 25 percent had more than 20 employees. Some 70 percent were concentrated in trade and services and only 18 percent were in manufacturing. As of mid-1994 more than 7,000 small-scale units had been put up for sale and about 3,000 were privatized, involving 13,500 employees. These units include retail outlets, workshops and hotels.

The Privatization Law provided an important adjunct to the formation of new private companies through the provision to sell off (normally at auction) "individual assets" of state properties. They are defined as excess parts of a commercial company that can be separated without affecting the company's main activity. As of January 1993 some 6105 such "assets" had been identified of which only 1436 had been sold (by July 1993 some 2,500). They involved 7800 employees and a sale price of about 15.1 billion lei.

By 1997 almost all small-scale trade and service activity was in the hands of private operators. Some 98 percent are privately owned. Joint private-state ownership covered 1.3 percent and state ownership another 0.7 percent.

Large-scale privatization The first privatization law of 1991 established five "private ownership funds" (POF), which were legally established as joint-stock companies, and one "state ownership fund" (SOF). The latter held 70 percent of the shares in 6,300 "commercial companies" (those legally reorganized under the commercial code) while the rest of the share were turned over to one of the POFs. In 1992 vouchers representing shares in the POFs were distributed to all adult citizens. The management of the POFs were appointed by the government.

About 270 small companies were privatized under this scheme in 1993 and another 250 during the first four months of 1994, mostly by management/employee buy-outs. The government intends to amend the voucher scheme before the end of 1994. A new voucher program was launched in 1995 (see below).

The organizational framework for privatization included the National Agency for Privatization (NAP), the State Ownership Fund (SOF), and the five Private Ownership Funds (POFs). The NAP was to be the main organizer of privatization, including the sale of "assets" and whole companies and some oversight functions with respect to the SOF and POFs. The SOF soon became the most powerful force as ownership agent for 70 percent of the shares of state-owned commercial companies, concentrating on very large companies. Under the law, it was required to liquidate its holdings in seven years (as is scheduled for 1998). The POFs were assigned to manage, as "mutual funds", the remaining 30 percent which has been distributed to citizens under the mass privatization program. They were located in five different cities in Romania and are semi-specialized by branch of industry (some branch holdings are assigned to all five). Also, their focus is more on medium-sized companies.

The latter manage the "mass privatization" program in which "certificates of ownership" were distributed to more than 15 million Romanians. Each certificate has five coupons or claims on each of the five POFs. The coupons could be sold for cash or invested in a POF or one of its constituent companies. The certificates could be offered, for example, for up to 30 percent of a company in a MEBO (management-employee buyout), which has been the most common form of privatization so far.

As might be expected, the privatization program has not been easy because of problems both in the lack of Romania expertise for such activity and in the combination of difficult economic conditions and company structures. Beginning in the summer of 1992 a PHARE-assisted program supported the help of western consultants for the evaluation of the first companies. Furthermore, setting up of the five POFs is now assisted on a bilateral basis by five different western countries (Germany, Holland, US, UK, France).

By the end of January 1993 some 16 companies had been privatized from a list of 30 candidates. Of these, 11 were by employees (MEBOs) and 5 were by outside investors, including at least 3 foreign companies.[9] By April 1993 some 19 companies were privatized. By August only 3 more had been sold, including one more foreign investor.[10] By branch, they included: 7 construction; 1 design-construction; 4 agricultural, meat, or vegetable processing; 1 brewery; 1 printing; 2 furniture; 3 clothing; 1 ceramics; and 1 foreign trade. They employed some 19,000 persons.[11]

Share distribution under the new voucher program of 1995 completed only in October 1996. Most vouchers were exchanged against enterprise shares directly, with only 14 percent exchanged against shares in the POFs, which were converted to so-called private investment funds (PIFs) in November 1996.

"The success of the new program was mixed." By the end of 1996, only 45 percent of all enterprises scheduled for privatization were privatized. This included about 70 percent of the eligible small enterprises, only 24 percent of medium enterprises, and 13 percent of large enterprises.

The new government attempted to accelerate privatization. In the first eight months of 1997, according to the EBRD, a further 1,100 companies were privatized, including 140 medium and large enterprises. This raised the privatized rate to about 60 percent of the original plan.

In 1997 the SOF started selling its large minority ownership stakes through the stock exchange. Larger companies with 51 percent or more SOF holdings are to be sold through open tender. Significant problems remain. Sale of majority state owned, large enterprises is subject to delay partly because of overly bureaucratic procedures applied by the SOF whose employees, of course, seek to protect their positions or ensure a place in the best privatized companies. The status of the POFs is uncertain and the interests are similar. Trading on the over-the-counter market and the stock exchange has not yet reached a volume sufficient to establish the concentration of ownership necessary to alleviate corporate governance problems. Interest in strategic investors outside Romania rose with the new regime in 1997. Incentives were offered by the SOF as cash rebates of up to 60 percent to potential buyers if the funds are reinvested in the company.

The SOF was restructured and put under direct government control in April 1997. It is legally required to cease operations in 1999, the date specified in the initial law for completion of the privatization program.

Overall statistics Private sector of GDP estimated at 16 percent at end of 1990 grew to over 31 percent by end of 1993. According to government estimates, the private sector share of GDP then rose from 35 percent in 1994 to 55 percent in 1997. These estimates include firms with a minority stake held by the state.

Private sector employment was about 42 percent of employment at the end of 1993 according to the EBRD [1994]. The private sector accounted for about 23 percent of employment in 1995 and 47 percent in 1996 [EBRD 97].

The share of private ownership varies considerably across sectors. In 1996, the private sector share in GDP was about 87 percent in agriculture, 24 percent in industry, 71 percent in construction and 75 percent in trade and services. The private sector accounted for about 52 percent of foreign trade during the first six months of 1997.

As of March 1994 there were 2.4 million private farmers (although many were waiting for full rights to land property) and 334,000 other registered firms (up from 200,000 at the end of 1992). The average size of private units remained small and some new company registrations are for the purpose of extending tax holidays for new companies.

Between 1992 and October 1996, the number of state-owned companies fell slightly, from about 8,000 to 6,000, and the number of private companies rose from 200,000 to 500,000. Self-employment, family businesses and foreign-held companies also increased by about 50 percent.

Restructuring and Financial Reforms

The approach has been gradual and erratic. The main restructuring tool has been subsidy reduction and attempts to introduce market-oriented credit conditions. Two occasions saw this interrupted by massive credit injections from the central bank aimed at "clearing" a rapidly growing stock of inter-enterprise arrears. A renewed effort at strengthening financial discipline in enterprises was initiated in the second half of 1993 and is still being pursued (mid-1994). This involved tightening of credit, establishment of a restructuring agency (with EC-Phare support) and financial supervision intensified for 25 enterprises that account for the bulk of inter-enterprise arrears.

A draft bankruptcy law had been long under debate in parliament with an anti-trust law not submitted until much later. Finally in March 1995 a bankruptcy law was passed (see description in EBRD 1997). Arrears continued to be a major problem throughout 1996 under the former governing regime partly because the bankruptcy law does not apply to the "Regies Autonomes", the autonomous state enterprises operating mostly in the public utilities area. In their case, a special bankruptcy law applies. In any event, in spite of having targeted about 150 loss-making enterprises, the previous regime hardly made any progress.

The new government in February 1997 launched a new program with proposals for merging, restructuring, and/or liquidating unprofitable enterprises and autonomous state enterprises (RAs). Special measures were set out for dismantling the National Oil Company, which had been set up only in August 1996. Production is to be concentrated in two refineries with associated retail networks. Measures are also being taken to restructure transportation. In the enterprise sector, a group of enterprises accounting for about 75 percent of the total state enterprises losses has been targeted. They include 42 commercial companies and 20 RAs. Initial concentration was to be on eight enterprises, covering various sectors, and then another group of 17 enterprises. In June 1997 all RAs were reorganized as joint-stock companies under the Commercial Code and are to be privatized.

Measures in the agricultural sector Agriculture is potentially a major contributor to Romania's development and has required special measures. Quasi-fiscal support in the form of credit advances to state companies and RAs were refinanced by the National Bank and in 1996 were estimated to have reached 2.1 percent of GDP (EBRD 1997). Other distortions came from administered wholesale and retail prices, monopolistic state-owned intermediaries, storage facilities, and distribution networks.

The reform program has focused on price liberalization, tariff reduction, and privatization and demonopolization of intermediaries, distributors, and large farm units. Prices were liberalized early in 1997. By mid-1997 11 large livestock farms had been liquidated, while the other loss makers were targeted for privatization and division in the course of 1997 and 1998.

Improved conditions for leasing land have been set out in a new land law. Tariffs on agricultural imports have been reduced from a product weighted average of 67 percent to only 22 percent, which is below the level required by the international agencies. Export bans have been abolished. A new subsidy system for purchase of inputs by private farmers was introduced in the fall of 1997. From now on the subsidy system is supposed to be a transparent component of the state budget.

Conditions for Foreign Investors

Foreign investment is allowed in all sectors provided not against environment, national security, and public order, health, and good morals. Special authorization is required for banking, insurance, and securities transactions. No restrictions face profit or capital repatriation, but a 10 percent withholding tax on dividends and profits transferred was established. Corporate tax rate is 30 percent for profit up to 1 million lei and 45 percent thereafter. If foreign ownership is greater than 20 percent or $10,000 taxes are exempt 2-5 years depending on sector. Reductions may be extended for activities with certain characteristics (exports, R&D, etc.). Additional special tax incentives in petroleum and industrial sectors.

Also free economic zones have been established. They provide exemption of up to two years on custom duties on raw materials used for production purposes. Special import duty exemptions can be obtained in petroleum and industry sectors. Exemption is provided from import duties on equipment if contributed in kind or financed by foreign cash contribution.

A Romanian registered company may theoretically buy land for business activity, but in practice the most accepted vehicle is long-term lease or concession. May lease agricultural land. But in June 1993 parliament refused to confirm foreigners' right to buy land. Participation in privatization permitted with approval from the State Ownership Fund and, as the case may be, the POF. Foreign participation is not allowed in natural resources, public utilities and transportation, and infrastructure, and arms production.

Participation of foreign investors was at first rather low (only 3 companies up to the summer of 1993). By contrast, the number of joint ventures set up in Romania was initially very high, but most were small companies and some were reorganizations seeking new benefits. By April 1993 there were reported 23,706 companies and social capital of $642 million (not actual foreign asset contributions). A major impediment was a common practice of Romanian managers attempting to obtain both ownership shares and a place in the management of companies having a strong foreign partner or government officials seeking tips and other favors.

Conditions have since improved as investors learned how to work in Romanian conditions. At the end of 1997 the Romanian Economic Newsletter reported that investments had reached $3.4 billion and included a total of 55,694 investors. In terms of the origins by capital, France stood first ($427 million), followed by Korea ($368 million), and then the Netherlands, Germany and the U.S. From the Balkan neighborhood came $124 million from Turkey, $63 million from Greece, and even $7 million from Bulgaria. Italy provided the greatest number of investors, 5913, followed by Germany 5726, and Turkey 4732. Unfortunately, the numerical basis of this report is such that international comparisons can not be made with it.

The UN Economic Commission for Europe estimated that the FDI flow in Romania in the first half of 1997 was 3.5 percent of GDP which ranked it sixth in the region. The cumulative inflow in June 1997 is estimated $79 per capita, far below the $1430 figure for Hungary and ranking behind even Albania and Bulgaria (Economic Bulletin for Europe, 49:1997, p. 93).[12] The Commission remarked that "Bulgaria and Romania received more FDI in the first half of 1997 than in any previous year, Romania emerging as one of the largest recipients of FDI among the transition countries." This is a hard fact which demonstrates the author's emphasis on political conditions in the region. It can only be hoped that 1998 will still have the same attraction for Romania even though the glitter on the new political regime is worn off.

415

Economic Structure

When looking at data on changes in economic structure of a transition country, one must keep in mind several different causes or sources of the structural change: the correction of distortions of the former system, the impact of a decline in aggregate demand and then possibly a rise in aggregate demand, the shift in foreign trade relations from the CMEA to the world and especially the EU economies with new sources of market opportunities and new forms of competition, and finally the different pace of transition institutional and policy reforms across the main sectors of the economy and the branches within the sectors. The author and other colleagues have been looking for relatively straight forward ways to identify the simultaneous effects of all of these forces, but so far have not succeeded. Until more comparative modeling has been done, any ad hoc explanation is likely to be in error.

Broad Sectors

Labor force data (defined in Romania as "populatia ocupata") provides a broad measure of economic structure in terms of the relative important of the broad sectors. Unfortunately the available data, shown in Table 5, do not provide comparable data for 1989 because some sectors such as finance and real estate were not identified in the communist system. The overall labor force declined more than 12 percent from 1989 to 1995. Nevertheless, some sectors such as finance and trade grew absolutely and others, less expected, experienced some growth (public administration, education, health). There is instability shown in some new sectors. Real estate and related activities grow at first and then decline. Even trade in 1993 and agriculture in 1995 exhibit declines. There is, of course, a chance that changes in classification have been introduced.

As happens in other transition countries, the share of industry and construction in the occupied population declines steadily, from 45 percent at the end of 1989 to 33.6 percent at the end of 1995 (Table 5). It would not be a surprise if Romania and Bulgaria, compared to transition countries in Central Europe, would exhibit a larger relative decline in share of industrial employment and industrial output because relative to their capacities to manage industry they might have been more "over industrialized". In the same time period, end of 1989 to end of 1995, labor shares in agriculture and forestry rise from 28 percent to 34.4 percent. This increase in shares

416

Table 5 Change and Structure of the Labor Force

	1989	1990	1991	1992	1993	1994	1995
			Change (1989 = 100.0)				
Agriculture	100.0	101.4	103.4	111.6	117.4	118.2	105.8
Forestry	100.0	202.3	202.3	184.1	175.0	195.5	177.3
Industry	104.1	100.0	95.0	82.4	75.7	72.0	67.8
Construction	108.6	100.0	71.0	82.0	81.3	79.7	67.8
Trade	89.6	100.0	126.0	128.3	98.9	106.6	136.5
Transportation	101.2	100.0	89.1	83.4	74.5	69.3	68.7
Communications	84.3	100.0	99.0	95.9	97.9	96.9	101.0
Finance	100.0	112.8	146.2	169.2	151.3	182.1	
Real estate & other	137.5	100.0	108.5	113.7	107.5	112.9	83.5
Public administration	61.1	100.0	112.5	128.4	133.0	142.0	148.9
Education	90.7	100.0	103.6	105.1	105.1	106.3	106.3
Health	91.3	100.0	97.2	95.6	96.3	104.1	104.1
Other	117.6	100.0	149.0	82.9	78.1	79.3	77.7
Total	101.0	100.0	99.5	96.5	92.8	92.4	87.6
			Structure				
Agriculture	27.5	28.2	28.9	32.1	35.2	35.6	33.6
Forestry	0.4	0.8	0.8	0.8	0.8	0.9	0.8
Industry	38.1	36.9	35.3	31.6	30.1	28.8	28.6
Construction	7.0	6.5	4.6	5.5	5.7	5.6	5.0
Trade	5.9	6.7	8.5	8.9	7.1	7.7	10.4
Transportation	6.2	6.2	5.5	5.3	4.9	4.6	4.8
Communications	0.7	0.9	0.9	0.9	0.9	0.9	1.0
Finance	0.4	0.4	0.5	0.7	0.6	0.7	
Real estate & other	4.9	3.6	3.9	4.2	4.1	4.4	3.4
Public administration	0.5	0.8	0.9	1.1	1.2	1.2	1.4
Education	3.4	3.8	3.9	4.1	4.3	4.4	4.6
Health	2.7	3.0	2.9	2.9	3.1	3.3	3.5
Other	2.7	2.3	3.5	2.0	1.9	2.0	2.1
Total	100.0	100.0	100.0	100.0	100.0	100.0	100.0
			1000 persons				
Agriculture	3012.3	3055.0	3116.0	3362.0	3537.0	3561.0	3187.0
Forestry	44.0	89.0	89.0	81.0	77.0	86.0	78.0
Industry	4169.0	4005.0	3803.0	3301.0	3030.0	2882.0	2714.0
Construction	766.7	706.0	501.0	579.0	574.0	563.0	479.0
Trade	648.9	724.0	912.0	929.0	716.0	772.0	988.0
Transportation	675.3	667.0	594.0	556.0	497.0	462.0	458.0
Communications	81.8	97.0	96.0	93.0	95.0	94.0	98.0
Finance	39.0	44.0	57.0	66.0	59.0	71.0	
Real estate & other	533.6	388.0	421.0	441.0	417.0	438.0	324.0
Public administration	53.8	88.0	99.0	113.0	117.0	125.0	131.0
Education	372.8	411.0	426.0	432.0	432.0	437.0	437.0
Health	292.3	320.0	311.0	306.0	308.0	333.0	333.0
Other	295.2	251.0	374.0	208.0	196.0	199.0	195.0
Total	10945.7	10840.0	10786.0	10458.0	10062.0	10011.0	9493.0

417

exceeds that of all remaining sectors together (roughly "services") which increased from 27 percent to 32 percent. Compared to other transition countries this is not a big increase in "services".

Table 6 on economic structure shows GDP by main sectors. As with labor force, GDP shares of industry fall and that of agriculture rises. The

Table 6 Change and Structure of GDP

	1989	1990	1991	1992	1993	1994	1995
	Change in constant prices (1989 = 100.0)						
Agriculture	100.0	139.4	122.8	106.7	121.9	125.4	131.7
Forestry	100.0	93.7	68.9	64.8	59.3	61.1	62.6
Industry	100.0	83.3	72.6	62.6	63.3	65.1	70.2
Construction	100.0	101.1	81.5	76.9	95.9	121.6	131.1
Trade	100.0	109.3	81.4	73.9	67.2	69.1	74.8
Transportation	100.0	78.2	65.1	61.1	61.4	61.5	62.0
Communications	100.0	81.2	112.3	121.6	147.2	161.6	172.1
Finance	100.0	117.3	117.0	163.4	164.3	167.0	171.7
Real estate & other	100.0	104.0	101.8	121.3	113.9	118.4	132.6
Public administration	100.0	114.0	104.8	116.2	118.4	129.8	130.1
Education	100.0	105.4	122.8	121.9	126.1	126.5	127.2
Health	100.0	124.4	121.9	118.5	121.1	130.4	133.3
Gross value added	100.0	97.6	86.1	78.4	81.0	84.5	90.3
GDP	100.0	94.4	82.2	75.0	76.1	79.1	84.7
	Structure in current prices						
Agriculture	13.7	21.2	18.3	18.6	20.6	19.3	19.4
Forestry	0.7	0.6	0.5	0.5	0.4	0.5	0.4
Industry	46.2	40.5	37.9	38.3	33.8	35.6	34.6
Construction	5.5	5.4	4.4	4.8	5.2	6.4	6.5
Trade	5.8	6.2	13.5	14.3	10.3	9.9	10.2
Transportation	5.8	4.9	5.7	7.6	8.8	6.6	6.2
Communications	1.0	0.8	1.0	0.9	1.3	1.3	1.4
Finance	2.1	2.7	2.6	5.3	5.1	4.7	5.2
Real estate & other	4.5	4.4	3.9	4.3	4.2	4.3	5.0
Public administration	2.5	2.8	3.1	3.4	3.1	3.2	3.5
Education	2.2	2.6	2.8	2.7	2.5	2.5	2.5
Health	1.7	2.0	2.3	2.1	1.8	1.9	1.7
Gross value added	90.1	91.9	93.7	98.1	92.7	92.3	93.0
GDP	100.0	100.0	100.0	100.0	100.0	100.0	100.0
	1000 persons						
Agriculture	109.8	181.6	404.3	1119.9	4124.3	9620.6	14112.5
Forestry	5.4	5.5	11.6	28.0	81.5	243.7	313.0
Industry	369.3	347.6	834.6	2311.0	6781.4	17733.4	25095.0
Construction	43.9	46.0	96.1	290.1	1040.0	3171.8	4746.7
Trade	46.0	53.2	296.5	859.5	2057.7	4907.7	7431.9
Transportation	46.2	42.2	125.2	457.2	1759.3	3304.3	4521.2
Communications	7.6	7.2	21.9	57.1	255.3	636.4	1013.4
Finance	16.7	23.2	57.9	322.2	1014.5	2330.2	3768.7
Real estate & other	36.0	37.9	85.9	260.8	839.5	2129.5	3648.3
Public administration	20.2	23.9	68.1	203.3	620.2	1611.1	2508.0
Education	17.9	22.3	61.3	159.8	491.6	1260.1	1789.0
Health	13.7	17.4	49.9	127.3	361.8	943.5	1261.0
Gross value added	721.1	788.1	2066.1	5916.2	18579.2	45949.0	67457.7
GDP	800.0	857.9	2203.9	6029.2	20035.7	49767.6	72559.7

other sectors together, "services" increase from 39.4 percent of the total to 45.6 percent.

Using information from both tables we can see that GDP per occupied person in agriculture and forestry is only about half that of industry. It turns out the GDP per occupied person in the other "service" sectors is about the same as in industry.

Industrial Structure

There are at least two ways to compare industrial structure by component branches. One would be to look at the shares of branch output in current prices (and this could be done in terms of either value added or gross output). Another would be to look at changes in real output or output in constant prices. The first way actually shows the results of two, often offsetting effects: changes in relative prices and changes in relative real output. Having done such a comparison across seven transition countries of changes from 1989 to 1995 for both gross industrial output and value added (Jackson and Repkin 1997), the author has decided to avoid the comparison here because it is inconclusive without some form of modeling (Table 7).

It is useful to compare the indices of real change in gross industrial output by main branches (1989=100), as in Table 7. Romania and Bulgaria share the distinction of having the largest real fall in total industrial output and manufacturing output during the transition period. The branches that have lost the most output since 1989 are food & beverages (shared with Slovakia), fuels, chemicals, rubber & plastic, metallurgy & metal products, and transport equipment (shared with Bulgaria). The branches doing better in terms of real output are textiles & clothing (although not as good as in Poland), printing & publishing (as in Poland), radio, TV, & communication equipment and, especially furniture.

Before one draws conclusions from such a comparison it is important to consider if maintaining output is necessarily a good thing. The answer would be, no, if it were done on the basis of subsidies and other market distortions. The answer would be, yes, if it were done by improving labor productivity and the quality of output, as measured by success on international markets. Investigations of these issues are underway, but not completed.[13]

Table 7 Comparison of Changes in Gross Industrial Output

(1989 = 1.00)

NACE	Branch / Category	Czech Rep 95	96	97p	Poland 95	96	97p	Hungary 95	96	Sloven. 95	96	Slovak. 95	96	Romania 95	96	97p	Bul 95
C,D,E	Total Industry	0.64	0.67	0.70	0.93	1.01	1.13	0.72	0.74	0.72	0.72	0.60	0.61	0.55	0.57	0.53	0.55
C	Extraction	0.57	0.60	0.59	0.96	0.98	0.96	0.43	0.44	0.65	0.66	0.33	0.35	0.53	0.54	-	0.70
D	Total Manufacturing	0.63	0.67	0.71	0.97	1.07	1.23	0.71	0.74	0.71	0.72	0.58	0.59	0.53	0.55	0.46	0.54
DA	Food, Beverage, Tobacco	0.72	0.75	0.78	1.08	-	-	0.83	0.83	0.80	0.84	0.53	0.56	-	-	-	0.46
15	Food & Beverages	-	-	-	1.08	1.18	1.34	0.83	0.83	-	-	0.52	-	0.63	0.50	0.42	0.44
15.1-8	Food Products	-	-	-	-	-	-	0.81	0.80	0.80	0.83	0.47	-	-	-	-	0.36
15.9	Beverages	-	-	-	-	-	-	1.05	1.04	0.88	0.97	1.03	-	-	-	-	1.18
16	Tobacco	-	-	-	2.22	2.04	2.23	0.84	0.95	0.67	0.72	0.90	-	0.79	0.85	0.87	0.61
DB	Textiles & Products	0.51	0.47	0.46	1.03	-	-	0.52	0.50	0.63	0.60	0.40	0.39	-	-	-	0.54
17	Textiles	-	-	-	0.62	0.64	0.68	0.43	0.40	0.64	0.65	0.37	-	0.82	0.39	0.34	0.47
18	Apparel	-	-	-	2.26	2.39	2.79	0.75	0.76	0.65	0.64	0.45	-	0.57	0.95	0.96	0.70
DC	Leather & Products	0.43	0.38	0.28	0.75	0.85	0.89	0.49	0.47	0.55	0.44	0.37	0.38	0.61	0.52	0.43	0.50
19.1-2	Leather Products	-	-	-	-	-	-	0.39	0.32	0.61	0.58	0.42	-	0.61	-	-	0.44
19.3	Footwear	-	-	-	-	-	-	0.55	0.54	0.53	0.40	0.36	-	0.61	-	-	0.55
DD(20)	Wood Products	0.53	0.50	0.53	1.45	1.64	1.76	1.26	1.27	0.70	0.71	0.44	0.43	0.33	0.36	0.32	0.49
DE	Paper, Printing, Publishing	0.95	0.92	1.03	2.15	-	-	0.95	0.88	0.73	0.71	0.99	1.05	0.78	-	-	1.06
21	Paper & Products	-	-	-	1.53	1.68	2.03	0.79	0.75	0.75	0.72	1.08	-	0.41	0.39	0.35	0.70
22	Printing & publishing	-	-	-	3.59	4.05	5.22	0.92	0.84	0.78	0.75	0.78	-	1.97	3.50	3.47	2.57
DF(23)	Fuels Production	0.59	0.44	0.44	0.72	0.72	0.73	-	-	1.11	0.85	0.83	0.81	0.43	0.41	0.39	0.73
23.1	Coke Oven Products	-	-	-	-	-	-	-	-	-	-	0.73	-	0.54	-	-	-
23.2	Petroleum Refining	0.75	-	-	-	-	-	-	-	1.11	0.85	0.83	-	0.41	-	-	0.81
DG(24)	Chemicals, products, fibers	0.75	1.06	1.07	0.83	0.88	0.96	0.55	0.52	0.66	0.69	0.65	0.67	0.44	0.41	0.31	0.61
DH(25)	Rubber & Plastic Products	0.87	0.94	1.09	1.72	2.00	2.49	1.01	1.04	0.91	0.90	0.85	0.87	0.37	0.33	0.25	0.46
25.1	Rubber Products	-	-	-	-	-	-	0.45	0.50	1.10	1.09	0.86	-	0.62	-	-	0.31
25.2	Plastic Products	-	-	-	-	-	-	1.47	1.50	0.00	0.00	0.84	-	0.33	-	-	0.59
DI(26)	Mineral Materials& Prod.	0.70	0.72	0.78	1.11	1.22	1.36	0.74	0.75	0.79	0.84	0.51	0.51	0.45	0.39	0.34	0.55
26.1	Glass Products	-	-	-	-	-	-	0.80	0.95	-	-	0.55	-	0.72	-	-	0.80
26.2-3	Pottery, China, Earthware	-	-	-	-	-	-	0.76	-	0.83	0.81	0.49	-	0.88	-	-	0.97
26.4	Other Mineral Products	-	-	-	-	-	-	0.41	-	0.76	0.88	0.35	-	0.44	-	-	0.45
DJ	Basic Metals & Fab prod	0.70	0.69	0.72	0.77	-	-	0.66	0.65	0.76	0.71	0.86	0.79	-	-	-	0.75
27	Basic Metals	-	-	-	0.59	0.59	0.67	0.58	0.63	-	-	0.84	-	0.46	0.40	0.40	0.71
27.1-3	Ferrous Metals	-	-	-	-	-	-	0.54	0.54	0.66	0.54	0.85	-	0.46	-	-	0.66
27.4	Non-ferrous Metals	-	-	-	-	-	-	0.49	0.99	1.06	1.02	0.78	-	0.72	-	-	0.67
27.5	Castings	-	-	-	-	-	-	1.26	1.11	1.07	1.07	0.87	-	0.40	-	-	0.50
28	Fab Metal Products	-	-	-	1.41	1.69	1.96	0.91	0.77	0.61	0.59	0.99	-	0.36	0.38	0.40	0.55
DK(29)	Machin.. excluding electrical	0.43	0.44	0.50	0.95	1.05	1.14	0.69	0.65	0.65	0.60	0.29	0.31	0.48	0.62	0.57	0.32
29.3	Agri.. & Forest Machinery	-	-	-	-	-	-	-	-	-	-	0.24	-	0.46	-	-	-
29.7	Domestic appliances	-	-	-	-	-	-	-	-	-	-	0.23	-	0.34	-	-	-
DL	Electr.& Optical Equipment	0.53	0.57	0.71	-	-	-	0.74	1.08	0.77	0.89	0.44	0.51	0.59	-	-	0.26
30	Office Machines & Comp.	-	-	-	-	-	-	-	-	-	-	0.38	-	0.22	0.28	0.13	0.27
31	Electr.. Mach. & Equipment	-	-	-	-	-	-	-	-	0.87	0.96	0.46	-	0.77	1.02	1.33	-
32	Radio, TV, Comm Equipm	-	-	-	-	-	-	-	-	-	-	0.49	-	1.48	2.47	3.17	-
33	Professional-Scientific Equip	-	-	-	-	-	-	-	-	-	-	0.38	-	0.52	0.74	0.70	0.11
DM	Transport Equipment	0.56	0.72	0.83	0.86	-	-	0.62	0.78	0.53	0.49	0.61	0.74	-	-	-	0.35
34	Motor Vehicles & Trailers	-	-	-	0.65	0.87	1.16	-	-	0.54	0.51	0.65	-	0.43	0.54	0.54	-
35	Other Vehicles	-	-	-	1.93	1.81	1.95	-	-	0.36	0.31	0.53	-	0.44	0.31	0.33	-
DN(36)	Other Manufactured Prod.	0.69	0.72	0.75	2.50	2.79	3.63	0.66	0.57	0.80	0.80	0.56	0.62	1.16	1.37	1.30	0.79
36.1	Furniture	-	-	-	-	-	-	0.66	0.59	-	-	0.55	-	1.09	-	-	0.64
E(40.41)	Utilities	0.85	0.88	0.85	1.13	1.13	1.15	0.83	0.87	0.99	1.00	1.03	1.08	0.95	0.83	-	0.73

Foreign Trade Structure

Table 8 presents a comparison of the relative change in exports and imports measured in USD and real GDP. Most countries in the sample have experienced a significant increase in real foreign trade dependence. That is their exports and imports in dollars grew relative to their GDPs measured in constant internal prices. Romania and even more so Bulgaria are exceptions. Both have had exports shrink more than GDP and Bulgaria also had relative imports decline. Romania's relative increase in imports must be judged in terms of the extreme import deprivation of the economy in 1989. As already indicated it had been forced into a high state of autarchy at that point.

Table 8 Changes in Dollar Trade Compared to Real GDP

	1989	1990	1991	1992	1993	1994	1995	1996
	Exports based in dollars relative to real GDP							
Bulgaria	1.00	0.80	0.57	0.69	0.65	0.68	0.87	0.74
Czech Rep.	1.00	0.97	1.26	1.42	2.19	2.23	3.30	3.18
Hungary	1.00	1.04	1.24	1.34	1.12	1.31	1.55	1.57
Poland	1.00	1.41	1.24	1.07	1.11	1.28	1.58	1.59
Romania	1.00	0.60	0.64	0.72	0.79	0.96	1.16	1.13
Slovakia	1.00	0.92	1.13	1.34	2.04	2.39	2.87	2.76
Slovenia	1.00	1.31	1.36	2.48	2.19	2.34	2.73	2.65
	Imports based on dollars relative to real GDP							
Bulgaria	1.00	0.77	0.40	0.72	0.76	0.67	0.83	0.66
Czech Rep.	1.00	1.08	1.24	1.65	2.10	2.30	3.79	3.97
Hungary	1.00	1.03	1.52	1.52	1.74	1.94	2.03	2.11
Poland	1.00	1.10	1.46	1.48	1.65	1.81	2.28	2.75
Romania	1.00	1.25	1.21	1.43	1.47	1.54	2.08	2.22
Slovakia	1.00	1.03	1.12	1.55	2.72	2.65	3.31	3.91
Slovenia	1.00	1.60	1.53	2.41	2.48	2.65	3.31	3.18

Next, Table 9 gives a brief glance at the commodity structure of Romania's exports and imports. This time the other transition countries have been left out, although their numbers can be found in the source of the table, the UN/ECE, Economic Bulletin. One of the main features of such a comparison is the low share in both exports and imports of food, beverages, and agricultural products. Romania's share is about the same as the Czech Republic, Slovakia and Slovenia. It is much smaller than shares for Poland, and

Table 9 Growth and Structure of Romania's Trade by Main Commodities

		Structure				Growth		
Romania (see change in classification below)	1992	1994	1997a	1993	1994	1995	1996	1997a
agricultural produce (I-III)	6	-	-	16.5	17.0	-	-	-
food. beverage. tobacco (IV)	1	-	-	-2.1	44.7	-	-	-
mineral products (V)	13	-	-	0.3	24.4	-	-	-
chemical & allied products (VI)	10	-	-	-18.3	41.6	-	-	-
plastics & rubber (VII)	2	-	-	-3.5	74.4	-	-	-
textiles & products (XI)	10	-	-	72.5	47.3	-	-	-
base metals & products (XV)	17	-	-	30.5	11.1	-	-	-
machinery & equipment (XVI)	12	-	-	-13.6	18.2	-	-	-
vehicles & trans equip (XVII)	11	-	-	-14.4	-3.5	-	-	-
Total above	81	-	-	10.7	24.4	-	-	-
Total trade	100	-	-	12.1	25.7	-	-	-
Romania (new classification)								
food. beverage and tobacco (0+1)	-	6.2	6.0	-	-	33.9	33.5	-44.1
raw materials except fuel (2+4)	-	4.5	3.8	-	-	7.2	4.7	23.5
fuel products (3)	-	10.0	8.0	-	-	2.4	-5.1	-0.4
chemical products (5)	-	33.9	33.6	-	-	39.1	-9.0	6.8
machinery and transport equipment (7)	-	14.3	14.1	-	-	18.0	6.1	14.1
other manufactured goods (6+8)	-	31.1	31.1	-	-	32.5	8.6	10.5
Total	-	100.0	100.0	-	-	28.6	2.2	3.3

a January-September
b Jan.-Sep.over same period previous year

		imports						
Romania	1992	1994	1997a	1993	1994	1995	1996	1997a
agricultural produce (I-III)	9	-	-	2.0	-51.9	-	-	-
food. beverage. tobacco (IV)	7	-	-	-9.5	-2.0	-	-	-
mineral products (V)	32	-	-	-7.7	18.8	-	-	-
chemical & allied products (VI)	7	-	-	24.3	9.2	-	-	-
plastics & rubber (VII)	3	-	-	13.3	11.3	-	-	-
textiles & products (XI)	9	-	-	17.3	22.9	-	-	-
base metals & products (XV)	4	-	-	2.2	26.6	-	-	-
machinery & equipment (XVI)	15	-	-	25.7	26.2	-	-	-
vehicles & trans equip (XVII)	5	-	-	-3.7	17.3	-	-	-
Total above	90	-	-	4.7	6.4	-	-	-
Total trade	100	-	-	4.2	9.0	-	-	-
Romania (new classification)								
food. beverage and tobacco (0+1)	-	8.7	5.2	-	-	38.3	-7.8	-29.1
raw materials except fuel (2+4)	-	5.8	4.3	-	-	32.0	12.8	-24.0
fuel products (3)	-	23.6	23	-	-	30.7	8.9	0.2
chemical products (5)	-	27.6	31.6	-	-	59.1	14.6	-4.0
machinery and transport equipment (7)	-	25.3	25.5	-	-	41.5	15.0	3.8
other manufactured goods (6+8)	-	8.9	10.4	-	-	59.4	11.6	5.5
Total	-	100.0	100.0	-	-	44.6	11.3	-3.1

Croatia and much smaller than shares for Hungary and Bulgaria. Romania's natural endowment should result in a larger share of these commodities in both exports and imports. Romania (and even more so, Bulgaria) has much smaller shares of exports in machinery and equipment than any of the other CEFTA countries (remember Romania became a member July 1997).

The final comparison of economic structure is in terms of the ratio of exports (measured in domestic currencies and prices) to gross output of the main branches of industry (Table 10). The table suggests how difficult it is to make meaningful comparisons. Romania shows up as having the largest

Table 10 Shares of Exports in Sales or Gross Output

NACE	Category	Hungary		Poland		Czech R.		Slovakia		Romania		
		89	95	89	93	89	94	89	95	89	95	96p
C.D.E.	Total industry	0.26	0.32	0.19	0.18	0.17	0.27	0.45	0.41	0.12	0.30	0.19
C	Extraction	0.04	0.06	0.46	0.19		0.27	0.13	0.14	0.00	0.05	0.01
D	Total manufacuring	0.30	0.37	0.16	0.23	0.18	0.31	0.57	0.45	0.13	0.37	-
DA	Food, beverage, tobacco	0.22	0.19	0.09	0.08	0.05	0.09	0.02	0.11	0.04	0.05	-
15	Food & beverages	0.22	0.19	-	-	-	-	-	-	0.04	0.05	0.05
15.1-8	Food products	0.23	0.20	-	-	-	-	-	-	0.04	-	-
15.9	Beverages	0.16	0.10	-	-	-	-	-	-	0.03	-	-
16	Tobacco	0.05	0.11	-	-	-	-	0.03	0.11	0.00	0.00	-
DB,DC	Textiles, Apparel, Leather	-	-	-	-	-	-	0.71	0.14	0.14	-	-
DB	Textiles & textile products	0.32	0.56	0.10	0.42	0.26	0.45	0.62	0.46	0.15	0.21	-
17	Textiles	0.27	0.47	-	-	-	-	-	-	0.08	0.22	0.23
18	Apparel, exc footwear	0.43	0.70	-	-	-	-	-	-	0.26	0.21	0.47
DC	Leather & leather products	0.41	0.55	0.09	0.29	0.24	0.38	0.95	0.40	0.11	1.08	0.32
19.1-2	Leather products	0.35	0.54	-	-	-	-	-	-	0.11	-	-
19.3	Footwear, exc rub. or plas (FT)	0.45	0.56	-	-	-	-	-	-	0.11	-	-
DD,DE	Wood & paper products	-	-	-	-	-	-	0.49	0.44	-	-	-
DD(20)	Wood products	0.08	0.29	0.27	0.62	0.20	0.44	0.39	0.44	0.16	0.47	0.39
DE	Paper, Printing, Publishing	0.08	0.11	0.06	0.04	0.13	0.23	0.53	0.44	0.06	0.11	
21	Paper & products	0.10	0.17	-	-	-	-	0.54	0.44	0.07	0.21	0.16
22	Printing, publishing	0.07	0.05	-	-	-	-	0.52	0.44	0.01	0.01	0.00
DF (23)	Fuels production	0.28	-	0.04	0.02	0.13	0.23	0.55	0.49	0.37	0.28	0.18
23.1	Coke oven products	-	-	-	-	-	-	0.56	0.50	-	-	-
23.2	Petroleum refining	-	-	-	-	-	-	0.55	0.49	0.41	-	-
23.3	Nuclear fuel	-	-	-	-	-	-	0.54	0.50	-	-	-
DG(24)	Chemicals	0.38	0.45	0.21	0.27	0.17	0.41	0.75	0.64	0.17	0.30	0.36
24.1	Industrial chemicals	-	0.50	-	-	-	-	-	-	0.46	-	-
24.2-6	Chemical products	-	0.41	-	-	-	-	-	-	0.03	-	-
24.7	Manmade fibers	-	-	-	-	-	-	-	-	0.20	-	-
DH(25)	Rubber & plastic prod	0.32	0.38	0.36	0.12	0.12	0.32	0.76	0.55	0.08	0.31	0.14
25.1	Rubber products	0.52	0.57	-	-	-	-	-	-	0.19	-	-
25.2	Plastic products	0.17	0.34	-	-	-	-	-	-	0.03	-	-
DI(26)	Mineral materials	0.12	0.21	0.08	0.17	0.20	0.39	0.41	0.51	0.06	0.15	0.23
26.1	Glass & products	0.22	0.50	-	-	-	-	0.41	0.51	0.16	-	-
26.2-3	Pottery, china, earthware	0.10	0.14	-	-	-	-	0.42	0.51	0.39	-	-
26.4	Other mineral products	0.04	0.10	-	-	-	-	0.41	0.51	0.03	-	-
DJ	Basic metals & fab prods	0.15	0.27	0.19	0.39	0.16	0.40	0.62	0.56	0.12	0.39	-
27	basic metals	0.97	0.26	0.18	0.47	-	-	-	-	0.18	0.44	0.30
27.1-3	Ferrous metals	0.97	0.23	-	-	-	-	-	-	0.26	-	-
27.4	Non-ferrous metals	0.60	0.32	-	-	-	-	-	-	0.14	-	-
27.5	Castings	-	0.29	-	-	-	-	-	-	-	-	-
28	Fab metal products	3.94	0.28	0.21	0.25	-	-	-	-	0.02	0.22	0.27
DK(29)	Machinery, exc electrical	0.15	0.28	0.58	0.61	0.28	0.36	1.30	0.41	0.10	0.24	0.28
29.3	Agricul. & forest machinery	-	0.52	-	-	-	-	1.33	0.41	0.09	-	-
29.7	Domestic appliances	-	0.33	-	-	-	-	6.36	2.55	0.17	-	-
29.1-2,4-5	Other not above	-	0.24	-	-	-	-	-	-	0.10	-	-
DL	Electrical & optical equip (EO)	0.14	0.35	0.06	0.17	0.20	0.25	0.43	0.52	0.04	0.17	0.19
30	office mach & computer	-	0.46	-	-	-	-	-	-	0.01	0.08	0.08
31	electrical mach & equip	-	0.46	-	0.26	-	-	-	-	0.06	0.41	0.25
32	radio, tv, comm equip	-	0.19	-	-	-	-	-	-	0.01	0.06	0.05
33	profess.-scientific equip (EQ)	-	0.26	-	0.20	-	-	-	-	0.05	0.13	0.14
DM	Transport equipment	0.25	0.28	0.22	0.36	0.34	0.38	0.52	0.83	0.24	0.31	0.19
34	motor vehicles & trailers	1.00	0.29	-	-	-	-	-	-	0.25	0.21	0.07
35	other vehicles	-	0.20	-	-	-	-	-	-	0.23	0.51	0.47
DN(36)	Other manufactures	0.13	0.22	0.18	0.07	0.26	0.41	0.47	0.39	0.44	0.75	0.43
36.1	furniture	1.64	0.22	-	-	-	-	-	-	0.55	-	-
36.2-6, 37	other misc manufactures	0.77	0.20	-	-	-	-	-	-	0.07	-	-
E(40,41)	Utilies	0.00	0.01	0.05	0.01	0.04	0.01	0.01	0.20	0.00	-	-

increase in export:output ratios from 1989 to 1994 or 1995. Also, it has comparatively high ratios in textiles, leather goods, and other manufactures (probably accounted for by furniture). What is also interesting is that in most other branches its export ratio is the smallest only in the case of general machinery (but it is 24 percent compared to Hungary 28 percent). It remains to do a systematic analysis of the relations between changes in foreign trade and changes in industrial structure (for a review of the transition literature see Jackson 1997).

International Economics

Trade Agreements and Trade Regimes

As is known, in the 1960s communist Romania turned away from the Soviet Bloc in a move to reduce its dependency on Moscow and to diversify its opportunities for favorable trade and credit arrangements. This also involved special political relationships with West Germany and Israel linked to emigration of the Romanian German and Jewish minorities. Bilateral trade and credit agreements were signed with individual West European countries and the United States granted MFN status in 1975. An economic cooperation agreement was concluded with the European Community, the second after the former Yugoslavia which goes back to the earlier 1960s. In 1971 Romania became a GATT contracting member and in 1992 a member of the IMF and the World Bank.

In the 1970s political and economic relations were pushed with China and the Third World. At the same time relations with the West cooled and much of the economic advantage of the earlier agreements was lost. When the country could no longer meet its debt service obligations to either the London or Paris Clubs in the early 1980s the political leadership pushed the country towards autarchy. Only absolutely necessary imports were permitted and these only when they could be acquired on barter. General consumption standards and public use of energy were severely cut until health and welfare standards suffered. At the same time, at attempt at self-supply of both basic and more complex industrial equipment was undertaken. The quality of the capital stock surely deteriorated during these years in spite of what statistics might show.

After 1989 the new regime had to repair international economic relations. Romania's status in the GATT was revived. In mid-1994 an official "working party" of other contracting countries was set up for renegotiating of GATT accession terms for the new system and in 1994 Romania formally joined the WTO[14]. The European Free Trade Agreement (EFTA) came into force May 1993. All other OECD countries have granted MFN and/or general preference (GSP) status. In July 1997 Romania joined the Central European Free Trade Association (CEFTA), a symbolically important move even though its share of trade with CEFTA countries does not reach even 5 percent.

Table 11 Directions of Romanian Foreign Trade (1989-1996)

Shares in percent	1989	1990	1991	1992	1993	1994	1995	1996
Total EU								
Exports	30.6	33.9	36.9	35.2	41.4	48.2	54.1	56.5
Imports	13.0	21.8	28.7	41.3	45.3	48.2	50.5	52.3
Total CEFTA								
Exports	-	-	-	-	3.4	4.5	3.5	3.6
Imports	-	-	-	-	4.1	4.1	4.9	4.7
Total Balkan								
Exports	8.2	8.7	-	15.2	10.6	9.3	9.3	10.5
Imports	5.8	6.2	-	8.0	5.1	4.8	5.2	4.7
Europe minus FSU								
Exports	46.6	-	-	-	-	-	-	-
Imports	34.6	-	-	-	-	-	-	-
FSU								
Exports	22.6	24.6	23.0	13.9	9.1	6.7	5.7	-
Imports	31.5	23.1	18.2	17.4	15.7	17.9	15.8	-
Asia minus FSU								
Exports	17.9	16.0	18.8	28.5	30.6	23.8	20.6	-
Imports	28.6	23.2	23.8	19.0	18.7	13.5	13.3	-
America								
Exports	8.9	8.3	4.2	4.0	4.1	5.8	5.1	-
Imports	4.8	7.2	6.3	6.0	8.7	9.5	6.7	-
Africa								
Exports	3.8	3.7	4.0	4.0	5.3	6.8	7.2	-
Imports	2.7	6.9	8.8	4.6	2.8	2.4	4.7	-
Total Trade								
Exports, fob	100.0	100.0	100.0	100.0	100.0	100.0	100.0	100.0
Imports, cif	100.0	100.0	100.0	100.0	100.0	100.0	100.0	100.0

Sources: Calculated from the Romanian statistical yearbook and the Romanian foreign trade yearbook.

The Europe Agreement (EA) with the European Union was signed in February 1993. The Interim Agreement covering trade components came into force May 1993. The full version became operational in February 1995. It provides for the gradual introduction of free trade in industrial products between Romania and the EU by 2003. Romania applied for membership in 1995, but has been put into the second tier of five countries (along with neighboring Bulgaria) in the Agenda 2000 decisions following the Amsterdam Treaty in 1997.

Economic and political relations with the EU and its associated organizations and forums have become the dominant considerations of Romania's policy makers. So has Romania's trade relations with the EU assumed a dominant impact on the country's economic development. Table 11 brings out the feature that has dominated all transition countries' foreign trade relations and that is the shift towards the EU as both market and source of supply. Its share of Romanian exports has nearly doubled while its share of imports has more than tripled. In the case of imports, again it should be emphasized than imports from the West in 1989 had been slashed by the Ceausescu regime. CEFTA and the Balkan countries take together about 10 percent of Romania's trade, a share that probably has not changed since 1989. Africa has increased its shares roughly by the same percentage points as trade with the Americas has decreased. The big losers as trade shifted toward the EU is the FSU and, in terms of imports, the other Asian countries.

Romania's Early Experience with the EU

While Romania's economy in the future faces the prospect of virtual free access to the EU for industrial products it, of course, also must be able to meet increasing competition from exporters and investors from the EU countries. At the same time, it should be remembered that during the transition period which has been the focus of this paper Romania has not had free access to EU markets and this condition deserves some further elaboration (Jackson and Biesbrouck 1994).

Schumacher and Mobius (1994) remark that Romania and Poland faced some increasing protection from the EC after 1988 and until the European Agreement started to provide better market access. In 1991, Romania had the largest share of its exports to the EC subject to quota restrictions and the highest average MFN duty rate of the original six countries with

European Agreements. In both cases, average EC protection was up from 1990 and earlier years. Romania fared better in the case of other non-tariff barriers (along with Poland).

Romania's exports to the EU could have faced relatively higher protection for several reasons. One reason might be that it tended to export commodity groups facing high average protection. Another reason could be that within a given commodity group it tended to export the more protected varieties of the commodity.

Romania's export success in wooden furniture has been assisted by a past of having been one of the world's leading exporters. Certainly it reflected some diversion of exports from former CMEA countries, but also reflects long-term relationships from some Western European companies (like IKEA, for example). Romania's large clothing exports also benefits from older cooperation agreements with Western Europe manufacturers in which Romania essentially worked according to the western partner's specifications.

The relationship between Romanian trade coverage ratios (simply the ratio of exports to imports for each commodity) and the factor intensity of commodity groups in the EC was investigated more formally by Jackson and Biesbrouck (1994). The chief conclusions were that Romanian trade coverage ratios were strongly negatively correlated with EC skill intensive commodity groups, positively correlated with EC labor intensity, and negatively correlated with EC R&D intensity. Unlike other transition countries, Romanian trade coverage seemed to have little relationship with commodities that are energy intensive in the EC.

In terms of EC protection the following findings are important. Some 65 percent of Romania's exports to the EC were in commodities that are labor intensive by EC standards. High EC protection of labor intensive industries such as footwear, knitting and clothing affected some 33 percent of Romania's exports, medium protection affected 11 percent of the exports of the commodities in this group, and low protection 21 percent of the exports of the commodities in this group. Only medium and low levels of EC protection affected the relatively small proportion of Romanian exports of commodities that by EC standards are skill intensive, R&D intensive, and capital intensive. Thus, given EC protection in labor intensive branches Romania would face difficulties in finding markets for its traditional exports there. These barriers were in 1994 the highest faced by any of the six EA countries.

The other important aspect of EU trade barriers faced by Romania has been for agricultural and food products. While there is no available evidence that the EU has discriminated in any special way against Romanian exports in this area, the facts of Romania's comparatively heavy dependence on agriculture and its traditional assortment of products in the more supported and protected categories of the Common Agricultural Policy makes EU discriminate more against Romania's present economy than those of other European Agreement countries.

Two General Indicators of Romania's Comparative International Competitiveness

As the EU market has been opening for Romanian exporters there remain important questions about their general competitive position during the transition period. A common way of looking at a country's general "competitiveness" is to compare movements in wage costs per unit of output measured in a standard foreign currency (Table 12). This is a summary of the effects of three important factors: 1) changes in the ratio of labor to output (or labor productivity), 2) changes in the nominal wage rate, and 3) changes in the

Table 12 Unit Wage Costs in Foreign Currency*

	Bulgaria	Czech R.	Hungary	Poland	Romania	Slovakia	Slovenia
1989	1.00	1.00	1.00	1.00	1.00	1.00	-
1990	0.62	0.83	1.14	0.91	0.75	0.83	-
1991	0.40	0.70	1.48	1.52	0.61	0.70	-
1992	0.75	0.94	1.59	1.38	0.54	0.80	-
1993	0.91	1.18	1.44	1.26	0.59	0.89	-
1994	0.62	1.31	1.40	1.19	0.57	0.93	-
1995	0.65	1.33	1.13	1.22	0.54	0.98	-
1996	0.46	1.46	1.09	1.37	0.50	1.12	-
1993	1.00	1.00	1.00	1.00	1.00	1.00	1.00
1994	0.68	1.11	0.97	0.94	0.96	1.04	0.99
1995	0.72	1.13	0.78	0.97	0.92	1.10	1.03
1996	0.50	1.24	0.76	1.09	0.85	1.25	1.02

Sources: Calculated from EBRD, Transition Report and UN/ECE, Economic Bulletin for Europe.
* Bulgaria, Slovakia and Slovenia for industrial wages. Others are wages in manufacturing.

exchange rate of the domestic currency into the standard foreign currency. In Table 12 the author has assembled information on changes from 1989 to 1996 in unit wage costs measured in foreign currency, the USD from 1989 to 1993 and the DM from 1993 to 1996 (the change in currency of comparison from dollars to DM was made in order to more fully reflect competitiveness in EU markets during a time of important fluctuations of the dollar exchange rate).

Romania and Bulgaria have had a remarkably different experience than the other countries in the table. Their average unit wage costs in industry measured in a relevant standard foreign currency have fell to half of the 1989 levels by 1996. By contrast, those in the Czech Republic rose by 50 percent. Thus, if we can assume that these countries were producing export commodities of a constant quality (see below) while making constant quality efforts to serve the markets, then Romania and Bulgaria should have improved their market positions.

During the period under observation Romania tended to maintain these low levels since 1992. In contrast, Bulgaria had increasing costs from 1991 to 1993 so Romania's average competitiveness should have been better.

It is important to stress again that the combination of factors leading to the same relative change can be quite different. The preferred source of increasing competitiveness would be rising labor productivity on the basis of better organization and management, not by labor shedding. Also, the incomes of the population can suffer if nominal wages and exchange rates are depreciated. Finally it is also important to consider changes at the level of branches of industry. The same overall averages labor costs could hide much different experiences in terms of individual commodities in which, for example, one country could have large reductions in comparative wage costs in some highly competitive branches while also having large increases in comparative wage costs in uncompetitive branches, suggesting increasing international specialization. Another country could have the same overall change in comparative wage costs as the first, but without great differences across its own industrial branches.

The measurement of output in constant prices that is the basis of productivity measurements assumes that changes in quality are adequately taken into consideration. But it does not show changes in quality relative to one's international competitors. Table 13 is based on work by Landesmann and Bergstaller (1997) in which they use unit export values at the eight-digit level as proxies for price. They assume that relative price reflects relative quality in highly competitive international markets.

Table 13 Estimated Quality Gaps for Exports to the EU *

Country	Engineering		Clothing, textiles & footwear	
	1988-90	1992-94	1988-90	1992-94
Romania	0.12	0.14	0.53	0.51
Bulgaria	0.40	0.24	0.39	0.57
Yugoslavia/Slovenia	0.50	0.60	0.89	1.08
Greece	0.57	0.51	1.07	1.16
Turkey	0.38	0.48	1.08	1.12
CFSR/Czech Rep	0.41	0.52	0.61	0.79
Hungary	0.38	0.44	0.74	1.03
Poland	0.34	0.42	0.60	0.76
USSR/Russia	0.44	0.25	0.40	0.42
China	-	0.35	-	0.60
India	0.59	0.45	0.89	0.88
Portugal	0.83	0.90	1.04	1.05

Sources: EBRD, Transition Report 1997, p.68, and Landesmann M. and Bergstaller I. 1997.
* Trade weighted average of country prices compared to average prices for all exporters to the EU at the eight digit level of EU data.

The table is based on the values obtained by exports to the EU. By this calculation, Romania has exported the lowest quality of engineering products of all of the countries in the sample by a wide margin, receiving only 12 percent of the average price in 1988-90 and 14 percent in the later period, 1992-94. In this case, the only good thing that might be said is that Romania did not experience the sharp quality declines of Bulgaria and the FSU/Russia. Romania does relatively better in the case of clothing, textiles and footwear, roughly matching Bulgaria's performance. Both countries, unfortunately, fall slightly below China in this ranking.

A conclusion can be drawn on the basis of both tables. Romanian exporters should have improved their competitiveness in EU markets through lower unit wage costs. There is little evidence that quality might have deteriorated during this time. Similarly it should be noted that Romanian exporters seem to perform in the low quality niches of the EU market with such low wage countries as China and India. Thus, even while it will have better access to the EU market than do these very low wage countries it is not yet using the opportunity to improve competitiveness.

Romanian Trade with the Balkans

A final consideration in this paper is Romania's trade with its Balkan neighbors which has already been seen in international comparison. Table 11 gives data from Romania's own statistical yearbook for each country in the region.

The only clear trend is the increasing share of trade with Turkey which has been taking more exports from Romania. There are well known reasons why trade with the more eastern parts of the former Yugoslavia amounts to little or nothing. It is not clear why trade with Albania should have declined to almost nothing by 1993. Apparently open markets did not attract each other's traders as much as buying elsewhere in Europe. But why trade with Bulgaria and Greece should also be so low needs further investigation.

Is history the problem? Greece should have been more attractive to Romania's policy of seeking non-aligned countries during the Cold War even through often Greek governments were hard to the right. After all there was little known support of the Greek Communists by Romania, as was the case with Bulgaria and Yugoslavia? During the communist period, Romania and Bulgaria had quite different official positions regarding political loyalty to the former Soviet Union and economic loyalty to the CMEA trade and cooperation programs. Yet this did not prevent seemingly friendly relations between the two countries' leaders, who often met on one side of the border or the other. Cultural relations were officially quite close, as well, and there was no basic cause for animosity. Still, the border between these two countries remained one of the least developed in Europe. The single "Friendship" bridge, built with Soviet assistance was never strained by steams of lorries or freight trains. According to Hewett (1976) Romania-Bulgaria commodity trade flows were only 59 percent of those that would be expected to take place between countries having their location and development parameters.[15] Otherwise, only occasional mostly local trade passed over the Danube by water. This heritage needs further investigation. It, of course, is an even worse impediment today when cross-Balkan freight is diverted from its routes through Bulgarian and the former Yugoslavia. Also, it is a tragic joke that the two countries are taking so long to agree on new routes even when international financial assistance is available. Possibly the domestic crises in both countries in 1996-1997 have detracted attention, but more seems to be at work. There seems to be little economic attraction on either side. This reflects both historical development patterns

431

and probably the fact that both countries are the obvious laggards among the ten countries that have European Agreements and the prospect of membership in the EU. The latter is not just an accident in the opinion of the author but reflects historical factors which led in both countries to the weak development of middle class institutions up to the communist period and to the greater destruction of the fiber of society during the communist period. This is not the place to argue the connections between the two or the possible consequences of Ottoman Turkish control of the region, but it does suggest that developing the institutional fiber necessary for successful transition is very difficult if it was lacking in the pre-communist period. Nevertheless, it is necessary to reconnect Romania to its Balkan neighbors so intra-regional trade and investment can stimulate transition on a level more accessible to the many small- and medium-sized businesses that are trying to launch themselves in the region.

Summary Comments

With the disintegration of former Yugoslavia, Romania is by far the largest country of the European "Balkans". This identity can be questioned, of course. Romanians generally strongly prefer to see themselves as "Southeast Europeans" and clearly the northern parts of the country show strong Central European cultural and geographic orientations. Also, one can argue that Turkey is properly part of any regional identity encompassing Romania.[16] As pointed out, Turkey with its large market took slightly more of Romania's 1993 than all its Balkan neighbors together or its new CEFTA partners.

The latter situation must be seen in the light of several important qualifications that make it likely to be possibly a temporary condition. First, Romania's trade shares with Bulgaria defy the normal "gravity" factors that should attract economic relations of two countries sharing such a long common border. As pointed out this condition persisted and even become exaggerated in the period of communist "forced industrialization" of the two countries.

Second, the transition has been accompanied by the unusually strong pull of the EU market and the penetration of imports from the EU. The strength of both factors must be seen relative to the pronounced weakness of the Romanian economy and its economic agents, as well as those also of its immediate neighbors compared to the counterparts in the EU. Add to this the pull of political and cultural factors, especially the strong sense of Romanian identification with France and Italy. Here are the ingredients of a possibly exaggerated shift towards the present EU.

Third, Romania, like Bulgaria and other neighbors (FYR Macedonia and those to the north and east), had developed both non-complementary industrial structures under communist rule. They also created institutional arrangements for the conduct of international economic relations that limited possibilities for the discovery of mutually beneficial trading and investment opportunities (Jackson 1987). Structural adjustment, especially downsizing some industrial capacities and modernizing others consumes enormous human, financial, and political resources. Replacing institutions of central administration and planning by strong enough financial and business services sectors demand similar efforts. Both essentially inward looking efforts hardly leave resources for a most difficult building of regional economic cooperation and the infrastructure necessary to support it.

Finally, getting the tasks of transition done, which are probably intrinsically larger in the less developed countries of Central and Eastern (for reasons identified in the previous paragraph), have proved especially difficult politically for both Romania and Bulgaria. Note that they are the only two European Agreement countries to suffer significant reversals of their apparent initial recoveries. This is not to insist that they had similar political patterns because on the surface at least Bulgaria has suffered from too much instability while Romania has suffered from too much stability under a regime that succeeded in perverting transition processes until it was voted out at the end of 1976. Unfortunately the period of six years was long enough for special interests of the old regime (meaning before 1990) to get deep into the framework of transition institutions. The result is that both time and resources for a necessarily difficult transition have been wasted if not permanent institutional and social damage permitted to the country.

All four of these powerful forces have worked against regional cooperation growing in the same measure as has cooperation with the EU, other economic powers, and international agencies. Nevertheless, from now on it is unlikely that the latter relations can continue to expand at the rapid rates characteristic of the early transition. At the same time, it may be hoped that the worst period of industrial and institutional restructuring is over and that present political configurations, although far from idea, can move the countries forward in the rebuilding of social and institutional structures. Unfortunately, this cannot be said yet for Romania's neighbors in the former Soviet Union.

It would now seem that the most ready opportunities for both economic and political progress is the development of neglected relations with neighbors, both Balkan and Central European. For the unfortunate moment and possibly a longer period such development will not include areas of the new Yugoslav Republic, although greater participation by Balkan neighbors (Greece, Bulgaria, and not excluding Romania) in a peace and stabilization process should not be neglected. As many point out, more intense regional cooperation requires great investments in transportation and communications infrastructures. Similar help is needed for cross-border business development between Romania and Bulgaria (and between Romania and Moldova) where some of the least developed Romanian counties are found. At the same time, the initiation and promotion of such measures should not be left only to the EU and the international agencies. As is evidenced by this paper and others in this volume, it is now time for regional forces and not only those of the governments to take strong initiatives. It is time that transition should turn next door.

Notes

1 The author has lived several years in Romania. He has been a consultant to governments and the European Commission on Romania and has a long list of published research, some of which is cited in the references. In recent years this research has especially emphasized the comparative aspects of countries in the region, something which is some times lacking in the work of local researchers.

2 As cited in GATT, Romania Trade Policy Review, Vol. II.

3 World Bank, Romania Economic Report, March 29, 1993.

4 The Romanian currency unit is the leu (singular - plural in Romanian is lei).

5 As reported in Finance East Europe, August 5, 1993.

6 According to a Romanian survey of enterprises in 1991, the chief reasons for the decline in output, according to enterprises themselves, were as follows:

- financial difficulties	40 percent
- raw materials shortages	
- domestic stocks	15 percent
- imports	16 percent
- energy shortage	10 percent
- shortage of demand	7 percent
- shortage of production capacity	1 percent
- other reasons	11 percent

434

At the end of 1991 stocks of industrial products rose to 227.4 billion lei, 107.9percent of 1990 levels. This compared to a GDP in industry of 973.1 billion lei, or 23percent. That is a large "product overhang" that could be dumped on foreign markets. Also, there was 162.5 billion lei in unhonoured contracts, including 36.3 billion lei for exports by foreign customers, probably mostly in the former Soviet Union.We assume that the major reason for financial difficulties, given that "shortage of demand" is less of a problem, is that Romanian companies are not being paid for goods delivered or orders supplied. This suggests that customers either have no cash funds or can not obtain credits. Also, the inability to find sound buyers may indicate that Romanian companies have customers only because they do not ask for payment. Shortages of raw materials and energy may also indicate that companies simply do not have the means of payment necessary.

7 Tom Hoopengardner, "Enterprise Arrears in Romania: How to Cope with Unpaid Debts?" Transitions, 3:10 (November 1992).

8 National Agency for Privatisation, Privatisation in the Sequence of the Romanian Reform, Bucharest, April 1993.

9 Romania Economic Newsletter, January-March 1993, and Privatisation in the Sequence of the Romanian Reform provide lists of the companies.

10 Finance Eastern Europe, 19 August 1993.

11 The numbers reported by the western business publications are always confusing, per haps because confusing information is given to them. PlanEcon Business Report reported 1 September 1993 that the SOF had sold its first company and then on 29 September report ed that it had sold 97 companies so far in 1993.

12 One of the best comparative surveys of FDI which includes sector and branch of industry data is the UN/ECE, Statistical Survey of Recent Trends in Foreign Investment in East European Countries, 1996.

13 See, for example, Landesmann and Bergstaller (1997).

14 In the GATT system, participating countries are known as "a contracting party" because the GATT was a legal agreement and not an organization with members, as such.

15 Worth pointing out is that Hewett also estimated that Romanian-Hungarian trade was only 70 percent of "normal" levels, but that both Romania and Bulgaria had larger trade flows than "normal" with other CMEA partners.

16 And so would such identity also include Moldova, the Ukraine, and probably also other countries bordering the Black Sea.

References

Cosmos (various issues), Romania: Economic Newsletter.

EBRD (various issues), Transition Report and Transition Report Update.

EIU (various issues), *Country Studies: Romania,* Economics Inteligent Unit.

European Commission (1995), *Agricultural Situation and Prospects in the Central and Eastern European Countries: Romania.* DGVI (Directorate General for Agriculture), VI/1112/95. Brussels, 63pp.

European Commission (1997), *Agenda 2000 Commission opinion on Romania's application for membership of the European Union.* Supplement 8/97 - Bulletin of the European Union, 105pp.

GATT (1993), *Romania 1992, Trade Policy Review*. Geneva.

Government of Romania (1991), *Memorandum on economic policies of the Government of Romania to the IMF*, Bucharest.

Government of Romania (1993), *The Governing Programme: Strategy for Economic and Social Reform*, Bucharest.

Hewett, E. (1976), A Gravity Model of CMEA Trade. In Josef. C. Brada, ed., *Quantitative and Analytical Studies in East-West Economic Relations*, Bloomington, IN: Indiana University.

Hoopengardner, T. (1992), Enterprise Arrears in Romania: How to Cope with Unpaid Debts? *Transitions*, 3:10, November.

Jackson, M. (1987), Economic Development in the Balkans Since 1945 Compared to Southern and East-Central Europe. *Eastern European Politics and Societies*. 1:3 (Fall).

Jackson, M. (1990a), The Romanian Economy in the Wake of the Revolution. *Report on Eastern Europe*, February 2, 1990.

Jackson, M. (1990b), Restructuring the Romanian Economy. *Berichte des Bundesinstituts für ostwissenschaftliche und internationale Studien*, 1990. 53pp.

Jackson, M. (1991), The Politics and Economics of Post-Communist Bulgaria and Romania. *Nato's Sixteen Nations*, September 1991.

Jackson, M. (1994a), The Economic Penetration between the EC and Eastern Europe: the Case of Romania. *European Economies*, No. 6, 1994, pp. 283-336.

Jackson, M. (1994b), Political Incredibility and Weak Transformation in Romania. *East-Central European Economies in Transition*. Papers submitted to the *Joint Economic Committee, Congress of the United States*. U.S. Government Printing Office: Washington, DC.

Jackson, M. (1997), Restructuring or Structural Change in Industry of Transition Countries: a Review of Issues. *LICOS Discussion Papers on the Economic Transformation: Policy, Institutions, and Structure*. No. 64.

Jackson, M. and A. Repkin (1997), A Comparison of Structural Change among the Branches of Industry in Seven Transition Countries. *LICOS Discussion Papers on the Economic Transformation: Policy, Institutions, and Structure*. No. 63.

Landesmann, M. and Bergstaller, I. (1997), Vertical Product Differentiation in EU Markets: The Relative Position of East European Producers. *Vienna Institute for Comparative Economic Studies:* Research Report, No. 234a. February.

Population and Housing Census January 7, 1992 (1994), *Romanian National Commission for Statistics*, Bucharest.

Privatization in the Sequence of the Romanian Reform (1993), *National Agency for Privatization*, Bucharest, April.

Romania libera (various issues), A daily newspaper.

Romanian National Commission for Statistics (various years), *Romanian Statistical Yearbook*. Bucharest.

Romanian National Commission for Statistics (1997), *Romanian Foreign Trade Yearbook*. Bucharest.

Schumacher, D. and Mobius, U. (1994), Community trade barriers facing Central and East European countries (CEECs): Impact of the Europe Agreements. *European Economies*, No. 6, 1994, pp. 17-76.

UN/ECE (1996), *Statistical Survey of Recent Trends in Foreign Investment in East European Countries.* Trade/R.647, 3 December.

UN/ECE, *Economic Bulletin for Europe,* various issues.

UN/ECE, *Economic Survey of Europe,* various issues.

World Bank, Aide Memoire, November 1990.

World Bank, Romania - Industrial Restructuring Project, 1993.

World Bank, Romania Economic Report, 1993.

14 Greece and the Balkans: Geography Lost and Found

GEORGE PETRAKOS
Associate Professor, Department of Planning and Regional Development, University of Thessaly, Greece

Introduction

The post-1989 conditions in Central and East European Countries (CEEC) give rise to a number of interesting questions concerning the impact of changing geography on economic performances and outcomes on both sides of the East-West frontier. Although positive answers will have to wait until a substantial body of empirical literature becomes available, several hypotheses have been put forward and some initial evidence seems already to be available. On the regional scale, for example, there is now sufficient evidence that transition has increased disparities in CEEC, as western regions and metropolitan areas, in general, fare better (Haussermann 1993, Balaz 1996, Downes 1996, Fazekas 1996, Raagmaa 1996). On a larger scale, the economic gravity centre of Europe shifts gradually to the East and new spheres of economic influence and co-operation are appearing. In this new setting, several "border conditions" are changing, as Germany for example is transformed from the eastern border to the central part of the new Europe, and Greece, the most distant and peripheral member of the EU, finds neighbours to trade with after decades of isolation (Petrakos 1996a).

Geography also seems to be an important factor affecting the allocation of costs and benefits from the expansion of the European market. Transition generates pressures and opportunities for the European Union (EU) members that are not equally distributed among states and regions. Distant southern European countries, such as Spain or Portugal, find, on the one hand, new competitors in their effort to attract mobile investment from the north and, on the other, limited accessibility to the new markets. On the other side of the spectrum, EU states close to the EU-CEEC frontier are in a more favourable position to benefit from the rising opportunities for trade and economic interaction (Petrakos 2000).

439

Similarly, the regional implications of transition also seem to be favourable for EU regions which are lagging behind (Brocker and Jager-Roschko 1996). Mainly due to favourable locational effects, average gains from trade with CEE countries are greater for Greece and Southern Italy. As a result, trade threats to the regions which are lagging behind in the EU seem to arise much more from the more prosperous regions of the EU, Japan and the NICs, than from transition economies. Fears that Objective One regions in the EU and transition countries will have antagonistic structures do not seem valid.

In addition economic performance and structure in both the EU and the CEEC seem to have a clear geographical dimension. There is now sufficient evidence that in terms of economic structure and performance, a North-South divide is present in both EU and CEE countries (Mertzanis and Petrakos 1998, Petrakos and Totev 2000). Within the EU, Northern and Western European countries have a better performance and a more sustainable economic structure than Southern European ones. Within the CEEC, the Visegrad countries have a better performance and a better economic structure than the Balkan ones. As a result, the new divide in Europe may take on a Northwest-Southeast character, where the Southwest and the Central countries will take the intermediate positions (Petrakos 2000).

Although several other instances can be identified where post-1989 developments have a clear spatial dimension, our interest in this paper is to examine how the changing geography in the Balkans has affected in the past and is once affecting the performance of the Greek economy. To this end we present the main findings concerning the changing economic environment and the changing "border conditions" of Greece in the Balkans. The Greek economic relations in the Balkans and the future developments in this region assume a special analytical and policy making interest as they concern: (a) relations between EU and CEE countries with an East-West character, (b) relations between countries with relatively lower levels of development compared to the other EU or CEE countries respectively, (c) relations between countries that are in various degrees perimetric with respect to the geographical and economic gravity centre of Europe and (d) relations between countries that have adjusted in a relatively poor way to the pressures of EU economic integration (Greece) and transition (the other BCs) respectively. In this paper it is argued that the new economic environment generates opportunities for development for the entire Balkan region, which are related to the intensity and structure of commodity and factor

440

flows between Greece and the other countries in the region. These flows provide the missing link in the recent integration experience of Greece and can be a good basis for regional co-operation and development.

This paper is organised as follows: In the next section we examine the pre-1989 conditions in Greece with respect to its international environment, and discuss possible factors that have affected its admittedly weak integration performance. In the third section we look at the new conditions that have prevailed in the post-1989 period and especially its relations with the other Balkan countries, while in the last section we draw the conclusions and present the policy implications of our analysis.

The Pre-1989 Conditions in Greece and the Balkans

The integration experience of Greece, a country that is peripheral to the European Union (EU) gravity and development centre in both geographical and economic terms, has been (until recently) considered, among economists and policy makers, to be a disappointing case of failure.

The analysis of a number of economic indicators such as GDP growth, labour productivity, industrial production and gross fixed capital formation for the period 1961-1995 shows that Greece had a considerably better performance than the EU average in the 1960s and the 1970s (showing a catching up process), but a weaker (and in fact diverging) performance than the EU thereafter (Petrakos and Pitelis 1997). For example, Real GDP has been growing in Greece at an average rate of 7.6% in the 1961-70 period and 4.7% in the 1971-1981 period, better than the EU average, which was 4.8% and 3.0% respectively for the same periods. In the 1980s, however, this picture changed and Greece (growing at an average rate of 1.5%) had a weaker performance than the EU (which experienced a 2.4% growth rate), a trend that also continued in the early 1990s. Interestingly, in the 1981-1990 period, Greece is in a unique situation with a performance in all indicators which is not simply worse than the EU average, but also worse than any other single member state of the EU (EC 1995).

This weak performance, which lasted from the late 1970s until the mid 1990s, has affected relative welfare levels, as GDP per capita compared to the EU average has also declined. Relative GDP per capita (EU=100), measured in purchasing power parity (ppp), increased in the 1960s and the 1970s and decreased thereafter, with some signs of stability in the 1990s. In

1995 however, Greek GDP per capita in ppp was equal to 57.3% of the EU average, a figure considerably lower than that of 1978 (64.6%), which was the highest in the entire period.

Other symptoms of this weak performance have been the decline of the industrial sector of the economy and the increasing trade deficits. The decline of Greek manufacturing in the last period is expressed with a shift of investment and employment towards traditional activities and a contraction of the already weak and undeveloped intermediate and capital goods sector. In general, capital, R&D and technology intensive sectors have a considerably lower share in total industrial employment in Greece than in the EU (Petrakos and Totev 2000). In addition, industrial activity in Greece takes place in production units which are very small by international standards (Petrakos 1996b, Petrakos and Zikos 1996). In the last two decades, for example, about 93% of industrial firms employed 1-9 persons. As a result, for the entire period the average size of firms has remained equal to the very small figure of 5 employees per firm, which is by far the lowest in Europe. This industrial structure has, as expected, a negative impact on the export performance of the economy. Total exports, as a share of GDP were 18.1% for Greece and 31.3% for the EU in 1995. This difference of about 13 percentage points, which is maintained in the entire 1960-1995 period, is responsible for the increasing trade deficit of the economy.

What factors have contributed to the disappointing performance of the Greek economy during the last two decades and its poor integration record? And how will the changing economic environment in the Balkans affect (or has already affected) this performance? Although several hypotheses have been advanced to answer the first question, the most commonly shared views among economists consider two factor responsible for this poor performance:

(a) The shock of opening the economy through its membership in the EU, which is conceived - at least partially - as a process of integration among unequal partners (Petrakos and Zikos 1996) and

(b) The expansion of the public sector in the 1980s, which accumulated an unmanageable public debt and had a "crowding out" effect on the economy (Alogoskoufis 1993).

In the remainder of this section we are going to advance a third explanation for the poor integration performance of the Greek economy, which pays attention to the pre-1989 conditions in the Balkans. It is argued here that the shock of integration was stronger for Greece, due to the special conditions that prevailed on the northern borders of the country throughout the post-War period. The third section of this paper attempts, on the basis of available evidence, to provide an answer to the second question: that is, how the changing environment in the Balkans is expected to affect the performance of the Greek economy.

According to a recent view (Petrakos and Christodoulakis 1997), Greece was confronted in the post World War II period with a uniquely unfavourable situation not found anywhere else in Europe. This situation results from the interaction of:

(a) a perimetric location in Southeastern Europe, away from major markets and the European development centre and

(b) distorted economic relations, as the northern borders of the country were (due to the post war realities) meant to be real barriers to communication and trade with neighbouring countries. This type of "border condition", where practically the entire continental borderline of the country operated as a barrier to economic and social relations, is a rare situation in the history of international relations.

These two conditions generated an overall unfavourable index of geographic location within the post-war European economic space, with serious long-term implications for the economic structure and performance of the country. The isolation and distance from the European core and the other EU members implied, in general, limited accessibility of domestic products to large foreign markets which (by definition of the EU) were supposed to be accessible, explaining the low export-to-GDP ratios, while the "missing factor" in the trade relations with its neighbours generated serious disadvantages. Theoretical and empirical research has shown the importance of geographical factors such as adjacency and proximity in trade relations (Krugman 1994, 1992). As a result, it is only natural that the "missing factor" in the trade relations of Greece has caused a significant reduction in the trade potential of the country, limiting market accessibility for exporting industries and limiting the prospects for export-led growth.

Because of these conditions the trade relations of Greece necessarily took on an inter-industry character with the more advanced and distant countries of Western Europe, with serious impact on the industrial structure of the country. Trade theory indicates (Grimwade 1989) that trade with neighbouring countries is more intensive and usually assumes an intra-industry character, implying greater room for more industries to develop, as international specialisations are not mutually exclusive and the division of labour takes place within and not between sectors.

Therefore, the lack of trade relations with the other Balkan countries pushed Greece further towards an inter-industry type of specialisation with the technologically more advanced western European countries[1], which was rather unfavourable for the industrial development of the country. In that respect, the post-war "border conditions" of the country have generated a "missing factor" in trade relations which, in turn, has imposed additional constraints on the already weak structure of the economy. In addition, due to the small size of the country and the lack of accessible markets of a critical size, industrial firms could not benefit from economies of scale. As a result, the industrial base of the country became the most fragmented in Europe, with firms that are very small by international standards (Petrakos and Zikos 1996, Petrakos 1996b), which aggravated the structural problems of the economy and reduced overall economic efficiency.

Due to the ongoing conflict in the Middle East, and the Greek-Turkish dispute, Greece lost significant markets in this region in the early 1970s. As a result, the operation of these two factors (limited accessibility to European markets and no economic relations with neighbouring countries) may explain some aspects of the Greek economic performance during the last decades. Distance and the "missing factor" in trade relations may explain, for example, why the dynamism of the economy in the 1950s and the 1960s was exhausted so quickly afterwards, or why the public sector in the 1970s and the 1980s became so popular and so large. As export-led growth was not possible due to limited accessible markets and the predominantly inter-industry structure of trade, the industrial sector unavoidably assumed an inward looking character. Unavoidably, it became more fragmented, less efficient and, of course, smaller in size, leaving to the public sector the principal responsibility for absorbing the labour force which was expanding due to strong urban migration flows.

Overall, it is claimed here that the pre-1989 period performance of the Greek economy has been affected by the restrictions imposed on the structure and level of the external economic relations of the country by the limitations of geography and the artificial division of Europe into two camps. Although there is no direct empirical evidence to support it, we are confident that a simple spatial trade model would predict for Greece a very different level, direction and structure of trade from the existing one, had barriers to interaction with the neighbouring countries not been imposed.

Greece and the New Geography of the Balkans

The post-1989 developments in the Central and East European Countries (CEEC) have changed European geography dramatically and have affected the position and the relations of Greece in the Balkans. Of course, it will take some time before the impact is fully appreciated. Initial evidence, however, concerning factor flows and the trade relations of Greece with the other Balkan countries (Petrakos and Christodoulakis 1997) indicates that, despite the historically explained fragmentation of the economic potential of the region (Petrakos 1997a), the new environment generates opportunities that were not available before.

The Trade Relations of Greece in the Balkans

Greek trade in the Balkans[2] changed significantly in the 1989-1997 period. The Balkan share of Greek exports has increased from 3.16% in 1989 to 11.43% in 1997, while the Balkan share of the volume of trade (exports and imports) has increased from 2.72% in 1989 to 5.58% in 1997. Clearly, the 1997 figures would have been much higher than the ones presented, in the absence of the conflict in the former Yugoslavia and the embargoes imposed in the area. As a result of the transition process and the severe structural difficulties in the Balkan countries, their share in total Greek imports increased slightly in the same period.

Bulgaria[3], FYROM[4] and Albania[5] appear to be, in 1997, the most important trading partners of Greece in the Balkans, followed by Romania[6] while trade with the other States in the territory of the former Yugoslavia was, as expected, virtually non-existent until 1997. The export and import shares of Greece with Albania, FYROM, Bulgaria and Romania show the impact on trade relations of factors such as country (and market) size, distance and non-economic preference factors. Clearly, the adjacency and proximity factors explain the higher shares of Bulgaria, FYROM and Albania, compared to that of Romania, in total Greek trade, while the size and the capacity of the market explain the higher share of Bulgaria compared to those of FYROM and Albania. Other factors, such as religious or historical ties, the existence of minorities and various types of implemented policies of external relations have certainly affected, in various ways, the level and the growth rate of trade between Greece and the other Balkan countries (Petrakos 1997a).

445

As we can see in Table 1, in the period 1989-1997 the share of Greek exports which goes to the rest of the European Union (EU) countries has declined significantly, from 65,22% to 49.81%. In the same period, the share of Greek imports that come from the rest of the EU countries has decreased slightly from 64,72% to 62.58%. As a result, in the 1989-1997 period we have two opposite trends with respect to the geographical distribution of Greek trade relations. On the one hand, we observe the declining performance of Greek products in the EU markets, as indicated by falling exports (but relatively stable import shares) and on the other, the improving performance of Greek products in the Balkan markets, indicated by increasing export (and again rather stable import) shares. These differences in performance are certainly very important and deserve further examination.

Table 1 The Geographical Composition of Greek Trade in the Balkans, 1989-97

	EXPORTS		IMPORTS		VOLUME OF TRADE	
	1989	1997	1989	1997	1989	1997
BALKANS	3.16%	11.43%	2.50%	3.17%	2.72%	5.58%
EU	65.20%	49.81%	64.72%	62.58%	64.88%	58.85%
WORLD	100.00%	100.00%	100.00%	100.00%	100.00%	100.00%

Sources: Petrakos (1997b) and own estimates from the Hellenic Exporters Association database.

The evolution of Greek trade with the BCs is given in Table 2. From the examination of the data we observe that the value of Greek exports to the BCs in USD has increased by 429% in the period 1989-1997 accounting, in 1997, on 11.43% of total Greek exports. This indicates a major development in the structure of Greek exports in a short period of time when compared to the 1989 figure. This impressive increase comes in at a period when Greek exports to the EU have been almost constant in dollar value but declining as a share of total exports. This development indicates the declining competitiveness of Greek products in the EU markets, which is partly attributed to the structural difficulties of Greek industry and partly to the strength of the drachma. The latter is the outcome of anti-inflationary policies applied in accordance with the convergence criteria of Maastricht.

Table 2 Trade of Greece with Balkans, 1989-97

YEAR	EXPORTS INDEX	EXPORTS Share	IMPORTS INDEX	IMPORTS Share	VOLUME OF TRADE INDEX	BALANCE OF TRADE Value	EXPORT-IMPORT RATIO
1989	100.00	3.16%	100.00	2.50%	100.00	-144.627	0.62
1990	129.67	3.88%	121.09	2.41%	124.39	-154.623	0.67
1991	144.16	3.98%	119.03	2.21%	128.68	-112.043	0.75
1992	163.31	3.96%	83.30	1.41%	114.02	70,872	1.22
1993	289.60	8.21%	85.85	1.60%	164.07	363.090	2.10
1994	314.11	8.00%	121.42	2.23%	195.40	285.189	1.61
1995	420.63	9.18%	186.73	2.76%	276.52	289,275	1.40
1996	519.83	10.48%	184.67	2.47%	313.34	534,417	1.75
1997	529.98	11.43%	222.02	3.17%	340.25	415.338	1.49

Trade of Greece with the EU 1989-97

YEAR	EXPORTS INDEX	EXPORTS Share	IMPORTS INDEX	IMPORTS Share	VOLUME OF TRADE INDEX	BALANCE OF TRADE Value	EXPORTS IMPORTS
1989	100.00	65.20%	100.00	64.72%	100.00	-4.998,360	0.50
1990	103.12	63.73%	127.04	65.55%	119.10	-7.532,522	0.40
1991	111.41	63.51%	129.47	62.36%	123.47	-7,363,539	0.43
1992	130.49	65.39%	147.36	64.56%	141.76	-8,199,406	0.44
1993	95.48	55.95%	132.52	63.96%	120.22	-8,454,041	0.36
1994	102.59	54.03%	138.92	66.19%	126.86	-8,739,338	0.37
1995	127.67	57.56%	173.77	66.61%	158.46	-10,964,025	0.37
1996	123.69	51.51%	177.88	61.63%	159.88	-11.568.868	0.35
1997	111.78	49.81%	169.25	62.58%	150.17	-11,299,493	0.33

Total Trade of Greece, 1989-97

YEAR	EXPORTS INDEX	EXPORTS Share	IMPORTS INDEX	IMPORTS Share	VOLUME OF TRADE INDEX	BALANCE OF TRADE Value	EXPORTS IMPORTS
1989	100.00	100.00%	100.00	100.00%	100.00	-7,780,578	0.49
1990	105.51	100.00%	125.43	100.00%	118.84	-11.268,527	0.42
1991	114.38	100.00%	134.35	100.00%	127.75	-11.967.531	0.42
1992	130.12	100.00%	147.73	100.00%	141.91	-12.828,412	0.43
1993	111.28	100.00%	134.08	100.00%	126.55	-12.161,013	0.41
1994	123.82	100.00%	135.83	100.00%	131.86	-11,478,478	0.45
1995	144.62	100.00%	168.82	100.00%	160.83	-14,969,591	0.42
1996	156.57	100.00%	186.79	100.00%	176.81	-16,824,536	0.41
1997	146.34	100.00%	175.03	100.00%	165.55	-15,792,430	0.41

Sources: Petrakos (1997b) and own estimates from the Hellenic Exporters Association database.

As a result of the expansion of exports and imports of Greece with the BCs, the volume of trade (VOT) increased by 240% in the 1989-1997 period. The magnitude of this increase can be better appreciated if compared to the 50% and 65% increase in the Greek VOT with the EU and the rest of the world respectively. This explosive expansion of trade indicates that the economic, geographical, historical, cultural or other factors in operation favour cross-border interaction and trade in the area. As expected, due to the difficulties of the transition process, but also due to the conflict in the territory of the former Yugoslavia, Greece has increased its exports faster than its imports. As a result, its balance of trade (BOT) in the period 1989-1997 has turned from negative to positive, in the case of trade with the BCs.

The export/import ratio measures the degree of relative penetration of a foreign market by Greek products. Looking at the export/import ratio in Table 2, we see first, that the Greek export/import ratio with the BCs has turned from smaller than one to greater than one, and it keeps increasing. Second, the Greek export/import ratio with the EU has dropped from 0.50 in 1989 to 0.33 in 1997, indicating that for each dollar of imports from the EU, Greece manages to export to the EU countries products worth only $ 0.37. Similarly, and to a certain extent, affected by the relative weight of the Greek-EU trade, the export/import ratio of Greece with the rest of the world has declined from 0.49 in 1989 to 0.41 in 1997.

The observations made above indicate that in the post-1989 period two processes which are different in direction take place, with respect to the Greek performance in international markets. On the one hand, there is the deteriorating position of Greek exports in the EU and World markets and on the other hand, there is an export performance in the neighbouring Balkan countries which is successful in all terms. Interpreting these facts, it becomes obvious that the competitiveness of the Greek economy in the EU and world markets is quite low and declining, while its competitiveness in the Balkan countries is at high levels and increasing. Although higher competitiveness in the Balkans is certainly affected by the difficulties of transition in these countries, the fact remains that Greece has managed to improve its overall export performance in the region, while other Southern European countries have not.

There is also another interesting observation in these figures. Despite the existence of the single European market and the fact that the Greek products no longer face tariff or non-tariff barriers in the EU, their ability to penetrate the EU market is lower, compared to their ability to penetrate the Balkan and world markets, where certain barriers to trade exist. This may be an indication of the difficulties of integration among basically unequal partners and the fact that the qualitative standards of the EU market are higher and more difficult to meet than those of the World (and certainly the Balkan) markets. It may also be an indication that geography is, after all, an important factor which affects the trade performance of a country.

A. Sectoral trends in the trade of Greece with the BCs Besides the examination of the evolution of exports, imports, export/import ratios and the VOT, a question that frequently arises is related to the sectoral structure and composition of trade between two countries. The issues usually examined are those of inter-industry or intra-industry specialisation: that is whether two countries tend to specialise and trade products that belong to different industries or tend to trade more intensively products within the same industry. The first is known as inter-industry or Heckscher-Ohlin (H-O) type of trade, while the second, as intra-industry type of trade (IIT).

Standard international trade theory has shown that in the case of the H-O type of trade, where countries specialise in different products and then exchange them, there are well defined welfare gains, known as gains from specialisation and gains from exchange (Caves and Jones 1981). H-O types of relations, however, have also been criticised as suitable only for countries with comparable levels of development. This is because in the case of trade between a developed and a developing country, the second will necessarily specialise in labour-intensive or resource-intensive products, missing the opportunity to industrialise, and therefore, missing the opportunity to develop. Also the H-O type of trade relations are considered to cause, in several cases, severe adjustments to the productive base of a country, as some sectors shrink and some others expand, a process that is not always free of social friction.

On the other hand, trade within the same industry is usually associated with welfare gains (Grimwade 1989) to the extent that consumer preference functions have an additive form: that is, consumers derive more satisfaction when offered a greater selection of similar products. IIT is not associated with major structural adjustment (as adjustment takes place within the industry or even within the firm), and it usually characterises neighbouring countries with similar levels of development and similar tastes.

Table 3 Trade of Greece with the Balkans, the EU and the World by 1-digit SITC Sector

		GREEK EXPORTS					
		BALKANS		EU		WORLD	
SITC	SECTORS	1989-97 value in '000 US$	1989-97 (% structure)	1989-97 value in '000 US $	1989-97 (% structure)	1989-97 value in '000 US $	1989-97 (% structure)
0	Food and live animals	1,215,548	19.5%	11,350,802	22.8%	16,654,640	19.4%
1	Beverages and tobacco	537,972	8.6%	2,038,757	4.1%	4,994,466	5.8%
2	Crude materials, inedible	557,740	8.9%	2,676,984	5.4%	5,259,930	6.1%
3	Mineral fuels, etc.	1,007,885	16.1%	1,252,699	2.5%	6,564,059	7.6%
4	Animal. vegetab.oils, fats	46,713	0.7%	3,485,501	7.0%	3,851.016	4.5%
5	Chemicals, etc.	400,170	6.4%	1,489,025	3.0%	3,930.089	4.6%
6	Manuf.goods,class.by mat.	1,051,903	16.8%	10,533,399	21.2%	18,513,357	21.6%
7	Machinery and transp.equip.	664,678	10.6%	2,380,038	4.8%	5,367,990	6.3%
8	Misc.manufactured articl.	729,251	11.7%	13,521,071	27.2%	18,985,845	22.1%
9	Commod.not elsewhere clas	32,554	0.5%	989,033	2.0%	1,719,271	2.0%
-9	Total	6,244,414	100.0%	49,717,310	100.0%	85,840,664	100.0%

		GREEK IMPORTS					
		BALKANS		EU		WORLD	
SITC	SECTION	1989-97 value in '000 US $	1989-97 (% structure) structure)	1989-97 value in '000 US $	1989-97 (% structure)	1989-97 value in '000 US $	1989-97 (% structure)
0	Food and live animals	564,207	11.8%	20,344,567	15.7%	24,975,264	12.2%
1	Beverages and tobacco	15,048	0.3%	3,460,733	2.7%	3,966,207	1.9%
2	Crude materials, inedible	418,017	8.8%	2,223,623	1.7%	7,720,805	3.8%
3	Mineral fuels, etc.	397,398	8.3%	1,118,820	0.9%	18,252,995	8.9%
4	Animal. vegetab.oils, fats	11,148	0.2%	638,545	0.5%	837,784	0.4%
5	Chemicals. etc.	645,181	13.5%	18,418,893	14.3%	24,109,371	11.8%
6	Manuf.goods,class.by mat.	1,859,075	39.0%	26,332,541	20.4%	39,344,860	19.2%
7	Machinery and transp.equip.	492,006	10.3%	40,648,400	31.5%	62,980,116	30.7%
8	Misc.manufactured articl.	368,795	7.7%	15,820,967	12.2%	22,290,692	10.9%
9	Commod.not elsewhere clas	99	0.0%	225,548	0.2%	502,513	0.2%
-9	Total	4,770,975	100.0%	129,232,638	100.0%	204,980,608	100.0%

Sources: Petrakos (1997b) and own estimates from the Hellenic Exporters Association database.

IIT is also often used as a measure of economic integration (Grimwade 1989). That is, the higher the level of IIT between two countries, the greater the similarities in their productive bases, the more homogeneous their consumer preferences and therefore, the greater the degree of economic integration. On the other hand, the higher the level of H-O type of trade between two countries, the higher the possibility of having dissimilar productive bases and development levels.

In Table 3 we present sectoral data for the trade of Greece with the BCs and the EU, as well as total trade by one-digit International Standard Trade Classification (ISTC) categories. The first observation in this table is that the Greek exports to the BCs are more evenly distributed to sectors than exports to the rest of the EU countries. In the case of the BCs, seven sectors have significant shares close to or greater than 10% of total exports to the region. In the case of the EU, however, three sectors concentrate more than 70% of Greek exports. Turning to Greek imports, we see that differences in sectoral structures among the BCs and the EU are less important.

B. Measures of revealed comparative advantage (RCA) In an attempt to further analyse the 1-digit SITC data of Greek trade with the BCs, we have estimated in Table 4 the sectoral coefficients of Revealed Comparative Advantage (RCA) for the Greek exports to the BCs and the EU. The RCA coefficients are measured as a share of a sector i's exports to a country j, divided by the share of sector i's total exports $\{RCA=(Xij/Xj)/(Xi/X)\}$. A value of RCA coefficient greater than one $(RCA>1)$ in a sector, indicates a better exporting performance than average, and therefore, a specialisation and a possible comparative advantage (CA).

From the examination of the table, we can see first, that Greek exports to the Balkan countries appear to have a CA in sectors 1 (beverages and tobacco), 2 (crude materials), 3 (fuels), 5 (chemicals) and 7 (machinery and transportation equipment). Second, this specialisation appears to be complementary to that developed with the EU, where Greece appears to have a CA in sectors 0 (food), 4 (oils and fats) and 8 (miscellaneous manufacturing articles).

Table 4 The Coefficient of Revealed Comparative Advantage (RCA) for the Trade of Greece with the Balkans and the EU

RCA SECTORS	BALKANS 1989-97	EU 1989-97
0	1.00	1.18
1	1.48	0.70
2	1.46	0.88
3	2.11	0.33
4	0.17	1.56
5	1.40	0.65
6	0.78	0.98
7	1.70	0.77
8	0.53	1.23
9	0.26	0.99
TOTAL	1.00	1.00

Sources: Petrakos (1997b) and own estimates from the Hellenic Exporters Association database.

Therefore, on the basis of one-digit ISTC data, Greece appears to have a potential CA in more sectors when trading with the BCs than when trading with EU countries. This observation is also verified from the examination of two-digit ISTC data. Table 5 presents summary information for the number of two-digit sectors that appear to have weak (RCA>1.0), moderate (RCA>1.5) and strong (RCA>2.0) comparative advantage in the trade of Greece with the Balkans and the EU. As we can see, trade with the two different regions exhibits both quantitative and qualitative differences in terms of sectoral specialisations. Firstly, in the 1990-97 period, Greece appears to have a CA in 42 sectors when trading with the BCs and in only 18 sectors when trading with the EU. Secondly, in the same period, Greece appears to have a strong CA (RCA>2.0) in 18 sectors when trading with the BCs, but none when trading with the EU.

Table 5 The Coefficient of Revealed Comparative Advantage (RCA) for the Trade of Greece with the Balkans and the EU (2-digit ISTC Sectors)

	RCA Coefficients based on 2-digit ISTC Sectors Data					
	Trade With The Balkans			Trade With The EU		
Year	RCA>1.0	RCA>1.5	RCA>2.0	RCA>1.0	RCA>1.5	RCA>2.0
1990	12	5	9	18	1	0
1991	7	5	14	18	1	0
1992	9	6	17	21	0	0
1993	10	9	16	13	4	0
1994	11	10	16	16	3	0
1995	14	10	15	19	3	0
1996	39	7	20	16	4	0
1997	15	8	16	14	4	1
1990-97	13	11	18	15	3	0

Source: Own estimates from the Hellenic Exporters Association database.

This analysis reveals two points with significant long-term implications for the trade relations of Greece. First, it indicates that Greece has developed its trade in the Balkans in such a way that more sectors can take the opportunity and expand their activities because of trade, finding a CA in a new market that was not available before. Second, Greece appears to have a CA in more sectors when trading with its Balkan neighbours than when trading with the other EU members.

C. Measures of intra-industry trade (IIT) As discussed earlier, measures of IIT are usually estimated in an attempt to find the share of the total trade of a country with another country or a group of countries which takes place within sectors (rather than between sectors). On the basis of these estimates, conclusions can be drawn about the existing type of trade relations, with all the implications about the structure and the required adjustments in the production base, as well as the type and the strength of the ongoing process of economic integration. Table 6 presents IIT coefficients for Greek trade by 1-digit SITC sectors with the BCs, EU and total trade, estimated from the standard Grubel-Lloyd (1975) equation.

Table 6 The Intra-Industry Trade (IIT) Coefficient for the Trade of Greece with the Balkans, the EU and World (1-digit SITC Sectors)

SECTORS	BALKANS 1989-97	EU 1989-97	WORLD 1989-97
0	63	72	80
1	5	74	89
2	86	91	81
3	57	94	53
4	39	31	36
5	77	15	28
6	72	57	64
7	85	11	16
8	67	92	92
9	1	37	45
TOTAL	68	51	55

Sources: Petrakos (1997b) and own estimates from the Hellenic Exporters Association database.

From the examination of the data, we see that for the entire 1989-97 period, 68% of the Greek-Balkan, 51% of the Greek-EU and 55% of the total Greek trade was of an intra-industry character: that is, trade within (1-digit SITC) sectors. The trade of Greece with the BCs is characterised by a higher IIT coefficient. About two-thirds of the Greek-BCs trade takes place within industries in the 89-97 period, while only a little more than half of the Greek-EU trade takes place within sectors.

Table 7 presents similar information based on two-digit ISTC data. Although the IIT coefficients based on two-digit data are (as expected) lower, the general picture is maintained. In the 1990-97 period, Greece had 42% of its trade with the BCs and 32% of its trade with the EU taking place within two-digit sectors. Paradoxically, the IIT figure for the Greek-EU trade is consistently lower than those for the Greek-Balkan countries and for total Greek trade. To the extent that the IIT coefficient is an indication of economic integration, this means that 17 years of membership in the EU (EC) has not brought the Greek economy closer to the EU than to the World economy, since Greek-EU trade relations basically retain an inter-industry character. This type of integration is probably explained by the large distance (and the lack of adjacency) separating Greece from the other EU members (Petrakos and Zikos 1996) as well as by the significant Greek deviations from the production structure of the average EU country (Petrakos and Totev 2000).

Table 7 The Intra-Industry Trade Coefficient for the Trade of Greece with the Balkans, the EU and World (2-digit ISTC Sectors)

	IIT Coefficients estimated from 2-digit ISTC Sectors Data		
Year	The Balkans	The EU	The World
1990	31	31	37
1991	36	33	38
1992	31	31	35
1993	30	30	37
1994	37	32	42
1995	37	32	42
1996	39	31	42
1997	41	31	44
1990-1997	42	32	40

Source: Own estimates from the Hellenic Exporters Association database.

These figures also indicate that the Greek trade relations in the Balkans have a greater intra-industry component than the Greek-EU or the total Greek trade relations. Proximity, similar consumer preferences and tastes, or the technology level and the requirements of the two markets probably explain this fact. Although it is rather early to draw any firm conclusions, and further examination of this issue is certainly necessary, it seems that this development in Greek-Balkan trade relations has two significant implications.

First, it allows for the expansion of economic relations in a sectorally more diversified manner, without exerting pressure for a strict H-O type of specialisation that would perhaps require severe structural adjustments in the Balkan region. This leaves some room for restructuring policies in order to reorganise productive resources within sectors, maintaining existing specialisations and avoiding major sectoral shifts of resources that could generate structural unemployment and reduce the diversity of the production base. Secondly, it offers Greece the missing component in its trade relations: that is, cross-border trade of strong intra-industry character that would balance and ameliorate the implications of the existing inter-industry type of specialisation and trade with the distant EU markets.

Factor Mobility between Greece and the Other Balkan Countries

A. Cross-border labour mobility in the Balkan region Besides trade relations that imply cross-border flows of goods and services, another important characteristic of the level of interaction between different countries is the level and the direction of production factor flows. It can be stated that factor mobility in the Greek-Albanian and Greek-Bulgarian borders has followed, in general terms, the predictions of a simple neo-classical model applied for transition economies. Under the pressure imposed on labour markets and labour relations by the transition and restructuring process, intensive labour emigration has been recorded, mainly in Albania but also in Bulgaria, while capital has followed the opposite route, flowing into these countries from various directions, to various destinations and at various rates.

Cross-border labour migration from Albania to Greece has been much more massive, persistent and mostly illegal (although in most of the period, with the tolerance of the Greek State). Estimations of the level of migration range, depending on the source, from 300 to 400 thousand people. This number increases during the summer months, when border crossing is easier, and decreases during the winter. A small proportion of this number enters Greece with a tourist visa (usually for a month) which is violated, since most of the visa holders stay either for a longer period of time or permanently. The rest of them cross the borders illegally in remote mountainous sites.

On the other hand, labour migration from Bulgaria to Greece has been much less and it is estimated at about 50 thousand people, mostly concentrated in Northern Greece. The Bulgarian migrants are, in fact, long-term commuters who stay for a few months in Greece with a tourist visa, "bending" the rules, probably with the "understanding" or the tolerance of the State. Most of them work in the fields, having rather stable contacts with employers in N. Greece. A very small number of them obtain a work permit. Overall, there are estimated to be more than 500 thousand migrants in Greece from the former Socialist countries. Besides Albanians (who are by far the majority) and Bulgarians, migrants from Romania, Poland, the former Soviet Union and the former Yugoslavia are found in significant numbers in Greece. In general, it can be claimed that the relatively homogeneous and mono-cultural Greek society has reacted to the shock of the new post-1989 conditions of population inflows from other Balkan countries in a relatively modest way. Anti-migration, racist or ultra-nationalist movements scarcely exist, and of course have no influence on public opinion, which seems to consider migration flows as an unavoidable by-product of an overall positive development (the transition process) in the region.

Despite fears of labour displacement in a period when unemployment is rising in Greece, there are no official reports or documentation providing any evidence in support of that allegation. On the contrary, sporadic reports in the press indicate that the migrants have been absorbed in the informal sector of the economy (irregular or sporadic work, repairs, painting, housekeeping, gardening, hauling, construction, etc.) or in the fields, where in several cases, their assistance has been gratefully acknowledged by the farmers.

While a significant proportion of migrants (legal and illegal) consider their stay in Greece permanent, another (perhaps larger) number consists, in fact, of long-distance commuters in a continuous, but irregular, in-and-out of the country motion. Incomes and remittances from Albanian migrants in Greece is estimated to be a significant supplement to the disposable income of Albania. Overtime, labour mobility is expected to have beneficial effects for the entire region. Migration reduces the pressure on limited production resources in Albania and Bulgaria, while in Greece, given the dual structure of the economy, labour immigration has resulted in cost related advantages and has rather improved the efficiency of the informal sector.

B. Greek-Balkan capital mobility Following the predictions of a simple West-East Neo-classical model of capital flows, inward Foreign Direct Investment (FDI) in transition economies has increased significantly, but in a geographically unbalanced way. Recent data compiled by the Economist Intelligent Unit for the period 1990-1997 indicates that the Balkan countries in transition have managed to attract only 13.5% of cumulative FDI. On the other hand, the Visegrad countries have managed to attract 86.5% of the FDI directed in the CEE region (Petrakos and Christodoulakis 1998). Most FDI flows originate from EU countries, with Germany (by far the first), the Netherlands, France and Italy being the most significant investors (Petrakos 2000). This geographical pattern is expected to continue in the future, driven by cultural and geographical proximity, access to large markets, economic recovery and political stability (UNCTAD 1996, Collis et al 1997). Should this be the case, the Balkan transition countries will be benefit only marginally from the west-east flows of capital in the post-transition period.

One positive and significant factor that offsets some of the consequences of the weak prospects of the Balkan transition countries with respect to FDI, is the rapidly increasing presence of Greek outward investment in the region. Although until recently Greece was more a host to FDI than an investing country, it is estimated that in the post-transition period Greek firms have invested more than 1 billion USD in the region (Petrochilos 1997). Despite the dominance of hundreds of small Greek firms investing in the area (which, however, increase economic and social mobility in Greece), a significant number of large projects have also been present in virtually all sectors of economic activity. As a result, Greece appears to be a serious investor in the Balkan region, ranking in the top-four position in Albania, Bulgaria and probably FYROM, in terms of its share in the total invested foreign capital.

Here again, the role of geography (adjacency and proximity) seems to be a decisive factor affecting the allocation of Greek investment in the region. Greek investors more often select Albania, Bulgaria (and with an increasing frequency FYROM) as a host country than they do the more distant Romania. Within each country however, spatial investment patterns differ. In Albania the majority of Greek investment is located close to the Greek borders and in an area with a significant presence of the Greek minority. This geographical pattern is explained by the convenience of a Greek speaking population, the incentives provided by Greek investment law and the re-exporting character of many activities (Petrakos 1996c). In

Bulgaria the spatial pattern is different, as the majority of Greek investment is located in the metropolitan area of Sofia, taking advantage of the larger and more developed domestic market. Nevertheless, a significant (and perhaps increasing) share of investment is taking place near the Greek borders. To the extent that market dynamics and local or national policies result in an increasing presence of cross-border type of investment, this may improve the development prospects of the border regions. This may have a significant long-term impact on the regional patterns of development, as, due to the post-war realities and the multiple divisions in the Balkans, border regions have been the least developed of all countries (Petrakos 1996c, 1997a).

Overall, Greek FDI is expected to have multiple long-term beneficial effects for the entire region, as Greek capital flows (in the absence of interest by more developed EU countries) generate much needed working positions, incomes and entrepreneurial capacity and know-how.

Policy Implications and Conclusions

After some 40 years of separation by military blocks (and assuming that peace in Bosnia and Kosovo will be permanent) a large regional market of 60-70 million people in South-eastern Europe is formed. This includes Greece (a EU member), Albania, Bulgaria, Romania and the territory of the former Yugoslavia, where significant opportunities for co-operation, specialisation and trade exist. To the extent that geography plays a role in shaping preferences in economic interaction (which is clearly evident by the bulk and type of relations between countries in North-western Europe), a regional market will gradually emerge in the Balkans, driven by distance (of the countries in the region from the European core), size and proximity (to each other).

This market seems to provide Greece with opportunities for rapid expansion of its trade, relatively high diversification in sectoral specialisation and a relatively high share of IIT compared to its figures with the EU and the world. Over time, factor mobility is also expected to have beneficial effects for the entire region. Migration reduces the pressure on limited production resources in Balkan transition economies, while capital inflows generate jobs, incomes and entrepreneurial capacity and know-how. For Greece, given the dual structure of its economy, labour immigration has resulted in cost related advantages and has rather improved the efficiency of the informal sector. On the other hand, capital outflows are associated in most cases with an expansion (and not dislocation) of activities to new markets which are easier to enter than the western European markets which are congested and difficult to compete with. The operation of regional multipliers also guarantees that incomes generated by Greek investment in Bulgaria will have a positive impact on incomes and work positions in Greece, to the extent that the positive business climate encourages the promotion of Greek exports. In other words, an advantageous cycle may be in operation, where the higher level of interaction leads to greater long-term benefits for all the countries in the region.

From this analysis, two points emerge which deserve consideration from the policy making point of view, the first one concerning Greece and the second, all the countries in the region. Perhaps for the first time after its membership in the EU, a real opportunity is given to Greece to deal effectively with the difficulties and the pressures imposed on its economic structure by the process of European integration. This opportunity is related to the prospect of gradually re-composing the economic space in its vicinity with the creation of a regional Balkan market, in which it will have a central and highly influential role. For the first time also, in the post-war period, a real opportunity is given to the Balkan countries to interact and co-operate without systemic or military block barriers, leaving the level and type of their relations to be an affair of markets, preferences and geography.

From the strategic point of view, the long-term interests of Greece and the other countries in the region require stable relations and successful implementation of the policies of transition. They also require a policy mix promoting the unification and coherence of the European economic space, the development of the European South-eastern region and the facilitation of cross-border co-operation. Since Greece, of all the other Balkan countries, has the highest "degrees of freedom" in influencing policies for the region, it also has the greatest responsibility for promoting them.

The appropriate policy mix should include steady and energetic support of the efforts of all Balkan countries to join the EU in the future, according to the progress they make in the requirements and the criteria set. This policy is a cornerstone for the future of the Balkan region and it is the only one that allows, in the long run, the unification of the Balkan and European space and better accessibility and connection of Southern with Northern and Western Europe. Secondly, it should include the promotion of an EU

459

strategic development plan for the Balkan region at various spatial, operational and sectoral levels with the active participation of Greece and a special emphasis on the issues of intra-regional co-operation and integration. This development plan should include effective transportation and telecommunication networks which will allow for the integration of the existing development axes, or areas in the Balkans and reveal the special weight of South-eastern Europe as an emerging regional market with significant size, strong intra-regional relations and a strategic advantage for the expansion of the EU economic relations in the Black Sea region and the Middle East.

Notes

1 This may explain why of all the EU countries, Greece has the lowest share of intra-industry trade.
2 Although Turkey (at least in part) certainly belongs to the Balkans, it is not included in the analysis, as the emphasis is on the Greek economic relations with the transition economies in the Balkans, where significant changes have occurred in the last years.
3 Bulgaria accounted for 2.85% of total Greek exports and 1.47% of total Greek imports in 1997.
4 The Former Yugoslav Republic of Macedonia (FYROM) accounted for 2.45% of Greek exports and 0.22% of Greek imports in 1997
5 Albania accounted for 2.24% of total Greek exports and 0.13% of total Greek imports in 1997.
6 Romania accounted for 1.57% of total Greek imports and 0.74% of total Greek imports in 1997.

References

Alogoskoufis G.(1993) How to escape crisis?, *Economikos Tahidromos,* No 2025, 25-2-93, pp 29-32 (in Greek).
Balaz V. (1996) "The wild East"? Capital markets in the V4 countries, *European Urban and Regional Studies,* Vol. 3, No 3, pp. 251-266.
Brocker J. and Jager-Roschko O. (1996) Eastern reforms, trade and spatial changes in the EU, *Papers in Regional Science,* Vol. 75, No 1, pp. 23-40.
Caves R., and Johnes R. (1981) *"World trade and payments",* 3rd edition, Little Brown, Boston.
Collis C., Berkeley N. and Noon D. (1997) Attracting foreign direct investment to east European economies: can lessons be learned from the UK experience? Paper presented in the *Regional Studies Association Regional Frontiers Conference* in Frankfurt (Oder), September 1997.

Downes R. (1996) Economic transformation in Central and Eastern Europe: the role of regional development, *European Planning Studies,* Vol. 4, No 2, pp. 217-224.

Fazekas K. (1996) Types of Microregions, Dispersion of Unemployment and Local Employment Development in Hungary, *Eastern European Economics,* Vol. 34, No. 3, pp. 3-48.

Greenway, D. and Milner, C. (1986) *"The economics of intra-industry trade",* Oxford, Blackwell.

Grimwade, N. (1989) *"International trade: new patterns of trade, production and investment",* Routledge, London.

Grubel, H. and Lloyd, P. (1975) *"Intra-industry trade: the theory and measurement of international trade in differentiated products",* Macmillan, London.

Haussermann, H.(1993) Regional Perspectives of East-Germany after the Unification of the Two Germanies, *TOPOS,* URDP, Special Edition, Athens.

Krugman P. (1986) Introduction: New Thinking about Trade Policy, in Krugman P. (Editor) Strategic Trade Policy and the New International Economics, MIT Press.

Krugman P.(1994) *Geography and Trade,* MIT Press.

Mertzanis H. and Petrakos G. (1998) Changing landscapes of economic structure in Europe, *Transition,* Volume 9, No. 2, pp. 12-13, The World Bank.

MNE (1996) Greek enterprise activity in the Balkans, General Secretariat, *Ministry of National Economy,* Greece.

Petrakos G.(1996a) The regional dimension of transition in Eastern and Central European countries: An assessment, in Jackson and Petrakos (editors), Regional Problems and SME development in transition countries, *Eastern European Economics,* Vol. 34, No 5, pp. 5-38.

Petrakos G.1996b Small enterprise development and regional policy, *Eastern European Economics,* Vol. 34, No. 2, pp. 31-64.

Petrakos G. (1996c) The New Geography of the Balkans: Cross-border co-operation between Albania, Bulgaria and Greece, *Series on Transition in the Balkans,* Vol. 1, University of Thessaly, Department of Planning and Regional Development.

Petrakos G. (1997a) The regional structure of Albania, Bulgaria and Greece: implications for cross-border cooperation and development, *European Urban and Regional Studies,* Vol. 4, No. 3, pp. 195-210.

Petrakos G. (1997b) A European macro-region in the making? The Balkan trade relations of Greece, *European Planning Review,* Vol. 5, No. 4, pp. 515-533.

Petrakos G. (2000) The spatial impact of East-West integration in Europe, in G. Petrakos, G. Maier and G. Gorzelak (eds) *"Integration and Transition: The Economic Geography of Interaction",* London: Routledge, pp. 38-68.

Petrakos G. and Pitelis C. (1997) Peripherality and integration: The experience of Greece as a member of the EU and its implications for the Balkan economies in transition, Paper presented at the Conference *Economic Co-operation in the Balkans: A Regional Approach to European Integration,* supported by the European Commission's Phare-ACE Program, 11-14 January 1997, Volos, Greece.

Petrakos G., Zikos S. (1996) "European Integration and Industrial Structure in Greece, Prospects and Possibilities for Convergence", in Paraskevopoulos C., Grinspun R. and Georgakopoulos T. (eds) *Economic Integration and Public Policy,* Edward Elgar, London, pp. 247-259.

Petrakos G. and Christodoulakis N. (1997) "Economic Development in the Balkan Countries and the Role of Greece: From Bilateral Relations to the Challenge of Integration", Discussion Paper No 1620, *CEPR,* University of London.

Petrakos G. and Christodoulakis N. (1998) "Transition in the Balkans: Patterns of Change and Policies to Overcome Marginalisation and Disintegration", Phare-ACE Program *"Structural Changes and Spillovers in the East European Reform Process",* Final Report, Imperial College Management School, University of London.

Petrakos G. and Totev S. (2000) Economic structure and change in the Balkan region: implications for integration, transition and economic co-operation, *International Journal of Urban and Regional Research.,* Vol. 24, No. 1, pp. 95-113.

Petrochilos G. (1997) Explaining Greek outward foreign direct investment: a case of regional economic integration, Paper presented in the *Regional Studies Association Regional Frontiers Conference* in Frankfurt (Oder), September 1997.

Raagmaa G. (1996) Shifts in regional development in Estonia during the transition, *European Planning Studies,* Vol. 4, No. 6, pp. 683-703.

UNCTAD (1996) *World Investment Report:* investment, trade and international arrangements, United Nations, Geneva.

15 Geographical Proximity Matters in the Orientation of FDI: The Case of Greek FDI in the Balkans

LOIS LABRIANIDIS
Professor, Department of Economic Sciences, University of Macedonia, Greece

Introduction

This paper is concerned with the role of geographic proximity in influencing the orientation of Foreign Direct Investment (FDI) to particular countries. It advances its arguments on the one hand through the analysis of FDI world-wide and on the other hand by focusing more thoroughly on the particular development of Greek FDI. It is a theoretically informed work based on three main research projects (Labrianidis et al., 1997, 1998 and 1999).

Greek FDI is a quite recent phenomenon and it concerns almost exclusively the expansion of Greek companies in the Central and Eastern European Countries (CEECs). The conditions created in the CEECs after the collapse of the communist regimes led many Greek companies to invest there. This article attempts to interpret this novel phenomenon, where in a very short time a large number of investment projects were initiated abroad.

This recent opening of Greek firms is seen as an outcome of the increasing importance of FDI in the world economy (see section 2). Moreover, this opening is attributed to the trend of SMEs world-wide to go international in the 1990s (which has been analysed in other works see among others - Kalantaridis and Labrianidis, 1999 and Labrianidis and Karagianni, 2000). Finally, this trend is attributed to more conjectural events i.e. the sweeping changes that occurred in the CEECs in the 1990s which presented an "easy" target for Greek companies mainly because of geographical proximity.

Before proceeding in our analysis we must point out that there are significant problems in trying to study the FDI activities (FDI= Equity capital + other capital + reinvested earnings). As it is stated in UNCTAD (1994,

12) the levels of world-wide inward and outward FDI flows and stocks should balance; but in practice they do not. The causes of the discrepancy include differences in the definition and valuation of FDI; the treatment of unremitted branch profits and of unrealised capital gains and losses; the recording of transactions of "offshore" enterprises and of reinvested earnings; the treatment of real estate and construction investment; and the share-in-equity threshold.

Moreover, in certain cases such as Greece it is extremely difficult to find accurate data regarding inward and even more so outward FDI. One of the most significant problems that was faced by the researchers while conducting the research was the lack of systematic data collected by official agencies regarding FDI in the CEECs. Such lack is particularly intense in the Greek case where the investment activity is through a multitude of relatively small investment plans. It should be stressed that, during the last few years, all the CEECs have created FDI promotion agencies. Some of these agencies, in co-operation with the statistical services of these countries, are partly responsible for the collection of the relative data. However, in many cases (e.g. Romania and Bulgaria) even that data are highly problematic.

The aim was the analysis of a new phenomenon but because of the above-mentioned problems it has been decided to form our own database set. In this context an extensive database of 1,269 Greek companies operating in the CEECs was created. Moreover, a fieldwork covering all investments of Greek interest in Bulgaria, which can be used as a guideline to, test generalisations concerning Greek investment interests all over the CEECs was conducted. This database cannot obviously be considered to be exhaustive. Moreover, since a large number of sources were used[1], the data was often incompatible. Nevertheless, we still believe that that these data allow us to arrive to some basic conclusions concerning the very nature of Greek entrepreneurial activities in the CEECs.

In this paper we do not focus on Greece's trade relations with the Balkans which, as has been argued elsewhere (Labrianidis, 2000b), have considerably increased since the opening of the CEECs markets. However, they still constitute a secondary trade partner of Greece since their trade relations have started from a very low point. In 1997, trade (imports and exports) with the Balkans constituted 6 percent of the total Greek trade compared to 61 of trade with the European Union (EU) countries. Greek trade with the Balkans in the 1990s was highly dynamic and its importance in the total Greek trade increased steadily, basically in relation to exports where it almost increased four times since 1989. What is warring is that the increase of the relative importance of the CEECs as export markets coincided with a deterioration of Greek exports to the EU (Figure 1). In fact the share of Greek exports to the EU decreased by around 20 percent during the same period.

Figure 1 Breakdown of Greek Exports

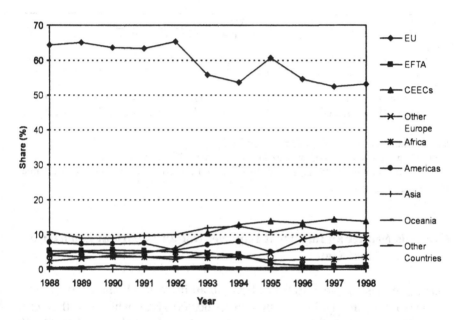

Source: NNSG.

What is of outmost importance, however, is that Greece has significantly more Intra Industry Trade -IIT- with the CEECs than with the EU, which is an indication that there is greater resemblance of the Greek economy to those of the CEE than to those of the EU countries (Table 1). The importance of Greece's trade with the CEECs and the fact that this is to a great extend IIT calls for the creation of a "Balkan economic area", as we have argued extensively elsewhere (Labrianidis, 2000c). The need for the formation of a "Balkan economic area" is further enhanced by the fact that "we are all in the same boat" (the Balkans) which has very negative associations as the "other" Europe whose inhabitants do not care to conform to the standards of behaviour devised as normative by the "civilised" world (Todorova, 1997). Hence, it is to the interest of all to have socio-political and economic stability in the area, which could minimise migration from these countries to Greece; avert conflicts; minimise pollution, etc.

Table 1 G-L Indices of Aggregate Greek and German Trade with the EU and the CEECs (1985 - 1996)

Country	Year											
	1985	1986	1987	1988	1989	1990	1991	1992	1993	1994	1995	1996
Greek												
EU	0.22	0.22	0.22	0.21	0.21	0.23	0.24	0.22	0.22	0.24	0.23	0.21
CEECs[1]	0.07	0.05	0.06	0.10	0.12	0.17	0.26	0.32	0.35	0.27	0.26	0.31
German												
EU	0.59	0.62	0.61	0.61	0.62	0.67	0.71	0.70	0.70	0.71	0.71	0.72
CEECs[1]	0.21	0.22	0.24	0.25	0.27	0.30	0.33	0.34	0.33	0.36	0.43	0.31

Source: Statistics Canada World Trade Analyzer.
Note: Calculations by the author, based on fourth digit SITC classification.
(1): Includes Albania, Bulgaria, Fr. Czechoslovakia, Fr. GDR, Hungary, Poland, Romania, Fr. USSR, Fr. Yugoslavia.

Greece is Neither an Important Importer Nor an Important Exporter of FDI on a Global Scale

During the last decades FDI has become an increasingly important aspect of the world economy. In 1998 there were 60,000 TNCs, which together with their 500,000 subsidiaries presented a total sales volume that reached 11,450 billion $USA (UNCTAD, 1999). Moreover, according to UNCTAD (1998), the ratio of inward plus outward FDI stocks to global GDP was 21 percent in 1997; foreign affiliate exports were one-third of world exports; and GDP attributed to foreign affiliates accounted for 7 percent of world total.

These impressive figures, however, disguise the existing differences between regions. In this sense developed countries are still the main recipients as well as the sources of FDI. However, one of the main characteristics of the last decade is the increasing importance of underdeveloped countries as regards both inward and outward FDI. Specifically, while in 1990 the volume of inward FDI stocks in the underdeveloped countries was 20.6 percent (UNCTAD, 1998) of the total, in 1997 the respective number reached 30.2 percent. On the other hand the volume of stock of outward FDI from underdeveloped countries during the 1990-97 period more than doubled (from 4.4 percent to 9.7 percent). The regions of the world, which presented the largest increase in their share of FDI, were Southeast Asia and Latin America.

The single most important characteristic of the last decade is that, with the exception of few countries, for the first time in history there is no continent, wider regional area or coalition of countries, that is excluded from this world system. The most recent accession to this world market were the CEECs.

More specifically, Western Europe was the largest recipient of FDI yearly in the 1982-1998 period (ranging from 30 to 50 percent - UNCTAD, 1999). USA had the second largest share of world inflows during the same period (ranging from 11 to 40 percent). Western Europe had also the largest share of world inflows stocks throughout the 1980-1998 period (ranging from 31 to 44 percent). Once again the USA was second with a share ranging from 17 to 25 percent (Figure 2).

Figure 2 Share of Total FDI Stock by Host Country/Region

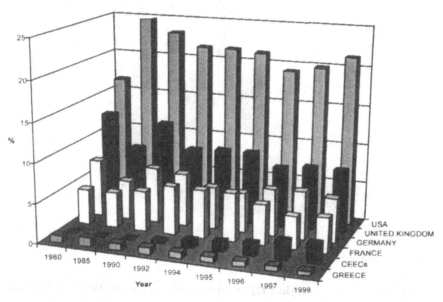

Sources: United Nations. 1999. World Investment Report, 1999.

Regarding World FDI outflows, Western Europe again had the biggest share yearly in the 1982-1998 period (ranging from 51 to 63 percent - UNC-TAD, 1999), significantly higher than its share in inflows. The USA had the second biggest share of world inflows yearly in the 1982-1998 period (ranging from 9 to 21 percent), lower than its share in inflows. Japan's role in FDI outflows is very distinct, though decreasing (from 13.4 percent in 1982-87 to 3.8 percent in 1998). Moreover, Western Europe had the biggest share of world outflow stocks during the late 1990s (50 percent). The importance of Western Europe in terms of both FDI inflows and outflows should primarily be attributed to the UK, Germany, the Netherlands, France and Belgium-Luxembourg. The USA had the second biggest share of world outflow stocks during the late 1990s (25 percent -Figure 3).

Figure 3 Share of FDI Stock by Country/Region of Origin

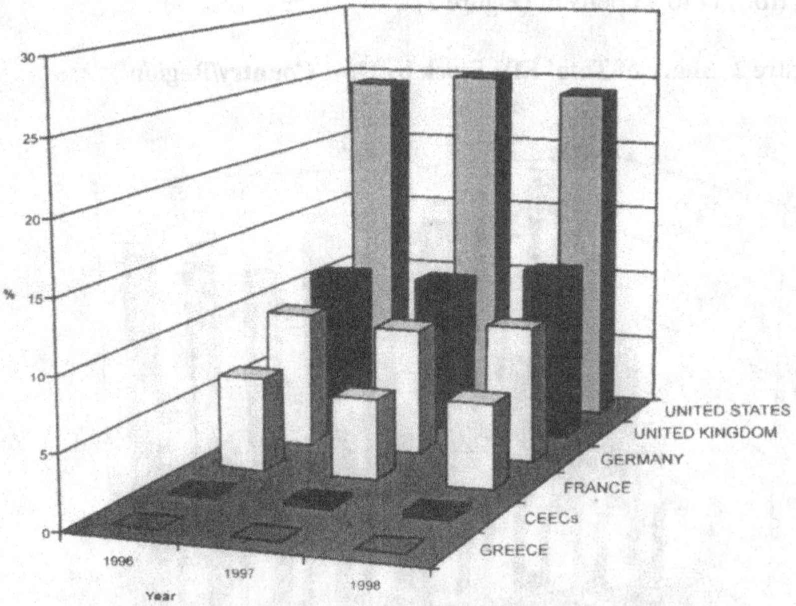

Sources: United Nations. 1999. World Investment Report, 1999.

Greece's share in world FDI inflows is not significant. While in 1982-87 it constituted the 0.732 percent of the share, it was gradually reduced to

0.483 in 1990, 0.283 in 1995 and to 0.109 in 1998). Greece's share in world FDI inflows stocks is less than 1 percent throughout the 1980-98 period with a decreasing tendency (i.e. 0.900 in 1980, 0.822 in 1990 0.720 in 1995 and 0.538 in 1998 -Figure 2). Greece's share in world FDI outflows was insignificant throughout the 1996-98 period and its share in world FDI outflow stocks was around 0.03 percent (Figure 3).

In 1998 Greece was ranked 21st on a world level in terms of its inflow stocks which were 22 billion $USA while those of the country with the largest stocks (USA) were 875,600 billion $USA. Moreover, Greece was ranked 19th in terms of its FDI outflows per capita. That is 2,094 $USA /capita, while the Netherlands which was ranked first had 64,791 $USA /capita i.e. Greece's FDI inflows have a relation of 1/31 to the country with the most important inflows (Figure 4 and Table 2).

Figure 4 FDI Inflows Per Capita

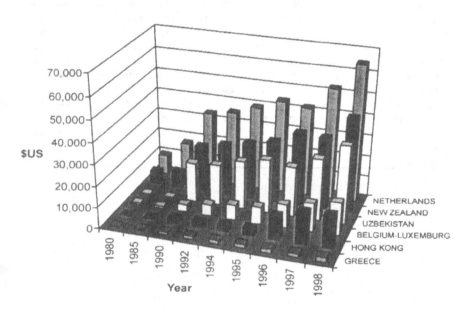

Sources: United Nations. 1999. World Investment Report, 1999.

Table 2 FDI Inflows Per Capita ($USA)

Country	1980	1985	1990	1992	1994	1995	1996	1997	1998
1 NETHERLANDS	9.519	17,046	33,709	35.642	39,644	44.085	42,408	52,502	64,791
2 NEW ZEALAND	6,034	7,566	21,847	24,601	26.750	29,173	34.934	34,106	44,933
3 UZBEKISTAN	-	-	18,611	19.556	22,971	25,497	23.721	29,222	36,726
4 BELGIUM-LUXEMBURG	712	861	3,564	5,549	7,326	8.164	11,228	13.734	15,692
5 HONG KONG	342	645	2,351	2,731	3,285	3.559	11.387	15,113	15,317
6 SWEDEN	619	1,071	7,715	11,262	13,712	14.567	12,659	11,370	13,352
7 NORWAY	578	491	1,176	1,339	5,344	6.032	5.976	7,136	7,694
8 SWITZERLAND	521	738	1,752	2.058	2,731	4,650	4,389	5,967	7,511
9 IRELAND	1,102	1,313	1,419	1,458	1,494	1,515	3,330	4,851	6,758
10 DENMARK	818	706	1,788	2.275	3.555	4,177	4,183	4.755	6,017
11 AUSTRALIA	896	1,586	4,194	4,547	5,062	5.720	5,440	5.397	5,554
12 CANADA	2,104	2,409	3,934	4.284	3,638	3.975	4,147	4,583	4,670
13 SINGAPORE	0	0	0	248	693	1.326	1.736	4.545	4.196
14 AUSTRIA	419	459	1,281	1,487	1,619	1,744	2,172	2,206	3,134
15 FRANCE	421	606	1,537	2,100	2,487	2.826	2,491	2,436	3,082
16 FINLAND	231	273	1,030	733	1,132	1,305	1,674	1,864	3,031
17 GERMANY	474	482	1,507	1,608	1,536	1,642	2,027	2,550	2,793
18 PORTUGAL	9	18	33	138	521	787	840	1.789	2,339
19 GREECE	469	837	1,395	1,585	1,753	1,835	1,846	2,032	2,094
20 ITALY	158	336	1,018	1,102	1,073	1,148	1,125	1,433	1,862
21 HUNGARY	0	0	0	286	628	974	1,169	1.568	1,811
22 ISRAEL	188	267	420	478	714	786	790	1.253	1,560
23 CZECH REPUBLIC	-	-	-	0	344	587	718	894	1,311
24 UNITED STATES	277	262	816	678	822	928	805	1.031	1,209
25 ESTONIA	-	-	0	37	292	418	456	719	1,182
26 SLOVENIA	-	-	-	0	202	328	503	804	1,055
27 THAILAND	183	195	549	565	693	724	950	928	979

Table 2 continued

Country	1980	1985	1990	1992	1994	1995	1996	1997	1998
28 ROMANIA	26	35	275	469	241	303	760	801	935
29 POLAND	88	107	209	221	370	403	504	535	626
30 LATVIA	-	-	0	5	110	208	234	511	593
31 CROATIA	-	-	-	0	36	54	88	332	533
32 SPAIN	431	285	288	287	286	285	384	472	481
33 LITHUANIA	-	-	0	3	19	32	106	266	426
34 KAZAKHSTAN	-	-	0	6	26	43	181	328	395
35 AZERBAIJAN	-	-	0	0	0	15	24	242	382
36 JAPAN	269	274	281	312	142	142	267	215	240
37 CHINA,P.R.: MAINLAND	-	3	12	25	76	107	108	175	210
38 BULGARIA	0	0	0	11	29	44	38	107	152
39 UKRAINE	-	-	25	57	81	102	100	131	147
40 ALBANIA	0	0	0	0	37	57	59	96	108
41 MACEDONIA, FYR	-	-	-	0	0	0	0	46	91
42 KYRGYZ REPUBLIC	-	-	0	0	2	5	31	59	79
43 GEORGIA	-	-	0	0	0	0	2	31	78
44 SOUTH AFRICA	0	0	0	0	7	11	40	49	52
45 BELARUS	-	-	0	1	3	5	0	29	49
46 UNITED KINGDOM	0	0	0	3	10	13	15	36	47
47 RUSSIA	-	-	0	1	4	6	8	24	29
48 TURKEY	0	0	0	0	0	0	0	1	1
49 MOLDOVA	-	-	0	4	12	20			
50 SLOVAK REPUBLIC	-	-	-	7.953	9,402	10,376			
51 TAIWAN PROV.OF CHINA	55	104	392	584	684	784			

Sources: UNCTAD, 1999, IMF, 1999, own calculations.

In 1998 Greece was ranked 28th on a world level in terms of its outflow stocks and these were 0.9 billion $ USA while those of the country with the largest stocks (USA) were 993,600 billion $USA. Moreover, Greece was ranked 26th in terms of its FDI outflows per capita. That is 86 $USA/capita, while Switzerland which was ranked first had 24,669 $USA/capita, a ratio of 1/287 (Figure 5 and Table 3).

Figure 5 FDI Outflows Per Capita

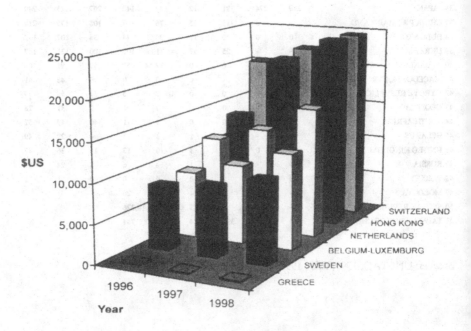

Sources: United Nations. 1999. World Investment Report, 1999.

Table 3 FDI Outflows Per Capita ($US)

Country	1996	1997	1998
1 SWITZERLAND	20,182	22,419	24,669
2 HONG KONG	13,665	21,744	24,664
3 NETHERLANDS	11,572	13,430	16,758
4 BELGIUM-LUXEMBOURG	8,515	10,137	12,317
5 SWEDEN	8,255	8,922	10,500
6 UNITED KINGDOM	5,303	6,358	8,444
7 NORWAY	5,132	6,910	7,446
8 DENMARK	4,297	6,024	6,774
9 FINLAND	2,955	3,983	6,414
10 CANADA	4,046	4,789	5,158
11 GERMANY	3,279	3,705	4,763
12 FRANCE	3,196	3,275	4,167
13 UNITED STATES	2,622	3,212	3,676
14 AUSTRALIA	2,557	3,030	3,290
15 ITALY	1,718	2,211	3,016
16 JAPAN	1,897	2,158	2,345
17 AUSTRIA	1,452	1,574	2,073
18 IRELAND	1,139	1,645	1,838
19 SPAIN	942	1,227	1,760
20 NEW ZEALAND	2,171	1,499	1,458
21 ISRAEL	685	910	1,051
22 PORTUGAL	269	496	808
23 SOUTH AFRICA	535	616	637
24 SLOVENIA	251	213	219
25 CROATIA	88	133	155
26 ESTONIA	0	131	131
27 HUNGARY	49	89	129

Table 3 continued

Country	1996	1997	1998
28 LATVIA	78	79	119
29 GREECE	86	86	86
30 CZECH REPUBLIC	29	49	68
31 SLOVAK REPUBLIC	0	37	56
32 RUSSIA	20	43	50
33 POLAND	13	18	21
34 ALBANIA	13	19	19
35 CHINA,P.R.: MAINLAND	13	17	18
36 TURKEY	4	10	14
37 ROMANIA	5	5	5
38 BULGARIA	1	4	4
39 UKRAINE	2	2	2
40 AZERBAIJAN	0	0	0
41 BELARUS	0	0	0
42 GEORGIA	0	0	0
43 KAZAKHSTAN	0	0	0
44 KYRGYZ REPUBLIC	0	0	0
45 LITHUANIA	0	0	0
46 MACEDONIA, FYR	0	0	0
47 MOLDOVA	0	0	0
48 SINGAPORE	0	0	0
49 THAILAND	0	0	0
50 TAIWAN PROV.OF CHINA	0	0	0
51 TAJIKISTAN	0	0	0

Sources: UNCTAD, 1999, IMF, 1999, own calculations.

CEECs have not yet managed to attract a significant portion of the world's FDI. However, there has been a steady increase of FDI inflows to the CEECs mainly since 1989 and from being an absolutely insignificant percentage in the 1982-87 0.027 percent, it reached 0.177 in 1990, 4.012 in 1995 and 3.309 in 1998. Contrary to the widely held belief that the ex communist countries were not integrated in the world economy, they were. In fact, their integration has accelerated abruptly during the last decade (the inward investment in seven countries of CEE which was 1,179 million $USA in 1976-80 reached 60,076 million $ USA in 1997 - Lankes and Stern, 1998). There is also a steady increase of FDI inflow stocks to the CEECs mainly since 1990 and from being an absolutely insignificant percentage of 0.045 percent in 1980 it reached 0.123 in 1990, 1.240 in 1995 and 2.428 in 1998. The three most significant FDI hosts in CEE have been Hungary, Poland and the Czech Republic (Figure 2).

CEECs' share in world FDI outflows is absolutely insignificant (0.012 percent in 1982-87 and 0.311 percent in 1998) as well as its outflow stocks (around 0.3 percent -Figure 3). FDI in the CEECs are concentrated in few countries i.e. Poland, Russia, Hungary, Czech Republic and Kazakhstan. CEECs can be classified in three main groups according to the volume of FDI per inhabitant. The first group, with the lowest ratio of FDI/inhabitant comprises of Balkan countries. Greek investments are located almost exclusively in this group. The second group comprises of all the ex USSR republics. The last group, with the highest ratio of FDI/inhabitant, comprises of the remaining CEECs (Lankes and Stern, 1998).

Investment Activity of Greek Companies in the CEECs

An Overview

The Greek capital has no experience in trade or production activities at the international level. Historically, the number of companies with production activities abroad was insignificant, the two exceptions being the shipping capital and the trading of oriental tobacco leaves. Things have changed abruptly recently and now there is a flourishing of international production activities mainly in the CEECs though not exclusively (e.g. Chipita, Thrace Paper Mills, Delta, in Cyprus, Lebanon, Egypt and Spain). Greek companies going multinational constitute a novel phenomenon, where in a very short time a large number of investment projects have been initiated abroad. Indeed, until the opening of the CEECs there were fewer than ten Greek companies with investments abroad, while in the 1960s and mainly the 1970s a number of construction companies showed some activity in the Middle Eastern countries. Since then the situation has changed drastically and now we are dealing with a very large number of Greek companies with activities abroad (Labrianidis, 2000a).

475

There are 1,269 investment projects of Greek companies in 20 of the 27 CEECs. The great majority (81.7 percent) is concentrated in just 3 countries (i.e. Bulgaria 41.1 percent, Albania 20.3 percent and Romania 20.3 percent). The majority of Greek investment projects in the CEECs are in trade (47.2 percent) and industry (36 percent) while there is a significant percentage of service related companies (13.3 percent). Industrial companies are mainly in garments and textiles (47.9 percent) and food-beverages (25.5 percent - Labrianidis, 2000a). It is worth mentioning that these four branches are of utmost importance for Greek manufacturing (40 percent of value added and 44 percent of the labour force- NSSG, 1996).

Investment activities with Greek interests in the CEECs have gone through three different phases:

1989-1993: During this first period of the opening of the CEECs there was a widely held view that has been codified as the "El Dorado" approach, where these countries were considered as areas where one could enjoy high profits. In this period many attempted to exploit the supposedly existing opportunities available, they were mainly micro SMEs and in certain cases "entrepreneurs" who thought that they could enjoy quick profits with no long-term investment perspective. There were many cases of such entre-preneurs, which in fact enjoyed extremely high profit rates (Success stories). However, in most of the cases they soon realised that the situation was much harder than they had expected and many quit and returned home.

1994-97: In this period the "catch phrase" is that of "Mafia". This connotes the proliferation of illegal practices in the economic sphere, the lack of market institutions, lack of intra state agreements for the protection of investments, etc. Greek businessmen realised the hardships of investing in a country with socio-political instability (high rates of inflation, wide spread use of semi-illegal practises) in many cases through the bankruptcy of their own businesses.

1997- today: It is a period where one can notice a "rationalisation" of the internationalisation process. There are large investments with long term prospects mainly by established companies in Greece. This opening is supported by Greek firms of the public sector (such as the Hellenic Telecommunications Organisation (OTE), Hellenic Petroleum (ELPE) and the National Bank of Greece).

In April 1999 the Greek FDI amounted to 2.4 billion $USA and was concentrated in the Federal Republic of Yugoslavia (47 percent), Romania

(37.4 percent), Bulgaria (7.9 percent), FYROM (4.6 percent)[2], and Albania (3.1 percent) (YPETHO, 1999b).

Though there are numerous investment projects in the CEECs the bulk of capital invested is owned by a handful of companies. Specifically, 32 companies have more than 67.3 percent of total Greek investments in five Balkan countries, while 10 companies have 64.1 percent of the total Greek investments. However, what is of most importance is that the few publicly owned Greek firms that invested in the CEECs account for much more than half of the total capital invested (in fact OTE on its own has the 45.6 percent! -YPETHO, 1999a). For example in Bulgaria at the end of 1998 there were 1,282 Greek companies registered with a total capital of 68.6 million $USA invested. Only 12 firms invested 85.4 percent of the total amount (BFIA, 1998).

The Recent Shift in the Greek Government's Policy Towards the Opening of Firms to the Balkans

Since the opening of the markets of the CEECs the Greek government has tried to encourage entrepreneurs to grasp the opportunities offered there. However, they did not do much to support such an effort because during the 1990s were preoccupied with pursuing an intensive macroeconomic and structural adjustment program aiming to decrease inflation, budget deficit, etc. During the last three years the government's primary aim has been to secure the country's accession to the European Monetary Union.

It anticipated that the intensification of the privatisation process was likely to inject more dynamism in the growth process by spreading a competitive culture and higher efficiency in several protected areas of the economy. Several state enterprises and banks have been privatised (OTE, Ionian Bank, etc.). In fact, the business community in Greece is showing signs of renewed dynamism and is gradually becoming more outward looking. The Athens Stock exchange has become the focus for increased activity as all major companies are now listed and privatisation has gathered momentum. Finally, the government promotes mergers and acquisitions as well as co-operation of companies, in order to grasp the anticipated opportunities in the Balkans. For instance, Greek construction companies, - recognising that the reconstruction process in the Balkans will entail large infrastructure projects - are currently going through a process of mergers and the creation of alliances in order to consolidate their competitive position[3].

The Greek government has recently changed its strategy[4] towards the Balkan countries. It realised that there is a vital need to support democratisation - security, socio-political stability and economic development of the Balkan area aiming to its future accession to the EU because it recognised that all these are of paramount importance for Greece itself. It has also encouraged investments from public owned firms. In this context it is the first country that in practice decided to financially support the reconstruction of the Balkans (YPETHO, 1999b). However, what is of outmost importance is that, recognising that Greek private capital is very small by international standards, it encouraged the wider public sector companies and Banks to go international. Furthermore, the Greek government promotes the idea of Public companies investing in the Balkans with the co-operation of Greek private capital. Already, there are quite a few such examples[5].

The Great Bulk of Companies with Greek Interests in the CEECs are Very Small and are not Directly Related to a Parent Company in Greece

There are two basic types of companies with Greek interests operating in the CEECs, according to whether they have a parent company in Greece:

I. Companies with a parent company in Greece:
I.1.There is a great number of small companies with activities in the CEECs, most of which are mainly trading or subcontracting companies. A significant proportion of the industrial companies in the CEECs belongs to industrial companies in Greece, which operate exclusively as subcontractors on behalf of large foreign firms, mainly in the garment industry.
I.2. The medium size Greek companies exhibited the smallest dynamism regarding the penetration of the CEEC markets. It seems that they feel quite safe at the home market and do not want to take risks.
I.3. There are some large companies in Greece that have invested in the CEECs. These are: a). few TNCs that have assigned to their subsidiaries or their trade agents in Greece the task of operating in the CEECs. They are assigned by TNCs the task of "entering" the Balkans, since this is a rather small market and therefore not of interest to a T.N.C. yet, whereas the Greek agent can benefit from economies of scale in distribution. Furthermore, the Balkans is a difficult market in which "informal" relations and practices are predominant and the Greek businessman is experienced in operating in such an environment. Working within such markets is also facilitated by the Greek tax legislation. Finally, geographic

proximity is of great importance. b). A significant proportion of the productive companies in the CEECs belongs to companies in Greece that have foreign capital in their structure. The above figure is rather high in relation to the average in Greece, and indicates an increasing dynamism by this type of companies. c). The majority of large companies investing in the CEEC's are of Greek ownership, of the private or public sector (banks, OTE, etc. -see Section 3.b). A significant number of large companies operating in the Balkans had previously strengthened their positions through the Stock Exchange or through a process of mergers and acquisitions.

II. Companies with no parent company in Greece:
What is of outmost importance however is that there are many companies of Greek interests which do not have a parent company in Greece. That is, there is a very significant proportion of firms of Greek interests with no connection/relation to the Greek economy. In fact, in Bulgaria where the total number of firms with Greek interests that have been registered at any time with the Bulgarian National Statistical Institute (where all firms have to register) was analysed, some more solid conclusions can be drawn. That is, up to April 1999 2,475 companies with Greek interests were registered. 12 percent of them are no longer in operation, while another 64.8 percent seem to have registered but never operated. Moreover, of the companies that are still in operation (573) and replied to the questionnaire, 62 percent do not have a parent company in Greece (Labrianidis et al., 1999).

Firms with no parent company in Greece have been established in the CEECs a) by entrepreneurs that left Greece because they failed there (they had a company that went bankrupt; they ceased operating because it wasn't profitable anymore, etc.). b) in search for better opportunities, the emigrant entrepreneur type who decides to try his fortune abroad. That is, businessmen who migrate carrying with them their skills and sometimes, capital; c) by Greeks - mainly students, political refugees, etc- who lived there. They operate there mainly as subcontractors for garment manufacturing firms in Greece, in trade (they import fruits from Greece, etc.). The main question is what sort of influence such companies might have on the development of the Greek economy.

However, what is of most importance in order to grasp the implications of the investment activity in the CEECs for the Greek economy is the classification of such Greek investments according to their relations with the

Greek economy. a.) No affiliation with a company in Greece. This is a very significant percentage of the total number of Greek investments. In the case of Bulgaria - where it was estimated to be 60 percent of total investments with Greek ownership. In such a case one must not expect benefits to the Greek economy apart for the repatriation of profits, which however has the prerequisite that profitability in Greece will be higher than in the country of the CEE. b.) Affiliation with a company in Greece, which can be affiliation with: b1.) Extremely loose relations, as in the case of small firms in Greece or subcontracting companies in Greece), b2.) Loose relations as in the case of medium size companies and finally b3.) Strong relations as in the case of large companies (especially I.3.b. and c.).

The Restricted Volume of FDI Coming from Greece Must be Attributed, Among Other Reasons, to its Geographical Isolation

The extremely restricted role of Greece in terms of its FDI outflows (which is particularly low compared to its level of development) is undoubtedly due to the structure of Greek economy. That is, the extremely high percentage of micro companies - companies with less than 10 employees constitute 97.3 percent of firms in non-primary sector, etc. (European Observatory for SMEs, 1994). However, another significant explaining factor is the geographic isolation of Greece. In the sense that it neighbours with Turkey with which it traditionally has uncomfortable relations that were deteriorated since the 1950s and three ex-socialist countries (i.e. Albania, FYROM and Bulgaria) which up to a certain time meant "iron curtain" borders. This has been a major handicap because the new TNCs expand their investments first in countries with a lower level of development than their own country and countries which are close geographically (Dunning, 1988 and Wells, 1983).

In fact a great number of countries have a very significant percentage of FDI outflows going to neighbouring countries. For example the average for the 1980-1997 period was 66.3 percent for Belgium-Luxembourg, Austria 46.4 percent, Denmark 39.5 percent, France 38.5 percent, Germany 37.3 percent, the Netherlands 33.7 percent, Portugal 31.7 percent and UK 27.3 percent. There are however, some countries (such as USA, Japan and Italy with small percentages of FDI outflows that go to their neighbouring countries, something that it is related to the fact that they are world leaders in FDI outflows (Figure 6 and Table 4).

Figure 6 Share of Total FDI Outflows of Austria, Denmark, Germany and the Netherlands to Their Neighbouring Countries

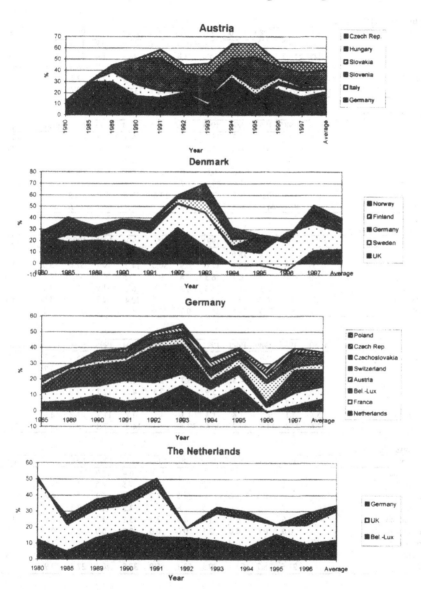

Sources: United Nations. 1999. World Investment Report, 1999.

481

Table 4 FDI Outflows from the Most Important Sources of FDI to Their Neighbouring Countries

Outflows of Belgium-Luxembourg %

Country	1980	1985	1989	1990	1991	1992	1993	1994	1995	1996	1997	Average
UK	150.0	64.2	8.2	1.9	7.6	-10.9	33.1	-47.4	10.8	-10.5	27.6	21.3
France	-222.2	53.3	1.9	11.7	-5.0	21.8	7.8	93.7	1.4	25.1	17.3	0.6
Germany	11.1	2.9	34.7	94.4	104.4	52.6	-12.0	349.0	22.7	-16.5	3.6	58.8
Netherlands	-105.6	-84.7	13.2	-5.5	-2.4	9.2	20.8	-63.4	23.4	12.1	23.9	-14.4
Total	-166.7	35.8	58.0	102.4	104.7	72.7	49.7	332.0	58.3	10.2	72.4	66.3

Outflows of Austria %

Country	1980	1985	1989	1990	1991	1992	1993	1994	1995	1996	1997	Average
Germany	12.5	30.0	29.8	17.3	15.3	20.1	9.0	29.9	26.6	22.9	16.0	20.9
Italy	0.0	0.0	8.8	10.3	6.7	1.7	3.2	1.0	-11.9	4.7	6.2	2.8
Slovenia	0.0	0.0	0.0	0.0	0.0	0.7	3.0	2.2	3.5	2.6	1.9	1.3
Slovakia	0.0	0.0	0.0	0.0	0.0	0.0	1.8	4.4	5.7	4.0	1.9	1.6
Hungary	0.0	0.0	6.1	21.6	29.3	15.7	16.8	13.5	28.2	9.6	12.0	13.9
Czech Rep.	0.0	0.0	0.0	1.1	7.3	6.9	12.6	12.6	12.0	3.9	9.3	6.0
Total	12.5	30.0	44.7	50.3	58.7	44.9	46.3	63.7	64.2	47.6	47.4	46.4

Outflows of Denmark %

Country	1980	1985	1989	1990	1991	1992	1993	1994	1995	1996	1997	Average
UK	23.4	18.6	20.2	18.6	9.8	31.2	15.0	-1.5	-1.2	-5.8	11.5	12.7
Sweden	-5.6	6.9	3.6	12.2	17.6	20.9	30.0	14.2	10.7	32.6	23.0	15.1
Germany	5.9	13.0	7.1	6.4	6.3	0.8	-0.2	2.2	14.7	-8.2	12.2	5.5
Finland	1.0	2.3	0.3	-1.1	1.3	4.3	10.9	6.2	-1.9	2.1	0.4	2.3
Norway	2.9	-1.7	1.7	2.6	2.2	2.5	14.2	10.4	2.7	1.2	4.0	3.9
Total	27.6	39.1	32.9	38.8	37.1	59.7	70.0	31.5	25.0	21.9	51.1	39.5

Outflows of France %

Country	1980	1985	1989	1990	1991	1992	1993	1994	1995	1996	1997	Average
UK	6.6	4.6	10.8	14.0	6.8	5.2	5.6	0.9	11.3	5.4	18.8	8.2
Spain	7.6	2.6	6.7	8.1	10.6	5.3	7.2	0.0	3.8	3.4	3.7	5.4
Italy	14.1	4.5	7.1	4.8	5.4	6.3	5.5	4.0	9.9	7.3	5.6	6.8
Germany	7.5	4.3	5.2	5.9	5.9	7.6	5.4	4.2	12.7	8.6	11.6	7.2
Bel.-Lux	0.0	2.2	11.1	5.3	6.6	11.7	2.3	5.7	18.8	12.4	10.2	7.8
Switzerland	5.8	4.1	2.5	1.8	1.3	1.1	1.3	-0.7	11.3	1.8	4.9	3.2
Total	41.6	22.3	43.4	39.9	36.6	37.1	27.3	14.2	67.8	38.9	54.8	38.5

Outflows of Germany %

Country		1985	1989	1990	1991	1992	1993	1994	1995	1996	1997	Average
Netherlands		5.2	6.1	9.7	5.8	7.8	15.8	6.4	14.8	-0.8	3.4	7.4
France		6.1	9.0	6.0	13.5	10.1	7.5	7.5	8.8	3.2	8.2	8.0
Bel.-Lux		3.9	10.5	13.6	11.9	22.5	18.8	5.0	5.1	2.9	14.2	10.8
Austria		2.7	2.1	2.6	2.5	2.8	4.6	3.2	4.7	12.3	2.3	4.0
Switzerland		3.6	1.1	6.1	3.4	4.5	3.6	5.2	3.3	1.9	7.9	4.1
Czechoslovakia		0.0	0.0	0.0	2.1	0.0	0.0	0.0	0.0	0.0	0.0	0.2
Czech Rep.		0.0	0.0	0.0	0.0	1.9	2.8	4.1	2.1	3.0	1.0	1.5
Poland		0.0	0.0	0.0	0.2	0.6	1.9	1.5	1.5	4.8	2.9	1.3
Total		21.5	28.7	37.9	39.3	50.1	55.0	32.8	40.1	27.2	39.9	37.3

Table 4 continued

Outflows of Netherlands %

Country	1980	1985	1989	1990	1991	1992	1993	1994	1995	1996	Average
Bel.-Lux	12.4	5.0	13.5	18.2	13.8	13.8	11.7	7.4	15.6	9.7	12.1
UK	39.3	16.8	17.8	15.9	30.9	5.9	16.8	18.2	6.1	11.6	17.9
Germany	-2.8	5.5	6.1	6.7	6.1	0.0	4.1	4.1	0.2	7.2	3.7
Total	48.9	27.2	37.4	40.8	50.7	19.6	32.6	29.7	21.9	28.5	33.7

Outflows of Portugal %

Country	1980	1985	1989	1990	1991	1992	1993	1994	1995	1996	1997	Average
Spain	0,0	4.5	14.1	26.7	51.4	54.4	93.5	25.4	50.5	11.1	16.6	31.7
Total	0,0	4.5	14.1	26.7	51.4	54.4	93.5	25.4	50.5	11.1	16.6	31.7

Outflows of Japan %

Country	1980	1985	1989	1990	1991	1992	1993	1994	1995	1996	Average
Singapore	3.0	2.8	2.8	1.5	1.5	2.0	1.8	2.6	2.3	2.3	2.2
Indonesia	11.3	3.3	0.9	1.9	2.9	4.9	2.3	4.3	3.1	5.0	4.0
Hong Kong	3.3	1.1	2.8	3.1	2.2	2.2	3.4	2.8	2.2	3.1	2.6
China	0.3	0.8	0.6	0.6	1.4	3.1	4.7	6.2	8.7	5.2	3.2
Australia	9.2	3.8	6.3	6.4	6.1	6.3	5.3	3.1	5.2	1.6	5.3
Total	27.0	11.8	13.5	13.6	14.1	18.5	17.5	18.9	21.5	17.2	17.4

Outflows of Italy %

Country	1980	1985	1989	1990	1991	1992	1993	1994	1995	1996	1997	Average
France	0.0	5.1	21.5	10.6	1.1	23.0	17.0	17.0	14.4	3.7	2.1	10.5
Austria	0.0	0.0	0.0	-0.2	0.0	-6.2	0.2	0.2	0.2	0.9	2.5	-0.2
Switzerland	0.0	0.0	0.0	2.2	0.0	0.0	9.6	1.3	0.4	-4.6	2.0	1.0
Slovenia	0.0	0.0	0.0	0.0	0.0	0.0	0.1	0.1	0.1	0.1	0.1	0.1
Slovakia	0.0	0.0	0.0	0.0	0.0	0.0	0.0	0.0	0.0	0.1	0.1	0.0
Greece	0.0	0.1	0.9	0.2	0.8	0.1	0.7	1.0	2.5	0.1	0.3	0.6
Total	0.0	5.2	22.4	12.8	1.9	17.0	27.6	19.5	17.7	0.3	7.1	12.0

Outflows of USA %

Country	1980	1985	1989	1990	1991	1992	1993	1994	1995	1996	1997	Average
Canada	0.0	0.6	3.4	12.6	4.1	4.8	4.6	8.3	9.3	9.7	9.4	6.1
Mexico	0.0	1.1	4.4	6.2	7.1	3.1	3.2	6.1	3.2	3.6	5.2	3.9
Total	0.0	1.7	7.8	18.8	11.2	7.9	7.8	14.3	12.6	13.3	14.6	10.0

Source: IMF (1999).

Regarding Greek FDI one can understand the importance of geographical proximity on the one hand by the fact that the great majority of FDIs have been materialised in their neighbouring countries (Bulgaria, Albania, Romania and FYROM). The sweeping changes in 1989 that occurred in the neighbouring socialist countries meant that Greece finally could normalise its economic relations with its northern neighbours.

The Greek companies in the CEECs tend to concentrate spatially in the capital cities (i.e. Bucharest 91.2 percent, Moscow 83.3 percent, Skopia 80 percent, Warsaw 71.4 percent and Tirana 41.4 percent). This spatial concentration is not the outcome of a proportional concentration of economic activity and population in the capital cities. Concentration in the capital cities is even more accute for the trading companies. In Sofia in particular there is a concentration of 62.4 percent of trading firms and 25.7 percent of manufacturing firms while in Bucurest the related percentages are 76.2 percent and 41.9 percent (Labrianidis et al., 1998).

The reason why in Tirana, Sofia and Skopia it is only a relatively small percentage of Greek investment projects that is located there must be attributed to the fact that high percentages of Greek investment projects are located in the southern part of these countries that is bordering with Greece. That is, companies coming from Greece are taking advantage of their comparative advantage (i.e. geographical proximity) and they tend to concentrate in the southern parts of Albania and Bulgaria. Moreover, in these investment projects there is an over representation of companies that have a parent company in Northern Greece.

Moreover within each country the majority of Greek FDIs is concentrated in the areas along the Greek borders. In Bulgaria in particular, the location pattern of companies with Greek ownership differs from the pattern of total FDI In both cases there is a huge concentration in Sofia (52.7 percent), a city with no more than 13.4 percent of the county's population. However there is a huge discrepancy otherwise. That is, total FDI is concentrated in the north (34.8 percent), while Greek companies in the southern part (38.2 percent). Cities like Plovdiv, Stara Zagora, Santanski, Gotze Delchev, Blagoevgrad, Petric, Yabol and Kioustentil have attracted most of the Greek investments, because proximity with Greece was an essential factor for their success (Table 5). In southern Bulgaria in particular in a zone of 60-80 Kms from its boders with Greece there is a heavy concentration of Greek garment manufacturing firms. This was facilitated by the existence of high unemployment rates in this area of people that were before 1989 engaged in agriculture an activity that was almost destroyed.

In Albania, there is no extremely high percentage of Greek companies in Tirana (41.4 percent), because there is a strong concentration in the Southern part of the country bordering with Greece (i.e. 55 percent) a good part of which is within the areas where a population of Greek origin is located (Argyrokastro, 10.3 percent, Korca 31 percent, Ag. Saranta 6.9 percent - Labrianidis et. al., 1998). This tendency to locate in these areas was financially facilitated by the Greek legislation (L. 1892/90 -Labrianidis, 1997).

Table 5 Distribution of Total FDI and Greek FDI by City (1992-1997)

City	Location	Total FDI[1]	Greek FDI Own data[2]	BNSI[3]
I. Sofia/ Greater Sofia		52.7	56.8	48.5
1. Gabrovo	N	3.9	0.7	
2. Lovetch	N	3.4	0.7	
3. Pazgrad	N	3.3		
4. Pleven	N	2.1	.1.4	
5. Veliko Tirnovo	N	0.2	0.7	
6. Rouche	N	0.2		
7. Varna	NE	16.2	1.4	0.8
8. Shoumen	NE	0.8		
9. Dobric	NE	0.7	2.2	
10. Terkovic	NE	0.4		
11. Kotel	NE		0.7	
12. Neglanci. Tervel	NE		0.7	
13. Tervel	NE			0.8
14. Vratsa	NW	2.5		
15. Montana	NW	0.7		
16. Vidin	NW	0.4		
17. Potevgrad	NW			0.8
II. Northern Bulgaria		34.8	8.63	2.31
18. Stara Zagora	S	2.4	2.2	4.6
19. Plovdiv	S	2.2	10.1	10.0
20. Haskovo	S	1.7	1.4	2.3
21. Pazartsik	S	0.5	1.4	1.5
22. Smolian	S	0.1		
23. Kartzali	S	0		0.8
24. Assenovgrad	S			0.8
25. Dimitrovgrad	S			1.5
26. Kazanlak	S		1.4	0.8
27. Peshtera	S			0.8
28. Svilangrad	S		2.2	1.5
29. Bourgas	SE	2.3	0.7	0.8
30. Yambol	SE	0	0.7	2.3
31. Sliven	SE	0	3.6	1.5
32. S.E. Bulgaria	SE			2.3
33. Blagoevgrad	SW	1.1	1.4	0.8 ·
34. Kioustentil	SW	0		1.5
35. Pernik	SW	0		0.8
36. Gotse Delchev	SW		0.7	1.5
37. Kresna	SW			0.8
38. Petritch	SW		1.4	3.8
39. Razlog	SW		1.4	
40. Sandanski	SW		2.9	3.1
41. Stromiani	SW			0.8
III. Southern Bulgaria		10.3	31.7	44.6
42. Silistren		0.1		
43. Damianicha				0.8
44. Devin				0.8
45. Garmanli				0.8
46. Giazodovo				0.8
47. Koprivshsitsa			0.7	
48. Dupnitsa			0.7	
49. Pomorie			0.7	0.8
50. Provgiat				0.8
51. Velingrad			0.7	
52. Others		2.2		
IV. Remaining Bulgaria		2.3	2.88	4.62
TOTAL		100.0	100.0	100.0

Sources:(1) Bulgarian Foreign Investment Agency, (2) see note of Table 2., (3) Field Work, Sept. - Nov. 1999. Based on data provided by the National Statistical Institute of Bulgaria.

Needless to say, apart from spatial proximity, which is important for FDI (as well as for international trade); there are other important aspects, such as historic and cultural ties between countries. For example, the FDI of the USA are realised mainly in Canada and in the UK; while those of Spain mainly in Latin America; finally those of France and the UK in most parts of the world due to their colonial past (Caves et al., 1996, 206-214).

Geographic proximity is a crucial factor in determining the destination of FDI. In this context, there is an extremely high concentration of companies of Greek as well as Turkish interests in Bulgaria, Romania and FYROM. Similarly, in the Czech Republic the two closest neighbours, Germany and Austria, account for around 60 percent of all investing firms (CzechInvest, 1998), while Hungary, Germany and Austria are again among the three most significant investors. The proximity argument is valid mainly for the smaller firms and to a great extend for the less developed economies. In this context, Greek and Turkish investments in countries other than the Balkans are quite insignificant. The opposite is not true, since for example German investments are of primary importance throughout the CEECs while USA and S. Korea are significant investors.

Concluding Remarks

Geographical proximity is a very important factor in relation to the orientation of FDI. This has been argued through the analysis of FDI world-wide focusing in great detail on the analysis of Greek FDI In fact most of the European countries tend to invest heavily in their neighbouring countries.

As for Greek FDI these are almost exclusively in the CEECs. The recent changes in the CEECs have led many companies with Greek interests to invest there. This novel phenomenon of Greek firms investing abroad is seen as an outcome of three main factors. That is, the increasing importance of FDI in the world economy; the trend of SMEs world-wide to go international in the 1990s; and the sweeping changes that occurred in the CEECs which presented an "easy" target for Greek companies mainly because of the geographical proximity.

The companies with Greek interests in the CEECs - which are of the "emigrant type entrepreneur", or SMEs and only a handful of them "new" TNCs - can be very important for both Greece and the Balkan economies, all depending on the form that this will take. That means that the great bulk of them are small firms, and this renders geographical proximity an even more important factor. In particular Greek FDI are directed almost exclusively to Bulgaria, Albania and Romania, among other reasons (i.e. of the least developed countries of the CEECs, etc.) because of their geographical proximity. Furthermore, within these neighbouring countries Greek FDI are directed to the southern parts of these countries that are neighbouring to Greece.

Notes

1 These sources were the following:
   a. Reports of the Greek Embassies' Trade Attaches.
   b. Law I. 1892 regarding the realisation of investments in CEECs.
   c. Catalogue of the Exporters' Association of Northern Greece of firms exporting to at least one CEE country.
   d. ICAP catalogue, with information on 5000 firms exporting to at least one CEE country.
   e. Economic Chamber of Greece (1993).
   f. Indexing of the daily press and journals.
   g. Interviews (snow ball sampling).
2 This relatively small investment activity in FYROM is mainly due to the embargo imposed upon the country by the Greek government, due to the dispute over the name of " Macedonia" in the period.....
3 Nine Greek construction companies formed an alliance in order to enter the Balkan market and furthermore they proceed to an alliance with 10 Portuguese companies - press release November 4th 1999).
4 This shift was pointed out explicitly in Papantoniou's speech at the think tank of Woodrow Wilson Centre in Washington DC.
5 a). In 1999 ELPE acquired 54% of "OKTA" the petroleum company of FYROM. To do that it formed a joint venture with a private company (METON) where the ELPE owns 80% of the shares.
   b). OTE in collaboration with Intracom is involved in several international projects and
   c). HELLASCOM is a collaboration of a public (OTE) with private companies.

References

Buckley P., Newbould G. and Thurwell J. (1988). *Foreign direct investment by smaller UK firms.* Macmillan, London.
Bulgarian Foreign Investment Agency (BFIA) (1999). *Data on Greek companies.* (unpublished).
d'Amboise G. and Muldowney M. (1988). "Management theory for small businesses", *Academy of Management Review, vol. 13 (2)*, pp. 226-240.
Dicken P. (1992). Global shift. P. Chapman, London.

Dunning J. (1988). "The investment development cycle and third world multinationals", In: J. Dunning *Explaining international production.* Unwin Hyman, London, pp. 140-168.

- (1993). "The prospects for Foreign Direct Investment in Eastern Europe", In: P. Artoisen, M. Rojec and M. Svetlicic (eds.) *Foreign investment in Central and Eastern Europe.* Macmillan, London, pp. 16-33.

- (1993). *Multi-national enterprises and the global economy.* Addison-Wesley, Wokingham England.

European Commission (1989). "Horizontal mergers and competition policy in the European Community", *European Economy, vol. 40.*

European Observatory for SMEs (1994). Second annual report, *European Network for SME Research,* Brussels.

Fiegenbaum A. V. and Karnani A. (1991). "Output flexibility - A competitive advantage for small firms", *Strategic Management Journal, vol. 12,* pp. 101-114.

Fotopoulos T. (1985). *Dependent development.* Exantas, Athens (in Greek).

Helpman E. and Krugman P. (1985). *Market structure and foreign trade.* Harvester Wheatsheaf, Brighton.

IMF (1999). *World economic outlook, International Monetary Fund.*

Kalantaridis Ch. and Labrianidis L. (1999). "The internationalisation of SMEs from countries of intermediate development", *Social Science Tribune vol.* (forthcoming) (in Greek).

Karagozoglu N. and Lindell M. (1998). "Internationalization and small and medium-sized technology-based firms: an exploratory study" *Journal of Small Business Management, vol. 36,* pp. 44-59.

Katsos G. and Lekakis J. (1991). "Trends and causes of mergers and acquisitions in Greece", *Spoudai vol. 41(1),* pp. 26-39

Kobrin S. (1997). "Comment". In: T. Agmon and C.P. Kindelberger (eds.) *Multinationals from small countries.* MIT Press, pp. 157-165.

Krugman P. [1994] (1995). *The age of diminishing returns.* Polis, Athens (in Greek).

Labrianidis L. (1996a). "The opening of the Balkan markets and consequent economic problems in Greece", *Modern Greek Studies vol. 12/13,* pp. 211-235.

- (1996b). "Subcontracting in Greek manufacturing and the opening of the Balkan markets", *Cyprus Journal of Economics vol. 9(1),* pp. 29-45.

- (1997). "The opening of the Greek companies to the Balkan markets might have important negative consequences in the development of the country", *The Hellenic Review of Political Sciences, vol. 9,* pp. 65-101 (in Greek).

- (2000a). "Are Greek companies that invest in the Balkans in the 1990s Transnational Companies?" In: A. Mitsos and E. Mossialos (eds.) *The contribution of a changing Greece to the European Union,* LSE / Ashgate Press, London.

- (2000b). "The investment activity of Greek companies in the CEE Countries: The situation beyond the myth". In: E. Andrikopoulou and G. Kafkalas (eds.) *Greece and the new European Space* Themelio, Athens (in Greek) (forthcoming).

- (2000c). "The reconstruction of the Balkans and the role of Greece: a critical approach", In: G. Petrakos (ed.) *The development of the Balkans.* University of Thessaly Publications, Volos (forthcoming) (in Greek).

Labrianidis L., Kalantaridis Ch., Karagianni St., Katsikas I, Kourtessis Ar. (1997). *The Greek industry and developments in Central and Eastern Europe.* Research Report for the Ministry of Industry (in Greek).

Labrianidis L., Kalogeresis Th., Karagianni St., Katsikas I., Mavroudeas St. (1998). *The eco-*

nomic implications for the development of Greece and Northern Greece in particular, due to the opening of the Greek industry to the Balkans. Research Report for the General Secretary of Research and Technology (in Greek).

Labrianidis L., Kalogeresis Th., Argyropoulos Sp. (1999). *Inventory of Greek firms active in Bulgaria.* Research Report for the Inter-Balkan and Black Sea Business Centre (DIPEK) (in Greek).

Labrianidis L. and Karagianni St. (2000). "The pros and cons of SMEs going international: Greek companies in Bulgaria", Proceedings of Conference "*Integration and Economies in Transition*", Chios, December 16-18.

Lall S. (1983). "The theoretical background", In: Lall S. (ed.) (1983). *The new multinationals* J. Wiley & Sons, pp. 1-20.

Lankes P.H. and Stern N. (1998). Capital flows to Eastern Europe and the former Soviet Union. EBRD *Working Paper No. 27.*

Meyer K. (1995). "Foreign direct investment in the early years of transition", *Economics of Transition, vol. 3(3),* pp. 301-320.

NSSG (1996). *Statistical research of industry.* NSSG, Athens.

OECD (1998). *International direct investment statistics yearbook.* OECD, Paris.

OECD (1999). Statistical compendium. OECD, Paris.

Papantoniou Y. (1999). "Restructuring South East Europe", Speech at the Woodrow Wilson Centre Washington DC, 27.9.99.

Petrakos G. (1996). *The new geography of the Balkans. University of Thessaly,* Volos.

Petrakos G. (1997). "A European macro region in the making? The Balkan trade relations of Greece", *European Planning Studies vol. 5(4),* pp. 515- 533.

Petrakos G. and Pitelis C. (1996). "Peripherality and integration", Paper presented to the Conference on "*Economcic Cooperation in the Balkans*", University of Thessaly -Phare ACE program.

Petrakos G. and Zikos S. (1996) "European integration and industrial structure in Greece", In: Paraskevopoulos et al. (eds). *Economic integration and public policy.* Edward Elgar, London, pp. 247-259.

Sadler D. and Swain A. (1994). "State and market in Eastern Europe", *Transactions of the Institute of British Geographers vol. 19,* pp. 387-403

Smallbone D. and Wyer P. (1995). "Export activity in SMEs", CEEDR Working Paper Series, No 9.

Smith A. and Ferencikova S. (1998). "Inward investment, regional transformations and uneven development in Eastern and Central Europe", *European Urban and Regional Studies vol. 5(2),* pp. 155-173

UNCTAD (1995). *World investment report,* UN, N. York.

UNCTAD (1998). *World investment report,* UN, N. York.

UNCTAD (1999). *World investment report,* UN, N. York.

UNCTC (1978). *Transnational corporations in world development.* UN, N. York.

Wells L.T. (1977). "The internationalisation of firms from developing countries". In: T. Agmon, C.P. Kindelberger (eds.) ibid., pp. 133-156.

Wells L.T. (1983). *Third World multinationals.* MIT Press, Cambridge Mass.

Wells L.T. (1993). "New and old multinationals", In: S. Lall (ed.) op.cit.

World Bank (1996). *From plan to market: world development report 1996.* Oxford, Blackwell.

YPETHO (Ministry of National Economy and Finance), Division of CEECs (1999a). *The most important Greek investments in the Balkans,* April. (mimeo).

YPETHO (1999b). *The Greek plan for the economic reconstruction of the Balkans.* (mimeo).

16 Bulgaria and Romania: The Changing Patterns of Trade Specialisation with the European Union

RUMEN DOBRINSKY
President, Centre for Economic and Strategic Research, Sofia, Bulgaria

Introduction

The opening-up of the economies of central and eastern Europe in the aftermath of the political changes that took place at the end of the 1980s dramatically altered the direction and composition of their trade flows. Regarding European East-West trade, these changes were broadly in line with the theoretical conclusion that, if countries with different levels of economic development liberalise trade among themselves, the degree of measured trade specialisation can be expected to increase (Landesmann, 1995). Recently, a number of studies focused on the nature of the ongoing changes in the patterns of trade between the transition economies of central and eastern Europe and the developed economies of western Europe and more specifically, with the European Union (see Landesmann and Burgstaller, 1997; Landesmann, 1996; Dobrinsky and Landesmann, 1995; European Commission, 1994). These studies have uncovered a number of factors underlying this process, such as the interplay between trade creation and trade diversion, the fading of the distorted "revealed comparative advantages" of the past and the emergence of the actual comparative advantages of the countries as "revealed", the impact of natural and factor endowments, as well as of the geographical location.

One of the findings regarding trade performance of the transition countries vis-a-vis the European Union in a comparative aspect was that they are not homogeneous as a group: countries like Hungary and Czechoslovakia (later the Czech Republic) display changes that bring their trade structures closer to what is characteristic of the developed countries of western Europe while the gap remains in countries like Bulgaria and especially Romania

(Dobrinsky, 1995).

Landesmann (1995, 1996), using some derivations of recent growth theories, put forward the hypothesis that the emerging patterns of industrial and trade specialisation in the countries of central and eastern Europe may be a heterogeneous process in which some countries of this region may accelerate the process of catching-up with the West, while others may fall behind in terms of their developmental gap. According to his results based mainly on the recent changes in East-West inter- and intra-industry trade specialisation, Hungary and the Czech Republic again display more features typical of the first category, while the changes in the trade specialisation of Bulgaria and Romania suggest likely evolution of the second type. This proposition has been confirmed by the results of a later study (Landesmann and Burgstaller, 1997) which found that between 1989 and 1994 the process of differentiation between the central and eastern European transition countries widened further: while the "western" countries (the Czech Republic, Hungary, Poland and Slovenia) moved "upstream" (concerning their product quality and position in vertically differentiated product markets), the "eastern" countries (Bulgaria, Romania and Russia) have lagged far behind.

In a recent study, Petrakos and Totev (1997) analyse in a comprehensive manner the patterns of economic restructuring in the Balkan region. They argue convincingly that the locational disadvantages of the region (remoteness from the major European markets) have played (and are likely to play in the future as well) a very important role in the ongoing process of economic and trade restructuring in the peripheral south-eastern European transition countries. They use as a reference point the recent experience and performance patterns displayed by Greece after joining the EU in the mid-1980s: since that time the differences in Greek industrial and trade structures (and, hence, the developmental gap) vis-a-vis the European Union not only did not start to close but, on the contrary, widened.

Apart from the locational characteristics, it is important to note that policies pursued during the transition period obviously also had an impact on the patterns of industrial and trade restructuring. In this regard, there are also substantial differences between the rapidly reforming central European countries (Slovenia obviously also belongs to this category) and the countries of south-eastern Europe, where reforms encountered serious difficulties and delays (and, in general, these countries began their transition from a much more unfavourable starting point as compared to central European countries). The major financial crisis in Bulgaria in 1996, the collapse of the fraudulent financial investment schemes in Albania in 1997 and the chronic macroeconomic instability in Romania (which also escalated in 1997) are all symptoms of similar economic problems in these countries: they reflect the delays in structural reforms, the weak institutional environment in these countries, as well as the lack of consistent and coherent reform policies.

While it may still be too early for any definitive conclusions about the nature of the emerging industrial and trade patterns in the transition countries and, in particular, those of south-eastern Europe, it might be instructive to analyse in more depth the different aspects of the changes in the trade performance of these countries. Such an analytical insight might provide a better understanding of both the character of the underlying economic processes and their future trends.

This paper addresses some aspects of the changing patterns of the trade specialisation in trade between Bulgaria and Romania, on the one hand, and the EU, on the other. One of its main focal points is the interlinks between trade specialisation and the quality of traded goods (as measured by the value-added content of the traded goods) in these two transition economies. Apart from analysing the dynamics of the changes that have taken place in the first phase of transition, the paper seeks to reveal similarities and differences in the trade patterns of the two countries in comparison with the average trade patterns of central and eastern Europe (CEE) as a whole.

The coverage and scope of the study are essentially limited by the availability of trade data: it is based on the mirror statistics as reported by the EU member countries. Unfortunately, the national statistical offices of the transition countries still do not provide data in format and quality that would permit a similar study on the basis of national data. Thus, the changing patterns of trade with the neighbouring Balkan states, which might provide an interesting point of reference, are left out of consideration, hopefully not for long when data become available.

Notes on Methodology

The study reported in this paper is based on data about the trade flows (exports and imports) between Bulgaria and Romania and the European Union (total) as reported by the EU member states. The actual data source is the UN COMTRADE database.

The level of disaggregation of the source data used is SITC 3-digit level. The time points taken for the analysis are 1988, 1991, 1993 and 1994. Thus, the period under consideration covers the starting point (the last year before the start of economic and political transformation), an interim point and the last two available full years in COMTRADE (at the moment of writing).

COMTRADE provides two cross-sections of the data: values of the trade flows by the SITC categories (in current US dollars) and volume indicators by these categories in the form of physical weight (metric tons) of merchandise exported or imported. These source items make it possible to estimate price measures of the trade flows in the form of "unit values" defined as dollar values divided by physical weights (e.g., $/kg of merchandise). Throughout the text, the term "unit values" of Bulgarian and Romanian export and import flows is used in the above context, on the SITC 3-digit level. It has been suggested in the literature that in cross-country comparisons by commodity groups, the unit value within a given category can be regarded as a proxy for the relative value-added content of the goods and, hence for its quality (see Landesmann and Szıkely, 1995 and, more recently, Landesmann and Burgstaller, 1997).

As the unit values in our case are defined for the same commodity groups in different countries (SITC 3-digit), their absolute values can be used for direct cross-country comparisons of the quality level of the trade (export and import) flows in the different countries. Besides, if we consider a group of countries (such as the group of CEE countries[1]) we can eventually identify for each country the subset of commodity groups for which the country displays a level of quality of exports (or imports) which is above (or below) the average for the group as a whole, or subsets for which the country has the highest (or the lowest) level of quality of exports (or imports) within the group of countries.

Furthermore, the study makes use of the notion "unit value ratio" as defined in EBE (1995), namely as the ratio between the unit value of exports and the unit value of imports (or vice versa) within the same commodity group (SITC 3-digit). The unit value ratio compares the value-added content of one physical unit of exported and imported merchandise in one and the same commodity group. It has been suggested (EBE, 1995) that a higher "export/import unit value ratio" (EIUVR) may reflect a quality advantage of exported goods over imported ones in the same commodity category or that it may be the result of exporting goods which are technologically different from (and superior to) the imported ones. Thus, if the EIUVR within a given commodity group is greater than one (the unit value of one kg of exported merchandise is higher than the unit value of one kg of imported merchandise within the same commodity group), then it can be assumed that the country is specializing in exporting high value-added goods and thus has a competitive advantage in this commodity group (see EBE, 1995, p.48). This interpretation should be reversed if we define "import/export unit value ratios" (IEUVR).

EIUVRs and IEUVRs are defined at a certain level of disaggregation of the trade flows for which the physical weights can be assumed to have a non-controversial economic interpretation (in our case this is SITC 3-digit level). If we want to employ similar measures at a higher level of aggregation (e.g., SITC 1-digit) we can eventually compose trade weighted EIUVRs or IEUVRs, in which the weights are the shares of export (respectively import) flows within the aggregated commodity group. Trade weighted unit value ratios have analogous interpretation within the broader commodity group.

The unit value ratio analysis can be juxtaposed with the conventional measures of trade specialisation. Following Balassa (1965), we can define export specialisation index (export performance ratio) for commodity (sector) j of country i, denote it as ESI_{ij}, within a group of countries (the CEE transition economies), as:

$$ESI_{ij} = \frac{x_{ij}}{X_i} : \frac{M_j}{M}, \tag{1}$$

where x_{ij} is country i's exports of commodity (sector) j to the EU;

$X_i = S_j x_{ij}$ is country i's total exports to the EU;

$M_j = S_i x_{ij}$ is the EU's total imports of commodity (sector) j from all CEE countries (which is the same as the total exports of commodity (sector) j by the group of CEE countries to the EU);

$M = S_i S_j x_{ij}$ is the EU's total imports from all CEE countries (which is the same as the total exports of the group of CEE countries to the EU).

An import specialisation index MSI_{ij} can be defined in a similar manner as:

$$MSI_{ij} = \frac{m_{ij}}{M_i} : \frac{X_j}{X}, \tag{2}$$

where m_{ij} is country i's imports of commodity (sector) j from the EU;

$M_i = S_j m_{ij}$ is country i's total imports from the EU;

$X_j = S_i x_{ij}$ is the EU's total exports of commodity (sector) j to all CEE countries (which is the same as the total imports of commodity (sector) j by the group of CEE countries from the EU);

$X = S_i S_j m_{ij}$ is the EU's total exports to all CEE countries (which is the same as the total imports of the group of CEE countries from the EU).

The Commodity Composition of Bulgarian and Romanian Trade with the EU and Its Value Added Contents

Bulgarian and Romanian trade with the EU underwent significant changes in recent years both in terms of the volumes and value of trade and in terms of its commodity structure. During the communist period trade with the west was, by and large, determined by the general economic policies of the central authorities. However, the two countries followed quite different strategies in the 1980s. During this period, the Bulgarian authorities were making some attempts to modernize the manufacturing industry, and in this context, they regarded the EU as one of the main sources of high technologies, capital goods and sophisticated intermediate goods; in fact Bulgaria was, in that period, a major importer of these commodities among the CEE countries. As for exports, Bulgaria placed more emphasis on exports to less demanding markets, whereas the exports to the EU were not a main policy target. Romanian trade in the 1980s was dominated by the weird push of the communist regime to repay the foreign debt of the country: the country was exporting practically anything that could be exported, at any cost, while imports were reduced to the minimum (for details see Dobrinsky, 1994 and Jackson and Wiesbrouck, 1994).

The two countries thus had a different starting point in terms of their relative position within the group of the CEE countries: in 1988 Bulgaria accounted for 15.1 percent of total CEE imports from the EU but only for 4.6 percent of CEE exports; conversely, in the same year Romania was responsible for 21.4 percent of the total CEE exports to the EU but only for 6.7 percent of the imports (Table 1). In the course of the transition period, with the demise of the CMEA, the liberalisation of trade and the signing of the association agreements, the EU became the main market for both countries and these disproportionate trade flows gradually leveled off. At present, the shares of the two countries in the total CEE trade with the EU seem to reflect the size of the two economies (Table 1).

In terms of aggregated commodity groups, Bulgaria is a major exporter and importer (within CEE) to the EU of beverages and tobacco (SITC 1); while Romania specialises in the exports of miscellaneous manufactures (SITC 8) and in the imports of manufactured goods classified by material (SITC 6) and energy (SITC 3).

Table 1 Bulgarian and Romanian Trade with the EU: Shares in CEE Total Trade Flows by SITC 1-digit

(percentages)

A. Bulgaria		Exports				Imports			
Commodity groups	SITC	1988	1991	1993	1994	1988	1991	1993	1994
Food and live animals	0	4.8	5.4	5.6	4.7	16.0	9.7	7.3	4.3
Beverages and tobacco	1	43.8	45.6	47.6	45.4	24.6	6.9	27.8	15.7
Crude materials except fuels	2	4.6	6.3	6.3	6.6	13.3	5.1	5.2	4.2
Fuels, energy	3	4.7	6.3	6.3	6.6	13.3	5.1	5.2	4.2
Animal and vegetable oils	4	5.2	3.1	4.2	4.2	7.3	3.4	3.0	3.3
Chemicals	5	8.1	5.3	7.0	5.8	14.2	5.5	4.9	4.3
Manufactured goods by material	6	3.5	3.8	4.3	4.0	14.9	5.1	4.2	4.2
Machinery and transport equipment	7	3.8	4.2	2.4	2.4	16.9	5.5	4.2	4.2
Miscellaneous manufactures	8	2.8	3.9	4.8	4.4	11.1	3.8	6.4	3.9
Commodities not classified elsewhere	9	15.4	6.1	4.3	2.4	9.0	7.3	9.4	5.4
Total		4.6	4.6	4.8	4.3	15.1	5.5	5.3	4.1
B. Romania		Exports				Imports			
Commodity groups	SITC	1988	1991	1993	1994	1988	1991	1993	1994
Food and live animals	0	6.7	2.7	3.3	3.8	4.8	13.7	13.6	6.6
Beverages and tobacco	1	10.7	6.9	7.7	7.4	2.8	10.5	13.8	8.4
Crude materials except fuels	2	7.2	3.5	4.0	4.5	14.0	10.7	8.1	6.1
Fuels, energy	3	48.1	18.4	4.0	6.0	30.7	14.0	11.2	10.4
Animal and vegetable oils	4	2.9	3.7	9.4	11.5	2.0	21.9	6.2	2.6
Chemicals	5	12.8	4.8	5.3	7.4	6.3	7.0	5.7	5.6
Manufactured goods by material	6	18.7	6.9	5.3	7.8	12.2	9.5	10.6	11.2
Machinery and transport equipment	7	12.4	5.6	3.7	3.9	2.1	5.0	8.2	7.4
Miscellaneous manufactures	8	35.3	18.6	18.1	19.4	9.5	6.8	8.1	9.3
Commodities not classified elsewhere	9	1.3	7.8	6.0	3.5	2.8	16.6	19.3	16.2
Total		21.4	9.1	8.4	9.5	6.7	7.6	9.0	8.2

Source: UN COMTRADE database.

Some quantitative characteristics of the commodity composition of Bulgarian and Romanian trade with the EU, as well as a comparison with the average CEE trade structure, are presented in Tables 2 to 5.

On average, the commodity composition of Bulgarian trade is more evenly structured than that of Romania. This is especially pronounced on the export side: thus, the cumulative share of the five largest SITC 3-digit commodity groups in the total Romanian exports to the EU in 1994 was 50.8 percent, whereas the corresponding share in Bulgaria was 32.4 percent (Tables 4 and 5). Both countries have specialised in the light industry branches - textiles, clothing, footwear (this is especially pronounced in Romania), metals and metal products; besides, Romania is a major exporter of furniture and Bulgaria specialises in the export of wines.

Table 2 Bulgarian and Romanian Trade with the EU: Breakdown by SITC 1-digit

(percentages)

A. Bulgaria		Exports				Imports			
Commodity groups	SITC	1988	1991	1993	1994	1988	1991	1993	1994
Food and live animals	0	14.4	15.8	9.7	8.1	6.5	13.3	10.5	6.8
Beverages and tobacco	1	6.1	6.9	7.1	6.0	1.2	2.3	5.8	2.7
Crude materials except fuels	2	9.3	10.2	8.2	9.2	4.3	2.6	2.0	2.1
Fuels, energy	3	12.5	2.5	4.6	1.3	0.3	1.8	5.8	0.8
Animal and vegetable oils	4	0.4	0.1	0.2	0.1	0.2	0.2	0.2	0.4
Chemicals	5	15.0	10.8	10.0	9.3	21.3	12.5	11.7	13.8
Manufactured goods by material	6	17.2	19.7	21.6	25.7	20.2	16.3	16.1	18.8
Machinery and transport equipment	7	9.7	13.3	9.8	11.8	38.9	41.0	30.9	41.0
Miscellaneous manufactures	8	12.1	19.3	28.6	28.2	6.4	8.0	15.7	12.7
Commodities not classified elsewhere	9	3.4	1.4	0.2	0.5	0.8	2.0	1.1	1.0
Total		100.0	100.0	100.0	100.0	100.0	100.0	100.0	100.0
B. Romania		**Exports**				**Imports**			
Commodity groups	SITC	1988	1991	1993	1994	1988	1991	1993	1994
Food and live animals	0	4.3	4.1	3.3	2.9	4.4	13.6	11.6	5.1
Beverages and tobacco	1	0.3	0.5	0.7	0.4	0.3	2.5	1.7	0.7
Crude materials except fuels	2	3.1	2.9	3.0	2.7	10.1	3.9	1.9	1.5
Fuels, energy	3	27.8	12.8	2.2	2.3	2.4	5.3	3.4	2.2
Animal and vegetable oils	4	0.0	0.1	0.2	0.2	0.1	1.1	0.3	0.1
Chemicals	5	5.1	5.0	4.3	5.3	21.5	11.5	8.0	8.9
Manufactured goods by material	6	19.7	18.0	15.3	22.2	37.3	22.0	24.3	29.4
Machinery and transport equipment	7	6.7	9.1	8.6	8.4	10.9	27.1	35.7	35.7
Miscellaneous manufactures	8	32.9	46.5	62.3	55.2	12.5	10.5	11.8	14.8
Commodities not classified elsewhere	9	0.1	0.9	0.2	0.3	0.5	2.5	1.3	1.5
Total		100.0	100.0	100.0	100.0	100.0	100.0	100.0	100.0

Source: UN COMTRADE database.

Since 1998 both Bulgaria and Romania have drastically reduced the exports of fuels and energy (SITC 3), which used to be a major export item in the past (partly based on cheap oil imports from the former USSR) and by 1994 Romania was already a net importer in this category (Table 2). Similarly, the importance of food exports (SITC 0) from Bulgaria to the EU declined in relative terms in this period. In both countries, the exports of manufactured goods to the EU gained in importance in recent years: from 1988 to 1994 the share of manufactured goods in total Bulgarian exports to the EU increased from 39.0 percent to 65.7 percent; the corresponding shares in Romania changed from 59.3 percent to 85.8 percent (Table 2).

Table 3 Total CEE Trade with the EU: Breakdown by SITC 1-digit

(percentages)

Commodity groups	SITC	Exports				Imports			
		1988	1991	1993	1994	1988	1991	1993	1994
Food and live animals	0	13.7	13.6	8.4	7.3	6.1	7.6	7.6	6.4
Beverages and tobacco	1	0.6	0.7	0.7	0.6	0.7	1.8	1.1	0.7
Crude materials except fuels	2	9.4	7.5	6.3	5.9	4.8	2.8	2.1	2.1
Fuels, energy	3	12.4	6.3	4.6	3.7	0.5	2.9	2.7	1.72
Animal and vegetable oils	4	0.3	0.3	0.2	0.1	0.4	0.4	0.4	0.4
Chemicals	5	8.5	9.5	6.9	6.8	22.6	12.5	12.6	13.2
Manufactured goods by material	6	22.5	23.7	24.2	27.1	20.3	17.6	20.6	21.7
Machinery and transport equipment	7	11.6	14.7	19.4	20.5	34.6	41.2	39.2	39.7
Miscellaneous manufactures	8	19.9	22.7	28.9	27.2	8.7	11.7	13.0	13.2
Commodities not classified elsewhere	9	1.0	1.1	0.3	0.8	1.3	1.5	0.6	0.8
Total		100.0	100.0	100.0	100.0	100.0	100.0	100.0	100.0

Source: UN COMTRADE database.

Important changes also took place on the import side, although they were not so pronounced as in exports. Due to the transitional depression, both countries reduced, both in relative and in absolute terms, the imports of some inputs and intermediates, such as crude materials (SITC 2) and chemicals (SITC 5) (Table 2). On the other hand, Romania substantially increased the imports of machinery and transport equipment (SITC); the share of this item in Bulgarian exports remained more or less the same but its internal composition changed (the proportion of investment goods declined whereas that of vehicles increased). In the first years of transition, both countries imported relatively large amounts of food (SITC 0) from the EU, but by 1994 this tendency seems to have faded.

Many of the changes which are observed on the import side are related to the changes in the industrial (and export) specialisation of the countries, especially in the case of Romania. Thus, six out of the ten largest SITC 3-digit import commodity groups embody imports of inputs and intermediates for the textile, clothing and footwear industry in which the country is now strongly specialising; in Bulgaria there are two such groups among the first ten largest import categories and four among the first twenty (Table 5). This partly reflects outward processing traffic (OPT) from and to the EU, which has intensified substantially in recent years.

Table 4 Ranking of Bulgarian Exports To and Imports From the EU by SITC 3-digit Categories in 1994

Rank	Commodity group	SITC	Share in total, %	Rank	Commodity group	SITC	Share in total, %
1	COPPER	682	7.397	1	PASS. MOTOR VEHCLS. EX. BUS	781	4.971
2	FLAT-ROLLED IRON	673	7.201	2	FABRICS, MAN-MADE FIBERS	653	3.973
3	WOMEN'S, GIRLS' CLOTHING	842	6.967	3	ENGINES, MOTORS NONELECT	714	3.601
4	FOOTWEAR	851	5.523	4	TELECOMM. EQUIP. PARTS NES	764	2.806
5	MEN'S, BOYS' CLOTHING	841	5.313	5	FOOTWEAR	851	2.426
6	ALCOHOLIC BEVERAGES	112	4.337	6	DOM. ELEC. NON-ELEC. EQUIPT	775	2.376
7	OTHER TEXTILE APPAREL	845	4.132	7	ROAD MOTOR VEHICLES NES	783	2.048
8	ENGINES, MOTORS NONELECT	714	3.102	8	OTH. MACHINE PARTS, SPECIAL	728	1.963
9	OTHER MEAT, MEAT OFFAL	012	2.993	9	SPECIAL TRANSP. VEHICLES	782	1.863
10	FERTILIZERS EXCEPT CRUDE	562	2.312	10	ALCOHOLIC BEVERAGES	112	1.836
11	COPPER ORES, CONCENTRATES	283	2.075	11	COTTON FABRICS, WOVEN	652	1.836
12	TOBACCO, UNMANUFACTURED	121	1.641	12	ELECTRIC. MACH. APPARTUS	778	1.788
13	METAL. SALTS. INORGAN. ACID	523	1.624	13	MEDICAMENTS	542	1.697
14	ELECTRIC. MACH. APPARTUS	778	1.482	14	MEASURE. CONTROL, INST.	874	1.660
15	FABRICS, MAN-MADE FIBERS	653	1.389	15	CHOCOLATE. OTH. COCOA PREP	073	1.583
16	TRUNKS, SUIT-CASES, BAGS. ETC	831	1.289	16	TEXTILE. LEATHER MACHINES	724	1.547
17	MEDICINES	541	1.289	17	HEATNG. COOLING EQUIP. PART	741	1.437
18	PETROLEUM PRODUCTS	334	1.126	18	OTH.NONELECTR. MACH, TOOLS	745	1.304
19	MECHANICAL HANDLING EQUIP	744	1.080	19	EDIBLE PROD. PREPARATIONS	098	1.240
20	PRESERVED FRUIT 058 1.068	058	1.068	20	INSECTICIDES, ETC.	591	1.213
	5 largest		32.401		5 largest		17.741
	10 largest		49.290		10 largest		27.828
	20 largest		63.345		20 largest		43.131

Sources: UN COMTRADE database; own calculations.

Compared to the average composition of CEE trade with the EU on the SITC 1-digit level (Table 3), the structure of Bulgarian trade in 1994 is much more similar to that of the CEE average than is the composition of Romanian trade, especially on the export side. Romanian exports are heavily dominated by the exports of miscellaneous manufactures (SITC 8), which in turn are governed by light industry.

Table 5 Ranking of Romanian Exports To and Imports From the EU SITC 3-digit Categories in 1994

Rank	Commodity group	SITC	Share in total, %	Rank	Commodity group	SITC	Share in total, %
1	MEN'S, BOY'S CLOTHING	841	13.205	1	FABRICS, MAN-MADE FIBERS	653	7.655
2	WOMEN'S, GIRLS' CLOTHING	842	12.309	2	OTH. TEXTILE FABRIC, WOVEN	654	3.529
3	FURNITURE, CUSHIONS, ETC.	821	10.300	3	LEATHER	611	3.328
4	FOOTWEAR	851	9.443	4	FOOTWEAR	851	3.312
5	FLAT-ROLLED IRON	673	5.594	5	OTHER MACH. PARTS, SPECIAL	728	3.236
6	OTHER TEXTILE APPAREL	845	5.128	6	COTTON FABRICS, WOVEN	652	3.024
7	ALUMINIUM	684	4.678	7	TEXTILE, LEATHER MACHINES	724	2.932
8	PETROLEUM PRODUCTS	334	1.930	8	AGRIC. MACHINES, EX. TRACTOR	721	2.808
9	ELECTR DISTRIBT. EQUIPMENT	773	1.768	9	TELECOMM. EQUIP. & PARTS	764	2.716
10	ALCOHOL, PHENOL, ETC. DERIV.	512	1.580	10	ELECTR. DISTRIBT. EQUIPMENT	773	2.645
11	CLOTHING ACCESSRS, FABRIC	846	1.136	11	HEATING, COOLING EQP.,PARTS	741	2.289
12	IRON, STL. BAR, SHAPES ETC.	676	1.109	12	PETROLEUM PRODUCTS	334	2.108
13	BALL OR ROLLER BEARINGS	746	1.101	13	PASS. MOTOR VEHICLES. EX. BUS	781	1.888
14	GLASSWARE	665	0.993	14	SPECIAL YARN, TXTL.FABRIC	657	1.659
15	ROTATING ELECTRIC PLANT	716	0.896	15	OTH. NONELEC MACH., TOOLS	745	1.604
16	TEXTILE YARN	651	0.844	16	CLOTHING ACCESSRS, FABRIC	846	1.603
17	LIME, CEMENT, CONSTR. MATRL	661	0.844	17	SPEC. TRANSACT. NOT CLASSD	931	1.430
18	LIVE ANIMALS	001	0.801	18	FOOD-PROCESS. MCH. NON DOM	727	1.412
19	TUBES, PIPES, ETC. IRON, STL.	679	0.729	19	MEASURE, CONTROL INSTRMNT	874	1.233
20	WOMEN'S, GIRLS' CLOTHNG. KNIT	844	0.751	20	MANUFACTURES BASE METALS	699	1.222
	5 largest		50.852		5 largest		21.060
	10 largest		65.935		10 largest		51.633
	20 largest		75.202		20 largest		35.185

Sources: UN COMTRADE database; own calculations.

We now turn to the dynamics of value-added contents of Bulgarian and Romanian trade with the EU as depicted by the unit value ratios. An aggregate assessment of the "value-added composition" of the trade of the two countries and a comparison with the CEE average is presented in Tables 6-7 and 4.1-4.2. The weighted average unit values by SITC 1-digit categories and those for the total trade flows (Tables 6 and 7) are calculated on the basis of the SITC 3-digit numbers which are then aggregated by using the shares of the flows as weights[2].

Table 6 Bulgarian and Romanian Trade with EU: Trade Weighted Unit Value Ratios

A. Bulgaria		Exports Export-weighted "export/ import" unit value ratios				Imports Import-weighted "import/ export" unit value ratios			
Commodity groups	SITC	1988	1991	1993	1994	1988	1991	1993	1994
Food and live animals	0	2.41	2.00	2.50	4.56	2.14	3.80	1.70	3.61
Beverages and tobacco	1	8.63	2.45	1.52	0.79	3.45	1.05	1.06	3.26
Crude materials except fuels	2	0.59	5.48	3.09	0.79	3.09	3.39	2.81	3.94
Fuels, energy	3	1.32	0.90	0.66	0.63	0.92	1.03	1.68	1.50
Animal and vegetable oils	4	0.18	0.23	0.52	0.66	3.40	2.72	2.65	2.80
Chemicals	5	0.86	0.67	0.28	0.61	2.72	2.32	2.45	3.10
Manufactured goods by material	6	0.57	0.50	0.42	0.46	3.14	2.63	3.40	3.17
Machinery and transport equipment	7	0.36	0.53	0.72	1.82	4.32	3.23	2.91	2.80
Miscellaneous manufactures	8	0.55	0.80	1.19	0.93	2.45	1.96	3.43	2.09
Commodities not classified elsewhere	9*	1.52	2.26	33.39	9.32	0.66	0.44	0.05	0.11
Total		1.50	1.44	1.25	1.20	3.43	2.95	2.69	2.86

B. Romania		Exports Export-weighted "export/ import" unit value ratios				Imports Import-weighted "import/ export" unit value ratios			
Commodity groups	SITC	1988	1991	1993	1994	1988	1991	1993	1994
Food and live animals	0	1.63	1.66	2.31	1.34	1.72	1.54	2.02	2.89
Beverages and tobacco	1	6.31	2.03	2.01	0.78	1.27	0.66	0.68	1.12
Crude materials except fuels	2	3.66	1.08	11.72	0.51	2.50	1.52	4.02	3.93
Fuels, energy	3	0.81	0.72	0.60	1.44	1.20	1.38	1.72	0.87
Animal and vegetable oils	4	0.50	0.40	0.44	0.56	3.38	2.26	2.20	1.93
Chemicals	5	0.50	0.59	0.41	0.41	5.55	2.88	4.12	3.38
Manufactured goods by material	6	0.35	0.72	0.52	0.53	3.93	3.39	3.40	3.01
Machinery and transport equipment	7	0.32	0.52	0.48	0.57	7.19	4.99	4.43	3.70
Miscellaneous manufactures	8	068	1.02	1.23	1.14	3.47	2.37	2.85	2.15
Commodities not classified elsewhere	9	2.25	9.16	0.66	0.32	0.44	0.11	1.50	3.09
Total		0.75	0.96	1.35	0.90	4.40	3.20	3.59	3.12

Sources: UN COMTRADE database; own calculations.

The weighted average unit value ratios by commodity groups have their meaning both separately for the export and for the import flows and concurrently for both flows. A weighted average unit value ratio larger than 1, for example, in an aggregate export category, means that on average the exports of the country tend to be concentrated in commodity groups in which the EIUVRs are greater than one (and thus the country eventually has a competitive edge). In other words, the country tends to export relatively more merchandise in commodity groups of the type "high value-added exports"[3], than merchandise in commodity groups of the type "low value-added exports". Conversely, a weighted average unit value ratio larger than

1 in an aggregate export category means that there is relatively larger concentration of export flows in commodity groups of the type "low value-added exports". The interpretation for the import side is a mirror image of the above.

Table 7 Total CEE trade with EU: Trade Weighted Unit Value Ratios

Commodity groups	SITC	Exports Export-weighted "export/ import" unit value ratios				Imports Import-weighted "import/ export" unit value ratios			
		1988	1991	1993	1994	1988	1991	1993	1994
Food and live animals	0	3.34	1.27	1.51	1.48	1.36	1.86	1.40	1.54
Beverages and tobacco	1	3.64	1.49	1.13	0.77	1.28	0.84	2.26	1.32
Crude materials except fuels	2	0.91	1.29	1.30	0.79	2.71	2.36	2.35	2.33
Fuels, energy	3	0.58	0.53	0.38	0.56	1.87	1.79	1.80	1.25
Animal and vegetable oils	4	0.52	0.42	1.08	0.83	1.89	1.83	1.55	1.31
Chemicals	5	0.55	0.67	0.68	0.71	3.32	2.30	2.01	1.80
Manufactured goods by material	6	0.42	0.46	0.44	0.45	3.71	3.00	2.91	2.86
Machinery and transport equipment	7	0.34	0.51	0.51	0.57	6.27	3.59	3.01	2.69
Miscellaneous manufactures	8	0.81	0.96	1.03	0.99	3.80	2.71	1.97	1.98
Commodities not classified elsewhere	9	0.60	1.45	2.95	1.22	1.99	1.61	1.77	1.36
Total		0.99	0.80	0.79	0.75	4.28	2.92	2.55	2.39

Sources: UN COMTRADE database; own calculations.

The comparison of the weighted average EIUVRs and IEUVRs (within the same trade categories) may provide some additional insights. If the weighted average EIUVR is larger than the weighted average IEUVR, this might be accepted as an indication of a strong competitive position of the country in the given trade category, as the concentration of export flows in commodity groups of the type "high value-added exports" is more pronounced than the concentration of import flows in commodity groups of the type "high value-added imports".

The actual estimations of the weighted average EIUVRs and IEUVRs and their dynamics in Bulgaria and Romania (Tables 6 and 7) present a mixed picture. Taken as a whole, the weighted average EIUVRs in Bulgaria are higher than those in Romania (with the exception of 1993), indicating a higher degree of concentration of export flows in "high value-added exports" commodity groups. On the other hand, there is a marked trend for deterioration of the weighted average EIUVR for total Bulgarian exports, whereas that of Romania tends to increase as compared to the pre-transition period. What is particularly unfavourable is the relatively low level of the weighted average EIUVRs in many of the aggregated manufacturing categories in both countries. This means that within the manufacturing sectors, which, in principle, are characterised by a relatively high degree of processing, the two countries tend to export either commodities which are in the lower range of processing, or products of lower quality (hence, lower price).

The fact that the weighted average EIUVR in SITC 8 has been greater than 1 in Romania since 1991 (and was greater in Bulgaria in 1993) should be assessed against the intensive OPT in this SITC category. The presence of OPT flows reported within a given commodity group practically pushes upward the value of the corresponding EIUVR[4]; consequently, large shares of OPT commodity groups in an aggregated category will lead to higher values of the weighted average EIUVR.

Thus, it is no surprise that on the import side, the absolute values of the weighted average IEUVRs are much higher. It is only natural to expect that the imports from these more developed countries tend to be concentrated in "high value-added imports" commodity groups, i.e. in the range of products for which EU producers have a competitive advantage.

In comparing the absolute values of the weighted average EIUVRs and IEUVRs within the same trade categories (Table 6), it is clear that EU producers have an overwhelming competitive edge over those of Bulgaria, in Romania. Within the SITC 1-digit categories, in 1994 both Bulgaria and Romania held a competitive position in only one category each: food (SITC 0) in the case of Bulgaria and fuels and energy (SITC 3) in the case of Romania[5]. Both cases can be regarded as representing natural endowments of the two countries.

It should be noted, however, that the situation of Bulgaria and Romania in terms of the values of the weighted average EIUVRs and IEUVRs is not unique within CEE; moreover the weighted average EIUVRs for total exports in the two countries is higher than the average for CEE as a whole (Table 7). It is only on the import side that the other CEE countries seem to have outperformed Bulgaria and Romania in recent years in terms of lower absolute levels of the weighted average IEUVRs. This means that the competitive edge of EU producers on the markets of the central European countries is relatively lower than it is on the markets of Bulgaria and Romania.

A further insight into the quality contents of exports and imports can be provided by estimating the portions of trade flows which are rated as "high value added" in the sense that the corresponding EIUVRs and IEUVRs are greater than 1. This is done in Tables 8 and 9 for Bulgarian and Romanian exports and imports by SITC 1-digit categories as well as for the CEE averages.

Table 8 Bulgarian and Romanian Trade with EU: Share of High Value Added Exports and Imports (unit value ratios > 1) in Total Exports and Imports by SITC 1-digit commodity groups

A. Bulgaria		Exports Shares of high value added export				Imports Shares of high value added imports			
Commodity groups	SITC	1988	1991	1993	1994	1988	1991	1993	1994
Food and live animals	0	61.91	64.68	62.50	75.00	25.19	70.70	54.91	54.69
Beverages and tobacco	1	41.87	28.19	24.88	27.50	79.78	84.18	51.96	97.81
Crude materials except fuels	2	1.69	43.37	27.59	28.79	99.82	90.52	92.89	92.70
Fuels, energy	3	93.02	0.09	7.75	0.00	14.05	96.31	99.35	100.0
Animal and vegetable oils	4	0.00	0.13	0.00	0.00	100.0	77.76	100.0	100.0
Chemicals	5	30.12	17.72	3.78	16.72	92.61	89.58	58.15	85.15
Manufactured goods by material	6	5.09	5.16	0.53	2.23	83.63	79.28	96.30	94.78
Machinery and transport equipment	7	12.98	9.49	18.06	19.90	84.91	87.85	71.87	65.83
Miscellaneous manufactures	8	2.06	34.75	81.34	24.85	86.46	66.00	62.90	57.23
Commodities not classified elsewhere	9	100.0	100.0	100.0	100.0	0.00	0.00	0.00	0.00
Total		34.37	28.40	37.35	22.12	84.21	81.33	76.61	73.30

B. Romania		Exports Shares of high value added export				Imports Shares of high value added imports			
Commodity groups	SITC	1988	1991	1993	1994	1988	1991	1993	1994
Food and live animals	0	69.64	65.45	57.84	46.43	29.12	35.22	37.99	60.68
Beverages and tobacco	1	25.14	100.0	99.95	3.70	49.58	0.00	4.98	66.31
Crude materials except fuels	2	13.71	50.25	43.52	11.32	62.90	40.36	89.41	91.94
Fuels, energy	3	0.02	0.01	0.00	92.74	93.73	97.54	100.0	2.34
Animal and vegetable oils	4	0.00	0.00	0.00	0.00	100.0	100.0	100.0	100.0
Chemicals	5	14.29	16.40	0.76	2.01	96.05	74.79	82.38	76.13
Manufactured goods by material	6	6.45	15.35	10.49	7.45	96.70	92.66	97.05	97.13
Machinery and transport equipment	7	1.29	10.58	4.41	23.16	97.40	83.70	93.20	86.37
Miscellaneous manufactures	8	7.39	51.68	63.02	66.54	87.94	59.05	52.17	52.31
Commodities not classified elsewhere	9	100.0	100.0	0.00	0.00	0.00	0.00	100.0	100.0
Total		7.98	34.11	45.00	44.12	91.54	72.85	84.38	81.07

Sources: UN COMTRADE database; own calculation.

Predictably, for both countries the share of "high value added" flows is much higher in their imports from the EU than in their exports to that region. In terms of dynamics, however, it can be noted that in 1993-1994, this share has decreased in comparison to 1988, which presumably reflects the reduction of imports of some more sophisticated investment goods and intermediates, due to the transitional depression and the process of industrial restructuring.

Table 9 Total CEE Trade with EU: Share of High Value Added Exports and Imports (unit value ratios > 1) in Total Exports and Imports by SITC 1-digit Commodity Groups

(percentages)

		Exports				Imports			
		Shares of high value added export				Shares of high value added imports			
Commodity groups	SITC	1988	1991	1993	1994	1988	1991	1993	1994
Food and live animals	0	53.29	48.28	53.81	52.42	41.48	55.16	50.72	52.59
Beverages and tobacco	1	23.74	20.93	15.28	15.87	73.52	35.64	81.14	59.60
Crude materials except fuels	2	17.85	45.07	37.18	31.37	87.50	74.56	81.57	82.25
Fuels, energy	3	1.46	0.00	0.00	0.55	99.25	100.0	100.0	97.49
Animal and vegetable oils	4	0.13	1.42	2.24	2.39	92.12	91.78	89.92	85.85
Chemicals	5	6.69	6.28	20.30	24.67	98.43	90.95	79.99	73.47
Manufactured goods by material	6	1.48	3.24	0.43	0.35	98.96	96.93	98.44	98.29
Machinery and transport equipment	7	0.00	4.68	0.42	1.57	100.0	90.96	98.07	98.64
Miscellaneous manufactures	8	49.76	52.29	58.88	57.70	87.82	82.58	72.45	72.29
Commodities not classified elsewhere	9	1.66	91.61	75.28	91.46	99.80	2.73	7.03	6.21
Total		20.26	24.94	25.73	24.23	93.99	85.84	87.86	87.56

Sources: UN COMTRADE database; own calculation.

On the contrary, the share of "high value added exports" in Romania increased dramatically (and systematically) in recent years (this share jumped from 8.0 percent in 1988 to 44.1 percent in 1994 - see Table 8). No stable trend can be noticed in Bulgaria where the value-added composition varies from year to year.

The relatively high shares of high value added exports in Romania (higher than those of Bulgaria in the period 1992-94) look somewhat confusing if we compare them to the weighted average EIUVRs (Table 6), which were lower in the case of Romania in two of these years (1992 and 1994). The possible explanation of this situation is that Bulgarian exporters had a relatively stronger competitive position in some, but few export commodities, whereas the Romanian exporters had a more broadly based competitive edge, but it was not so pronounced for the individual commodities.

A further insight can be gained by looking into the value added composition of the trade flows by commodity groups. On the Bulgarian export side, at the SITC 1-digit level in recent years, there is high concentration of high value added exports only in the sector of food (SITC 0) and above average values in some of the other low processed commodity groups, whereas in the manufacturing sectors, in most cases, this concentration is below the average. In contrast, the recently increasing overall share of high value added exports in Romania is mostly due to the increased concentration of high valued added exports in SITC 9 (miscellaneous manufactures). Again, a word of caution will be added to notify the eventual bias in these measures, which is caused by the existence of OPT flows of great intensity.

In comparing these measures for Bulgaria and Romania (Table 8) to the CEE average values (Table 9) we can note that they are broadly similar, with the exception of the fact that the Romanian shares of high value added exports in recent years have been considerably higher than the CEE averages. Again, Bulgaria performs better than the CEE average in the sectors of food and some other primary goods, whereas Romania is better positioned in some of the manufacturing sectors (especially SITC 8).

Trade Specialisation within the CEE Countries and the Quality Contents of Bulgarian and Romanian Trade with the EU

In accordance with the propositions of standard trade theory (the Heckscher-Ohlin theory) countries specialise in the exports of commodities for which they enjoy comparative advantages vis-a vis their trading partners: that is, those goods which embody relatively large amounts of the countries abundant and therefore (relatively) cheap factors, and will tend to import goods which embody relatively large amounts of on relatively scarce (and hence expensive) factors. However, in practical terms comparative advantages are difficult to measure and empirical economists have sought some alternative measures, such as the index of 'revealed' comparative advantage concept (Balassa, 1965).

As discussed in section 2, the indices of revealed comparative advantage provide indicators of the trade specialisation of a country within a given group of countries, and we have used, in this study, indices of the relative trade specialisation of Bulgaria and Romania within the group of CEE countries. If an export specialisation index of type (1) is greater than 1, this indicates that the country (e.g. Bulgaria or Romania) specialises in the exports of commodity (sector) j to the EU within the group of CEE countries, in the sense that the export share of that commodity of the country is greater than the export share of CEE as a whole. Similarly, the indices of type (2) provide indicators of the import specialisation of the country within the group of CEE countries.

A general assessment of the trade specialisation of Bulgaria and Romania within CEE is provided in Table 10. For both countries, the specialisation is more pronounced on the export than on the import side; however, whereas the degree of specialisation of Romanian exports to the EU has not changed too much since 1988, it has shown a tendency to increase in Bulgaria in recent years. The relatively higher level of specialisation of the exports of the two countries to the EU may suggest that comparative advantage plays a more important role as a determinant of exports to, than of imports from, the EU. The highest concentration of specialised exports in the case of Bulgaria is observed in SITC 2 (beverages and tobacco) and in Romania, in SITC 3 (fuels and energy) and in SITC 8 (miscellaneous manufactures).

Table 10 Bulgarian and Romanian Trade with EU: Shares of Exports and Imports in Sectors with RCA (specialisation indices >1) in Total Exports and Imports by SITC 1-digit

(percentages)

A. Bulgaria		Exports Shares of specialised export				Imports Shares of specialised imports			
Commodity groups	SITC	1988	1991	1993	1994	1988	1991	1993	1994
Food and live animals	0	66.5	72.2	78.2	91.2	63.9	88.2	89.9	84.8
Beverages and tobacco	1	100.0	100.0	100.0	99.9	99.3	81.8	100.0	98.5
Crude materials except fuels	2	86.6	80.8	79.5	88.4	47.1	72.6	71.3	66.2
Fuels, energy	3	99.5	0.0	95.1	87.0	0.0.4	3.7	99.3	97.7
Animal and vegetable oils	4	91.6	0.0	84.7	86.9	0.0	75.3	44.9	73.2
Chemicals	5	91.4	69.8	86.1	90.5	54.1	62.3	47.2	64.1
Manufactured goods by material	6	62.0	57.9	73.3	83.9	64.4	54.7	34.7	61.1
Machinery and transport equipment	7	81.9	77.3	39.2	51.1	74.3	55.3	17.6	63.7
Miscellaneous manufactures	8	33.9	28.9	91.4	89.0	16.6	19.1	67.3	54.2
Commodities not classified elsewhere	9	99.7	45.2	40.4	6.4	0.0	98.5	99.4	100.0
Total		76.3	62.0	80.2	83.7	61.8	58.6	50.8	65.1
B. Romania		Exports Shares of specialised export				Imports Shares of specialised imports			
Commodity groups	SITC	1988	1991	1993	1994	1988	1991	1993	1994
Food and live animals	0	25.2	15.3	41.2	32.2	91.1	94.2	81.9	72.0
Beverages and tobacco	1	0.5	0.0	92.7	0.0	39.2	88.7	95.0	36.6
Crude materials except fuels	2	31.0	26.9	50.4	52.9	98.4	78.9	66.6	56.9
Fuels, energy	3	100.0	100.0	99.5	93.5	100.0	100.0	99.4	98.1
Animal and vegetable oils	4	0.0	62.7	67.1	56.7	0.0	94.3	0.0	0.0
Chemicals	5	59.8	20.7	37.8	65.1	49.8	71.0	38.6	37.9
Manufactured goods by material	6	51.2	63.0	47.1	65.6	90.2	82.7	76.8	74.8
Machinery and transport equipment	7	51.1	39.4	45.8	31.3	35.0	36.8	62.4	61.4
Miscellaneous manufactures	8	96.5	96.5	95.9	95.2	77.7	63.0	55.8	66.6
Commodities not classified elsewhere	9	0.0	11.0	24.6	0.0	19.6	99.8	99.9	99.8
Total		78.1	75.3	78.3	77.8	74.4	69.9	67.6	65.6

Sources: UN COMTRADE database; own calculation.

While trade specialisation is a customary phenomenon, especially in trade between countries with different levels of economic development (where it often occurs in the form of intra-industry trade), it is interesting to address the issue of the determinants of the concrete form of specialisation which appears on the surface in the form of the composition of the trade flows. Indeed, this is a very broad issue and we can only discuss some of its specific aspects[6]. One of these aspects is the relative value-added composition of the specialised exports and imports, which can be assessed by the concentration of the "high value added exports" and "high value added imports" (in the sense discussed in the previous section), which is shown in Table 11.

Table 11 Bulgarian and Romanian Trade with EU: Shares of High Value Added Exports and Imports in Specialised Exports and Imports by SITC 1-digit

(percentages)

A. Bulgaria		Exports Shares of high value added export				Imports Shares of high value added import			
Commodity groups	SITC	1988	1991	1993	1994	1988	1991	1993	1994
Food and live animals	0	57.7	62.3	65.4	79.1	8.2	53.4	51.3	31.0
Beverages and tobacco	1	41.9	28.2	24.9	27.5	65.8	83.3	44.3	70.2
Crude materials except fuels	2	1.3	43.0	33.2	21.1	86.9	93.4	90.1	90.6
Fuels, energy	3	93.0	0.0	0.0	0.0	0.0	0.0	100.0	95.3
Animal and vegetable oils	4	0.0	0.0	0.0	0.0	0.0	100.0	100.0	100.0
Chemicals	5	30.4	16.4	3.4	18.5	93.1	93.0	47.5	82.2
Manufactured goods by material	6	7.1	0.3	0.0	0.0	76.8	63.8	85.0	96.4
Machinery and transport equipment	7	13.2	11.7	3.6	3.0	83.8	83.3	93.7	55.0
Miscellaneous manufactures	8	0.0	0.1	87.2	23.8	27.1	43.3	49.2	33.2
Commodities not classified elsewhere	9	94.1	0.0	72.1	0.0	0.0	0.0	0.0	0.0
Total		38.0	24.3	40.1	20.2	77.8	72.1	63.6	62.8
B. Romania		Exports Shares of high value added export				Imports Shares of high value added import			
Commodity groups	SITC	1988	1991	1993	1994	1988	1991	1993	1994
Food and live animals	0	61.7	27.2	52.0	49.4	4.4	20.8	9.7	41.1
Beverages and tobacco	1	0.0	0.0	100.0	0.0	0.0	0.0	0.0	24.2
Crude materials except fuels	2	0.0	15.2	56.9	14.4	32.1	22.7	52.0	80.9
Fuels, energy	3	0.0	0.0	0.0	88.6	79.9	56.8	99.4	0.4
Animal and vegetable oils	4	0.0	0.0	0.0	0.0	0.0	100.0	0.0	0.0
Chemicals	5	23.9	0.0	0.0	0.0	88.2	74.5	84.1	83.1
Manufactured goods by material	6	8.6	17.5	22.0	11.0	93.4	91.6	96.5	97.5
Machinery and transport equipment	7	0.9	1.9	8.3	5.5	90.4	87.7	90.0	83.6
Miscellaneous manufactures	8	6.8	52.8	64.7	68.7	85.0	45.3	15.7	24.8
Commodities not classified elsewhere	9	0.0	0.0	0.0	0.0	0.0	0.0	96.5	96.4
Total		5.7	34.6	54.5	52.0	77.7	60.0	70.7	74.3

Sources: UN COMTRADE database; own calculation.

As can be seen, the concentration of "high value added" commodities is more pronounced in the specialised imports of the two countries from the EU than in the specialised exports to the EU. This confirms that, as a rule, EU exporters specialise in more sophisticated and higher quality goods which yield relatively higher unit values of the merchandise (e.g. R&D- and skill- intensive goods; also some capital-intensive commodities). The opposite seems to hold true for exports from Bulgaria and Romania, where specialisation, as a rule, is based either on higher content of natural resources (mostly of local origin) or on the higher content of (cheap) local labour, both of which are not based on high value added content and do not lead to higher unit values of the merchandise. This is confirmed by the fact that in a number of SITC 1-digit sectors, the share of "high value added exports" in the specialised exports of Bulgaria and Romania is zero or close to zero (Table 11). The one obvious exception is again SITC 8 in Romania, but it will now become apparent that these high figures are also misleading.

One problem with these measures is that they only compare the value added contents of the trade flows of one selected country and it may well be that the value added of one unit of exports is higher than that of imports (EIUVR > 1), but that at the same time the absolute level of the value added contents of imports (and hence of exports) is very low. To adjust for this, we have computed the average unit value of CEE exports to, and CEE imports from, the EU by SITC 3-digit commodity groups and we have compared the absolute levels of Bulgarian and Romanian unit values with the CEE averages by these categories. The results, aggregated by SITC 1-digit commodity groups are shown in Table 12.

These results reveal a somewhat different picture of the value added/quality composition of Bulgarian and Romanian trade flows. By this token, (taking the absolute levels of the value added content by SITC 3-digit commodity groups) Bulgarian exports are superior to Romanian exports (with the exception of year 1991), but in both countries the relative standing vis-a-vis the other CEE countries in 1993-1994 deteriorated as compared to 1988.

In comparing the export performance of the two countries by this measure (and comparing it to other measures discussed before) we can identify one major difference: while there is high concentration of relatively "high quality" exports in on sectors in which Bulgaria specialises among the CEE countries (such as SITC 0 and SITC 1), the share of relatively "high quality" exports in the sector where Romania's specialisation is most pronounced (SITC 8) in 1993 and 1994 is close to 0. This means that in spite of the fact that the Romanian weighted average EIUVR in this commodity group is high (the valued added contents of exports is higher than that of imports), the absolute level of value added of Romanian exports is, as a rule, lower than the average absolute valued added level of CEE exports in that commodity group.

Table 12 Bulgarian and Romanian Trade with EU: Share of "High Quality" Exports and Imports (unit value > CEE average) by SITC 1-digit Commodity Groups

(percentages)

A. Bulgaria		Exports				Imports			
		Shares of "high quality" exports				Shares of "high quality" imports			
Commodity groups	SITC	1988	1991	1993	1994	1988	1991	1993	1994
Food and live animals	0	75.8	87.3	73.4	81.8	29.1	74.7	44.8	45.9
Beverages and tobacco	1	99.9	100.0	100.0	100.0	65.3	72.6	93.2	99.3
Crude materials except fuels	2	67.6	55.3	41.8	60.5	49.1	81.6	68.6	92.9
Fuels, energy	3	99.6	22.1	4.9	100.0	14.1	2.6	0.0	95.4
Animal and vegetable oils	4	93.1	100.0	1.5	0.0	100.0	78.5	100.0	100.0
Chemicals	5	36.1	23.0	13.2	34.7	44.5	44.3	71.2	75.8
Manufactured goods by material	6	36.7	18.2	46.1	44.7	41.7	25.6	38.4	37.7
Machinery and transport equipment	7	79.6	43.2	41.7	65.6	67.0	49.4	57.2	69.6
Miscellaneous manufactures	8	5.7	3.2	4.4	6.7	65.7	53.3	48.2	40.1
Commodities not classified elsewhere	9	99.7	92.5	49.0	91.5	0.0	95.4	100.0	4.5
Total		59.6	40.7	34.6	44.2	53.1	50.1	52.7	60.2
B. Romania		Exports				Imports			
		Shares of "high quality" exports				Shares of "high quality" imports			
Commodity groups	SITC	1988	1991	1993	1994	1988	1991	1993	1994
Food and live animals	0	43.0	49.3	45.0	43.0	10.3	74.4	56.5	55.4
Beverages and tobacco	1	0.5	92.8	0.9	0.0	60.8	9.7	0.0	17.5
Crude materials except fuels	2	81.2	74.2	50.0	39.9	37.0	58.4	48.8	63.7
Fuels, energy	3	0.9	100.0	99.5	82.9	12.4	0.1	99.4	1.9
Animal and vegetable oils	4	96.5	37.3	0.0	56.7	78.7	95.0	100.0	100.0
Chemicals	5	34.7	20.8	37.4	38.2	69.0	57.7	77.8	67.0
Manufactured goods by material	6	39.9	56.8	27.5	18.2	66.2	45.1	36.9	35.9
Machinery and transport equipment	7	70.2	22.4	12.5	31.9	86.0	59.9	68.2	47.9
Miscellaneous manufactures	8	13.8	43.0	3.6	0.9	27.8	39.6	40.7	18.1
Commodities not classified elsewhere	9	97.7	88.3	1.2	1.0	80.4	0.0	0.1	0.2
Total		23.6	51.6	14.3	13.6	57.5	50.6	55.5	40.4

Sources: UN COMTRADE database; own calculation.

As the CEE countries are competitors among themselves on the EU markets, this difference in the type of export specialisation of the two countries may also imply a different type of competitive behavior of the two countries: while the specialisation of Bulgaria (at least in the sectors where it is most pronounced) may be based on value added/quality superiority of the exported goods, the export specialisation of Romania seems rather to be driven by price competition in the lower range of quality spectrum.

To test this hypothesis and to gain a better insight into this type of inter-relation between specialisation and absolute value added/quality level in the Bulgarian and Romanian trade with the EU, we have computed the share of specialised exports (those for which the export specialisation indices are greater than 1) in "high quality" exports (those which have unit value higher than the CEE average) of the two countries (Table 13). As per this measure, the main difference between the export performance of the two countries is in the concentration of "specialised" exports in the "high quality" exports: it is much higher in the case of Bulgaria (with the exception of the year 1991)[7]. his concentration seems to be quite pronounced in the trade sectors where Bulgaria specialises within CEE, whereas it is quite low in the most impor-tant Romanian exporting sectors (in fact it is zero in commodity group SITC 8 in 1994) (Table 13). So these quantitative results seem to be in line with the above proposition about the type of export specialisation of the two countries in their trade with the EU.

Table 13 Bulgarian and Romanian Trade with EU: Share of Specialised Exports and Imports in "High Quality" Exports and Imports by SITC 1-digit Commodity Groups

(percentages)

A. Bulgaria		Exports Shares of specialised exports				Imports Shares of specialised imports			
Commodity groups	SITC	1988	1991	1993	1994	1988	1991	1993	1994
Food and live animals	0	55.3	70.9	62.2	75.5	15.0	68.7	40.2	36.8
Beverages and tobacco	1	99.9	100.0	100.0	99.9	65.3	68.1	40.2	36.8
Crude materials except fuels	2	62.1	48.7	37.7	51.2	19.6	70.9	42.5	60.0
Fuels, energy	3	99.5	0.0	0.0	87.0	0.0	0.0	0.0	93.1
Animal and vegetable oils	4	91.6	0.0	0.0	0.0	0.0	75.3	44.9	73.2
Chemicals	5	31.6	13.1	7.0	31.6	23.9	28.2	25.9	40.1
Manufactured goods by material	6	14.4	2.2	37.7	24.5	33.2	12.6	7.6	16.9
Machinery and transport equipment	7	67.5	35.4	8.4	41.0	53.6	29.9	2.1	37.8
Miscellaneous manufactures	8	2.9	1.1	3.4	1.8	6.4	13.1	33.9	18.0
Commodities not classified elsewhere	9	99.7	38.6	0.0	0.0	0.0	95.4	99.4	4.5
Total		50.1	30.4	26.8	35.0	35.7	33.5	21.9	33.9
B. Romania		Exports Shares of specialised exports				Imports Shares of specialised imports			
Commodity groups	SITC	1988	1991	1993	1994	1988	1991	1993	1994
Food and live animals	0	16.0	15.3	21.4	19.9	2.5	72.5	48.9	33.7
Beverages and tobacco	1	0.5	0.0	0.8	0.0	0.0	0.0	0.0	0.0
Crude materials except fuels	2	27.5	19.6	11.4	7.0	36.5	39.8	24.1	29.3
Fuels, energy	3	0.9	100.0	99.5	82.8	12.4	0.1	98.8	0.0
Animal and vegetable oils	4	0.0	0.0	0.0	56.7	0.0	94.3	0.0	0.0
Chemicals	5	14.3	1.8	8.5	14.2	26.6	42.3	36.1	21.8
Manufactured goods by material	6	13.7	31.5	16.4	10.8	56.8	31.2	21.2	19.4
Machinery and transport equipment	7	38.5	8.8	5.8	4.0	31.3	30.9	49.5	38.0
Miscellaneous manufactures	8	12.6	41.6	3.3	0.0	24.2	22.3	17.4	3.1
Commodities not classified elsewhere	9	0.0	0.0	0.0	0.0	0.0	0.0	0.0	0.0
Total		11.9	39.9	8.7	6.3	37.4	34.9	37.2	23.8

Sources: UN COMTRADE database; own calculation.

As far as imports are concerned, while in both countries the share of "high quality" imports is quite high, this does not seem to be a major driving force in determining the import specialisation of the two countries (Tables 12 and 13). Apart from commodity group SITC 7 (machinery and transport equipment) the other important import commodity groups are characterised by lower concentration of "high quality" imports than the country's average.

The comparison of the unit values of the countries' exports with the CEE averages, as it has been made so far, can be interpreted as a relative quality advantage in the quality of the exported merchandise within the group of CEE countries. Following this line, we have also analysed the quality composition of Bulgarian and Romanian trade flows in terms of absolute quality advantage or "highest quality" within the group of CEE countries. In turn, the latter was measured by the level of exports (or imports) in commodity groups which are characterised by highest absolute level of the unit value of merchandise within the group of CEE countries by SITC 3-digit commodity groups. These quantitative results are presented in Table 14 (aggregated on the SITC 1-digit level).

In terms of absolute quality advantage (measured as defined above) Bulgarian exports are superior to Romanian exports in the sense that a larger proportion of exports is identified as belonging to the "highest quality" category within CEE. However, in both countries the share of "highest quality" exports in 1993-1994 has declined drastically from its 1988 level, which indicates a deterioration in the overall quality composition of exports.

In Bulgaria there is a markedly large concentration of "highest quality" exports only in SITC 1-digit commodity group SITC 1 (food) and to some extent in groups SITC 2 (crude materials) and SITC 7 (machinery and transport equipment). The decline of the total share of "highest quality" exports is largely due to the loss of the absolute quality advantage in commodity group SITC 2 (beverages and tobacco), which took place in 1993. In Romania the drop in the total share of "highest quality" exports was caused by the declining share of such exports in some of the important manufacturing commodity groups, as well as in the energy sector (SITC 3).

There appears to be no systematic pattern in the concentration of "highest quality" imports, which is marked by high variability in both countries. However, it is worth noting that while in the case of Bulgaria the total shares of such imports are roughly comparable with the shares of "highest quality exports", in the case of Romania the latter are much lower than the former.

Table 14 Bulgarian and Romanian Trade with EU: Share of "Highest Quality" Exports and Imports (Highest Unit Value Exports and Imports Among CEECs) by SITC 1-digit Commodity Groups

(percentages)

A. Bulgaria		Exports Shares of "highest quality" exports				Imports Shares of "highest quality" imports			
Commodity groups	SITC	1988	1991	1993	1994	1988	1991	1993	1994
Food and live animals	0	45.4	46.8	59.5	66.2	9.9	44.7	21.0	13.6
Beverages and tobacco	1	41.9	71.8	0.0	0.0	65.3	0.0	0.0	69.1
Crude materials except fuels	2	13.4	23.4	16.5	25.6	0.4	59.8	30.8	62.3
Fuels, energy	3	92.5	1.5	38.0	0.0	14.1	0.0	0.0	2.1
Animal and vegetable oils	4	0.0	15.5	0.0	0.0	8.3	0.0	48.5	9.0
Chemicals	5	25.5	10.5	4.0	9.5	14.4	23.1	11.9	34.1
Manufactured goods by material	6	9.8	6.3	29.5	4.4	14.6	5.9	4.4	15.3
Machinery and transport equipment	7	16.0	34.0	17.7	33.6	9.7	34.0	13.9	38.9
Miscellaneous manufactures	8	4.5	2.7	0.4	0.7	5.3	31.5	20.9	23.1
Commodities not classified elsewhere	9	5.9	38.6	49.0	89.6	0.0	95.4	91.9	0.0
Total		29.7	22.8	17.6	14.3	11.6	29.7	13.6	30.6

B. Romania		Exports Shares of "highest quality" exports				Imports Shares of "highest quality" imports			
Commodity groups	SITC	1988	1991	1993	1994	1988	1991	1993	1994
Food and live animals	0	10.3	10.6	23.8	9.1	3.5	28.5	44.5	23.6
Beverages and tobacco	1	0.5	0.0	0.0	0.0	3.4	0.0	0.0	0.0
Crude materials except fuels	2	75.2	57.9	31.9	10.0	19.5	48.1	10.9	37.4
Fuels, energy	3	0.9	0.0	0.0	10.7	12.4	0.0	0.4	0.0
Animal and vegetable oils	4	96.5	15.1	0.0	0.0	0.0	0.1	6.2	10.4
Chemicals	5	20.1	15.8	0.0	0.0	0.1	0.1	6.2	10.4
Manufactured goods by material	6	12.0	33.4	10.9	7.8	26.8	32.6	29.8	18.0
Machinery and transport equipment	7	11.5	12.5	7.9	1.2	38.2	35.3	30.2	13.7
Miscellaneous manufactures	8	2.3	0.1	0.7	0.0	14.0	12.6	11.6	3.4
Commodities not classified elsewhere	9	0.0	88.3	0.0	0.0	80.4	0.0	0.0	0.0
Total		8.0	11.0	4.9	3.4	27.2	26.8	28.0	14.3

Sources: UN COMTRADE database; own calculation.

For the analysis to be complete, we have performed similar assessment of the other extreme end of the quality spectrum. Table 16 presents the shares of "lowest quality" exports and imports of Bulgaria and Romania as measured by the lowest absolute level of the unit value of merchandise within the group of CEE countries by SITC 3-digit commodity groups.

It is interesting to note that the total proportion of such exports is also higher in the case of Bulgaria than in the case of Romania, and this is especially pronounced in the exports of manufactured goods. In both countries the total proportion of "lowest quality" exports is higher than the proportion of "highest quality" exports (Tables 14 and 16). In Romania one can observe a substantial rise of this type of exports in 1994 compared to all previous years for which observations are available, but it remains to be seen whether this was a one time event or a point of structural change in Romanian export performance.

Table 15 Bulgarian and Romanian Trade with EU: Share of Specialised Exports and Imports in "Highest Quality" Exports and Imports by SITC 1-digit Commodity Groups

(percentages)

A. Bulgaria		Exports Shares of specialised exports				Imports Shares of specialised imports			
Commodity groups	SITC	1988	1991	1993	1994	1988	1991	1993	1994
Food and live animals	0	62.4	68.9	94.1	100.0	50.1	94.9	81.7	80.7
Beverages and tobacco	1	100.0	100.0	0.0	0.0	100.0	0.0	0.0	100.0
Crude materials except fuels	2	98.3	76.5	98.2	71.3	0.0	92.5	74.3	77.6
Fuels, energy	3	100.0	0.0	99.8	0.0	0.0	0.0	0.0	0.0
Animal and vegetable oils	4	0.0	0.0	0.0	0.0	0.0	0.0	92.5	100.0
Chemicals	5	100.0	46.3	57.2	69.1	15.7	50.4	0.7	89.8
Manufactured goods by material	6	67.6	5.5	93.1	33.5	93.9	52.7	70.1	65.8
Machinery and transport equipment	7	38.9	86.5	39.4	82.8	51.1	55.3	70.1	65.8
Miscellaneous manufactures	8	63.2	32.9	12.7	56.1	0.0	12.3	94.3	74.9
Commodities not classified elsewhere	9	100.0	100.0	0.0	0.0	0.0	100.0	100.0	0.0
Total		86.0	75.1	87.2	79.9	53.9	63.8	54.6	61.1

B. Romania		Exports Shares of specialised exports				Imports Shares of specialised imports			
Commodity groups	SITC	1988	1991	1993	1994	1988	1991	1993	1994
Food and live animals	0	0.6	0.0	11.8	66.4	0.0	99.2	98.2	94.6
Beverages and tobacco	1	100.0	0.0	0.0	0.0	0.0	0.0	0.0	0.0
Crude materials except fuels	2	36.5	19.8	18.7	70.2	98.5	81.4	30.0	55.0
Fuels, energy	3	97.5	0.0	0.0	99.9	100.0	0.0	0.0	0.0
Animal and vegetable oils	4	0.0	0.0	0.0	0.0	0.0	0.0	0.0	0.0
Chemicals	5	54.9	0.0	0.0	98.4	48.3	67.5	30.3	35.4
Manufactured goods by material	6	13.0	66.4	89.1	63.6	72.0	82.8	69.6	49.9
Machinery and transport equipment	7	67.2	64.7	48.0	0.0	11.9	30.8	71.7	64.4
Miscellaneous manufactures	8	99.4	63.9	100.0	0.0	94.2	73.8	16.5	65.2
Commodities not classified elsewhere	9	0.0	0.0	0.0	0.0	0.0	0.0	0.0	0.0
Total		40.5	46.6	50.8	73.0	57.6	64.4	68.2	57.5

Sources: UN COMTRADE database; own calculation.

Regarding imports, there is again a greater variability in the composition of the import flows. There seems to be a recent tendency of decline in the total proportion of "lowest quality" imports in Romania, whereas in Bulgaria there is a stable concentration of "lowest quality" imports in some of the manufacturing sectors.

Finally, we have analysed the interrelation between the specialisation of the countries in "highest quality" or "lowest quality" exports and imports and the general trade specialisation among the group of CEE countries, as measured by the export and import specialisation indices (1) and (2). This cross-section is presented in Tables 15 and 17.

On average, there appears to be a reverse relationship between the two types of specialisation in the two countries. In Bulgaria the share of specialised flows of "highest quality" exports is higher than the share in Romania, whereas on the import side, the share of specialised "highest quality" imports is higher in the case of Romania. In Bulgaria, for most of the available observations, the shares of specialised flows in both the "highest quality" and the "lowest quality" is higher on the export side than on the import side[8]. In Romania the situation was the opposite in the starting years but it reversed in recent years when it became similar to that in Bulgaria.

Table 16 Bulgarian and Romanian Trade with EU: Share of "Lowest Quality" Exports and Imports (Lowest Unit Value Exports and Imports Among CEECs) by SITC 1-digit Commodity Groups

(percentages)

A. Bulgaria		Shares of "lowest quality" Exports				Shares of "lowest quality" Imports			
Commodity groups	SITC	1988	1991	1993	1994	1988	1991	1993	1994
Food and live animals	0	12.0	0.3	6.2	0.6	6.8	2.1	29.0	20.5
Beverages and tobacco	1	0.0	0.0	0.0	0.0	17.2	13.7	0.0	0.0
Crude materials except fuels	2	10.0	27.0	23.7	3.1	19.0	4.5	1.1	5.0
Fuels, energy	3	0.0	0.0	0.0	0.0	85.9	97.4	100.0	0.0
Animal and vegetable oils	4	0.0	0.0	0.0	0.0	0.0	0.0	0.0	0.0
Chemicals	5	3.4	61.2	52.0	47.3	27.0	19.4	17.8	21.6
Manufactured goods by material	6	55.0	57.5	34.7	40.9	44.5	36.1	37.3	26.7
Machinery and transport equipment	7	1.3	11.1	10.3	9.8	11.4	17.5	15.0	18.9
Miscellaneous manufactures	8	49.2	41.5	59.4	46.1	6.6	18.2	15.3	6.0
Commodities not classified elsewhere	9	0.0	0.0	0.0	0.0	0.0	0.0	0.0	0.0
Total		18.7	30.2	33.2	29.3	22.1	19.4	24.1	18.0

B. Romania		Shares of "lowest quality" Exports				Shares of "lowest quality" Imports			
Commodity groups	SITC	1988	1991	1993	1994	1988	1991	1993	1994
Food and live animals	0	0.0	12.8	37.1	27.7	31.2	24.4	13.2	11.6
Beverages and tobacco	1	0.0	7.2	0.0	0.0	39.2	41.6	60.7	3.9
Crude materials except fuels	2	1.5	0.3	9.9	41.5	43.2	8.8	40.6	3.9
Fuels, energy	3	0.0	0.0	0.5	2.9	5.3	1.4	0.0	97.6
Animal and vegetable oils	4	3.5	0.0	0.0	0.0	21.3	5.0	0.0	0.0
Chemicals	5	29.0	8.4	44.2	32.3	3.6	32.7	4.2	17.5
Manufactured goods by material	6	7.8	7.6	13.6	12.3	12.0	11.0	7.9	7.7
Machinery and transport equipment	7	25.9	23.9	33.9	36.3	5.9	21.1	8.0	7.5
Miscellaneous manufactures	8	1.2	24.9	1.9	33.5	55.9	28.2	46.0	32.7
Commodities not classified elsewhere	9	0.0	11.0	74.2	97.2	0.0	97.6	99.9	0.0
Total		5.2	16.2	9.8	28.3	18.9	22.1	15.2	14.4

Sources: UN COMTRADE database; own calculation.

The magnitude of the shares of specialised flows may be interpreted as the degree to which one or another quality pattern plays the role of a systemic factor in determining the trade specialisation of the country. In these terms, quality has been a stronger systemic factor in Bulgaria than in

Romania[9]; and it now appears to play a more important role on the export than on the import side (but it used to be the opposite in the past for Romania).

Table 17 Bulgarian and Romanian Trade with EU: Share of Specialised Exports and Imports in "Lowest Quality" Exports and Imports by SITC 1-digit Commodity Groups

(percentages)

A. Bulgaria		Exports Shares of specialised exports				Imports Shares of specialised imports			
Commodity groups	SITC	1988	1991	1993	1994	1988	1991	1993	1994
Food and live animals	0	88.6	0.0	98.7	0.0	56.3	54.9	89.9	89.3
Beverages and tobacco	1	0.0	0.0	0.0	0.0	100.0	0.0	0.0	0.0
Crude materials except fuels	2	45.2	86.4	31.4	91.8	0.0	0.0	0.0	94.9
Fuels, energy	3	0.0	0.0	0.0	0.0	0.0	3.8	99.4	0.0
Animal and vegetable oils	4	0.0	0.0	0.0	0.0	0.0	0.0	0.0	0.0
Chemicals	5	0.0	81.5	99.6	94.4	51.9	78.6	100.0	98.8
Manufactured goods by material	6	73.5	80.3	99.6	94.4	51.9	78.6	100.0	98.8
Machinery and transport equipment	7	0.0	0.0	11.7	47.2	69.6	46.6	0.0	97.6
Miscellaneous manufactures	8	59.5	20.3	97.4	89.1	0.0	24.1	63.6	69.4
Commodities not classified elsewhere	9	0.0	0.0	0.0	0.0	0.0	0.0	0.0	0.0
Total		66.5	61.2	81.7	88.1	53.5	47.6	64.0	90.6

B. Romania		Exports Shares of specialised exports				Imports Shares of specialised imports			
Commodity groups	SITC	1988	1991	1993	1994	1988	1991	1993	1994
Food and live animals	0	0.0	0.0	53.4	0.0	96.7	87.1	45.5	63.6
Beverages and tobacco	1	0.0	0.0	0.0	0.0	100.0	96.2	100.0	100.0
Crude materials except fuels	2	0.0	0.0	0.0	86.2	100.0	83.1	88.6	0.0
Fuels, energy	3	0.0	0.0	0.0	0.0	100.0	100.0	0.0	100.0
Animal and vegetable oils	4	0.0	0.0	0.0	0.0	0.0	0.0	0.0	0.0
Chemicals	5	61.6	0.0	49.8	92.6	20.2	68.4	0.0	75.3
Manufactured goods by material	6	36.6	0.0	0.0	0.0	98.9	73.4	64.4	39.8
Machinery and transport equipment	7	48.3	10.3	54.1	34.0	0.0	25.8	0.0	0.0
Miscellaneous manufactures	8	30.2	94.6	0.0	94.2	67.1	42.0	65.7	86.7
Commodities not classified elsewhere	9	0.0	100.0	0.0	0.0	0.0	100.0	100.0	0.0
Total		46.7	69.6	32.6	74.3	80.5	62.2	56.1	62.8

Sources: UN COMTRADE database; own calculation.

Conclusions

Recent years brought no changes supported by data expressed in tables in the patterns of trade specialisation of the CEE countries in their trade with the developed market economies and, in particular, with the EU. This paper addressed some aspects of these changes in two of the south-eastern European transition countries: Bulgaria and Romania.

One general conclusion from this analysis, which is based on the results of a number of empirical quantitative assessments is that the quantitative expansion of the trade flows between these two countries and the EU, which has taken place since 1990, is accompanied by a marked deterioration in the quality composition of these flows, especially that concerning the exports of Bulgaria and Romania to the EU. This is consistent with the findings of other studies on this topic (see Landesmann and Burgstaller, 1997); they also confirm propositions by other scholars (Petrakos and Totev, 1997) that the re-integration of the south-eastern European transition countries into the European economy is likely to increase the differences in their industrial and trade structures vis-a-vis the European Union.

Such a deterioration is noticeable, both when analysing the trade flows of the individual countries separately, and when comparing their trade performance with the rest of the CEE countries, which is an even greater cause for concern. Although an overal deterioration of the quality composition of trade with the EU can be observed in all CEE countries, Bulgaria and Romania (which have the lowest per capita income level among the CEE countries considered in this study), have markedly worsened their relative standing within this group of countries. These findings are also consistent with the results of other empirical studies quoted above and in the Introduction, according to which some CEE countries (such as Hungary and the Czech Republic) may accelerate the process of "catching-up" with the West, while others (such as Bulgaria and Romania) may fall behind in terms of their developmental gap.

However, there are both similarities and differences in the patterns of trade performance of Bulgaria and Romania vis-a-vis the EU. Although the general trends are similar, there are important differences in both the trade specialisation and the quality contents and quality composition of the trade flows in the two countries. Although Bulgaria and Romania are geographical neighbours, they display quite different trade (and especially export) specialisation within the group of CEE countries, which presumably reflects the natural endowments and, to some extent, the historical patterns of industrial development of the two countries. On average, the share of exported goods of higher value-added content (interpreted as a sign of higher quality) is larger in the case of Bulgaria than in the case of Romania, but the quality content and the quality composition of Bulgarian exports has been rapidly deteriorating in recent years.

At the same time, Bulgarian exports to the EU seem to be more heterogeneous in their quality content than those of Romania: while Romania is specialising mostly in the below average range of quality among the CEE countries but not so much in the lowest quality segments of the spectrum, Bulgaria displays a more pronounced degree of export specialisation both in the higher quality segments, including the segment of "highest quality" among the CEE countries, and in the lowest segments of the quality spectrum. Thus, there may be some important and specific trade specialisation "niches" for the two countries, and it remains to be seen whether, and to what extent, they will be able to capitalise on them in the future.

Notes

1 Throughout the paper we define as CEE countries the group consisting of Bulgaria, Czechoslovakia (after 1993 the Czech Republic and Slovakia, respectively), Hungary, Poland and Romania.
2 Only the unit value ratios for the commodity groups where both exports and imports are non-zero flows are taken into account for this exercise.
3 That is, the value added of one physical unit of exports is higher than the value added of one physical unit of imports of the merchandise from the same commodity group.
4 Since the value added content of the exported merchandise is essentially higher than the value added content of the imported merchandise by definition.
5 The SITC 9 category should be disregarded in this case, as it contains the ambiguous item "transactions not classified elsewhere".
6 Some other aspects of this issue are addressed in Dobrinsky and Landesmann (1995) and European Commission (1994).
7 In many respects 1991 is an exception to the general trends. However, there are sound reasons to consider that 1991 was an abnormal year in terms of trade of the CEE countries as this was the first year after the disintegration of the CMEA and apart from the substantial trade restructuring and reorientation that was performed in that year, some "one time" transactions also took place (such as the liquidation of stocks previously planned for other markets).
8 The only exception is 1994 imports.
9 Note that in this case "quality" is regarded as a variable, i.e. we take into account the whole quality spectrum.

References

Balassa, B. (1965), Trade Liberalisation and "Revealed" Comparative Advantage. *The Manchester School of Economic and Social Studies* 33 (2), pp. 99-123.

Dobrinsky, R. (1994), The Economic Interpenetration Between the EC and Eastern Europe: The Case of Bulgaria. In: The Economic Interpenetration Between the EC and Eastern Europe, *European Economy Reports and Studies* No.6, 1994.

Dobrinsky, R. (1995), Economic Transformation and the Changing Patterns of European East-West Trade. In: Dobrinsky, R. and Landesmann, M. (eds), *Transforming Economies and European Integration*. Aldershot/ Brookfield: Edward Elgar, pp. 86-115.

Dobrinsky, R. and Landesmann, M. (eds) (1995), *Transforming Economies and European Integration*, Aldershot/ Brookfield: Edward Elgar.

EBE (1995), *Economic Bulletin for Europe*, v. 47.

European Commission (1994), The Economic Interpenetration Between the EC and Eastern Europe. *European Economy Reports and Studies* No.6, 1994.

Jackson, M. and Wiesbrouck, W. (1994), The Economic Interpenetration Between the EC and Eastern Europe: The Case of Romania. In: *The Economic Interpenetration Between the EC and Eastern Europe, European Economy Reports and Studies* No.6.

Landesmann, M. (1995) The Pattern of East-West Integration: Catching-Up or Falling Behind?. In: Dobrinsky, R. and Landesmann, M. (eds), *Transforming Economies and European Integration*, Aldershot/ Brookfield: Edward Elgar, pp. 116-140.

Landesmann, M. (1996), Emerging Patterns of European Industrial Specialisation: Implications for Labour Market Dynamics in Eastern and Western Europe. *WIIW Research Reports* No. 230, September.

Landesmann, M. and Burgstaller, J. (1997), Vertical Product Differentiation in EU Markets: The Relative Position of East European Producers. *WIIW Research Reports* No. 234a, February.

Landesmann, M. and Szıkely, I.P. (eds) (1995), *Industrial Restructuring and Trade Reorientation in Eastern Europe*, Cambridge: Cambridge University Press.

Petrakos, G. and Totev, S. (1997) Economic Structure and Change in the Balkan Region: Implications for Integration, Transition and Economic Cooperation. Paper Presented at the Conference on *"Economic Cooperation in the Balkans: A Regional Approach to European Integration"*, Volos, 16-18 January 1997.

Printed in the United States
by Baker & Taylor Publisher Services